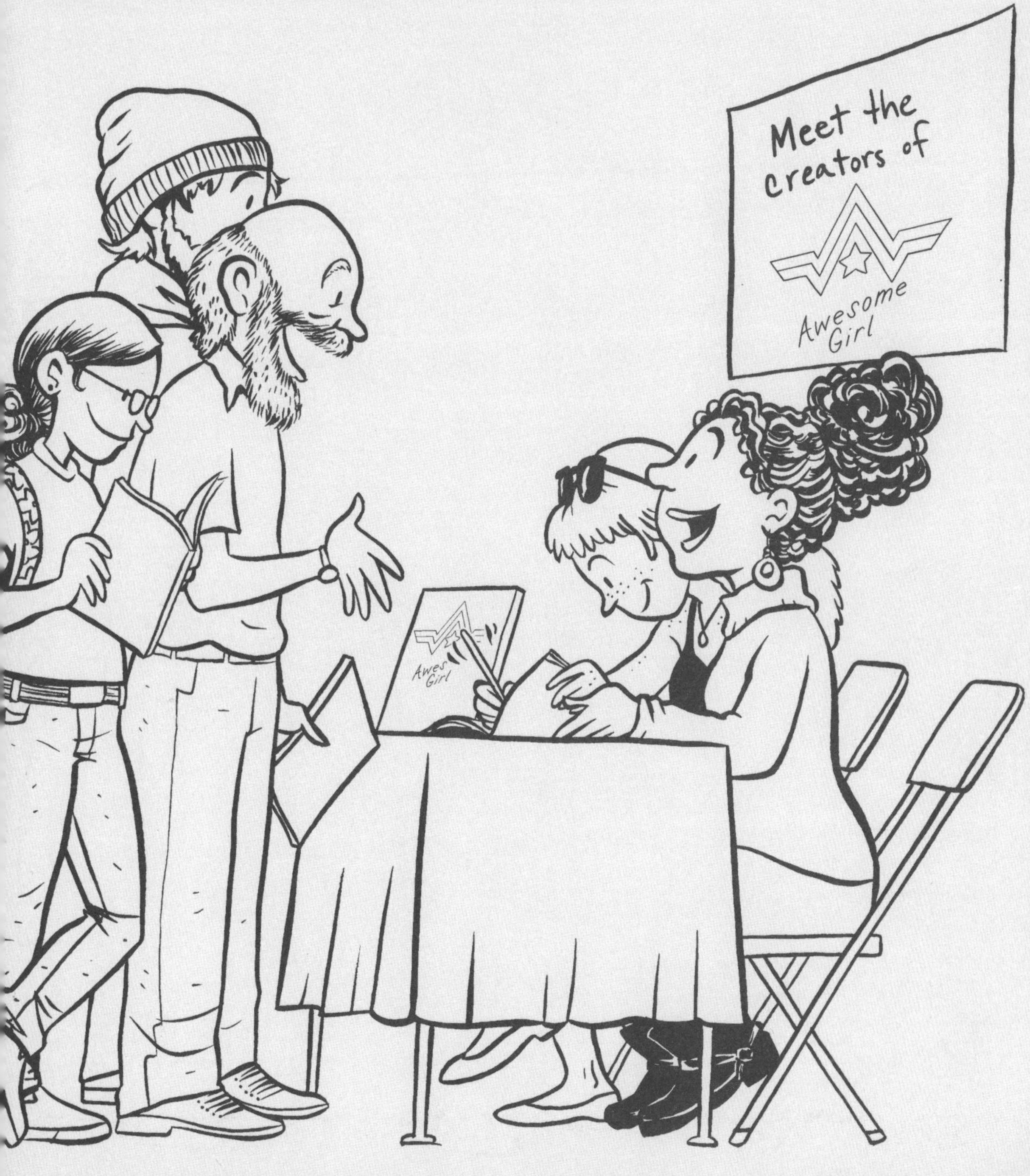
Meet the creators of
Awesome Girl

THE BEST AMERICAN

Comics 2014

GUEST EDITORS OF THE
BEST AMERICAN COMICS

2006 HARVEY PEKAR
2007 CHRIS WARE
2008 LYNDA BARRY
2009 CHARLES BURNS
2010 NEIL GAIMAN
2011 ALISON BECHDEL
2012 FRANÇOISE MOULY
2013 JEFF SMITH
2014 SCOTT McCLOUD

THE BEST AMERICAN

Comics

2014

EDITED *and* INTRODUCED
by Scott McCloud

BILL KARTALOPOULOS,
series editor

HOUGHTON MIFFLIN HARCOURT
BOSTON · NEW YORK   2014

www.hmhco.com

Library of Congress Cataloging-in-Publication Data is available.

ISBN 978-0-544-10600-0

Book design: David Futato
Endpaper art: Raina Telgemeier
Cover design: Jaime Hernandez
Cover art direction: Christopher Moisan
Cover color: Jordan Crane

PRINTED IN THE UNITED STATES OF AMERICA

DOC 10 9 8 7 6 5 4 3 2 1

Permissions credits are located on page 380.

Contents

Foreword

As the new series editor for the Best American Comics, I would assert that this series is, at its best, a utopian project.

Of course, I can also attest that working on a Best American series sometimes feels like a complicated juggling act, negotiating constraints of chronology, geography, time, access, page count, and subjectivity toward the difficult goal of representing the year's best work in one annual volume. But after all is said and done, the final result of this particular process remains astonishingly idealistic, especially in light of comics' recent history.

More often than not, ambitious, artistic comics have been a marginal endeavor. In the 1980s and 1990s, now-acclaimed artists, including Chris Ware, Dan Clowes, Joe Sacco, Julie Doucet, and the Hernandez brothers, worked in relative obscurity, their comics published by small, independent presses that, at the time, enjoyed little distribution or support outside of a network of specialty comic book stores. With only a few exceptions (particularly Art Spiegelman's *Maus*), this was the status quo until the turn of the new millennium. At that time, a number of progressive individuals within the established publishing industry (most notably Chip Kidd at Pantheon) championed the critical mass of truly great work that had blossomed in the margins and began to publish artistic, expressive comics in bookstore-friendly formats through mainstream channels. This push, combined with a contemporaneous enthusiasm for translated Japanese *manga*, had a number of positive, permanent effects that established comics (or "graphic novels") as a stable category of publishing and bookselling. The Best American Comics series is, itself, one of the happy products of this recent revolution.

The North American publishing industry's initial engagement with comics gave rise to a fertile, unpredictable period of experimentation that briefly saw many idiosyncratic, unconventional works enter the broader marketplace. For some, it felt as if comics had finally arrived, and in many key ways they had. But access to the marketplace of mainstream culture carries with it certain perceived requirements, and as the graphic novel category has stabilized, publishers have, as publishers do, analyzed successes and failures with an eye on an efficient bottom line. So in recent years corporate book publishers have increasingly focused on proven artists and genres, largely eschewing the wide-open experimentation that fundamentally created this category fourteen short years ago. Some of the smaller, long-standing independent presses have managed to sustain their growth and have gained more powerful bookstore distribution; they now continue to delicately balance artistic freedom with commercial viability on a larger, more public stage. Many aesthetically adventurous comics have simply gone back underground, available principally through selective comic book stores, at independent comics festivals, and directly to readers through online ordering. And for countless artists, online media platforms are currently the final word in low- (or no-) cost self-publishing.

Comics are fortunate to have been included in the Best American series for a number of reasons. For one thing, comics' ongoing inclusion in a larger project that also recognizes outstanding short fiction, essays, and more reaffirms comics' important and coequal status among culturally significant literary forms. Additionally, while networked technology has wonderfully democratized expressions of opinion, taste, and critical analysis (see the flood of year-end "best of" lists online), the Best American Comics, by virtue of its careful process, lush presentation, and visibility, articulates a particularly forceful notion of critical distinction that, at its best, can elevate the field.

Within all of that, the element that truly characterizes the Best American Comics series as a utopian project is the total and fundamental openness of its purview: any kind of work can make it into this book. The Best American Comics, as the project of a major book publisher, enjoys lavish production values, wide distribution, and noticeable publicity. But the works represented in the book might originate from any area of the comics field: from major publishing houses and newspaper pages to boutique specialty presses, self-published 'zines, and online media.

As a case in point, this year's volume includes self-published comics that have enjoyed limited distribution to date; it includes work that has, so far, only been published online via platforms like Tumblr; and it includes an excerpt from a one-of-a-kind book object that has, before now, only been visible to the general public as scans on a blog. In the Best American Comics, these works and more all take their place alongside comics by well-known artists from established publishers. It is a rare thing for a project with so much commercial support to enjoy such editorial freedom—especially now, as the publishing industry faces new challenges—and while it should be less rare, it should not be taken for granted.

The Best American Comics 2014 presents a selection of North American comics first published between September 1, 2012, and August 31, 2013. I believe that any reader who is closely familiar with contemporary comics would likely agree that this volume of Best

American Comics represents, as much as any individual volume can, a broad snapshot of the field over the past year. At the risk of sounding presumptuous, I would suggest that this particular volume may represent the aesthetic diversity of comics today even better than the graphic novel section of many stores in which this book might be found. Somewhat romantically, I hope that this book may plant a seed that will transform the landscape around it.

For years I've obsessively pursued the impossible goal of knowing about "all the good comics." My first public activity was a blog that tracked new developments in comics in the eventful early 2000s. This started me down a road that led to a variety of fruitful experiences, including assistant work for Art Spiegelman, critical writing, curating comics-related exhibits, lecturing around the world, and teaching about comics on the undergraduate and graduate levels. But the work that's been most directly applicable to my editing here has been my work organizing comics festivals. Since 2006 I've run programming for SPX: The Small Press Expo, and in 2009 I cofounded the Brooklyn Comics and Graphics Festival, which ran for four years and focused on the vital, international grassroots while tracing the places where fine arts and comics meet. In 2014 I directed programming for the MoCCA festival in New York City, which features a large and varied pool of established and developing comics artists. All of this activity and more has given me intimate contact with the wild diversity of the comics field, but even still, with more and more artists emerging every day in print and online, it's harder than ever to try to keep track of everything.

As series editor, I receive hundreds of submissions in the mail and in person at comics festivals; additionally, I keep my eyes open for new work at comic book stores, at events, online, and via recommendations from colleagues. It is my great privilege to read and consider all of the work that comes to me, and from this large pool I select a diverse body of excellent work to forward to each year's guest editor for consideration. From this selection, the guest editor must then choose the comparatively small number of pieces that will be published in the Best American Comics (while retaining the latitude to include some work they may have discovered on their own).

This year's volume so thoroughly demonstrates the series' ability to recognize quality across the entire field because of the unique contribution of this year's guest editor, Scott McCloud. Like every guest editor, Scott brings his own critical tastes to the book in making his final selections. But Scott has uniquely created a space for himself as American comics' most well-known and influential theorist. In his 1993 book, *Understanding Comics*, Scott articulated a broad and insightful analysis of the comics form, informed by a thorough knowledge of comics' past and suggesting a limitless sense of comics' inherent possibilities. Similarly, Scott has structured this year's volume to indicate vital areas of expression within the comics landscape as he sees it today, each represented by the work he responded to most strongly as an engaged reader.

I will continue to seek exciting new work to submit to future guest editors for upcoming volumes of the Best American Comics series, but I cannot stress enough that the best way to bring work to our attention is to submit material via our public postal address. All work that we receive will be read and considered, and the continued scope and diversity of the series is very much dependent upon this submission process. Any artist or publisher who wishes to submit material for consideration should please send work clearly labeled with publication date and contact information to the following address:

Bill Kartalopoulos
Series Editor
The Best American Comics
Houghton Mifflin Harcourt Publishing Company
215 Park Avenue South
New York, NY 10003

By the time this volume is published, we will have already collected work to consider for *The Best American Comics 2015* and will be actively seeking work published between September 1, 2014, and August 31, 2015, for the 2016 volume. More information about submission guidelines can be found online at: www.hmhbooks.com/hmh/bestamerican/comics.

Because we can represent only a sample of all of the great work published every year, each volume in this series also includes a lengthy list of additional notable comics. This list can be found in the back of this book, and all of the comics named there are worth seeking out and exploring if you have enjoyed any of the work presented here. Following a practice initiated in previous volumes, I have posted an online version of this list to my website (www.on-panel.com), which includes links to further information about this year's notable comics.

One additional custom I would like to observe is to thank some of the many people who made this book possible. First, I would like to thank my predecessors, Matt Madden and Jessica Abel, who shepherded this series admirably through six volumes and expressed a generous vote of confidence in my abilities by recommending me for the series editor position upon their departure. Jonathan Wilber was Houghton Mifflin Harcourt's in-house editor for the series when we made the transition, and I thank him as well for agreeing to bring me on board. After Jonathan moved on, his role was more than ably filled by Nicole Angeloro, an experienced Best American editor at Houghton Mifflin

Harcourt. Nicole graciously answered my many questions about the process behind this book and helped negotiate some of the trickier terrain involved in this year's volume. Many thanks as well to David Futato, who made the interior of this volume look so good, to Christopher Moisan, who art directed the book's cover and endpapers, to our very efficient production editor Beth Burleigh Fuller, and to Mary Dalton-Hoffman, who deftly handled the complexities of securing permissions for all of the work reprinted here.

I could not be more grateful to Jaime Hernandez for drawing this year's truly gorgeous cover. Jaime, with his brothers Gilbert (also in this volume) and Mario, began drawing beautiful, sophisticated comics for adult readers in their comic book series *Love and Rockets* in the early 1980s. *Love and Rockets* was bravely published by Fantagraphics—led by Gary Groth and Kim Thompson (who sadly passed away in 2013, while we were working on this volume)—at a time when almost no market or context for this kind of work existed in this country. Talk about a utopian project. Thanks as well to Jordan Crane (also a talented cartoonist and printmaker) for providing the brilliant color that makes Jaime's artwork pop. And I'm very grateful to Raina Telgemeier for drawing such lovely endpapers for this volume.

On my end, I'd like to thank Juliette Boutant, my intern from the École européenne supérieure de l'image (EESI) in Angoulême, France. I'm grateful to the organizers of the MoCCA, TCAF, and Autoptic comics festivals who facilitated my pursuit of work for consideration. I would like to thank as well the previous guest editors of this series, some of whom shared their experiences with me and provided helpful guidance. Many friends and colleagues contributed good advice and suggestions throughout this process, and I thank them all.

I extend my gratitude, of course, to the many artists and publishers who granted permission to reproduce the work in these pages. Without their cooperation we wouldn't be able to do this every year.

And lastly, I would like to thank this year's guest editor, Scott McCloud. Scott is generous, knowledgeable, thoughtful, funny, forthright, and a pleasure to work with. My periodic conversations with him about this volume and the work under consideration have been among my most cherished memories of the past year.

That's enough from me. Enjoy the comics. I'll see you here again next year with something completely different.

BILL KARTALOPOULOS

Please
READ

do not
BROWSE

The following comics selections and text explanations are meant to be read in the same order in which they're presented here. Please consider doing so, and honoring the affection, careful planning, and borderline obsessive-compulsive disorder that went into the creation of the book you hold in your hands.

Thank you.

Scott McCloud
Guest Editor

THE BEST AMERICAN

Comics 2014

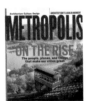

Great Comics—

Say their names with me: Harvey Pekar, Chris Ware, Lynda Barry, Charles Burns, Neil Gaiman, Alison Bechdel, Françoise Mouly, Jeff Smith. They're the past guest editors of the Best American Comics series; great cartoonists, writers, editors all. Yet every one of them had to capitulate to the same shameful ritual I must now reenact: the public recitation of the Ode to Futility. So here's mine in a concise, easily skipped paragraph.

"Best" is hopelessly subjective, good stuff was left out due to arbitrary circumstance, your editor meant well but probably shouldn't be trusted on critical matters of judgment, the idea that either Series Editor Bill Kartalopoulos or I actually read every single comic published between September 1, 2012, and August 31, 2013, is laughable (although Bill, mensch that he is, may have gotten close), the meaning of "American" would take about ten thousand words to explain, it's all a sham, woe is me, all human endeavor is meaningless.

That done, I want you to know, in all sincerity, that I *love* what we found for this volume, as I loved much of what we had to leave aside. And I'm grateful for the opportunity to paint this fleeting, accidental portrait of comics today through the alchemic pairings these stories produced.

This volume is a little different than in the past. I've divided our stories into ten sections, offering a short introduction for each. Each section is built around a unifying theme, and it's been fun watching the stories in each group talk to each other at night, find common ground, share a smoke, hook up in the broom closet—even when their authors arose from wildly different schools of writing and art. Take this first section, for example, the one I referred to in my notes as "The Usual Suspects."

After nearly a decade, we've grown accustomed to certain names, styles, and sensibilities when approaching each new volume of the Best American Comics. Y'know, the reliable, award-winning Mount Olympus of North American underground, alternative, and art comics. If R. Crumb, Chris Ware, or Daniel Clowes have major work out in a given year (two out of three this time), of course they'll be included. Ware doesn't stop being a great cartoonist just because he's been called one too often—despite what that dickhead in line at Starbucks might've said—and there's no reason an editor should resort to quotas to "keep things fresh" if it means bypassing inarguably great work.

But comics-watchers like myself sometimes worry that a kind of shadow genre is forming in the minds of some readers: "Great Comics" as a stylistic category of its own, some-

—Are Not a Genre

thing we can recognize at a glance, to speed our buying/surfing decisions and dismiss whatever doesn't fit the mold.

Is the story built around quiet everyday events or autobiography? Check. Does it have a dark satiric undercurrent? Check. Does our protagonist have a low opinion of him/herself? Check. Is there a complete absence of anything that might remotely remind you of a superhero comic? Check.

Some great comics do actually fit into this mold, but some mediocre comics do too. We can't categorically embrace or reject such qualities. These are just the markings of a tribe like any other, showing a rich family tree of influences: a little Kurtzman or Crumb here, a little Pekar or Spiegelman there, all contributing traits that have been passed down through generations.

Bill K. and I wanted to include a variety of tribes in this volume, to show a broader picture of comics, but even this first section is refreshingly resistant to categorization. Charles Burns's colorful nightmare visions are nothing like the backyard burlesque of the Kominsky & Crumb Show. Gilbert Hernandez's memories of growing up in Oxnard are nothing like Ben Katchor's "memories" of lands that never were. And Jaime Hernandez, well. . .

Bill and I were overjoyed when Jaime Hernandez agreed to do the cover for this volume—and even more so when the art came in. There've been rumblings in the comics press lately, thanks to Tom Spurgeon, that we've been taking this amazing artist for granted in recent years. Maybe we have.

While other great North American cartoonists have revved up then cooled down, gotten inspired then gotten sidetracked, Jaime Hernandez simply started making great comics thirty years ago and never, ever stopped—continuously, relentlessly, improving his mastery of the form every step of the way, to the point where he's simply one of the best draftsmen in comics history.

Together with brothers Gilbert and (occasionally) Mario, Los Bros Hernandez never quite conformed to anybody's preconceived checklist, but their comics remained undeniably great throughout the years. More, they were American originals in ways few artists can claim, and a Big Bang for the generation that followed them, as much as Crumb, Kirby, or Spiegelman were for theirs.

Pull out your telescopes and watch these crazy universes expand.

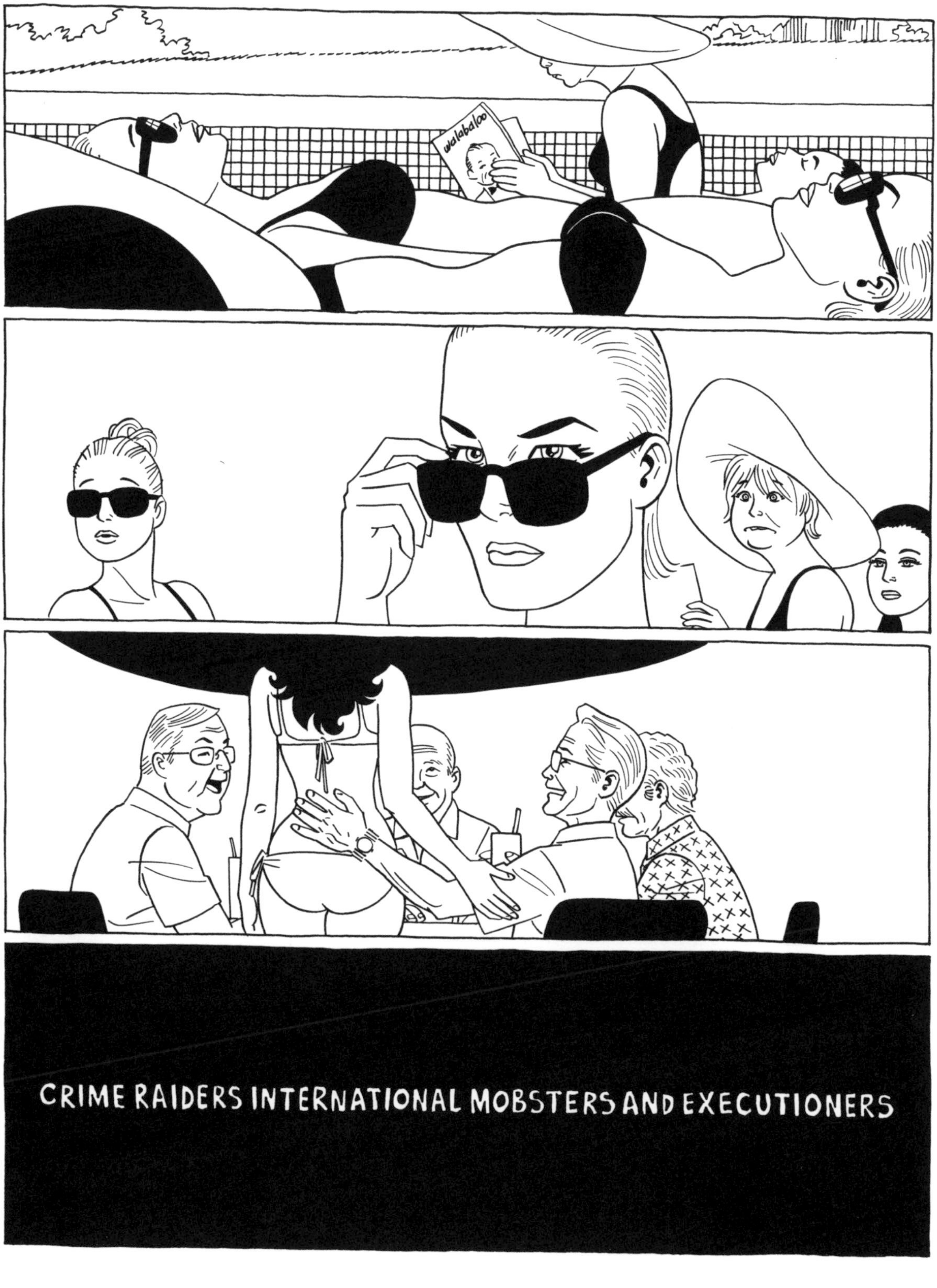
walabaloo
CRIME RAIDERS INTERNATIONAL MOBSTERS AND EXECUTIONERS

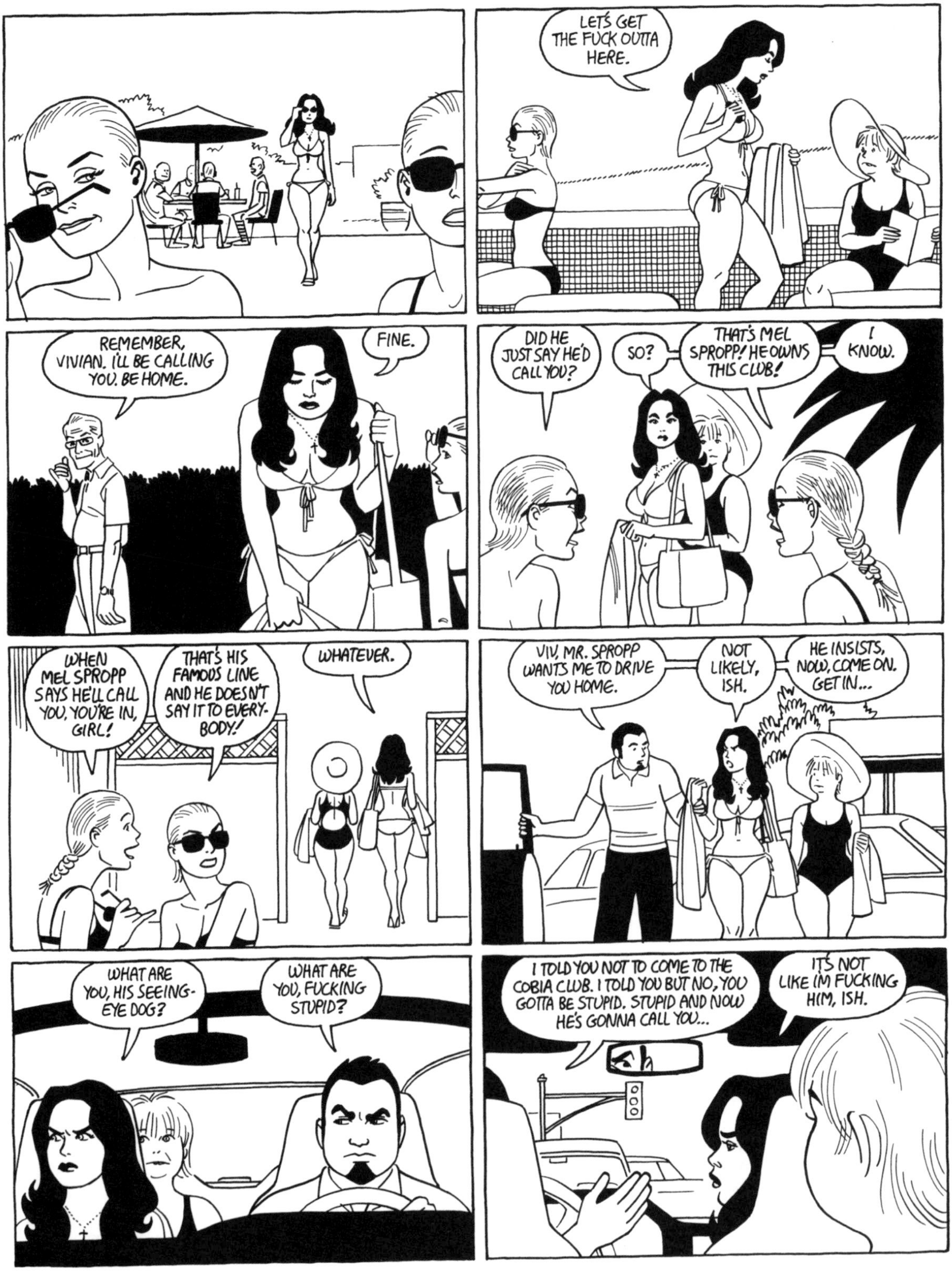
LET'S GET THE FUCK OUTTA HERE.
REMEMBER, VIVIAN. I'LL BE CALLING YOU. BE HOME.
FINE.
DID HE JUST SAY HE'D CALL YOU?
SO?
THAT'S MEL SPROPP! HE OWNS THIS CLUB!
I KNOW.
WHEN MEL SPROPP SAYS HE'LL CALL YOU, YOU'RE IN, GIRL!
THAT'S HIS FAMOUS LINE AND HE DOESN'T SAY IT TO EVERYBODY!
WHATEVER.
VIV, MR. SPROPP WANTS ME TO DRIVE YOU HOME.
NOT LIKELY, ISH.
HE INSISTS, NOW, COME ON. GET IN...
WHAT ARE YOU, HIS SEEING-EYE DOG?
WHAT ARE YOU, FUCKING STUPID?
I TOLD YOU NOT TO COME TO THE COBIA CLUB. I TOLD YOU BUT NO, YOU GOTTA BE STUPID. STUPID AND NOW HE'S GONNA CALL YOU...
IT'S NOT LIKE I'M FUCKING HIM, ISH.

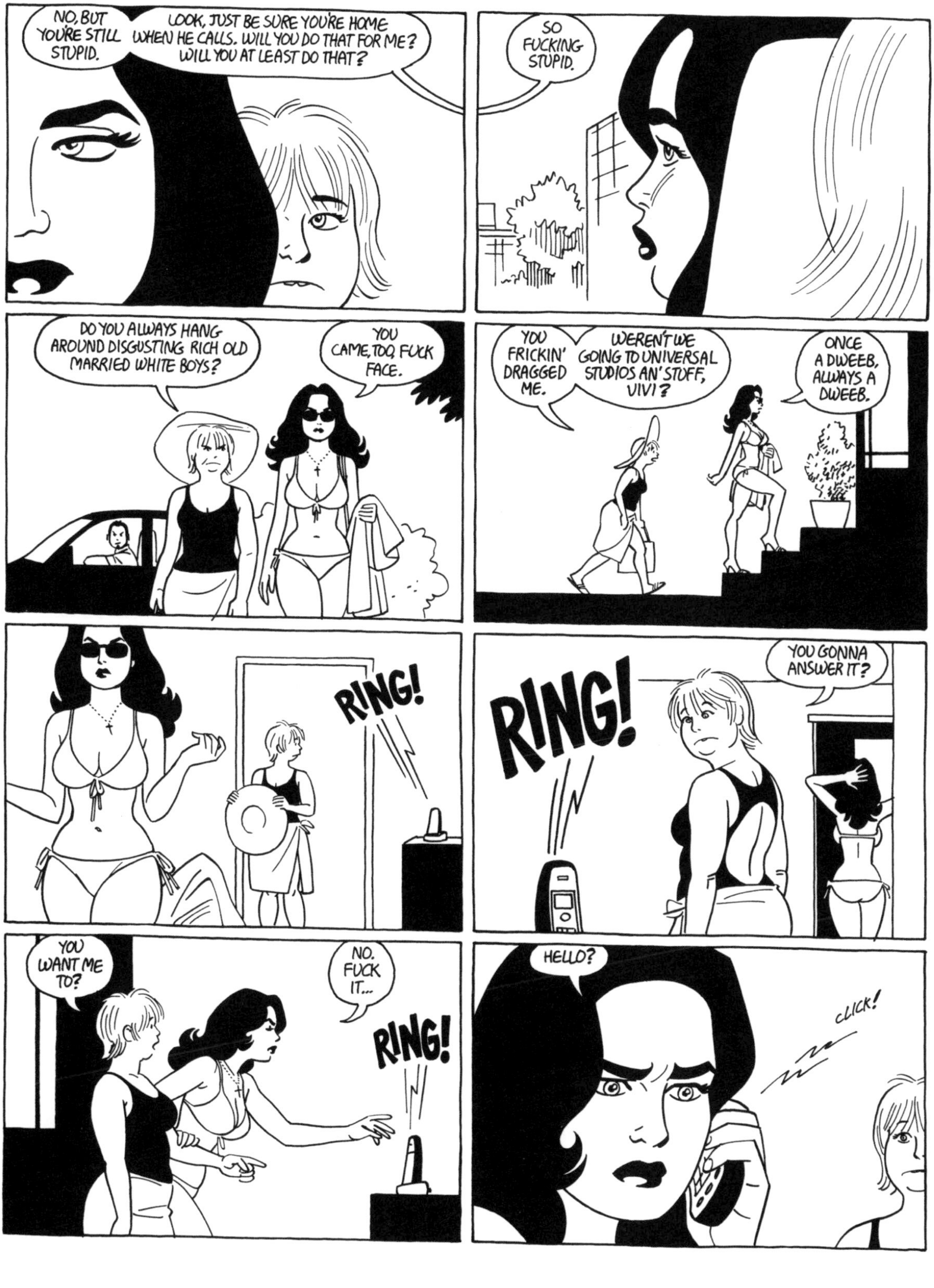
NO, BUT YOU'RE STILL STUPID.
LOOK, JUST BE SURE YOU'RE HOME WHEN HE CALLS. WILL YOU DO THAT FOR ME? WILL YOU AT LEAST DO THAT?
SO FUCKING STUPID.
DO YOU ALWAYS HANG AROUND DISGUSTING RICH OLD MARRIED WHITE BOYS?
YOU CAME, TOO, FUCK FACE.
YOU FRICKIN' DRAGGED ME.
WEREN'T WE GOING TO UNIVERSAL STUDIOS AN' STUFF, VIVI?
ONCE A DWEEB, ALWAYS A DWEEB.
RING!
RING!
YOU GONNA ANSWER IT?
YOU WANT ME TO?
NO. FUCK IT...
RING!
HELLO?
CLICK!

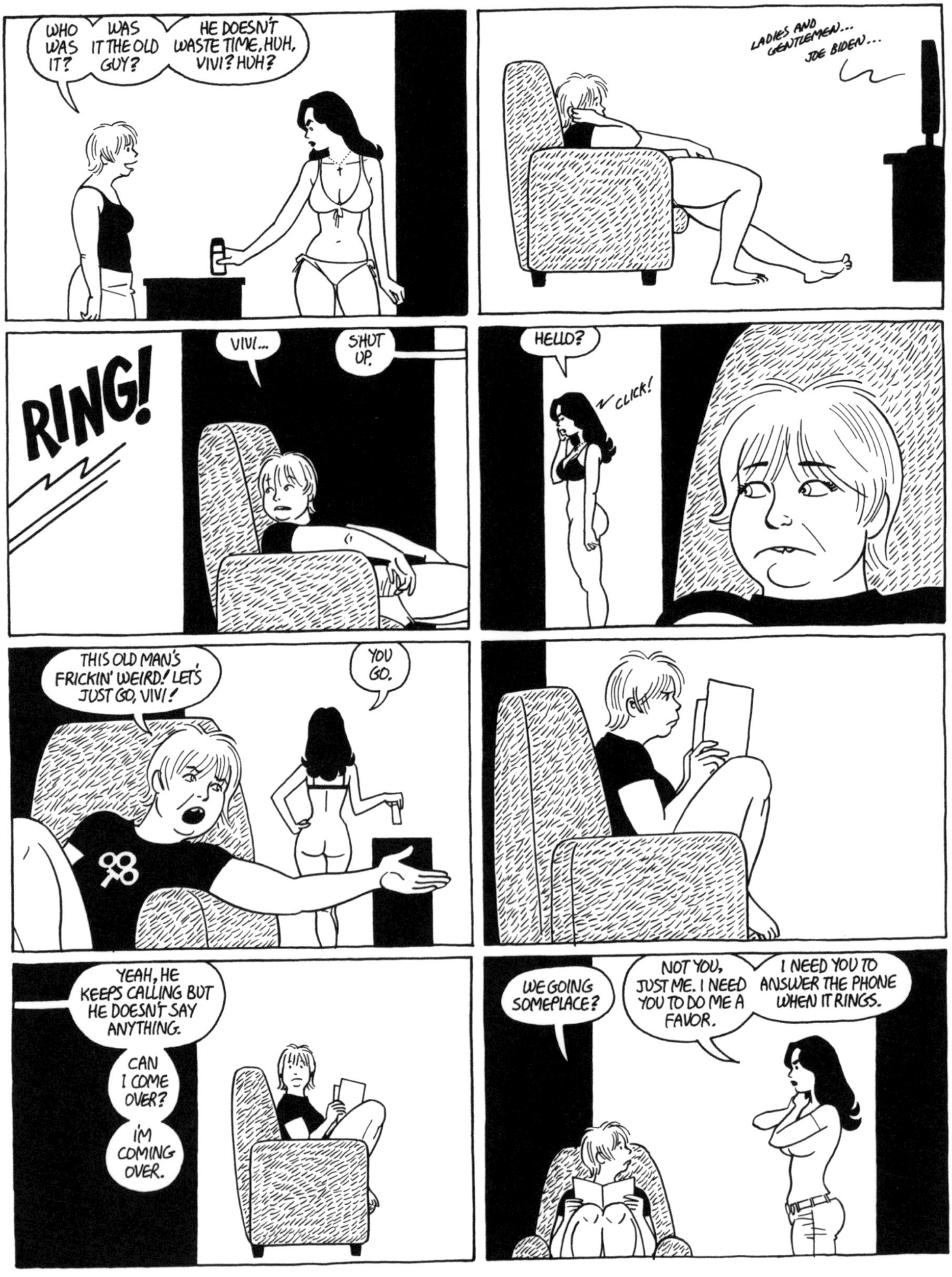
WHO WAS IT?
WAS IT THE OLD GUY?
HE DOESN'T WASTE TIME, HUH, VIVI? HUH?
LADIES AND GENTLEMEN... JOE BIDEN...
RING!
VIVI...
SHUT UP.
HELLO?
CLICK!
THIS OLD MAN'S FRICKIN' WEIRD! LET'S JUST GO, VIVI!
YOU GO.
YEAH, HE KEEPS CALLING BUT HE DOESN'T SAY ANYTHING.
CAN I COME OVER?
I'M COMING OVER.
WE GOING SOMEPLACE?
NOT YOU, JUST ME. I NEED YOU TO DO ME A FAVOR.
I NEED YOU TO ANSWER THE PHONE WHEN IT RINGS.

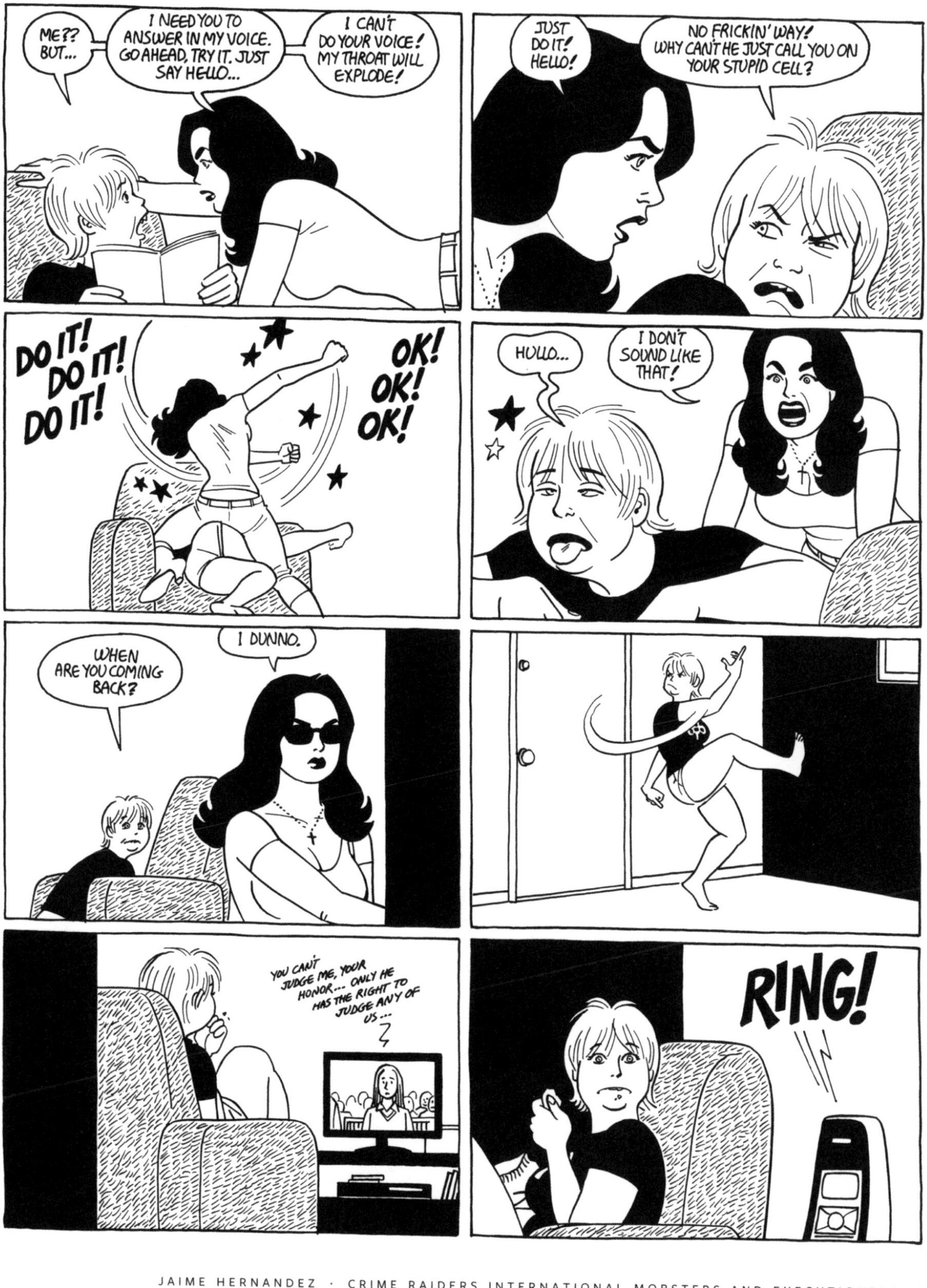
ME?? BUT...
I NEED YOU TO ANSWER IN MY VOICE. GO AHEAD, TRY IT. JUST SAY HELLO...
I CAN'T DO YOUR VOICE! MY THROAT WILL EXPLODE!
JUST DO IT! HELLO!
NO FRICKIN' WAY! WHY CAN'T HE JUST CALL YOU ON YOUR STUPID CELL?
DO IT! DO IT! DO IT!
OK! OK! OK!
HULLO...
I DON'T SOUND LIKE THAT!
WHEN ARE YOU COMING BACK?
I DUNNO.
YOU CAN'T JUDGE ME, YOUR HONOR... ONLY HE HAS THE RIGHT TO JUDGE ANY OF US...
RING!

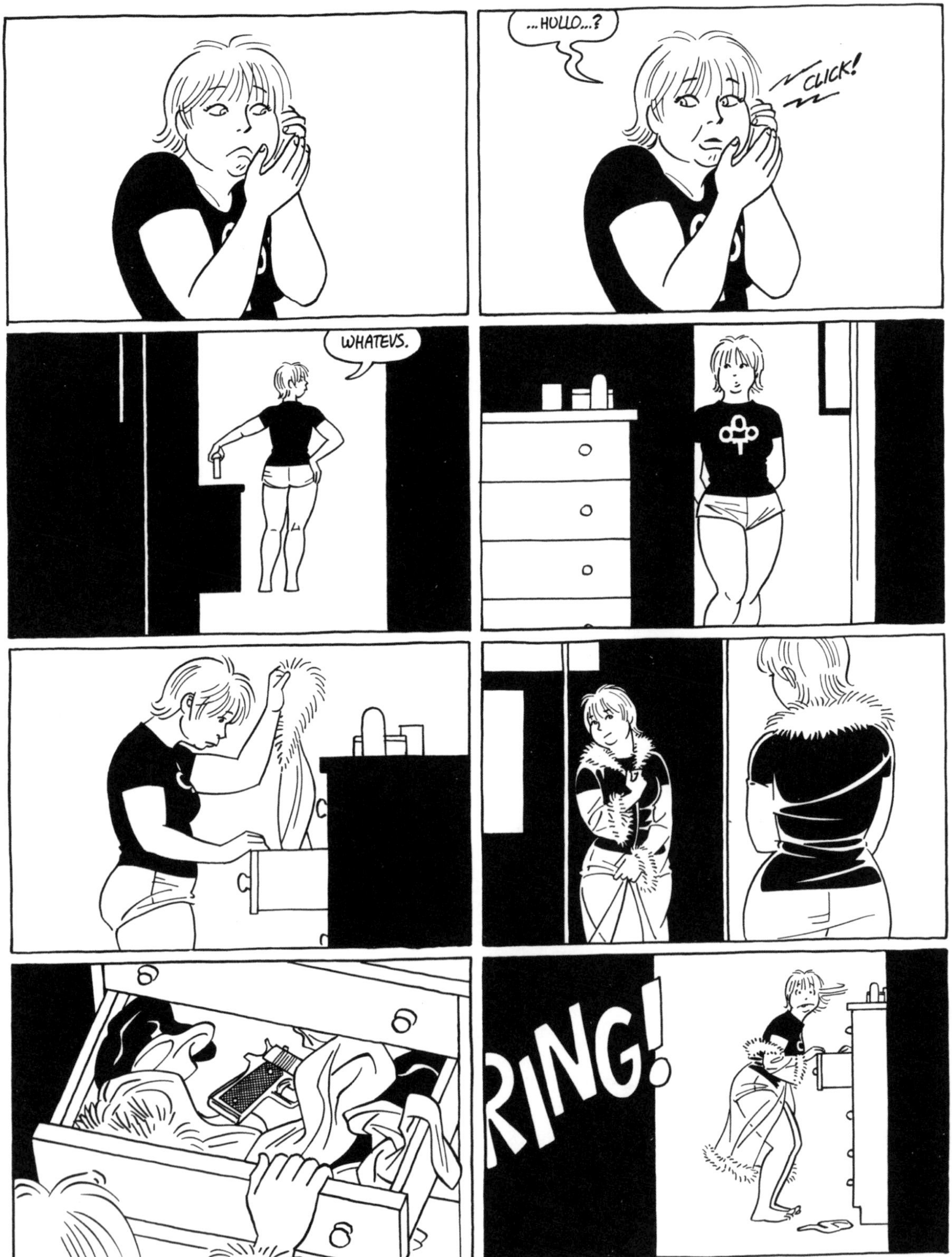
...HULLO...?
CLICK!
WHATEVS.
RING!

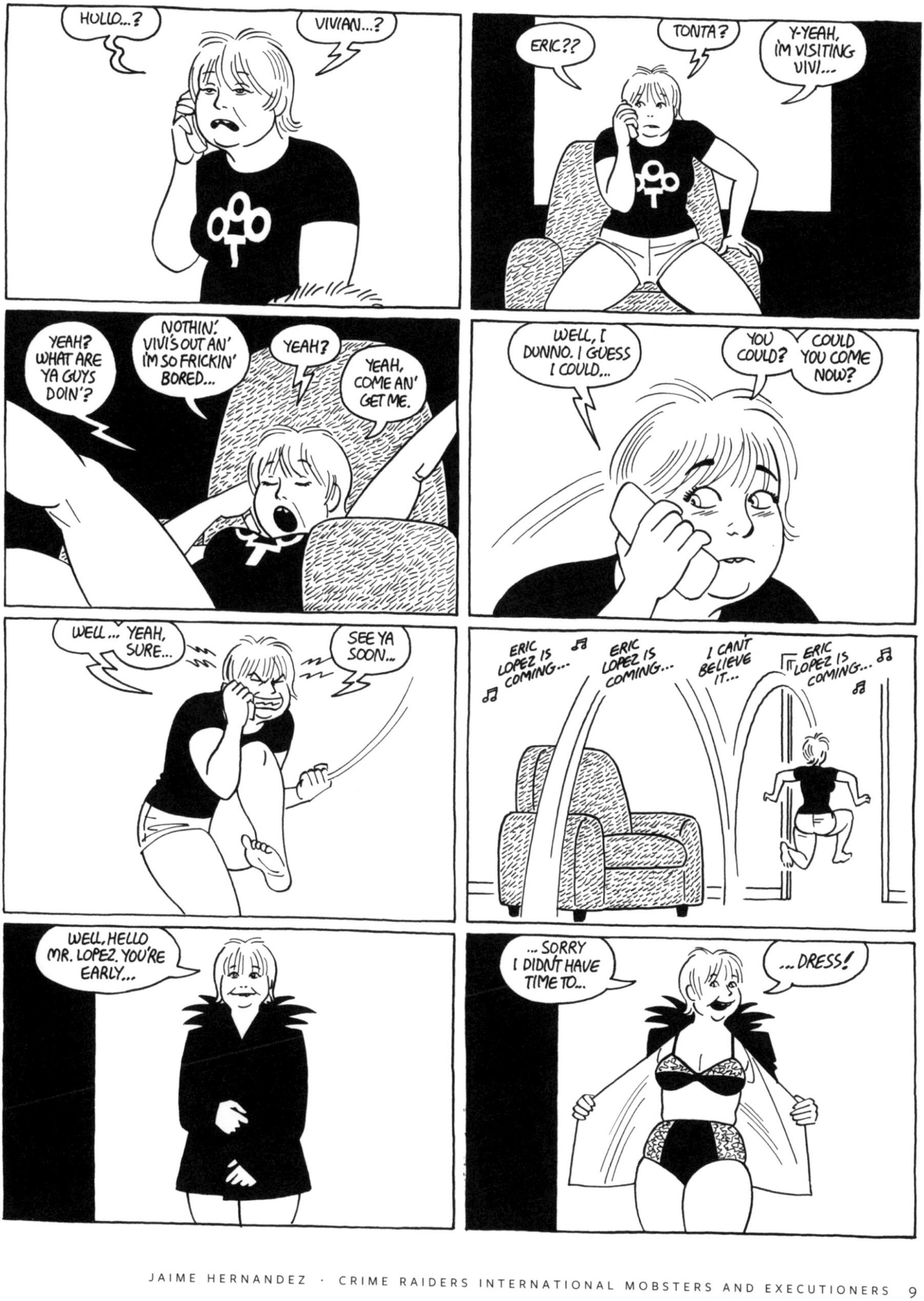
HULLO...?
VIVIAN...?
ERIC??
TONTA?
Y-YEAH, I'M VISITING VIVI...
YEAH? WHAT ARE YA GUYS DOIN'?
NOTHIN'. VIVI'S OUT AN' I'M SO FRICKIN' BORED...
YEAH?
YEAH, COME AN' GET ME.
WELL, I DUNNO. I GUESS I COULD...
YOU COULD?
COULD YOU COME NOW?
WELL... YEAH, SURE...
SEE YA SOON...
ERIC LOPEZ IS COMING...
ERIC LOPEZ IS COMING...
I CAN'T BELIEVE IT...
ERIC LOPEZ IS COMING...
WELL, HELLO MR. LOPEZ. YOU'RE EARLY...
...SORRY I DIDN'T HAVE TIME TO...
...DRESS!

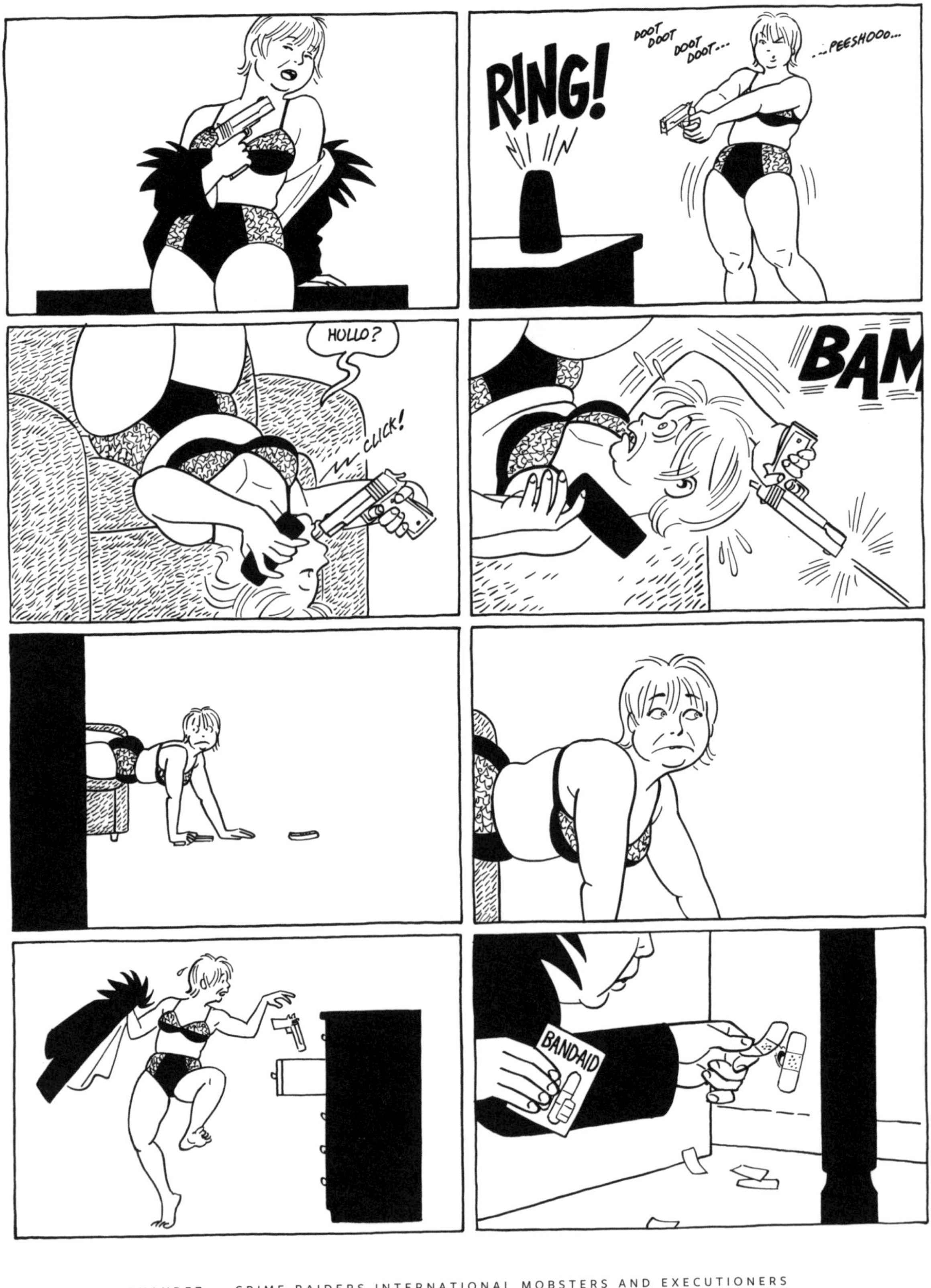
RING!
DOOT DOOT DOOT DOOT...
...PEESHOOO...
HULLO?
CLICK!
BAM
BANDAID

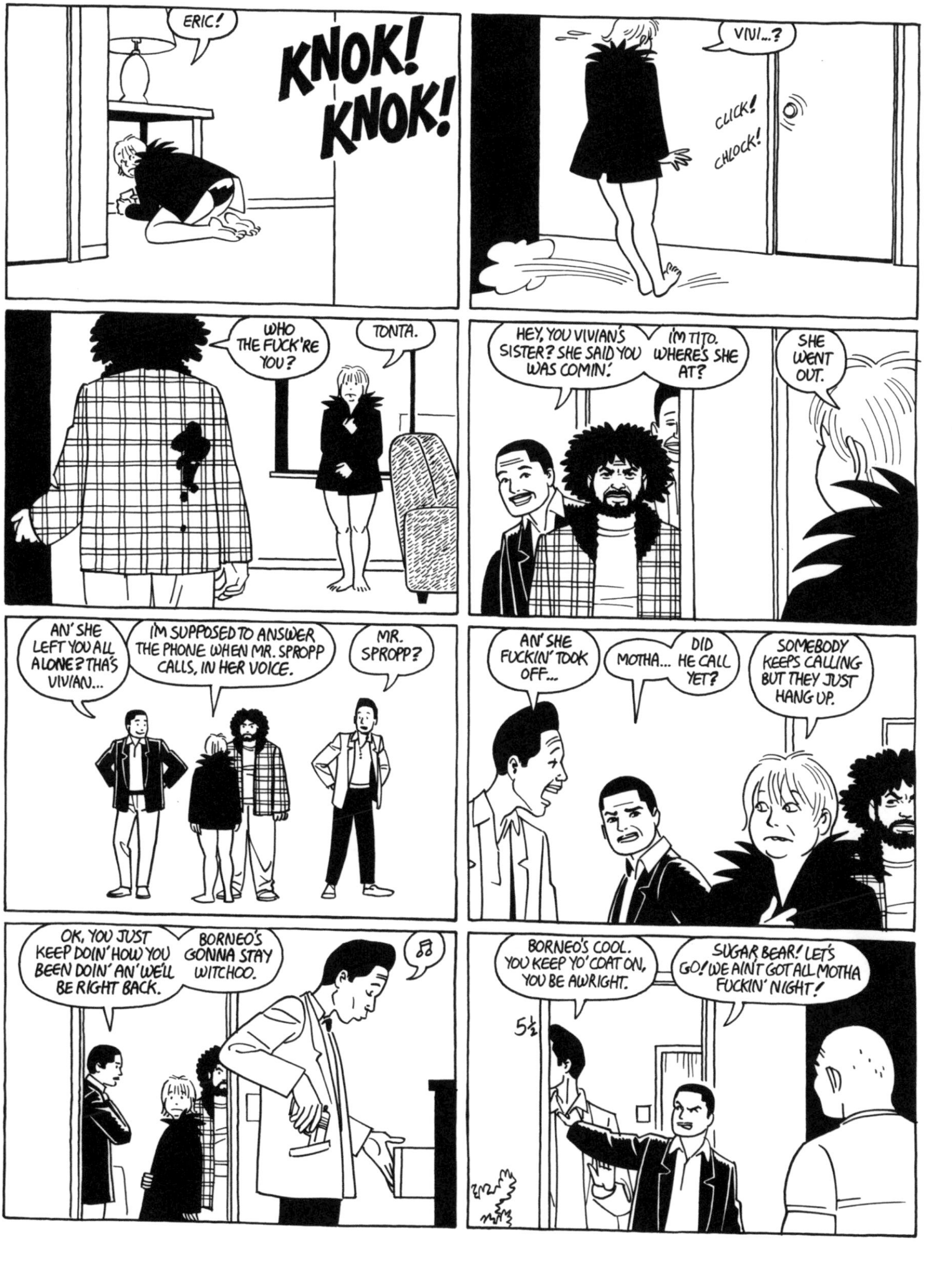
ERIC!
KNOK! KNOK!
VIVI...?
CLICK! CHLOCK!
WHO THE FUCK'RE YOU?
TONTA.
HEY, YOU VIVIAN'S SISTER? SHE SAID YOU WAS COMIN'.
I'M TITO. WHERE'S SHE AT?
SHE WENT OUT.
AN' SHE LEFT YOU ALL ALONE? THA'S VIVIAN...
I'M SUPPOSED TO ANSWER THE PHONE WHEN MR. SPROPP CALLS, IN HER VOICE.
MR. SPROPP?
AN' SHE FUCKIN' TOOK OFF...
MOTHA...
DID HE CALL YET?
SOMEBODY KEEPS CALLING BUT THEY JUST HANG UP.
OK, YOU JUST KEEP DOIN' HOW YOU BEEN DOIN' AN' WE'LL BE RIGHT BACK.
BORNEO'S GONNA STAY WITCHOO.
BORNEO'S COOL. YOU KEEP YO' COAT ON, YOU BE AWRIGHT.
SUGAR BEAR! LET'S GO! WE AIN'T GOT ALL MOTHA FUCKIN' NIGHT!
5½

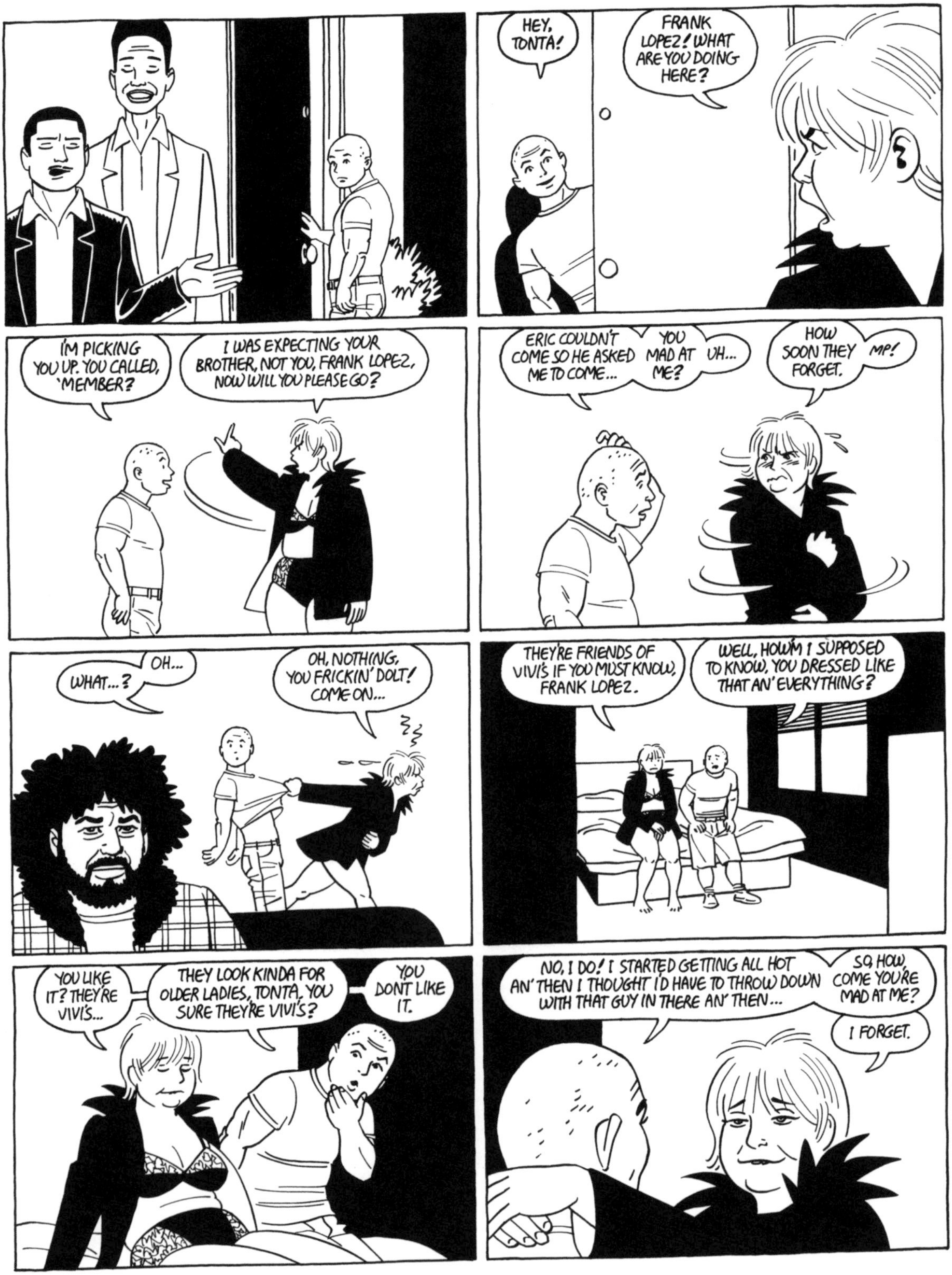
HEY, TONTA!
FRANK LOPEZ! WHAT ARE YOU DOING HERE?
I'M PICKING YOU UP. YOU CALLED, 'MEMBER?
I WAS EXPECTING YOUR BROTHER, NOT YOU, FRANK LOPEZ, NOW WILL YOU PLEASE GO?
ERIC COULDN'T COME SO HE ASKED ME TO COME...
YOU MAD AT ME?
UH...
HOW SOON THEY FORGET.
MP!
WHAT...?
OH...
OH, NOTHING, YOU FRICKIN' DOLT! COME ON...
THEY'RE FRIENDS OF VIVI'S IF YOU MUST KNOW, FRANK LOPEZ.
WELL, HOW'M I SUPPOSED TO KNOW, YOU DRESSED LIKE THAT AN' EVERYTHING?
YOU LIKE IT? THEY'RE VIVI'S...
THEY LOOK KINDA FOR OLDER LADIES, TONTA, YOU SURE THEY'RE VIVI'S?
YOU DONT LIKE IT.
NO, I DO! I STARTED GETTING ALL HOT AN' THEN I THOUGHT I'D HAVE TO THROW DOWN WITH THAT GUY IN THERE AN' THEN...
SO, HOW COME YOU'RE MAD AT ME?
I FORGET.

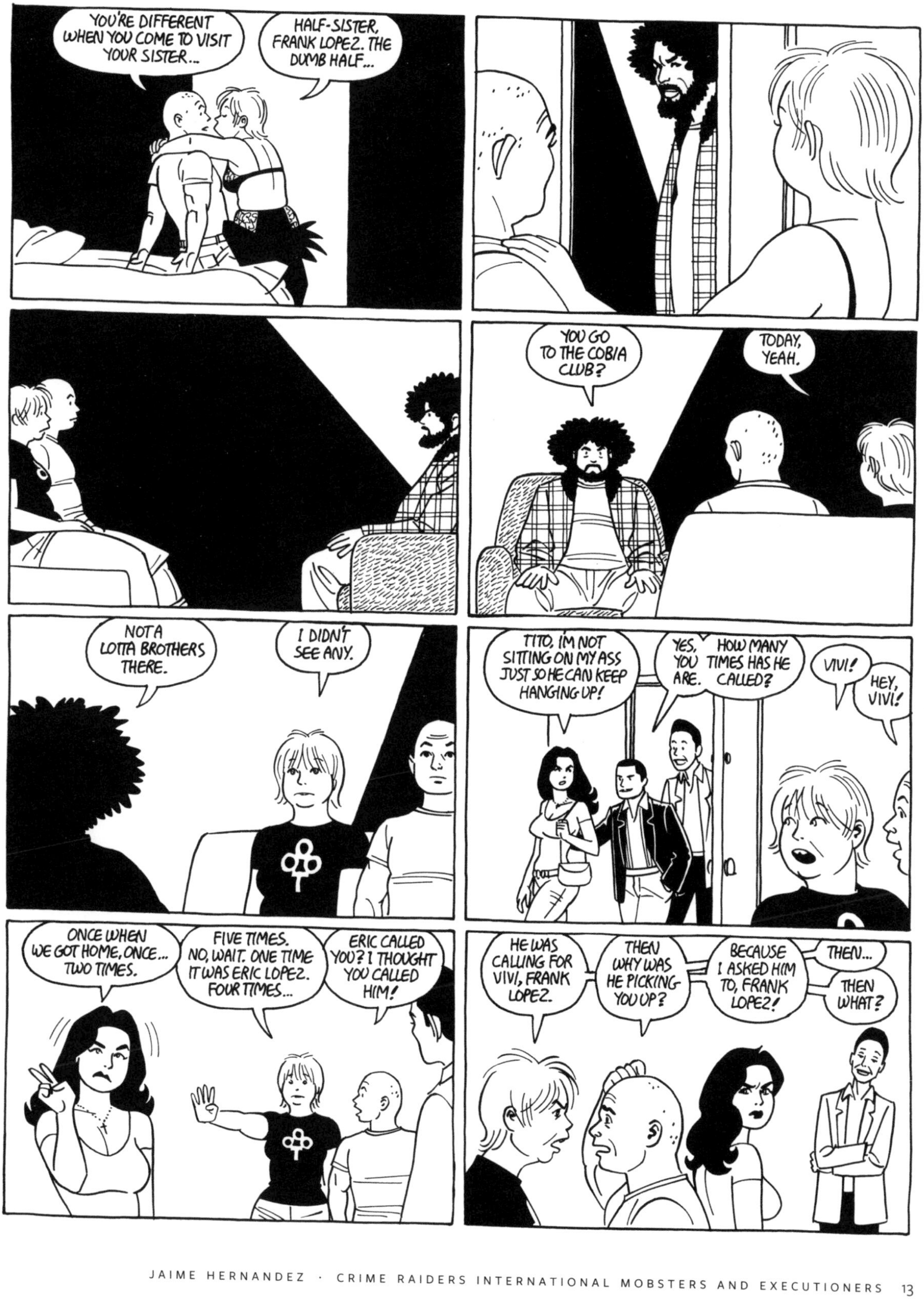
YOU'RE DIFFERENT WHEN YOU COME TO VISIT YOUR SISTER...
HALF-SISTER, FRANK LOPEZ. THE DUMB HALF...
YOU GO TO THE COBIA CLUB?
TODAY, YEAH.
NOT A LOTTA BROTHERS THERE.
I DIDN'T SEE ANY.
TITO, I'M NOT SITTING ON MY ASS JUST SO HE CAN KEEP HANGING UP!
YES, YOU ARE.
HOW MANY TIMES HAS HE CALLED?
VIVI!
HEY, VIVI!
ONCE WHEN WE GOT HOME, ONCE... TWO TIMES.
FIVE TIMES. NO, WAIT. ONE TIME IT WAS ERIC LOPEZ. FOUR TIMES...
ERIC CALLED YOU? I THOUGHT YOU CALLED HIM!
HE WAS CALLING FOR VIVI, FRANK LOPEZ.
THEN WHY WAS HE PICKING YOU UP?
BECAUSE I ASKED HIM TO, FRANK LOPEZ!
THEN...
THEN WHAT?

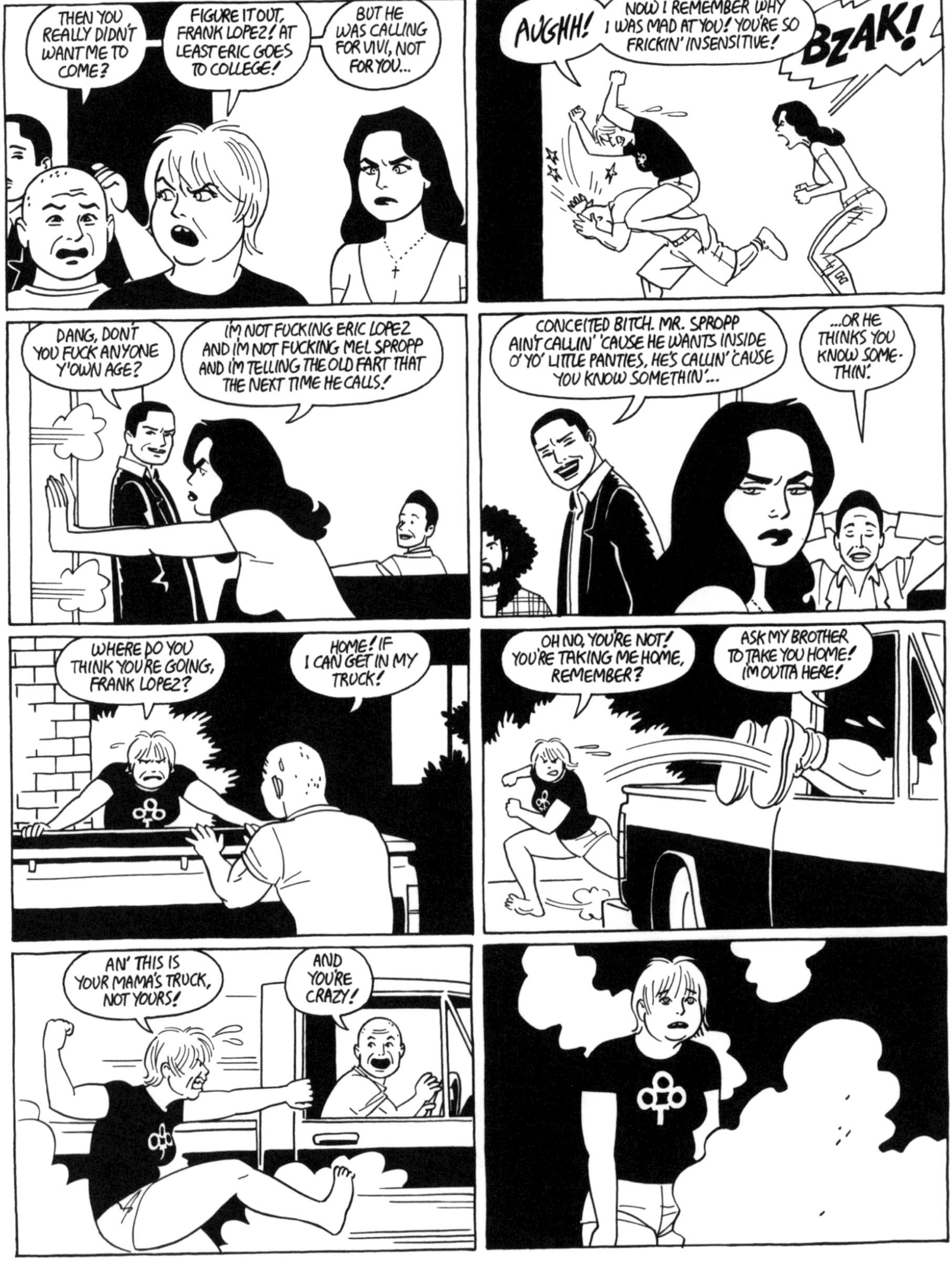
THEN YOU REALLY DIDN'T WANT ME TO COME?
FIGURE IT OUT, FRANK LOPEZ! AT LEAST ERIC GOES TO COLLEGE!
BUT HE WAS CALLING FOR VIVI, NOT FOR YOU...
AUGHH!
NOW I REMEMBER WHY I WAS MAD AT YOU! YOU'RE SO FRICKIN' INSENSITIVE!
BZAK!
DANG, DON'T YOU FUCK ANYONE Y'OWN AGE?
I'M NOT FUCKING ERIC LOPEZ AND I'M NOT FUCKING MEL SPROPP AND I'M TELLING THE OLD FART THAT THE NEXT TIME HE CALLS!
CONCEITED BITCH. MR. SPROPP AIN'T CALLIN' 'CAUSE HE WANTS INSIDE O' YO' LITTLE PANTIES. HE'S CALLIN' 'CAUSE YOU KNOW SOMETHIN'...
...OR HE THINKS YOU KNOW SOME-THIN'.
WHERE DO YOU THINK YOU'RE GOING, FRANK LOPEZ?
HOME! IF I CAN GET IN MY TRUCK!
OH NO, YOU'RE NOT! YOU'RE TAKING ME HOME, REMEMBER?
ASK MY BROTHER TO TAKE YOU HOME! I'M OUTTA HERE!
AN' THIS IS YOUR MAMA'S TRUCK, NOT YOURS!
AND YOU'RE CRAZY!

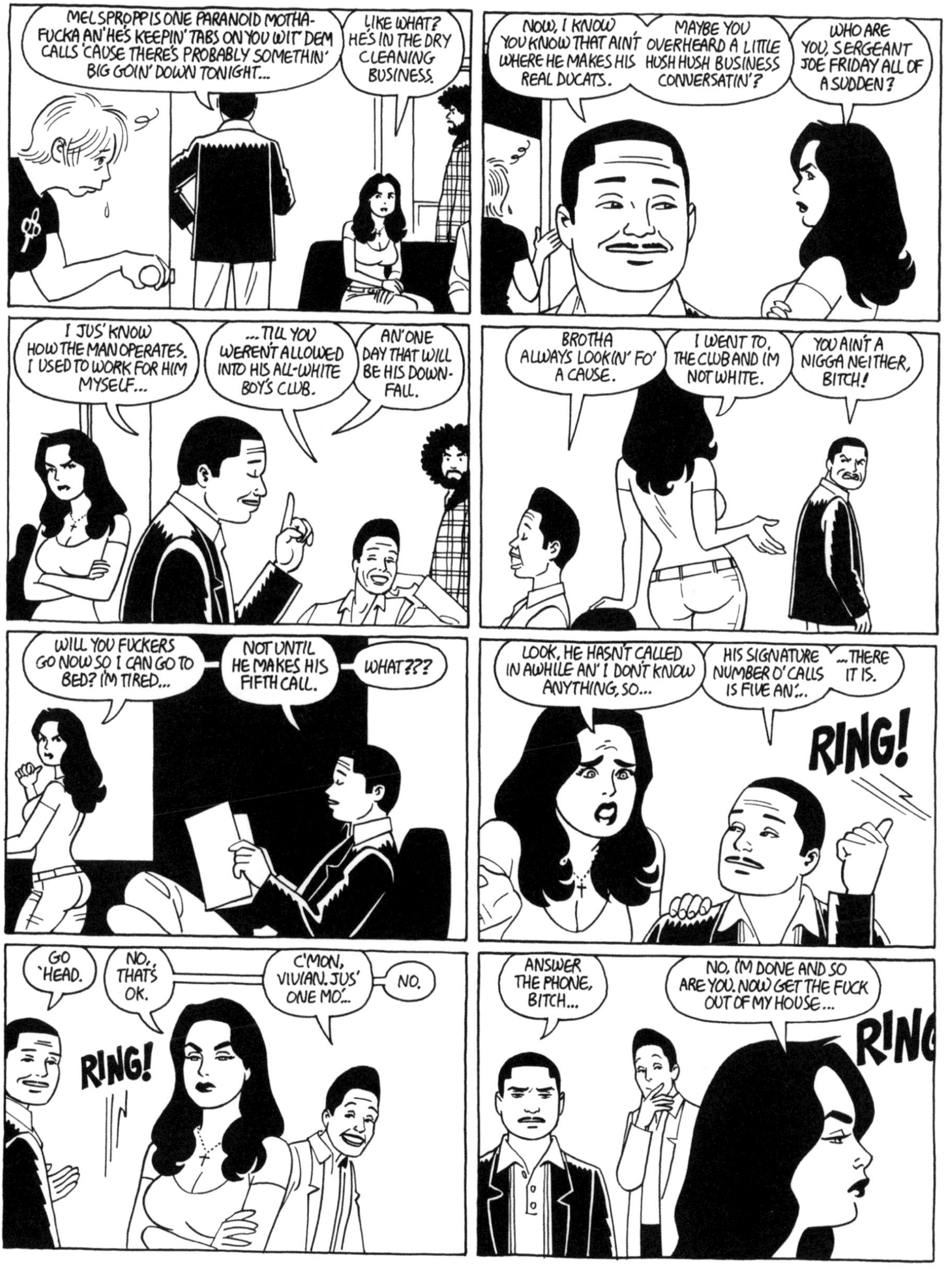
MELSPROPP IS ONE PARANOID MOTHA-FUCKA AN' HE'S KEEPIN' TABS ON YOU WIT' DEM CALLS 'CAUSE THERE'S PROBABLY SOMETHIN' BIG GOIN' DOWN TONIGHT...
LIKE WHAT? HE'S IN THE DRY CLEANING BUSINESS.
NOW, I KNOW YOU KNOW THAT AIN'T WHERE HE MAKES HIS REAL DUCATS.
MAYBE YOU OVERHEARD A LITTLE HUSH HUSH BUSINESS CONVERSATIN'?
WHO ARE YOU, SERGEANT JOE FRIDAY ALL OF A SUDDEN?
I JUS' KNOW HOW THE MAN OPERATES. I USED TO WORK FOR HIM MYSELF...
...TILL YOU WEREN'T ALLOWED INTO HIS ALL-WHITE BOY'S CLUB.
AN' ONE DAY THAT WILL BE HIS DOWN-FALL.
BROTHA ALWAYS LOOKIN' FO' A CAUSE.
I WENT TO THE CLUB AND I'M NOT WHITE.
YOU AIN'T A NIGGA NEITHER, BITCH!
WILL YOU FUCKERS GO NOW SO I CAN GO TO BED? I'M TIRED...
NOT UNTIL HE MAKES HIS FIFTH CALL.
WHAT???
LOOK, HE HASN'T CALLED IN AWHILE AN' I DON'T KNOW ANYTHING, SO...
HIS SIGNATURE NUMBER O' CALLS IS FIVE AN'...
...THERE IT IS.
RING!
GO 'HEAD.
NO, THAT'S OK.
C'MON, VIVIAN. JUS' ONE MO'...
NO.
RING!
ANSWER THE PHONE, BITCH...
NO, I'M DONE AND SO ARE YOU. NOW GET THE FUCK OUT OF MY HOUSE...
RING

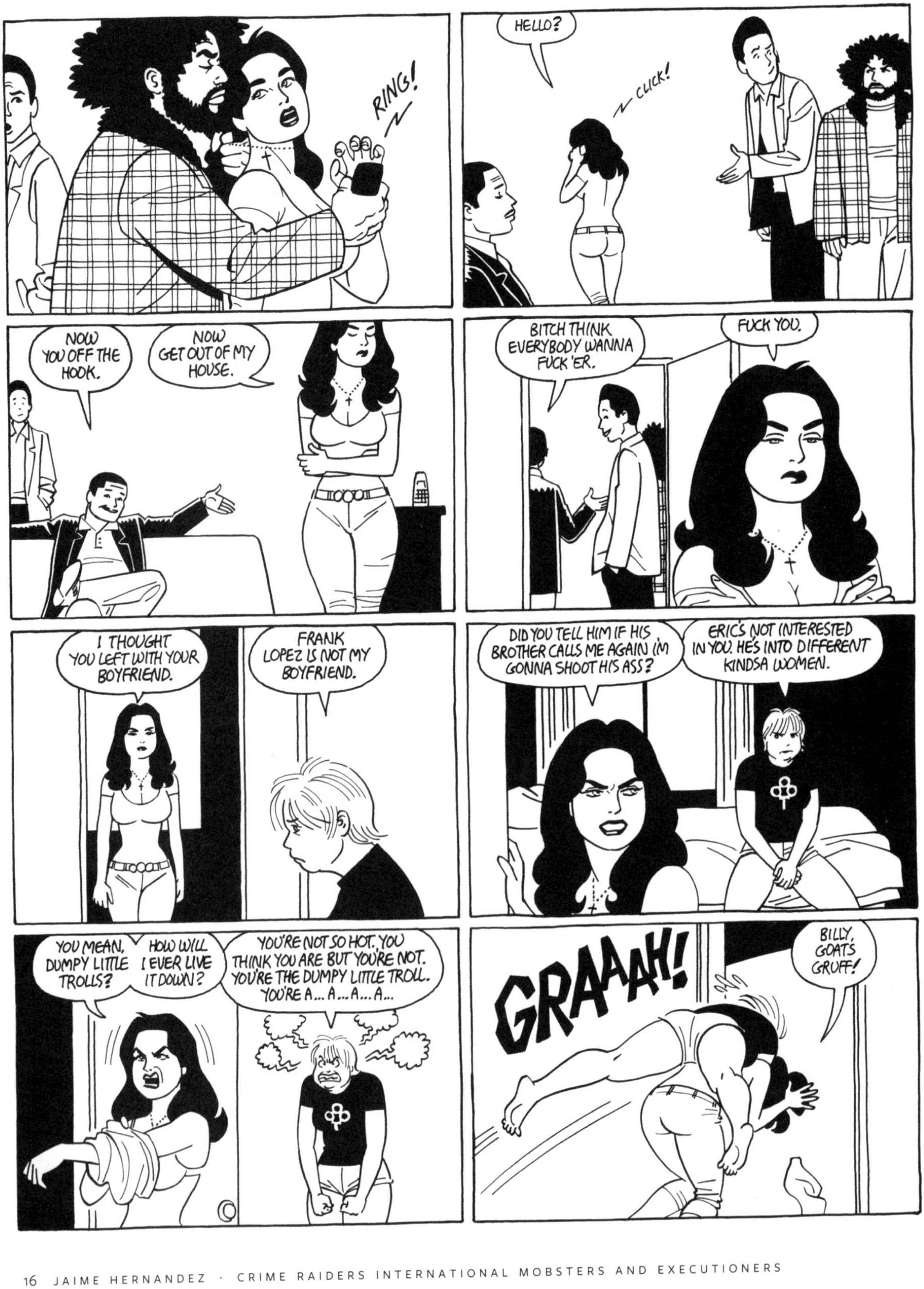
RING!
HELLO?
CLICK!
NOW YOU OFF THE HOOK.
NOW GET OUT OF MY HOUSE.
BITCH THINK EVERYBODY WANNA FUCK 'ER.
FUCK YOU.
I THOUGHT YOU LEFT WITH YOUR BOYFRIEND.
FRANK LOPEZ IS NOT MY BOYFRIEND.
DID YOU TELL HIM IF HIS BROTHER CALLS ME AGAIN I'M GONNA SHOOT HIS ASS?
ERIC'S NOT INTERESTED IN YOU. HE'S INTO DIFFERENT KINDSA WOMEN.
YOU MEAN, DUMPY LITTLE TROLLS?
HOW WILL I EVER LIVE IT DOWN?
YOU'RE NOT SO HOT. YOU THINK YOU ARE BUT YOU'RE NOT. YOU'RE THE DUMPY LITTLE TROLL. YOU'RE A... A... A... A...
GRAAAH!
BILLY, GOATS GRUFF!

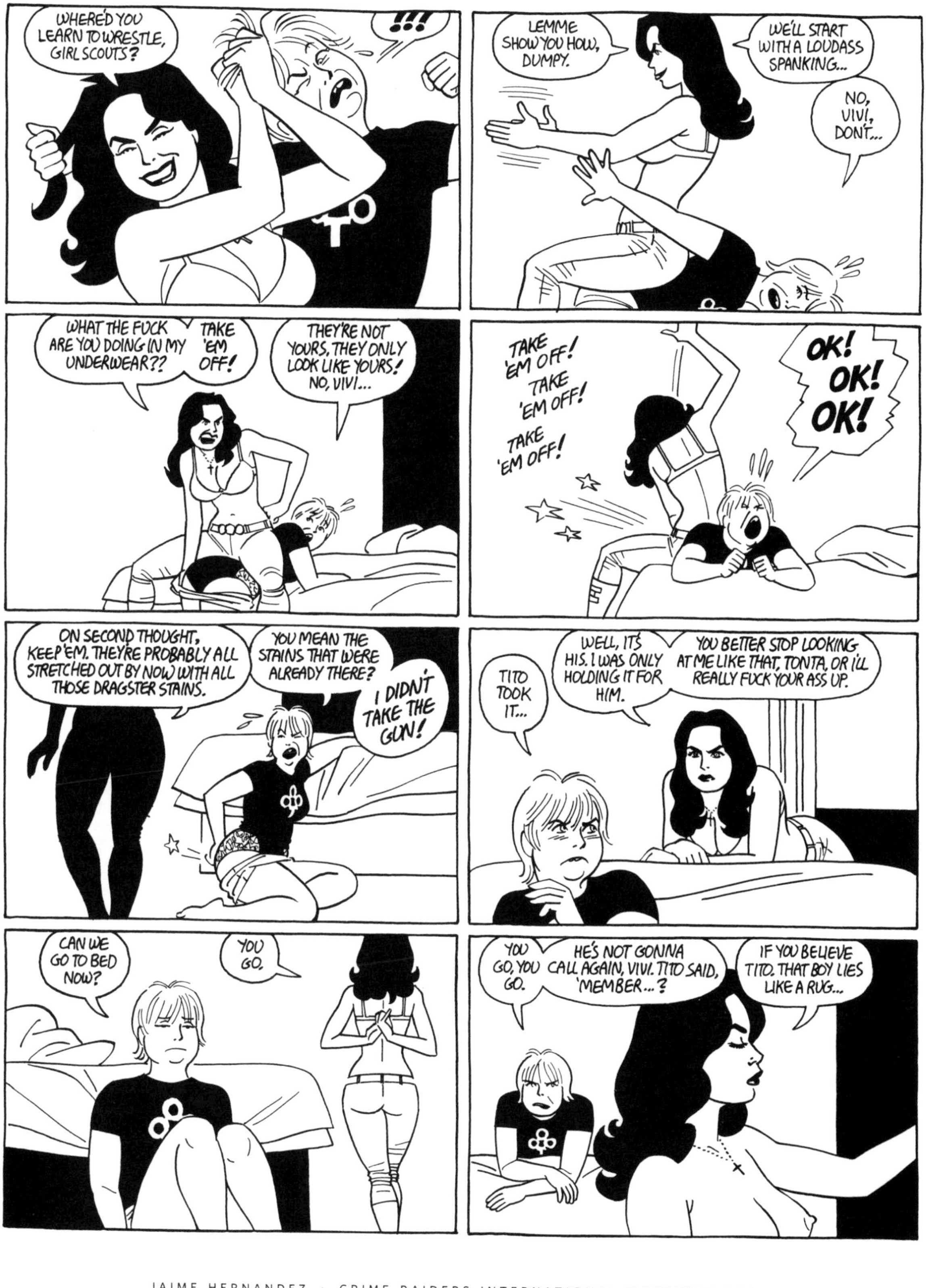
WHERE'D YOU LEARN TO WRESTLE, GIRL SCOUTS?
!!!
LEMME SHOW YOU HOW, DUMPY.
WE'LL START WITH A LOUDASS SPANKING...
NO, VIVI, DON'T...
WHAT THE FUCK ARE YOU DOING IN MY UNDERWEAR??
TAKE 'EM OFF!
THEY'RE NOT YOURS, THEY ONLY LOOK LIKE YOURS! NO, VIVI...
TAKE 'EM OFF!
TAKE 'EM OFF!
TAKE 'EM OFF!
OK! OK! OK!
ON SECOND THOUGHT, KEEP 'EM. THEY'RE PROBABLY ALL STRETCHED OUT BY NOW WITH ALL THOSE DRAGSTER STAINS.
YOU MEAN THE STAINS THAT WERE ALREADY THERE?
I DIDN'T TAKE THE GUN!
TITO TOOK IT...
WELL, IT'S HIS. I WAS ONLY HOLDING IT FOR HIM.
YOU BETTER STOP LOOKING AT ME LIKE THAT, TONTA, OR I'LL REALLY FUCK YOUR ASS UP.
CAN WE GO TO BED NOW?
YOU GO.
YOU GO, YOU GO.
HE'S NOT GONNA CALL AGAIN, VIVI. TITO SAID, 'MEMBER...?
IF YOU BELIEVE TITO. THAT BOY LIES LIKE A RUG...

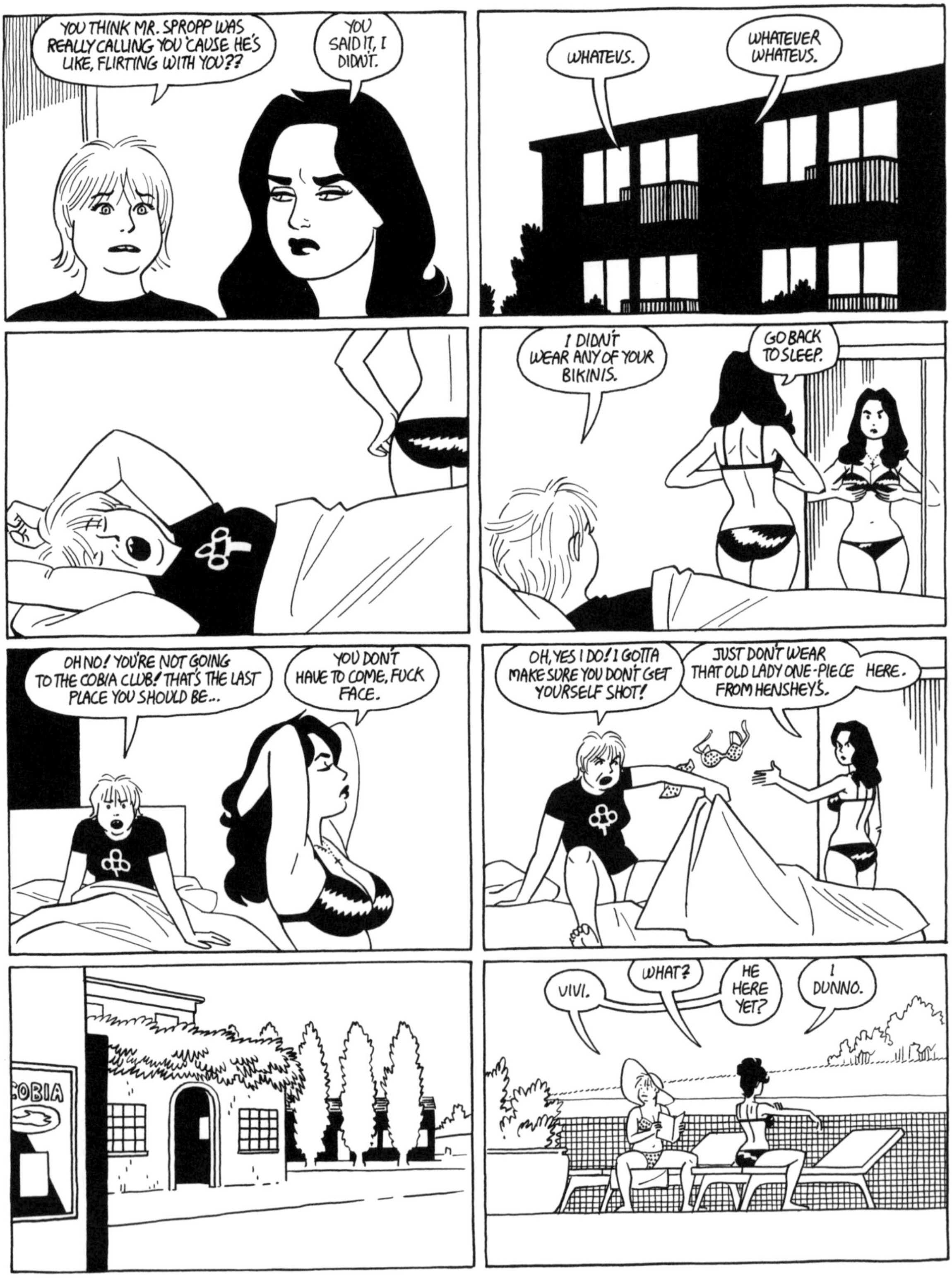

YOU THINK MR. SPROPP WAS REALLY CALLING YOU 'CAUSE HE'S LIKE, FLIRTING WITH YOU??
YOU SAID IT, I DIDN'T.
WHATEVS.
WHATEVER WHATEVS.
I DIDN'T WEAR ANY OF YOUR BIKINIS.
GO BACK TO SLEEP.
OH NO! YOU'RE NOT GOING TO THE COBIA CLUB! THAT'S THE LAST PLACE YOU SHOULD BE...
YOU DON'T HAVE TO COME, FUCK FACE.
OH, YES I DO! I GOTTA MAKE SURE YOU DON'T GET YOURSELF SHOT!
JUST DON'T WEAR THAT OLD LADY ONE-PIECE FROM HENSHEY'S.
HERE.
COBIA
VIVI.
WHAT?
HE HERE YET?
I DUNNO.

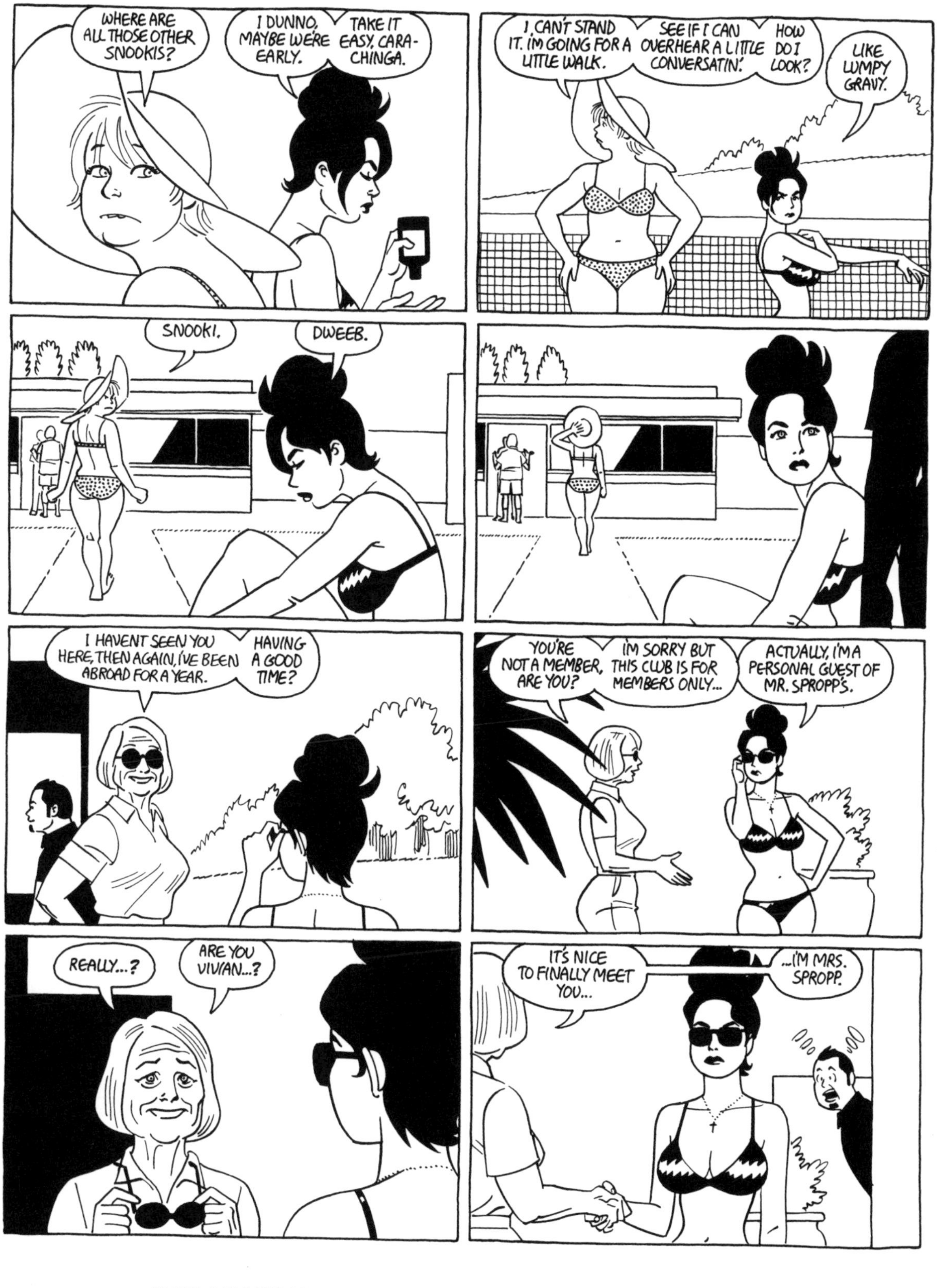
WHERE ARE ALL THOSE OTHER SNOOKIS?
I DUNNO, MAYBE WE'RE EARLY.
TAKE IT EASY, CARA-CHINGA.
I CAN'T STAND IT. I'M GOING FOR A LITTLE WALK.
SEE IF I CAN OVERHEAR A LITTLE CONVERSATIN'.
HOW DO I LOOK?
LIKE LUMPY GRAVY.
SNOOKI.
DWEEB.
I HAVEN'T SEEN YOU HERE, THEN AGAIN, I'VE BEEN ABROAD FOR A YEAR.
HAVING A GOOD TIME?
YOU'RE NOT A MEMBER, ARE YOU?
I'M SORRY BUT THIS CLUB IS FOR MEMBERS ONLY...
ACTUALLY, I'M A PERSONAL GUEST OF MR. SPROPP'S.
REALLY...?
ARE YOU VIVIAN...?
IT'S NICE TO FINALLY MEET YOU...
...I'M MRS. SPROPP.

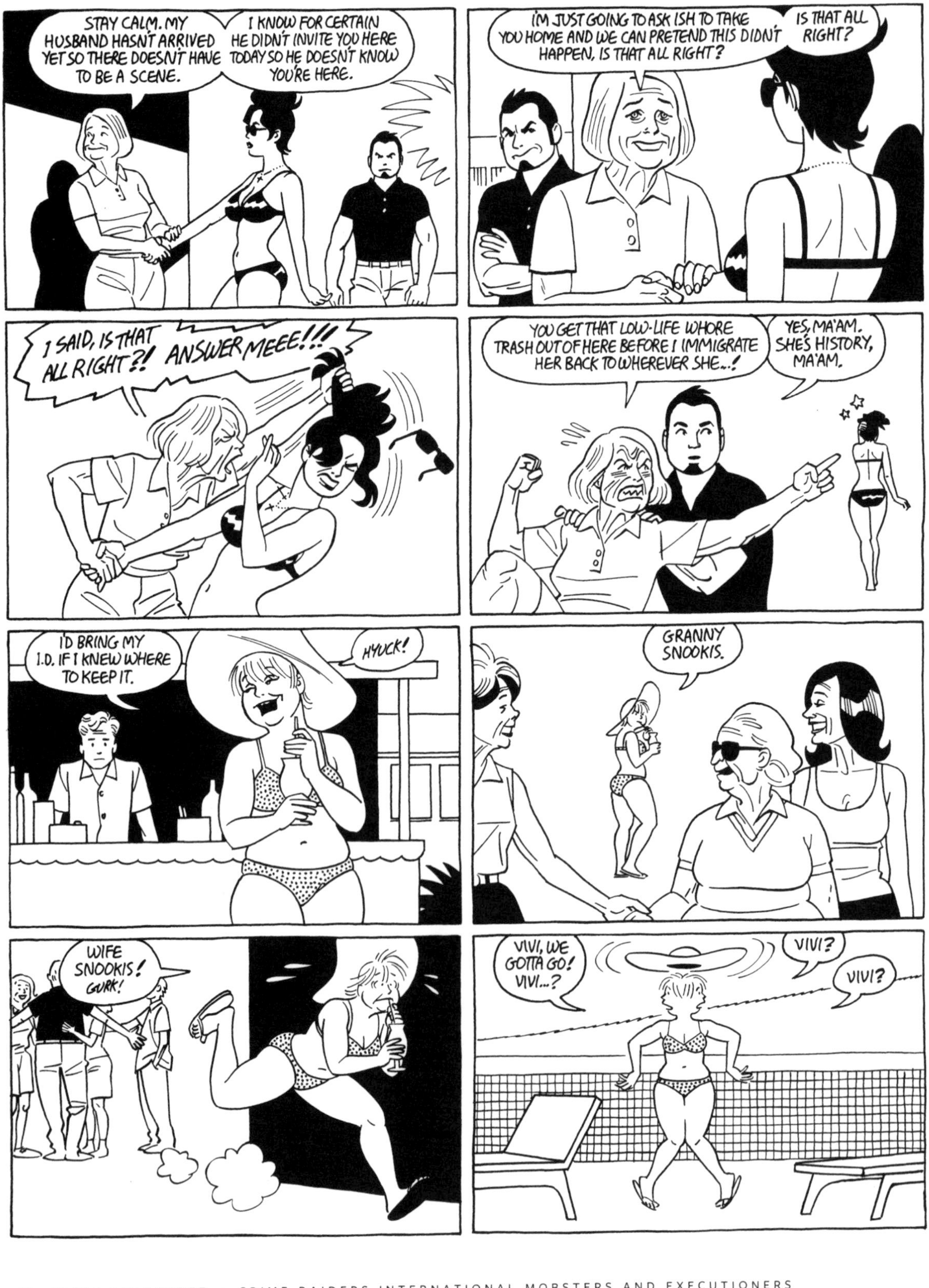
STAY CALM. MY HUSBAND HASN'T ARRIVED YET SO THERE DOESN'T HAVE TO BE A SCENE.
I KNOW FOR CERTAIN HE DIDN'T INVITE YOU HERE TODAY SO HE DOESN'T KNOW YOU'RE HERE.
I'M JUST GOING TO ASK ISH TO TAKE YOU HOME AND WE CAN PRETEND THIS DIDN'T HAPPEN, IS THAT ALL RIGHT?
IS THAT ALL RIGHT?
I SAID, IS THAT ALL RIGHT?! ANSWER MEEE!!!
YOU GET THAT LOW-LIFE WHORE TRASH OUT OF HERE BEFORE I IMMIGRATE HER BACK TO WHEREVER SHE...!
YES, MA'AM. SHE'S HISTORY, MA'AM.
I'D BRING MY I.D. IF I KNEW WHERE TO KEEP IT.
HYUCK!
GRANNY SNOOKIS.
WIFE SNOOKIS! GURK!
VIVI, WE GOTTA GO! VIVI...?
VIVI?
VIVI?

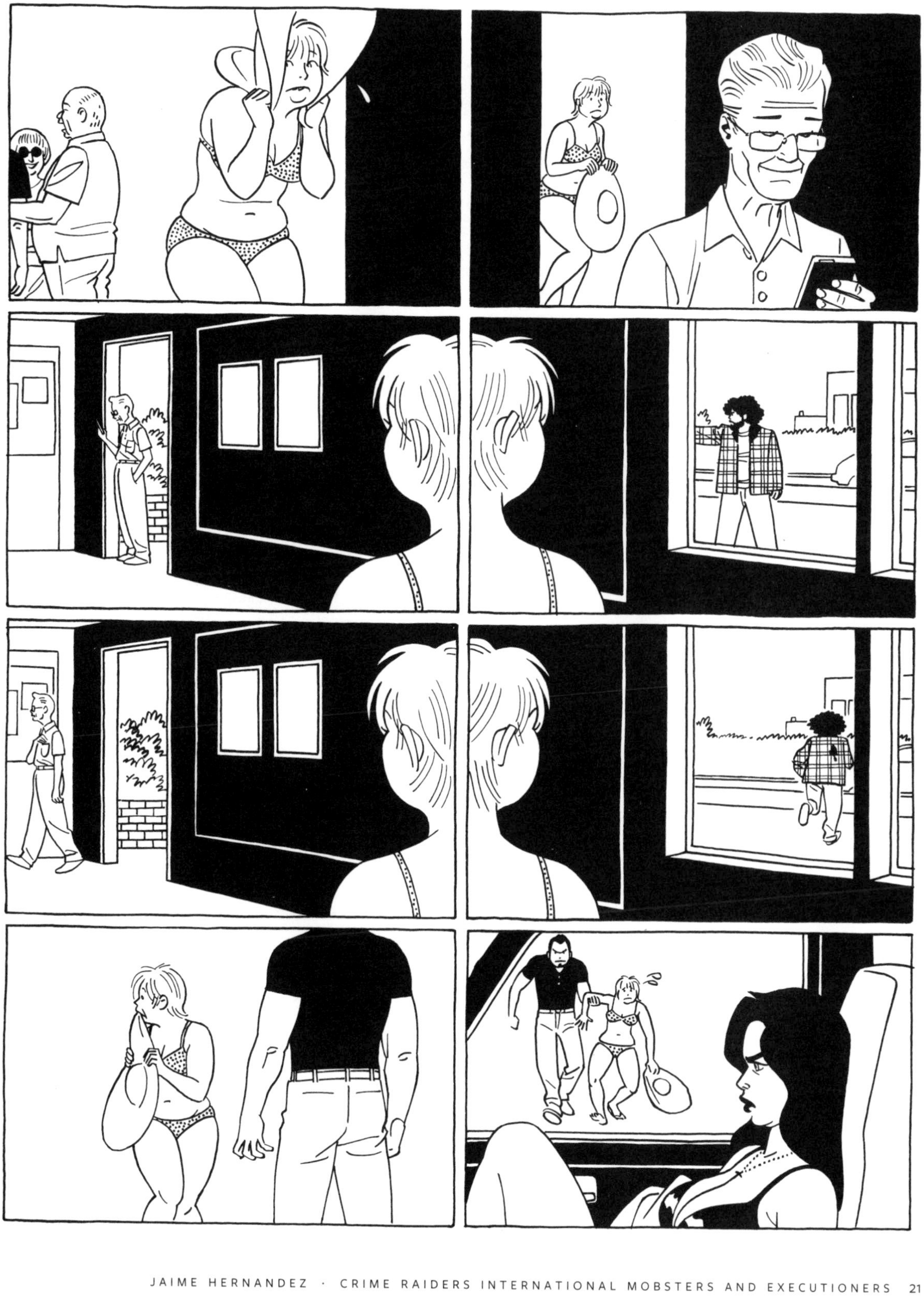

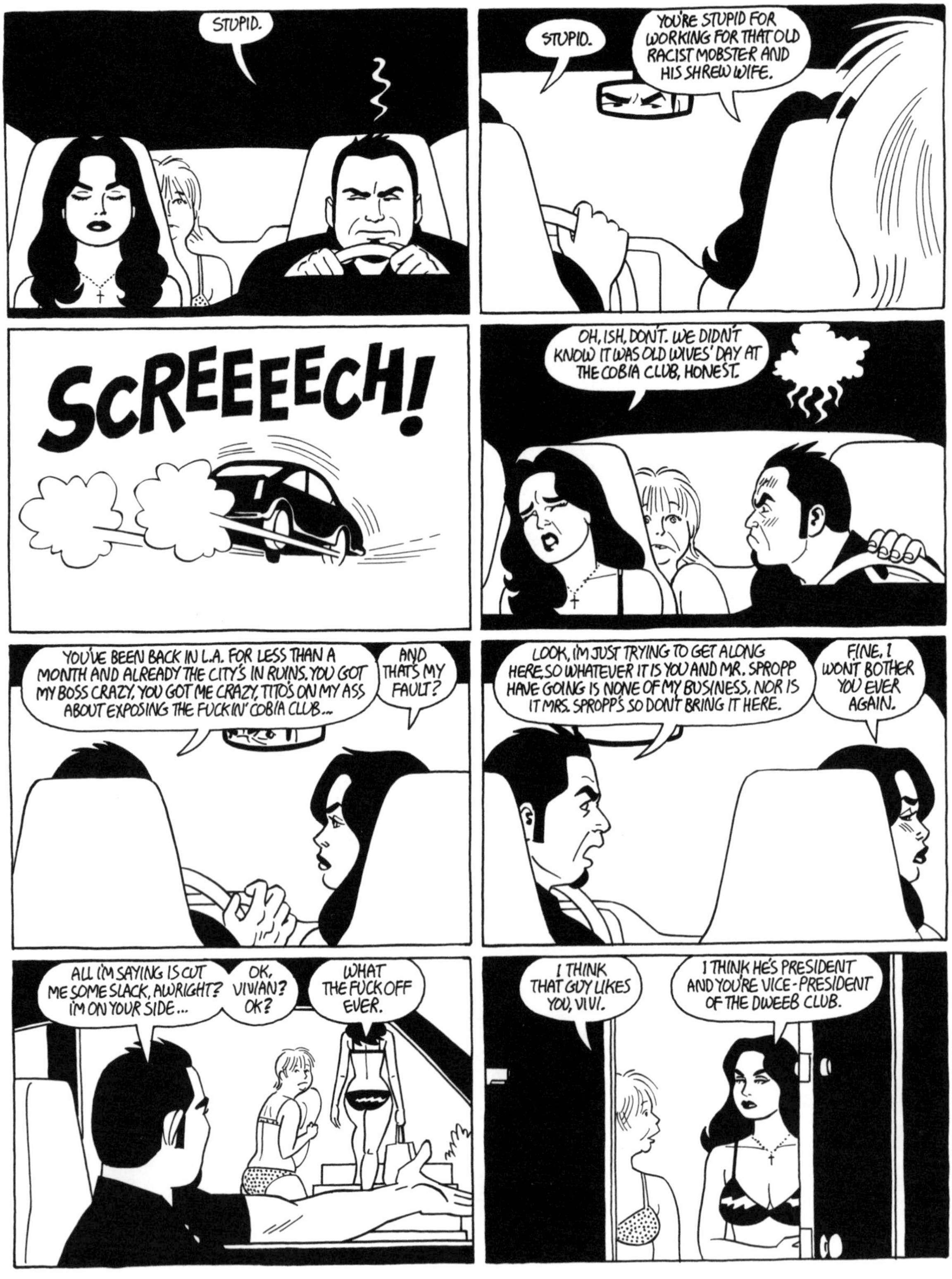
STUPID.
STUPID.
YOU'RE STUPID FOR WORKING FOR THAT OLD RACIST MOBSTER AND HIS SHREW WIFE.
SCREEEECH!
OH, ISH, DON'T. WE DIDN'T KNOW IT WAS OLD WIVES' DAY AT THE COBIA CLUB, HONEST.
YOU'VE BEEN BACK IN L.A. FOR LESS THAN A MONTH AND ALREADY THE CITY'S IN RUINS. YOU GOT MY BOSS CRAZY, YOU GOT ME CRAZY, TITO'S ON MY ASS ABOUT EXPOSING THE FUCKIN' COBIA CLUB...
AND THAT'S MY FAULT?
LOOK, I'M JUST TRYING TO GET ALONG HERE, SO WHATEVER IT IS YOU AND MR. SPROPP HAVE GOING IS NONE OF MY BUSINESS, NOR IS IT MRS. SPROPP'S SO DON'T BRING IT HERE.
FINE. I WON'T BOTHER YOU EVER AGAIN.
ALL I'M SAYING IS CUT ME SOME SLACK, AWRIGHT? I'M ON YOUR SIDE...
OK, VIVIAN? OK?
WHAT THE FUCK OFF EVER.
I THINK THAT GUY LIKES YOU, VIVI.
I THINK HE'S PRESIDENT AND YOU'RE VICE-PRESIDENT OF THE DWEEB CLUB.

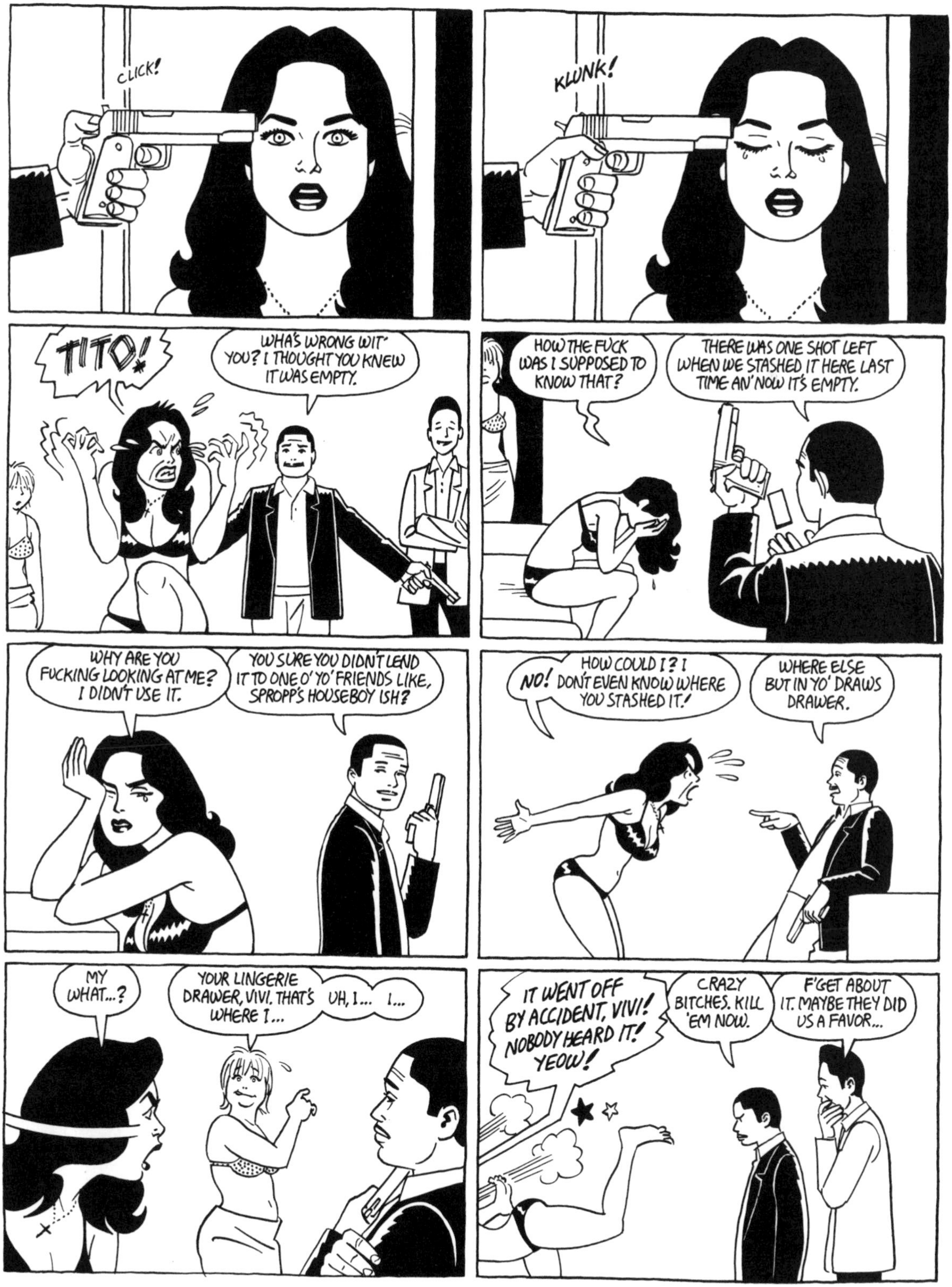
CLICK!
KLUNK!
TITO!
WHA'S WRONG WIT' YOU? I THOUGHT YOU KNEW IT WAS EMPTY.
HOW THE FUCK WAS I SUPPOSED TO KNOW THAT?
THERE WAS ONE SHOT LEFT WHEN WE STASHED IT HERE LAST TIME AN' NOW IT'S EMPTY.
WHY ARE YOU FUCKING LOOKING AT ME? I DIDN'T USE IT.
YOU SURE YOU DIDN'T LEND IT TO ONE O' YO' FRIENDS LIKE, SPROPP'S HOUSEBOY ISH?
NO! HOW COULD I?! I DON'T EVEN KNOW WHERE YOU STASHED IT!
WHERE ELSE BUT IN YO' DRAWS DRAWER.
MY WHAT...?
YOUR LINGERIE DRAWER, VIVI. THAT'S WHERE I...
UH, I... I...
IT WENT OFF BY ACCIDENT, VIVI! NOBODY HEARD IT! YEOW!
CRAZY BITCHES. KILL 'EM NOW.
F'GET ABOUT IT. MAYBE THEY DID US A FAVOR...

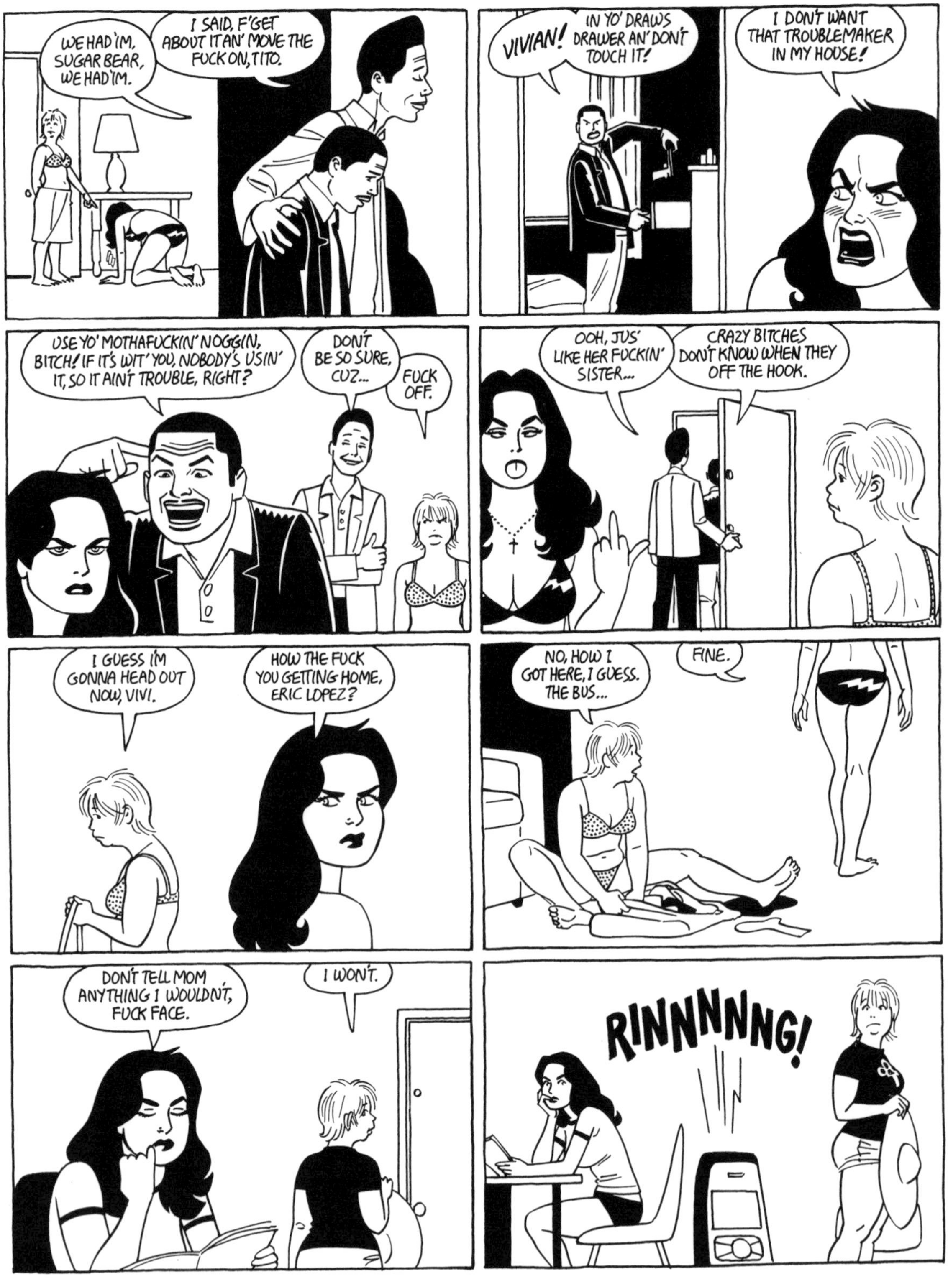
WE HAD 'IM, SUGAR BEAR, WE HAD 'IM.
I SAID, F'GET ABOUT IT AN' MOVE THE FUCK ON, TITO.
VIVIAN!
IN YO' DRAWS DRAWER AN' DON'T TOUCH IT!
I DON'T WANT THAT TROUBLEMAKER IN MY HOUSE!
USE YO' MOTHAFUCKIN' NOGGIN, BITCH! IF IT'S WIT' YOU, NOBODY'S USIN' IT, SO IT AIN'T TROUBLE, RIGHT?
DON'T BE SO SURE, CUZ...
FUCK OFF.
OOH, JUS' LIKE HER FUCKIN' SISTER...
CRAZY BITCHES DON'T KNOW WHEN THEY OFF THE HOOK.
I GUESS I'M GONNA HEAD OUT NOW, VIVI.
HOW THE FUCK YOU GETTING HOME, ERIC LOPEZ?
NO, HOW I GOT HERE, I GUESS. THE BUS...
FINE.
DON'T TELL MOM ANYTHING I WOULDN'T, FUCK FACE.
I WON'T.
RINNNNNG!

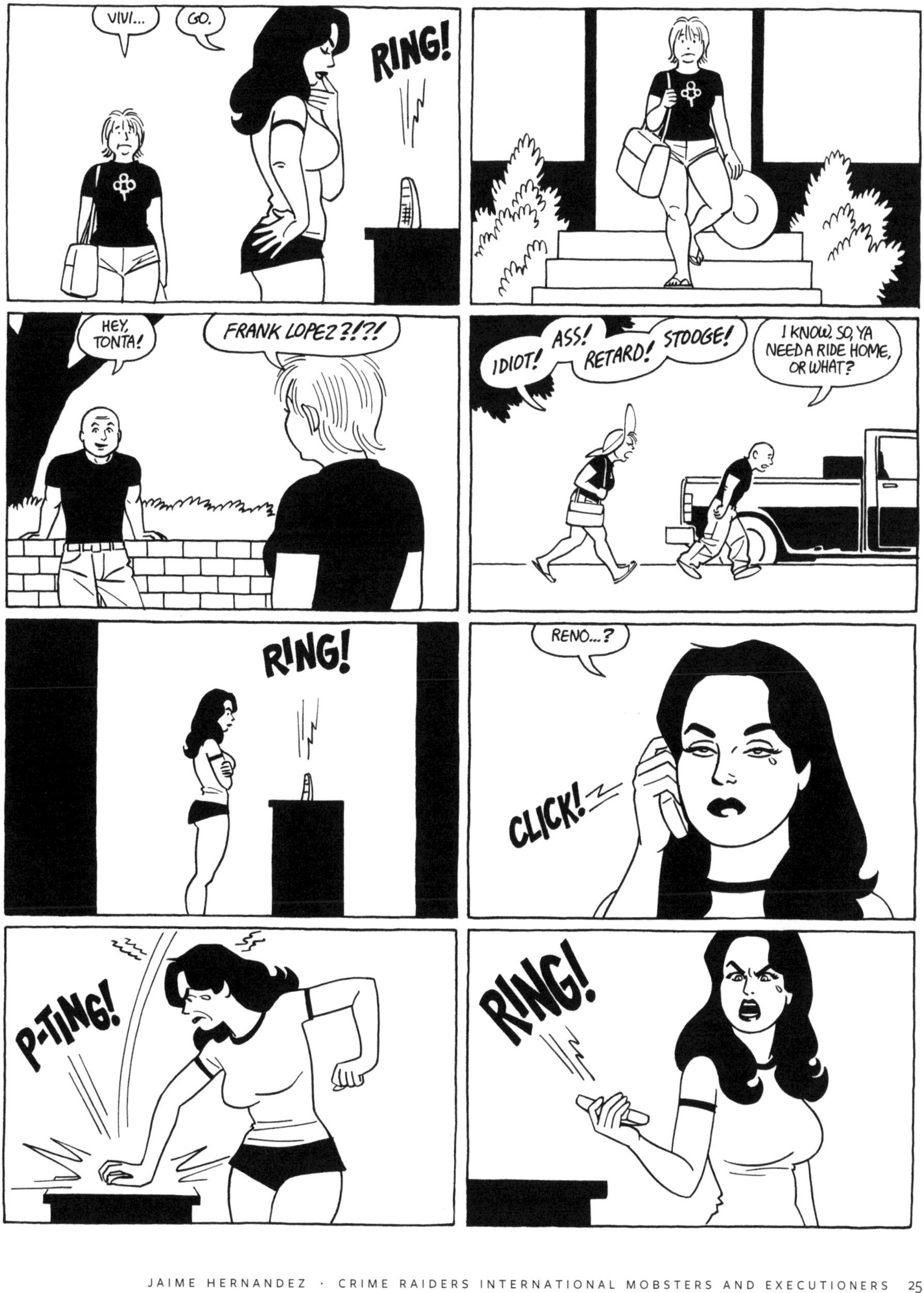
VIVI...
GO.
RING!
HEY, TONTA!
FRANK LOPEZ?!?!
IDIOT!
ASS!
RETARD!
STOOGE!
I KNOW. SO, YA NEED A RIDE HOME, OR WHAT?
RING!
RENO...?
CLICK!
P-TING!
RING!

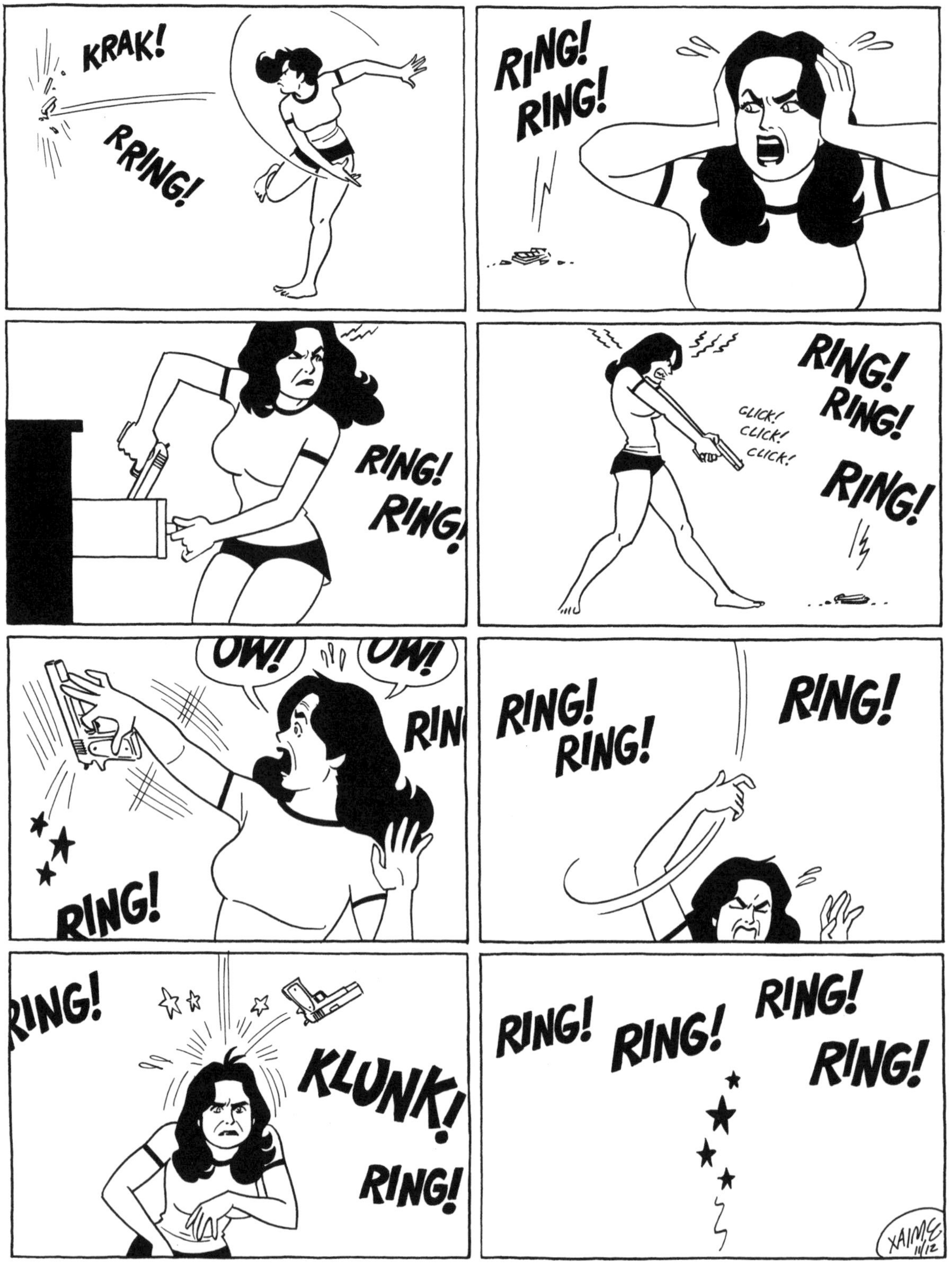
KRAK!
RRING!
RING! RING!
RING! RING!
RING! RING!
CLICK! CLICK! CLICK!
RING!
OW! OW!
RIN
RING!
RING! RING!
RING!
RING!
KLUNK!
RING!
RING!
RING!
RING!
RING!
XAIME 11/12

Picnic Now!

A GROWING NUMBER OF INDIVIDUALS HAVE ADOPTED PICNICKING AS A FORM OF NON-VIOLENT PROTEST...

AGAINST THE SYSTEM OF THREE SET MEALS A DAY...

AND THE INDIGESTION AND UNHAPINESS IT CAUSES.

WHENEVER AND WHEREVER THE IMPULSE TO EAT ARISES...

I THINK, I FEEL...

THEY STOP WHAT THEY'RE DOING...

MY PEPTIDES RISING.

SET UP A FOLDING TABLE AND BENCH...

PLEASE JOIN ME.

AND ENJOY A LEISURELY PICNIC.

COLD CUTS OF MEAT...

NO MORE PIOUS FAMILY DINNERS.

HARDBOILED EGGS...

NO MORE LUNCH HOUR CONSTRAINTS.

FRUIT, CHEESE, WINE AND BREAD...

NO MORE SURLY WAITERS.

HANDMADE PACKETS OF SALT AND PEPPER.

ONE RADICAL PICNICKER IS TORMENTED BY MOSQUITOS.

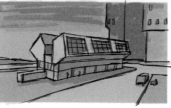

IN A SECRET COMMAND CENTER NEAR LAS VEGAS...

A BORED MAN PILOTS A MECHANICAL INSECT BY REMOTE CONTROL.

SQUITO, JUDY, JUDY I'M GOING IN FOR GUNS.

© BEN KATCHOR 2012

Sickroom Reading

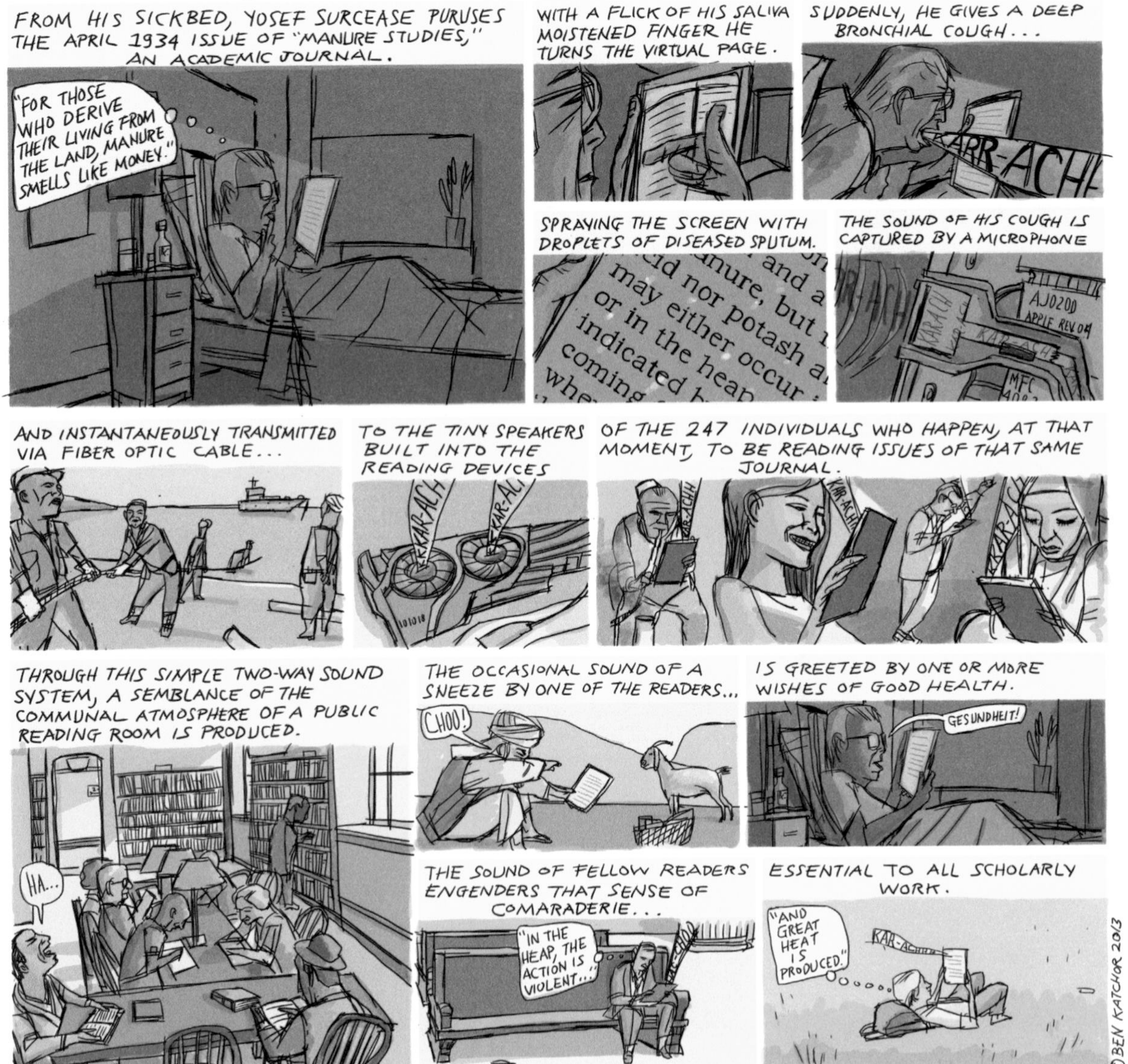
FROM HIS SICKBED, YOSEF SURCEASE PURUSES THE APRIL 1934 ISSUE OF "MANURE STUDIES," AN ACADEMIC JOURNAL.
"FOR THOSE WHO DERIVE THEIR LIVING FROM THE LAND, MANURE SMELLS LIKE MONEY."
WITH A FLICK OF HIS SALIVA MOISTENED FINGER HE TURNS THE VIRTUAL PAGE.
SUDDENLY, HE GIVES A DEEP BRONCHIAL COUGH...
KARR-ACHH
SPRAYING THE SCREEN WITH DROPLETS OF DISEASED SPUTUM.
THE SOUND OF HIS COUGH IS CAPTURED BY A MICROPHONE
AJ020D
APPLE REV 04
AND INSTANTANEOUSLY TRANSMITTED VIA FIBER OPTIC CABLE...
TO THE TINY SPEAKERS BUILT INTO THE READING DEVICES
KAR-ACH
OF THE 247 INDIVIDUALS WHO HAPPEN, AT THAT MOMENT, TO BE READING ISSUES OF THAT SAME JOURNAL.
THROUGH THIS SIMPLE TWO-WAY SOUND SYSTEM, A SEMBLANCE OF THE COMMUNAL ATMOSPHERE OF A PUBLIC READING ROOM IS PRODUCED.
HA...
THE OCCASIONAL SOUND OF A SNEEZE BY ONE OF THE READERS...
CHOO!
IS GREETED BY ONE OR MORE WISHES OF GOOD HEALTH.
GESUNDHEIT!
THE SOUND OF FELLOW READERS ENGENDERS THAT SENSE OF COMARADERIE...
"IN THE HEAP, THE ACTION IS VIOLENT..."
ESSENTIAL TO ALL SCHOLARLY WORK.
"AND GREAT HEAT IS PRODUCED."
KAR-ACHH
©BEN KATCHOR 2013

The Hand Laundry

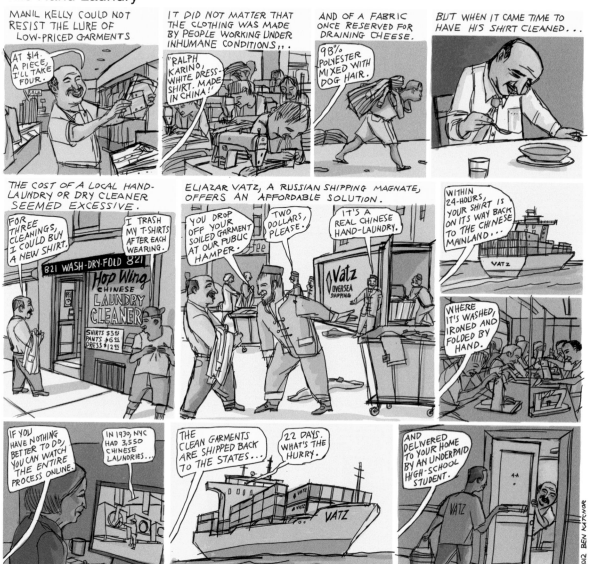

MANIL KELLY COULD NOT RESIST THE LURE OF LOW-PRICED GARMENTS

AT $14. A PIECE, I'LL TAKE FOUR.

IT DID NOT MATTER THAT THE CLOTHING WAS MADE BY PEOPLE WORKING UNDER INHUMANE CONDITIONS...

"RALPH KARINO, WHITE DRESS-SHIRT. MADE IN CHINA!!"

AND OF A FABRIC ONCE RESERVED FOR DRAINING CHEESE.

98% POLYESTER MIXED WITH DOG HAIR.

BUT WHEN IT CAME TIME TO HAVE HIS SHIRT CLEANED...

THE COST OF A LOCAL HAND-LAUNDRY OR DRY CLEANER SEEMED EXCESSIVE.

FOR THREE CLEANINGS, I COULD BUY A NEW SHIRT.

I TRASH MY T-SHIRTS AFTER EACH WEARING.

821 WASH-DRY-FOLD 821
Hop Wing
CHINESE
LAUNDRY
CLEANER
SHIRTS $3⁹⁵
PANTS $6⁹⁵
DRESS $12⁹⁵

ELIAZAR VATZ, A RUSSIAN SHIPPING MAGNATE, OFFERS AN AFFORDABLE SOLUTION.

YOU DROP OFF YOUR SOILED GARMENT AT OUR PUBLIC HAMPER.

TWO DOLLARS, PLEASE.

IT'S A REAL CHINESE HAND-LAUNDRY.

Vatz
OVERSEA SHIPPING

WITHIN 24-HOURS, YOUR SHIRT IS ON ITS WAY BACK TO THE CHINESE MAINLAND...

VATZ

WHERE IT'S WASHED, IRONED AND FOLDED BY HAND.

IF YOU HAVE NOTHING BETTER TO DO, YOU CAN WATCH THE ENTIRE PROCESS ONLINE.

IN 1930, NYC HAD 3,550 CHINESE LAUNDRIES...

THE CLEAN GARMENTS ARE SHIPPED BACK TO THE STATES...

22 DAYS. WHAT'S THE HURRY.

VATZ

AND DELIVERED TO YOUR HOME BY AN UNDERPAID HIGH-SCHOOL STUDENT.

VATZ

4-A

© 2012 BEN KATCHOR

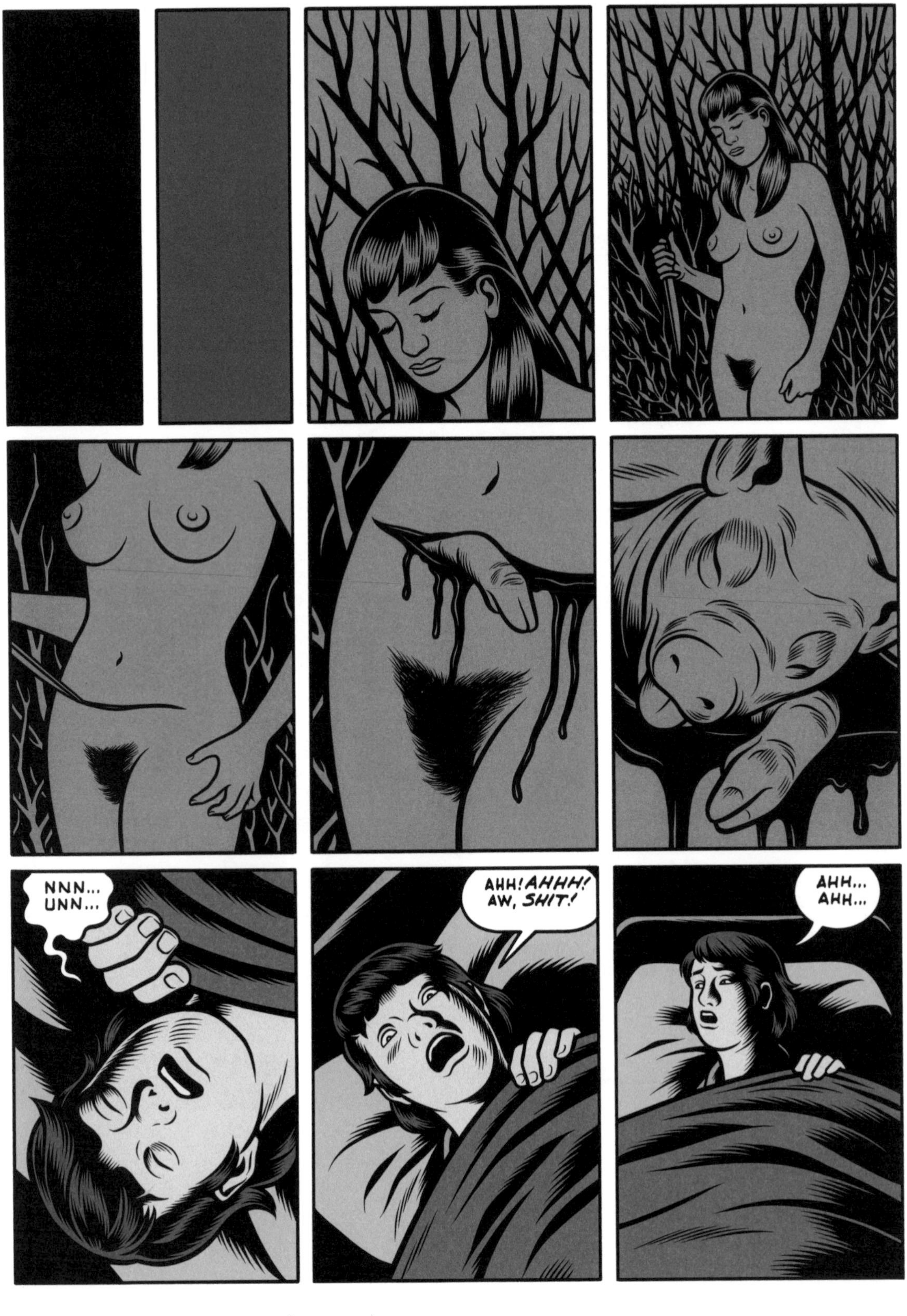
NNN... UNN...
AHH! AHHH! AW, SHIT!
AHH... AHH...

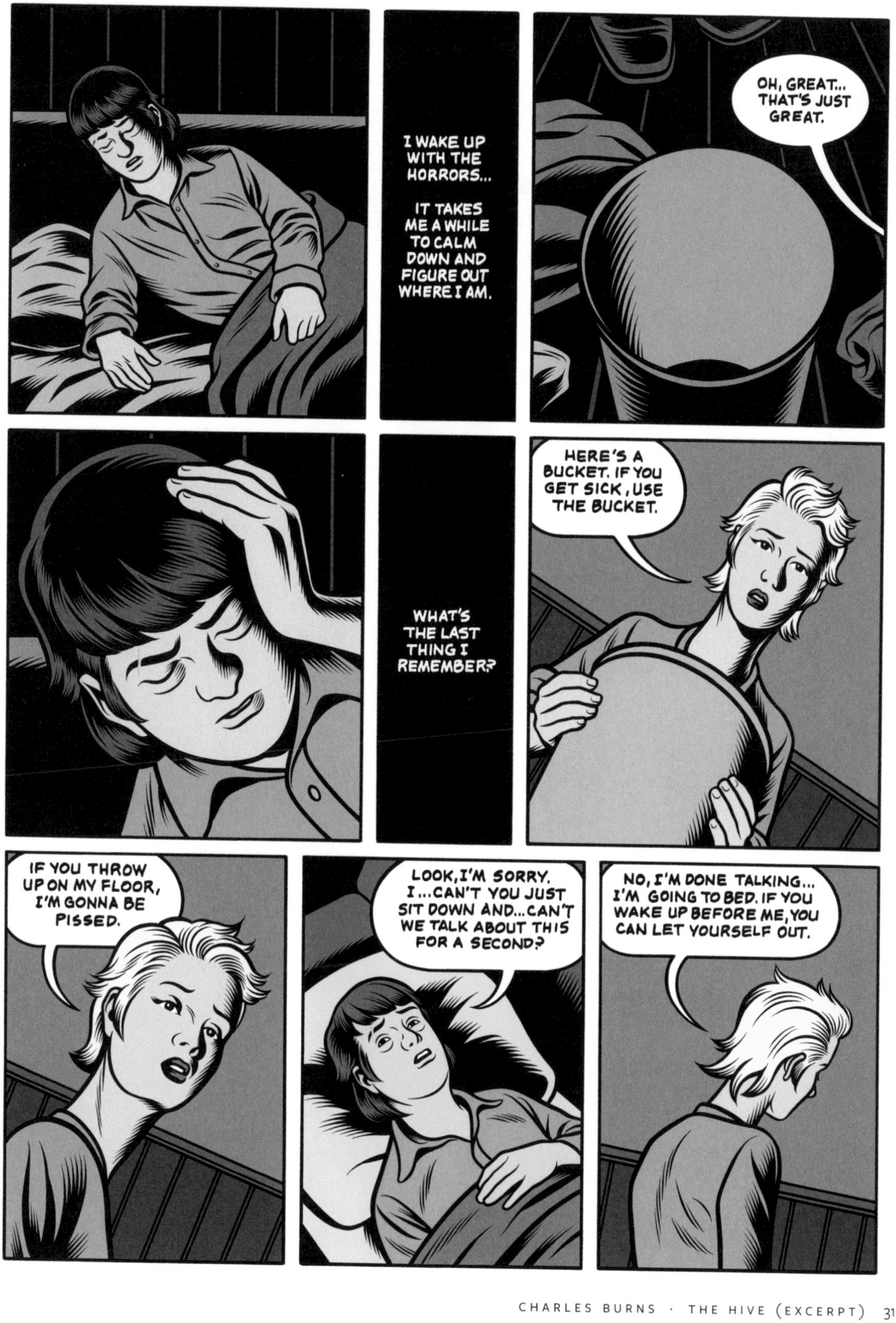
I WAKE UP WITH THE HORRORS...
IT TAKES ME A WHILE TO CALM DOWN AND FIGURE OUT WHERE I AM.
OH, GREAT... THAT'S JUST GREAT.
WHAT'S THE LAST THING I REMEMBER?
HERE'S A BUCKET. IF YOU GET SICK, USE THE BUCKET.
IF YOU THROW UP ON MY FLOOR, I'M GONNA BE PISSED.
LOOK, I'M SORRY. I...CAN'T YOU JUST SIT DOWN AND...CAN'T WE TALK ABOUT THIS FOR A SECOND?
NO, I'M DONE TALKING... I'M GOING TO BED. IF YOU WAKE UP BEFORE ME, YOU CAN LET YOURSELF OUT.

THE EVENING STARTED OUT OKAY.
I BROUGHT OVER A SIX-PACK OF
PABST AND A PINT OF JIM BEAM.
I DID MOST OF THE DRINKING.

I ALSO DID MOST OF THE TALKING.
I HAD IT IN MY HEAD THAT I WAS
GOING TO TELL HER EVERYTHING...
THE WHOLE STORY.

...AND I TRIED, I REALLY DID...BUT
IT CAME OUT ALL WRONG.

WHAT PARTS DID I LEAVE OUT?
WHAT DIDN'T I TELL HER?

I TOLD HER ABOUT THROWING MY
DAD'S ASHES OFF THE BRIDGE...

...AND THE COMICS...FINDING THOSE
ROMANCE COMICS WITH SARAH.

SO WHAT IS IT WITH YOU AND
SARAH? EVERYTHING YOU
TALK ABOUT ALWAYS COMES
BACK TO HER.

AW, SHIT...YEAH, I
GUESS YOU'RE RIGHT.
SORRY ABOUT THAT.

THERE'S SOMETHING YOU'RE
NOT TELLING ME ABOUT HER...
SOMETHING IMPORTANT. I
CAN HEAR IT IN YOUR VOICE.

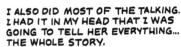

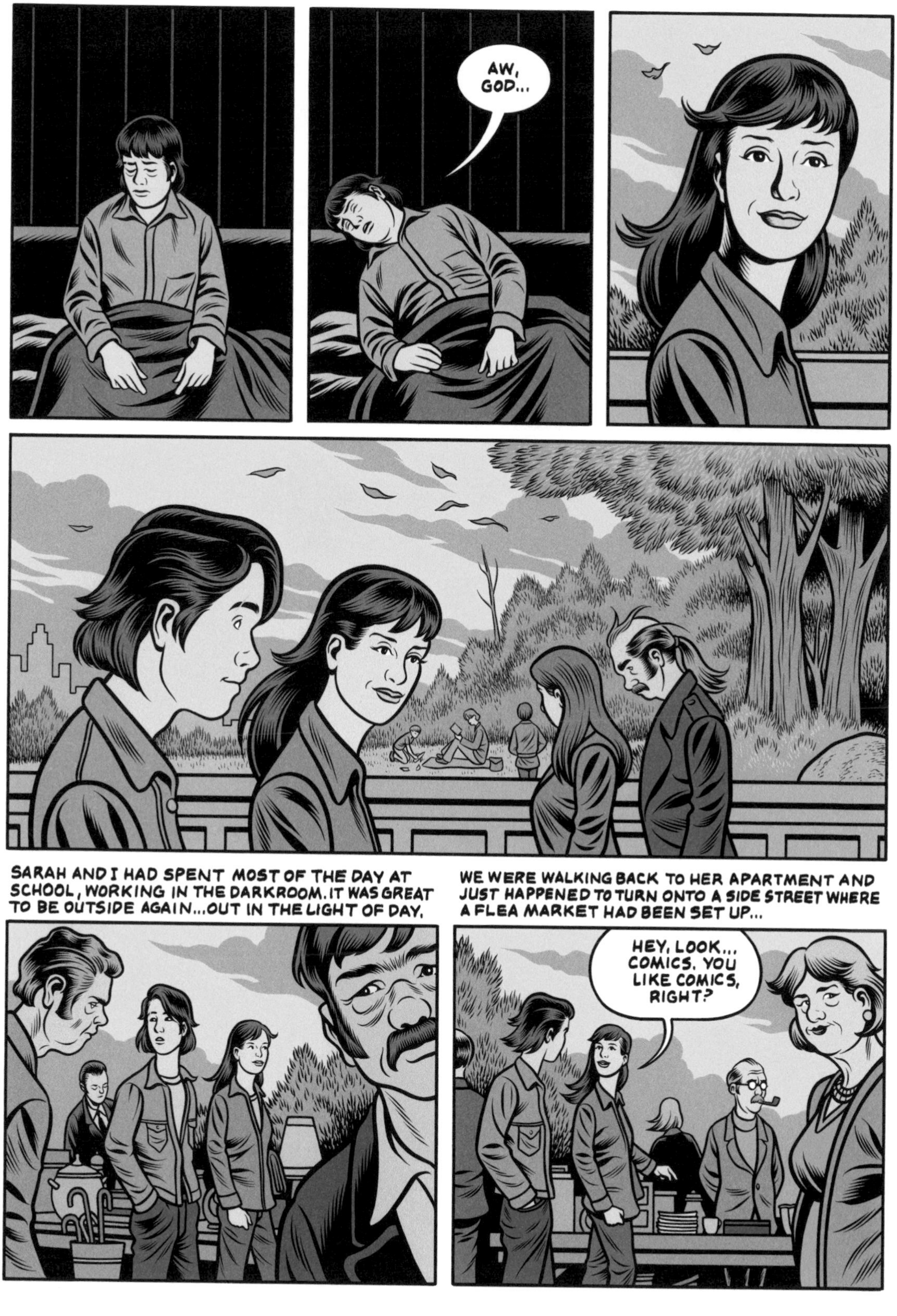
AW, GOD...
SARAH AND I HAD SPENT MOST OF THE DAY AT SCHOOL, WORKING IN THE DARKROOM. IT WAS GREAT TO BE OUTSIDE AGAIN...OUT IN THE LIGHT OF DAY.
WE WERE WALKING BACK TO HER APARTMENT AND JUST HAPPENED TO TURN ONTO A SIDE STREET WHERE A FLEA MARKET HAD BEEN SET UP...
HEY, LOOK... COMICS. YOU LIKE COMICS, RIGHT?

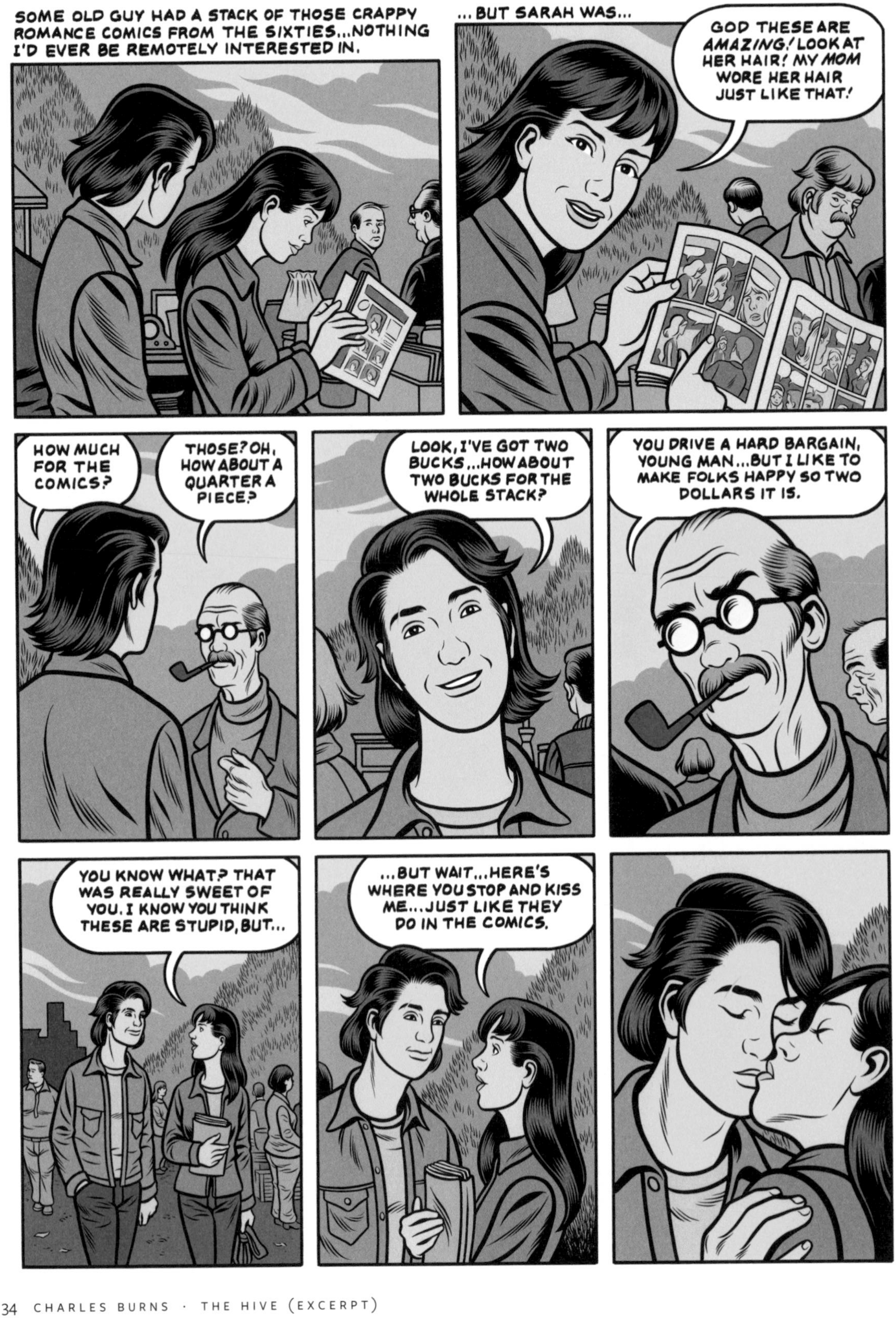
SOME OLD GUY HAD A STACK OF THOSE CRAPPY ROMANCE COMICS FROM THE SIXTIES...NOTHING I'D EVER BE REMOTELY INTERESTED IN.
...BUT SARAH WAS...
GOD THESE ARE AMAZING! LOOK AT HER HAIR! MY MOM WORE HER HAIR JUST LIKE THAT!
HOW MUCH FOR THE COMICS?
THOSE? OH, HOW ABOUT A QUARTER A PIECE?
LOOK, I'VE GOT TWO BUCKS...HOW ABOUT TWO BUCKS FOR THE WHOLE STACK?
YOU DRIVE A HARD BARGAIN, YOUNG MAN...BUT I LIKE TO MAKE FOLKS HAPPY SO TWO DOLLARS IT IS.
YOU KNOW WHAT? THAT WAS REALLY SWEET OF YOU. I KNOW YOU THINK THESE ARE STUPID, BUT...
...BUT WAIT...HERE'S WHERE YOU STOP AND KISS ME...JUST LIKE THEY DO IN THE COMICS.

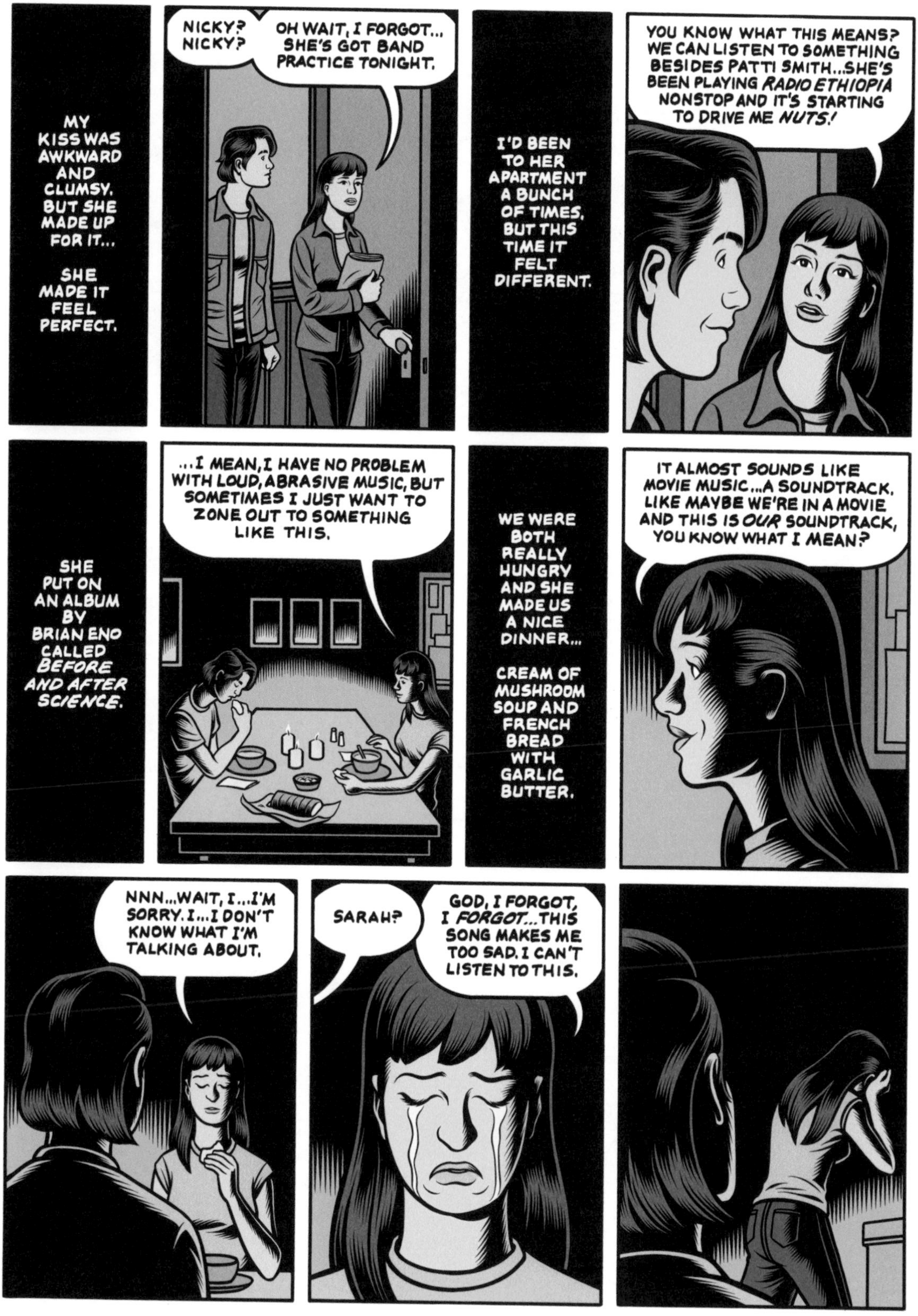
MY KISS WAS AWKWARD AND CLUMSY, BUT SHE MADE UP FOR IT...
SHE MADE IT FEEL PERFECT.
NICKY? NICKY?
OH WAIT, I FORGOT... SHE'S GOT BAND PRACTICE TONIGHT.
I'D BEEN TO HER APARTMENT A BUNCH OF TIMES, BUT THIS TIME IT FELT DIFFERENT.
YOU KNOW WHAT THIS MEANS? WE CAN LISTEN TO SOMETHING BESIDES PATTI SMITH...SHE'S BEEN PLAYING RADIO ETHIOPIA NONSTOP AND IT'S STARTING TO DRIVE ME NUTS!
SHE PUT ON AN ALBUM BY BRIAN ENO CALLED BEFORE AND AFTER SCIENCE.
...I MEAN, I HAVE NO PROBLEM WITH LOUD, ABRASIVE MUSIC, BUT SOMETIMES I JUST WANT TO ZONE OUT TO SOMETHING LIKE THIS.
WE WERE BOTH REALLY HUNGRY AND SHE MADE US A NICE DINNER...
CREAM OF MUSHROOM SOUP AND FRENCH BREAD WITH GARLIC BUTTER.
IT ALMOST SOUNDS LIKE MOVIE MUSIC...A SOUNDTRACK. LIKE MAYBE WE'RE IN A MOVIE AND THIS IS OUR SOUNDTRACK, YOU KNOW WHAT I MEAN?
NNN...WAIT, I...I'M SORRY. I...I DON'T KNOW WHAT I'M TALKING ABOUT.
SARAH?
GOD, I FORGOT, I FORGOT...THIS SONG MAKES ME TOO SAD. I CAN'T LISTEN TO THIS.

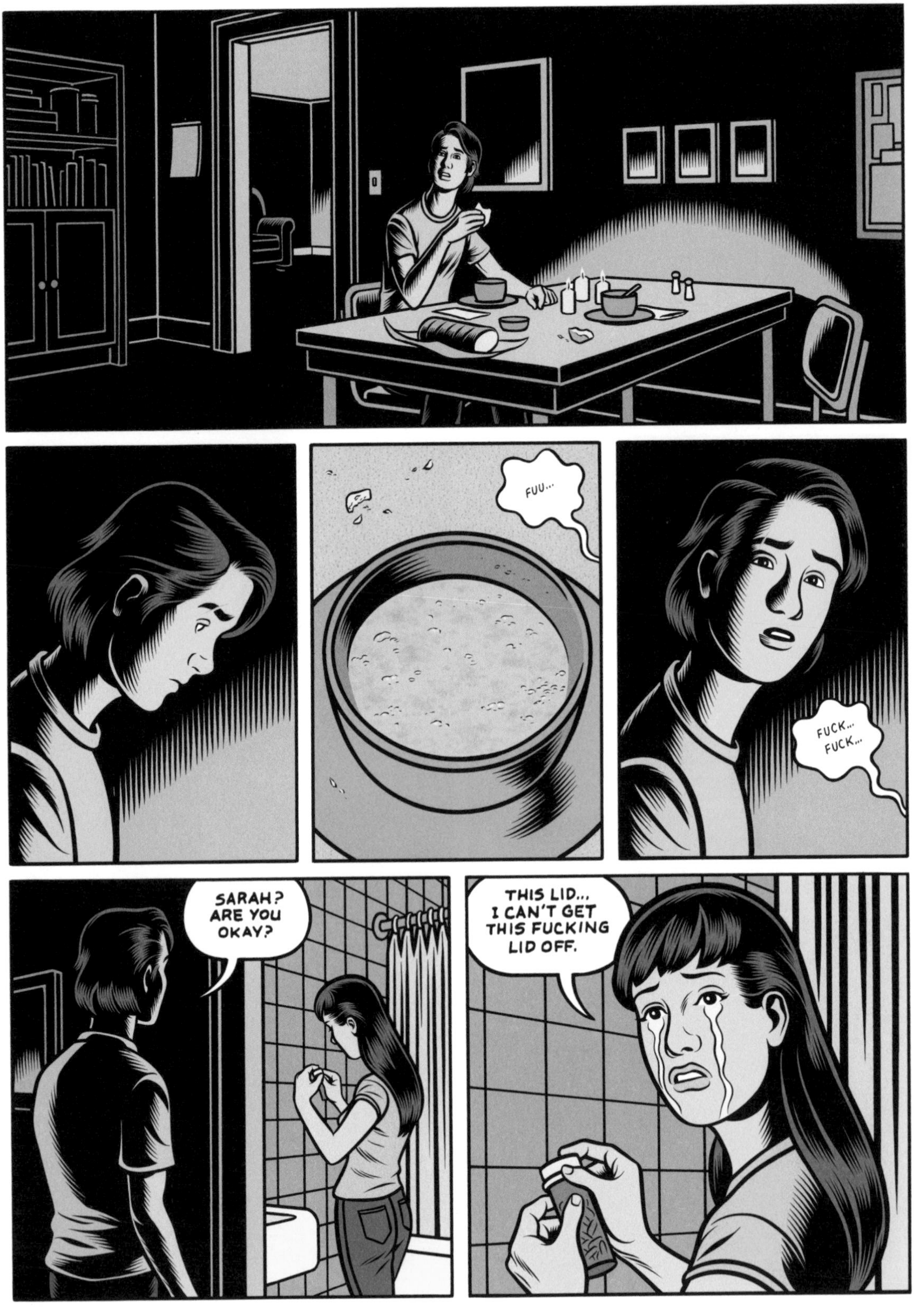
FUU...
FUCK... FUCK...
SARAH? ARE YOU OKAY?
THIS LID... I CAN'T GET THIS FUCKING LID OFF.

...SOME DAYS I JUST WANT TO JUMP OFF A FUCKING BRIDGE... BE DONE WITH IT ALL, BUT THEN A FEW HOURS LATER, IT ALL SLIPS AWAY AND I FEEL FINE AGAIN.

I MANAGED TO GET THE LID OFF AND SHE TOOK A COUPLE OF BIG, WHITE PILLS.

AFTER A WHILE, SHE STARTED TO CALM DOWN.

MY PARENTS HAD ME ON ALL KINDS OF MEDICATION FOR A WHILE, BUT IT KILLED EVERYTHING INSIDE OF ME.

...ALL OF MY HIGHS AND LOWS WERE GROUND DOWN TO THIS BORING, MONOTONOUS MIDDLE GROUND. I COULDN'T STAND IT.

I WAS A TOTAL ZOMBIE...I COULDN'T EVEN HAVE AN ORGASM.

LOOK, I'M SORRY ABOUT ALL THIS. YOU DON'T HAVE TO STAY IF YOU DON'T WANT TO. I'M OKAY NOW... REALLY.

BUT I WANT TO STAY. I WANT TO BE WITH YOU.

REALLY? WELL COME ON, LET'S GO LOOK AT SOME STUFF IN MY ROOM.

o safer.
d has no
n is like
That is,
TENSE NERVOUS
WOW. THESE ARE AMAZING.

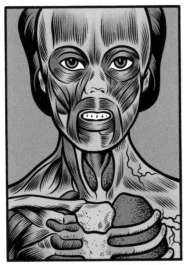

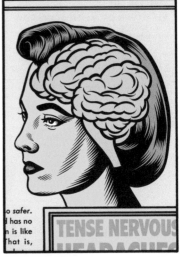

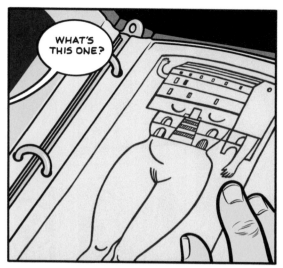

WHAT'S THIS ONE?

THAT'S BY LOUISE BOURGEOIS... SHE'S THIS AMAZING SCULPTOR, BUT THAT'S A DRAWING SHE DID BACK IN THE FORTIES WHEN SHE WAS RAISING A FAMILY.

IT'S CALLED FEMME MAISON. THE ENGLISH TRANSLATION WOULD BE HOUSE WOMAN OR HOUSEWIFE.

...SO YOU'VE GOT THIS BIG NAKED, ANONYMOUS WOMAN WITH A HOUSE FOR A HEAD...

...BUT WHAT'S SHE THINKING IN THERE? DOES SHE FEEL SAFE AND SECURE?

...OR DOES SHE FEEL TRAPPED?

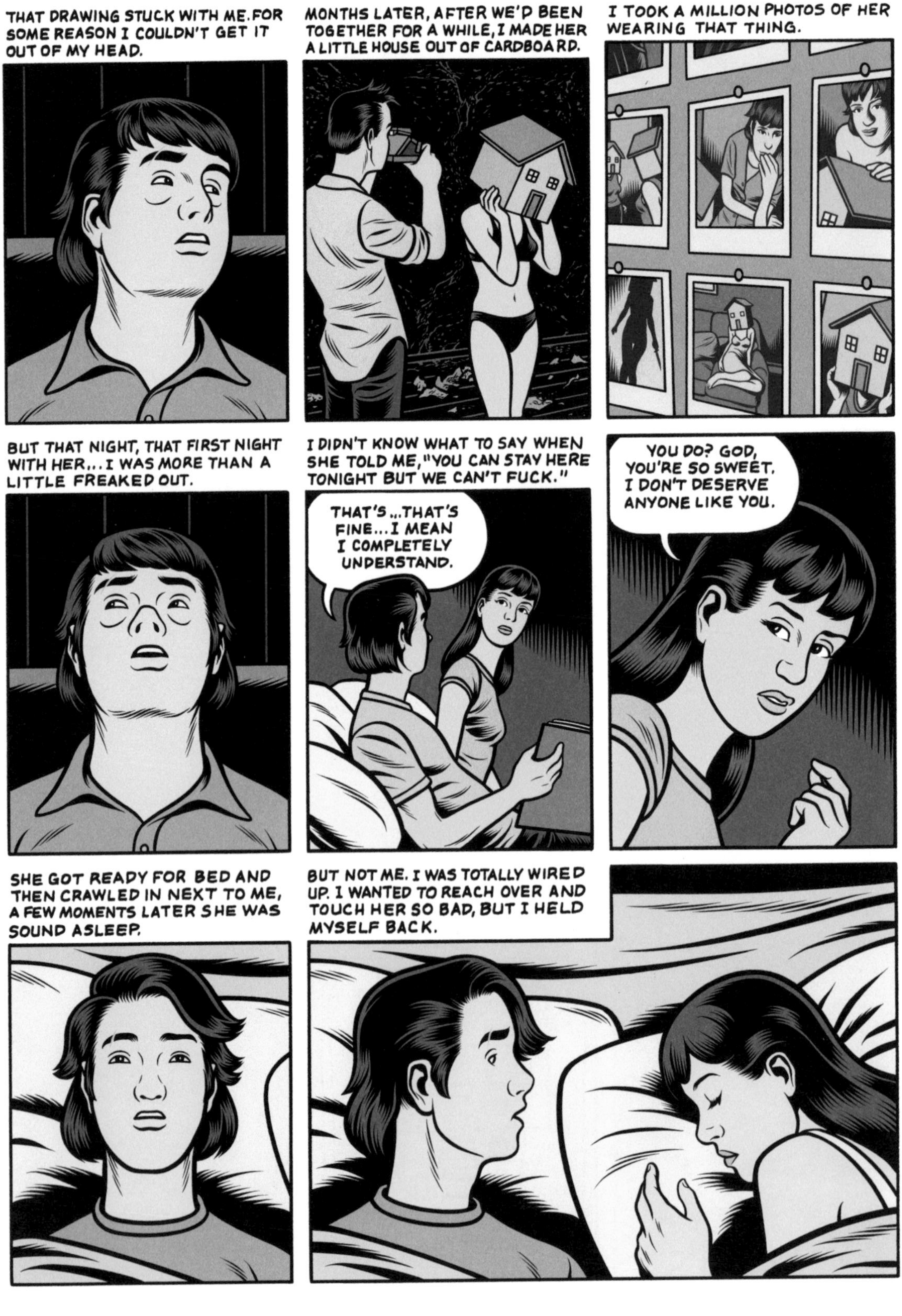
THAT DRAWING STUCK WITH ME. FOR SOME REASON I COULDN'T GET IT OUT OF MY HEAD.
MONTHS LATER, AFTER WE'D BEEN TOGETHER FOR A WHILE, I MADE HER A LITTLE HOUSE OUT OF CARDBOARD.
I TOOK A MILLION PHOTOS OF HER WEARING THAT THING.
BUT THAT NIGHT, THAT FIRST NIGHT WITH HER... I WAS MORE THAN A LITTLE FREAKED OUT.
I DIDN'T KNOW WHAT TO SAY WHEN SHE TOLD ME, "YOU CAN STAY HERE TONIGHT BUT WE CAN'T FUCK."
THAT'S...THAT'S FINE... I MEAN I COMPLETELY UNDERSTAND.
YOU DO? GOD, YOU'RE SO SWEET. I DON'T DESERVE ANYONE LIKE YOU.
SHE GOT READY FOR BED AND THEN CRAWLED IN NEXT TO ME. A FEW MOMENTS LATER SHE WAS SOUND ASLEEP.
BUT NOT ME. I WAS TOTALLY WIRED UP. I WANTED TO REACH OVER AND TOUCH HER SO BAD, BUT I HELD MYSELF BACK.

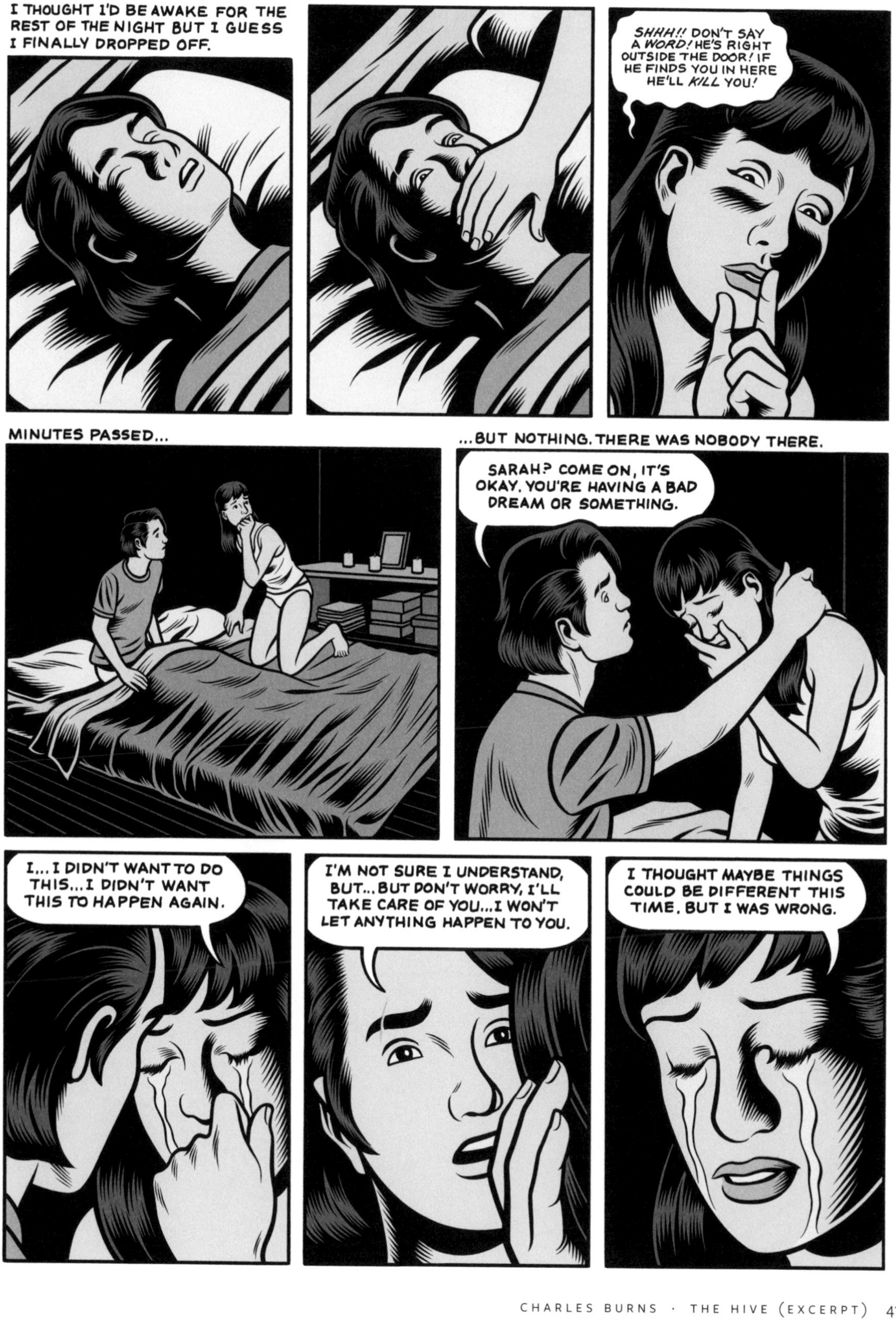
I THOUGHT I'D BE AWAKE FOR THE REST OF THE NIGHT BUT I GUESS I FINALLY DROPPED OFF.
SHHH!! DON'T SAY A WORD! HE'S RIGHT OUTSIDE THE DOOR! IF HE FINDS YOU IN HERE HE'LL KILL YOU!
MINUTES PASSED...
...BUT NOTHING. THERE WAS NOBODY THERE.
SARAH? COME ON, IT'S OKAY. YOU'RE HAVING A BAD DREAM OR SOMETHING.
I... I DIDN'T WANT TO DO THIS... I DIDN'T WANT THIS TO HAPPEN AGAIN.
I'M NOT SURE I UNDERSTAND, BUT... BUT DON'T WORRY, I'LL TAKE CARE OF YOU... I WON'T LET ANYTHING HAPPEN TO YOU.
I THOUGHT MAYBE THINGS COULD BE DIFFERENT THIS TIME, BUT I WAS WRONG.

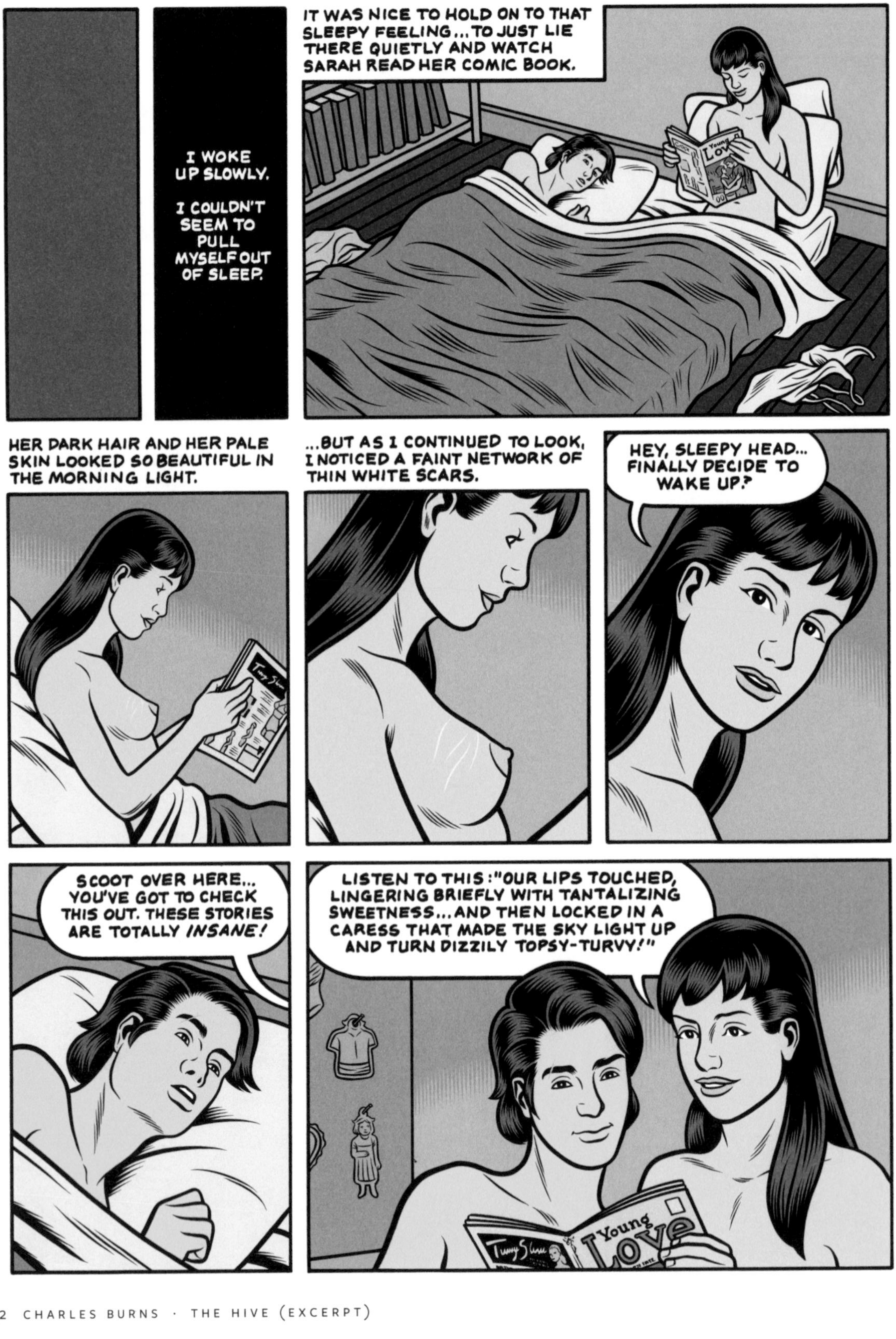
I WOKE UP SLOWLY.
I COULDN'T SEEM TO PULL MYSELF OUT OF SLEEP.
IT WAS NICE TO HOLD ON TO THAT SLEEPY FEELING... TO JUST LIE THERE QUIETLY AND WATCH SARAH READ HER COMIC BOOK.
Young Love
HER DARK HAIR AND HER PALE SKIN LOOKED SO BEAUTIFUL IN THE MORNING LIGHT.
...BUT AS I CONTINUED TO LOOK, I NOTICED A FAINT NETWORK OF THIN WHITE SCARS.
HEY, SLEEPY HEAD... FINALLY DECIDE TO WAKE UP?
SCOOT OVER HERE... YOU'VE GOT TO CHECK THIS OUT. THESE STORIES ARE TOTALLY *INSANE!*
LISTEN TO THIS: "OUR LIPS TOUCHED, LINGERING BRIEFLY WITH TANTALIZING SWEETNESS... AND THEN LOCKED IN A CARESS THAT MADE THE SKY LIGHT UP AND TURN DIZZILY TOPSY-TURVY!"
Young Love

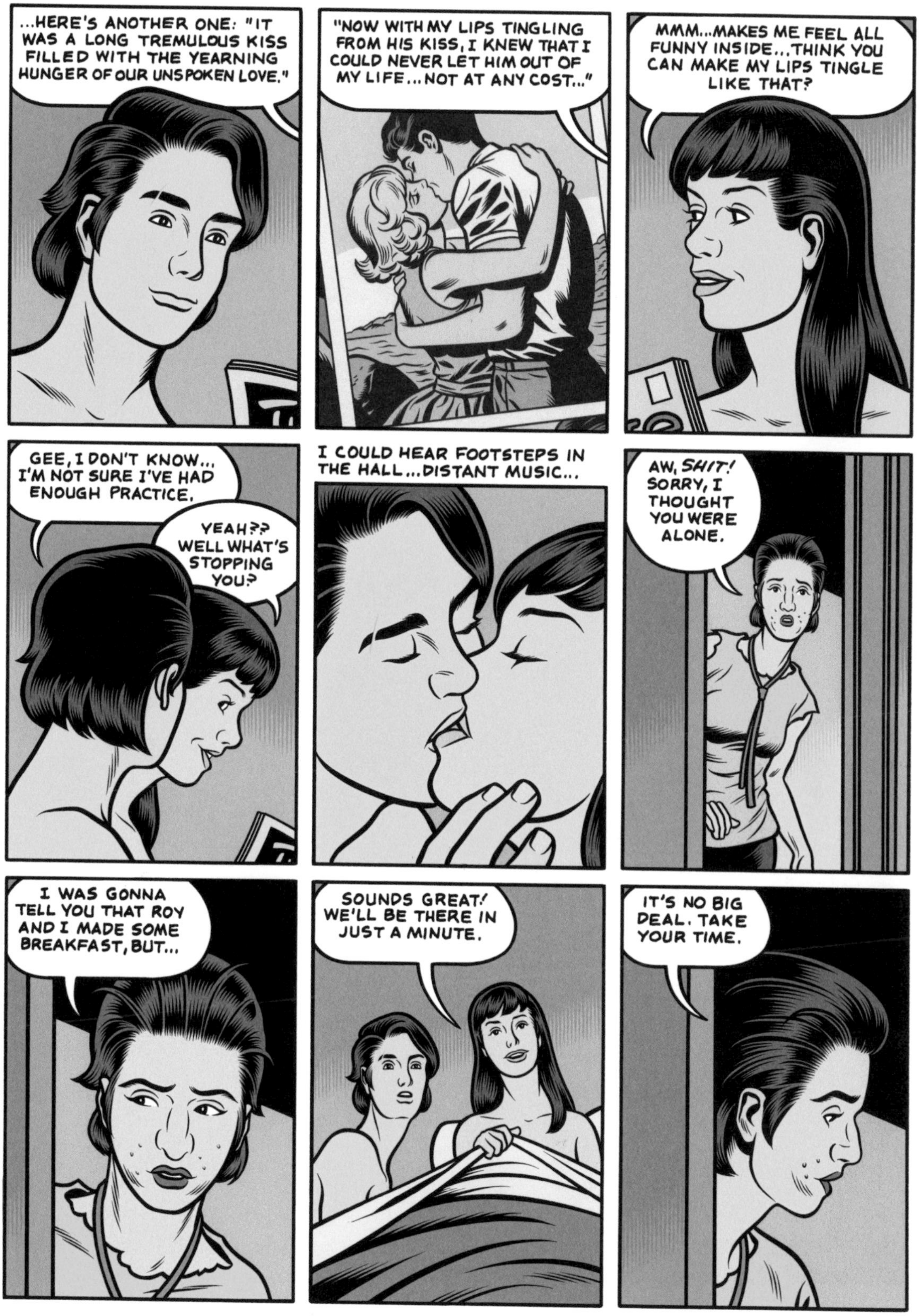
...HERE'S ANOTHER ONE: "IT WAS A LONG TREMULOUS KISS FILLED WITH THE YEARNING HUNGER OF OUR UNSPOKEN LOVE."
"NOW WITH MY LIPS TINGLING FROM HIS KISS, I KNEW THAT I COULD NEVER LET HIM OUT OF MY LIFE... NOT AT ANY COST..."
MMM...MAKES ME FEEL ALL FUNNY INSIDE... THINK YOU CAN MAKE MY LIPS TINGLE LIKE THAT?
GEE, I DON'T KNOW... I'M NOT SURE I'VE HAD ENOUGH PRACTICE.
YEAH?? WELL WHAT'S STOPPING YOU?
I COULD HEAR FOOTSTEPS IN THE HALL... DISTANT MUSIC...
AW, *SHIT!* SORRY, I THOUGHT YOU WERE ALONE.
I WAS GONNA TELL YOU THAT ROY AND I MADE SOME BREAKFAST, BUT...
SOUNDS GREAT! WE'LL BE THERE IN JUST A MINUTE.
IT'S NO BIG DEAL. TAKE YOUR TIME.

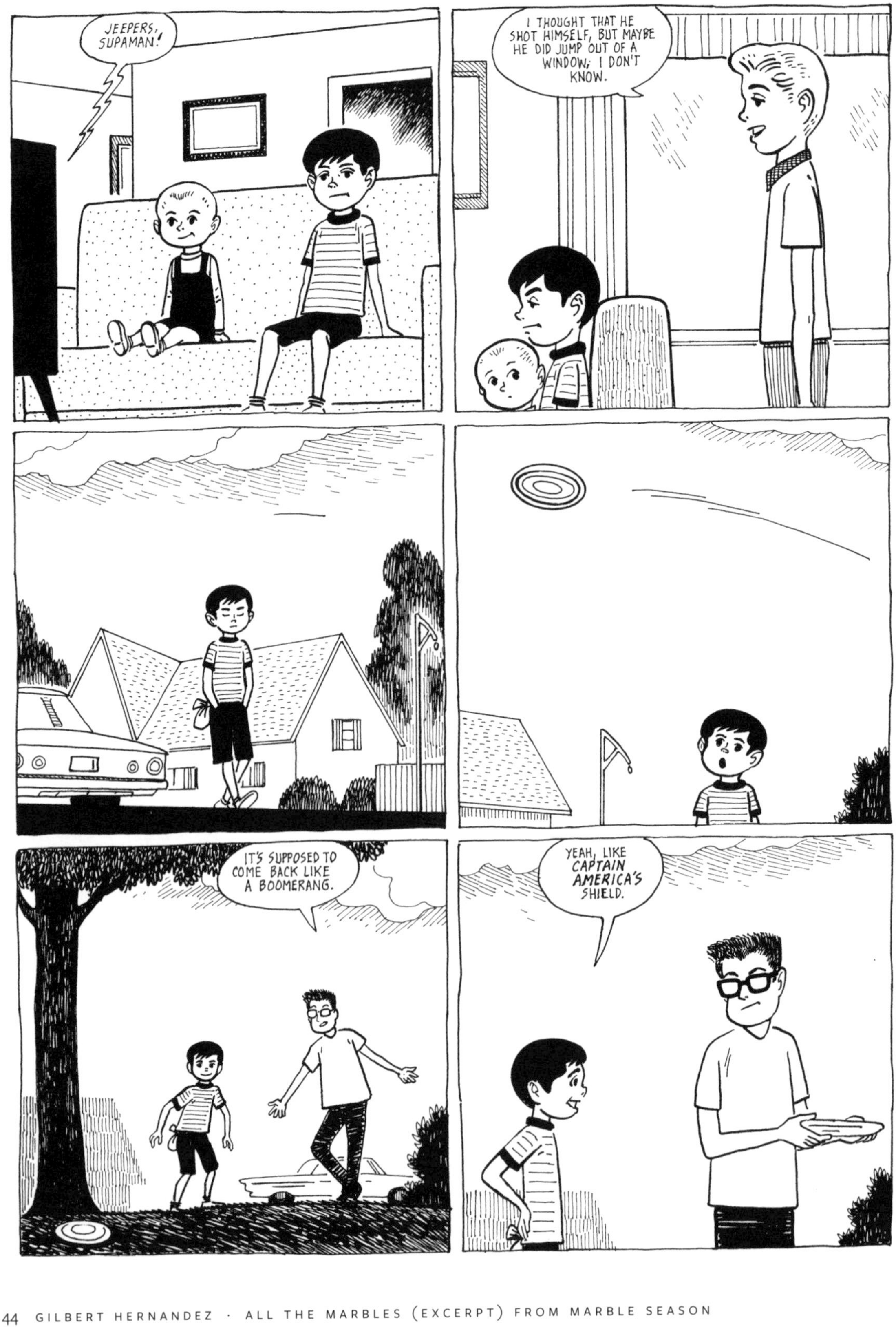
JEEPERS, SUPAMAN!
I THOUGHT THAT HE SHOT HIMSELF, BUT MAYBE HE DID JUMP OUT OF A WINDOW; I DON'T KNOW.
IT'S SUPPOSED TO COME BACK LIKE A BOOMERANG.
YEAH, LIKE CAPTAIN AMERICA'S SHIELD.

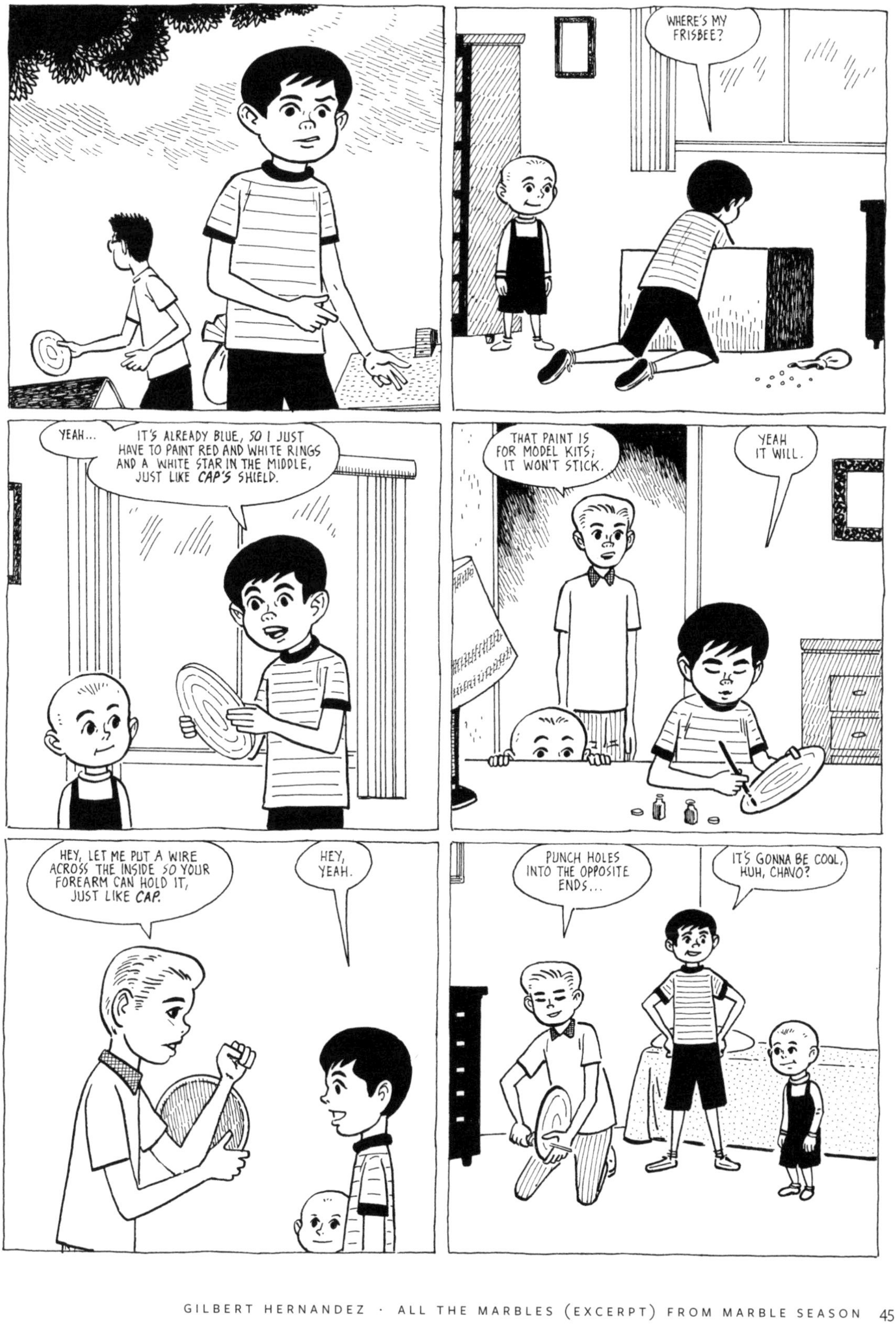
WHERE'S MY FRISBEE?
YEAH...
IT'S ALREADY BLUE, SO I JUST HAVE TO PAINT RED AND WHITE RINGS AND A WHITE STAR IN THE MIDDLE, JUST LIKE CAP'S SHIELD.
THAT PAINT IS FOR MODEL KITS; IT WON'T STICK.
YEAH IT WILL.
HEY, LET ME PUT A WIRE ACROSS THE INSIDE SO YOUR FOREARM CAN HOLD IT, JUST LIKE CAP.
HEY, YEAH.
PUNCH HOLES INTO THE OPPOSITE ENDS...
IT'S GONNA BE COOL, HUH, CHAVO?

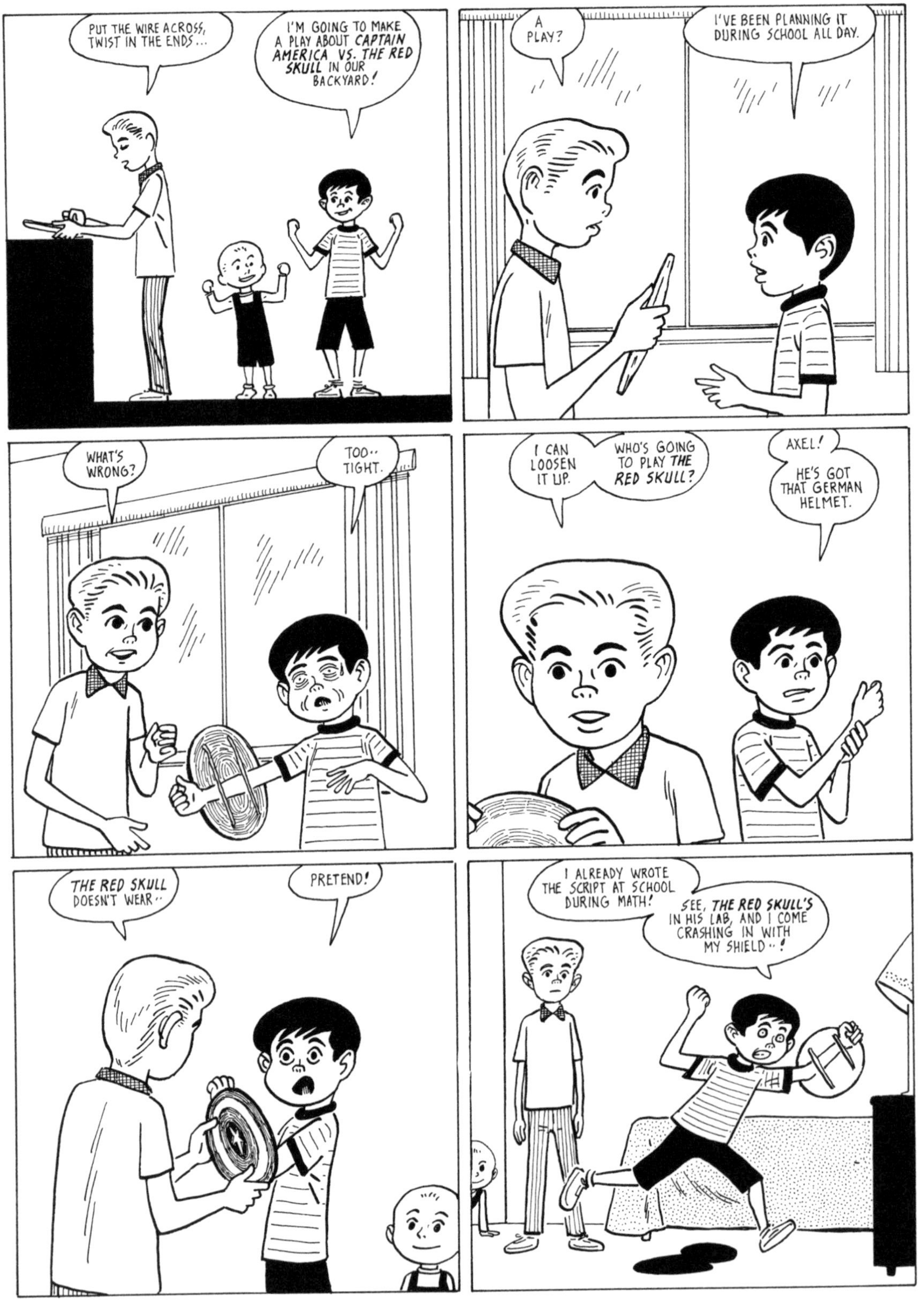
PUT THE WIRE ACROSS, TWIST IN THE ENDS...
I'M GOING TO MAKE A PLAY ABOUT CAPTAIN AMERICA VS. THE RED SKULL IN OUR BACKYARD!
A PLAY?
I'VE BEEN PLANNING IT DURING SCHOOL ALL DAY.
WHAT'S WRONG?
TOO.. TIGHT.
I CAN LOOSEN IT UP.
WHO'S GOING TO PLAY THE RED SKULL?
AXEL!
HE'S GOT THAT GERMAN HELMET.
THE RED SKULL DOESN'T WEAR..
PRETEND!
I ALREADY WROTE THE SCRIPT AT SCHOOL DURING MATH!
SEE, THE RED SKULL'S IN HIS LAB, AND I COME CRASHING IN WITH MY SHIELD..!

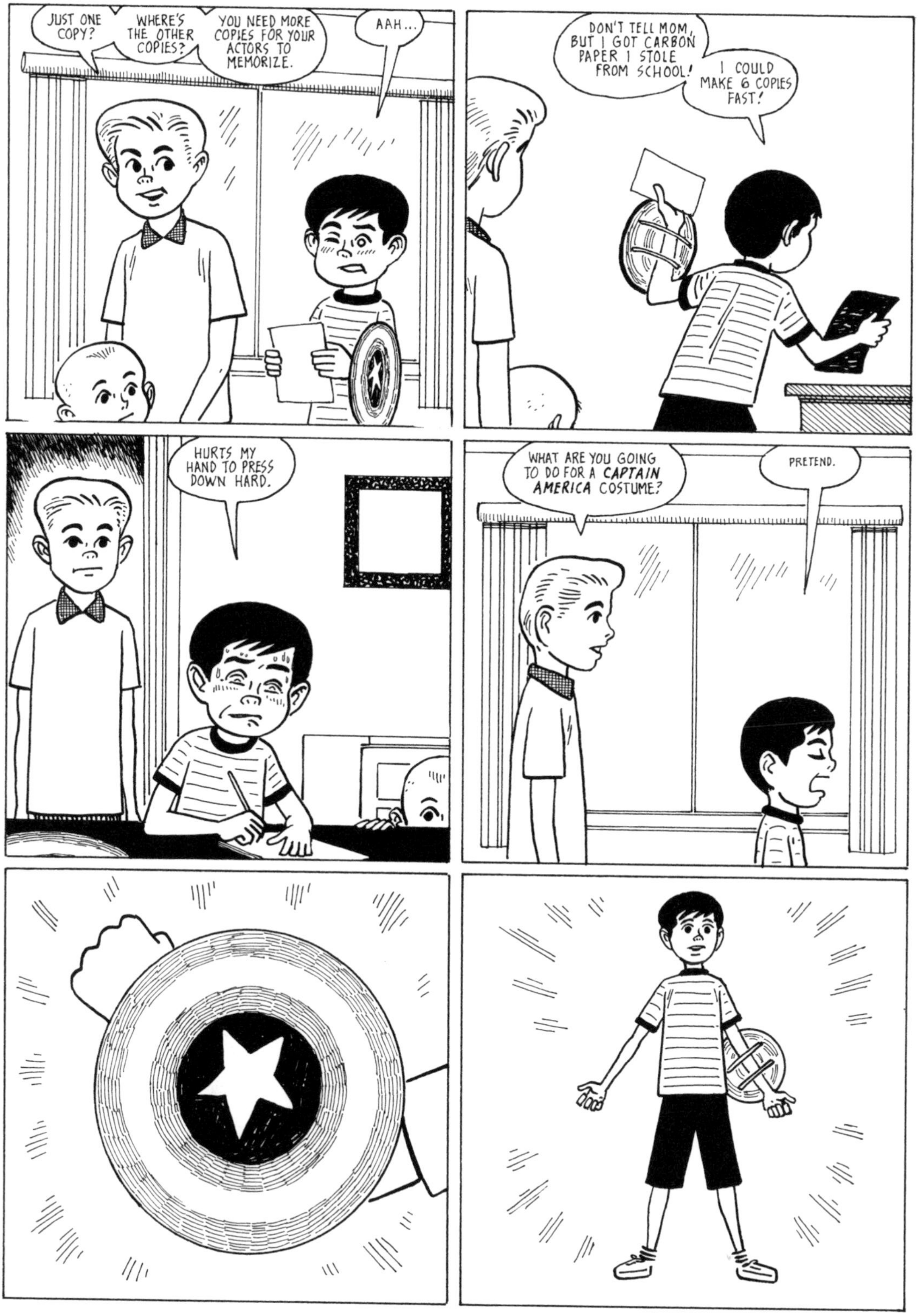
JUST ONE COPY?
WHERE'S THE OTHER COPIES?
YOU NEED MORE COPIES FOR YOUR ACTORS TO MEMORIZE.
AAH...
DON'T TELL MOM, BUT I GOT CARBON PAPER I STOLE FROM SCHOOL!
I COULD MAKE 6 COPIES FAST!
HURTS MY HAND TO PRESS DOWN HARD.
WHAT ARE YOU GOING TO DO FOR A **CAPTAIN AMERICA** COSTUME?
PRETEND.

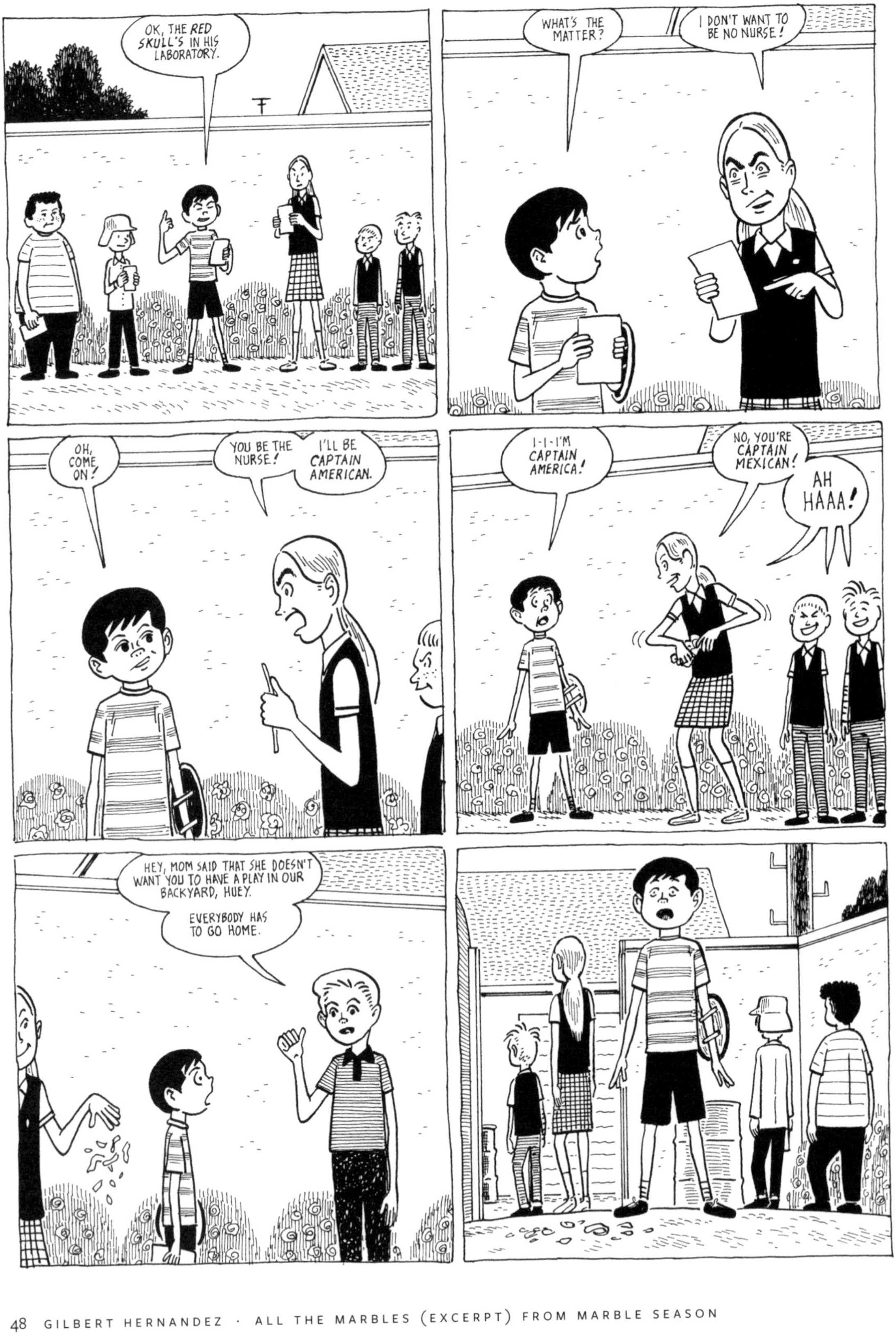
OK, THE RED SKULL'S IN HIS LABORATORY.
WHAT'S THE MATTER?
I DON'T WANT TO BE NO NURSE!
OH, COME ON!
YOU BE THE NURSE!
I'LL BE CAPTAIN AMERICAN.
I-I-I'M CAPTAIN AMERICA!
NO, YOU'RE CAPTAIN MEXICAN!
AH HAAA!
HEY, MOM SAID THAT SHE DOESN'T WANT YOU TO HAVE A PLAY IN OUR BACKYARD, HUEY.
EVERYBODY HAS TO GO HOME.

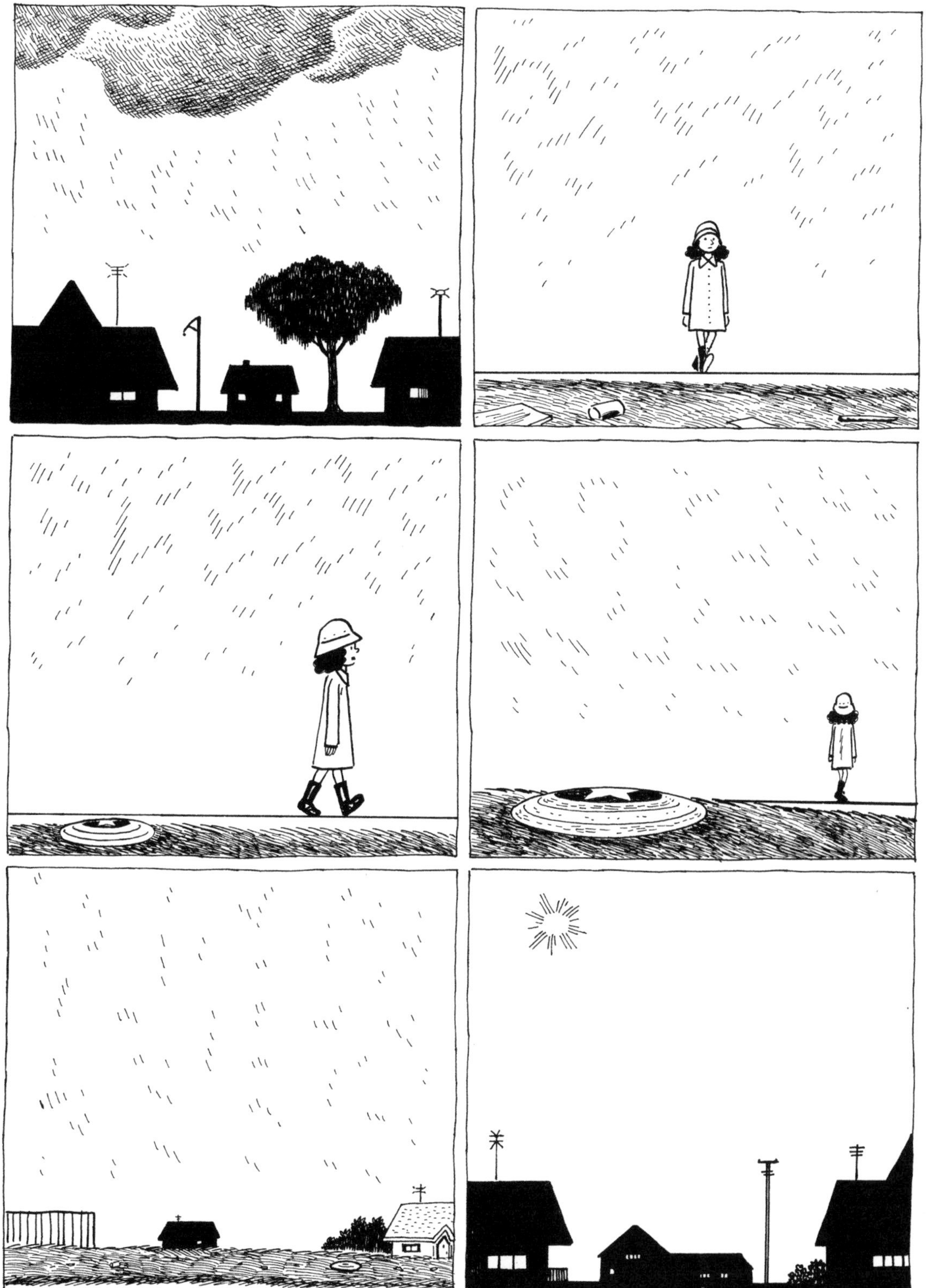

二月に気持ちの整理がついて全てを良く
考えられる様になった時には、カリフォルニア
に帰る事に決めました。あなたのお姿さん
と伯母さんと伯父さん達は皆この選択
には反対で、お互いに気まずいまま別れ
ました。でもそれは仕方のない事でした。

TRANSLATED,
from the JAPANESE,

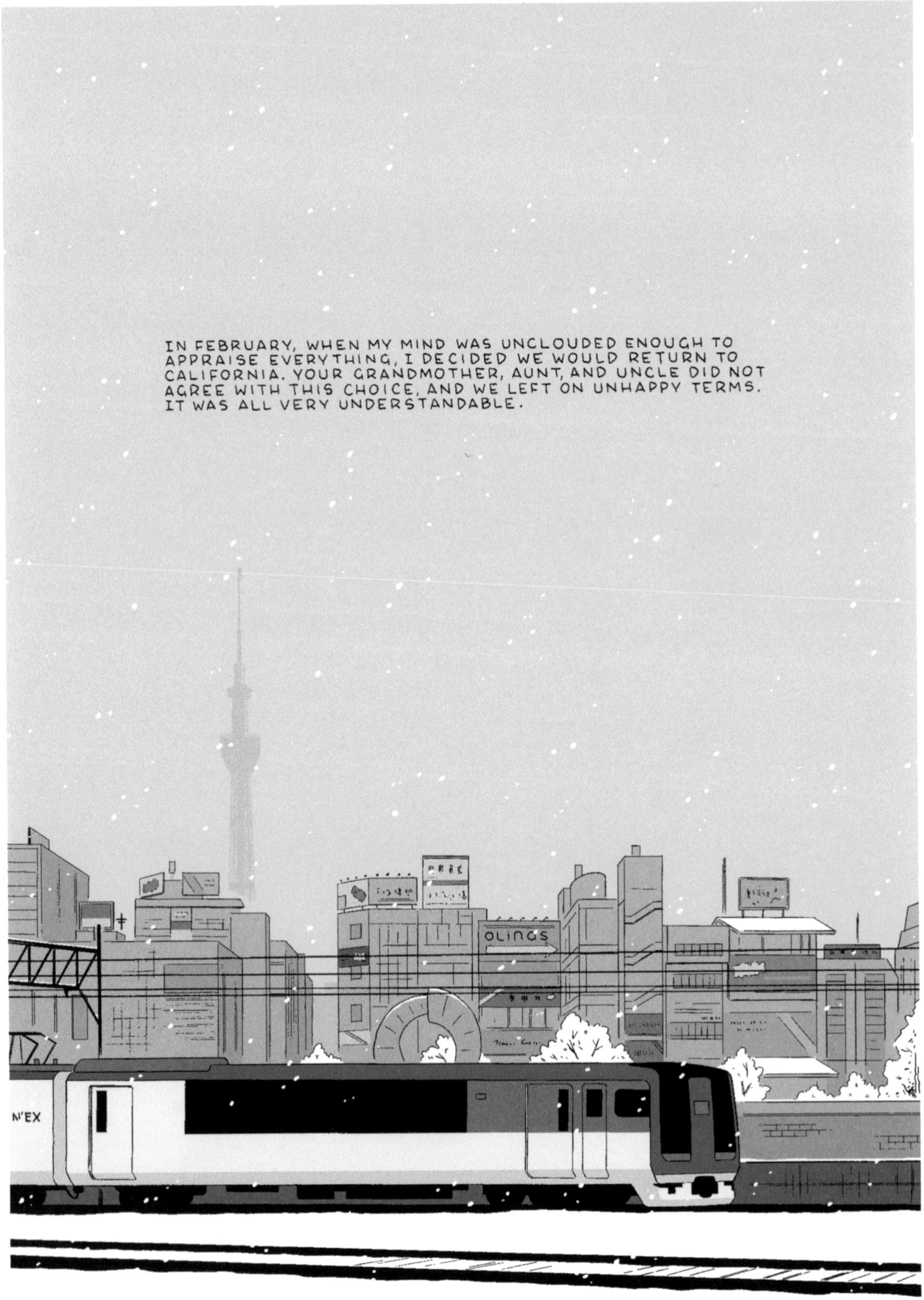
IN FEBRUARY, WHEN MY MIND WAS UNCLOUDED ENOUGH TO APPRAISE EVERYTHING, I DECIDED WE WOULD RETURN TO CALIFORNIA. YOUR GRANDMOTHER, AUNT, AND UNCLE DID NOT AGREE WITH THIS CHOICE, AND WE LEFT ON UNHAPPY TERMS. IT WAS ALL VERY UNDERSTANDABLE.
OLINGS
N'EX

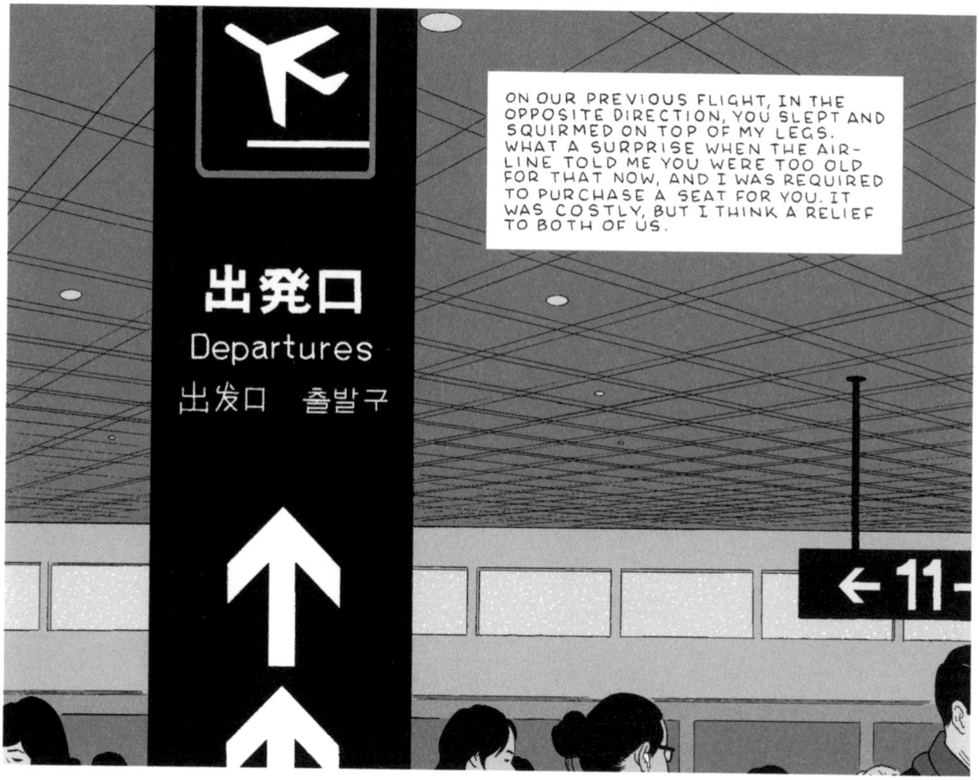
ON OUR PREVIOUS FLIGHT, IN THE OPPOSITE DIRECTION, YOU SLEPT AND SQUIRMED ON TOP OF MY LEGS. WHAT A SURPRISE WHEN THE AIRLINE TOLD ME YOU WERE TOO OLD FOR THAT NOW, AND I WAS REQUIRED TO PURCHASE A SEAT FOR YOU. IT WAS COSTLY, BUT I THINK A RELIEF TO BOTH OF US.
出発口
Departures
出发口 출발구
← 11

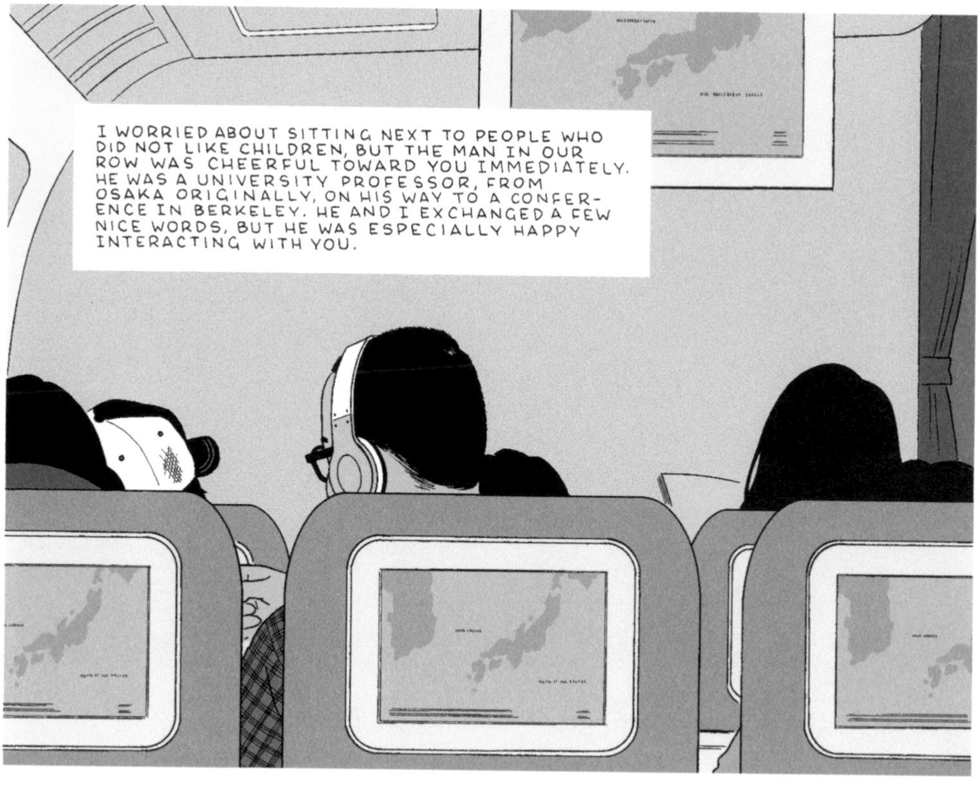
I WORRIED ABOUT SITTING NEXT TO PEOPLE WHO DID NOT LIKE CHILDREN, BUT THE MAN IN OUR ROW WAS CHEERFUL TOWARD YOU IMMEDIATELY. HE WAS A UNIVERSITY PROFESSOR, FROM OSAKA ORIGINALLY, ON HIS WAY TO A CONFERENCE IN BERKELEY. HE AND I EXCHANGED A FEW NICE WORDS, BUT HE WAS ESPECIALLY HAPPY INTERACTING WITH YOU.

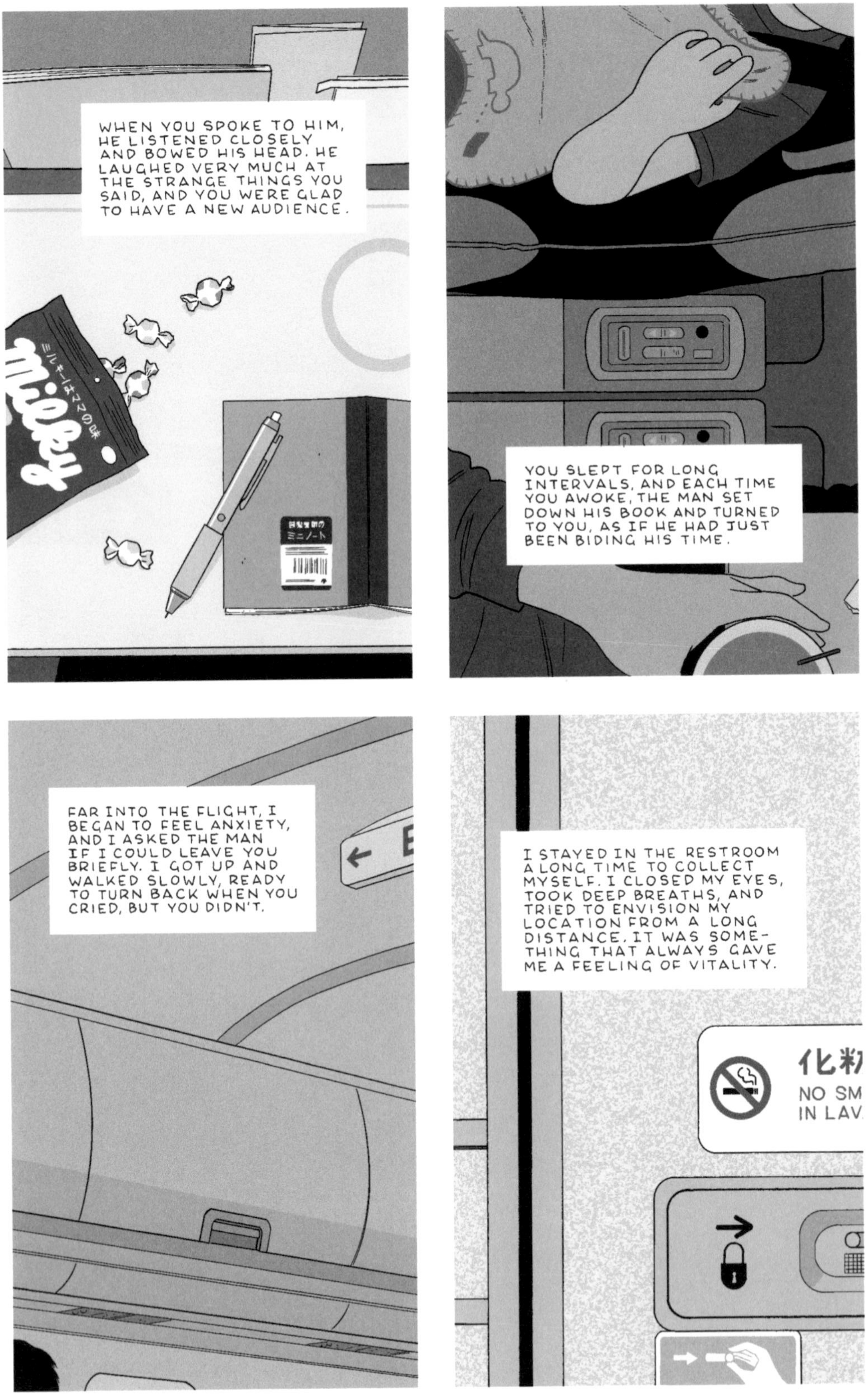
ミルキーはママの味
WHEN YOU SPOKE TO HIM, HE LISTENED CLOSELY AND BOWED HIS HEAD. HE LAUGHED VERY MUCH AT THE STRANGE THINGS YOU SAID, AND YOU WERE GLAD TO HAVE A NEW AUDIENCE.
YOU SLEPT FOR LONG INTERVALS, AND EACH TIME YOU AWOKE, THE MAN SET DOWN HIS BOOK AND TURNED TO YOU, AS IF HE HAD JUST BEEN BIDING HIS TIME.
FAR INTO THE FLIGHT, I BEGAN TO FEEL ANXIETY, AND I ASKED THE MAN IF I COULD LEAVE YOU BRIEFLY. I GOT UP AND WALKED SLOWLY, READY TO TURN BACK WHEN YOU CRIED, BUT YOU DIDN'T.
I STAYED IN THE RESTROOM A LONG TIME TO COLLECT MYSELF. I CLOSED MY EYES, TOOK DEEP BREATHS, AND TRIED TO ENVISION MY LOCATION FROM A LONG DISTANCE. IT WAS SOMETHING THAT ALWAYS GAVE ME A FEELING OF VITALITY.

BEFORE RETURNING TO MY
SEAT, I ASKED A STEWARDESS
FOR WATER. SHE HANDED ME
A BOTTLE AND ASKED IF I
WOULD ALSO LIKE SOME
SNACK FOR YOU, AND PERHAPS
A DRINK FOR MY HUSBAND.

I LAUGHED SLIGHTLY, BUT DID
NOT BOTHER TO CORRECT HER.
DID SHE NOT NOTICE YOUR
HAIR? MOVING SLOWLY DOWN
THE DARKENED AISLE, I HAD
THE STRANGE THOUGHT THAT
MAYBE SHE WAS NOT MISTAKEN
AFTER ALL.

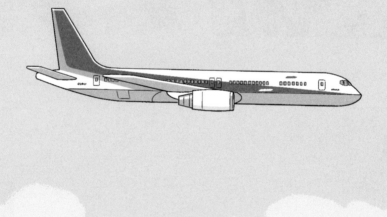

FOR THOSE MOMENTS, IT WAS VIVID TO ME. WE WERE GOING
ON VACATION TO AMERICA: ME, YOU, AND YOUR FATHER, A
UNIVERSITY PROFESSOR FROM OSAKA.

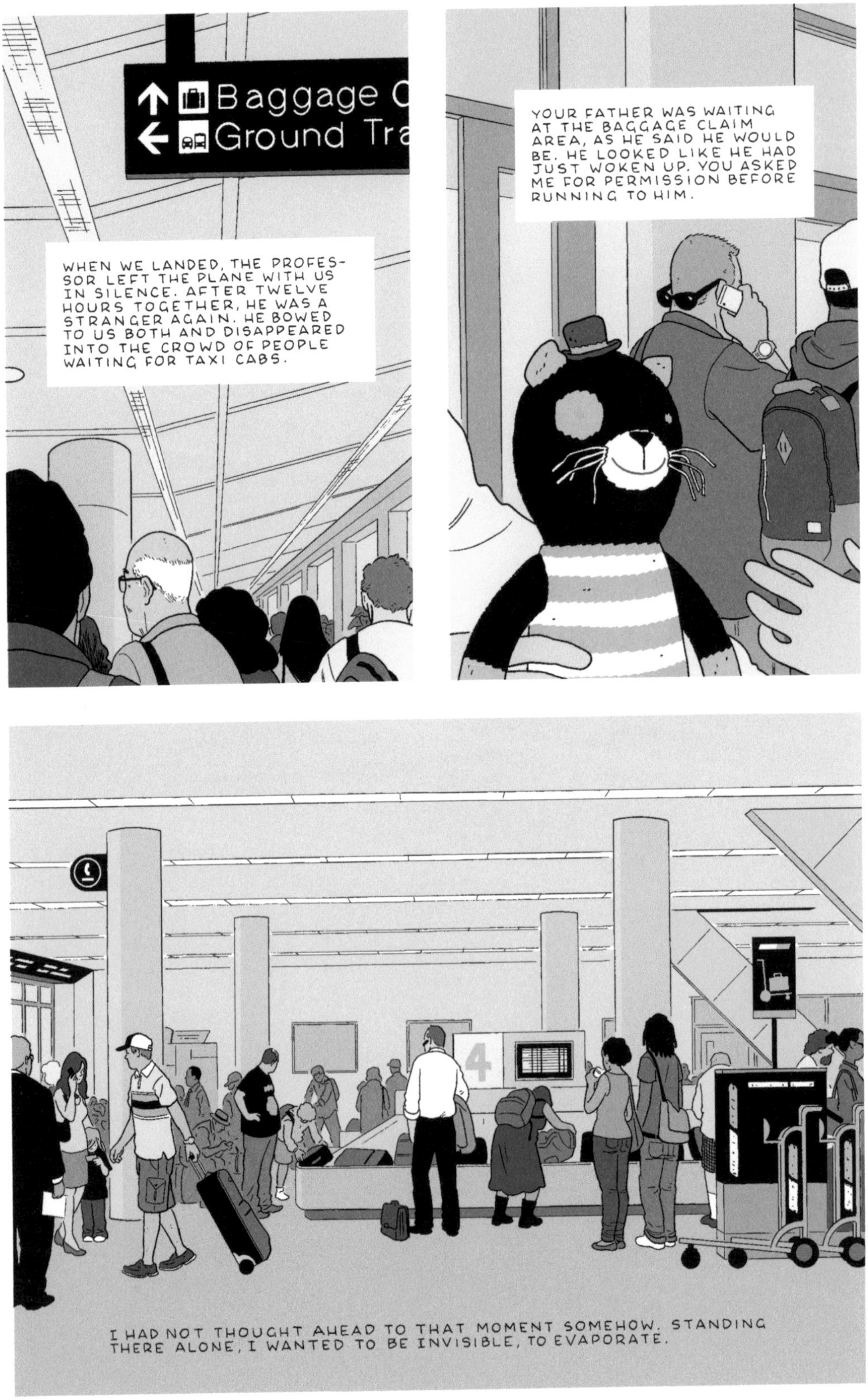
Baggage C
Ground Tra
WHEN WE LANDED, THE PROFESSOR LEFT THE PLANE WITH US IN SILENCE. AFTER TWELVE HOURS TOGETHER, HE WAS A STRANGER AGAIN. HE BOWED TO US BOTH AND DISAPPEARED INTO THE CROWD OF PEOPLE WAITING FOR TAXI CABS.
YOUR FATHER WAS WAITING AT THE BAGGAGE CLAIM AREA, AS HE SAID HE WOULD BE. HE LOOKED LIKE HE HAD JUST WOKEN UP. YOU ASKED ME FOR PERMISSION BEFORE RUNNING TO HIM.
4
I HAD NOT THOUGHT AHEAD TO THAT MOMENT SOMEHOW. STANDING THERE ALONE, I WANTED TO BE INVISIBLE, TO EVAPORATE.

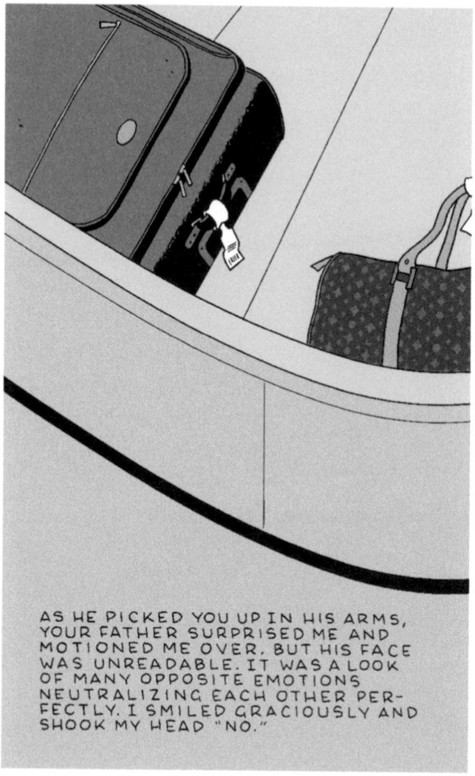
AS HE PICKED YOU UP IN HIS ARMS, YOUR FATHER SURPRISED ME AND MOTIONED ME OVER. BUT HIS FACE WAS UNREADABLE. IT WAS A LOOK OF MANY OPPOSITE EMOTIONS NEUTRALIZING EACH OTHER PERFECTLY. I SMILED GRACIOUSLY AND SHOOK MY HEAD "NO."

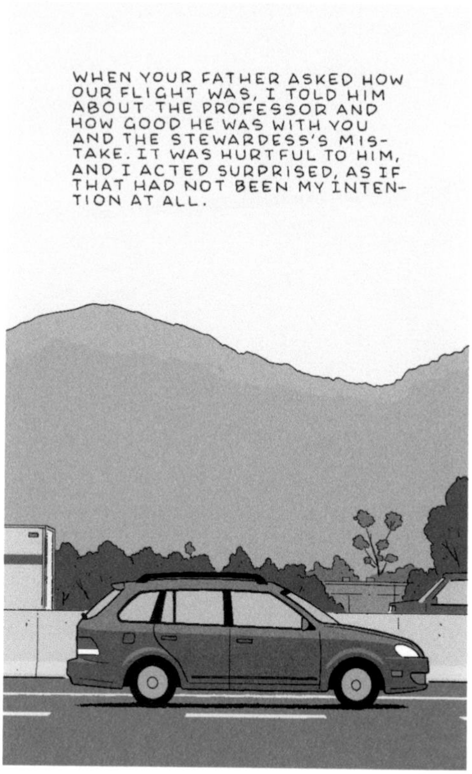
WHEN YOUR FATHER ASKED HOW OUR FLIGHT WAS, I TOLD HIM ABOUT THE PROFESSOR AND HOW GOOD HE WAS WITH YOU AND THE STEWARDESS'S MISTAKE. IT WAS HURTFUL TO HIM, AND I ACTED SURPRISED, AS IF THAT HAD NOT BEEN MY INTENTION AT ALL.

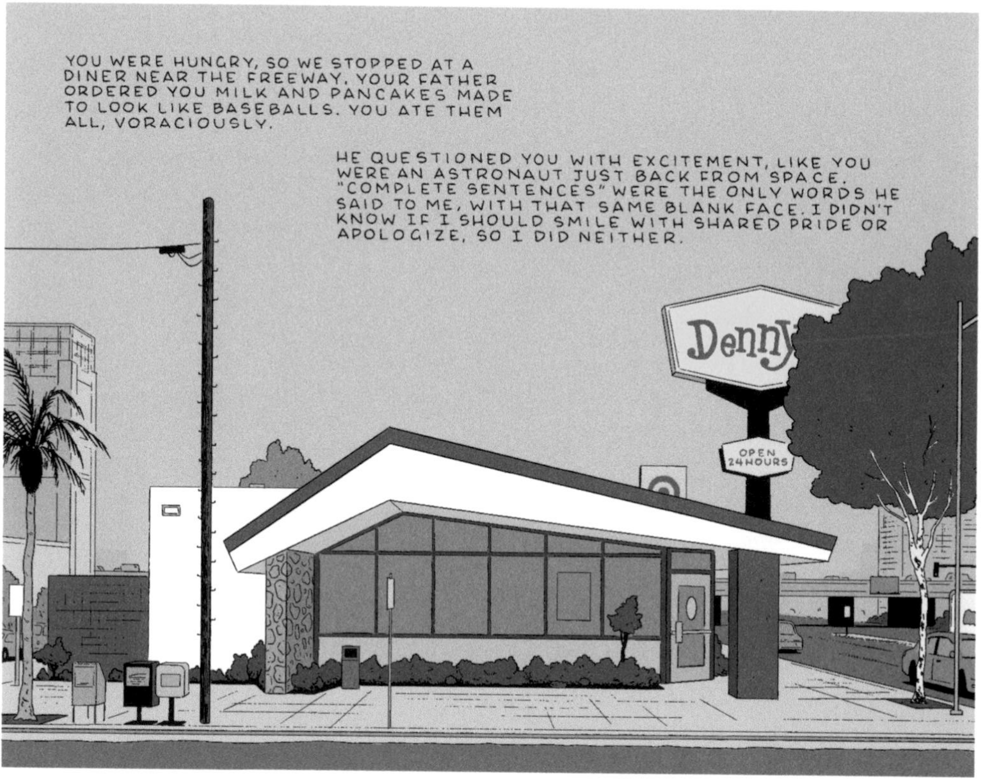
YOU WERE HUNGRY, SO WE STOPPED AT A DINER NEAR THE FREEWAY. YOUR FATHER ORDERED YOU MILK AND PANCAKES MADE TO LOOK LIKE BASEBALLS. YOU ATE THEM ALL, VORACIOUSLY.
HE QUESTIONED YOU WITH EXCITEMENT, LIKE YOU WERE AN ASTRONAUT JUST BACK FROM SPACE. "COMPLETE SENTENCES" WERE THE ONLY WORDS HE SAID TO ME, WITH THAT SAME BLANK FACE. I DIDN'T KNOW IF I SHOULD SMILE WITH SHARED PRIDE OR APOLOGIZE, SO I DID NEITHER.
Denny
OPEN 24HOURS

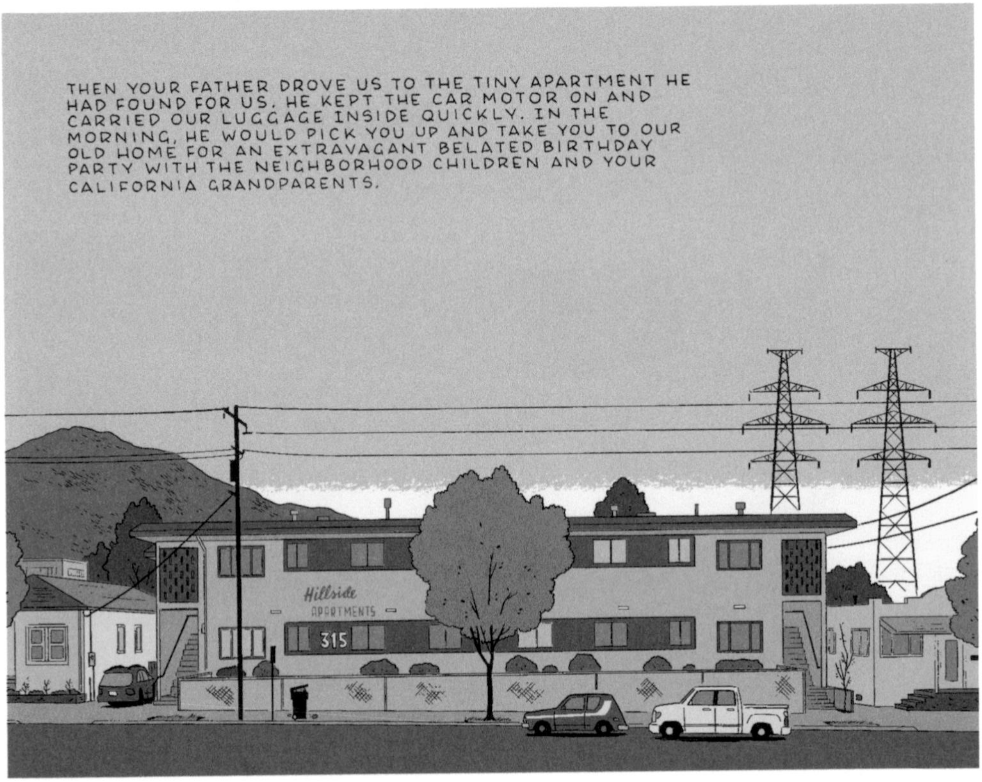
THEN YOUR FATHER DROVE US TO THE TINY APARTMENT HE HAD FOUND FOR US. HE KEPT THE CAR MOTOR ON AND CARRIED OUR LUGGAGE INSIDE QUICKLY. IN THE MORNING, HE WOULD PICK YOU UP AND TAKE YOU TO OUR OLD HOME FOR AN EXTRAVAGANT BELATED BIRTHDAY PARTY WITH THE NEIGHBORHOOD CHILDREN AND YOUR CALIFORNIA GRANDPARENTS.
Hillside
APARTMENTS
315

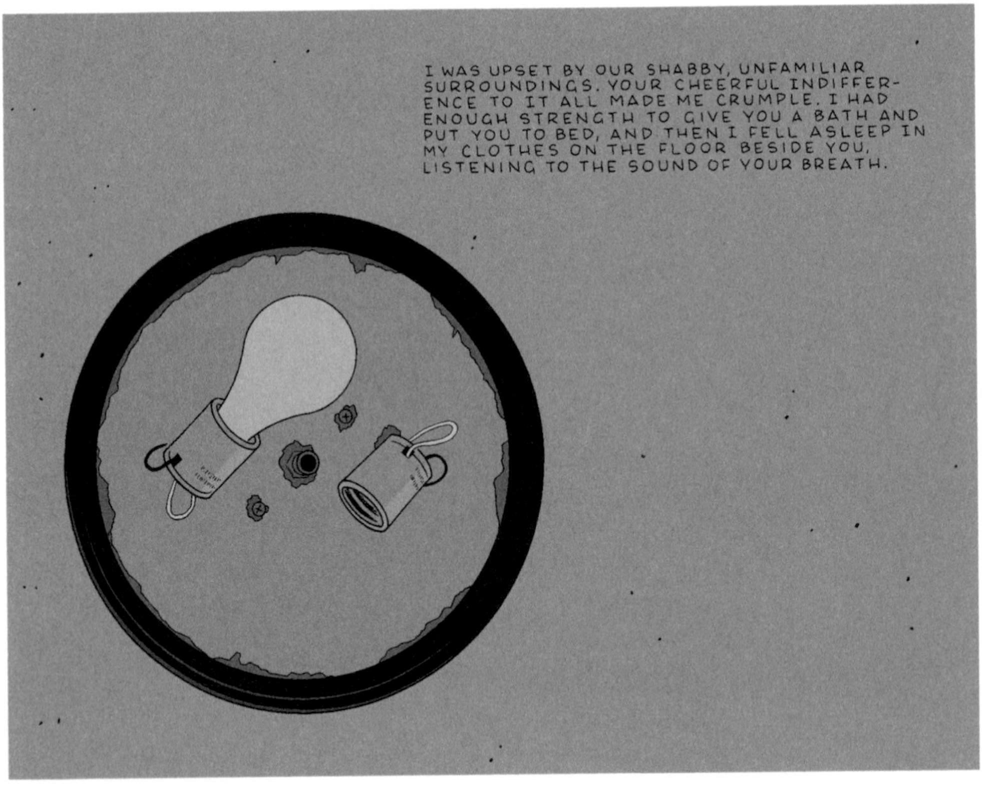
I WAS UPSET BY OUR SHABBY, UNFAMILIAR SURROUNDINGS. YOUR CHEERFUL INDIFFERENCE TO IT ALL MADE ME CRUMPLE. I HAD ENOUGH STRENGTH TO GIVE YOU A BATH AND PUT YOU TO BED, AND THEN I FELL ASLEEP IN MY CLOTHES ON THE FLOOR BESIDE YOU, LISTENING TO THE SOUND OF YOUR BREATH.

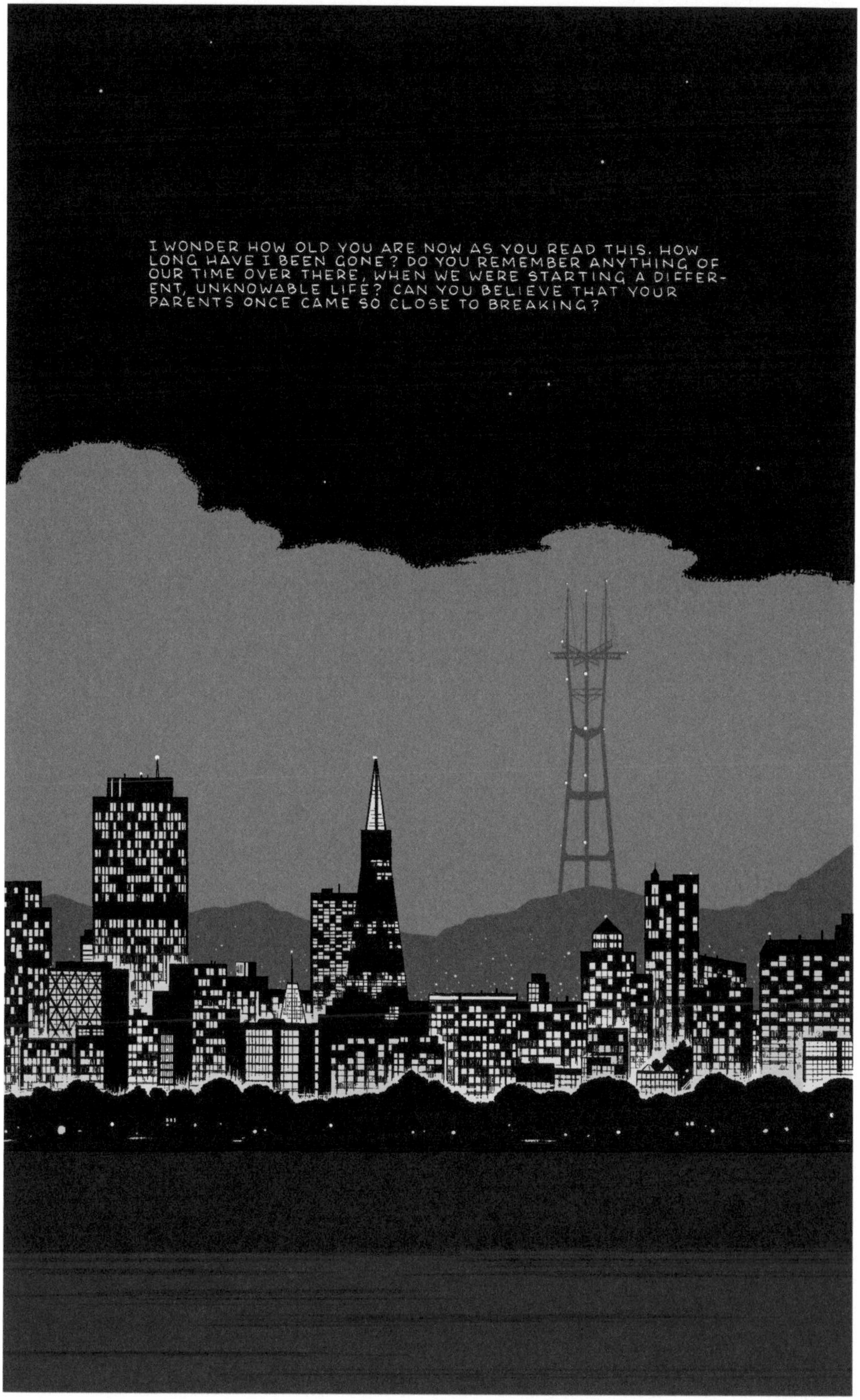
I WONDER HOW OLD YOU ARE NOW AS YOU READ THIS. HOW LONG HAVE I BEEN GONE? DO YOU REMEMBER ANYTHING OF OUR TIME OVER THERE, WHEN WE WERE STARTING A DIFFERENT, UNKNOWABLE LIFE? CAN YOU BELIEVE THAT YOUR PARENTS ONCE CAME SO CLOSE TO BREAKING?

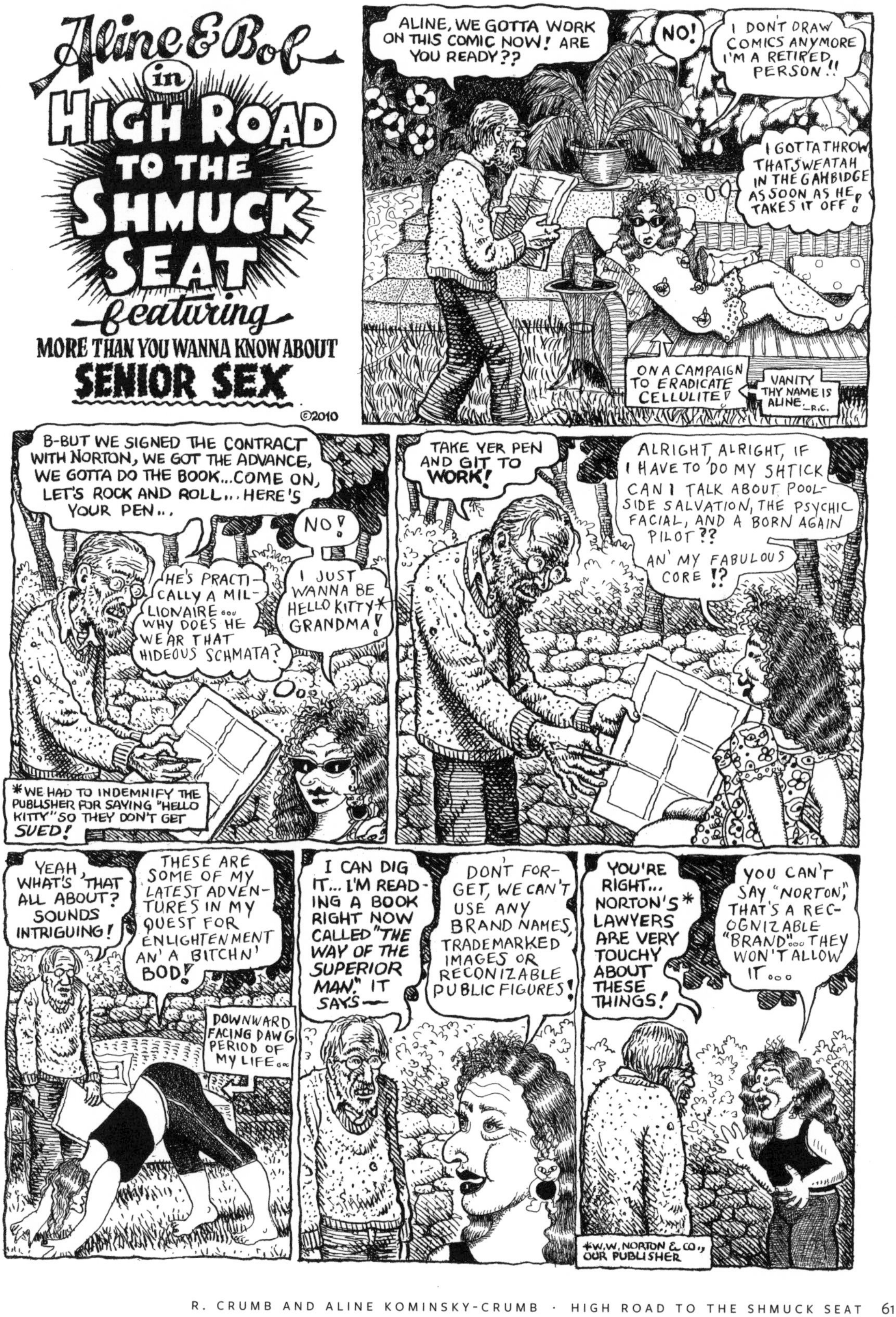

Aline & Bob in
HIGH ROAD TO THE SHMUCK SEAT
featuring
MORE THAN YOU WANNA KNOW ABOUT
SENIOR SEX
©2010
ALINE, WE GOTTA WORK ON THIS COMIC NOW! ARE YOU READY??
NO!
I DON'T DRAW COMICS ANYMORE I'M A RETIRED PERSON!!
I GOTTA THROW THAT SWEATAH IN THE GAHBIDGE AS SOON AS HE TAKES IT OFF!
ON A CAMPAIGN TO ERADICATE CELLULITE!
VANITY THY NAME IS ALINE. —R.C.
B-BUT WE SIGNED THE CONTRACT WITH NORTON, WE GOT THE ADVANCE, WE GOTTA DO THE BOOK... COME ON, LET'S ROCK AND ROLL... HERE'S YOUR PEN...
NO!
I JUST WANNA BE HELLO KITTY* GRANDMA!
HE'S PRACTICALLY A MILLIONAIRE... WHY DOES HE WEAR THAT HIDEOUS SCHMATA?
*WE HAD TO INDEMNIFY THE PUBLISHER FOR SAYING "HELLO KITTY" SO THEY DON'T GET SUED!
TAKE YER PEN AND GIT TO WORK!
ALRIGHT, ALRIGHT, IF I HAVE TO DO MY SHTICK CAN I TALK ABOUT POOL-SIDE SALVATION, THE PSYCHIC FACIAL, AND A BORN AGAIN PILOT??
AN' MY FABULOUS CORE!?
YEAH, WHAT'S THAT ALL ABOUT? SOUNDS INTRIGUING!
THESE ARE SOME OF MY LATEST ADVENTURES IN MY QUEST FOR ENLIGHTENMENT AN' A BITCHN' BOD!
DOWNWARD FACING DAWG PERIOD OF MY LIFE...
I CAN DIG IT... I'M READING A BOOK RIGHT NOW CALLED "THE WAY OF THE SUPERIOR MAN." IT SAYS—
DON'T FORGET, WE CAN'T USE ANY BRAND NAMES, TRADEMARKED IMAGES OR RECONIZABLE PUBLIC FIGURES!
YOU'RE RIGHT... NORTON'S* LAWYERS ARE VERY TOUCHY ABOUT THESE THINGS!
YOU CAN'T SAY "NORTON," THAT'S A RECOGNIZABLE "BRAND"... THEY WON'T ALLOW IT...
*W.W. NORTON & CO., OUR PUBLISHER

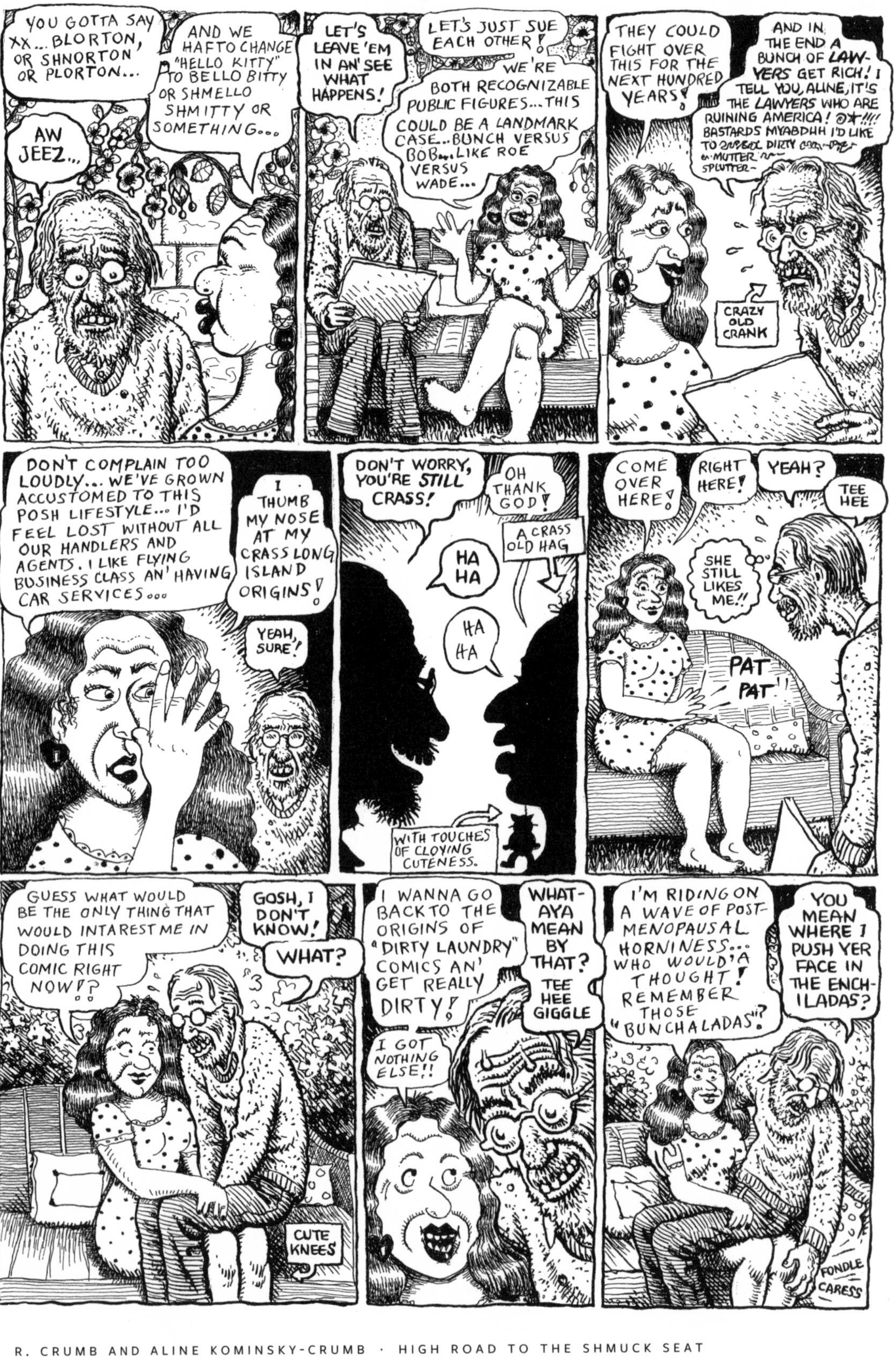
YOU GOTTA SAY XX... BLORTON, OR SHNORTON OR PLORTON...
AND WE HAFTO CHANGE "HELLO KITTY" TO BELLO BITTY OR SHMELLO SHMITTY OR SOMETHING...
AW JEEZ...
LET'S LEAVE 'EM IN AN' SEE WHAT HAPPENS!
LET'S JUST SUE EACH OTHER!
WE'RE BOTH RECOGNIZABLE PUBLIC FIGURES... THIS COULD BE A LANDMARK CASE... BUNCH VERSUS BOB... LIKE ROE VERSUS WADE...
THEY COULD FIGHT OVER THIS FOR THE NEXT HUNDRED YEARS!
AND IN THE END A BUNCH OF LAWYERS GET RICH! I TELL YOU, ALINE, IT'S THE LAWYERS WHO ARE RUINING AMERICA! @*!!!! BASTARDS MYABDHH I'D LIKE TO DIRTY MUTTER SPLUTTER-
CRAZY OLD CRANK
DON'T COMPLAIN TOO LOUDLY... WE'VE GROWN ACCUSTOMED TO THIS POSH LIFESTYLE... I'D FEEL LOST WITHOUT ALL OUR HANDLERS AND AGENTS. I LIKE FLYING BUSINESS CLASS AN' HAVING CAR SERVICES...
I THUMB MY NOSE AT MY CRASS LONG ISLAND ORIGINS!
YEAH, SURE!
DON'T WORRY, YOU'RE STILL CRASS!
OH THANK GOD!
A CRASS OLD HAG
HA HA
HA HA
WITH TOUCHES OF CLOYING CUTENESS.
COME OVER HERE!
RIGHT HERE!
YEAH?
TEE HEE
SHE STILL LIKES ME!!
PAT PAT
GUESS WHAT WOULD BE THE ONLY THING THAT WOULD INTAREST ME IN DOING THIS COMIC RIGHT NOW!?
GOSH, I DON'T KNOW!
WHAT?
CUTE KNEES
I WANNA GO BACK TO THE ORIGINS OF "DIRTY LAUNDRY" COMICS AN' GET REALLY DIRTY!
WHAT-AYA MEAN BY THAT?
TEE HEE GIGGLE
I GOT NOTHING ELSE!!
I'M RIDING ON A WAVE OF POST-MENOPAUSAL HORNINESS... WHO WOULD'A THOUGHT! REMEMBER THOSE "BUNCHALADAS"?
YOU MEAN WHERE I PUSH YER FACE IN THE ENCHILADAS?
FONDLE
CARESS

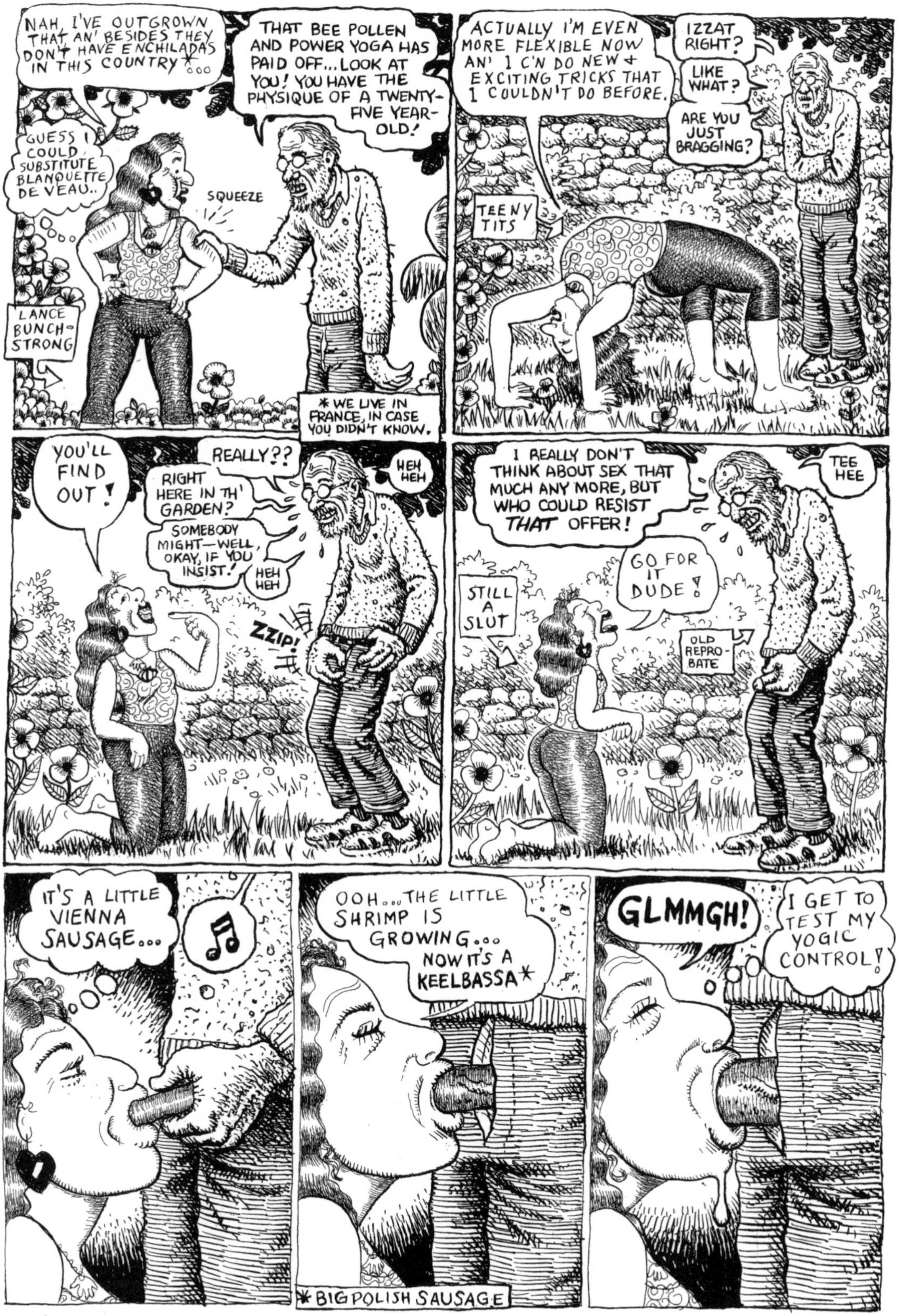
NAH, I'VE OUTGROWN THAT AN' BESIDES THEY DON'T HAVE ENCHILADAS IN THIS COUNTRY*...
THAT BEE POLLEN AND POWER YOGA HAS PAID OFF... LOOK AT YOU! YOU HAVE THE PHYSIQUE OF A TWENTY-FIVE YEAR-OLD!
GUESS I COULD SUBSTITUTE BLANQUETTE DE VEAU..
SQUEEZE
LANCE BUNCH-STRONG
*WE LIVE IN FRANCE, IN CASE YOU DIDN'T KNOW.
ACTUALLY I'M EVEN MORE FLEXIBLE NOW AN' I C'N DO NEW & EXCITING TRICKS THAT I COULDN'T DO BEFORE.
IZZAT RIGHT?
LIKE WHAT?
ARE YOU JUST BRAGGING?
TEENY TITS
YOU'LL FIND OUT!
REALLY??
RIGHT HERE IN TH' GARDEN?
SOMEBODY MIGHT—WELL, OKAY, IF YOU INSIST!
HEH HEH
HEH HEH
ZZIP!
I REALLY DON'T THINK ABOUT SEX THAT MUCH ANY MORE, BUT WHO COULD RESIST THAT OFFER!
TEE HEE
GO FOR IT DUDE!
STILL A SLUT
OLD REPROBATE
IT'S A LITTLE VIENNA SAUSAGE...
OOH... THE LITTLE SHRIMP IS GROWING... NOW IT'S A KEELBASSA*
*BIG POLISH SAUSAGE
GLMMGH!
I GET TO TEST MY YOGIC CONTROL!

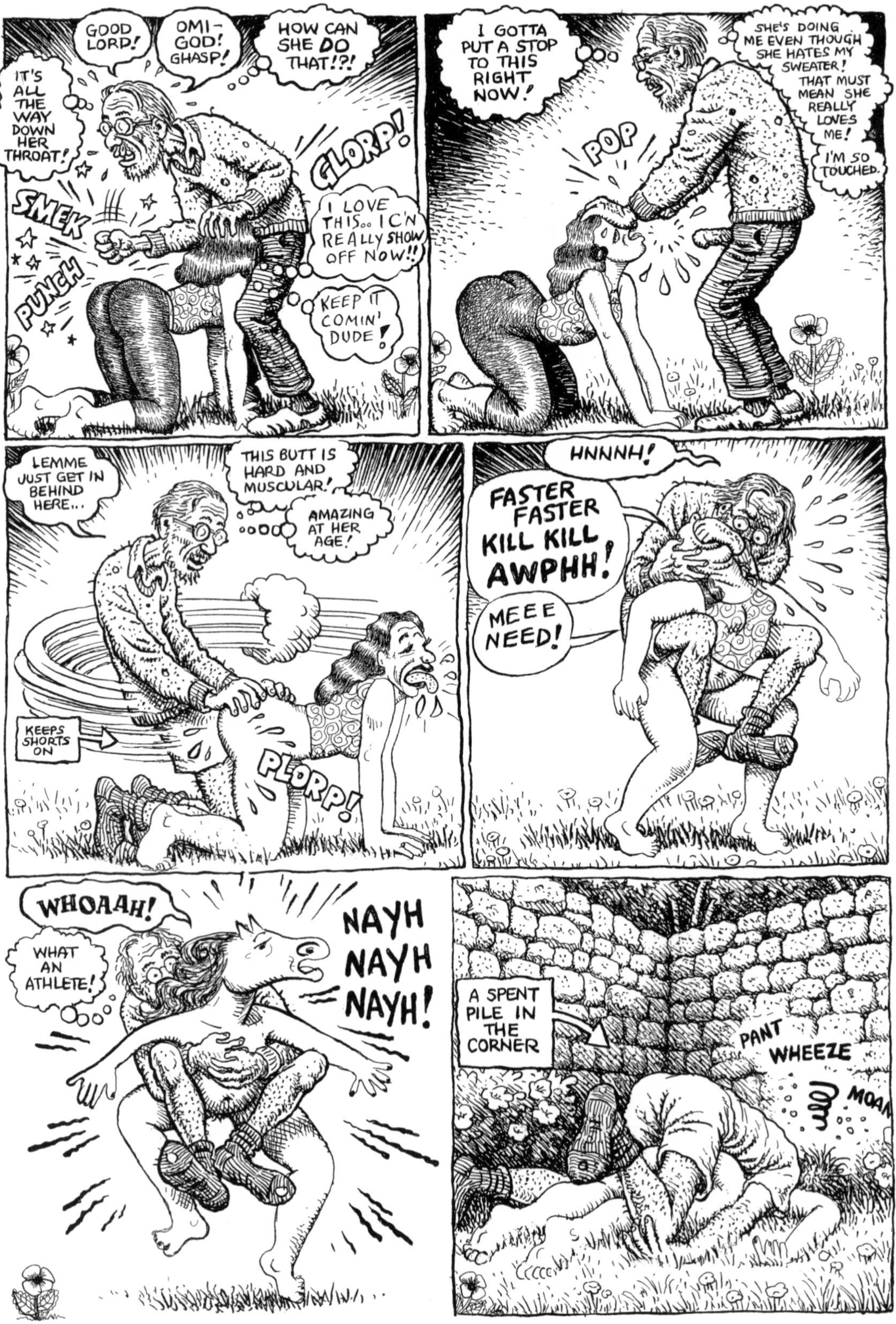
GOOD LORD!
OMI-GOD! GHASP!
HOW CAN SHE DO THAT!?!
IT'S ALL THE WAY DOWN HER THROAT!
GLORP!
SMEK
PUNCH
I LOVE THIS.. I C'N REALLY SHOW OFF NOW!!
KEEP IT COMIN' DUDE!
I GOTTA PUT A STOP TO THIS RIGHT NOW!
SHE'S DOING ME EVEN THOUGH SHE HATES MY SWEATER! THAT MUST MEAN SHE REALLY LOVES ME!
I'M SO TOUCHED.
POP
LEMME JUST GET IN BEHIND HERE...
THIS BUTT IS HARD AND MUSCULAR!
AMAZING AT HER AGE!
KEEPS SHORTS ON
PLORP!
HNNNH!
FASTER FASTER KILL KILL AWPHH!
MEEE NEED!
WHOAAH!
WHAT AN ATHLETE!
NAYH NAYH NAYH!
A SPENT PILE IN THE CORNER
PANT
WHEEZE
MOAN

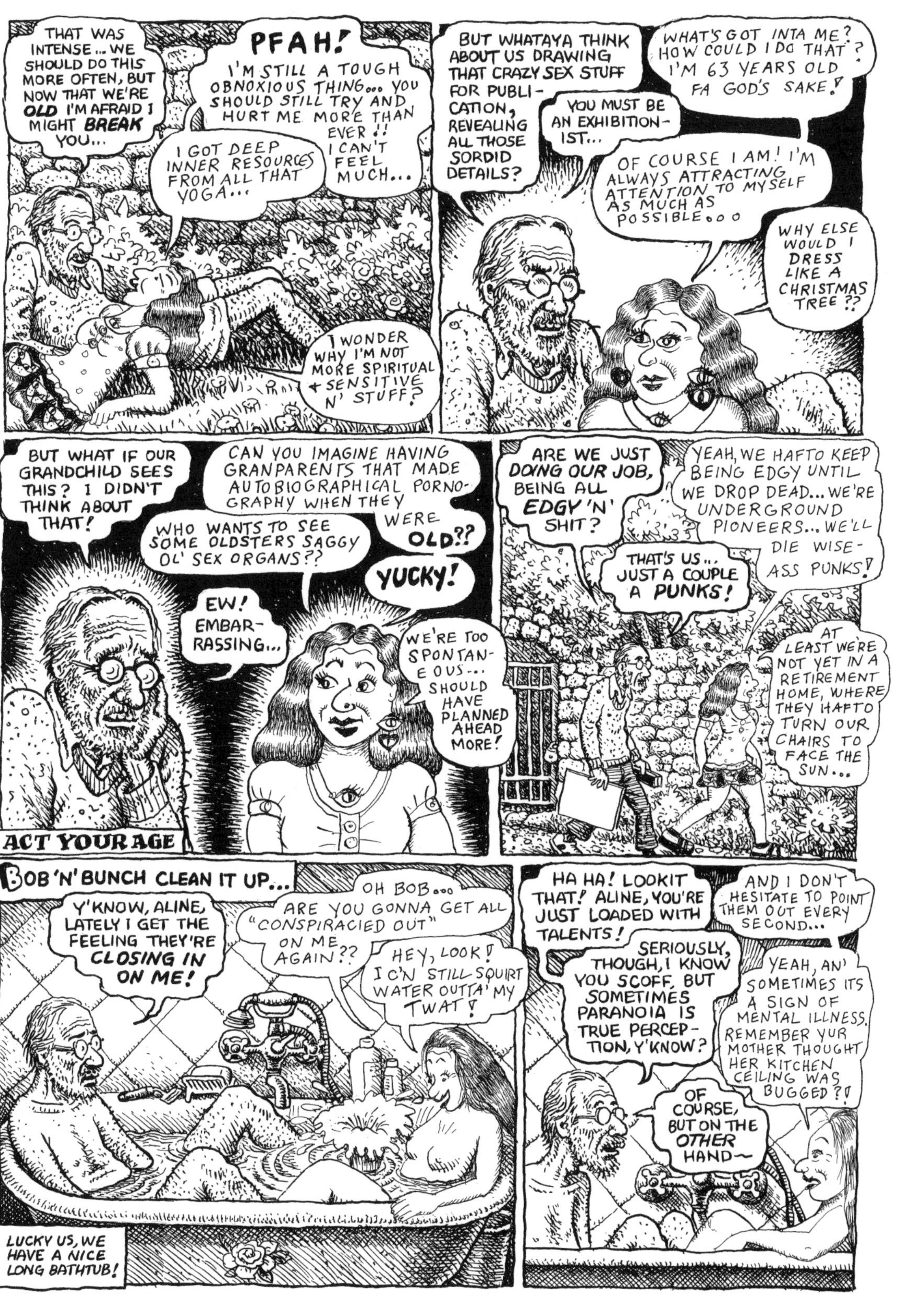
THAT WAS INTENSE... WE SHOULD DO THIS MORE OFTEN, BUT NOW THAT WE'RE OLD I'M AFRAID I MIGHT BREAK YOU...
PFAH! I'M STILL A TOUGH OBNOXIOUS THING... YOU SHOULD STILL TRY AND HURT ME MORE THAN EVER!! I CAN'T FEEL MUCH...
I GOT DEEP INNER RESOURCES FROM ALL THAT YOGA...
I WONDER WHY I'M NOT MORE SPIRITUAL + SENSITIVE N' STUFF?
BUT WHATAYA THINK ABOUT US DRAWING THAT CRAZY SEX STUFF FOR PUBLICATION, REVEALING ALL THOSE SORDID DETAILS?
WHAT'S GOT INTA ME? HOW COULD I DO THAT? I'M 63 YEARS OLD FA GOD'S SAKE!
YOU MUST BE AN EXHIBITIONIST...
OF COURSE I AM! I'M ALWAYS ATTRACTING ATTENTION TO MYSELF AS MUCH AS POSSIBLE...
WHY ELSE WOULD I DRESS LIKE A CHRISTMAS TREE??
BUT WHAT IF OUR GRANDCHILD SEES THIS? I DIDN'T THINK ABOUT THAT!
CAN YOU IMAGINE HAVING GRANPARENTS THAT MADE AUTOBIOGRAPHICAL PORNOGRAPHY WHEN THEY WERE OLD??
WHO WANTS TO SEE SOME OLDSTERS SAGGY OL' SEX ORGANS??
YUCKY!
EW! EMBARRASSING...
WE'RE TOO SPONTANEOUS... SHOULD HAVE PLANNED AHEAD MORE!
ACT YOUR AGE
ARE WE JUST DOING OUR JOB, BEING ALL EDGY 'N' SHIT?
YEAH, WE HAFTO KEEP BEING EDGY UNTIL WE DROP DEAD... WE'RE UNDERGROUND PIONEERS... WE'LL DIE WISE-ASS PUNKS!
THAT'S US... JUST A COUPLE A PUNKS!
AT LEAST WE'RE NOT YET IN A RETIREMENT HOME, WHERE THEY HAFTO TURN OUR CHAIRS TO FACE THE SUN...
BOB 'N' BUNCH CLEAN IT UP...
Y'KNOW, ALINE, LATELY I GET THE FEELING THEY'RE CLOSING IN ON ME!
OH BOB... ARE YOU GONNA GET ALL "CONSPIRACIED OUT" ON ME AGAIN??
HEY, LOOK! I C'N STILL SQUIRT WATER OUTTA' MY TWAT!
LUCKY US, WE HAVE A NICE LONG BATHTUB!
HA HA! LOOKIT THAT! ALINE, YOU'RE JUST LOADED WITH TALENTS!
AND I DON'T HESITATE TO POINT THEM OUT EVERY SECOND...
SERIOUSLY, THOUGH, I KNOW YOU SCOFF, BUT SOMETIMES PARANOIA IS TRUE PERCEPTION, Y'KNOW?
YEAH, AN' SOMETIMES ITS A SIGN OF MENTAL ILLNESS. REMEMBER YUR MOTHER THOUGHT HER KITCHEN CEILING WAS BUGGED?!
OF COURSE, BUT ON THE OTHER HAND~

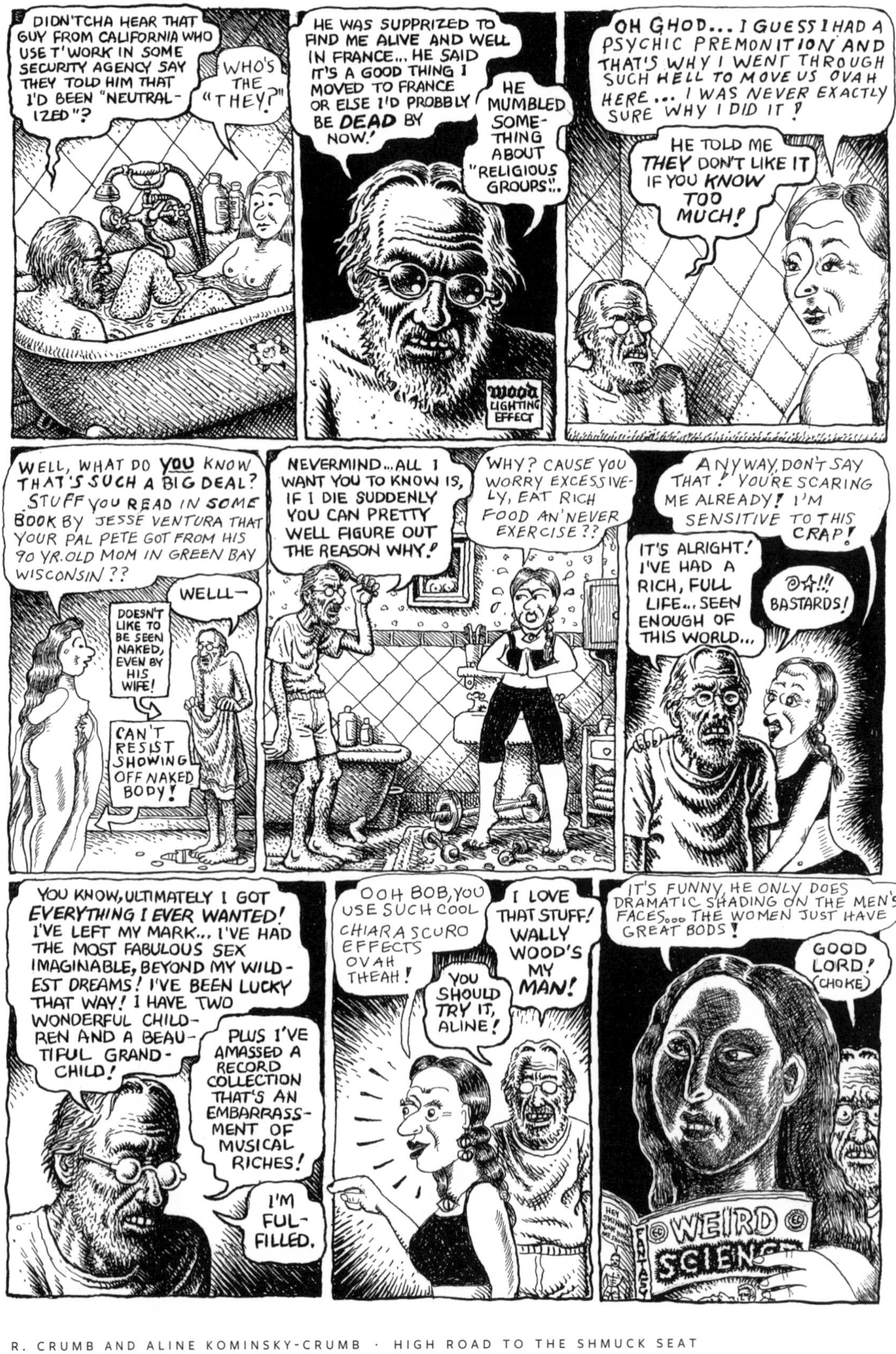
DIDN'TCHA HEAR THAT GUY FROM CALIFORNIA WHO USE T'WORK IN SOME SECURITY AGENCY SAY THEY TOLD HIM THAT I'D BEEN "NEUTRAL-IZED"?
WHO'S THE "THEY?"
HE WAS SUPPRIZED TO FIND ME ALIVE AND WELL IN FRANCE... HE SAID IT'S A GOOD THING I MOVED TO FRANCE OR ELSE I'D PROBBLY BE DEAD BY NOW!
HE MUMBLED SOME-THING ABOUT "RELIGIOUS GROUPS"...
WOOD LIGHTING EFFECT
OH GHOD... I GUESS I HAD A PSYCHIC PREMONITION AND THAT'S WHY I WENT THROUGH SUCH HELL TO MOVE US OVAH HERE... I WAS NEVER EXACTLY SURE WHY I DID IT!
HE TOLD ME THEY DON'T LIKE IT IF YOU KNOW TOO MUCH!
WELL, WHAT DO YOU KNOW THAT'S SUCH A BIG DEAL? STUFF YOU READ IN SOME BOOK BY JESSE VENTURA THAT YOUR PAL PETE GOT FROM HIS 90 YR.OLD MOM IN GREEN BAY WISCONSIN??
WELL—
DOESN'T LIKE TO BE SEEN NAKED, EVEN BY HIS WIFE!
CAN'T RESIST SHOWING OFF NAKED BODY!
NEVERMIND...ALL I WANT YOU TO KNOW IS, IF I DIE SUDDENLY YOU CAN PRETTY WELL FIGURE OUT THE REASON WHY!
WHY? CAUSE YOU WORRY EXCESSIVE-LY, EAT RICH FOOD AN' NEVER EXERCISE??
ANYWAY, DON'T SAY THAT! YOU'RE SCARING ME ALREADY! I'M SENSITIVE TO THIS CRAP!
IT'S ALRIGHT! I'VE HAD A RICH, FULL LIFE... SEEN ENOUGH OF THIS WORLD...
@☆!!! BASTARDS!
YOU KNOW, ULTIMATELY I GOT EVERYTHING I EVER WANTED! I'VE LEFT MY MARK... I'VE HAD THE MOST FABULOUS SEX IMAGINABLE, BEYOND MY WILD-EST DREAMS! I'VE BEEN LUCKY THAT WAY! I HAVE TWO WONDERFUL CHILD-REN AND A BEAU-TIFUL GRAND-CHILD!
PLUS I'VE AMASSED A RECORD COLLECTION THAT'S AN EMBARRASS-MENT OF MUSICAL RICHES!
I'M FUL-FILLED.
OOH BOB, YOU USE SUCH COOL CHIARASCURO EFFECTS OVAH THEAH!
I LOVE THAT STUFF! WALLY WOOD'S MY MAN!
YOU SHOULD TRY IT, ALINE!
IT'S FUNNY, HE ONLY DOES DRAMATIC SHADING ON THE MEN'S FACES... THE WOMEN JUST HAVE GREAT BODS!
GOOD LORD! (CHOKE)
WEIRD
FANTASY

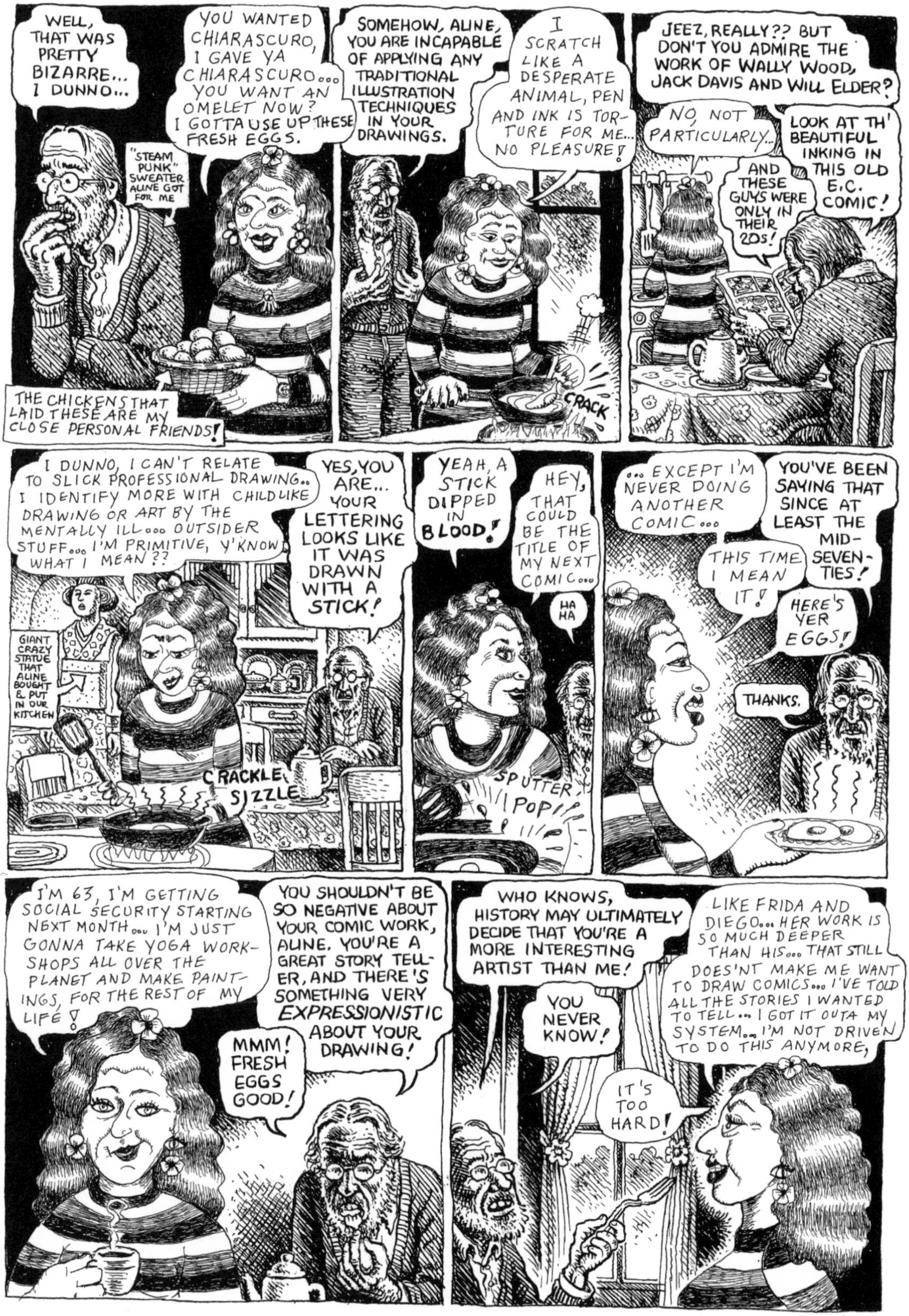
WELL, THAT WAS PRETTY BIZARRE... I DUNNO...
"STEAM PUNK" SWEATER ALINE GOT FOR ME
YOU WANTED CHIARASCURO, I GAVE YA CHIARASCURO... YOU WANT AN OMELET NOW? I GOTTA USE UP THESE FRESH EGGS.
THE CHICKENS THAT LAID THESE ARE MY CLOSE PERSONAL FRIENDS!
SOMEHOW, ALINE, YOU ARE INCAPABLE OF APPLYING ANY TRADITIONAL ILLUSTRATION TECHNIQUES IN YOUR DRAWINGS.
I SCRATCH LIKE A DESPERATE ANIMAL, PEN AND INK IS TORTURE FOR ME... NO PLEASURE!
CRACK
JEEZ, REALLY?? BUT DON'T YOU ADMIRE THE WORK OF WALLY WOOD, JACK DAVIS AND WILL ELDER?
NO, NOT PARTICULARLY...
LOOK AT TH' BEAUTIFUL INKING IN THIS OLD E.C. COMIC!
AND THESE GUYS WERE ONLY IN THEIR 20s!
I DUNNO, I CAN'T RELATE TO SLICK PROFESSIONAL DRAWING.. I IDENTIFY MORE WITH CHILDLIKE DRAWING OR ART BY THE MENTALLY ILL... OUTSIDER STUFF... I'M PRIMITIVE, Y'KNOW WHAT I MEAN??
GIANT CRAZY STATUE THAT ALINE BOUGHT & PUT IN OUR KITCHEN
CRACKLE SIZZLE
YES, YOU ARE... YOUR LETTERING LOOKS LIKE IT WAS DRAWN WITH A STICK!
YEAH, A STICK DIPPED IN BLOOD!
HEY, THAT COULD BE THE TITLE OF MY NEXT COMIC...
HA HA
SPUTTER POP!
... EXCEPT I'M NEVER DOING ANOTHER COMIC...
YOU'VE BEEN SAYING THAT SINCE AT LEAST THE MID-SEVENTIES!
THIS TIME I MEAN IT!
HERE'S YER EGGS!
THANKS.
I'M 63, I'M GETTING SOCIAL SECURITY STARTING NEXT MONTH... I'M JUST GONNA TAKE YOGA WORKSHOPS ALL OVER THE PLANET AND MAKE PAINTINGS, FOR THE REST OF MY LIFE!
YOU SHOULDN'T BE SO NEGATIVE ABOUT YOUR COMIC WORK, ALINE. YOU'RE A GREAT STORY TELLER, AND THERE'S SOMETHING VERY EXPRESSIONISTIC ABOUT YOUR DRAWING!
MMM! FRESH EGGS GOOD!
WHO KNOWS, HISTORY MAY ULTIMATELY DECIDE THAT YOU'RE A MORE INTERESTING ARTIST THAN ME!
YOU NEVER KNOW!
LIKE FRIDA AND DIEGO... HER WORK IS SO MUCH DEEPER THAN HIS... THAT STILL DOES'NT MAKE ME WANT TO DRAW COMICS... I'VE TOLD ALL THE STORIES I WANTED TO TELL... I GOT IT OUTA MY SYSTEM... I'M NOT DRIVEN TO DO THIS ANYMORE,
IT'S TOO HARD!

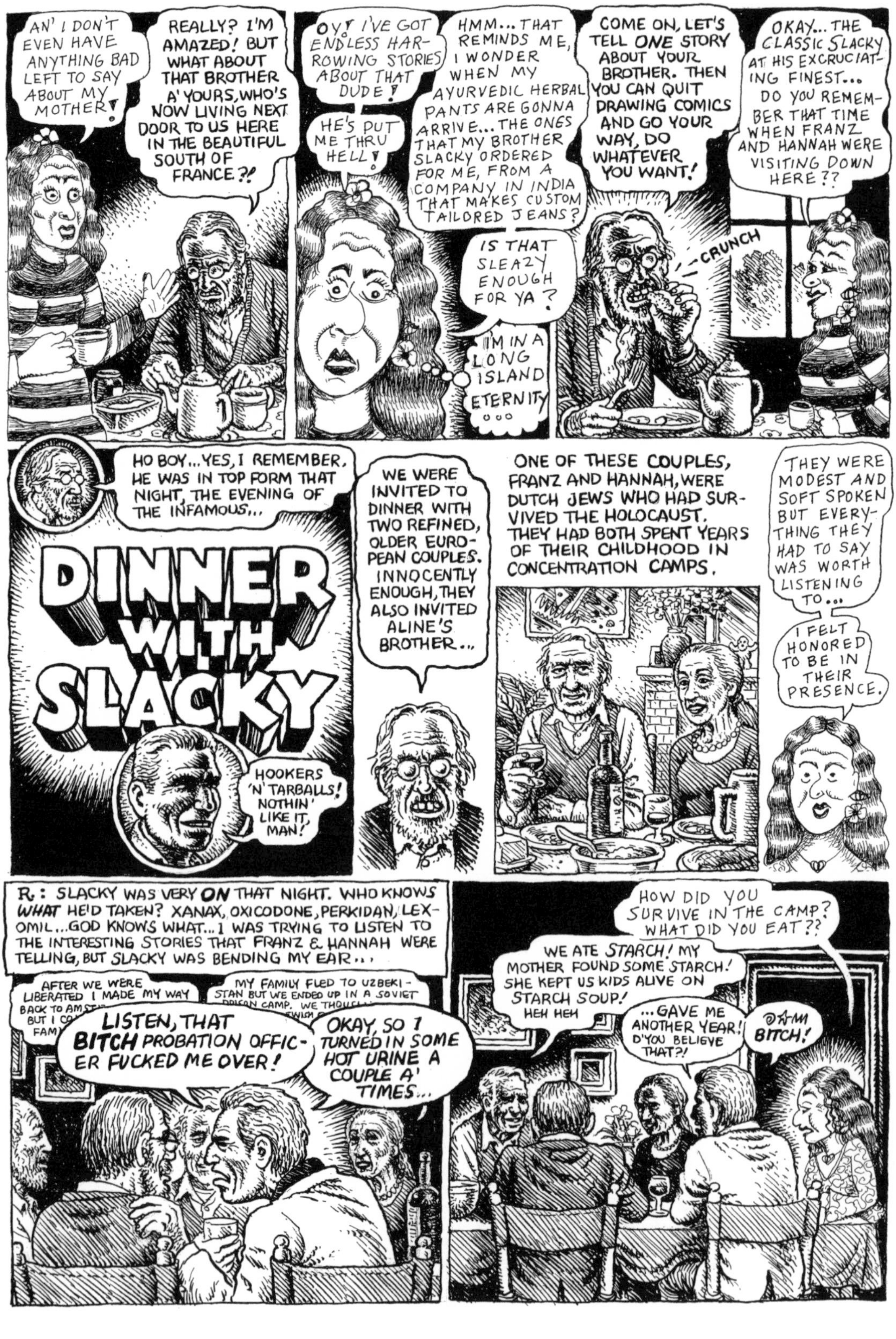
AN' I DON'T EVEN HAVE ANYTHING BAD LEFT TO SAY ABOUT MY MOTHER!
REALLY? I'M AMAZED! BUT WHAT ABOUT THAT BROTHER A' YOURS, WHO'S NOW LIVING NEXT DOOR TO US HERE IN THE BEAUTIFUL SOUTH OF FRANCE?!
OY! I'VE GOT ENDLESS HARROWING STORIES ABOUT THAT DUDE!
HE'S PUT ME THRU HELL!
HMM... THAT REMINDS ME, I WONDER WHEN MY AYURVEDIC HERBAL PANTS ARE GONNA ARRIVE... THE ONES THAT MY BROTHER SLACKY ORDERED FOR ME, FROM A COMPANY IN INDIA THAT MAKES CUSTOM TAILORED JEANS?
IS THAT SLEAZY ENOUGH FOR YA?
I'M IN A LONG ISLAND ETERNITY
COME ON, LET'S TELL ONE STORY ABOUT YOUR BROTHER. THEN YOU CAN QUIT DRAWING COMICS AND GO YOUR WAY, DO WHATEVER YOU WANT!
CRUNCH
OKAY... THE CLASSIC SLACKY AT HIS EXCRUCIATING FINEST... DO YOU REMEMBER THAT TIME WHEN FRANZ AND HANNAH WERE VISITING DOWN HERE??
HO BOY... YES, I REMEMBER. HE WAS IN TOP FORM THAT NIGHT, THE EVENING OF THE INFAMOUS...
DINNER WITH SLACKY
HOOKERS 'N' TARBALLS! NOTHIN' LIKE IT, MAN!
WE WERE INVITED TO DINNER WITH TWO REFINED, OLDER EUROPEAN COUPLES. INNOCENTLY ENOUGH, THEY ALSO INVITED ALINE'S BROTHER...
ONE OF THESE COUPLES, FRANZ AND HANNAH, WERE DUTCH JEWS WHO HAD SURVIVED THE HOLOCAUST. THEY HAD BOTH SPENT YEARS OF THEIR CHILDHOOD IN CONCENTRATION CAMPS.
THEY WERE MODEST AND SOFT SPOKEN BUT EVERYTHING THEY HAD TO SAY WAS WORTH LISTENING TO...
I FELT HONORED TO BE IN THEIR PRESENCE.
R.: SLACKY WAS VERY ON THAT NIGHT. WHO KNOWS WHAT HE'D TAKEN? XANAX, OXICODONE, PERKIDAN, LEXOMIL... GOD KNOWS WHAT... I WAS TRYING TO LISTEN TO THE INTERESTING STORIES THAT FRANZ & HANNAH WERE TELLING, BUT SLACKY WAS BENDING MY EAR...
AFTER WE WERE LIBERATED I MADE MY WAY
MY FAMILY FLED TO UZBEKISTAN BUT WE ENDED UP IN A SOVIET
LISTEN, THAT BITCH PROBATION OFFICER FUCKED ME OVER!
OKAY, SO I TURNED IN SOME HOT URINE A COUPLE A' TIMES...
HOW DID YOU SURVIVE IN THE CAMP? WHAT DID YOU EAT??
WE ATE STARCH! MY MOTHER FOUND SOME STARCH! SHE KEPT US KIDS ALIVE ON STARCH SOUP! HEH HEH
...GAVE ME ANOTHER YEAR! D'YOU BELIEVE THAT?!
DAMN BITCH!

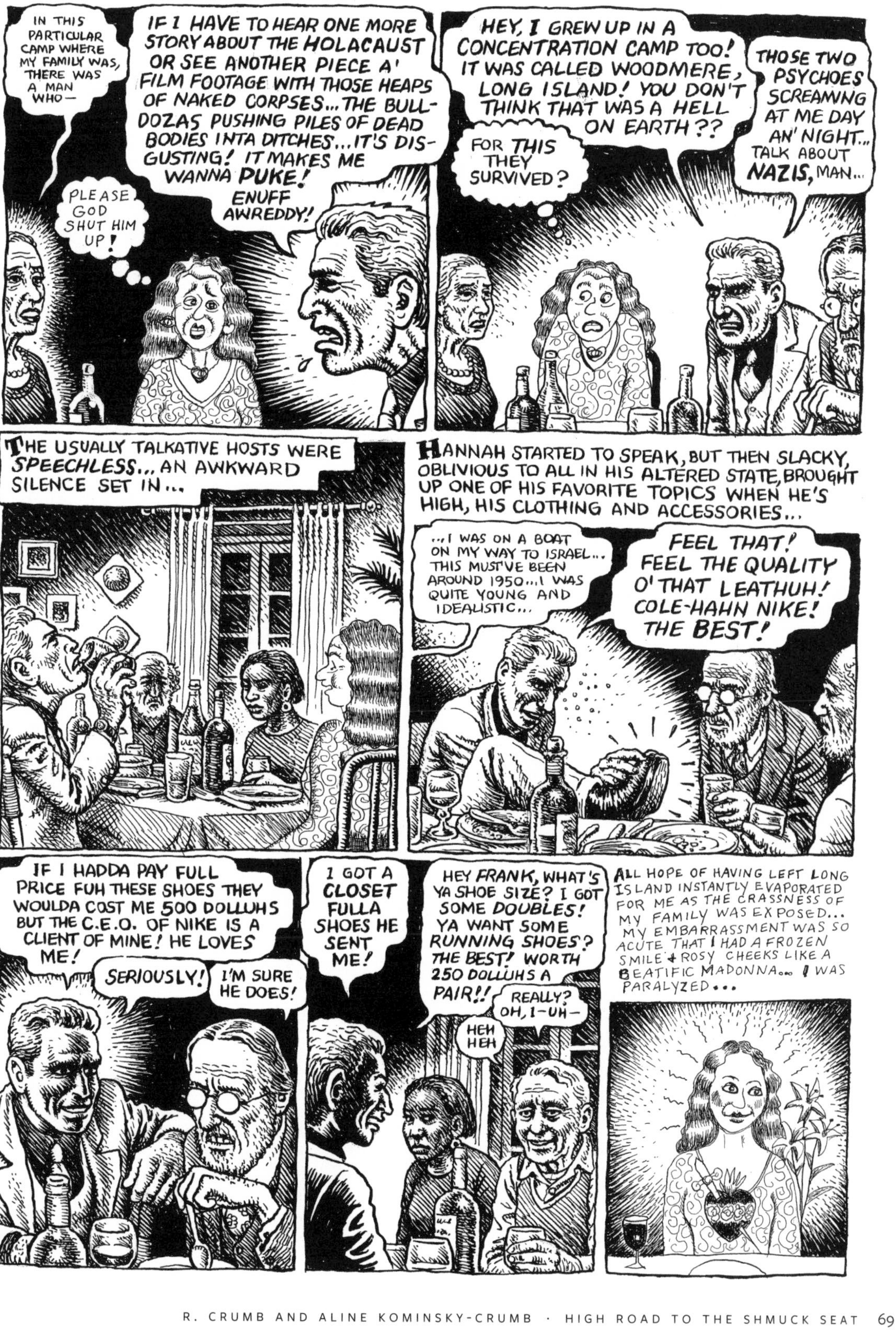

IN THIS PARTICULAR CAMP WHERE MY FAMILY WAS, THERE WAS A MAN WHO—
IF I HAVE TO HEAR ONE MORE STORY ABOUT THE HOLACAUST OR SEE ANOTHER PIECE A' FILM FOOTAGE WITH THOSE HEAPS OF NAKED CORPSES... THE BULL-DOZAS PUSHING PILES OF DEAD BODIES INTA DITCHES... IT'S DIS-GUSTING! IT MAKES ME WANNA PUKE!
PLEASE GOD SHUT HIM UP!
ENUFF AWREDDY!
HEY, I GREW UP IN A CONCENTRATION CAMP TOO! IT WAS CALLED WOODMERE, LONG ISLAND! YOU DON'T THINK THAT WAS A HELL ON EARTH??
FOR THIS THEY SURVIVED?
THOSE TWO PSYCHOES SCREAMING AT ME DAY AN' NIGHT... TALK ABOUT NAZIS, MAN...
THE USUALLY TALKATIVE HOSTS WERE SPEECHLESS... AN AWKWARD SILENCE SET IN...
HANNAH STARTED TO SPEAK, BUT THEN SLACKY, OBLIVIOUS TO ALL IN HIS ALTERED STATE, BROUGHT UP ONE OF HIS FAVORITE TOPICS WHEN HE'S HIGH, HIS CLOTHING AND ACCESSORIES...
...I WAS ON A BOAT ON MY WAY TO ISRAEL... THIS MUST'VE BEEN AROUND 1950... I WAS QUITE YOUNG AND IDEALISTIC...
FEEL THAT! FEEL THE QUALITY O' THAT LEATHUH! COLE-HAHN NIKE! THE BEST!
IF I HADDA PAY FULL PRICE FUH THESE SHOES THEY WOULDA COST ME 500 DOLLUHS BUT THE C.E.O. OF NIKE IS A CLIENT OF MINE! HE LOVES ME!
SERIOUSLY!
I'M SURE HE DOES!
I GOT A CLOSET FULLA SHOES HE SENT ME!
HEY FRANK, WHAT'S YA SHOE SIZE? I GOT SOME DOUBLES! YA WANT SOME RUNNING SHOES? THE BEST! WORTH 250 DOLLUHS A PAIR!!
HEH HEH
REALLY? OH, I-UH—
ALL HOPE OF HAVING LEFT LONG ISLAND INSTANTLY EVAPORATED FOR ME AS THE CRASSNESS OF MY FAMILY WAS EXPOSED... MY EMBARRASSMENT WAS SO ACUTE THAT I HAD A FROZEN SMILE + ROSY CHEEKS LIKE A BEATIFIC MADONNA... I WAS PARALYZED...

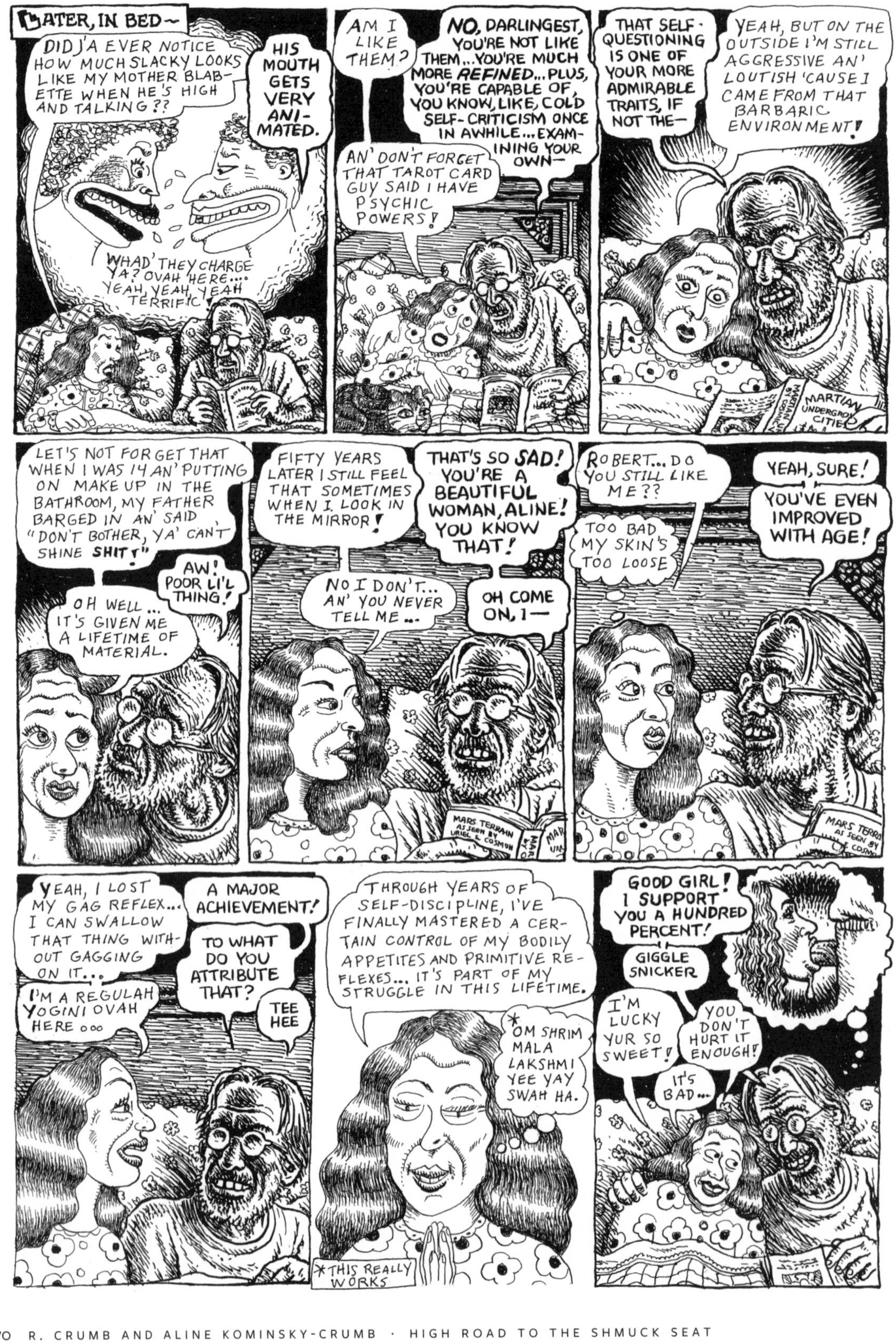
LATER, IN BED—
DIDJ'A EVER NOTICE HOW MUCH SLACKY LOOKS LIKE MY MOTHER BLABETTE WHEN HE'S HIGH AND TALKING??
HIS MOUTH GETS VERY ANIMATED.
WHAD' THEY CHARGE YA? OVAH HERE.... YEAH, YEAH, YEAH TERRIFIC!
AM I LIKE THEM?
NO, DARLINGEST, YOU'RE NOT LIKE THEM... YOU'RE MUCH MORE REFINED... PLUS, YOU'RE CAPABLE OF, YOU KNOW, LIKE, COLD SELF-CRITICISM ONCE IN AWHILE... EXAMINING YOUR OWN—
AN' DON'T FORGET THAT TAROT CARD GUY SAID I HAVE PSYCHIC POWERS!
THAT SELF-QUESTIONING IS ONE OF YOUR MORE ADMIRABLE TRAITS, IF NOT THE—
YEAH, BUT ON THE OUTSIDE I'M STILL AGGRESSIVE AN' LOUTISH 'CAUSE I CAME FROM THAT BARBARIC ENVIRONMENT!
MARTIAN UNDERGROUND CITIES
LET'S NOT FORGET THAT WHEN I WAS 14 AN' PUTTING ON MAKE UP IN THE BATHROOM, MY FATHER BARGED IN AN' SAID "DON'T BOTHER, YA' CAN'T SHINE SHIT!"
AW! POOR LI'L THING!
OH WELL... IT'S GIVEN ME A LIFETIME OF MATERIAL.
FIFTY YEARS LATER I STILL FEEL THAT SOMETIMES WHEN I LOOK IN THE MIRROR!
THAT'S SO SAD! YOU'RE A BEAUTIFUL WOMAN, ALINE! YOU KNOW THAT!
NO I DON'T... AN' YOU NEVER TELL ME...
OH COME ON, I—
MARS TERRAIN AS SEEN BY URIEL & COSMON
ROBERT... DO YOU STILL LIKE ME??
TOO BAD MY SKIN'S TOO LOOSE
YEAH, SURE!
YOU'VE EVEN IMPROVED WITH AGE!
YEAH, I LOST MY GAG REFLEX... I CAN SWALLOW THAT THING WITHOUT GAGGING ON IT...
A MAJOR ACHIEVEMENT!
TO WHAT DO YOU ATTRIBUTE THAT?
I'M A REGULAH YOGINI OVAH HERE...
TEE HEE
THROUGH YEARS OF SELF-DISCIPLINE, I'VE FINALLY MASTERED A CERTAIN CONTROL OF MY BODILY APPETITES AND PRIMITIVE REFLEXES... IT'S PART OF MY STRUGGLE IN THIS LIFETIME.
*OM SHRIM MALA LAKSHMI YEE YAY SWAH HA.
*THIS REALLY WORKS
GOOD GIRL! I SUPPORT YOU A HUNDRED PERCENT!
GIGGLE SNICKER
I'M LUCKY YUR SO SWEET!
YOU DON'T HURT IT ENOUGH!
IT'S BAD...

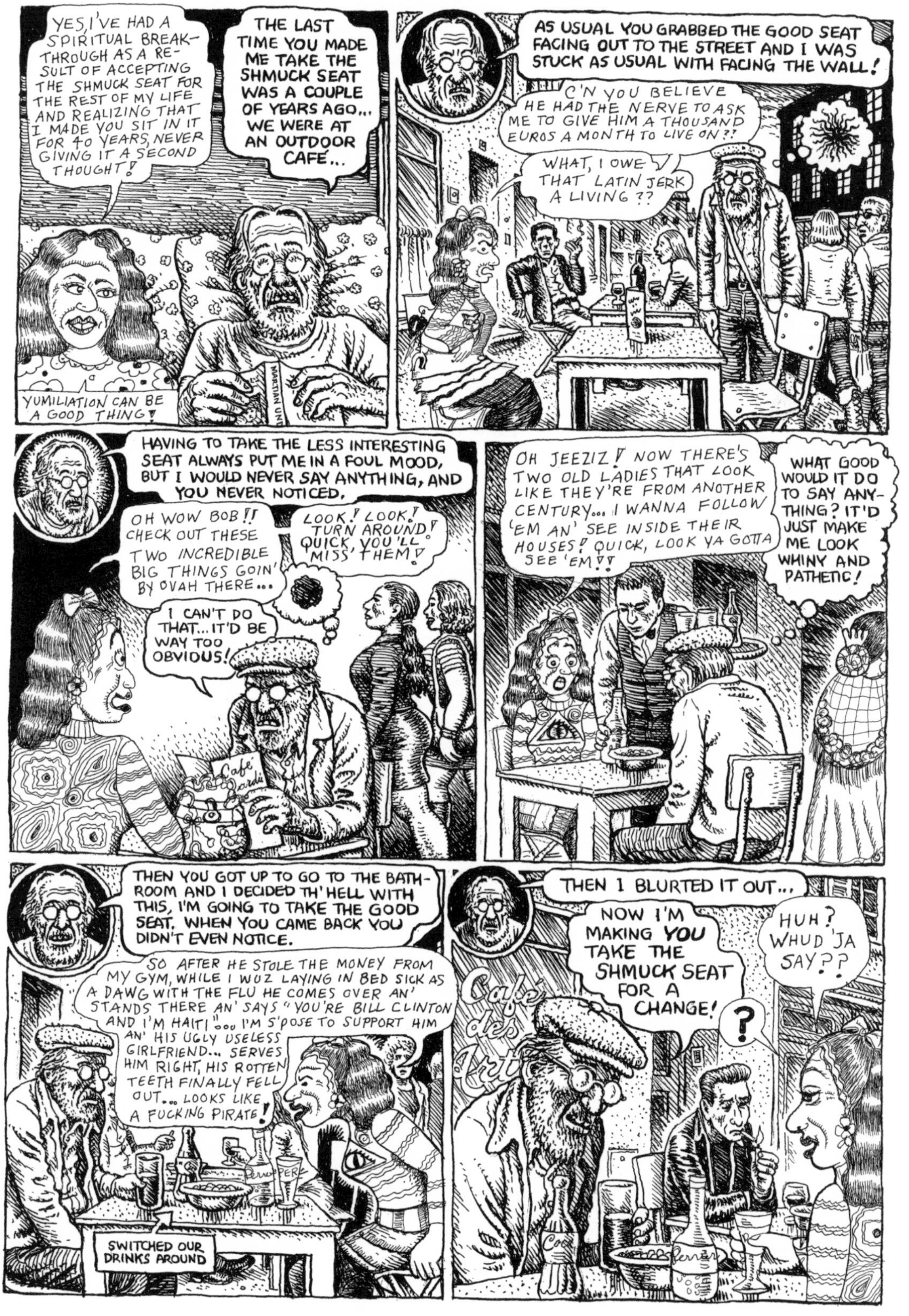

YES, I'VE HAD A SPIRITUAL BREAKTHROUGH AS A RESULT OF ACCEPTING THE SHMUCK SEAT FOR THE REST OF MY LIFE AND REALIZING THAT I MADE YOU SIT IN IT FOR 40 YEARS, NEVER GIVING IT A SECOND THOUGHT!
YUMILIATION CAN BE A GOOD THING!
THE LAST TIME YOU MADE ME TAKE THE SHMUCK SEAT WAS A COUPLE OF YEARS AGO... WE WERE AT AN OUTDOOR CAFÉ...
AS USUAL YOU GRABBED THE GOOD SEAT FACING OUT TO THE STREET AND I WAS STUCK AS USUAL WITH FACING THE WALL!
C'N YOU BELIEVE HE HAD THE NERVE TO ASK ME TO GIVE HIM A THOUSAND EUROS A MONTH TO LIVE ON?!
WHAT, I OWE THAT LATIN JERK A LIVING??
HAVING TO TAKE THE LESS INTERESTING SEAT ALWAYS PUT ME IN A FOUL MOOD, BUT I WOULD NEVER SAY ANYTHING, AND YOU NEVER NOTICED.
OH WOW BOB!! CHECK OUT THESE TWO INCREDIBLE BIG THINGS GOIN' BY OVAH THERE...
LOOK! LOOK! TURN AROUND! QUICK, YOU'LL MISS THEM!
I CAN'T DO THAT... IT'D BE WAY TOO OBVIOUS!
OH JEEZIZ! NOW THERE'S TWO OLD LADIES THAT LOOK LIKE THEY'RE FROM ANOTHER CENTURY... I WANNA FOLLOW 'EM AN' SEE INSIDE THEIR HOUSES! QUICK, LOOK YA GOTTA SEE 'EM!!
WHAT GOOD WOULD IT DO TO SAY ANYTHING? IT'D JUST MAKE ME LOOK WHINY AND PATHETIC!
THEN YOU GOT UP TO GO TO THE BATHROOM AND I DECIDED TH' HELL WITH THIS, I'M GOING TO TAKE THE GOOD SEAT. WHEN YOU CAME BACK YOU DIDN'T EVEN NOTICE.
SO AFTER HE STOLE THE MONEY FROM MY GYM, WHILE I WUZ LAYING IN BED SICK AS A DAWG WITH THE FLU HE COMES OVER AN' STANDS THERE AN' SAYS "YOU'RE BILL CLINTON AND I'M HAITI!"... I'M S'POSE TO SUPPORT HIM AN' HIS UGLY USELESS GIRLFRIEND... SERVES HIM RIGHT, HIS ROTTEN TEETH FINALLY FELL OUT... LOOKS LIKE A FUCKING PIRATE!
SWITCHED OUR DRINKS AROUND
THEN I BLURTED IT OUT...
NOW I'M MAKING YOU TAKE THE SHMUCK SEAT FOR A CHANGE!
?
HUH? WHUD 'JA SAY??
Café des Arts

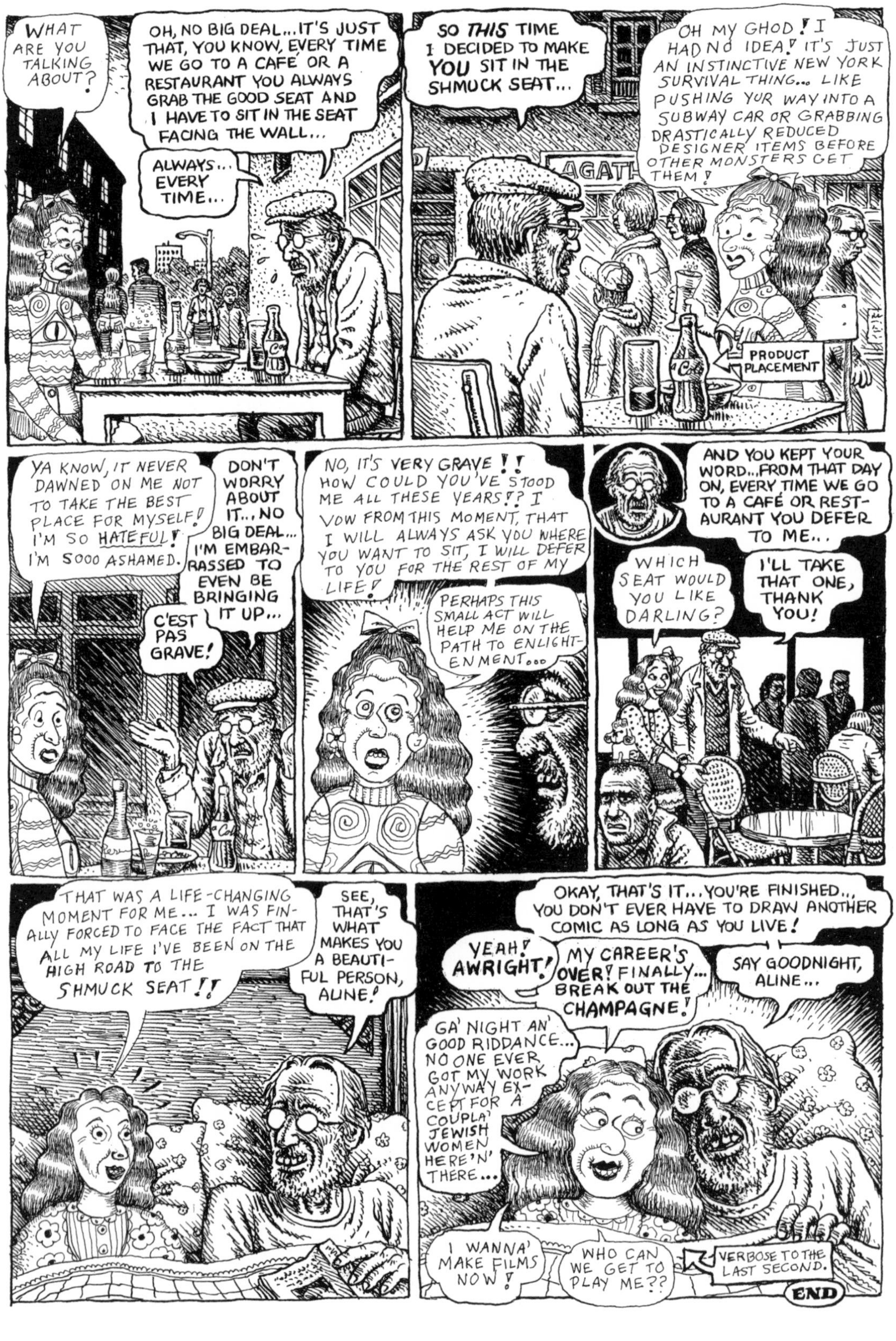
WHAT ARE YOU TALKING ABOUT?
OH, NO BIG DEAL... IT'S JUST THAT, YOU KNOW, EVERY TIME WE GO TO A CAFÉ OR A RESTAURANT YOU ALWAYS GRAB THE GOOD SEAT AND I HAVE TO SIT IN THE SEAT FACING THE WALL...
ALWAYS... EVERY TIME...
SO THIS TIME I DECIDED TO MAKE YOU SIT IN THE SHMUCK SEAT...
OH MY GHOD! I HAD NO IDEA! IT'S JUST AN INSTINCTIVE NEW YORK SURVIVAL THING... LIKE PUSHING YUR WAY INTO A SUBWAY CAR OR GRABBING DRASTICALLY REDUCED DESIGNER ITEMS BEFORE OTHER MONSTERS GET THEM!
AGATH
PRODUCT PLACEMENT
YA KNOW, IT NEVER DAWNED ON ME NOT TO TAKE THE BEST PLACE FOR MYSELF! I'M SO HATEFUL! I'M SOOO ASHAMED.
DON'T WORRY ABOUT IT... NO BIG DEAL... I'M EMBARRASSED TO EVEN BE BRINGING IT UP...
C'EST PAS GRAVE!
NO, IT'S VERY GRAVE!! HOW COULD YOU'VE STOOD ME ALL THESE YEARS!? I VOW FROM THIS MOMENT, THAT I WILL ALWAYS ASK YOU WHERE YOU WANT TO SIT, I WILL DEFER TO YOU FOR THE REST OF MY LIFE!
PERHAPS THIS SMALL ACT WILL HELP ME ON THE PATH TO ENLIGHTENMENT...
AND YOU KEPT YOUR WORD... FROM THAT DAY ON, EVERY TIME WE GO TO A CAFÉ OR RESTAURANT YOU DEFER TO ME...
WHICH SEAT WOULD YOU LIKE DARLING?
I'LL TAKE THAT ONE, THANK YOU!
THAT WAS A LIFE-CHANGING MOMENT FOR ME... I WAS FINALLY FORCED TO FACE THE FACT THAT ALL MY LIFE I'VE BEEN ON THE HIGH ROAD TO THE SHMUCK SEAT!!
SEE, THAT'S WHAT MAKES YOU A BEAUTIFUL PERSON, ALINE!
OKAY, THAT'S IT... YOU'RE FINISHED... YOU DON'T EVER HAVE TO DRAW ANOTHER COMIC AS LONG AS YOU LIVE!
YEAH! AWRIGHT!
MY CAREER'S OVER! FINALLY... BREAK OUT THE CHAMPAGNE!
SAY GOODNIGHT, ALINE...
GA' NIGHT AN' GOOD RIDDANCE... NO ONE EVER GOT MY WORK ANYWAY EXCEPT FOR A COUPLA' JEWISH WOMEN HERE'N' THERE...
I WANNA' MAKE FILMS NOW!
WHO CAN WE GET TO PLAY ME??
VERBOSE TO THE LAST SECOND.
END

Ooh, extra page! Let's throw in one more Katchor . . .

A 21st Century Still Life

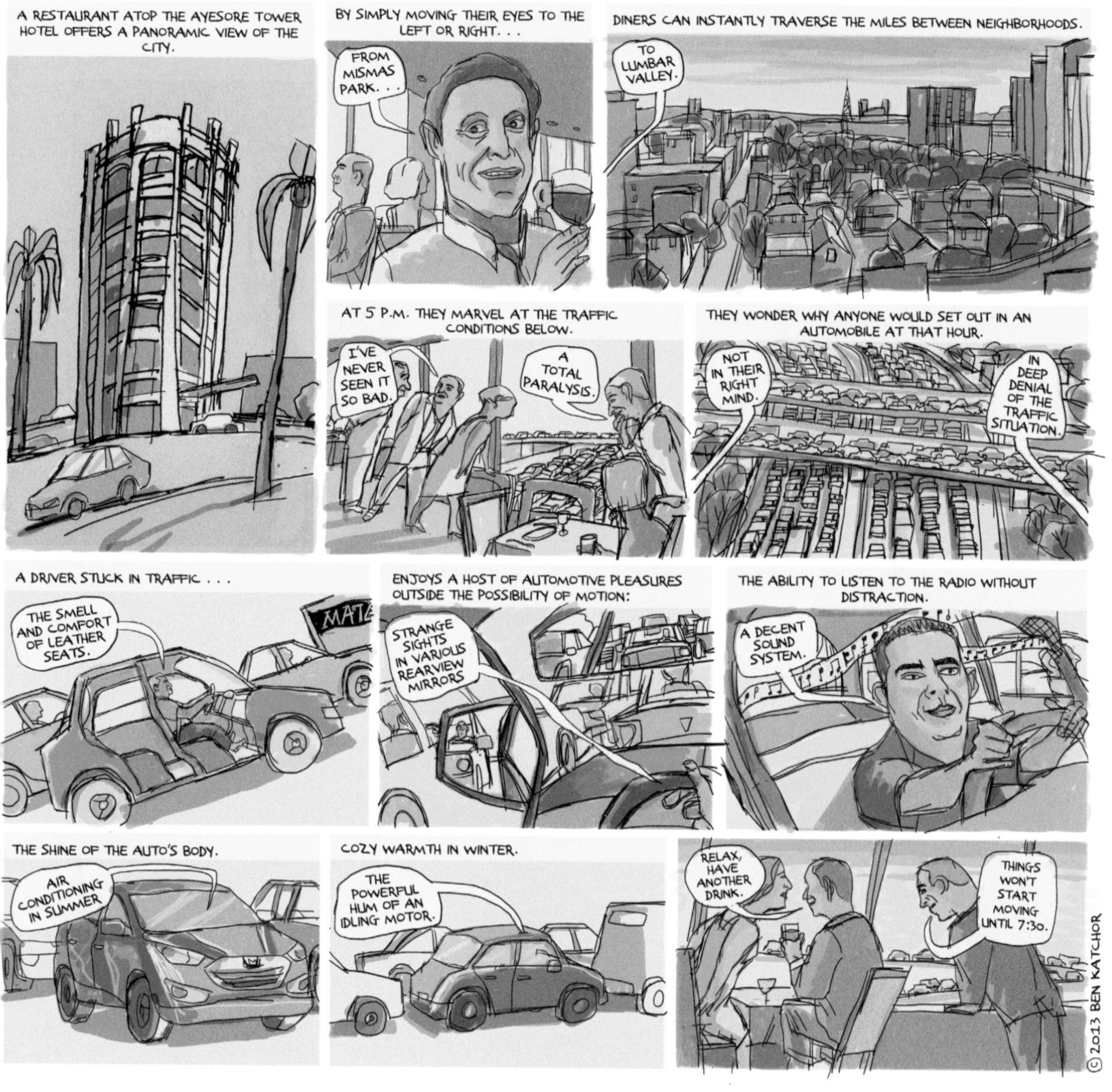

A RESTAURANT ATOP THE AYESORE TOWER HOTEL OFFERS A PANORAMIC VIEW OF THE CITY.
BY SIMPLY MOVING THEIR EYES TO THE LEFT OR RIGHT. . .
FROM MISMAS PARK. . .
DINERS CAN INSTANTLY TRAVERSE THE MILES BETWEEN NEIGHBORHOODS.
TO LUMBAR VALLEY.
AT 5 P.M. THEY MARVEL AT THE TRAFFIC CONDITIONS BELOW.
I'VE NEVER SEEN IT SO BAD.
A TOTAL PARALYSIS.
THEY WONDER WHY ANYONE WOULD SET OUT IN AN AUTOMOBILE AT THAT HOUR.
NOT IN THEIR RIGHT MIND.
IN DEEP DENIAL OF THE TRAFFIC SITUATION.
A DRIVER STUCK IN TRAFFIC . . .
THE SMELL AND COMFORT OF LEATHER SEATS.
ENJOYS A HOST OF AUTOMOTIVE PLEASURES OUTSIDE THE POSSIBILITY OF MOTION:
STRANGE SIGHTS IN VARIOUS REARVIEW MIRRORS
THE ABILITY TO LISTEN TO THE RADIO WITHOUT DISTRACTION.
A DECENT SOUND SYSTEM.
THE SHINE OF THE AUTO'S BODY.
AIR CONDITIONING IN SUMMER
COZY WARMTH IN WINTER.
THE POWERFUL HUM OF AN IDLING MOTOR.
RELAX, HAVE ANOTHER DRINK.
THINGS WON'T START MOVING UNTIL 7:30.
© 2013 BEN KATCHOR

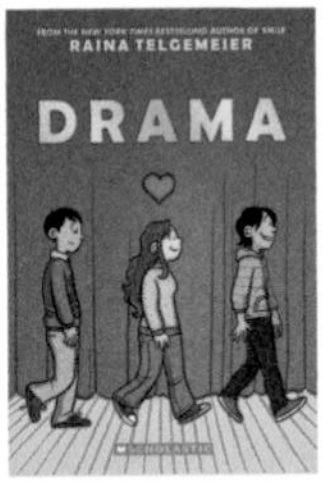
RAINA TELGEMEIER
DRAMA

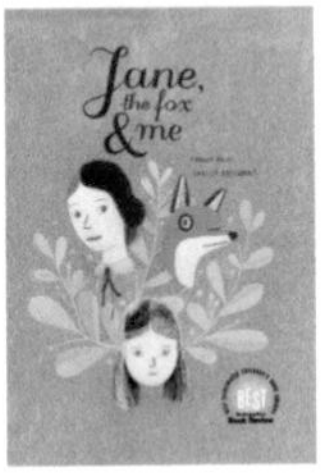
Jane, the fox & me

Raising Readers

Girls read.

There was a long sunny moment, early in this century, when it seemed at least possible that more girls were reading comics than boys. In large bookstores all over North America, translated *manga* (Japanese comics) exploded in popularity, eclipsing domestic comics and quite a few other categories of books in the bargain. Kids sitting cross-legged in the aisles would spend hours devouring Japanese titles such as *Fruits Basket*, *InuYasha*, *Naruto*, *Death Note*, anything by Clamp . . . and most of these kids happened to be girls.

The explosion dwindled in time, as did the stores, but not before a new generation had fallen in love with an art form. Some moved on to other interests, but a significant minority parlayed their love of reading comics into a love of making them, moved on to the Web, found an audience, and found each other.

At the height of that first wave, I made a bet. No one but me knew that it was a bet, but I figured I could tell everyone after the fact if I was right or let 'em forget about it if I was wrong. The bet was buried in a cheerfully deranged introduction I wrote for the first volume of a wonderful anthology called *Flight*, set to debut in 2004. Written in the voice of a distant, future, head-in-a-jar me, the intro made all kinds of predictions in the guise of references to the "past," including a glancing mention of "the male under-representation crisis of the late '20s." Basically, I was predicting (albeit, tongue-in-cheek) a majority female comics industry within twenty years.

Such a prediction was pure fantasy in 2004. Ten years later, in 2014 . . . okay, maybe it *still* sounds like pure fantasy to a lot of you, but I know some in art education and parts of the publishing industry (yes, there's still a publishing industry, don't be a wiseass) who are quietly nodding along with me right now.

Girls read. And guess what? They also write and draw.

And the young women I've had in my workshops usually write and draw just a little better than their male counterparts—in many cases, a lot better—and with every passing year, there are more of them. I know we recently passed the 50 percent mark at some schools with comics majors. I know that in a nine-week class I'll have finished teaching by the time you read this, the ratio will have been 72 percent.

Perhaps the real demographic time bomb in comics' future is the growing importance of all-ages comics. Here, many of the values of the *manga* generation are merging with homegrown sensibilities and homegrown settings and subjects to ensure a steady flow of new readers—again, mostly female—to help swell American comics' ranks. Talented all-ages creators like Vera Brosgol, Hope Larson, and Faith Erin Hicks are rewriting our conceptions of mainstream comics publishing and ensuring a new influx of potential comics creators down the road.

Numbers aside, just one cartoonist can make all the difference if she connects powerfully enough with a new generation of readers to instill the same love of comics in them that the previous generation instilled in her. And right now, there's no better cartoonist to fill that role than Raina Telgemeier.

Telgemeier was a Bay Area minicomics artist when most in the community got to know her, but soon she was tapped by Scholastic Books to create a comics adaptation of the wildly popular Baby-sitters Club series. The comics series didn't last nearly as long as the prose original, but it paved the way for a Scholastic edition of Telgemeier's own *Smile*, an all-ages comic about her childhood dental woes. *Smile* was a breakout hit, flying off tables at book fairs around the country, which led in turn to this year's selection, *Drama*.

Elsewhere in this collection, I'll pick a different title for "Book of the Year"—an easy choice, a slam dunk, you'll see—but if you asked me which book knocked my socks off last year, the one I had the strongest emotional connection to, I'd have to say *Drama*. And I'm a middle-aged guy; I can only imagine the effect it had on its grade-school target audience.

Even in the short excerpt on display here, you can get a sense of how Telgemeier's storytelling pulls the reader in. The principle of emotion-as-action is demonstrated on every page (as Wendy Pini demonstrated forty years ago in her underappreciated *Elfquest*), characters enlist readers into sharing their desires, and a sense of place combined with the power of silence delivers sensations I hope you'll recognize from your own childhood, as I did from mine.

Echoing some of Telgemeier's themes, and even amplifying some of her effects in places, is our other excerpt for this section: *Jane, the Fox and Me* by Fanny Britt and Isabelle Arsenault. It's a book that we might've missed entirely if not for Bill's superb detective work, since it comes more from the children's book world than the comics community, but it's pure comics (says the guy who supposedly "wrote the book") and a striking portrait of childhood isolation.

Get both of these books and read them in their entirety. You won't be sorry.

Oh, one more thing.

Around the same time as my fanciful "bet" in the pages of *Flight*, I remember a young woman approaching me with her portfolio at a convention in San Francisco. We looked at her work for a while. She asked a lot of questions and I tried to offer helpful answers. I don't remember her name or her work or what she looked like, but I remember that she seemed very dedicated to improving her craft.

I also remember that there was a nice young man standing next to her the whole time, quietly smiling, and listening to the conversation. When we were all done, the woman zipped up her portfolio and started to leave, at which point the young man started to follow her, caught my eye briefly, smiled, and waved.

"I'm just the boyfriend," he said.

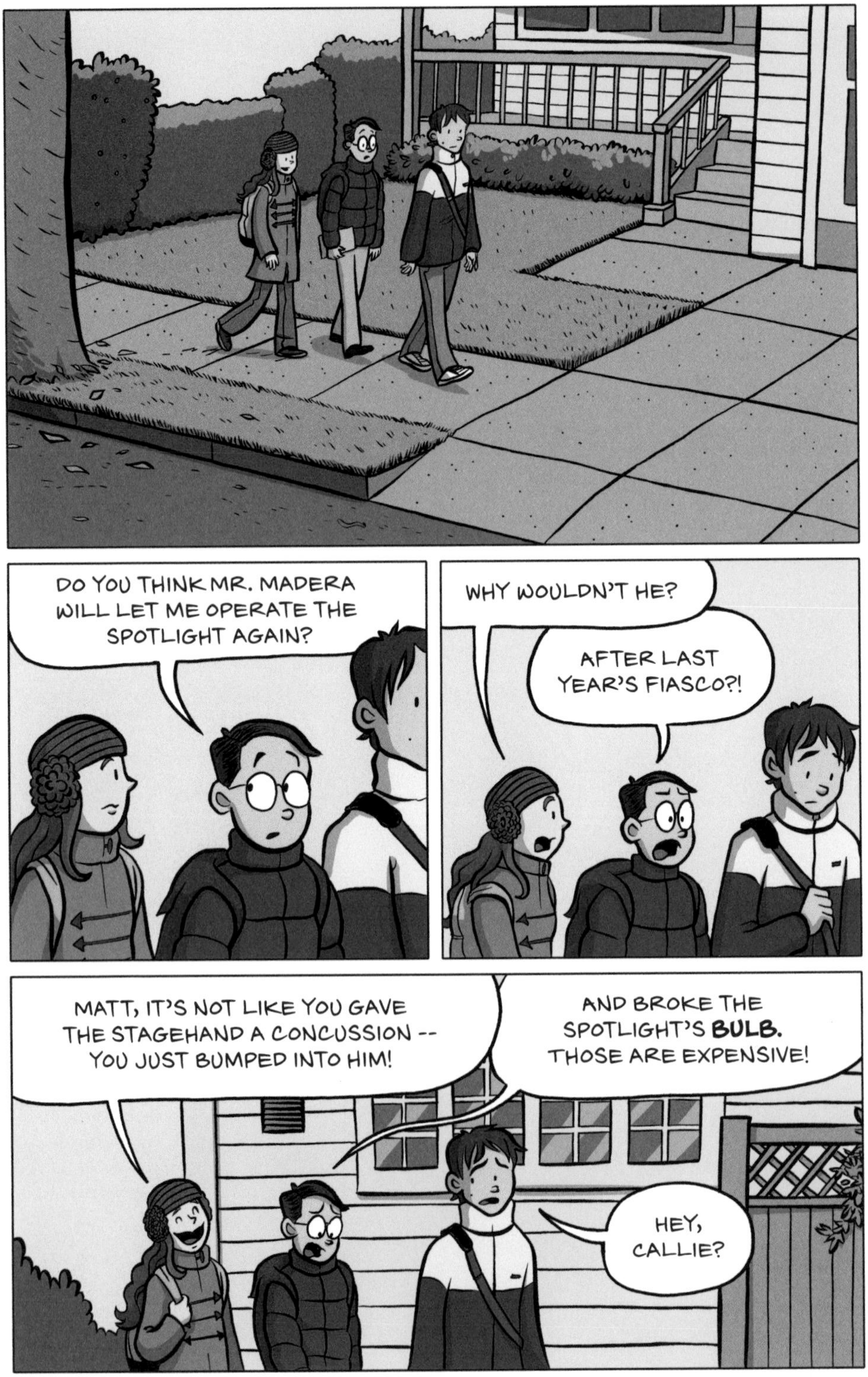
DO YOU THINK MR. MADERA WILL LET ME OPERATE THE SPOTLIGHT AGAIN?
WHY WOULDN'T HE?
AFTER LAST YEAR'S FIASCO?!
MATT, IT'S NOT LIKE YOU GAVE THE STAGEHAND A CONCUSSION -- YOU JUST BUMPED INTO HIM!
AND BROKE THE SPOTLIGHT'S **BULB.** THOSE ARE EXPENSIVE!
HEY, CALLIE?

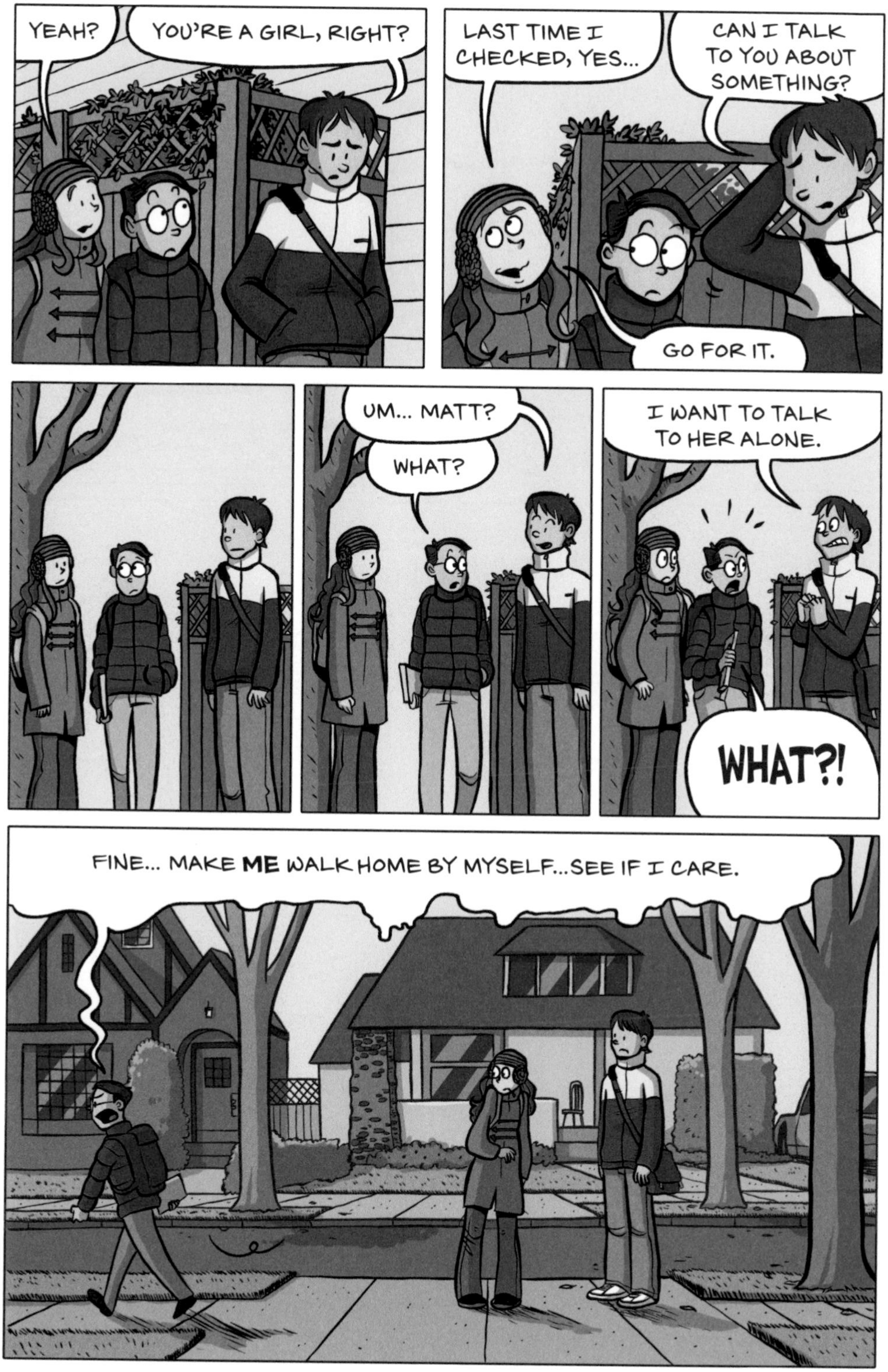
YEAH?
YOU'RE A GIRL, RIGHT?
LAST TIME I CHECKED, YES...
CAN I TALK TO YOU ABOUT SOMETHING?
GO FOR IT.
UM... MATT?
WHAT?
I WANT TO TALK TO HER ALONE.
WHAT?!
FINE... MAKE **ME** WALK HOME BY MYSELF...SEE IF I CARE.

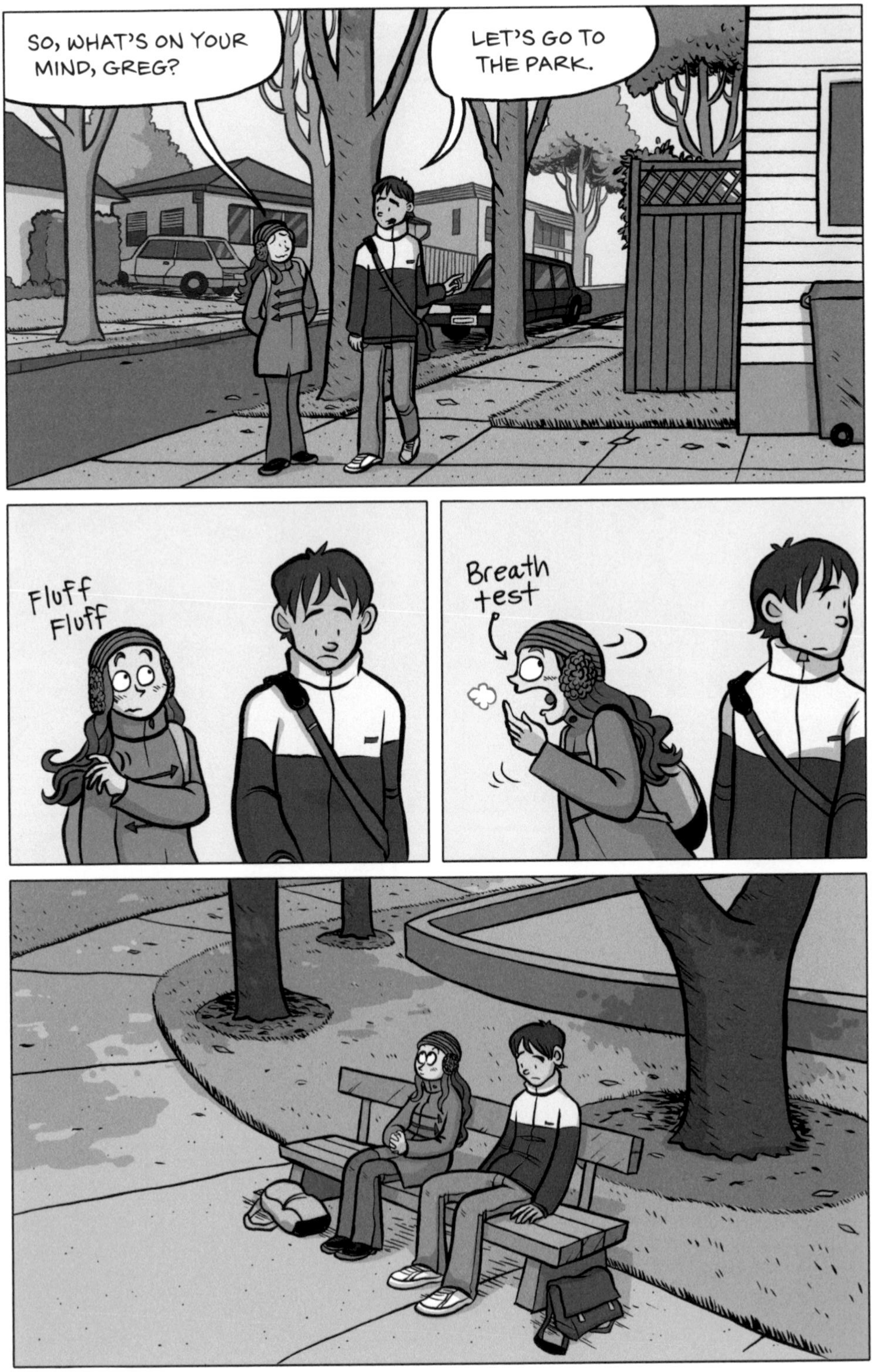
SO, WHAT'S ON YOUR MIND, GREG?
LET'S GO TO THE PARK.
Fluff Fluff
Breath test

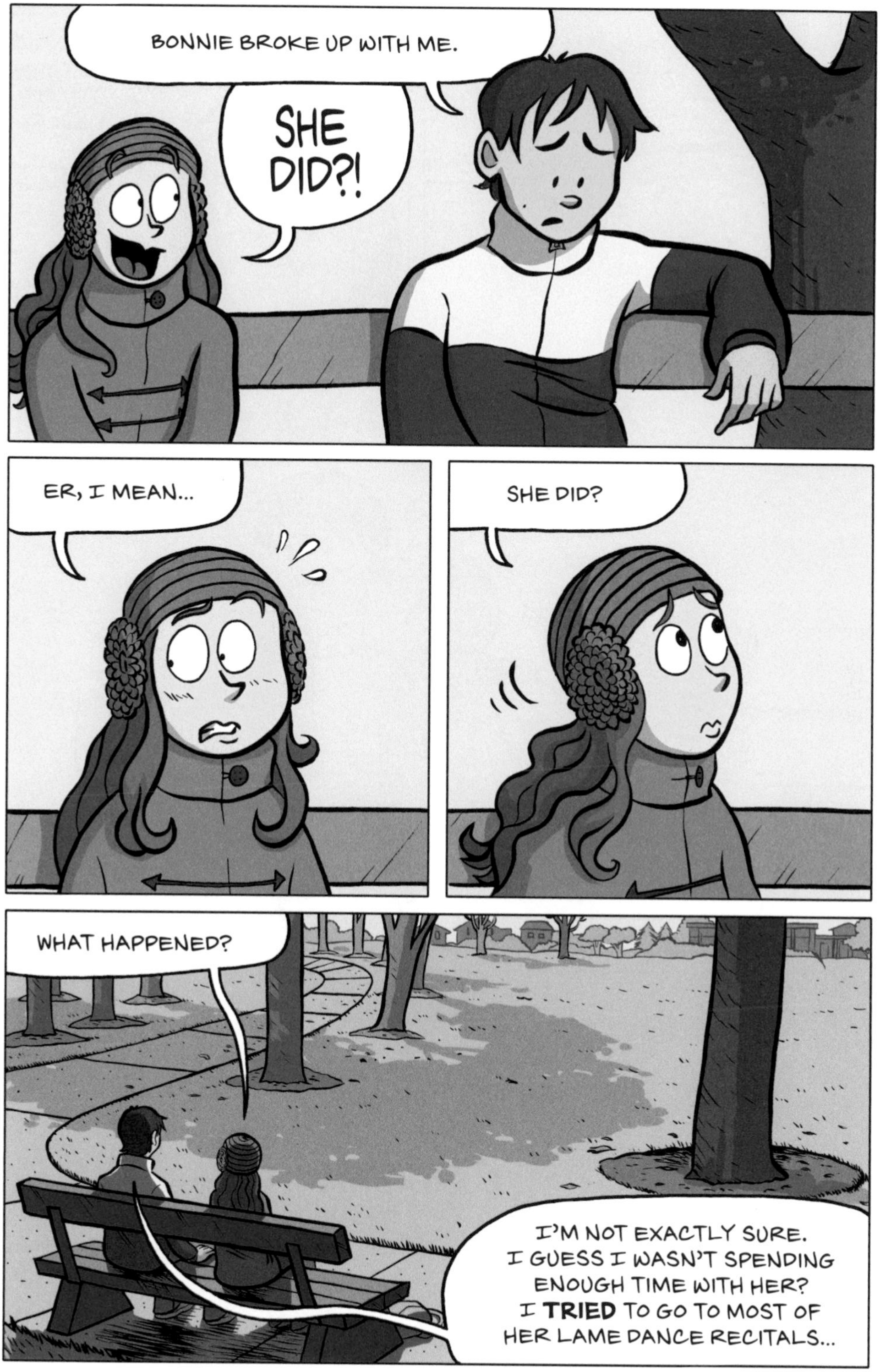
BONNIE BROKE UP WITH ME.
SHE DID?!
ER, I MEAN...
SHE DID?
WHAT HAPPENED?
I'M NOT EXACTLY SURE. I GUESS I WASN'T SPENDING ENOUGH TIME WITH HER? I **TRIED** TO GO TO MOST OF HER LAME DANCE RECITALS...

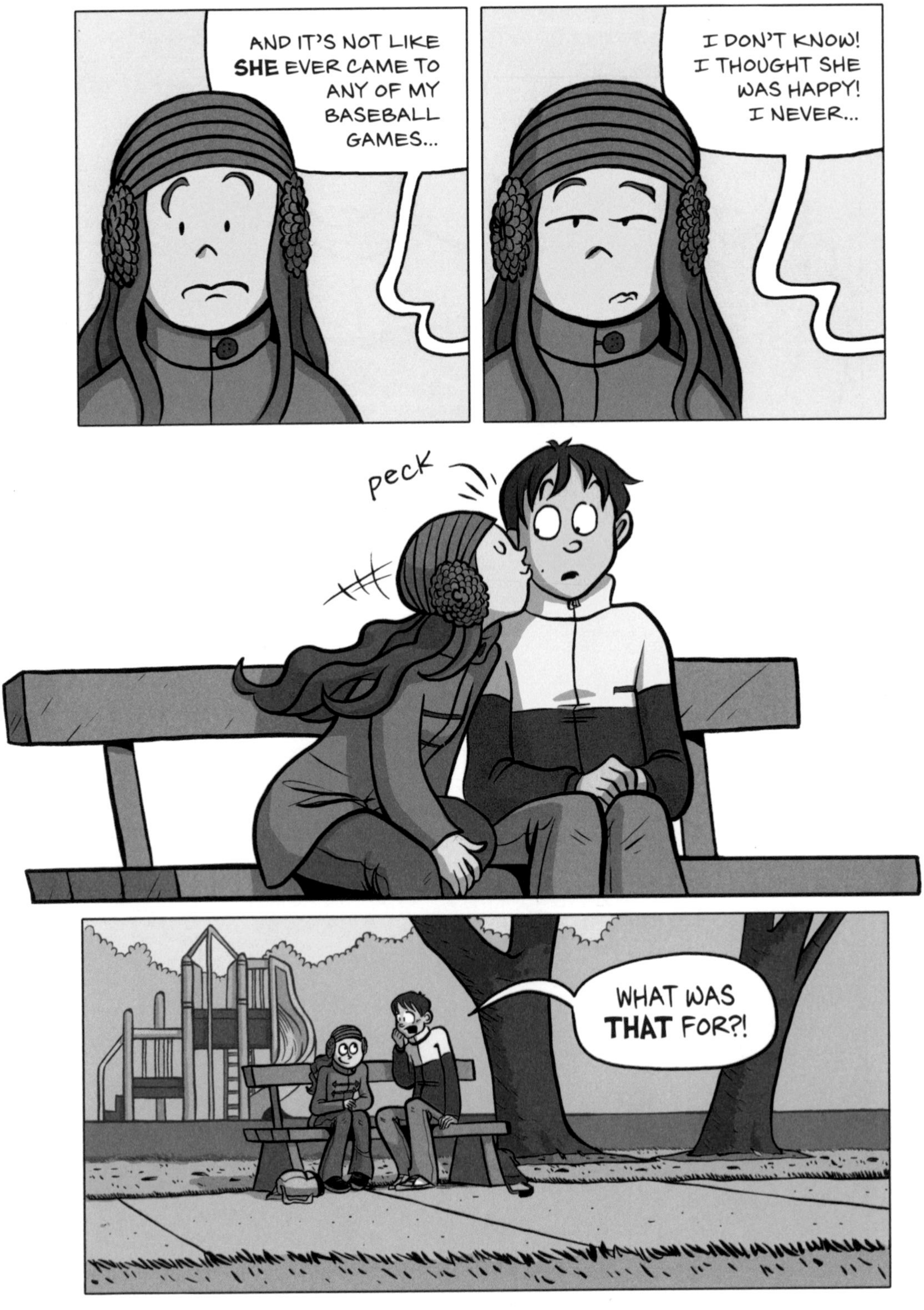
AND IT'S NOT LIKE **SHE** EVER CAME TO ANY OF MY BASEBALL GAMES...
I DON'T KNOW! I THOUGHT SHE WAS HAPPY! I NEVER...
peck
WHAT WAS **THAT** FOR?!

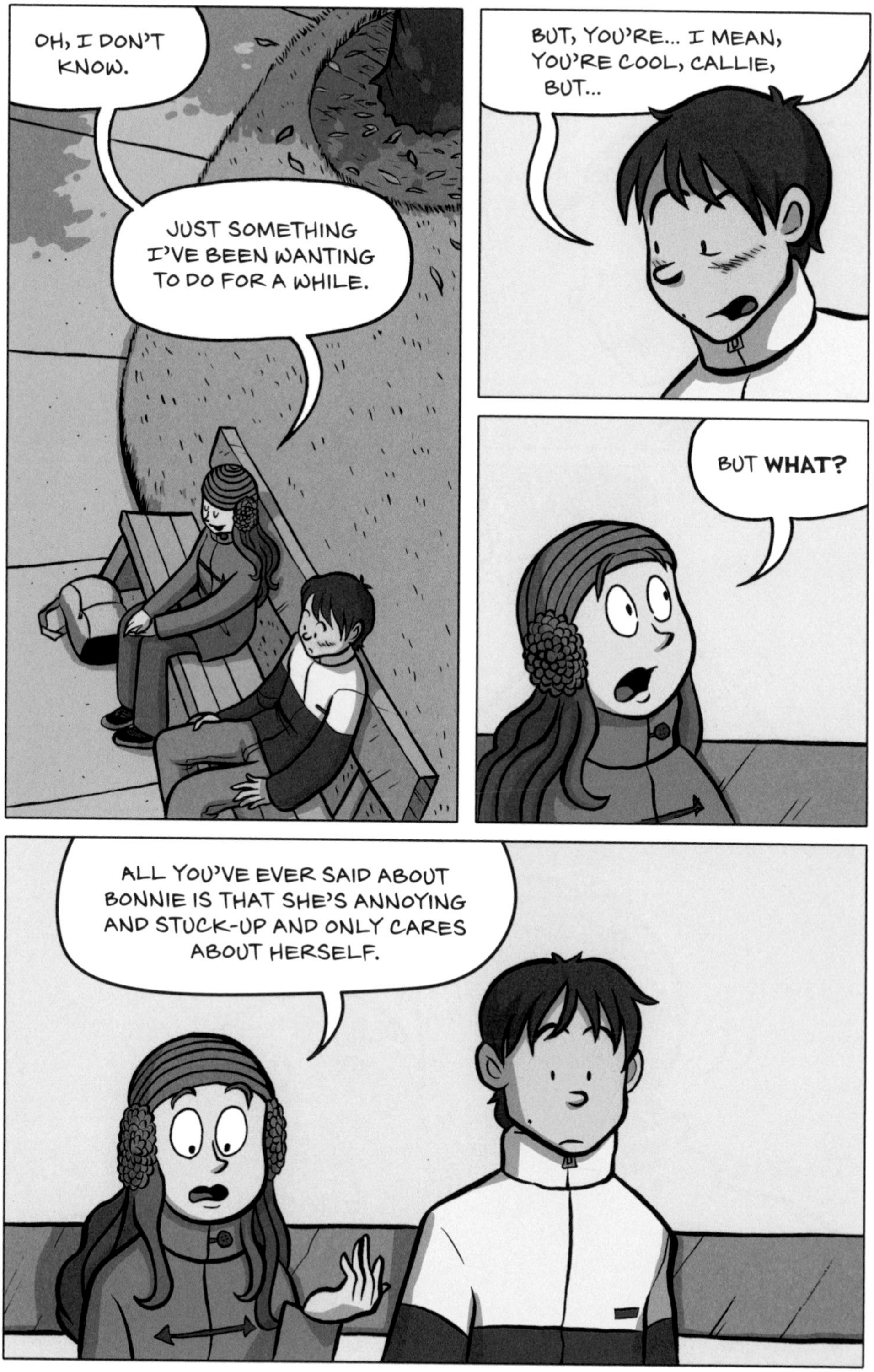
OH, I DON'T KNOW.
JUST SOMETHING I'VE BEEN WANTING TO DO FOR A WHILE.
BUT, YOU'RE... I MEAN, YOU'RE COOL, CALLIE, BUT...
BUT **WHAT?**
ALL YOU'VE EVER SAID ABOUT BONNIE IS THAT SHE'S ANNOYING AND STUCK-UP AND ONLY CARES ABOUT HERSELF.

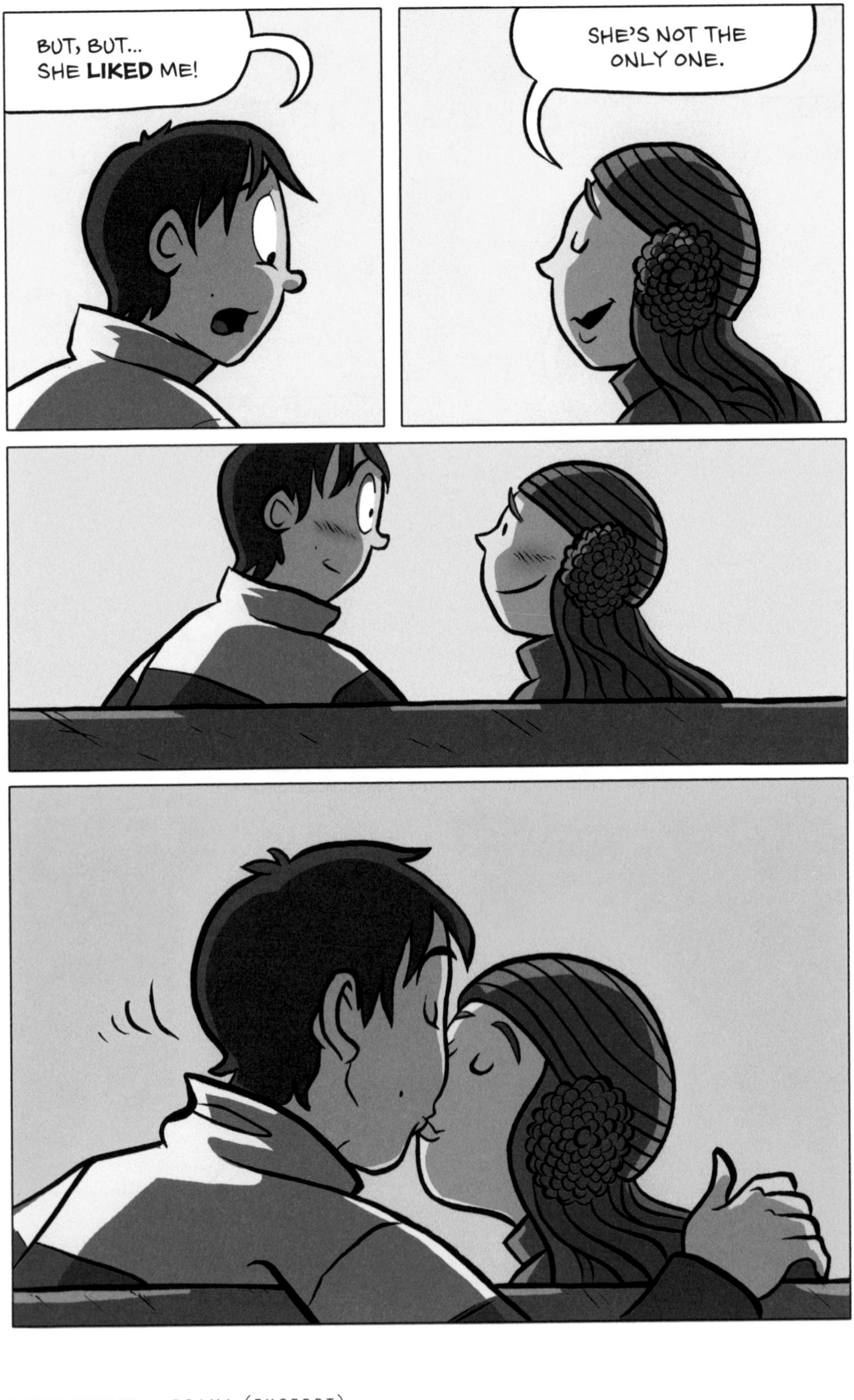
BUT, BUT...
SHE **LIKED** ME!
SHE'S NOT THE
ONLY ONE.

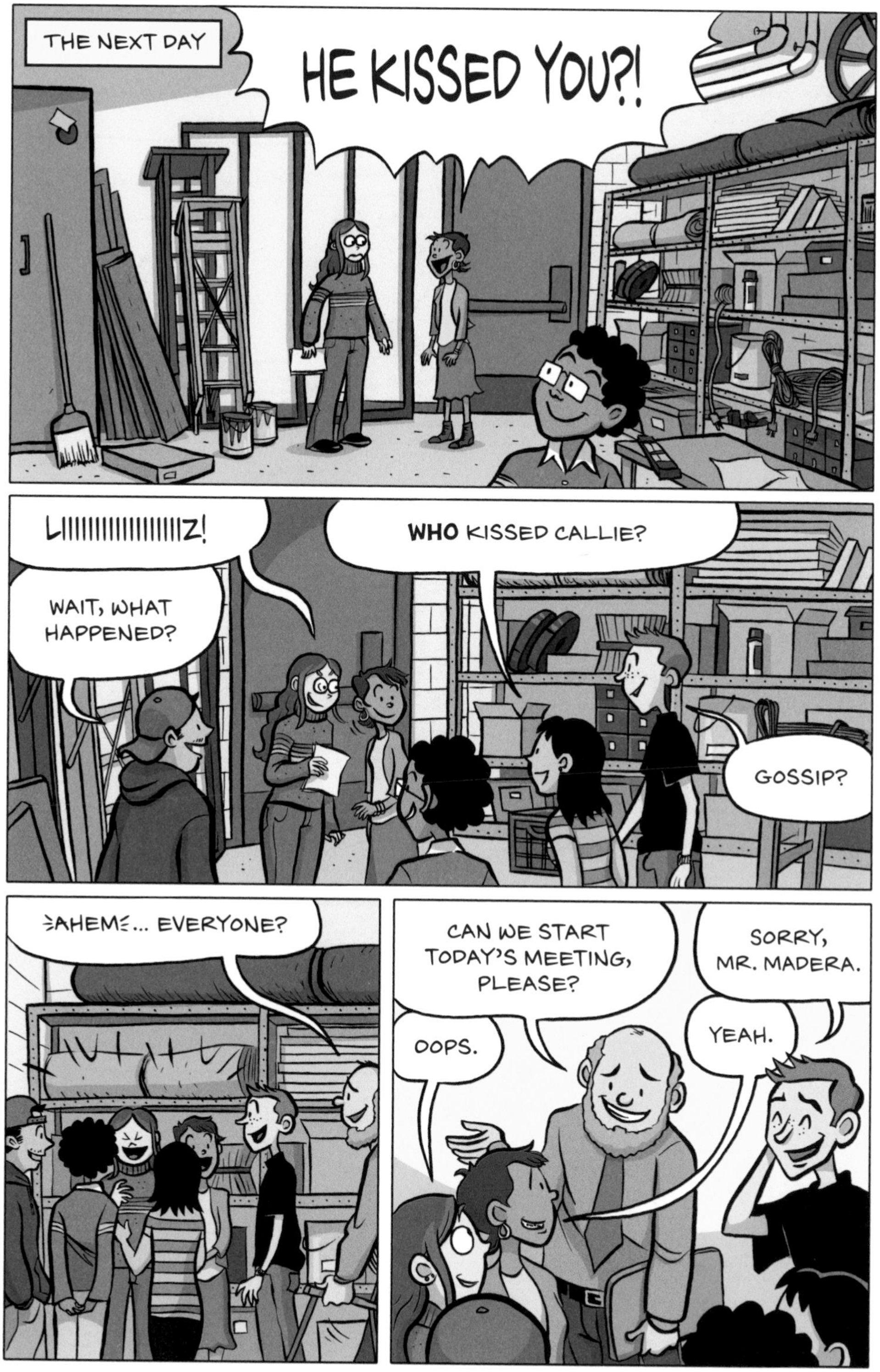
THE NEXT DAY
HE KISSED YOU?!
LIIIIIIIIIIIIIIIZ!
WAIT, WHAT HAPPENED?
WHO KISSED CALLIE?
GOSSIP?
≥AHEM≤... EVERYONE?
CAN WE START TODAY'S MEETING, PLEASE?
OOPS.
SORRY, MR. MADERA.
YEAH.

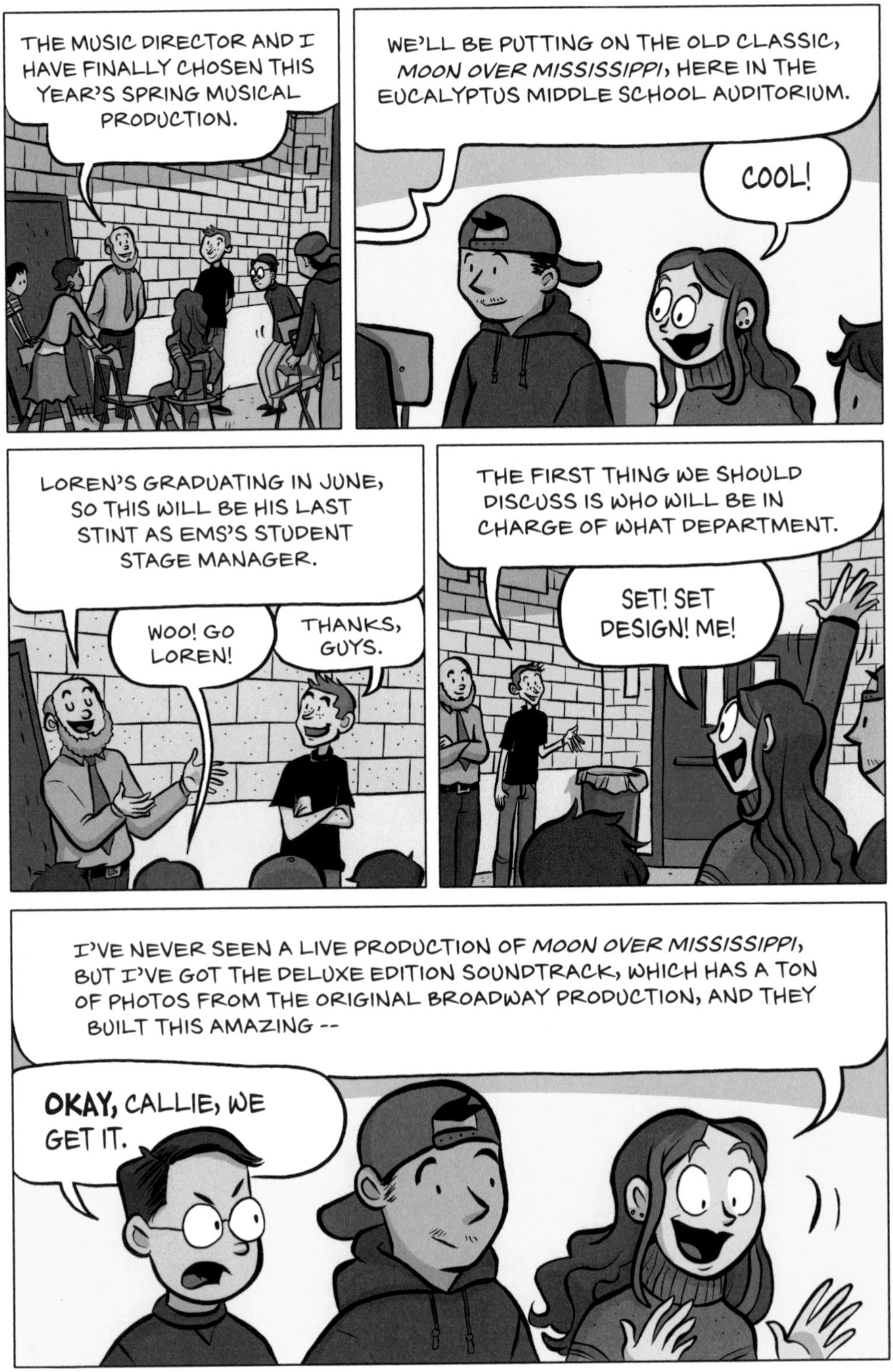
THE MUSIC DIRECTOR AND I HAVE FINALLY CHOSEN THIS YEAR'S SPRING MUSICAL PRODUCTION.
WE'LL BE PUTTING ON THE OLD CLASSIC, *MOON OVER MISSISSIPPI*, HERE IN THE EUCALYPTUS MIDDLE SCHOOL AUDITORIUM.
COOL!
LOREN'S GRADUATING IN JUNE, SO THIS WILL BE HIS LAST STINT AS EMS'S STUDENT STAGE MANAGER.
WOO! GO LOREN!
THANKS, GUYS.
THE FIRST THING WE SHOULD DISCUSS IS WHO WILL BE IN CHARGE OF WHAT DEPARTMENT.
SET! SET DESIGN! ME!
I'VE NEVER SEEN A LIVE PRODUCTION OF *MOON OVER MISSISSIPPI*, BUT I'VE GOT THE DELUXE EDITION SOUNDTRACK, WHICH HAS A TON OF PHOTOS FROM THE ORIGINAL BROADWAY PRODUCTION, AND THEY BUILT THIS AMAZING --
OKAY, CALLIE, WE GET IT.

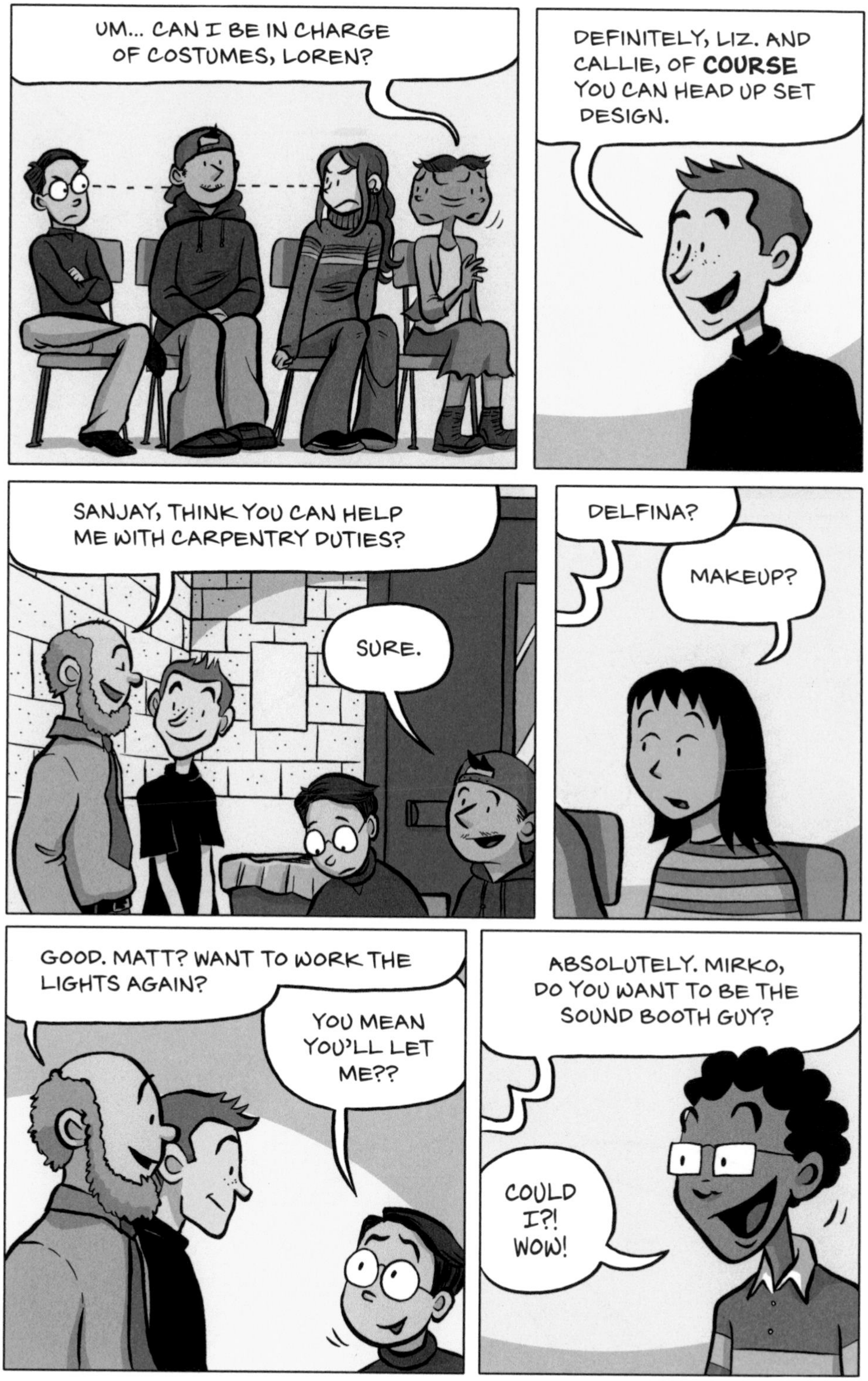
UM... CAN I BE IN CHARGE OF COSTUMES, LOREN?
DEFINITELY, LIZ. AND CALLIE, OF **COURSE** YOU CAN HEAD UP SET DESIGN.
SANJAY, THINK YOU CAN HELP ME WITH CARPENTRY DUTIES?
SURE.
DELFINA?
MAKEUP?
GOOD. MATT? WANT TO WORK THE LIGHTS AGAIN?
YOU MEAN YOU'LL LET ME??
ABSOLUTELY. MIRKO, DO YOU WANT TO BE THE SOUND BOOTH GUY?
COULD I?! WOW!

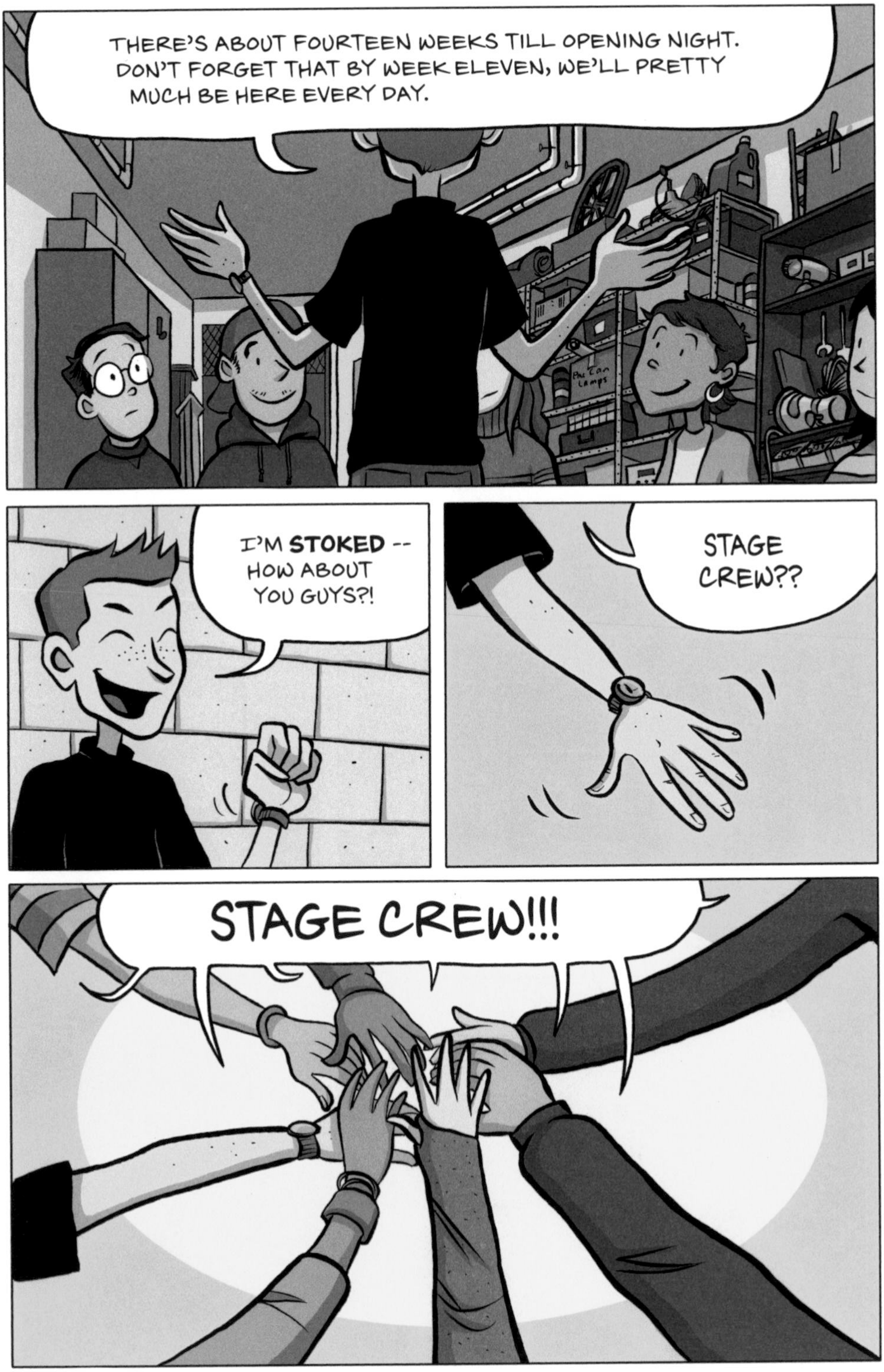
THERE'S ABOUT FOURTEEN WEEKS TILL OPENING NIGHT. DON'T FORGET THAT BY WEEK ELEVEN, WE'LL PRETTY MUCH BE HERE EVERY DAY.
I'M **STOKED** -- HOW ABOUT YOU GUYS?!
STAGE CREW??
STAGE CREW!!!

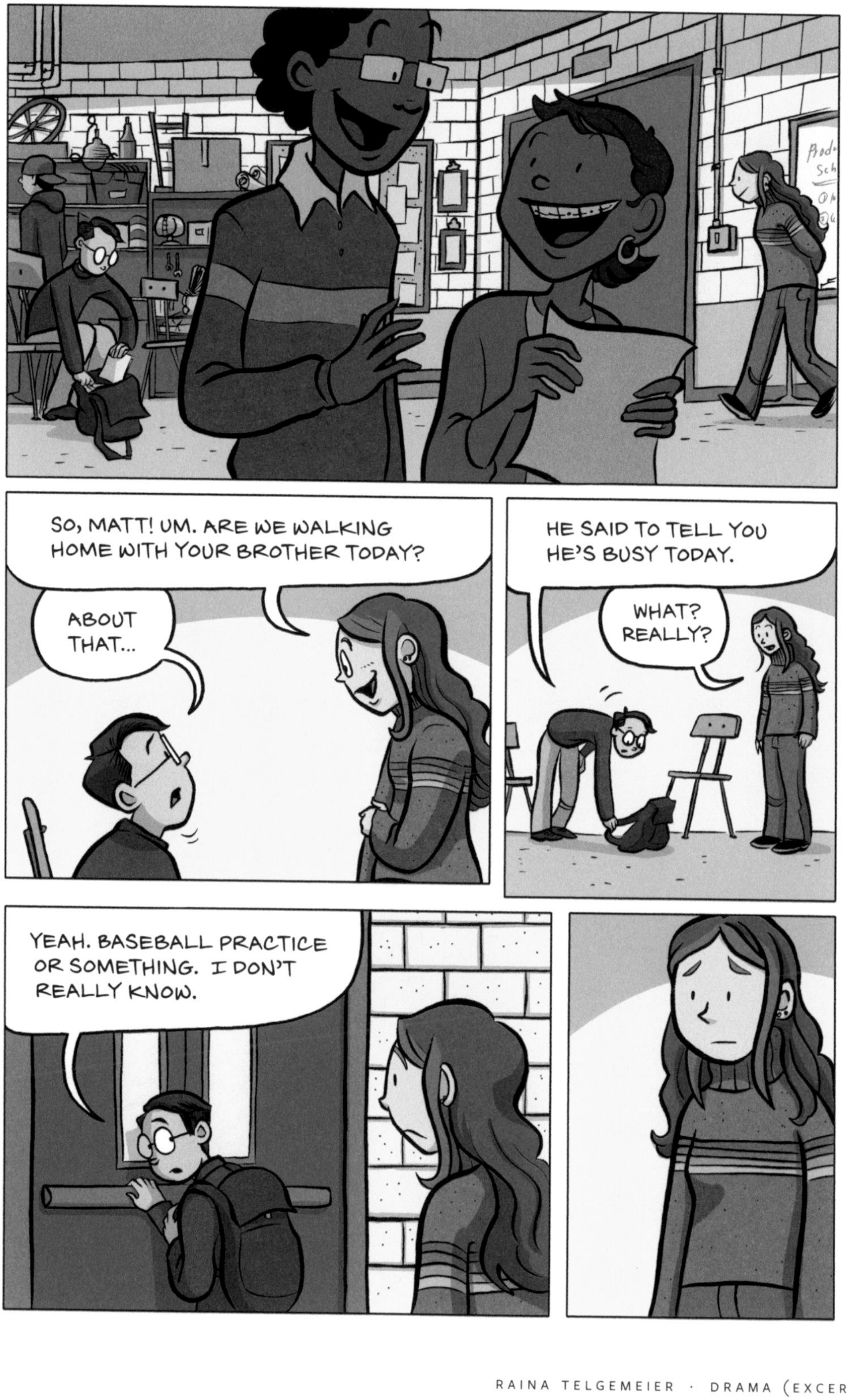
SO, MATT! UM. ARE WE WALKING HOME WITH YOUR BROTHER TODAY?
ABOUT THAT...
HE SAID TO TELL YOU HE'S BUSY TODAY.
WHAT? REALLY?
YEAH. BASEBALL PRACTICE OR SOMETHING. I DON'T REALLY KNOW.

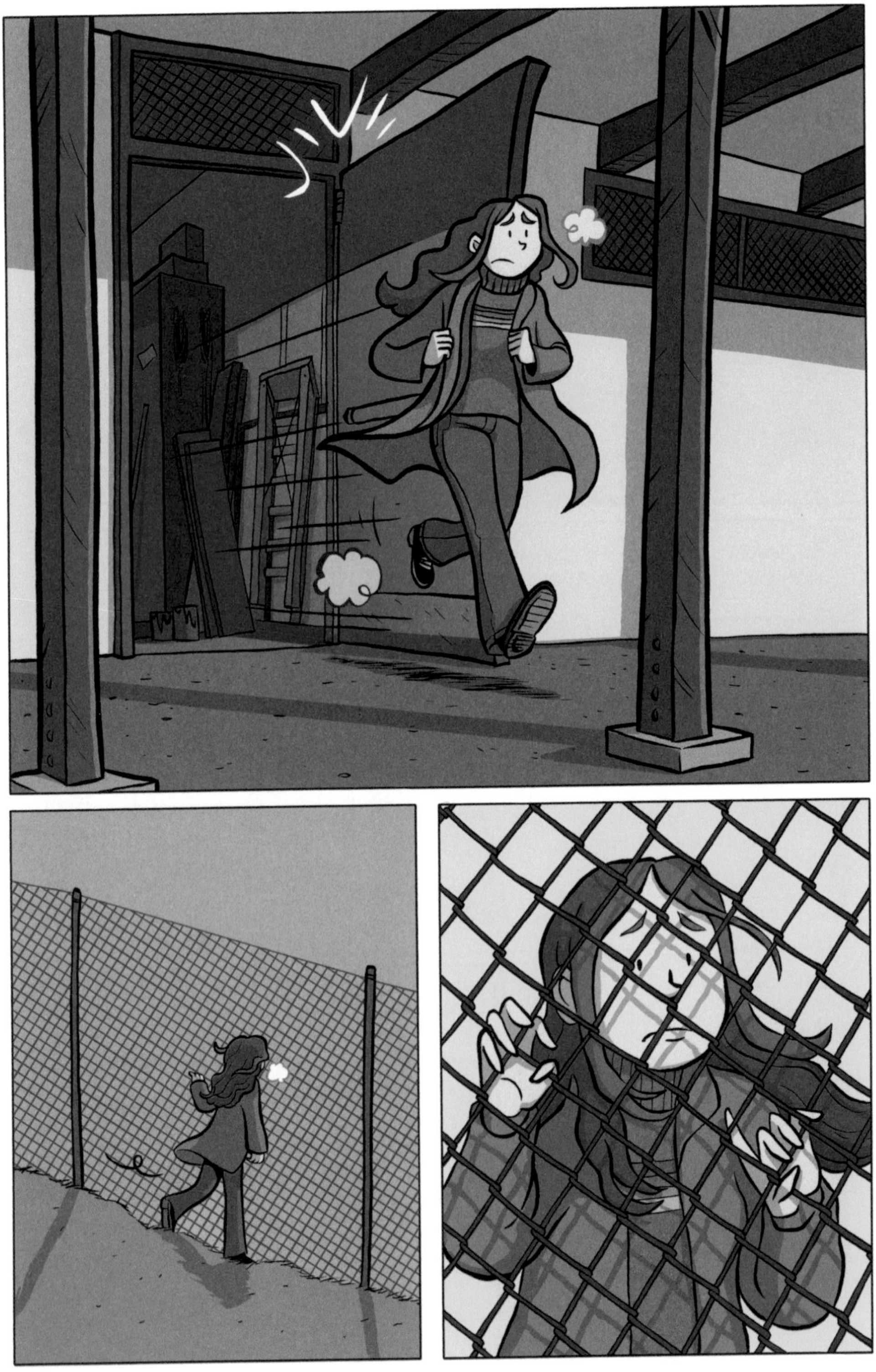

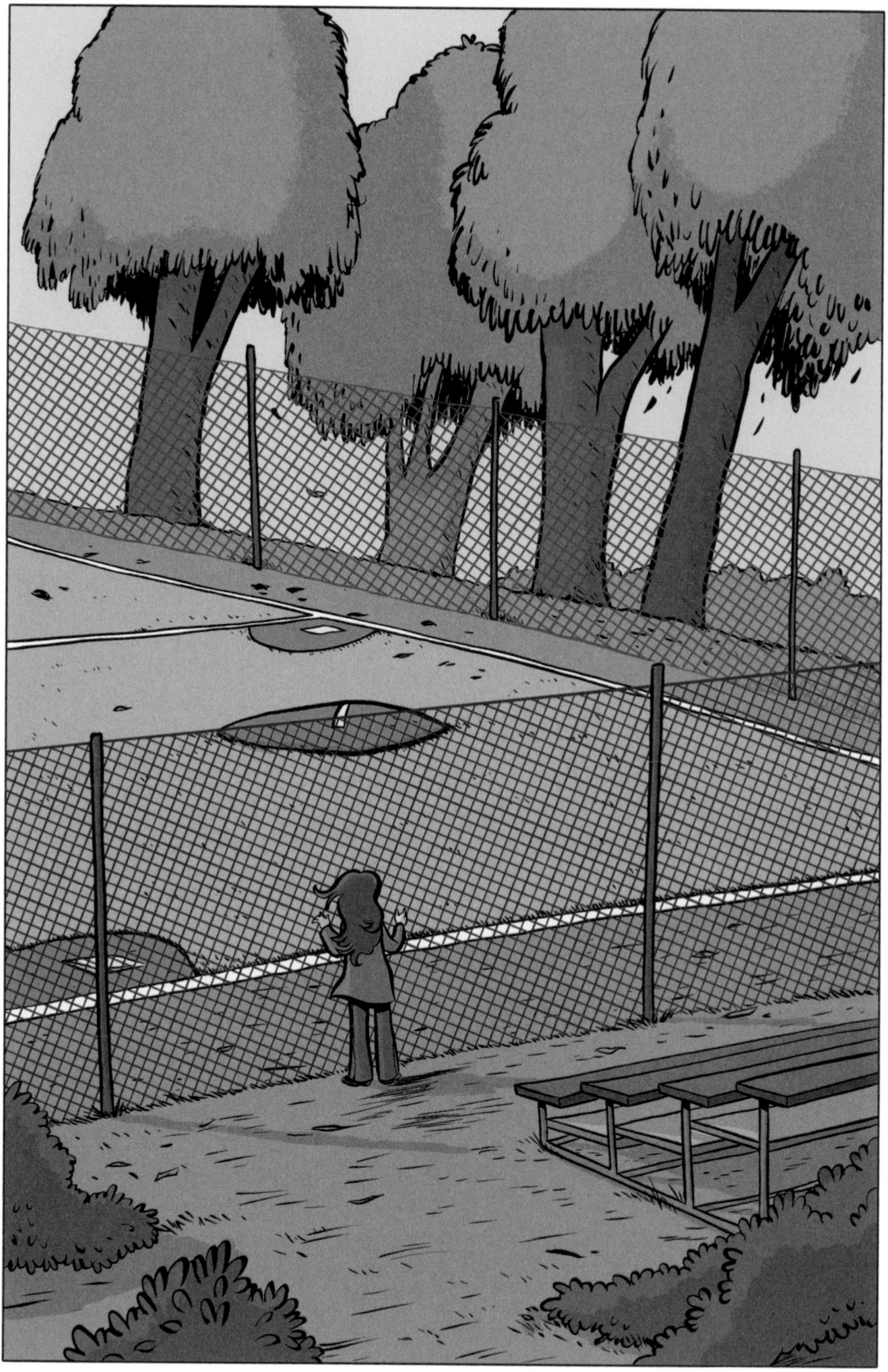

See what she did there?

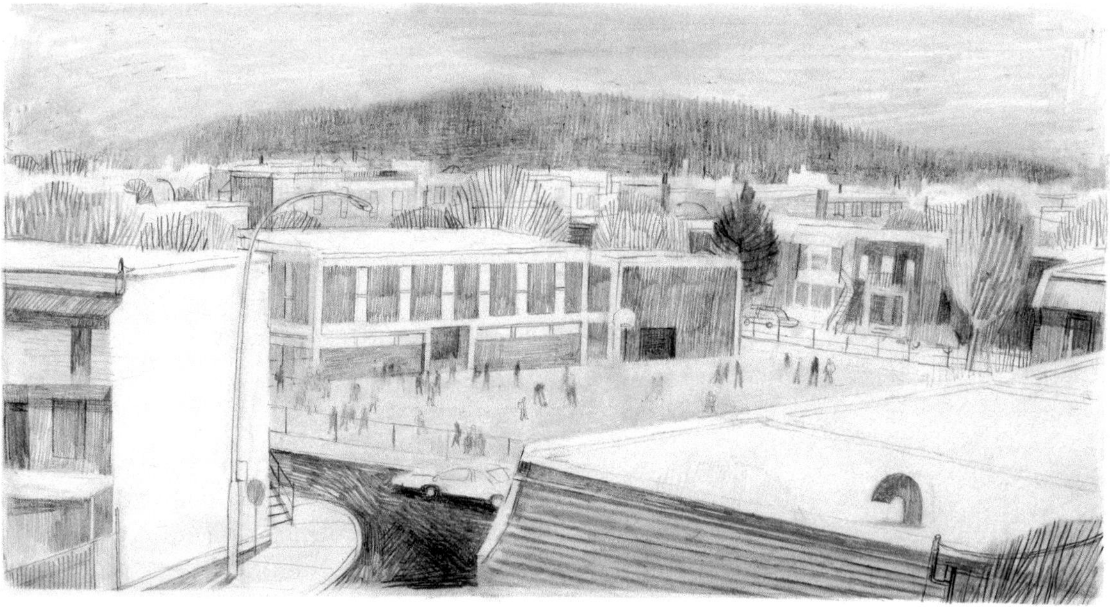

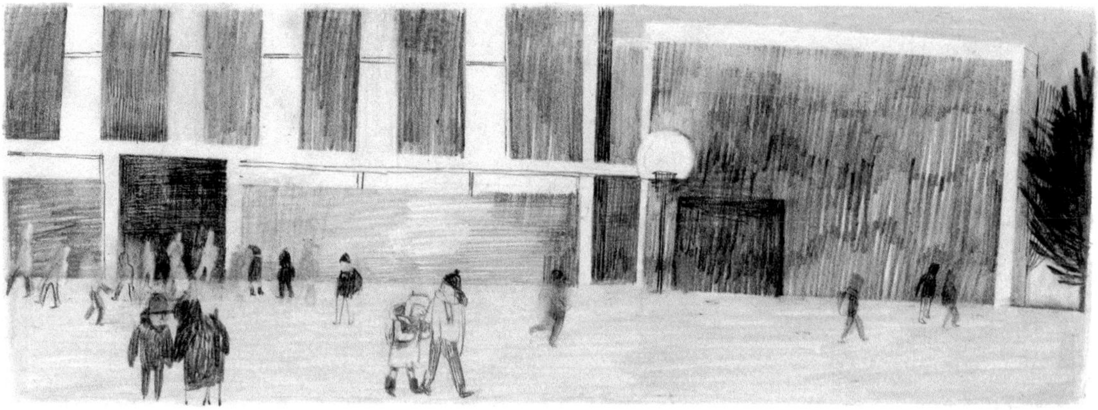

THERE WAS NO POSSIBILITY OF HIDING ANYWHERE TODAY.

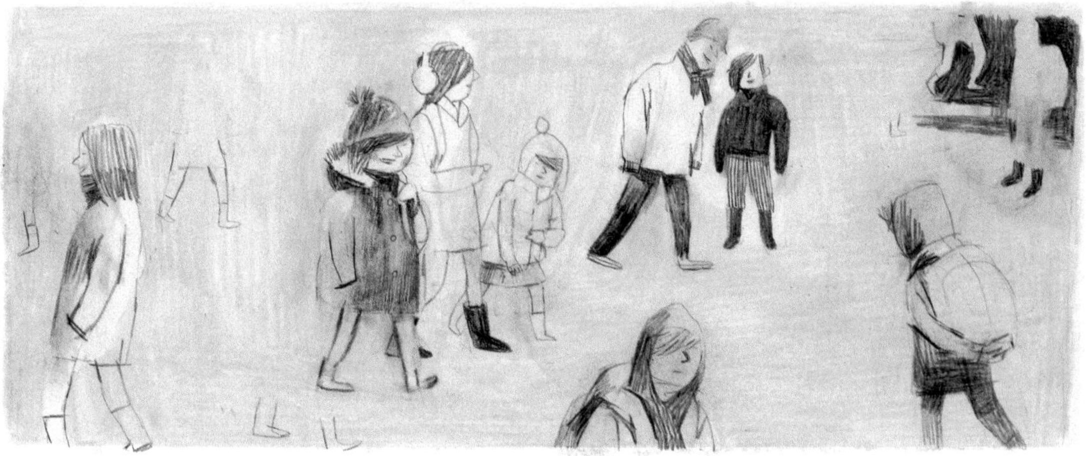

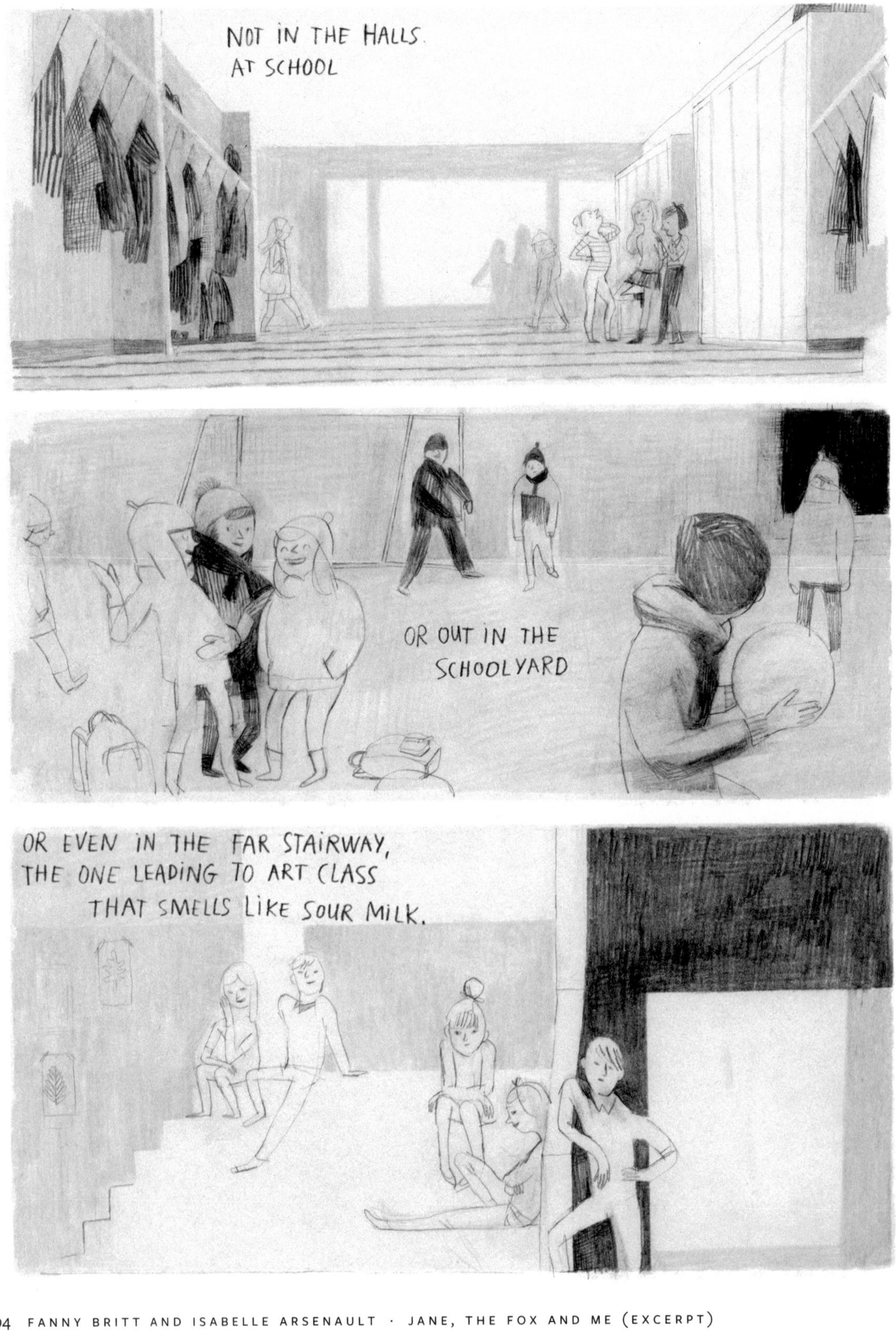
NOT IN THE HALLS
AT SCHOOL
OR OUT IN THE
SCHOOLYARD
OR EVEN IN THE FAR STAIRWAY,
THE ONE LEADING TO ART CLASS
THAT SMELLS LIKE SOUR MILK.

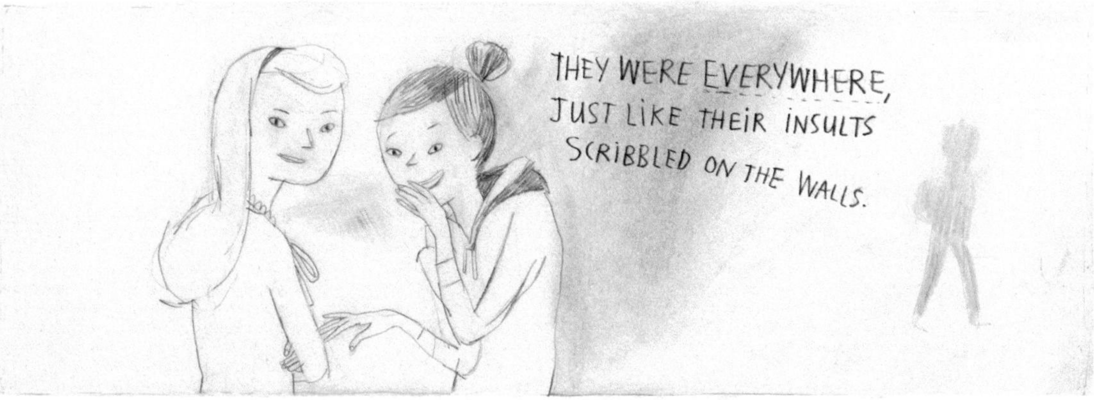
THEY WERE EVERYWHERE, JUST LIKE THEIR INSULTS SCRIBBLED ON THE WALLS.

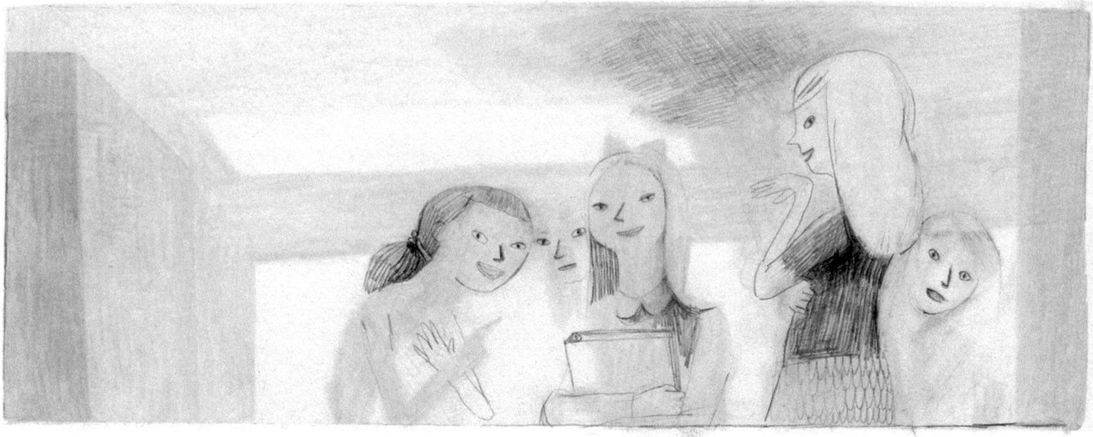

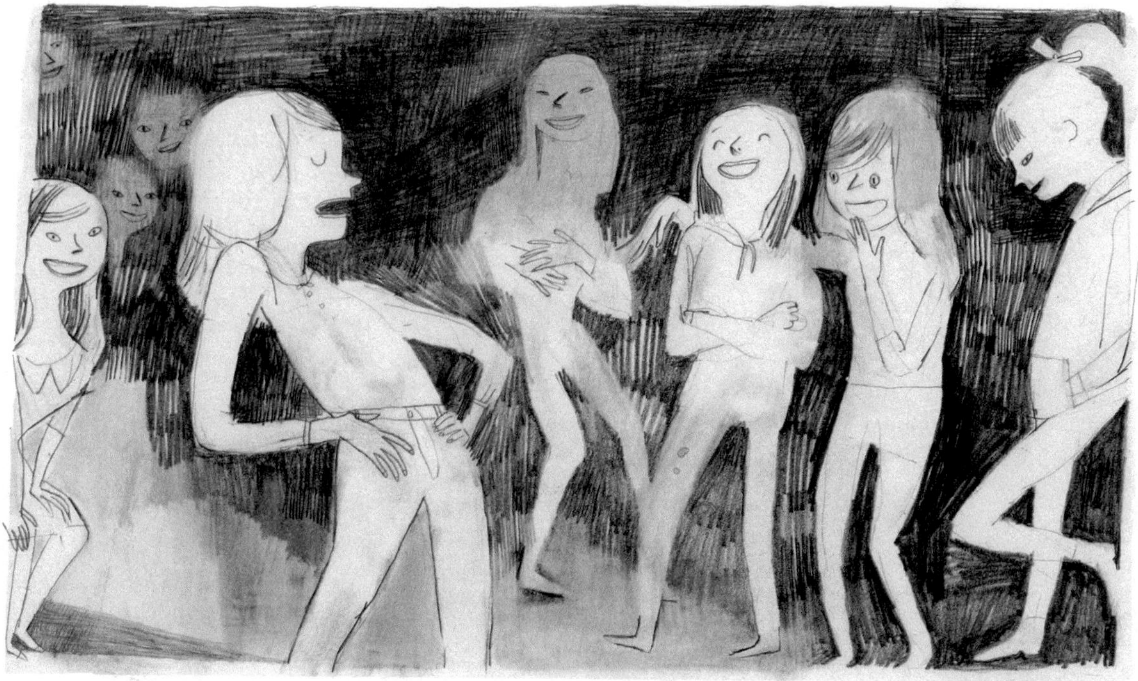

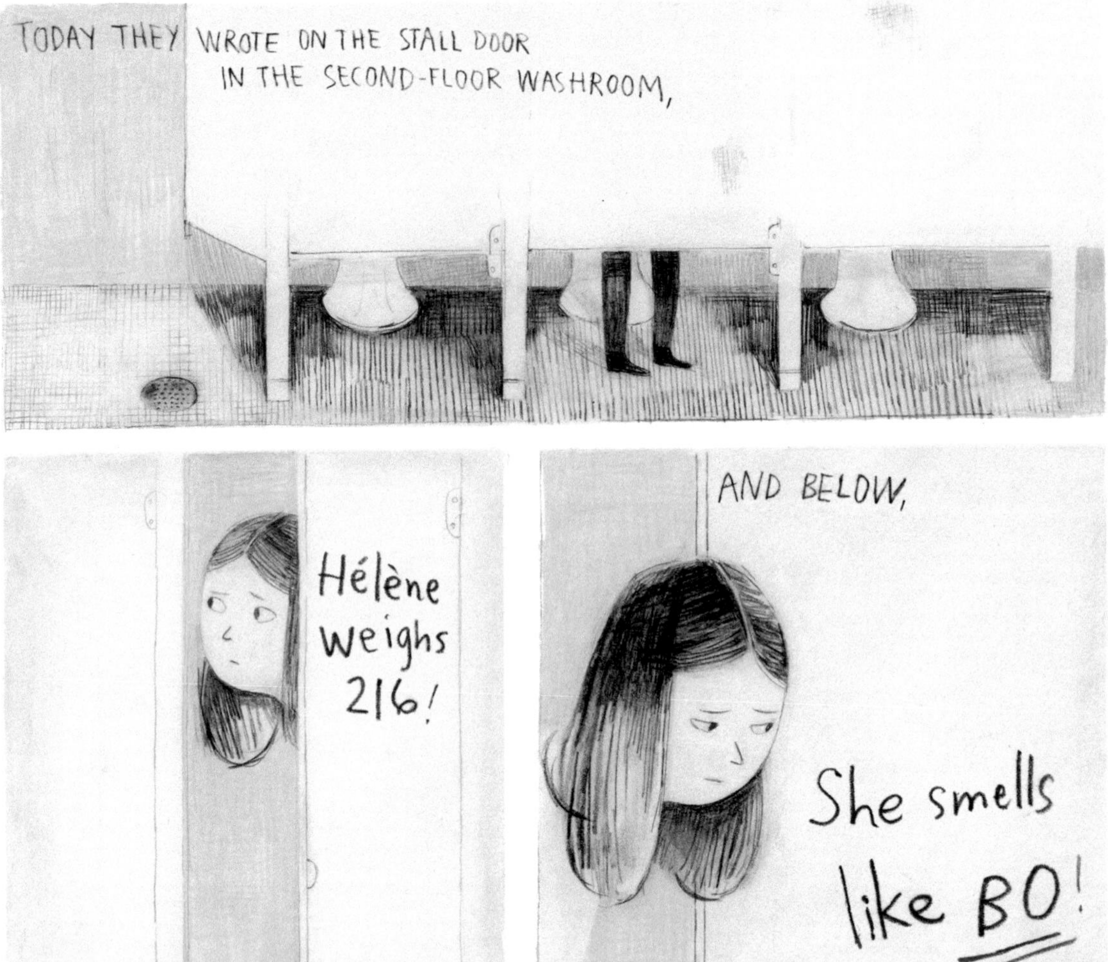
TODAY THEY WROTE ON THE STALL DOOR IN THE SECOND-FLOOR WASHROOM,
Hélène weighs 216!
AND BELOW,
She smells like BO!
THE SCRIBBLES ARE MOST CERTAINLY GENEVIÈVE'S DOING. SHE NEVER EVER MAKES MISTAKES. I ALWAYS KNOW WHEN IT'S HER.
IF IT HAD BEEN ANNE-JULIE, IT WOULD HAVE LOOKED MORE LIKE, "SHE SMELES LYKE BO."
MOST CERTAINLY.

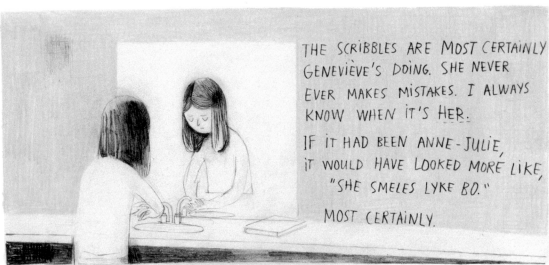

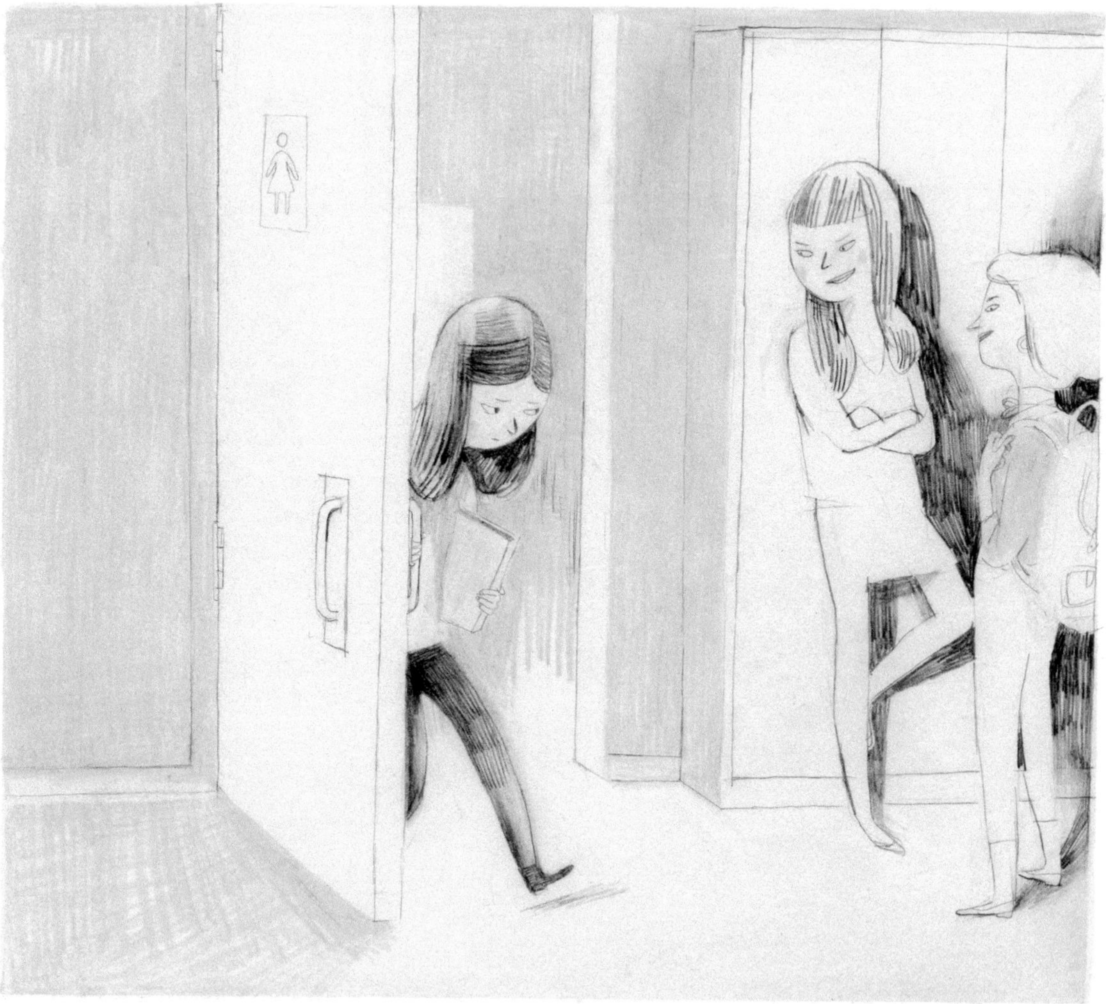

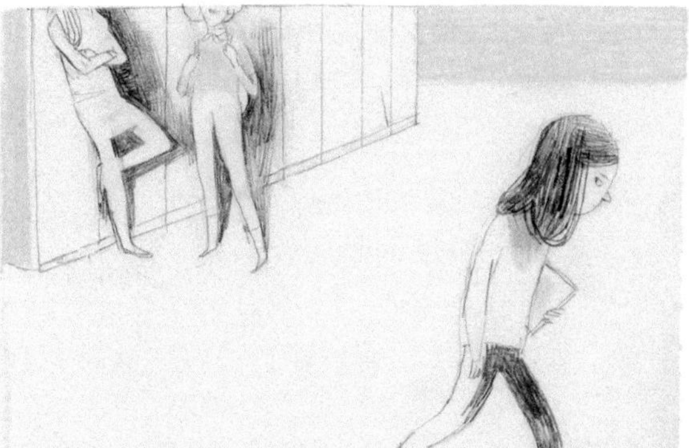

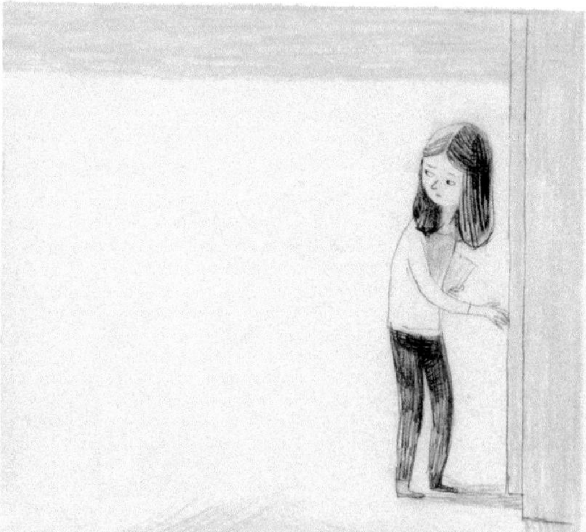

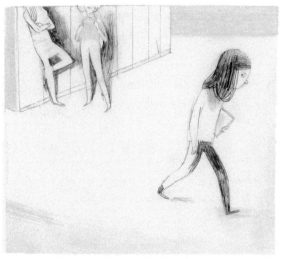

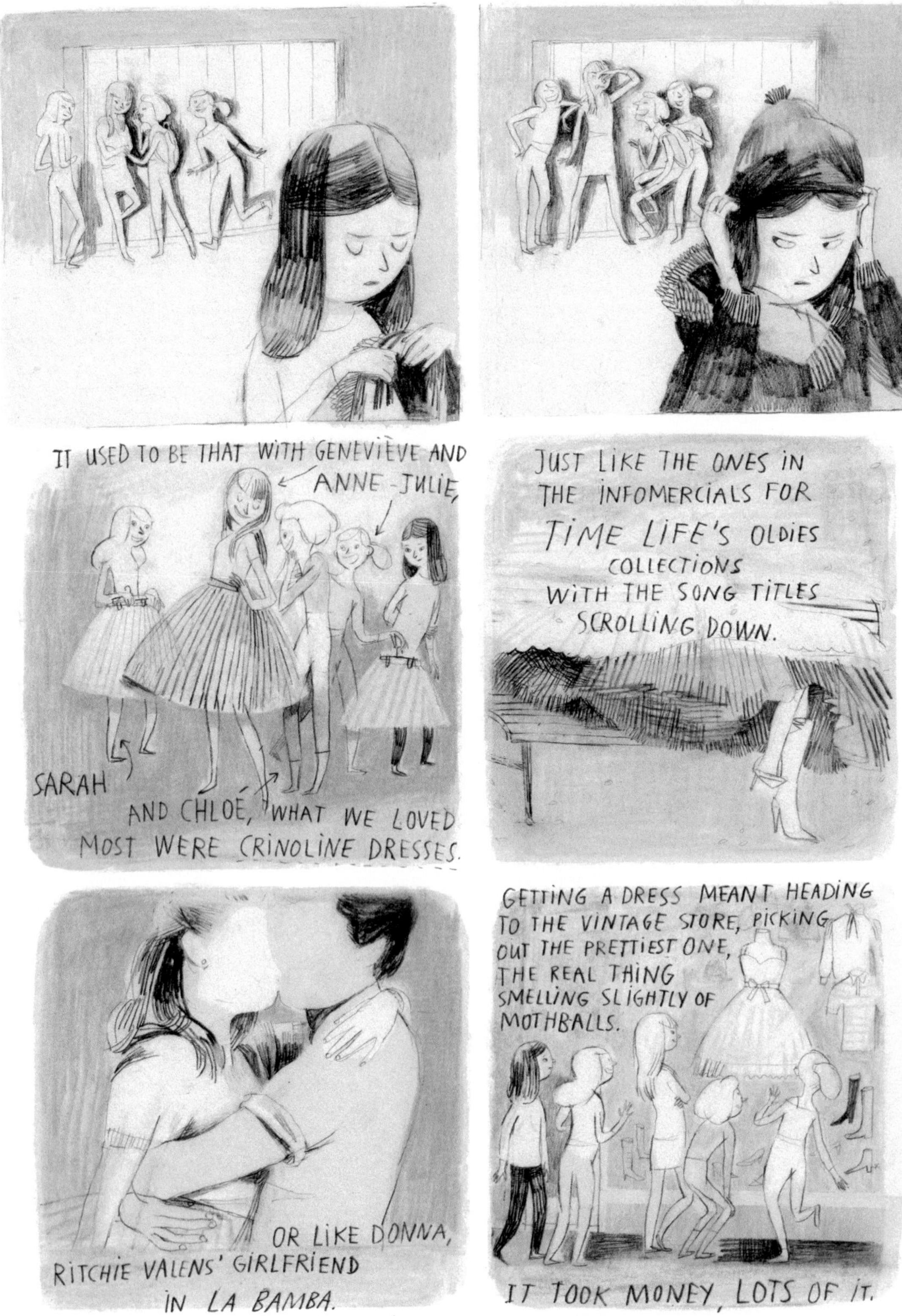
IT USED TO BE THAT WITH GENEVIÈVE AND
ANNE-JULIE,
SARAH
AND CHLOÉ, WHAT WE LOVED MOST WERE CRINOLINE DRESSES.
JUST LIKE THE ONES IN THE INFOMERCIALS FOR *TIME LIFE'S* OLDIES COLLECTIONS WITH THE SONG TITLES SCROLLING DOWN.
OR LIKE DONNA, RITCHIE VALENS' GIRLFRIEND IN *LA BAMBA*.
GETTING A DRESS MEANT HEADING TO THE VINTAGE STORE, PICKING OUT THE PRETTIEST ONE, THE REAL THING SMELLING SLIGHTLY OF MOTHBALLS.
IT TOOK MONEY, LOTS OF IT.

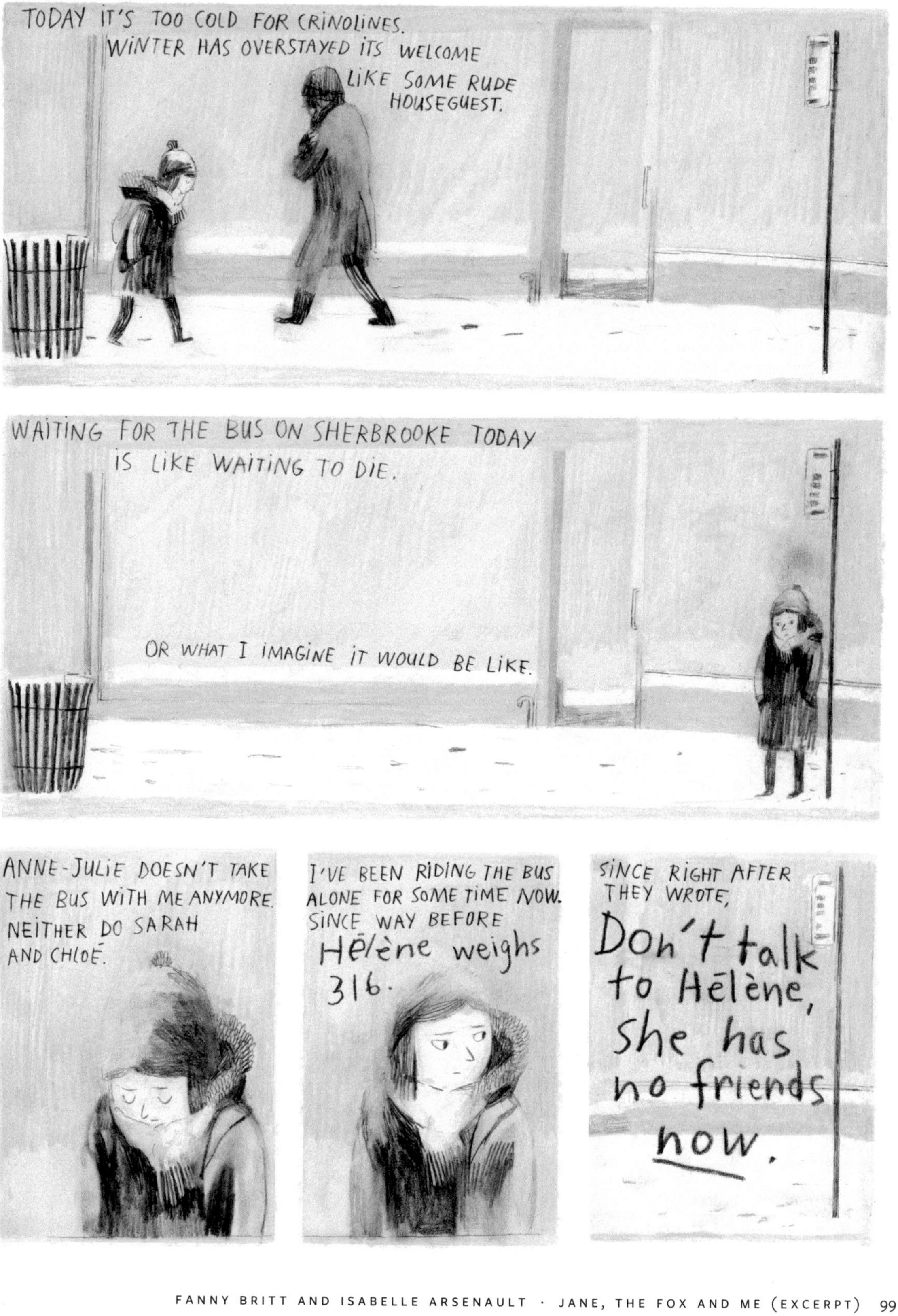
TODAY IT'S TOO COLD FOR CRINOLINES.
WINTER HAS OVERSTAYED ITS WELCOME
LIKE SOME RUDE HOUSEGUEST.
WAITING FOR THE BUS ON SHERBROOKE TODAY
IS LIKE WAITING TO DIE.
OR WHAT I IMAGINE IT WOULD BE LIKE.
ANNE-JULIE DOESN'T TAKE THE BUS WITH ME ANYMORE. NEITHER DO SARAH AND CHLOÉ.
I'VE BEEN RIDING THE BUS ALONE FOR SOME TIME NOW. SINCE WAY BEFORE
Hélène weighs 316.
SINCE RIGHT AFTER THEY WROTE,
Don't talk to Hélène, she has no friends now.

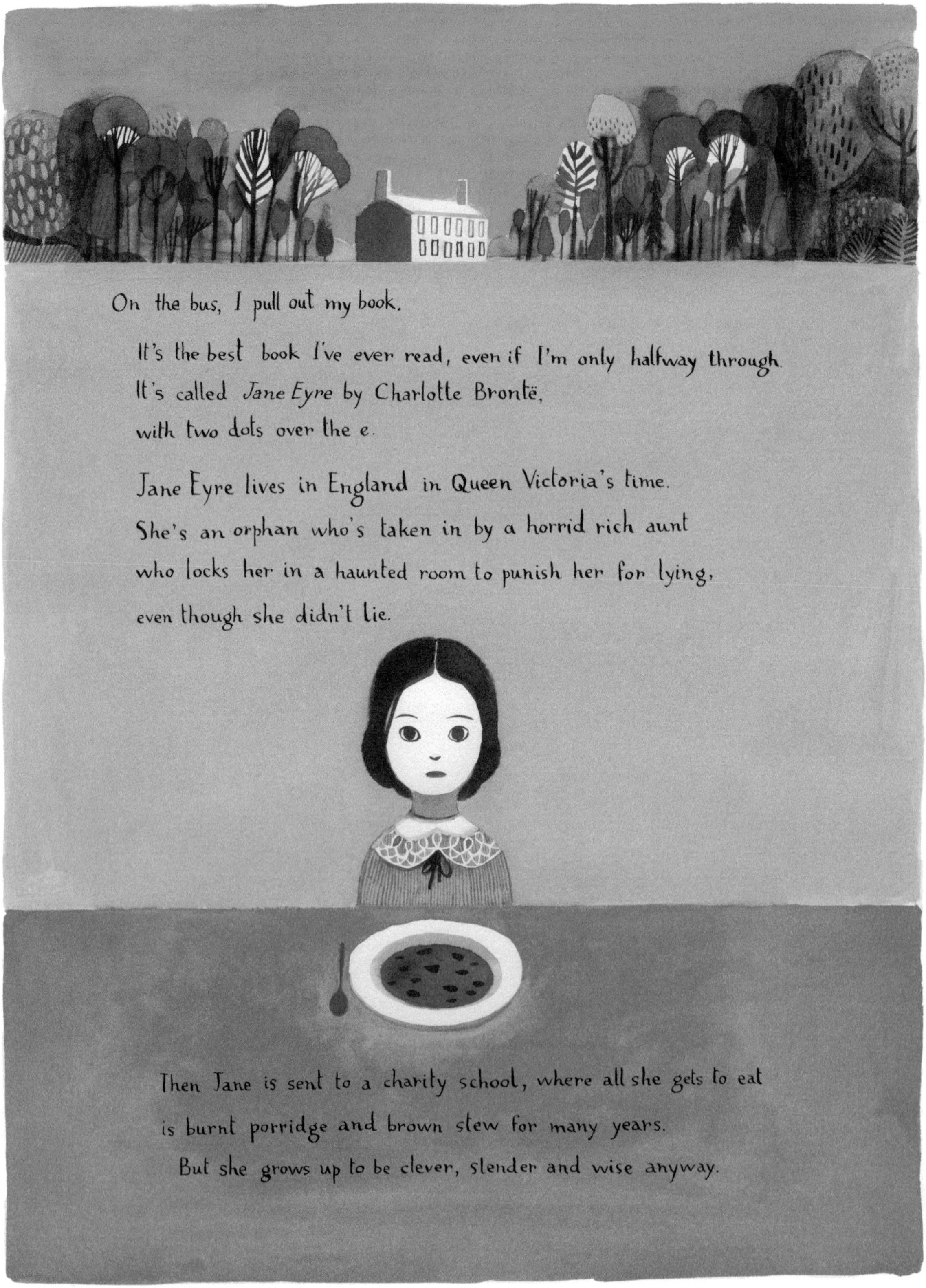
On the bus, I pull out my book.
It's the best book I've ever read, even if I'm only halfway through.
It's called *Jane Eyre* by Charlotte Brontë,
with two dots over the e.
Jane Eyre lives in England in Queen Victoria's time.
She's an orphan who's taken in by a horrid rich aunt
who locks her in a haunted room to punish her for lying,
even though she didn't lie.
Then Jane is sent to a charity school, where all she gets to eat
is burnt porridge and brown stew for many years.
But she grows up to be clever, slender and wise anyway.

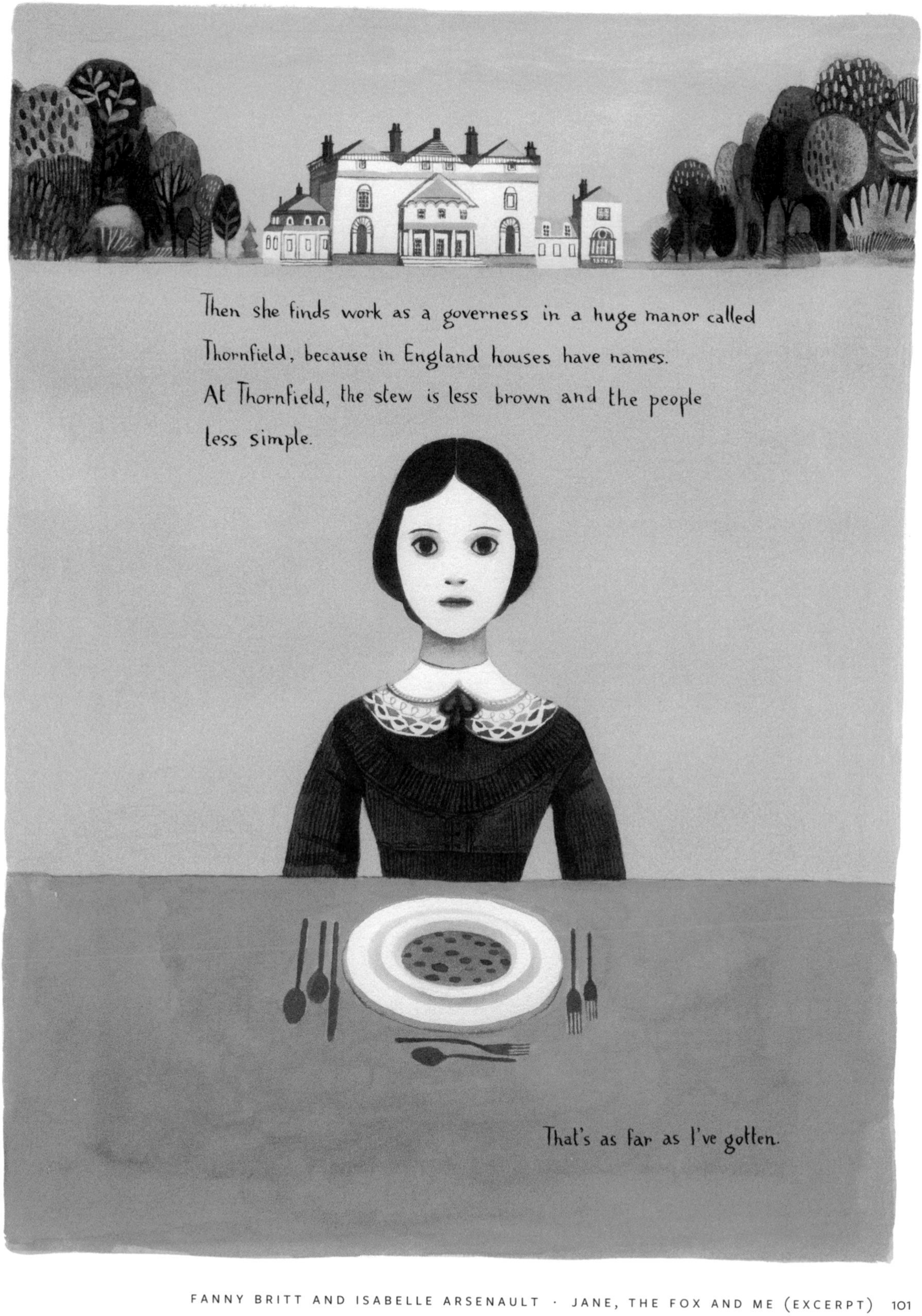
Then she finds work as a governess in a huge manor called Thornfield, because in England houses have names.
At Thornfield, the stew is less brown and the people less simple.
That's as far as I've gotten.

NORMALLY, I HAVE TIME TO READ SOMETHING LIKE THIRTEEN PAGES BETWEEN SCHOOL AND HOME.

IF GENEVIÈVE IS ON THE BUS, AND I CAN HEAR HER SNICKERING WITH THE BOYS NEAR THE BACK, I TURN PAGES WITHOUT REALLY SEEING THEM. I'M TOO DEAFENED BY THE HAMMERING OF MY HEART.

EVEN WITH MY CREEPING VINE OF AN IMAGINATION, I'M ALWAYS TAKEN OFF GUARD BY THE INSULTS SHE INVENTS.

THE SAME THING HAPPENS EVERY TIME — ANOTHER HOLE OPENS UP IN MY RIB CAGE.

HEARING EVERYTHING.

HEARING NOTHING.

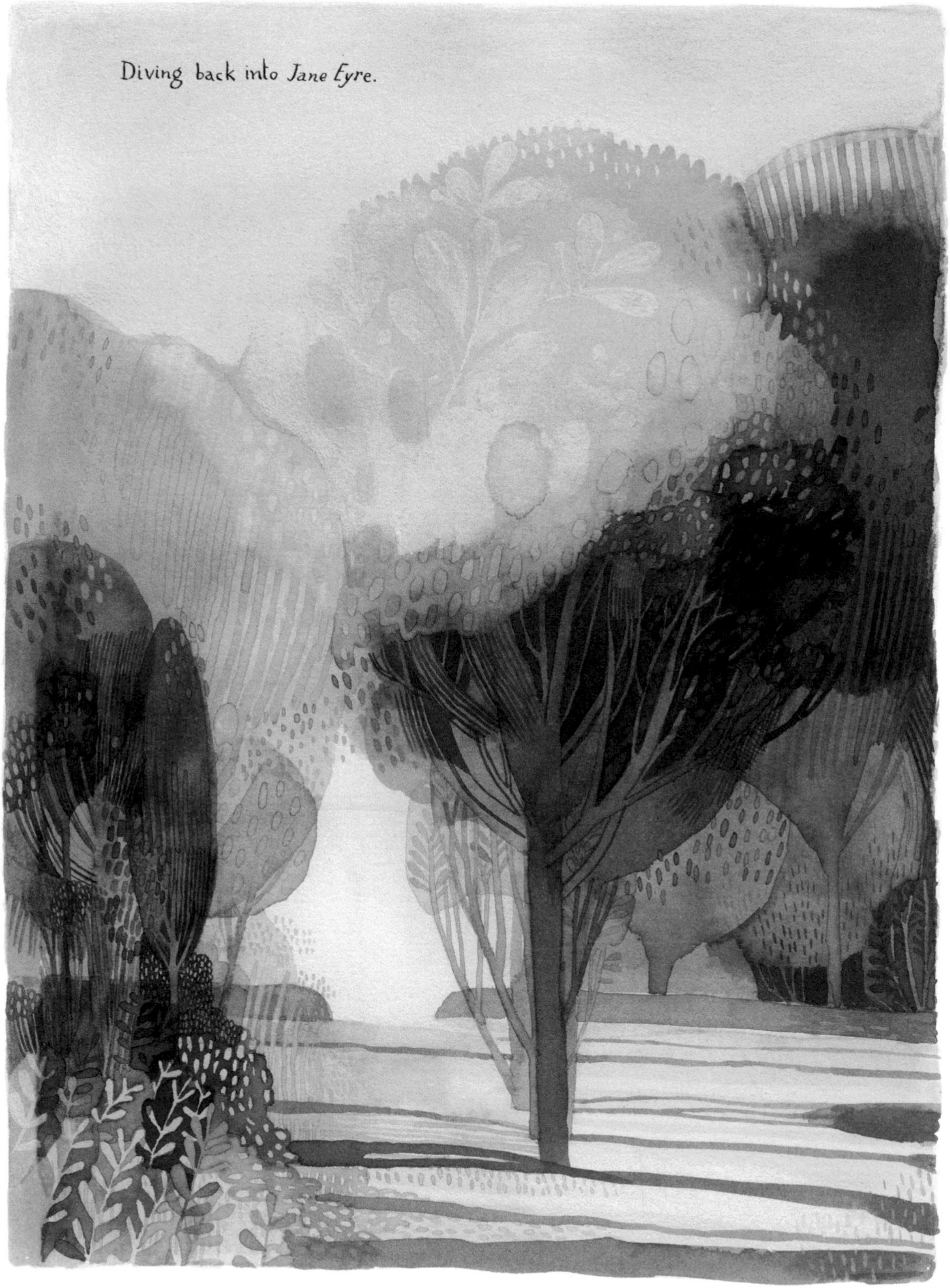
Diving back into *Jane Eyre*.

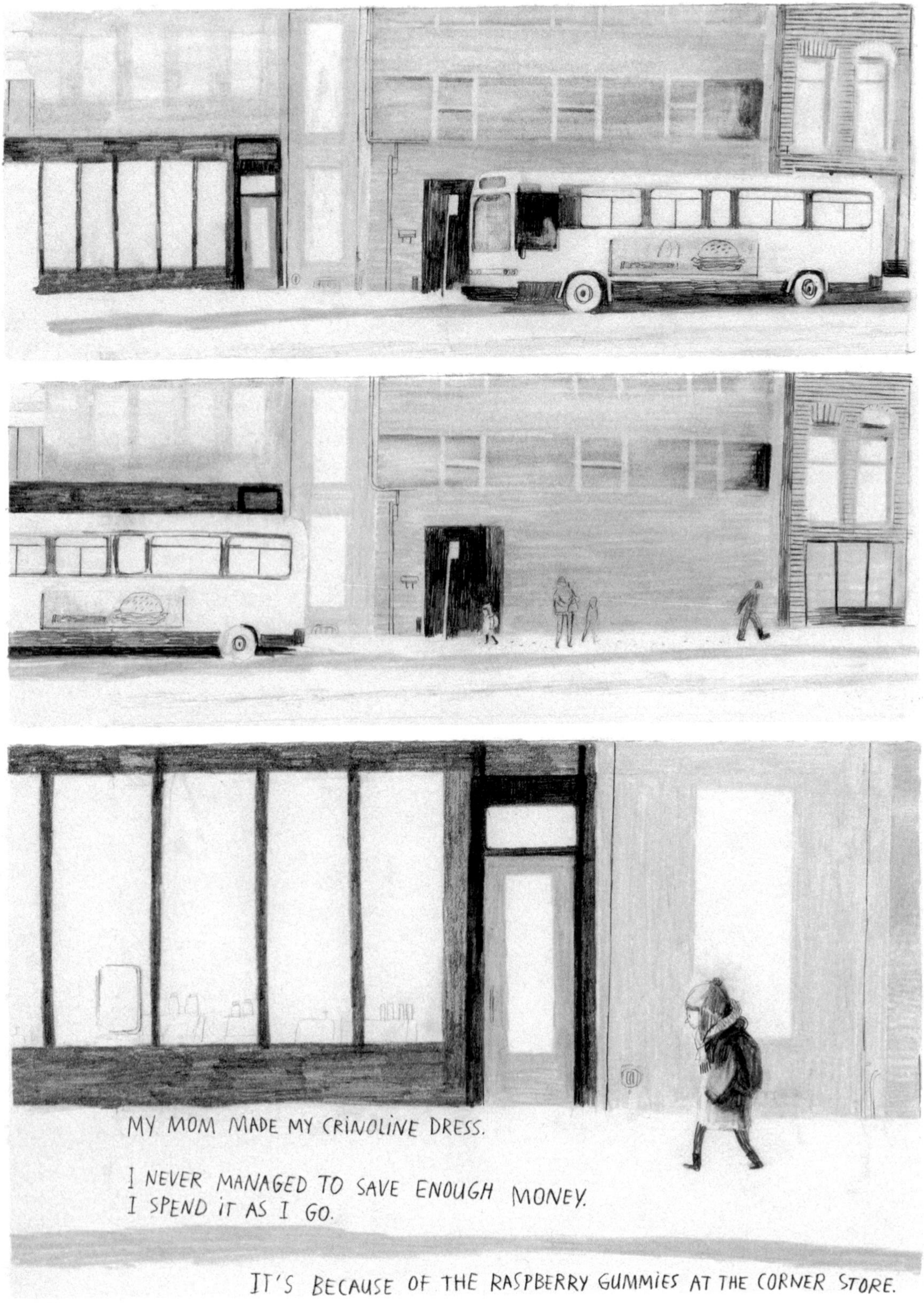
MY MOM MADE MY CRINOLINE DRESS.
I NEVER MANAGED TO SAVE ENOUGH MONEY.
I SPEND IT AS I GO.
IT'S BECAUSE OF THE RASPBERRY GUMMIES AT THE CORNER STORE.

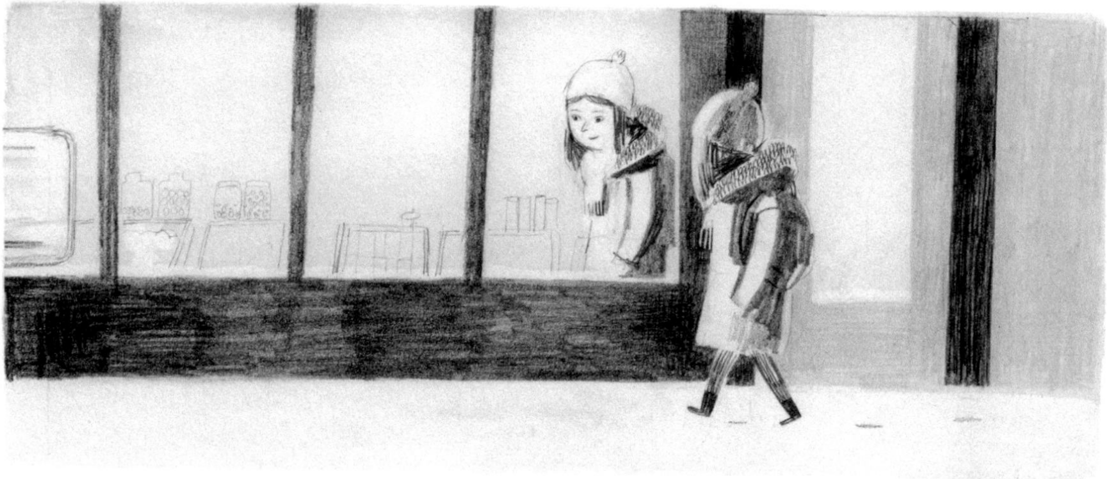

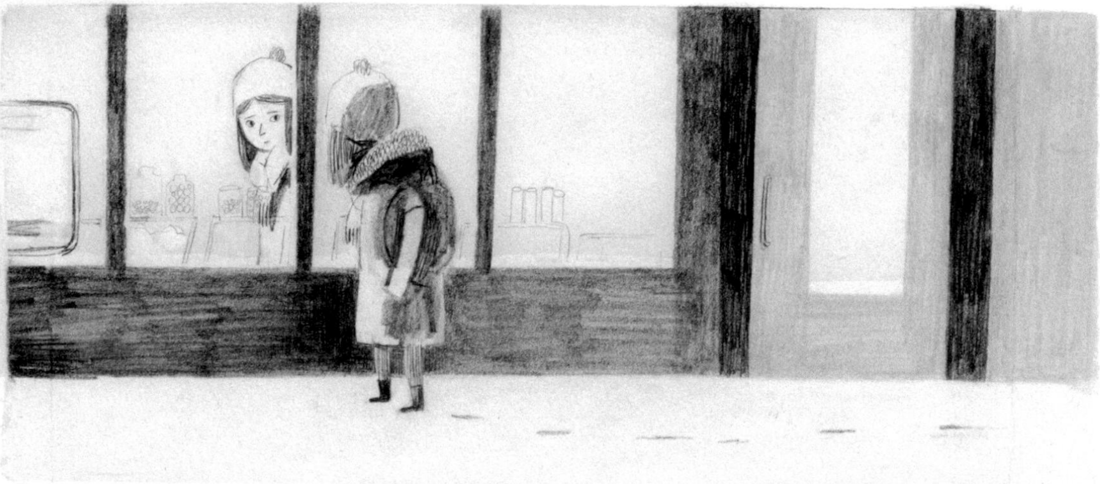

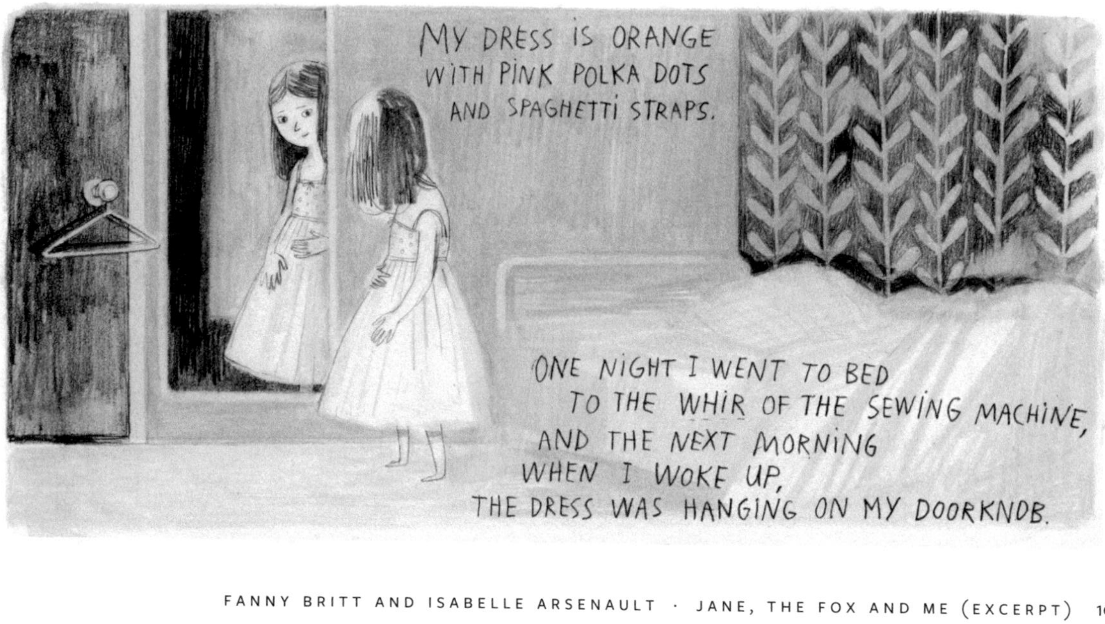
MY DRESS IS ORANGE WITH PINK POLKA DOTS AND SPAGHETTI STRAPS.
ONE NIGHT I WENT TO BED TO THE WHIR OF THE SEWING MACHINE, AND THE NEXT MORNING WHEN I WOKE UP, THE DRESS WAS HANGING ON MY DOORKNOB.

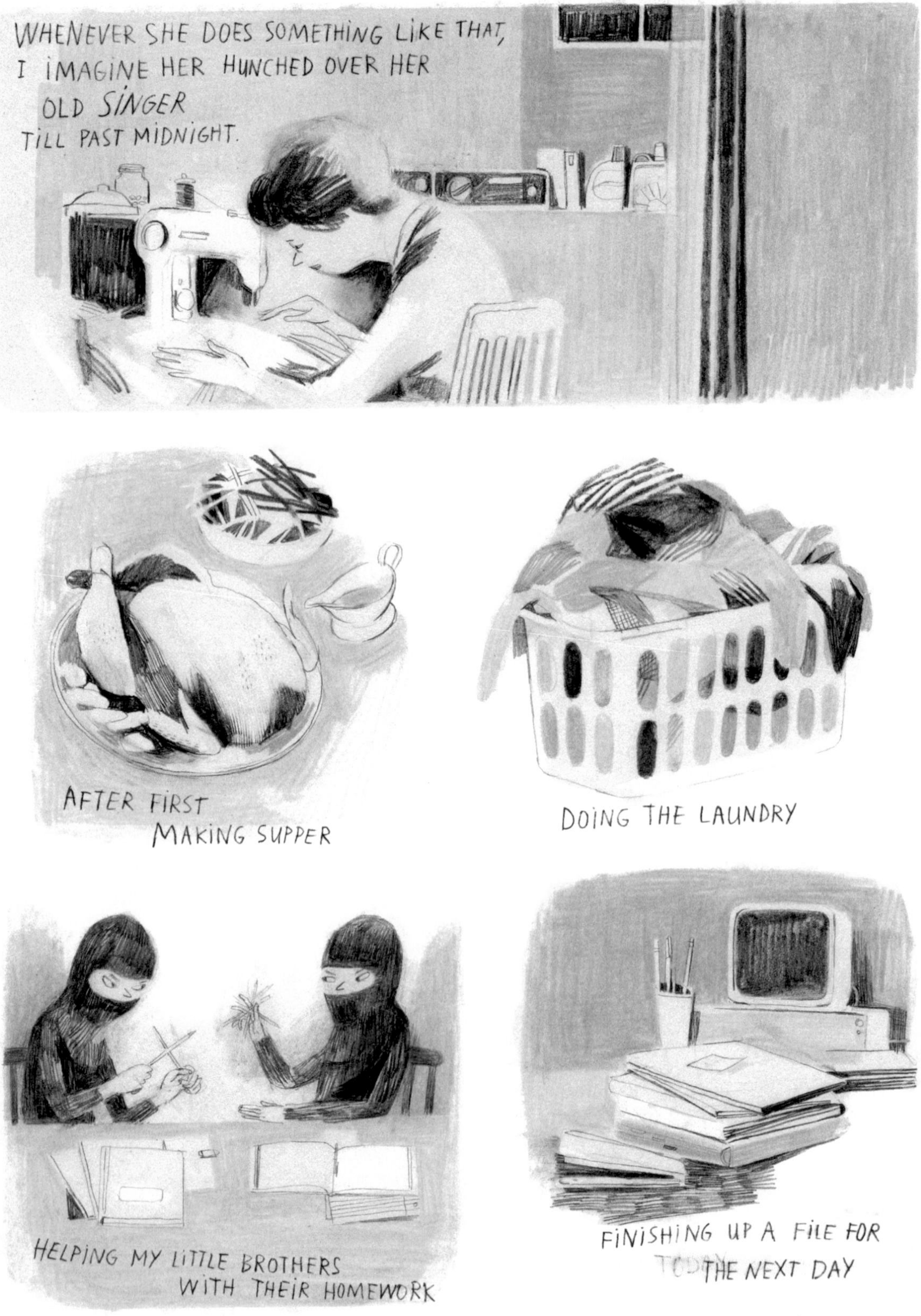
WHENEVER SHE DOES SOMETHING LIKE THAT, I IMAGINE HER HUNCHED OVER HER OLD SINGER TILL PAST MIDNIGHT.
AFTER FIRST MAKING SUPPER
DOING THE LAUNDRY
HELPING MY LITTLE BROTHERS WITH THEIR HOMEWORK
FINISHING UP A FILE FOR THE NEXT DAY

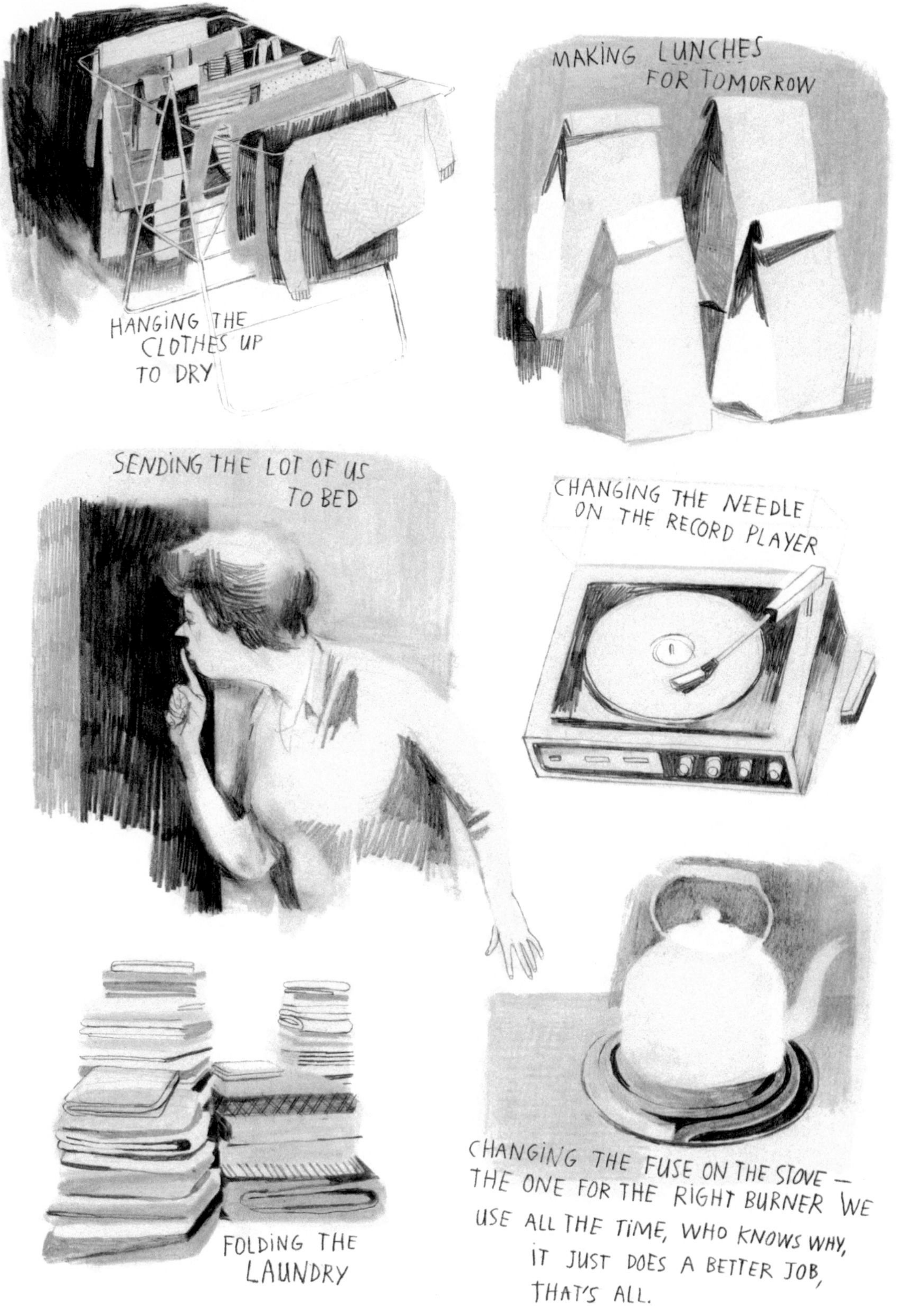
HANGING THE CLOTHES UP TO DRY
MAKING LUNCHES FOR TOMORROW
SENDING THE LOT OF US TO BED
CHANGING THE NEEDLE ON THE RECORD PLAYER
FOLDING THE LAUNDRY
CHANGING THE FUSE ON THE STOVE — THE ONE FOR THE RIGHT BURNER WE USE ALL THE TIME, WHO KNOWS WHY, IT JUST DOES A BETTER JOB, THAT'S ALL.

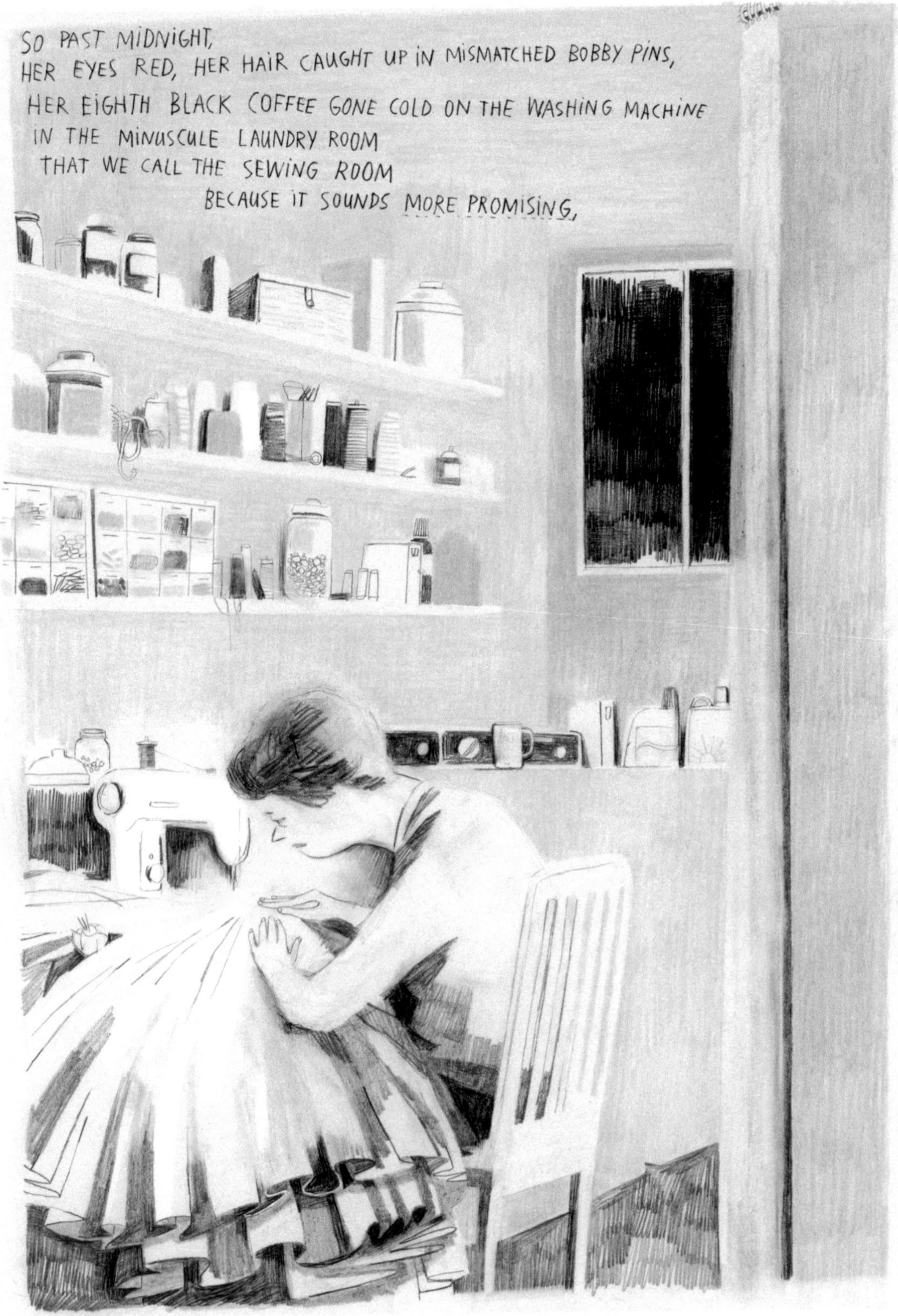
SO PAST MIDNIGHT,
HER EYES RED, HER HAIR CAUGHT UP IN MISMATCHED BOBBY PINS,
HER EIGHTH BLACK COFFEE GONE COLD ON THE WASHING MACHINE
IN THE MINUSCULE LAUNDRY ROOM
THAT WE CALL THE SEWING ROOM
BECAUSE IT SOUNDS MORE PROMISING,

I IMAGINE HER RUNNING OUT OF THREAD JUST BEFORE SHE'S DONE.

I IMAGINE HER HAVING TO CHANGE THE BOBBIN

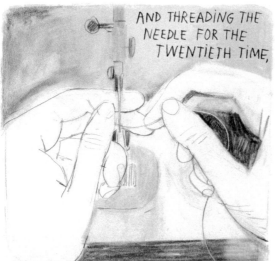

AND THREADING THE NEEDLE FOR THE TWENTIETH TIME,

SAYING TO HERSELF OUT LOUD SO JUST MAYBE SOMEONE WILL HEAR HER, EVEN THOUGH BY NOW EVERYONE'S IN BED,

I'm so tired I could die.

SO I STARE AT THE BEAUTIFUL BRAND-NEW CRINOLINE DRESS THAT'S MINE ALONE WITH NO WHIFF OF MOTHBALLS.

EVEN SO, IT DROOPS EVER SO SLIGHTLY.

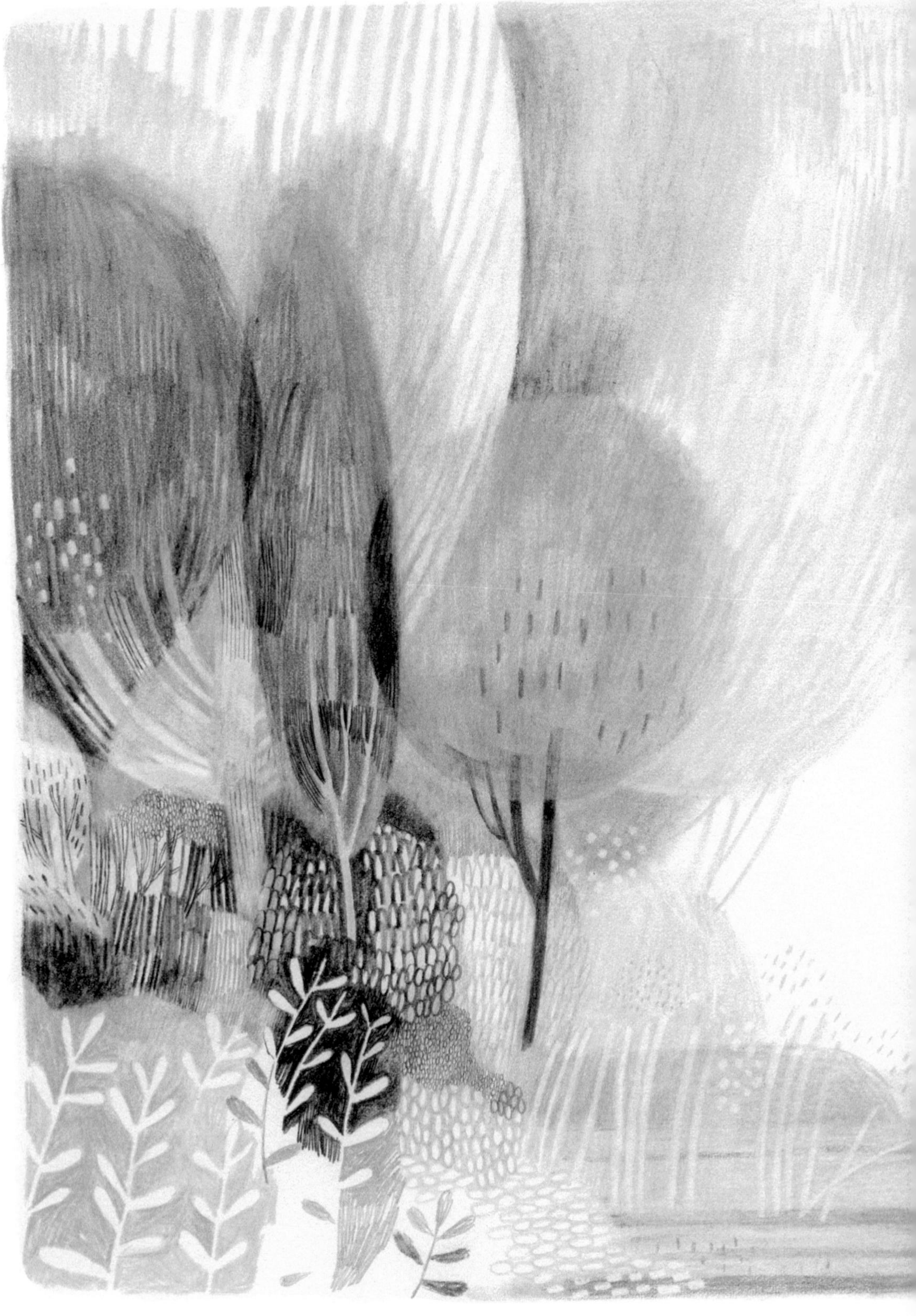

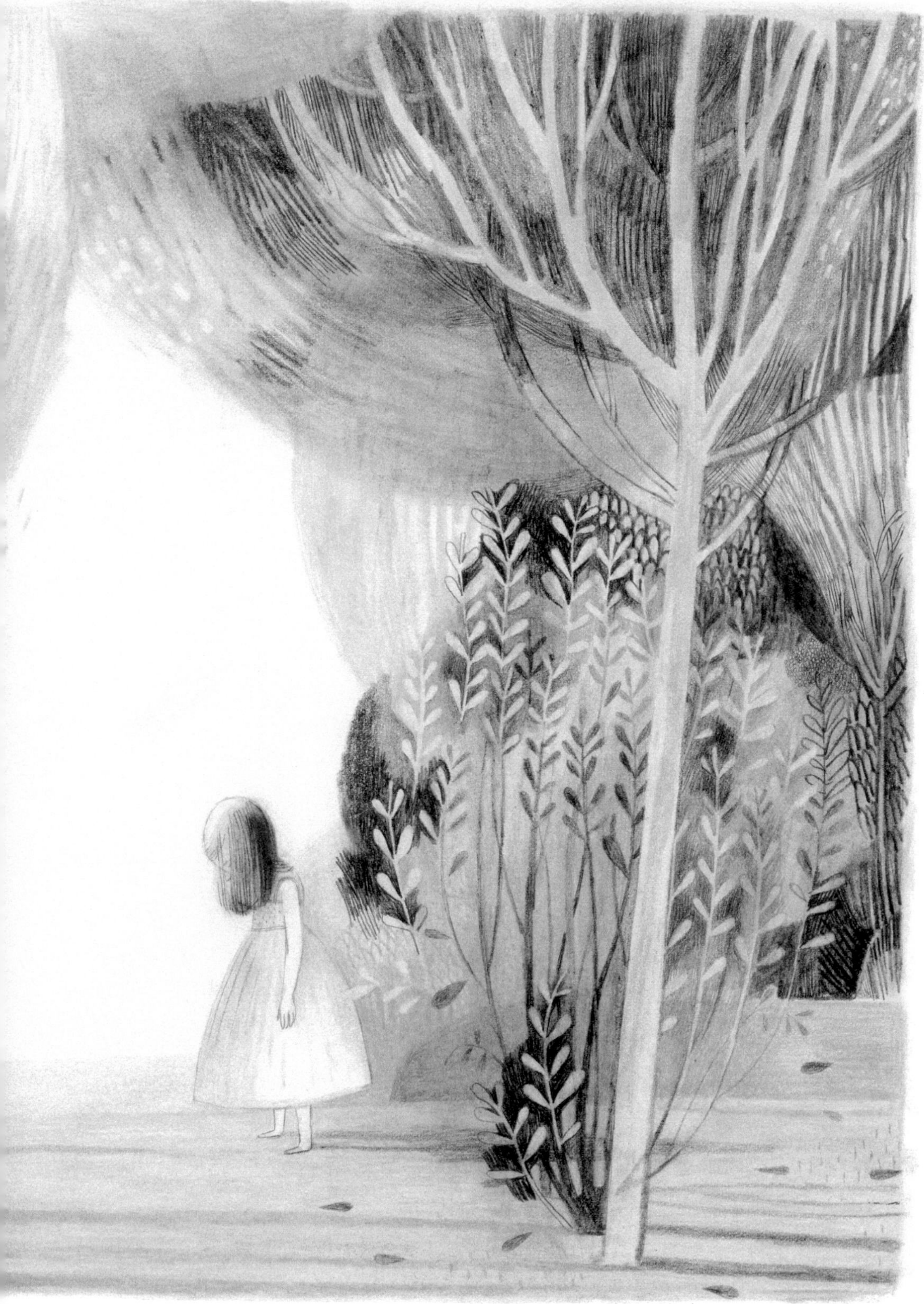

Family Tree

Comics is an intimate medium, well suited to stories of intimate relationships, and one of the most intimate relationships we experience as human beings is the bond between parent and child. I'd already put together these four stories under a vaguely autobiographical banner (although there are others in the book that might've qualified) when I noticed that all four stories were about that parental bond in one way or another.

The last of the four was the last to join. Nina Bunjevac's "August 1977" first caught my eye for its fierce, haunting artwork. Bill and I wanted to know more about its political context, so I did some digging and—

Wait, what do you mean, "Who's Bill?" Bill Kartalopoulos! Series editor of Best American Comics—I mentioned him in the last intro?

Ah, some of you have been browsing, haven't you? Don't browse! Read! This book is designed to be read in order. Trust me, I won't let you down.

Anyway, I found a great interview that Paul "The Man at the Crossroads" Gravett conducted with Bunjevac for *ArtReview* in 2012. Gravett writes:

> In 1977 Bunjevac lost her father, a Serbian nationalist exiled to Canada, where he died in a mysterious explosion. She finally began using comics to confront her unresolved issues about his death after visiting Serbia in 2009, where she learned of the humanitarian crisis and the rise of neofascist attacks on the LGBT, Roma, and other minorities. Her richly textural and shadow-filled panels in "August 1977," republished in Heartless, counterpoint the typewritten narration extracted from a real letter to her father by her mother, then an imaginary letter by the adult Nina herself. "I created 'August 1977' as a symbolic recreation of the last three hours of my father's life and as an attempt to reject his ideology, and patriarchy itself."

For much more information, try googling "Paul Gravett Nina Bunjevac." The article should be the first hit.

Miriam Katin's *Letting It Go* also combines the political and the personal, this time from the other side of the parental spectrum, as New York–based Holocaust survivor Miriam struggles with her son's decision to move to Berlin with his fiancée. We can offer only a brief excerpt—a visit to Lithuania taken by Miriam and her husband—from this wonderfully rich book, but I hope you'll seek out the whole story. It offers much more to its readers than anything we can parcel out here.

Sam Sharpe's story about reconnecting with his mentally ill mother ran in his smartly designed small-press comic book *Viewotron*. Sharpe, I'm guessing, is the youngest of our contributors, but he has a great ear for dialogue and a sharp eye for the small, repetitive dance steps of dysfunctional relationships.

Finally, nestled between Katin and Sharpe, is an excerpt from *RL* by Tom Hart. The initials stand for Rosalie Lightning, Tom Hart and Leela Corman's two-year-old daughter who died suddenly in November 2011. We're offering just a little slice of the ongoing story here. I'm not sure why I chose this part of it—it doesn't even deal with the central event at first, just with more prosaic issues of money and moving—but it connected with me as a parent on a very deep level. Maybe it felt crass somehow to get right to the point, to find the most direct awful statements of fact, I don't know. But you'll see enough of *RL*'s bleak power before you're done with it.

Thanks to our publisher, Houghton Mifflin Harcourt, we're offering a special feature in conjunction with this selection: while you read Tom's story, beginning at the second page and continuing until the last, all other pages in this book will turn temporarily blank out of respect.

Or so I like to tell myself.

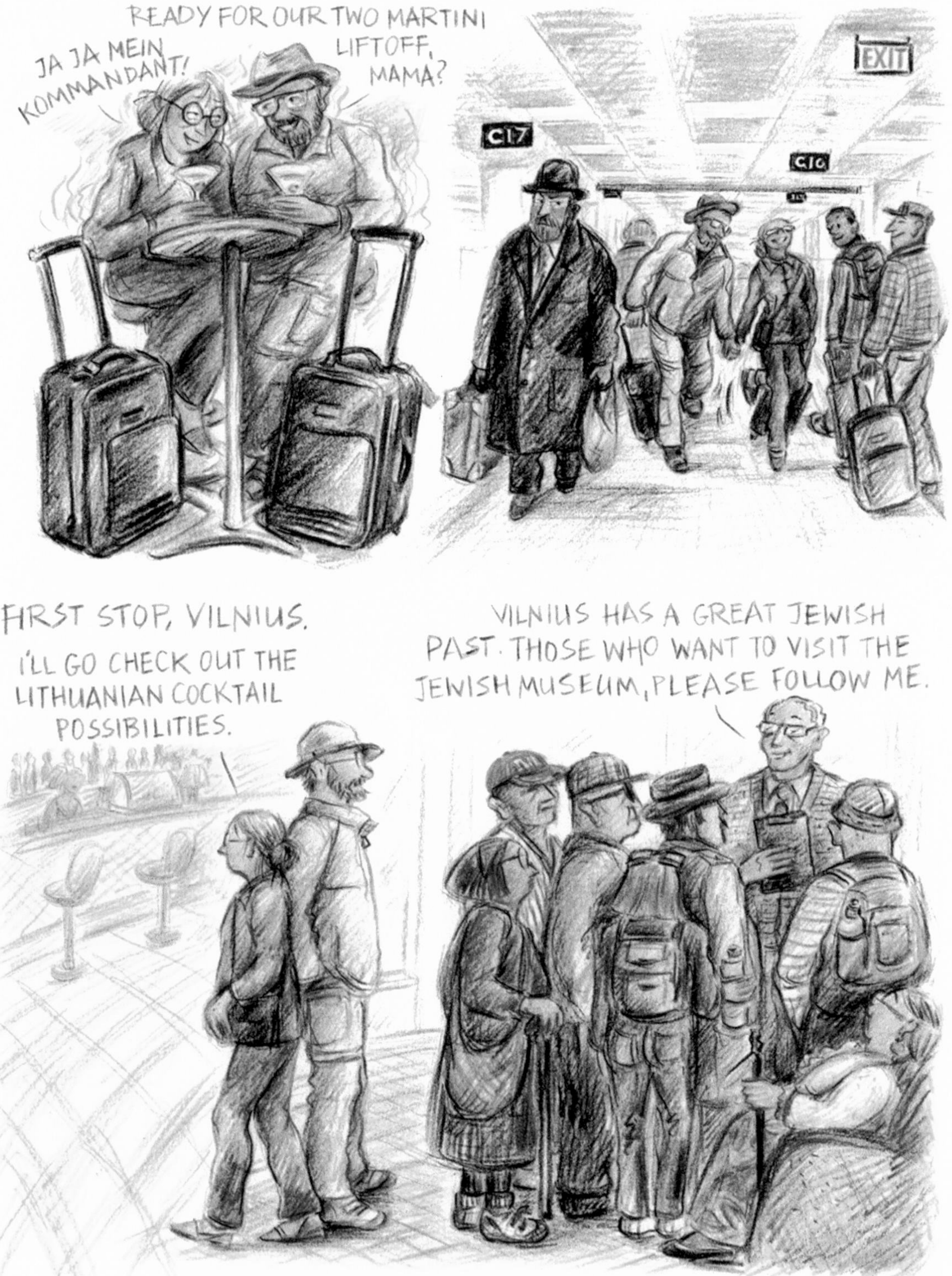
READY FOR OUR TWO MARTINI LIFTOFF, MAMA?
JA JA MEIN KOMMANDANT!
EXIT
C17
C16
FIRST STOP, VILNIUS.
I'LL GO CHECK OUT THE LITHUANIAN COCKTAIL POSSIBILITIES.
VILNIUS HAS A GREAT JEWISH PAST. THOSE WHO WANT TO VISIT THE JEWISH MUSEUM, PLEASE FOLLOW ME.

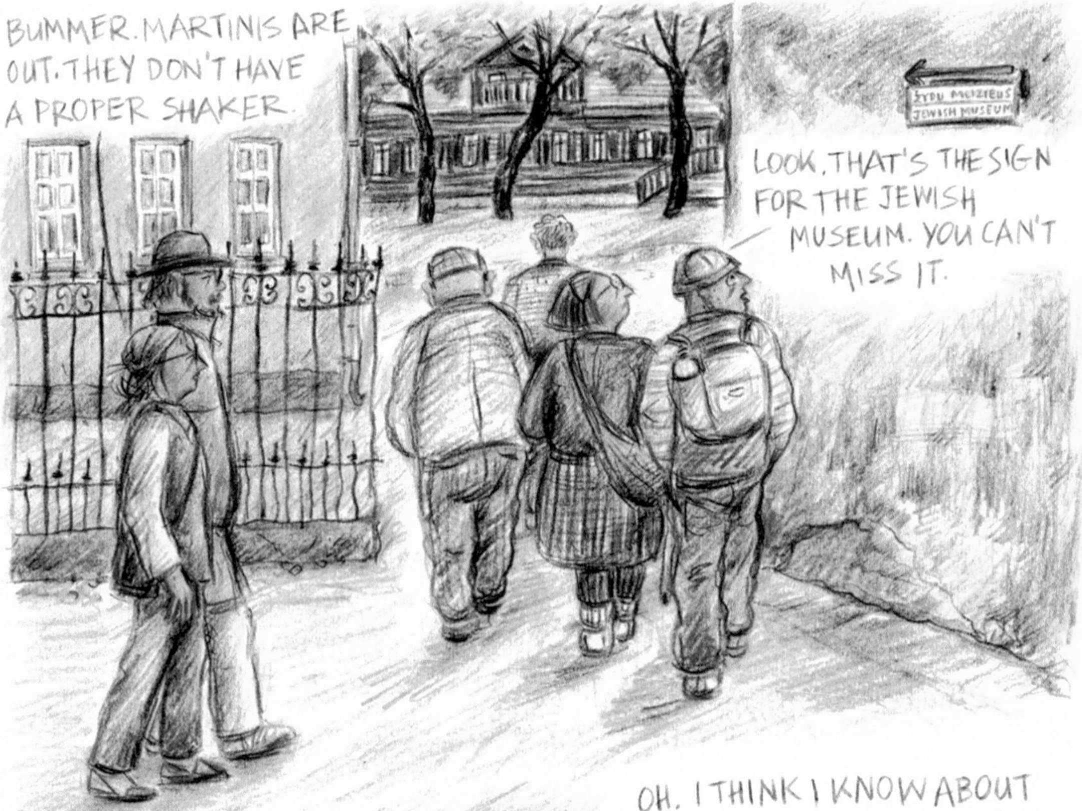
BUMMER. MARTINIS ARE OUT. THEY DON'T HAVE A PROPER SHAKER.
JEWISH MUSEUM
LOOK. THAT'S THE SIGN FOR THE JEWISH MUSEUM. YOU CAN'T MISS IT.

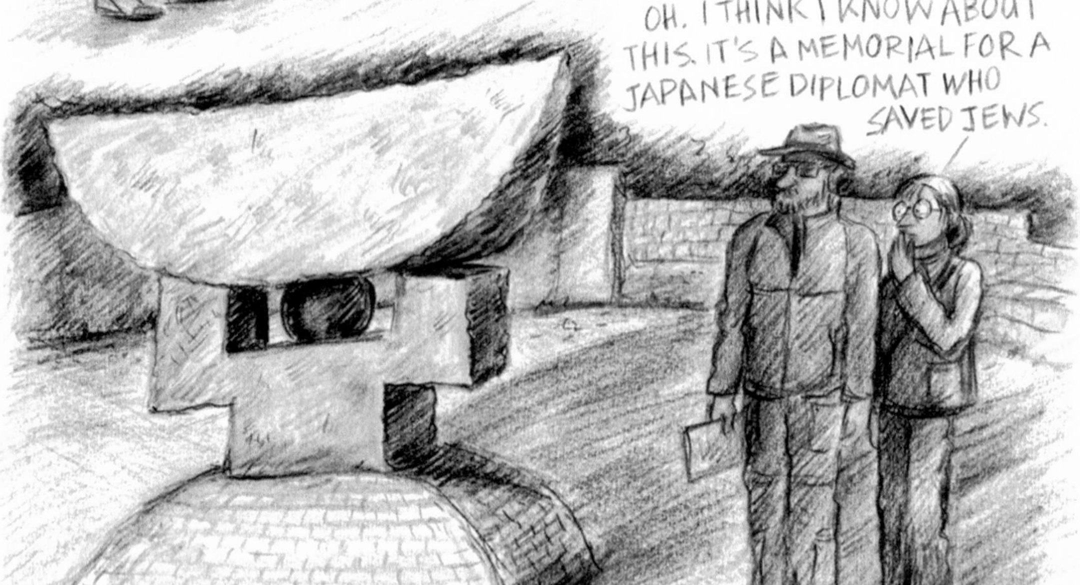
OH. I THINK I KNOW ABOUT THIS. IT'S A MEMORIAL FOR A JAPANESE DIPLOMAT WHO SAVED JEWS.

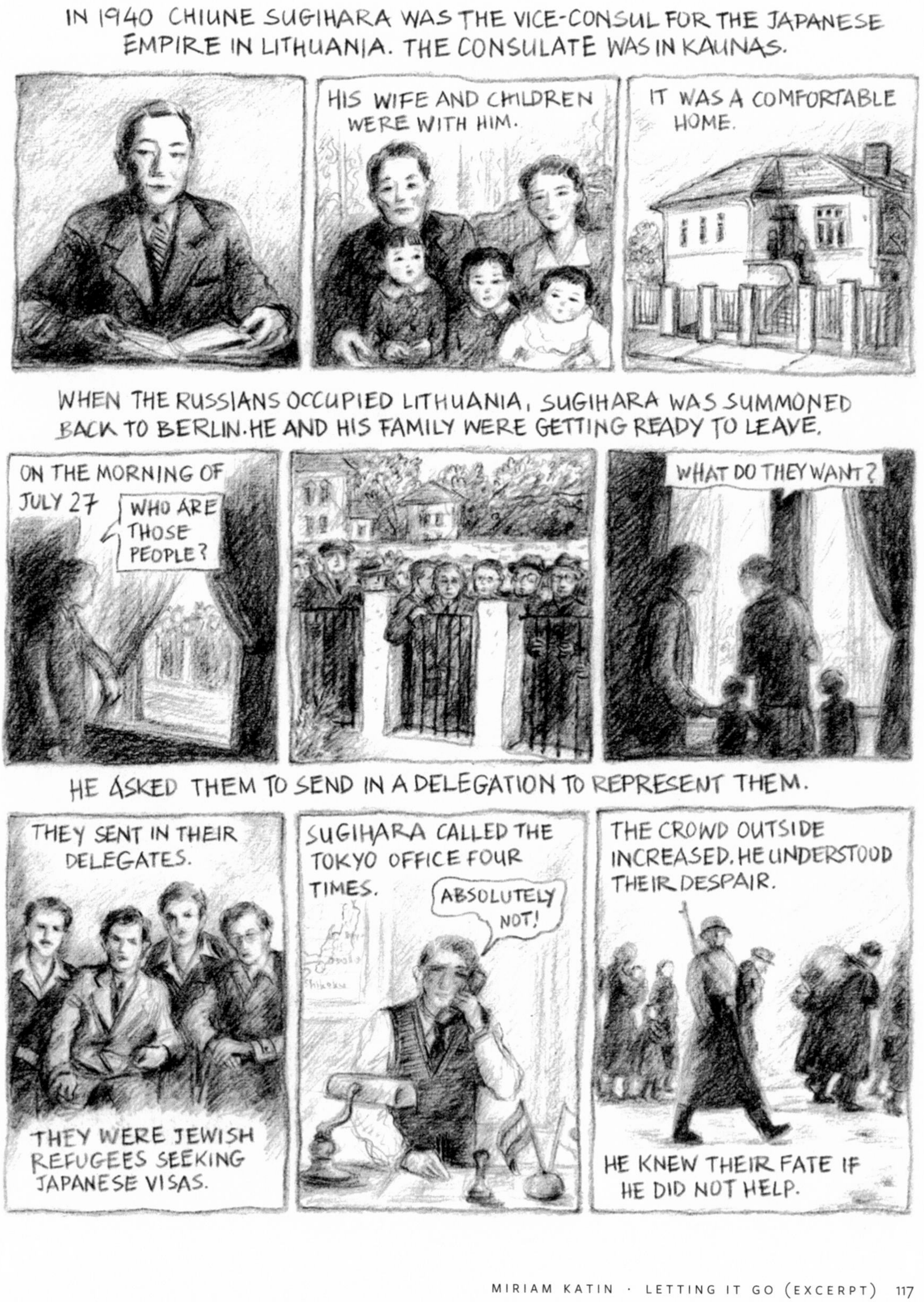

IN 1940 CHIUNE SUGIHARA WAS THE VICE-CONSUL FOR THE JAPANESE EMPIRE IN LITHUANIA. THE CONSULATE WAS IN KAUNAS.
HIS WIFE AND CHILDREN WERE WITH HIM.
IT WAS A COMFORTABLE HOME.
WHEN THE RUSSIANS OCCUPIED LITHUANIA, SUGIHARA WAS SUMMONED BACK TO BERLIN. HE AND HIS FAMILY WERE GETTING READY TO LEAVE.
ON THE MORNING OF JULY 27
WHO ARE THOSE PEOPLE?
WHAT DO THEY WANT?
HE ASKED THEM TO SEND IN A DELEGATION TO REPRESENT THEM.
THEY SENT IN THEIR DELEGATES.
THEY WERE JEWISH REFUGEES SEEKING JAPANESE VISAS.
SUGIHARA CALLED THE TOKYO OFFICE FOUR TIMES.
ABSOLUTELY NOT!
THE CROWD OUTSIDE INCREASED. HE UNDERSTOOD THEIR DESPAIR.
HE KNEW THEIR FATE IF HE DID NOT HELP.

SUGIHARA DECIDED TO DEFY HIS GOVERNMENT, TO RISK HIS CAREER AND HIS FUTURE. HIS WIFE, YUKIKO, AGREED. SHE WOULD HELP HIM.

29 DAYS THEY LABORED.

ISSUING UP TO 300 VISAS A DAY.

AT NIGHT YUKIKO MASSAGED HIS HAND.

AT LAST THEY HAD TO LEAVE THE CONSULATE.

ON THE WAY TO THE TRAIN STATION HE WAS STILL ISSUING VISAS.

I AM SORRY THAT I MUST LEAVE!

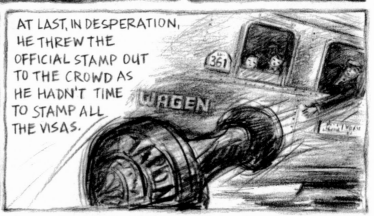
AT LAST, IN DESPERATION, HE THREW THE OFFICIAL STAMP OUT TO THE CROWD AS HE HADN'T TIME TO STAMP ALL THE VISAS.

THE MORE THAN 2000 VISAS SAVED 6000 JEWS. SUGIHARA AND HIS FAMILY WERE ARRESTED BY THE SOVIETS AND SPENT EIGHTEEN MONTHS IN A POW CAMP. AFTER HIS RETURN TO JAPAN HE WAS FIRED FROM THE FOREIGN MINISTRY.

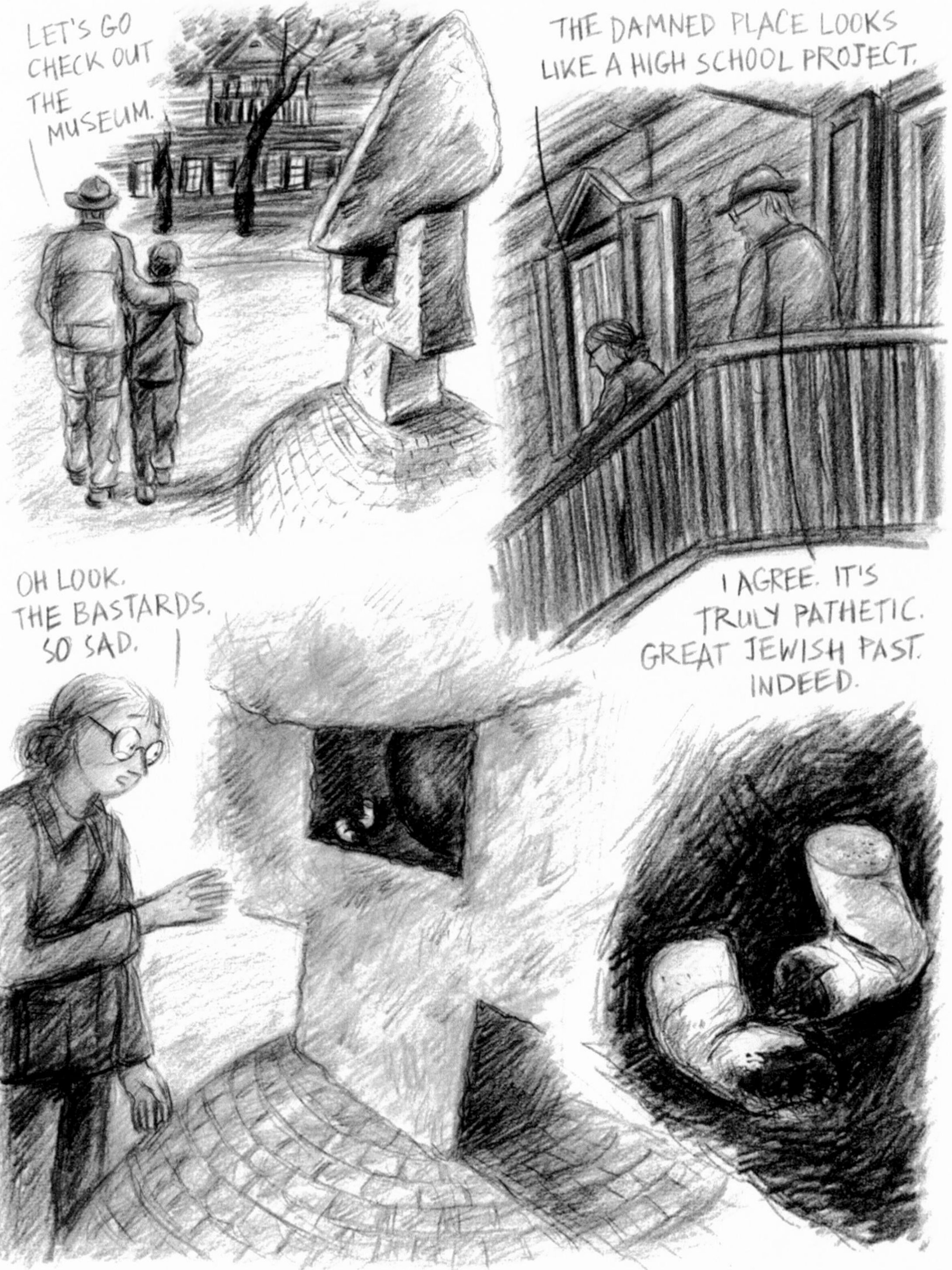
LET'S GO CHECK OUT THE MUSEUM.
THE DAMNED PLACE LOOKS LIKE A HIGH SCHOOL PROJECT.
I AGREE. IT'S TRULY PATHETIC. GREAT JEWISH PAST. INDEED.
OH LOOK. THE BASTARDS. SO SAD.

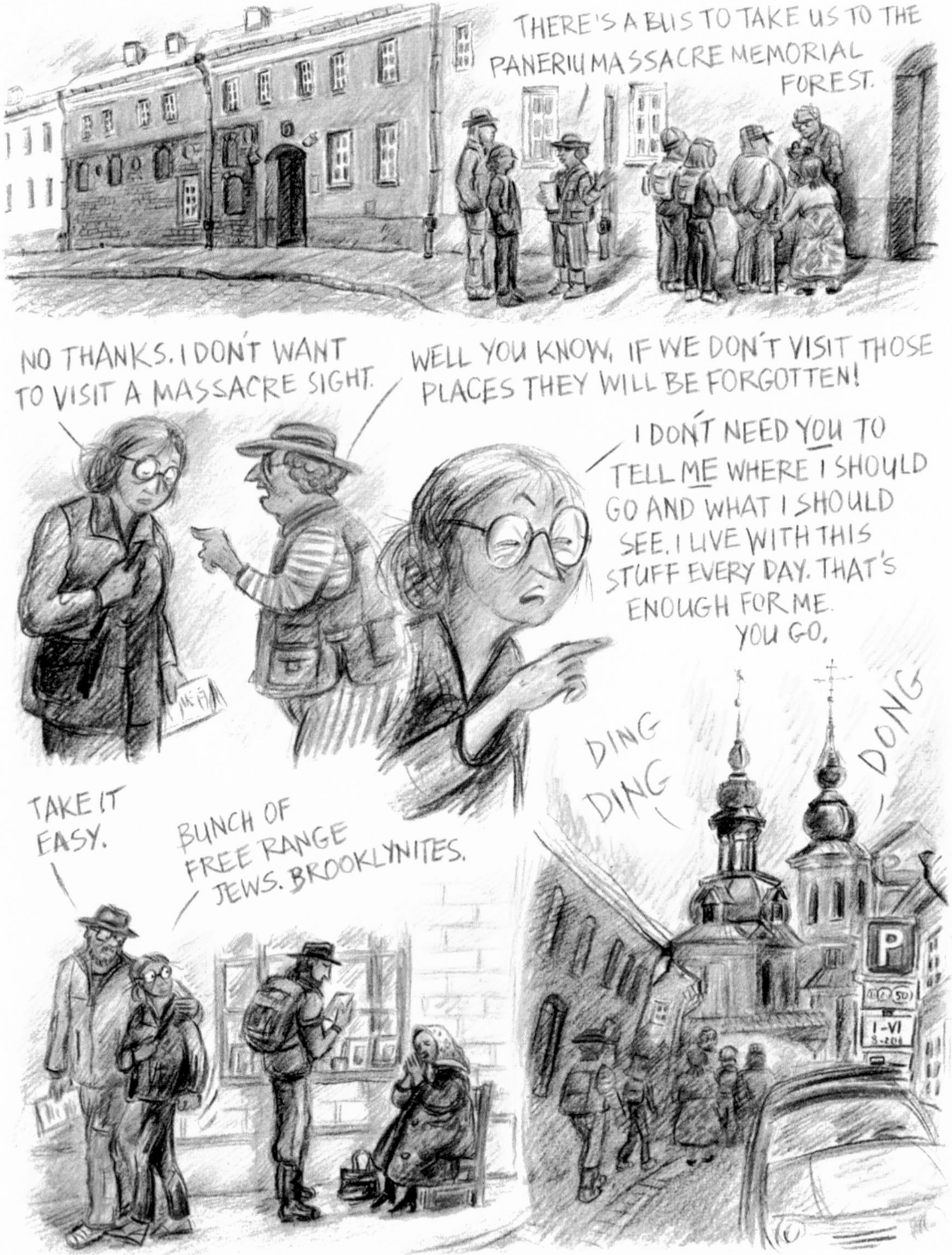
THERE'S A BUS TO TAKE US TO THE PANERIU MASSACRE MEMORIAL FOREST.
NO THANKS. I DON'T WANT TO VISIT A MASSACRE SIGHT.
WELL YOU KNOW, IF WE DON'T VISIT THOSE PLACES THEY WILL BE FORGOTTEN!
I DON'T NEED YOU TO TELL ME WHERE I SHOULD GO AND WHAT I SHOULD SEE. I LIVE WITH THIS STUFF EVERY DAY. THAT'S ENOUGH FOR ME. YOU GO.
TAKE IT EASY.
BUNCH OF FREE RANGE JEWS. BROOKLYNITES.
DING
DING
DONG
P

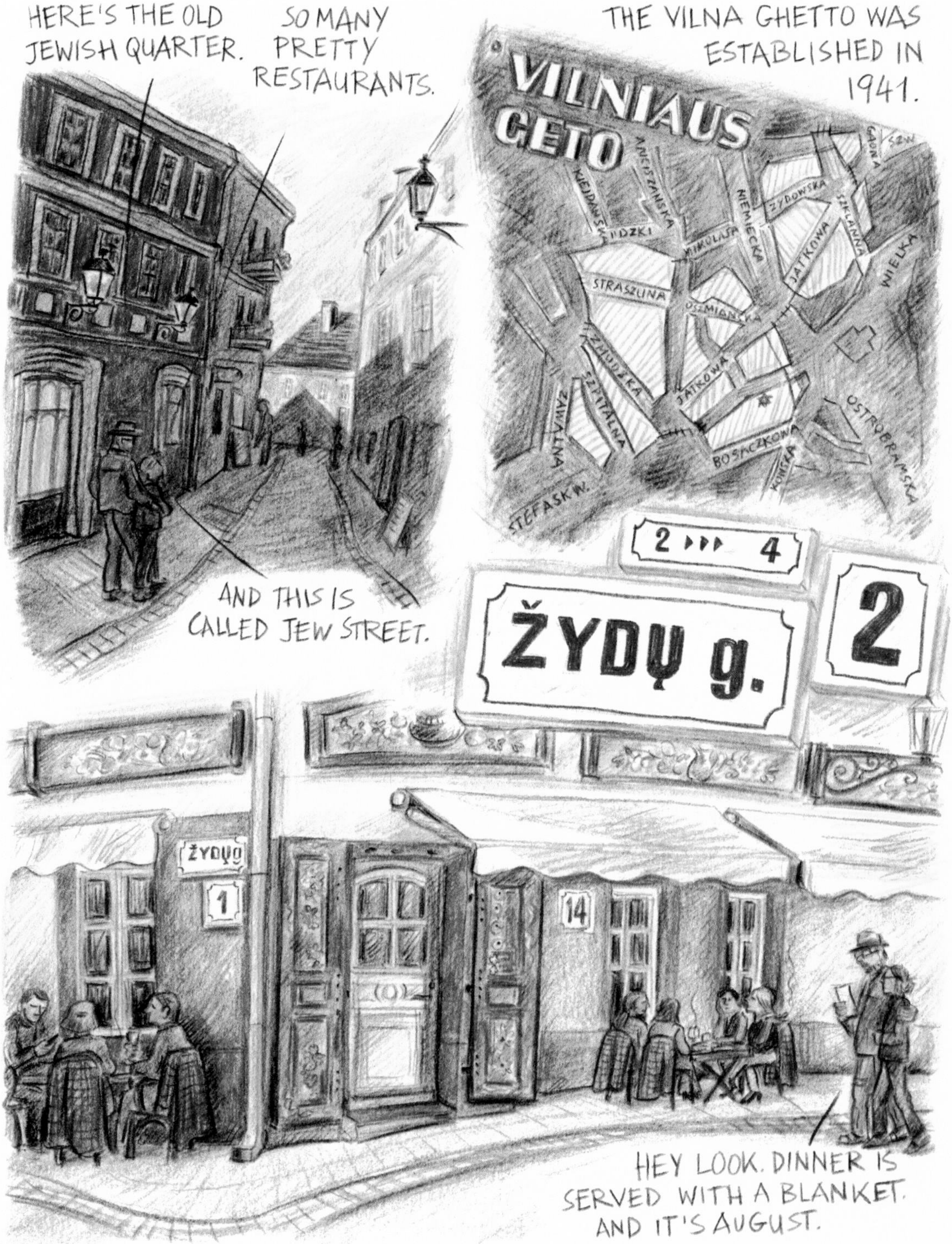
HERE'S THE OLD JEWISH QUARTER.
SO MANY PRETTY RESTAURANTS.
AND THIS IS CALLED JEW STREET.
THE VILNA GHETTO WAS ESTABLISHED IN 1941.
VILNIAUS GETO
ŽYDŲ g.
2
2 4
HEY LOOK. DINNER IS SERVED WITH A BLANKET. AND IT'S AUGUST.

ŽYDŲ: JEW (LITHUANIAN)

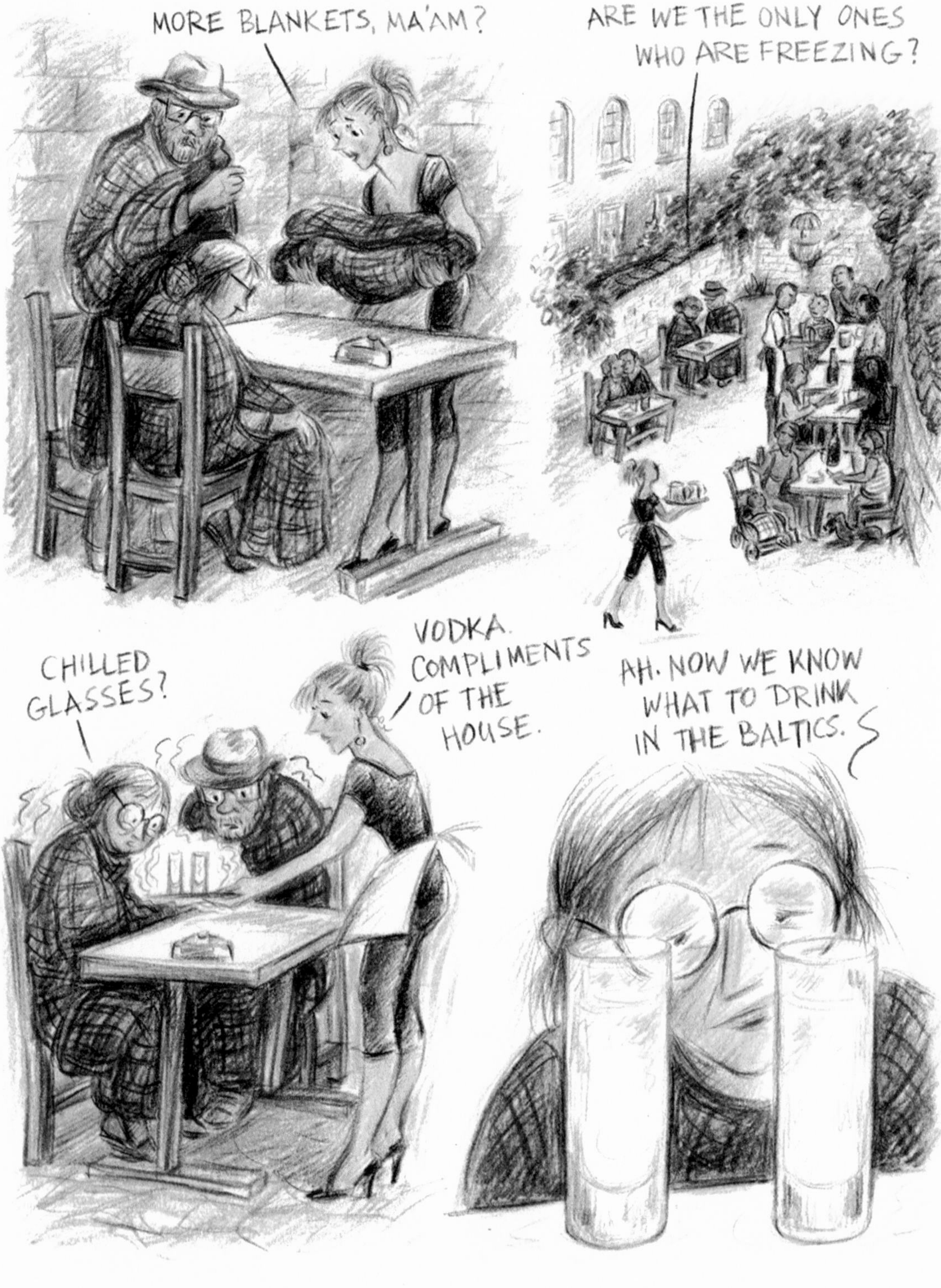
MORE BLANKETS, MA'AM?
ARE WE THE ONLY ONES WHO ARE FREEZING?
CHILLED GLASSES?
VODKA. COMPLIMENTS OF THE HOUSE.
AH. NOW WE KNOW WHAT TO DRINK IN THE BALTICS.

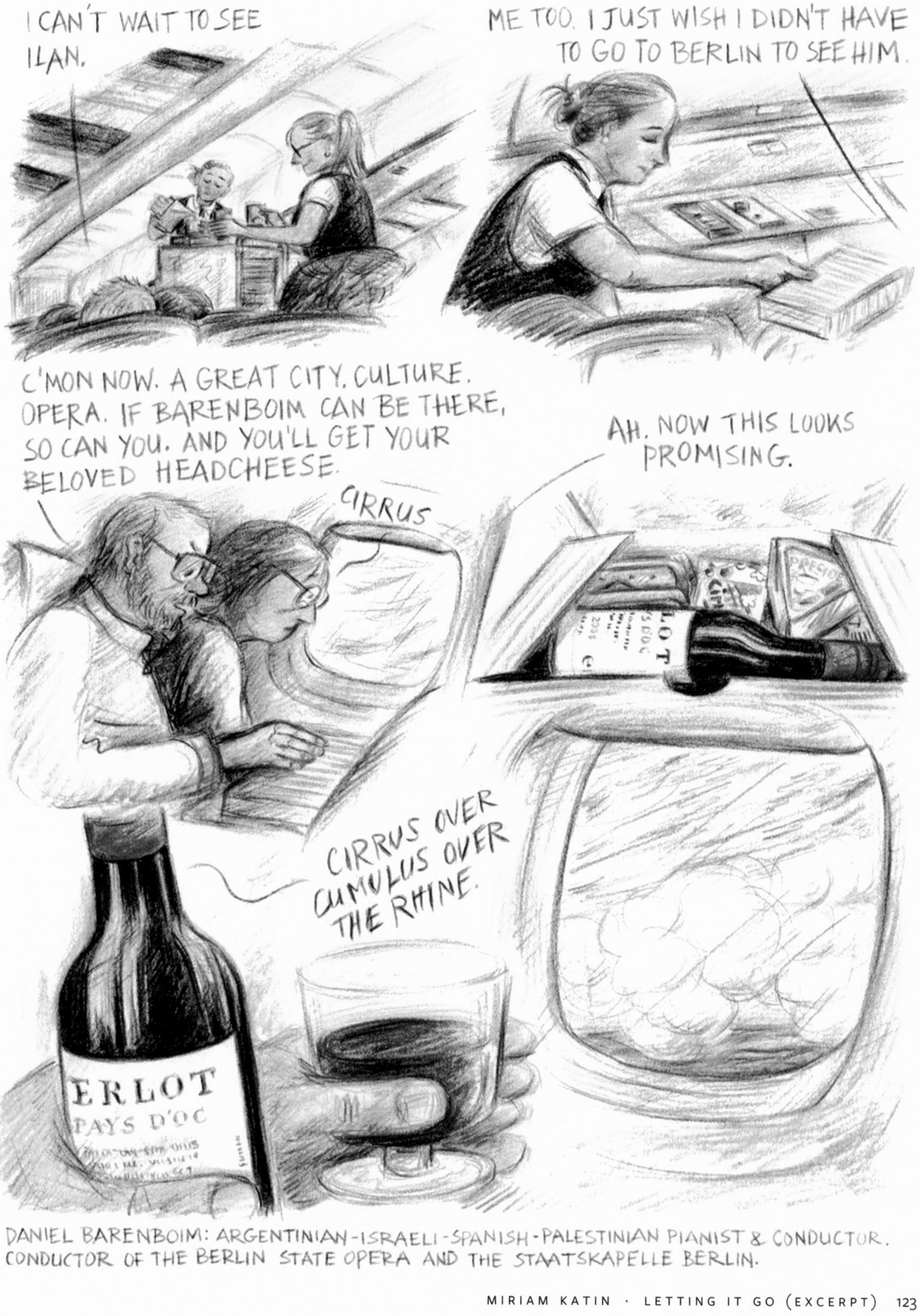

I CAN'T WAIT TO SEE ILAN.
ME TOO. I JUST WISH I DIDN'T HAVE TO GO TO BERLIN TO SEE HIM.
C'MON NOW. A GREAT CITY. CULTURE. OPERA. IF BARENBOIM CAN BE THERE, SO CAN YOU. AND YOU'LL GET YOUR BELOVED HEADCHEESE.
CIRRUS
AH. NOW THIS LOOKS PROMISING.
ERLOT
PAYS D'OC
CIRRUS OVER CUMULUS OVER THE RHINE.

DANIEL BARENBOIM: ARGENTINIAN-ISRAELI-SPANISH-PALESTINIAN PIANIST & CONDUCTOR. CONDUCTOR OF THE BERLIN STATE OPERA AND THE STAATSKAPELLE BERLIN.

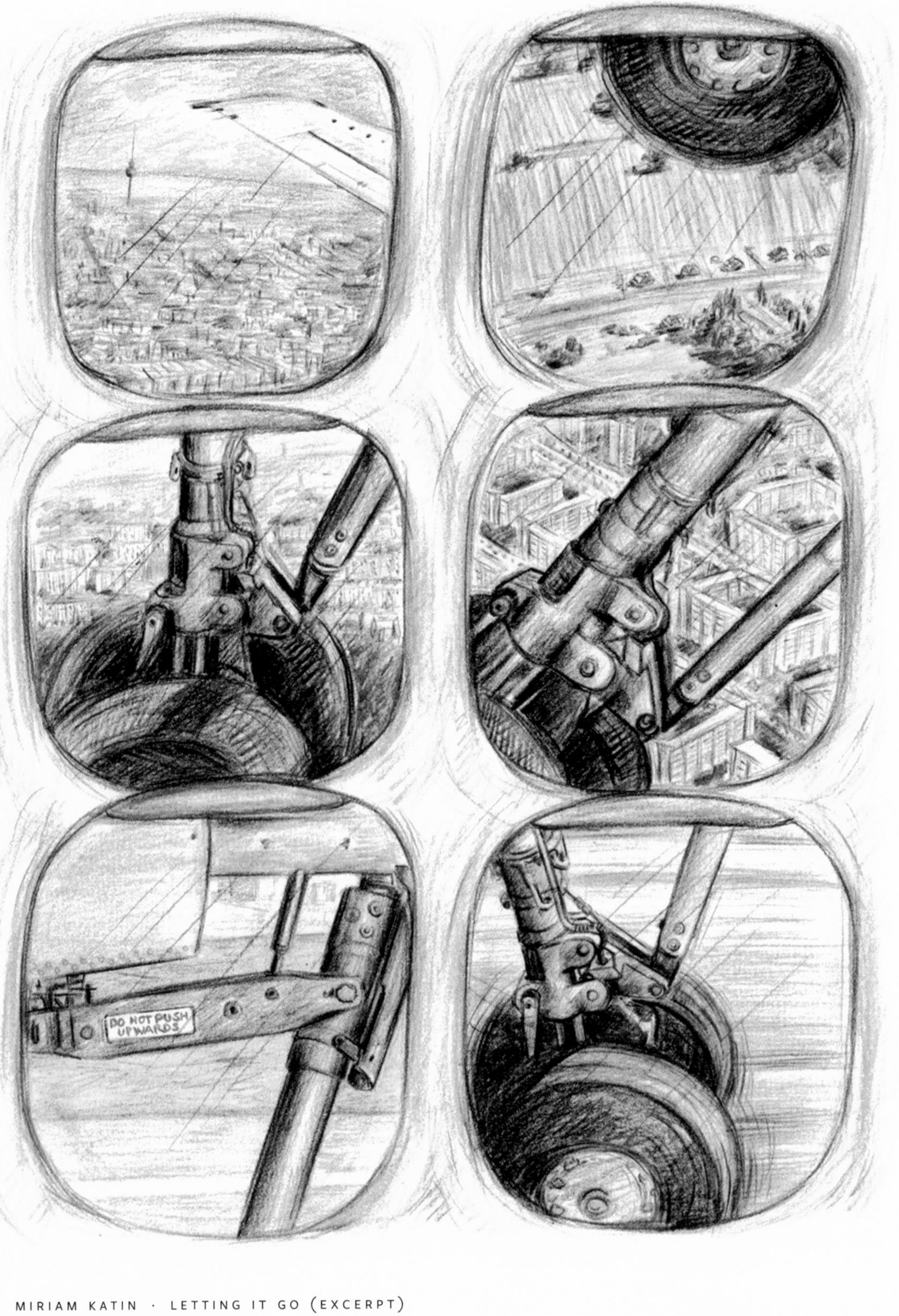
DO NOT PUSH UPWARDS

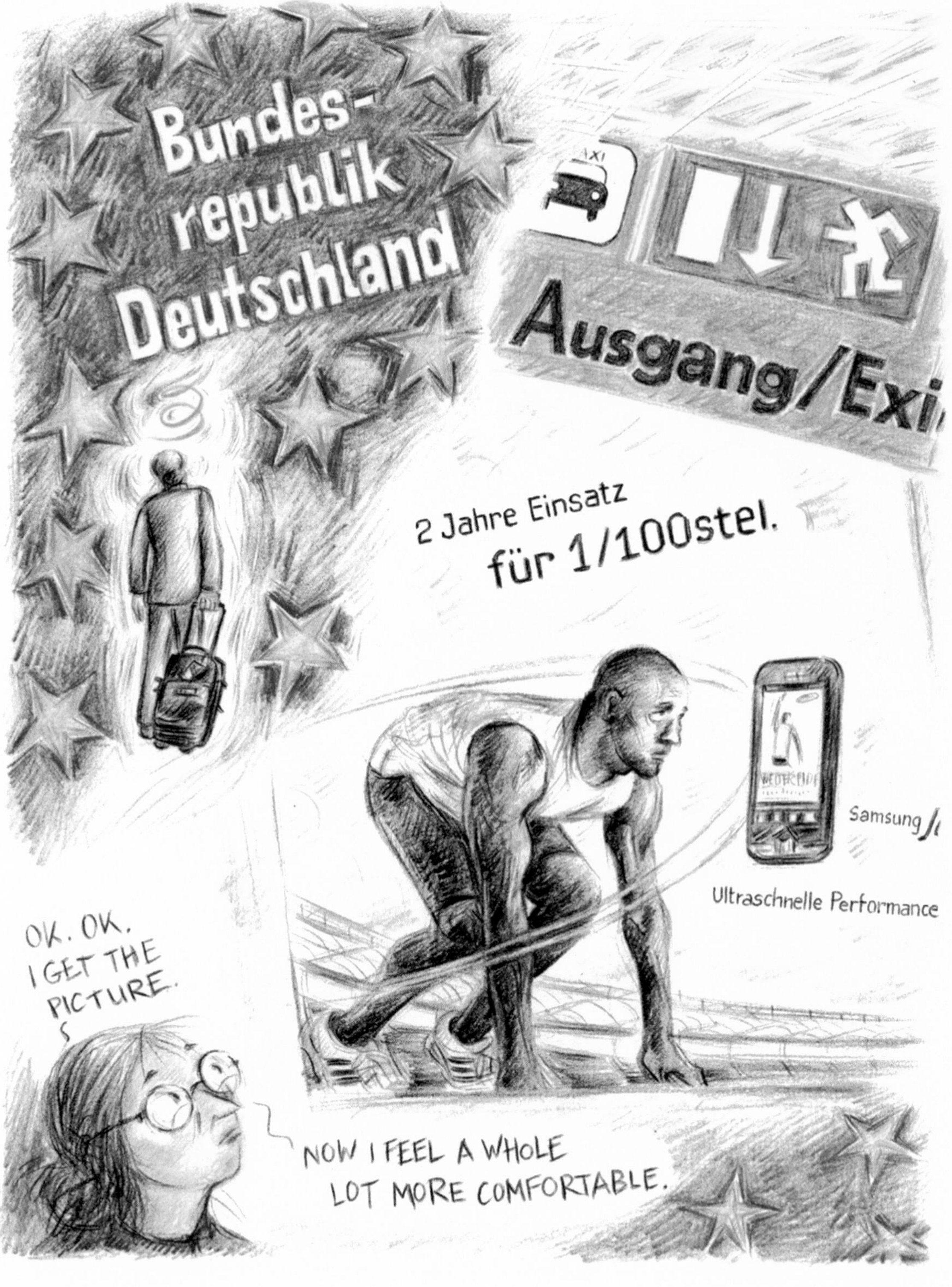
Bundes-
republik
Deutschland
TAXI
Ausgang/Exi
2 Jahre Einsatz
für 1/100stel.
Samsung
Ultraschnelle Performance
OK. OK.
I GET THE
PICTURE.
NOW I FEEL A WHOLE
LOT MORE COMFORTABLE.

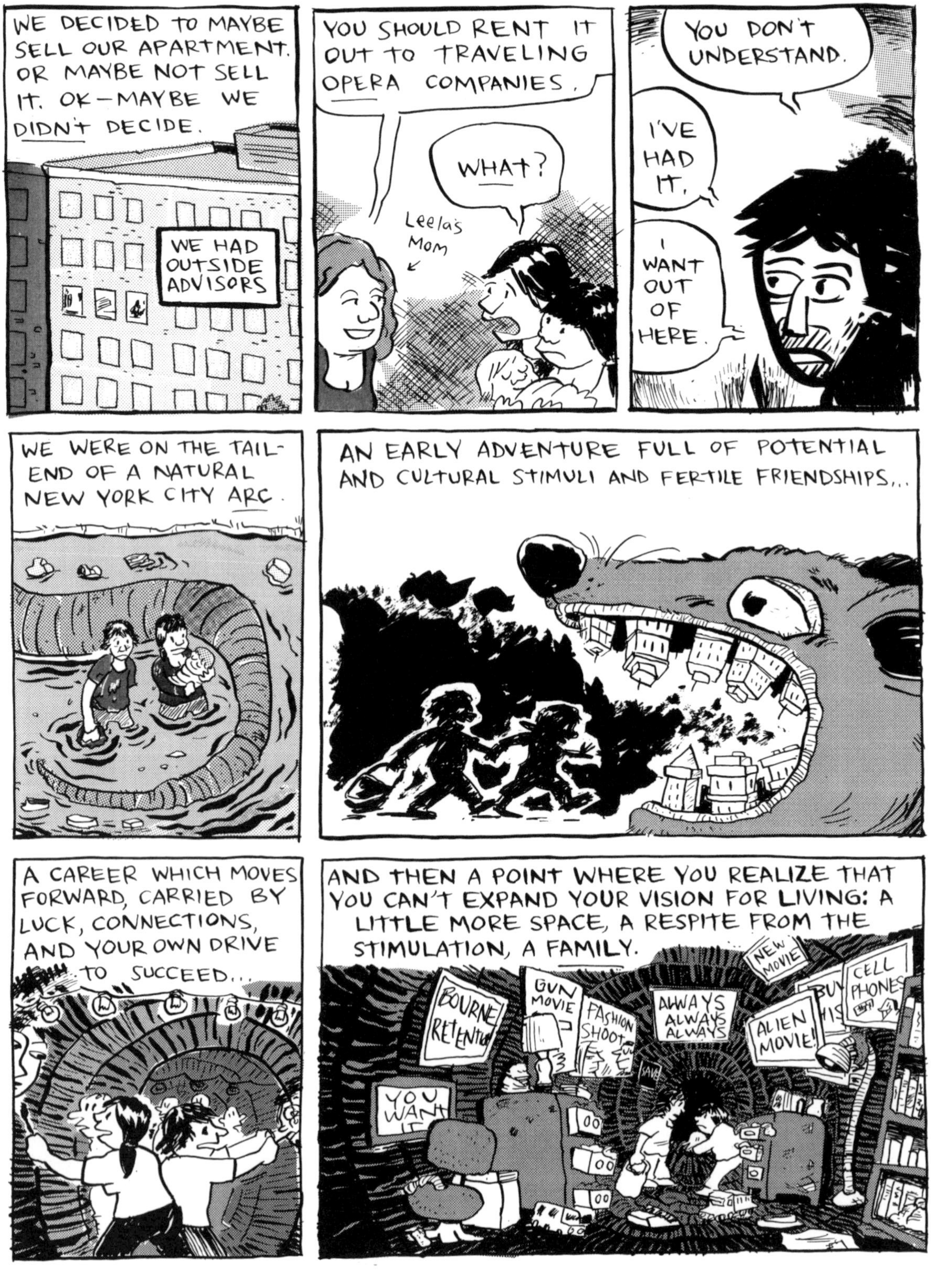
WE DECIDED TO MAYBE SELL OUR APARTMENT. OR MAYBE NOT SELL IT. OK—MAYBE WE DIDN'T DECIDE.
WE HAD OUTSIDE ADVISORS
YOU SHOULD RENT IT OUT TO TRAVELING OPERA COMPANIES.
WHAT?
Leela's Mom
YOU DON'T UNDERSTAND.
I'VE HAD IT.
I WANT OUT OF HERE.
WE WERE ON THE TAIL-END OF A NATURAL NEW YORK CITY ARC.
AN EARLY ADVENTURE FULL OF POTENTIAL AND CULTURAL STIMULI AND FERTILE FRIENDSHIPS...
A CAREER WHICH MOVES FORWARD, CARRIED BY LUCK, CONNECTIONS, AND YOUR OWN DRIVE TO SUCCEED...
AND THEN A POINT WHERE YOU REALIZE THAT YOU CAN'T EXPAND YOUR VISION FOR LIVING: A LITTLE MORE SPACE, A RESPITE FROM THE STIMULATION, A FAMILY.
NEW MOVIE
GUN MOVIE
FASHION SHOOT
ALWAYS ALWAYS ALWAYS
ALIEN MOVIE!
CELL PHONES
YOU WANT IT
SAVE

THE NEW YORK ARC REQUIRES YOU TO EITHER MAKE EXPONENTIALLY MORE MONEY — OR GET OUT.

WHERE IS UP TO YOU: NEW JERSEY, LONG ISLAND OR WESTCHESTER, ALL OF WHICH REQUIRE YOU TO RUTHLESSLY KEEP YOUR ATTENTION, MONEY, AND NERVES FOCUSED ON NEW YORK —

← SHITTY APARTMENTS, ROOMATES WHO VOMIT ON YOU AS YOU SLEEP

NICE BUT STILL COCKROACHES

MANHATTAN = 3K PER INCH

JERSEY = DULL AND TRAPPED

LAST CHANCE POWER DRIVE →

THE COMMUTE

THE GAP

DORITOS iPOD BEER

SWAN

WHOSE BLOODY, SWOLLEN, BILLBOARD EYES REMAIN FIXED ON YOU IN RETURN

COME BACK TO FASHION

STILL TIME TO SAVE

THE UNKNOWN

OR YOU REALLY LEAVE — YOU PACK UP YOUR DAUGHTER AND SET OFF...

SO WE DECIDED TO SELL OUR APARTMENT, TO PAY OFF OUR DEBTS AND MAYBE KEEP ENOUGH TO LIVE ON IN GAINESVILLE WHILE WE GOT OUR FOOTING THERE.

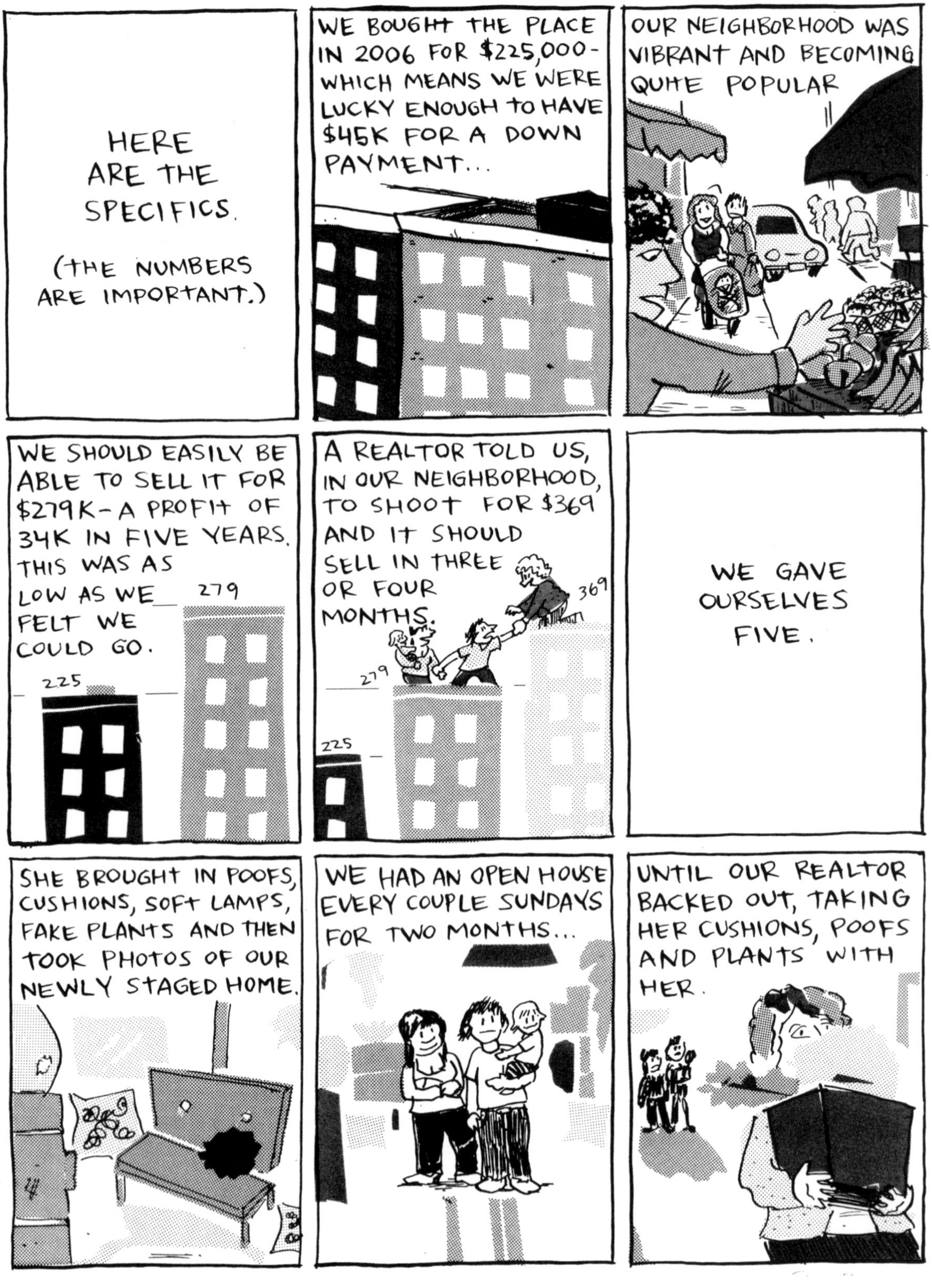
HERE ARE THE SPECIFICS.
(THE NUMBERS ARE IMPORTANT.)
WE BOUGHT THE PLACE IN 2006 FOR $225,000- WHICH MEANS WE WERE LUCKY ENOUGH TO HAVE $45K FOR A DOWN PAYMENT...
OUR NEIGHBORHOOD WAS VIBRANT AND BECOMING QUITE POPULAR
WE SHOULD EASILY BE ABLE TO SELL IT FOR $279K - A PROFIT OF 34K IN FIVE YEARS. THIS WAS AS LOW AS WE FELT WE COULD GO.
279
225
A REALTOR TOLD US, IN OUR NEIGHBORHOOD, TO SHOOT FOR $369 AND IT SHOULD SELL IN THREE OR FOUR MONTHS.
369
279
225
WE GAVE OURSELVES FIVE.
SHE BROUGHT IN POOFS, CUSHIONS, SOFT LAMPS, FAKE PLANTS AND THEN TOOK PHOTOS OF OUR NEWLY STAGED HOME.
WE HAD AN OPEN HOUSE EVERY COUPLE SUNDAYS FOR TWO MONTHS...
UNTIL OUR REALTOR BACKED OUT, TAKING HER CUSHIONS, POOFS AND PLANTS WITH HER.

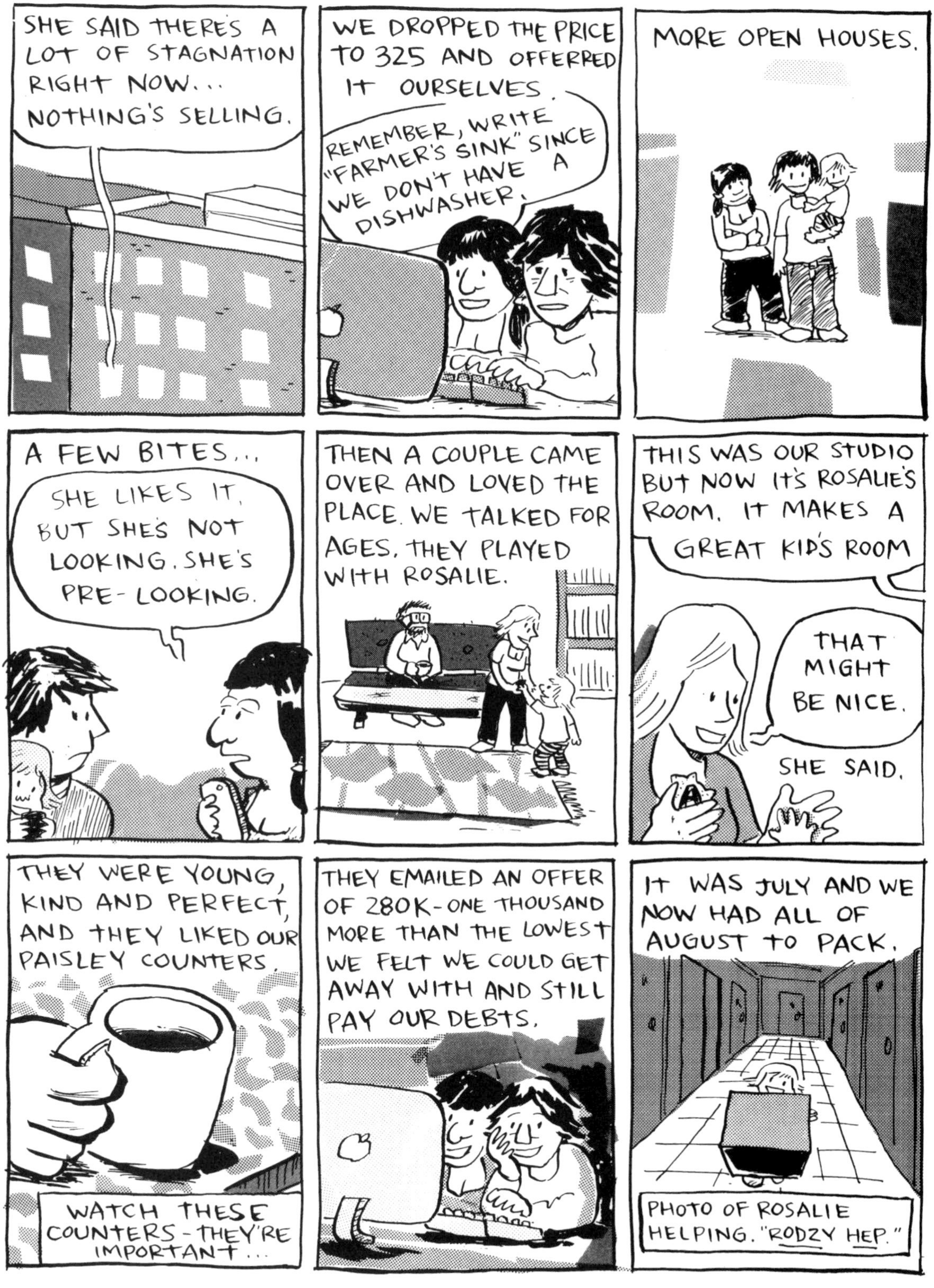
SHE SAID THERE'S A LOT OF STAGNATION RIGHT NOW... NOTHING'S SELLING.
WE DROPPED THE PRICE TO 325 AND OFFERRED IT OURSELVES.
REMEMBER, WRITE "FARMER'S SINK" SINCE WE DON'T HAVE A DISHWASHER.
MORE OPEN HOUSES.
A FEW BITES...
SHE LIKES IT, BUT SHE'S NOT LOOKING. SHE'S PRE-LOOKING.
THEN A COUPLE CAME OVER AND LOVED THE PLACE. WE TALKED FOR AGES. THEY PLAYED WITH ROSALIE.
THIS WAS OUR STUDIO BUT NOW IT'S ROSALIE'S ROOM. IT MAKES A
GREAT KID'S ROOM
THAT MIGHT BE NICE.
SHE SAID.
THEY WERE YOUNG, KIND AND PERFECT, AND THEY LIKED OUR PAISLEY COUNTERS.
WATCH THESE COUNTERS - THEY'RE IMPORTANT...
THEY EMAILED AN OFFER OF 280K - ONE THOUSAND MORE THAN THE LOWEST WE FELT WE COULD GET AWAY WITH AND STILL PAY OUR DEBTS.
IT WAS JULY AND WE NOW HAD ALL OF AUGUST TO PACK.
PHOTO OF ROSALIE HELPING. "RODZY HEP."

PAPERWORK WAS SUBMITTED TO THE BANKS, OUR CO-OP BOARD AND THE MANY VARIOUS LAWYERS

AGREEMENT

CONTRACT

ONCE THE CO-OP BOARD APPROVED THE SALE, IT WOULD ALL BE A MATTER OF SIGNING PAPERS AND GETTING OUT OF THERE.

WE PACKED.

MOVED

AND UNPACKED WHAT WE COULD IN FLORIDA.

THERE WILL BE LIGHT!

RODZY BOOK

RODZY HEP.

LEELA HAD A HUGE BOOK DEADLINE WHICH SHE FRANTICLY HAD TO WORK ON.

AND SLOWLY OTHER THINGS BECAME DIFFICULT...

WHY HASN'T THE BOARD APPROVED THE SALE?

WE CAN'T TELL YOU.

WHY CAN'T YOU TELL US?

THERE ARE COMPLICATIONS WITH THE SALE...

I KNOW THAT. I WANT TO KNOW WHAT THEY ARE.

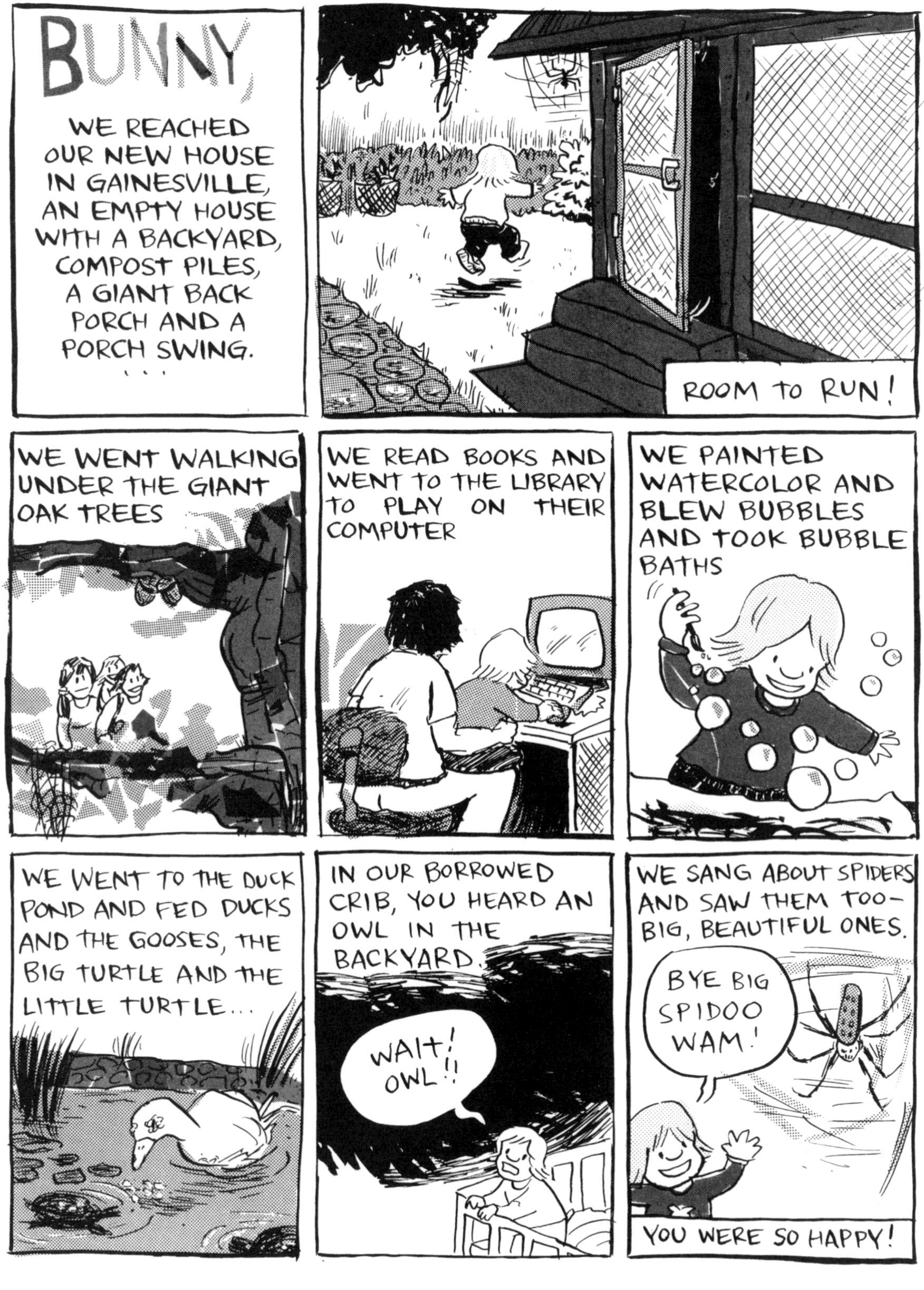
BUNNY,
WE REACHED OUR NEW HOUSE IN GAINESVILLE, AN EMPTY HOUSE WITH A BACKYARD, COMPOST PILES, A GIANT BACK PORCH AND A PORCH SWING. . . .
ROOM TO RUN!
WE WENT WALKING UNDER THE GIANT OAK TREES
WE READ BOOKS AND WENT TO THE LIBRARY TO PLAY ON THEIR COMPUTER
WE PAINTED WATERCOLOR AND BLEW BUBBLES AND TOOK BUBBLE BATHS
WE WENT TO THE DUCK POND AND FED DUCKS AND THE GOOSES, THE BIG TURTLE AND THE LITTLE TURTLE...
IN OUR BORROWED CRIB, YOU HEARD AN OWL IN THE BACKYARD.
WAIT! OWL!!
WE SANG ABOUT SPIDERS AND SAW THEM TOO– BIG, BEAUTIFUL ONES.
BYE BIG SPIDOO WAM!
YOU WERE SO HAPPY!

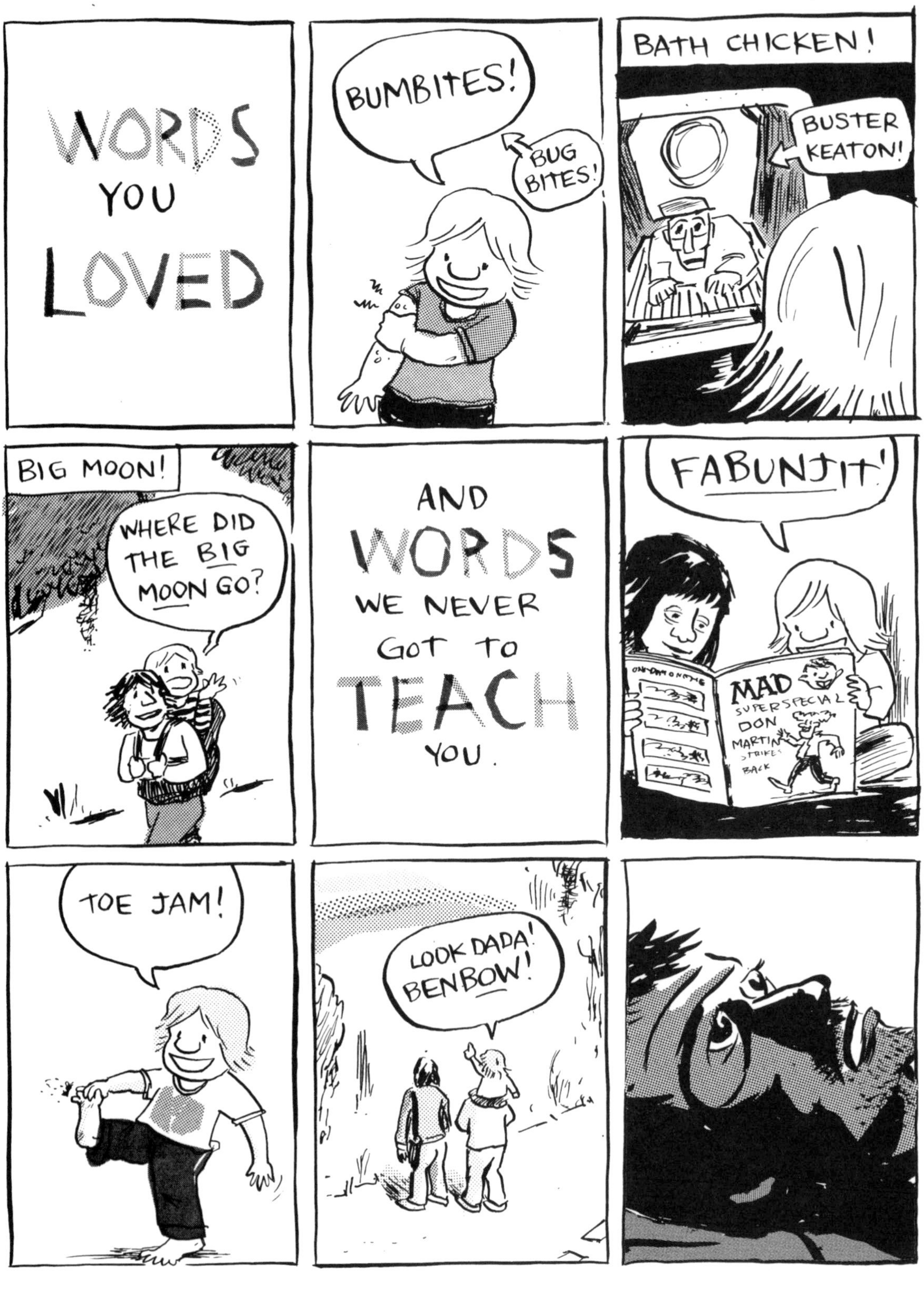
WORDS
YOU
LOVED
BUMBITES!
BUG BITES!
BATH CHICKEN!
BUSTER KEATON!
BIG MOON!
WHERE DID THE BIG MOON GO?
AND
WORDS
WE NEVER
GOT TO
TEACH
YOU.
FABUNJIT!
MAD
SUPERSPECIAL
DON
MARTIN
STRIKES
BACK
TOE JAM!
LOOK DADA! BENBOW!

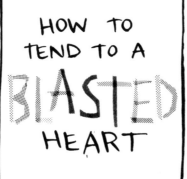

NOVEMBER. WE WALK THE CIRCUIT IN TRAVIS' NEIGHBORHOOD. WE GET TO KNOW THE CATS AND DOGS.

HOW TO TEND TO A **BLASTED** HEART

WALK.

SURROUND YOURSELF WITH NATURE.

HOLD THE WATER BOTTLE TO YOUR BELLY AND ROLL. ROLL

CHEST AND FACE. ROLL.

TRUST NATURE.

FIND EACH OTHER.

WALK.

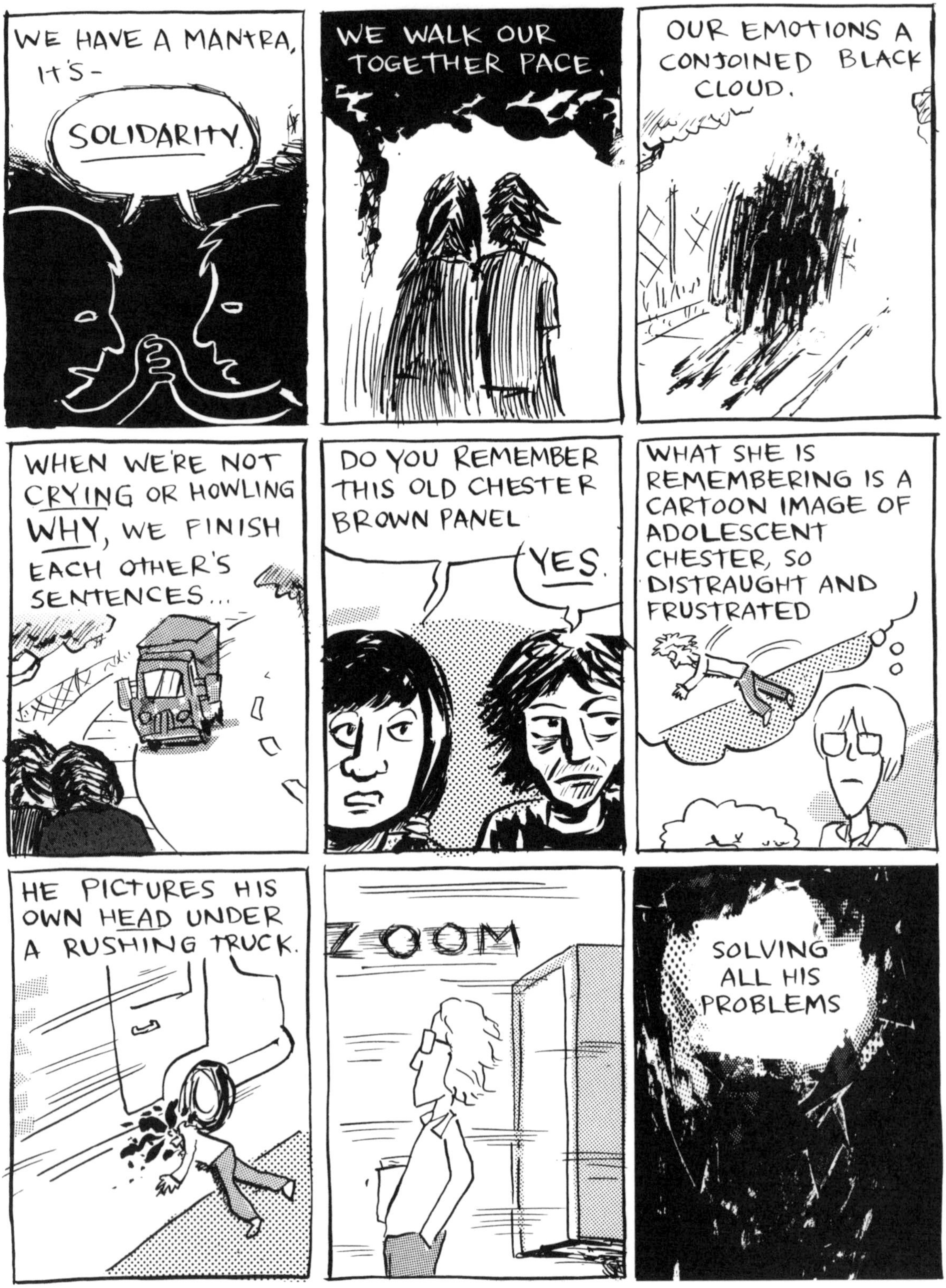
WE HAVE A MANTRA, IT'S-
SOLIDARITY.
WE WALK OUR TOGETHER PACE.
OUR EMOTIONS A CONJOINED BLACK CLOUD.
WHEN WE'RE NOT CRYING OR HOWLING WHY, WE FINISH EACH OTHER'S SENTENCES...
DO YOU REMEMBER THIS OLD CHESTER BROWN PANEL
YES.
WHAT SHE IS REMEMBERING IS A CARTOON IMAGE OF ADOLESCENT CHESTER, SO DISTRAUGHT AND FRUSTRATED
HE PICTURES HIS OWN HEAD UNDER A RUSHING TRUCK.
ZOOM
SOLVING ALL HIS PROBLEMS

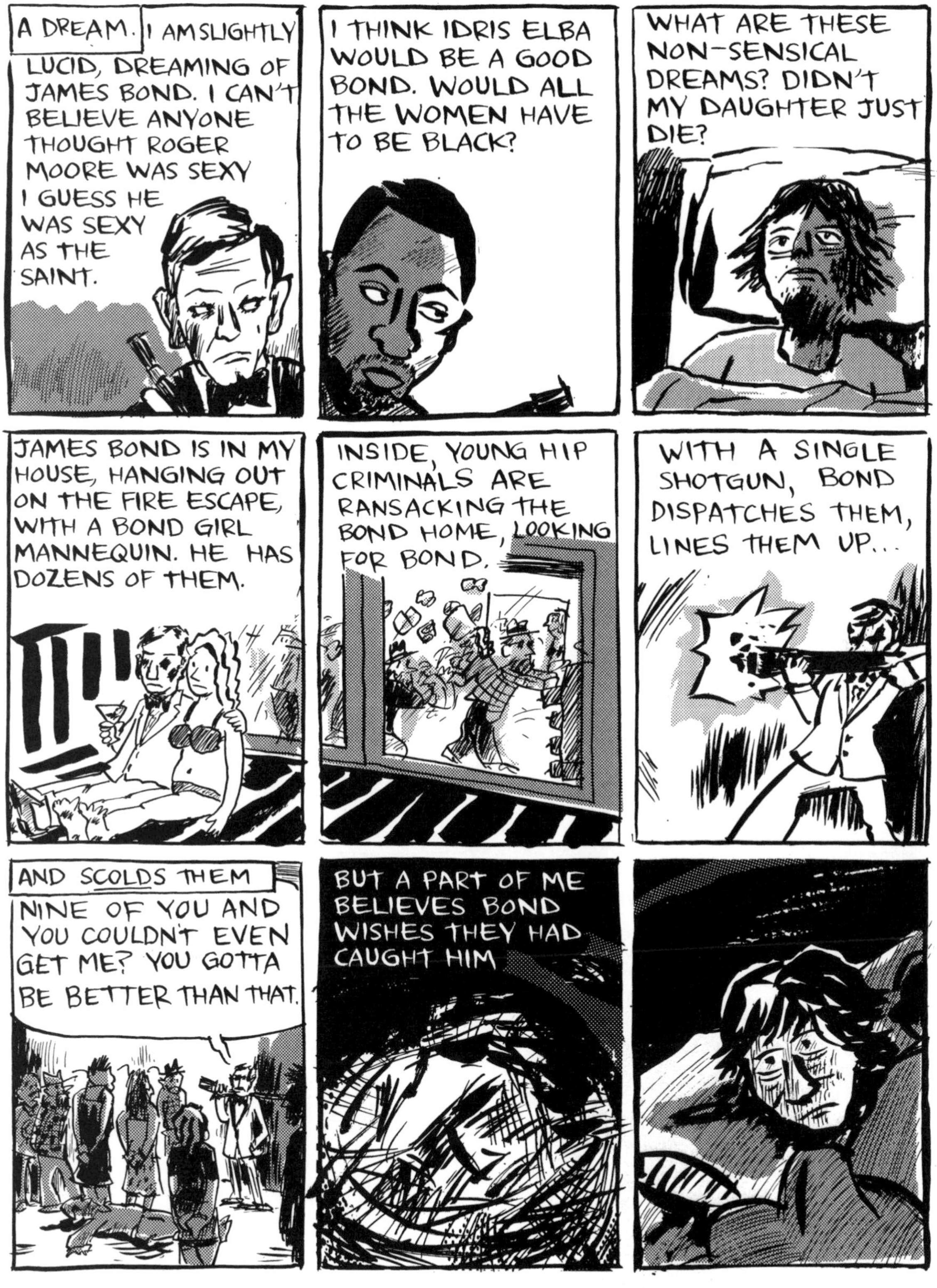
A DREAM.
I AM SLIGHTLY LUCID, DREAMING OF JAMES BOND. I CAN'T BELIEVE ANYONE THOUGHT ROGER MOORE WAS SEXY
I GUESS HE WAS SEXY AS THE SAINT.
I THINK IDRIS ELBA WOULD BE A GOOD BOND. WOULD ALL THE WOMEN HAVE TO BE BLACK?
WHAT ARE THESE NON-SENSICAL DREAMS? DIDN'T MY DAUGHTER JUST DIE?
JAMES BOND IS IN MY HOUSE, HANGING OUT ON THE FIRE ESCAPE, WITH A BOND GIRL MANNEQUIN. HE HAS DOZENS OF THEM.
INSIDE, YOUNG HIP CRIMINALS ARE RANSACKING THE BOND HOME, LOOKING FOR BOND.
WITH A SINGLE SHOTGUN, BOND DISPATCHES THEM, LINES THEM UP...
AND SCOLDS THEM
NINE OF YOU AND YOU COULDN'T EVEN GET ME? YOU GOTTA BE BETTER THAN THAT.
BUT A PART OF ME BELIEVES BOND WISHES THEY HAD CAUGHT HIM

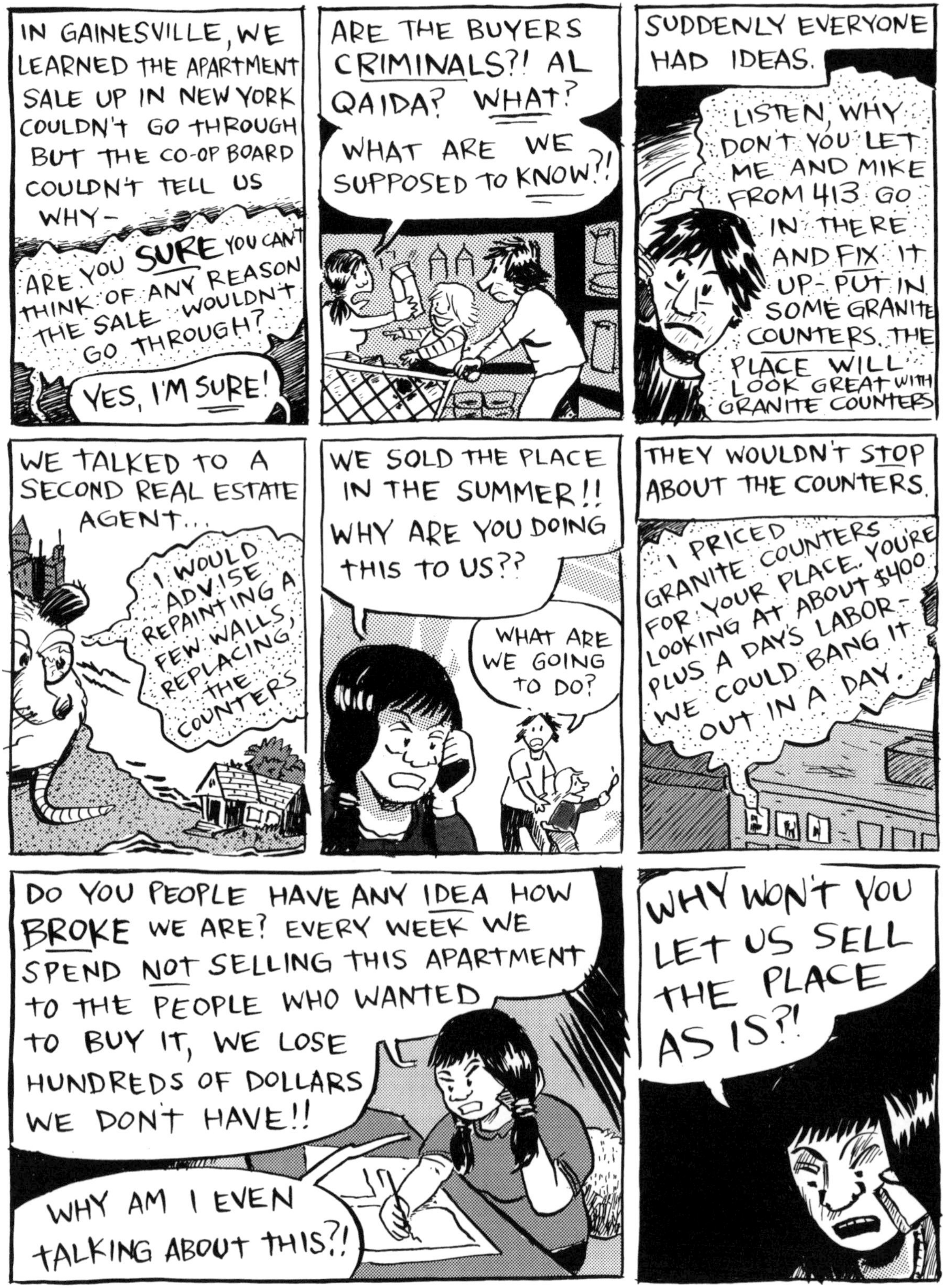
IN GAINESVILLE, WE LEARNED THE APARTMENT SALE UP IN NEW YORK COULDN'T GO THROUGH BUT THE CO-OP BOARD COULDN'T TELL US WHY-
ARE YOU SURE YOU CAN'T THINK OF ANY REASON THE SALE WOULDN'T GO THROUGH?
YES, I'M SURE!
ARE THE BUYERS CRIMINALS?! AL QAIDA? WHAT?
WHAT ARE WE SUPPOSED TO KNOW?!
SUDDENLY EVERYONE HAD IDEAS.
LISTEN, WHY DON'T YOU LET ME AND MIKE FROM 413 GO IN THERE AND FIX IT UP- PUT IN SOME GRANITE COUNTERS. THE PLACE WILL LOOK GREAT WITH GRANITE COUNTERS
WE TALKED TO A SECOND REAL ESTATE AGENT...
I WOULD ADVISE REPAINTING A FEW WALLS, REPLACING THE COUNTERS
WE SOLD THE PLACE IN THE SUMMER!! WHY ARE YOU DOING THIS TO US??
WHAT ARE WE GOING TO DO?
THEY WOULDN'T STOP ABOUT THE COUNTERS.
I PRICED GRANITE COUNTERS FOR YOUR PLACE. YOU'RE LOOKING AT ABOUT $400 PLUS A DAY'S LABOR- WE COULD BANG IT OUT IN A DAY.
DO YOU PEOPLE HAVE ANY IDEA HOW BROKE WE ARE? EVERY WEEK WE SPEND NOT SELLING THIS APARTMENT TO THE PEOPLE WHO WANTED TO BUY IT, WE LOSE HUNDREDS OF DOLLARS WE DON'T HAVE!!
WHY AM I EVEN TALKING ABOUT THIS?!
WHY WON'T YOU LET US SELL THE PLACE AS IS?!

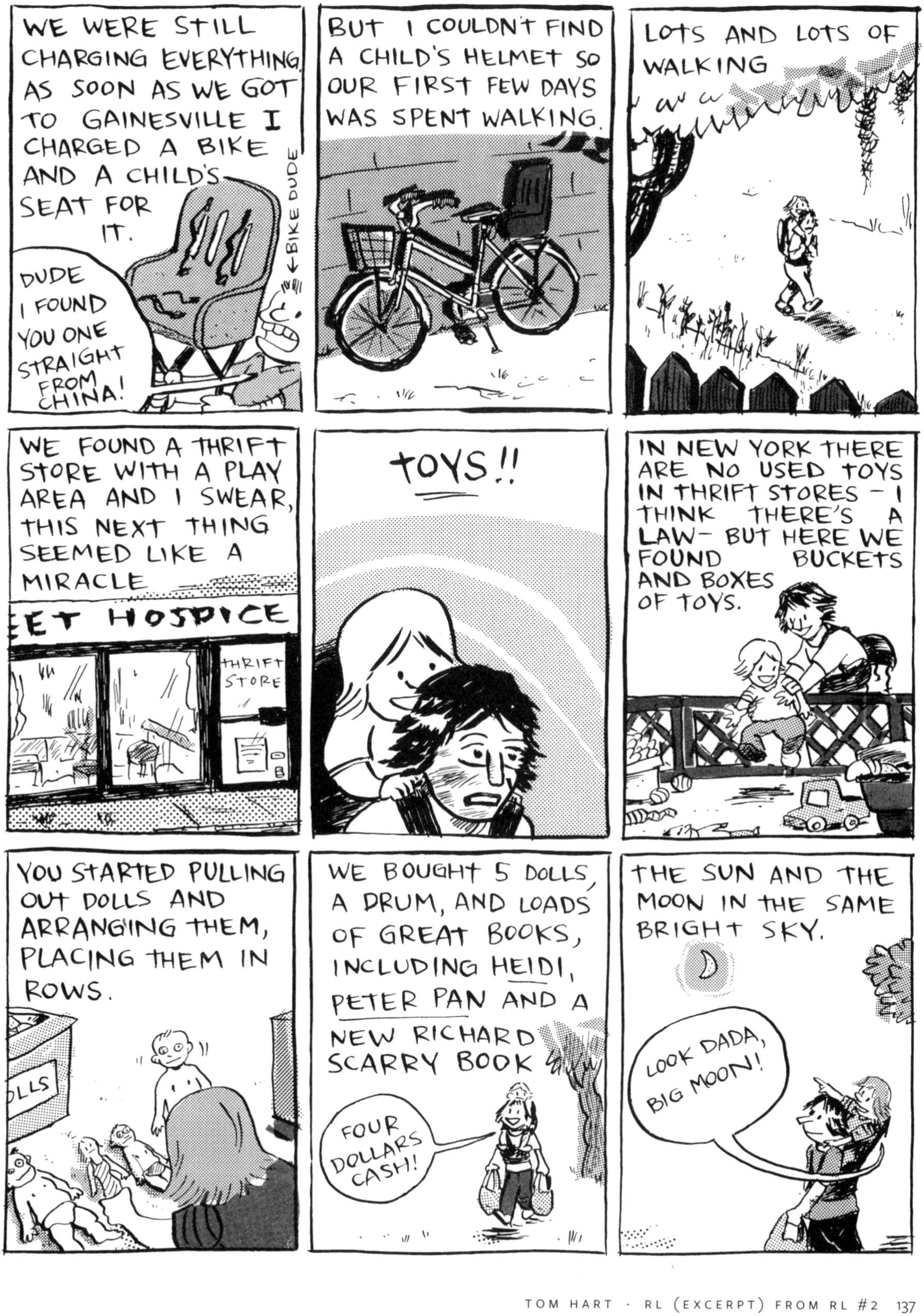
WE WERE STILL CHARGING EVERYTHING. AS SOON AS WE GOT TO GAINESVILLE I CHARGED A BIKE AND A CHILD'S SEAT FOR IT.
DUDE I FOUND YOU ONE STRAIGHT FROM CHINA!
← BIKE DUDE
BUT I COULDN'T FIND A CHILD'S HELMET SO OUR FIRST FEW DAYS WAS SPENT WALKING.
LOTS AND LOTS OF WALKING
WE FOUND A THRIFT STORE WITH A PLAY AREA AND I SWEAR, THIS NEXT THING SEEMED LIKE A MIRACLE
EET HOSPICE
THRIFT STORE
TOYS!!
IN NEW YORK THERE ARE NO USED TOYS IN THRIFT STORES – I THINK THERE'S A LAW– BUT HERE WE FOUND BUCKETS AND BOXES OF TOYS.
YOU STARTED PULLING OUT DOLLS AND ARRANGING THEM, PLACING THEM IN ROWS.
OLLS
WE BOUGHT 5 DOLLS, A DRUM, AND LOADS OF GREAT BOOKS, INCLUDING HEIDI, PETER PAN AND A NEW RICHARD SCARRY BOOK
FOUR DOLLARS CASH!
THE SUN AND THE MOON IN THE SAME BRIGHT SKY.
LOOK DADA, BIG MOON!

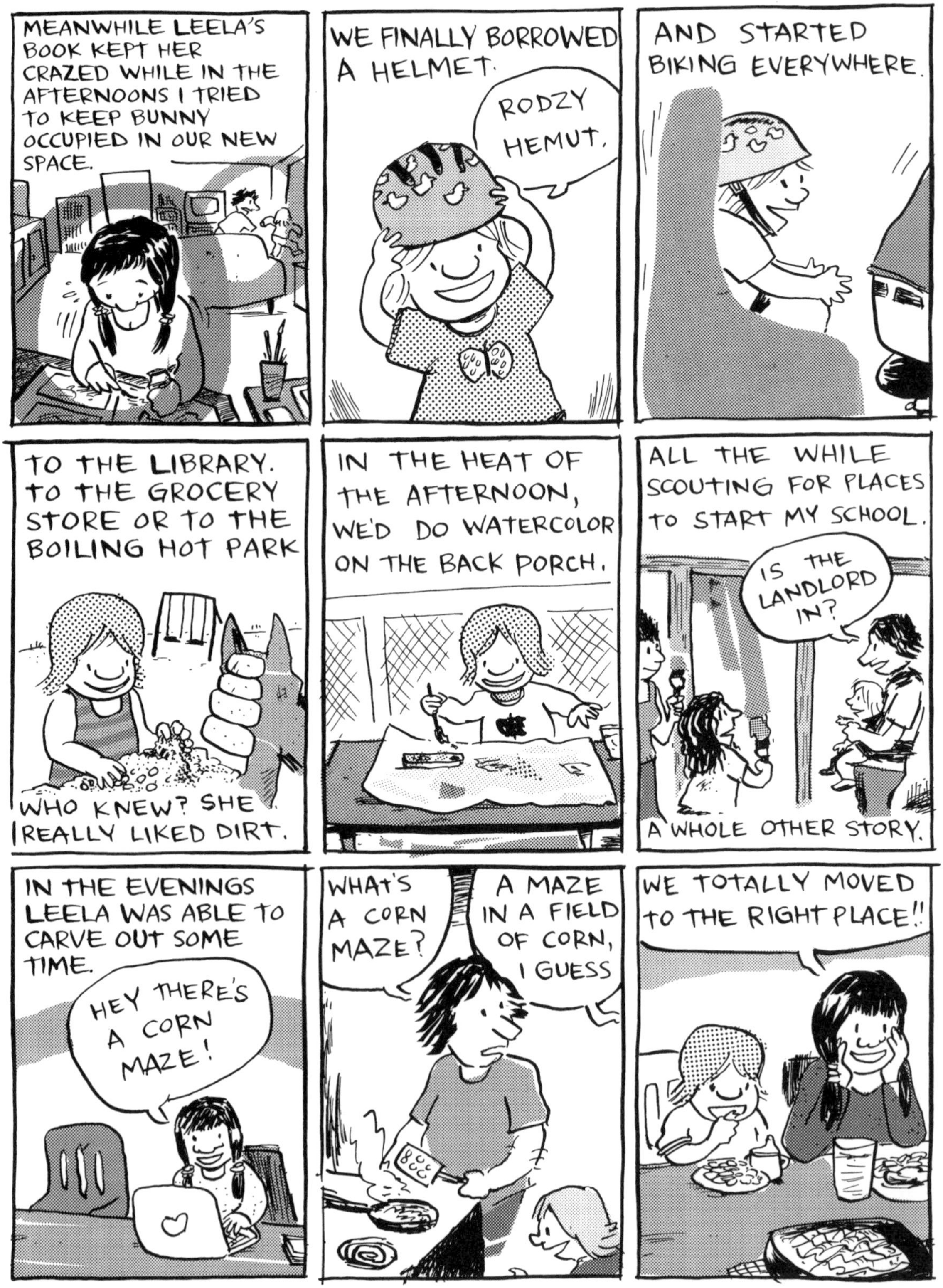
MEANWHILE LEELA'S BOOK KEPT HER CRAZED WHILE IN THE AFTERNOONS I TRIED TO KEEP BUNNY OCCUPIED IN OUR NEW SPACE.
WE FINALLY BORROWED A HELMET.
RODZY HEMUT.
AND STARTED BIKING EVERYWHERE.
TO THE LIBRARY. TO THE GROCERY STORE OR TO THE BOILING HOT PARK
WHO KNEW? SHE REALLY LIKED DIRT.
IN THE HEAT OF THE AFTERNOON, WE'D DO WATERCOLOR ON THE BACK PORCH.
ALL THE WHILE SCOUTING FOR PLACES TO START MY SCHOOL.
IS THE LANDLORD IN?
A WHOLE OTHER STORY.
IN THE EVENINGS LEELA WAS ABLE TO CARVE OUT SOME TIME.
HEY THERE'S A CORN MAZE!
WHAT'S A CORN MAZE?
A MAZE IN A FIELD OF CORN, I GUESS
WE TOTALLY MOVED TO THE RIGHT PLACE!!

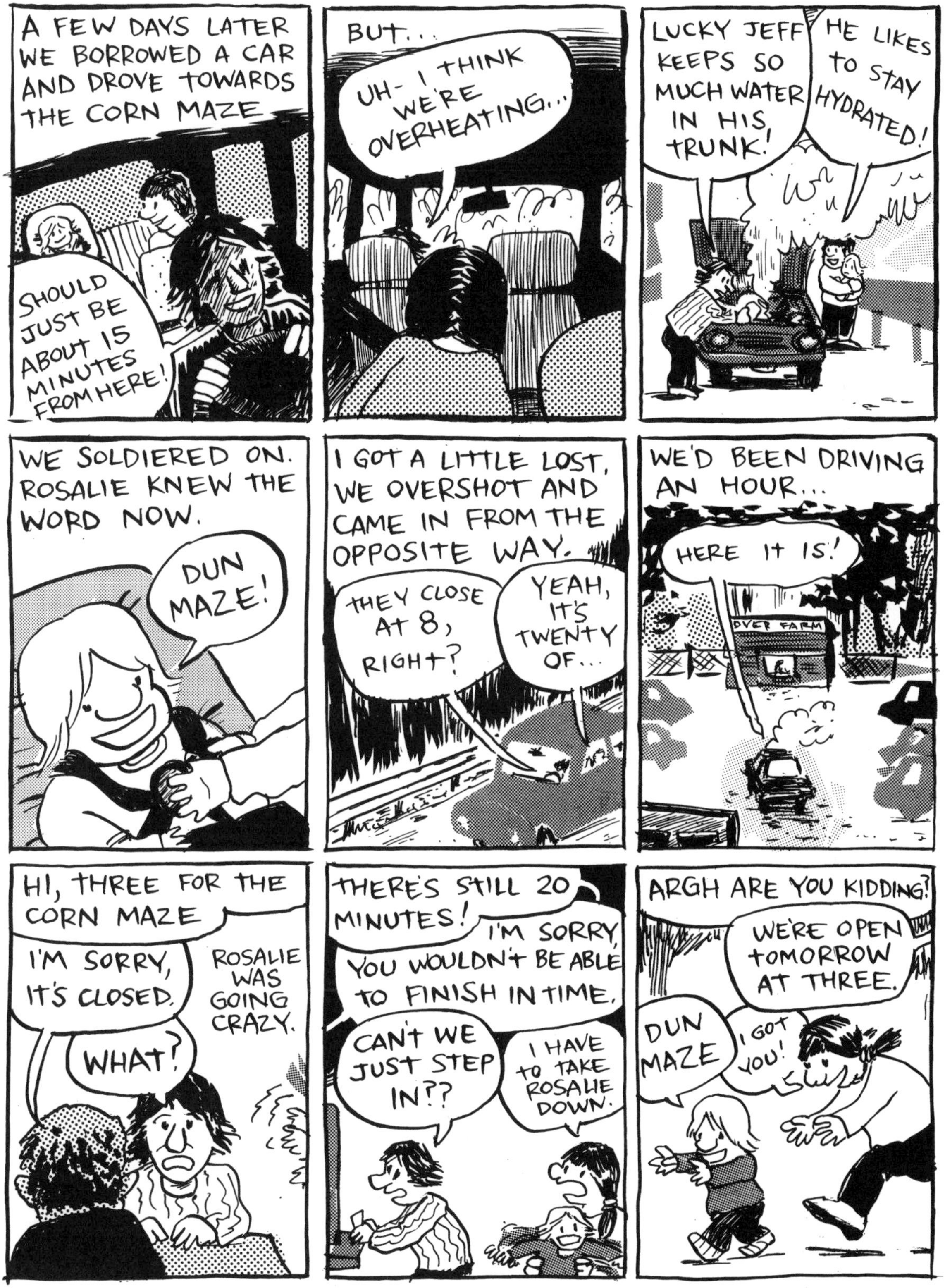
A FEW DAYS LATER WE BORROWED A CAR AND DROVE TOWARDS THE CORN MAZE
SHOULD JUST BE ABOUT 15 MINUTES FROM HERE!
BUT...
UH- I THINK WE'RE OVERHEATING...
LUCKY JEFF KEEPS SO MUCH WATER IN HIS TRUNK!
HE LIKES TO STAY HYDRATED!
WE SOLDIERED ON. ROSALIE KNEW THE WORD NOW.
DUN MAZE!
I GOT A LITTLE LOST, WE OVERSHOT AND CAME IN FROM THE OPPOSITE WAY.
THEY CLOSE AT 8, RIGHT?
YEAH, IT'S TWENTY OF...
WE'D BEEN DRIVING AN HOUR...
HERE IT IS!
HI, THREE FOR THE CORN MAZE
I'M SORRY, IT'S CLOSED.
ROSALIE WAS GOING CRAZY.
WHAT?
THERE'S STILL 20 MINUTES!
I'M SORRY, YOU WOULDN'T BE ABLE TO FINISH IN TIME.
CAN'T WE JUST STEP IN??
I HAVE TO TAKE ROSALIE DOWN.
ARGH ARE YOU KIDDING?
WE'RE OPEN TOMORROW AT THREE.
DUN MAZE
I GOT YOU!

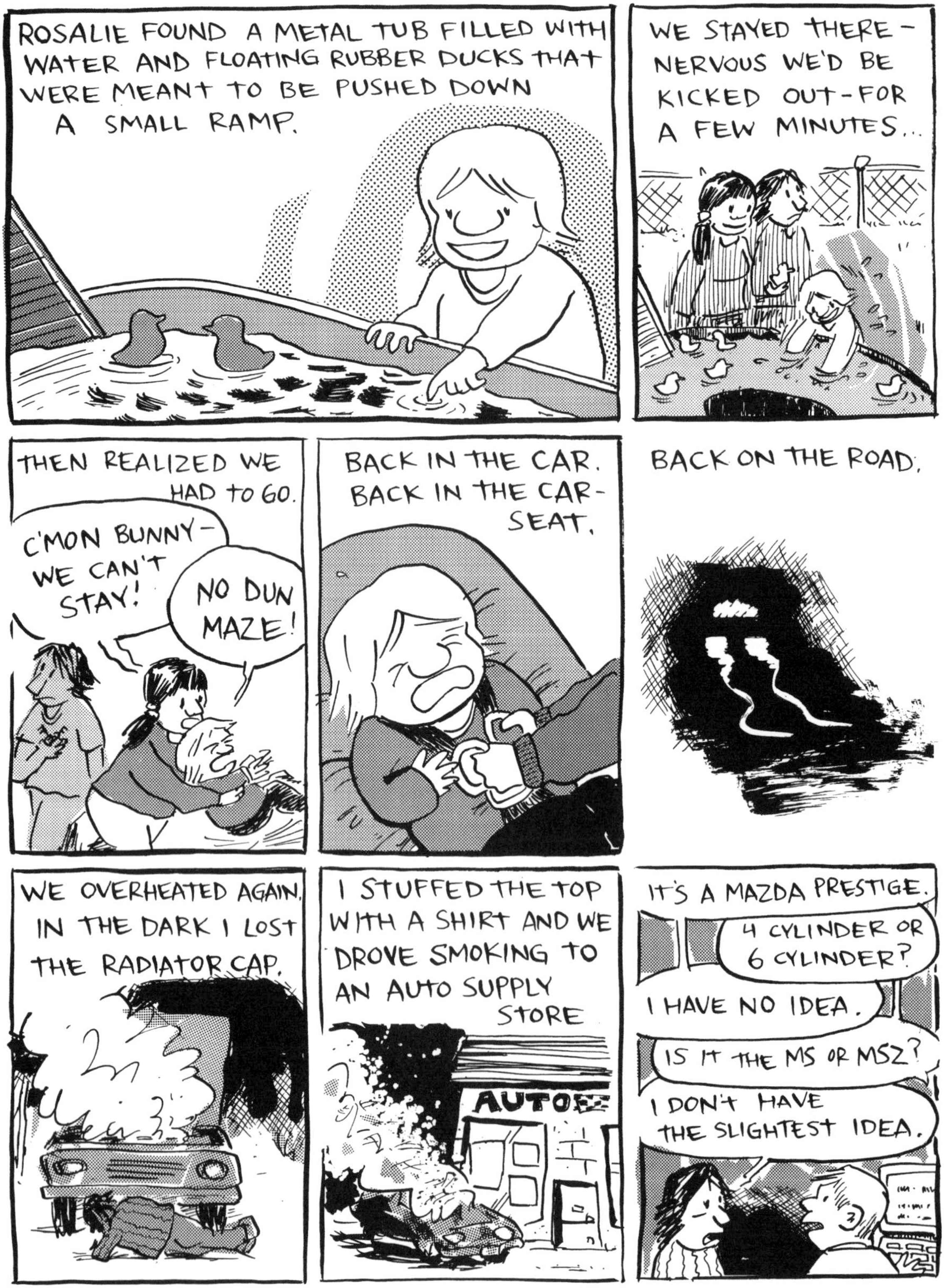
ROSALIE FOUND A METAL TUB FILLED WITH WATER AND FLOATING RUBBER DUCKS THAT WERE MEANT TO BE PUSHED DOWN A SMALL RAMP.
WE STAYED THERE - NERVOUS WE'D BE KICKED OUT - FOR A FEW MINUTES...
THEN REALIZED WE HAD TO GO.
C'MON BUNNY - WE CAN'T STAY!
NO DUN MAZE!
BACK IN THE CAR. BACK IN THE CAR-SEAT.
BACK ON THE ROAD.
WE OVERHEATED AGAIN. IN THE DARK I LOST THE RADIATOR CAP.
I STUFFED THE TOP WITH A SHIRT AND WE DROVE SMOKING TO AN AUTO SUPPLY STORE
AUTO
IT'S A MAZDA PRESTIGE.
4 CYLINDER OR 6 CYLINDER?
I HAVE NO IDEA.
IS IT THE MS OR MSZ?
I DON'T HAVE THE SLIGHTEST IDEA.

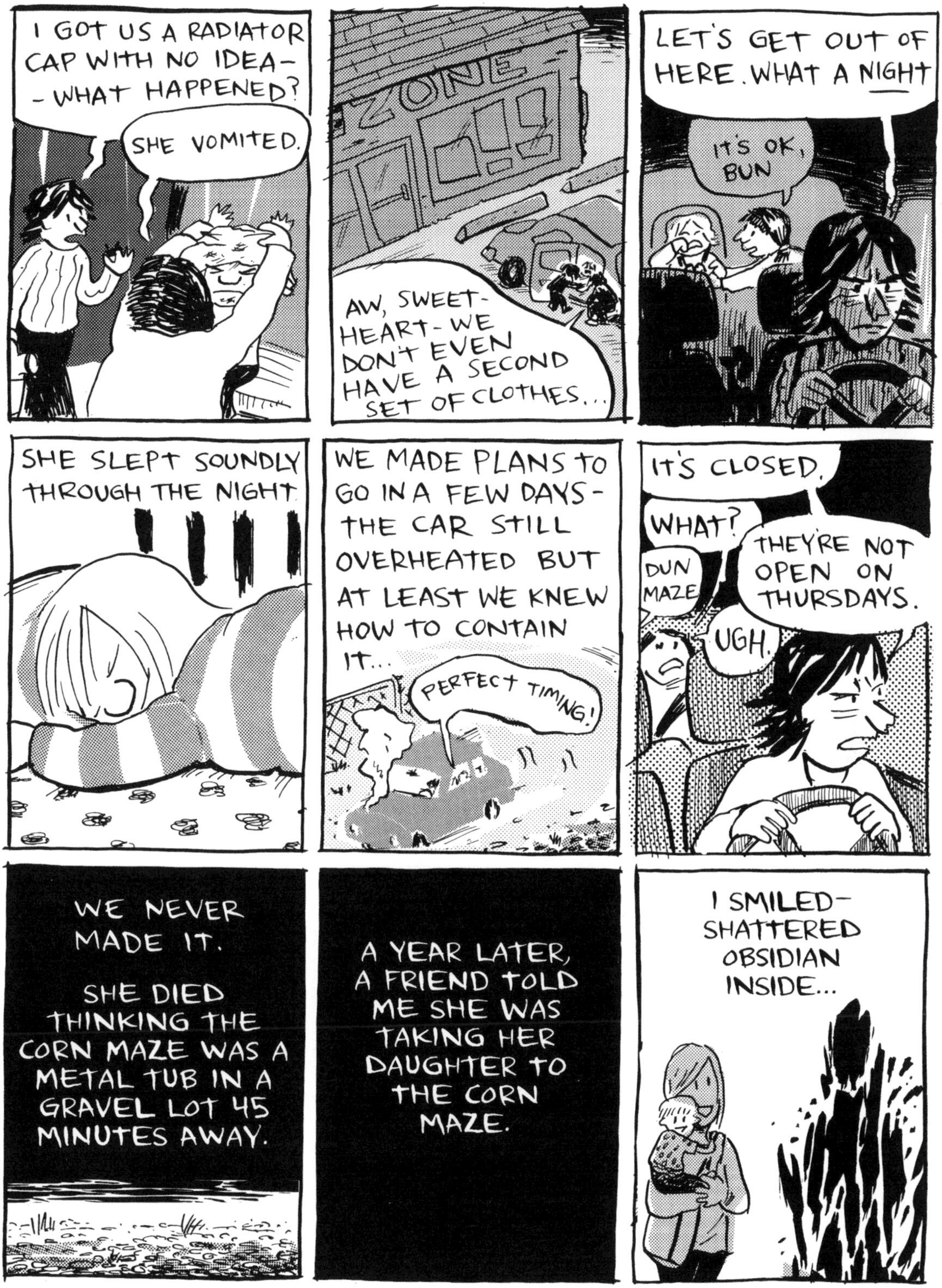
I GOT US A RADIATOR CAP WITH NO IDEA- - WHAT HAPPENED?
SHE VOMITED.
AW, SWEET-HEART- WE DON'T EVEN HAVE A SECOND SET OF CLOTHES...
LET'S GET OUT OF HERE. WHAT A NIGHT
IT'S OK, BUN
SHE SLEPT SOUNDLY THROUGH THE NIGHT
WE MADE PLANS TO GO IN A FEW DAYS- THE CAR STILL OVERHEATED BUT AT LEAST WE KNEW HOW TO CONTAIN IT...
PERFECT TIMING!
IT'S CLOSED.
WHAT?
DUN MAZE
THEY'RE NOT OPEN ON THURSDAYS.
UGH.
WE NEVER MADE IT.
SHE DIED THINKING THE CORN MAZE WAS A METAL TUB IN A GRAVEL LOT 45 MINUTES AWAY.
A YEAR LATER, A FRIEND TOLD ME SHE WAS TAKING HER DAUGHTER TO THE CORN MAZE.
I SMILED- SHATTERED OBSIDIAN INSIDE...

NOVEMBER.

LEELA ASKS ME ABOUT A WALKING MEDITATION I WAS DOING WHEN WE FIRST MET.

I LEARNED IT FROM A THICH NHAT HANH TAPE.

WHEN INHALING, SILENTLY SAYING WITH EACH STEP

YES.

YES.

YES

YES.

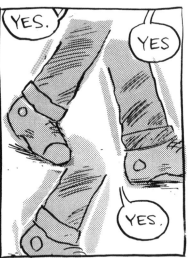

AND ON THE EXHALE,

THANK YOU.

THANK YOU.

THANK YOU.

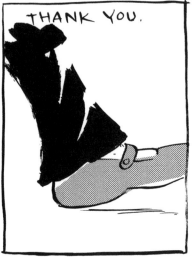

THANK YOU.

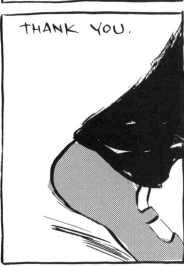

IT COMFORTS HER, THIS FOCUS ON THE MOMENT...

BUT I CAN'T DO IT.

I DO YES YES

YES

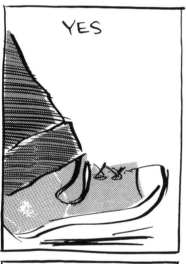

YES

YES

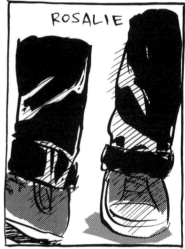

ROSALIE

ROSALIE.

ROSALIE

ROSALIE

I KNOW HER NAME HAS TO NOW TAKE ON A NEW MEANING.

I AM PRACTICING.

ROSALIE ROSALIE ROSALIE ROSALIE

WE ALWAYS HAD DREAMS—

THIS IS ROSALIE LIGHTNING FOR SUPER SATELLITE RADIO NEWS...

OR—

HI DAD! IT'S ROSALIE. I'M CALLING FROM—

YEAH— THE STATION!

IT'S FUNNY THAT YOU WOULD LIKE THE COLD SO MUCH! BEING THAT YOU GREW UP IN FLORIDA—

HA HA YEAH.

HELLO?

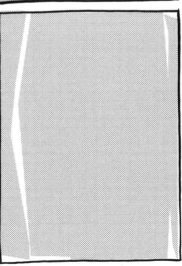

HELLO?

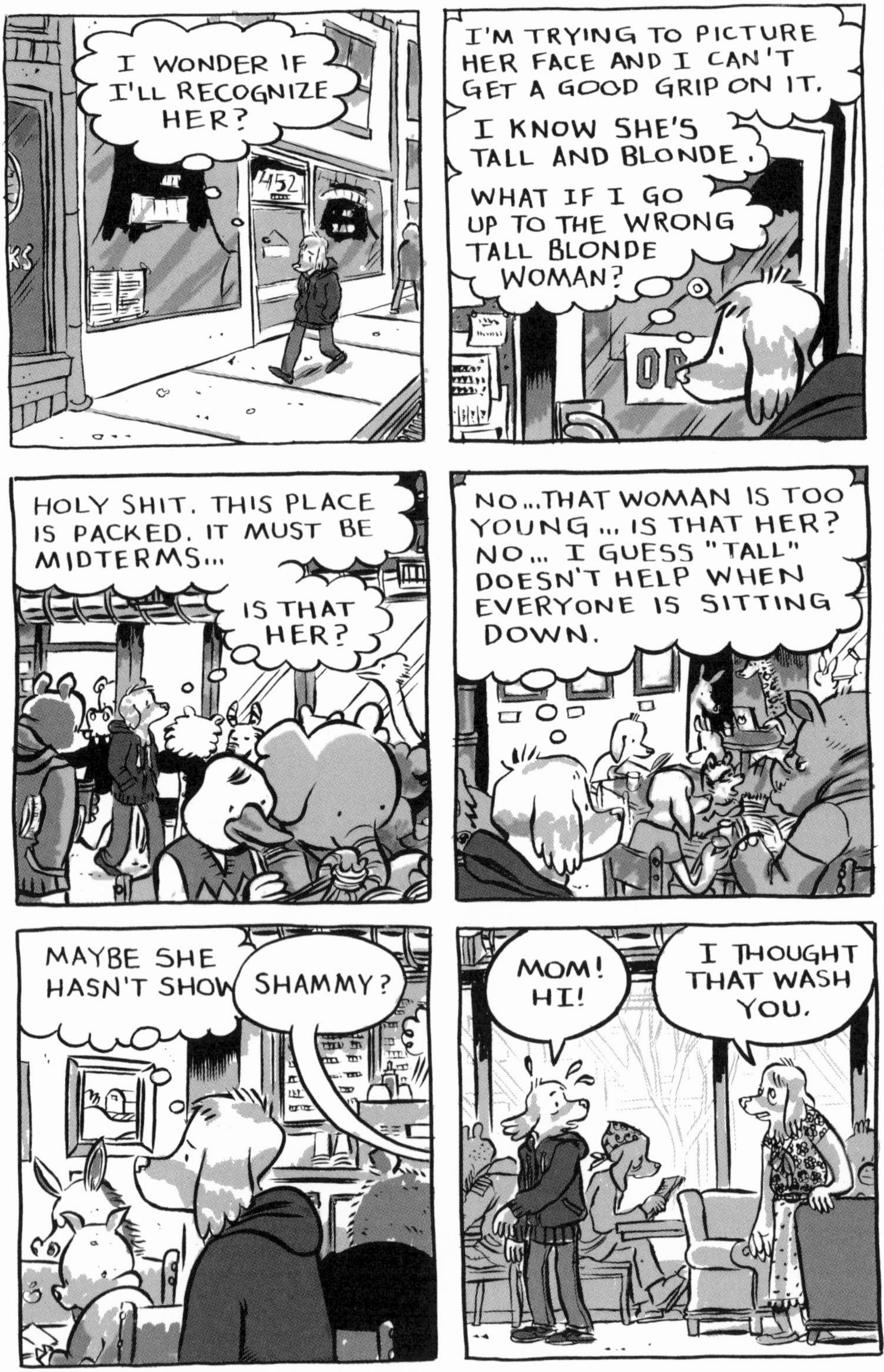
I WONDER IF I'LL RECOGNIZE HER?
452
I'M TRYING TO PICTURE HER FACE AND I CAN'T GET A GOOD GRIP ON IT.
I KNOW SHE'S TALL AND BLONDE.
WHAT IF I GO UP TO THE WRONG TALL BLONDE WOMAN?
HOLY SHIT. THIS PLACE IS PACKED. IT MUST BE MIDTERMS...
IS THAT HER?
NO...THAT WOMAN IS TOO YOUNG... IS THAT HER? NO... I GUESS "TALL" DOESN'T HELP WHEN EVERYONE IS SITTING DOWN.
MAYBE SHE HASN'T SHOW
SHAMMY?
MOM! HI!
I THOUGHT THAT WASH YOU.

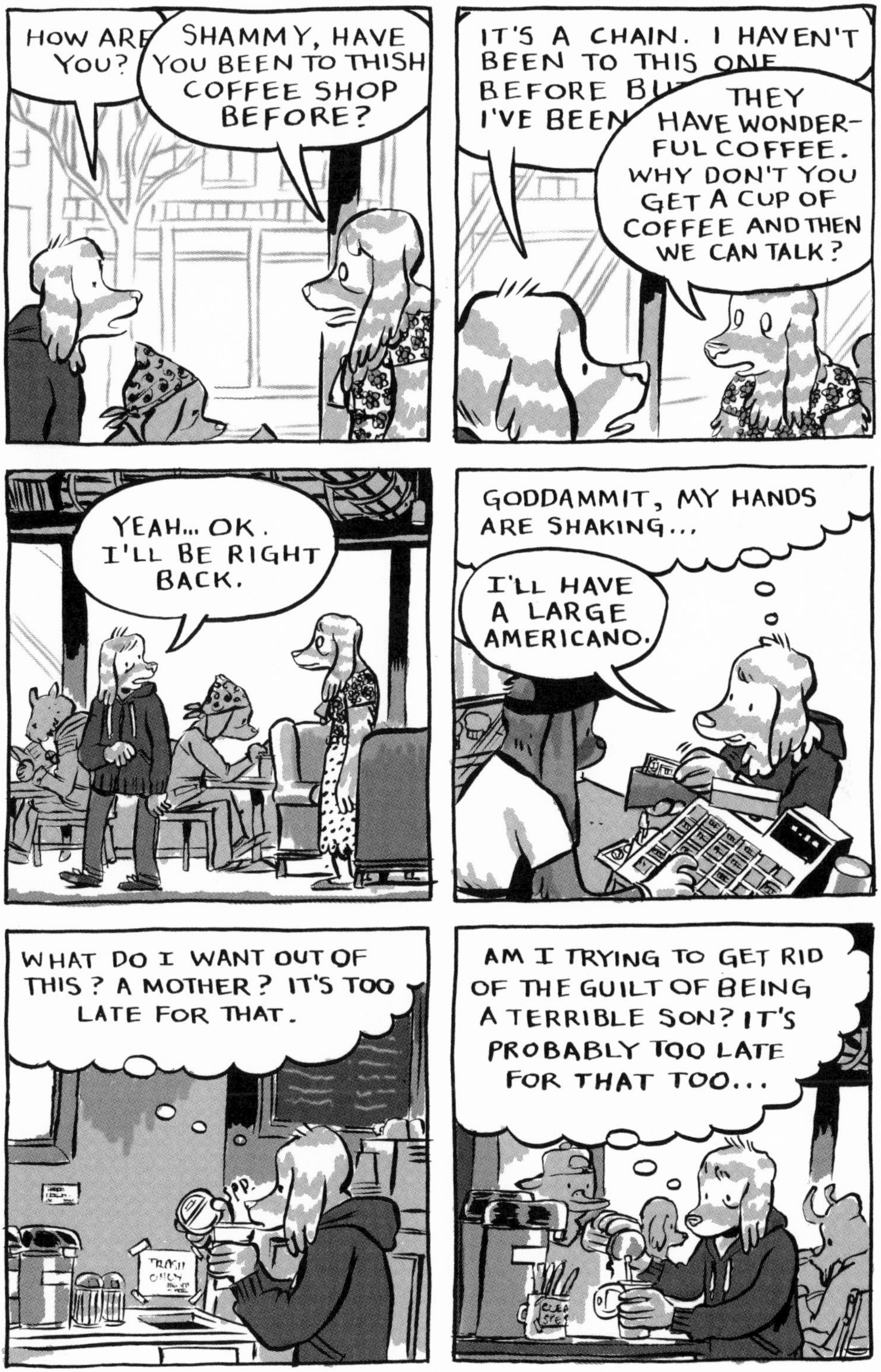
HOW ARE YOU?
SHAMMY, HAVE YOU BEEN TO THISH COFFEE SHOP BEFORE?
IT'S A CHAIN. I HAVEN'T BEEN TO THIS ONE BEFORE BU I'VE BEEN
THEY HAVE WONDERFUL COFFEE. WHY DON'T YOU GET A CUP OF COFFEE AND THEN WE CAN TALK?
YEAH... OK. I'LL BE RIGHT BACK.
GODDAMMIT, MY HANDS ARE SHAKING...
I'LL HAVE A LARGE AMERICANO.
WHAT DO I WANT OUT OF THIS? A MOTHER? IT'S TOO LATE FOR THAT.
AM I TRYING TO GET RID OF THE GUILT OF BEING A TERRIBLE SON? IT'S PROBABLY TOO LATE FOR THAT TOO...

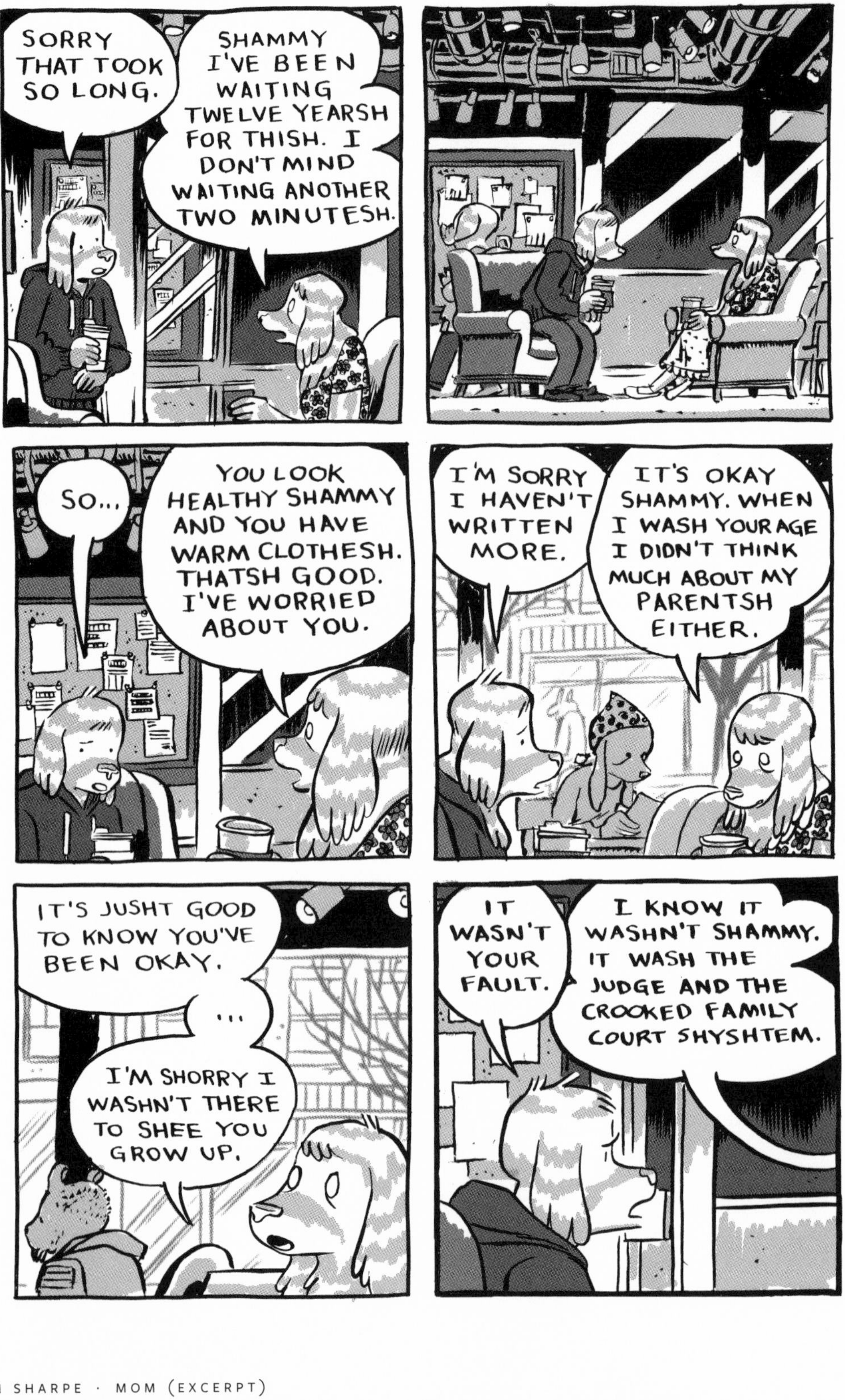
SORRY THAT TOOK SO LONG.
SHAMMY I'VE BEEN WAITING TWELVE YEARSH FOR THISH. I DON'T MIND WAITING ANOTHER TWO MINUTESH.
SO...
YOU LOOK HEALTHY SHAMMY AND YOU HAVE WARM CLOTHESH. THATSH GOOD. I'VE WORRIED ABOUT YOU.
I'M SORRY I HAVEN'T WRITTEN MORE.
IT'S OKAY SHAMMY. WHEN I WASH YOUR AGE I DIDN'T THINK MUCH ABOUT MY PARENTSH EITHER.
IT'S JUSHT GOOD TO KNOW YOU'VE BEEN OKAY.
...
I'M SHORRY I WASHN'T THERE TO SHEE YOU GROW UP.
IT WASN'T YOUR FAULT.
I KNOW IT WASHN'T SHAMMY. IT WASH THE JUDGE AND THE CROOKED FAMILY COURT SHYSHTEM.

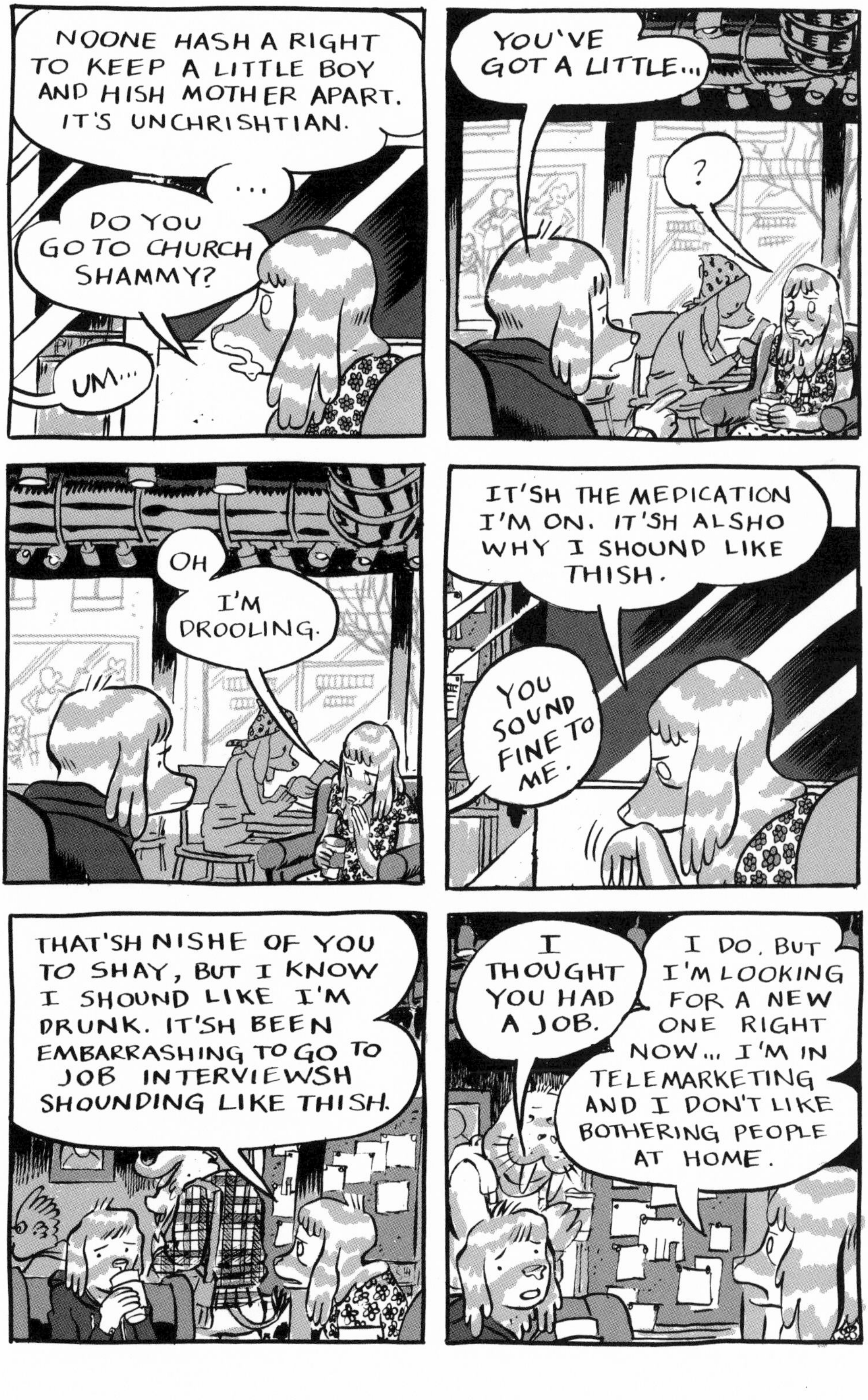
NOONE HASH A RIGHT TO KEEP A LITTLE BOY AND HISH MOTHER APART. IT'S UNCHRISHTIAN.
...
DO YOU GO TO CHURCH SHAMMY?
UM...
YOU'VE GOT A LITTLE...
?
OH
I'M DROOLING.
IT'SH THE MEDICATION I'M ON. IT'SH ALSHO WHY I SHOUND LIKE THISH.
YOU SOUND FINE TO ME.
THAT'SH NISHE OF YOU TO SHAY, BUT I KNOW I SHOUND LIKE I'M DRUNK. IT'SH BEEN EMBARRASHING TO GO TO JOB INTERVIEWSH SHOUNDING LIKE THISH.
I THOUGHT YOU HAD A JOB.
I DO, BUT I'M LOOKING FOR A NEW ONE RIGHT NOW... I'M IN TELEMARKETING AND I DON'T LIKE BOTHERING PEOPLE AT HOME.

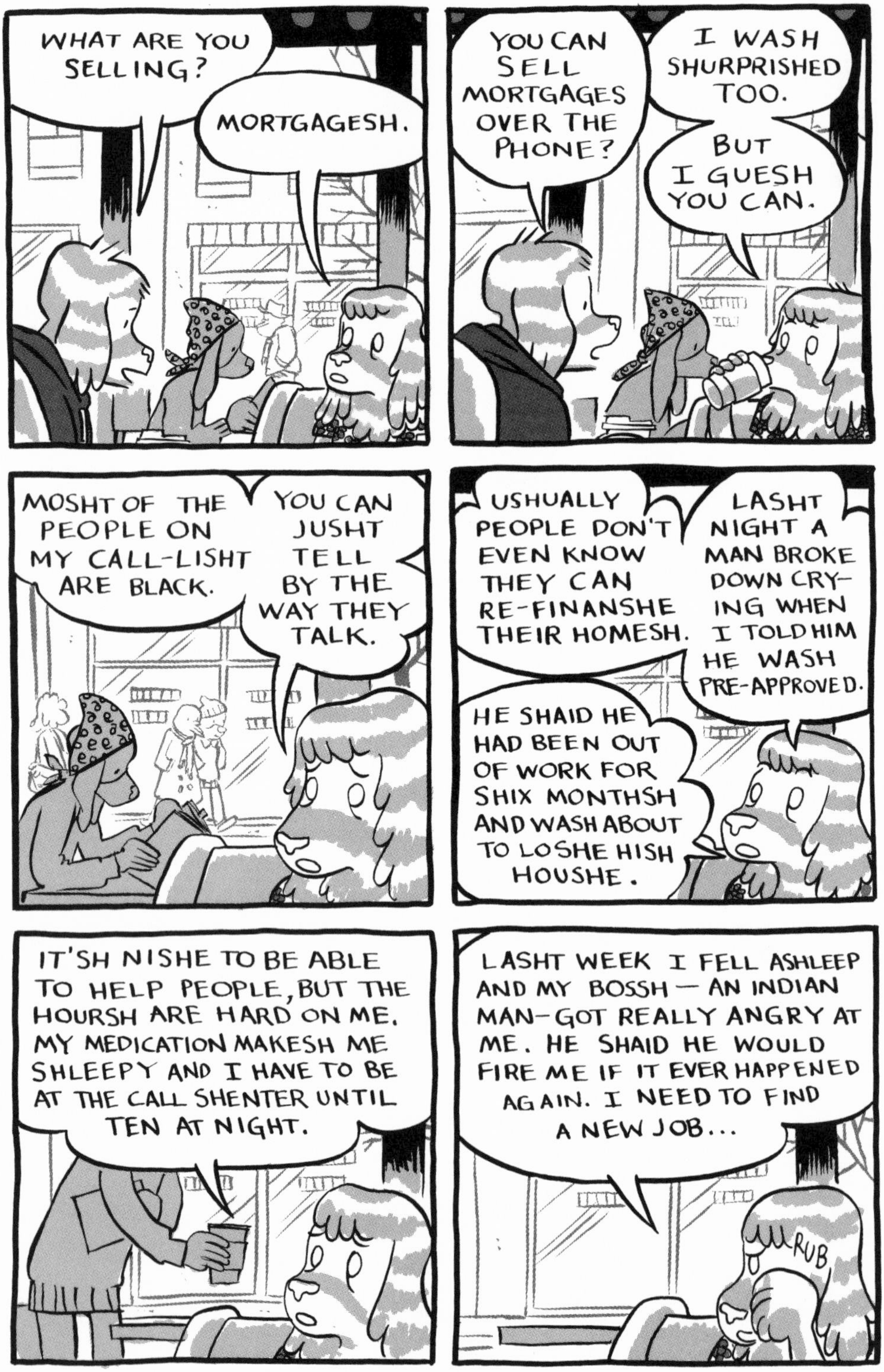
WHAT ARE YOU SELLING?
MORTGAGESH.
YOU CAN SELL MORTGAGES OVER THE PHONE?
I WASH SHURPRISHED TOO.
BUT I GUESH YOU CAN.
MOSHT OF THE PEOPLE ON MY CALL-LISHT ARE BLACK.
YOU CAN JUSHT TELL BY THE WAY THEY TALK.
USHUALLY PEOPLE DON'T EVEN KNOW THEY CAN RE-FINANSHE THEIR HOMESH.
LASHT NIGHT A MAN BROKE DOWN CRY-ING WHEN I TOLD HIM HE WASH PRE-APPROVED.
HE SHAID HE HAD BEEN OUT OF WORK FOR SHIX MONTHSH AND WASH ABOUT TO LOSHE HISH HOUSHE.
IT'SH NISHE TO BE ABLE TO HELP PEOPLE, BUT THE HOURSH ARE HARD ON ME. MY MEDICATION MAKESH ME SHLEEPY AND I HAVE TO BE AT THE CALL SHENTER UNTIL TEN AT NIGHT.
LASHT WEEK I FELL ASHLEEP AND MY BOSSH — AN INDIAN MAN — GOT REALLY ANGRY AT ME. HE SHAID HE WOULD FIRE ME IF IT EVER HAPPENED AGAIN. I NEED TO FIND A NEW JOB...
RUB

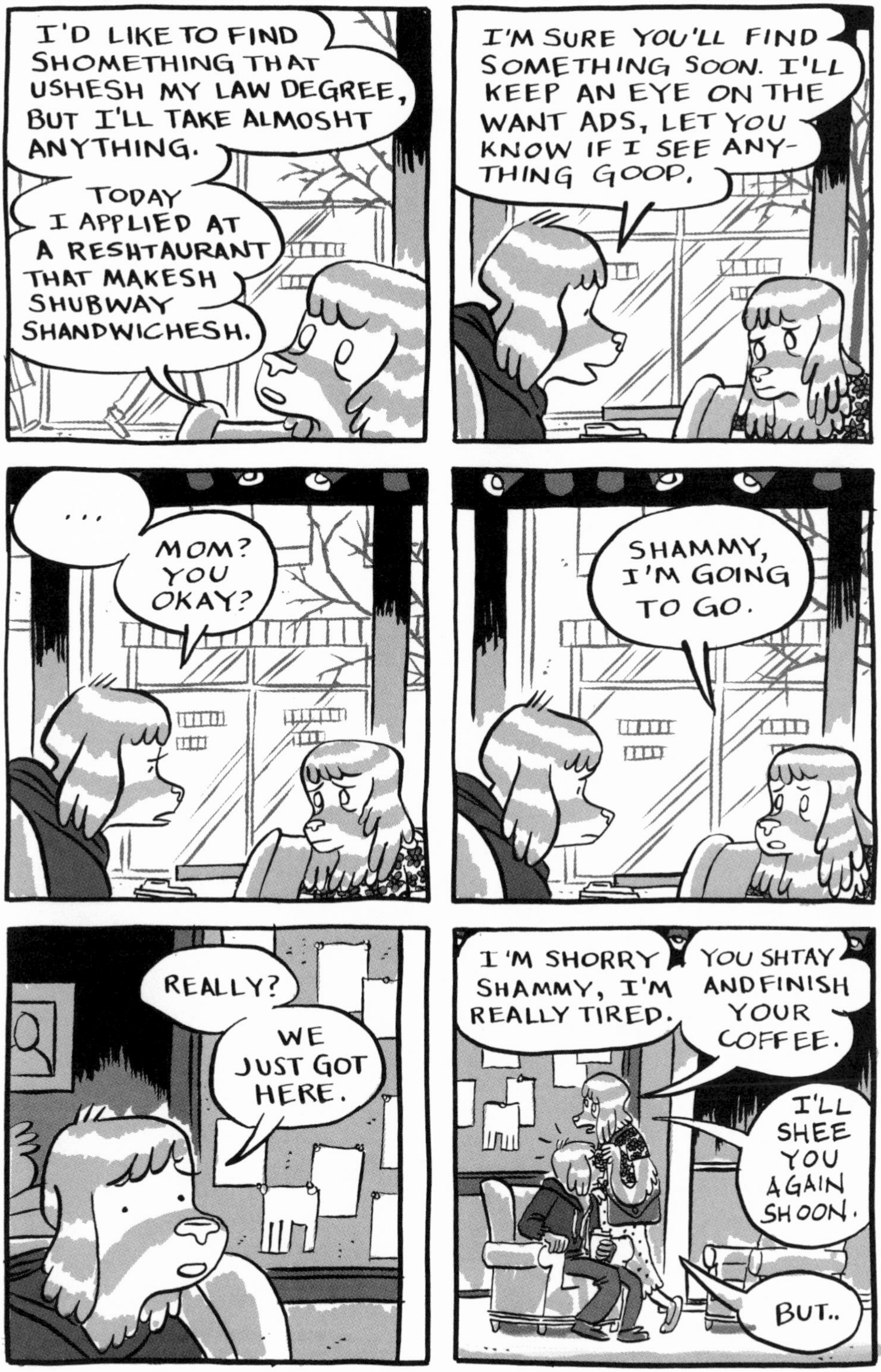
I'D LIKE TO FIND SHOMETHING THAT USHESH MY LAW DEGREE, BUT I'LL TAKE ALMOSHT ANYTHING.
TODAY I APPLIED AT A RESHTAURANT THAT MAKESH SHUBWAY SHANDWICHESH.
I'M SURE YOU'LL FIND SOMETHING SOON. I'LL KEEP AN EYE ON THE WANT ADS, LET YOU KNOW IF I SEE ANY-THING GOOD.
...
MOM? YOU OKAY?
SHAMMY, I'M GOING TO GO.
REALLY?
WE JUST GOT HERE.
I'M SHORRY SHAMMY, I'M REALLY TIRED.
YOU SHTAY AND FINISH YOUR COFFEE.
I'LL SHEE YOU AGAIN SHOON.
BUT..

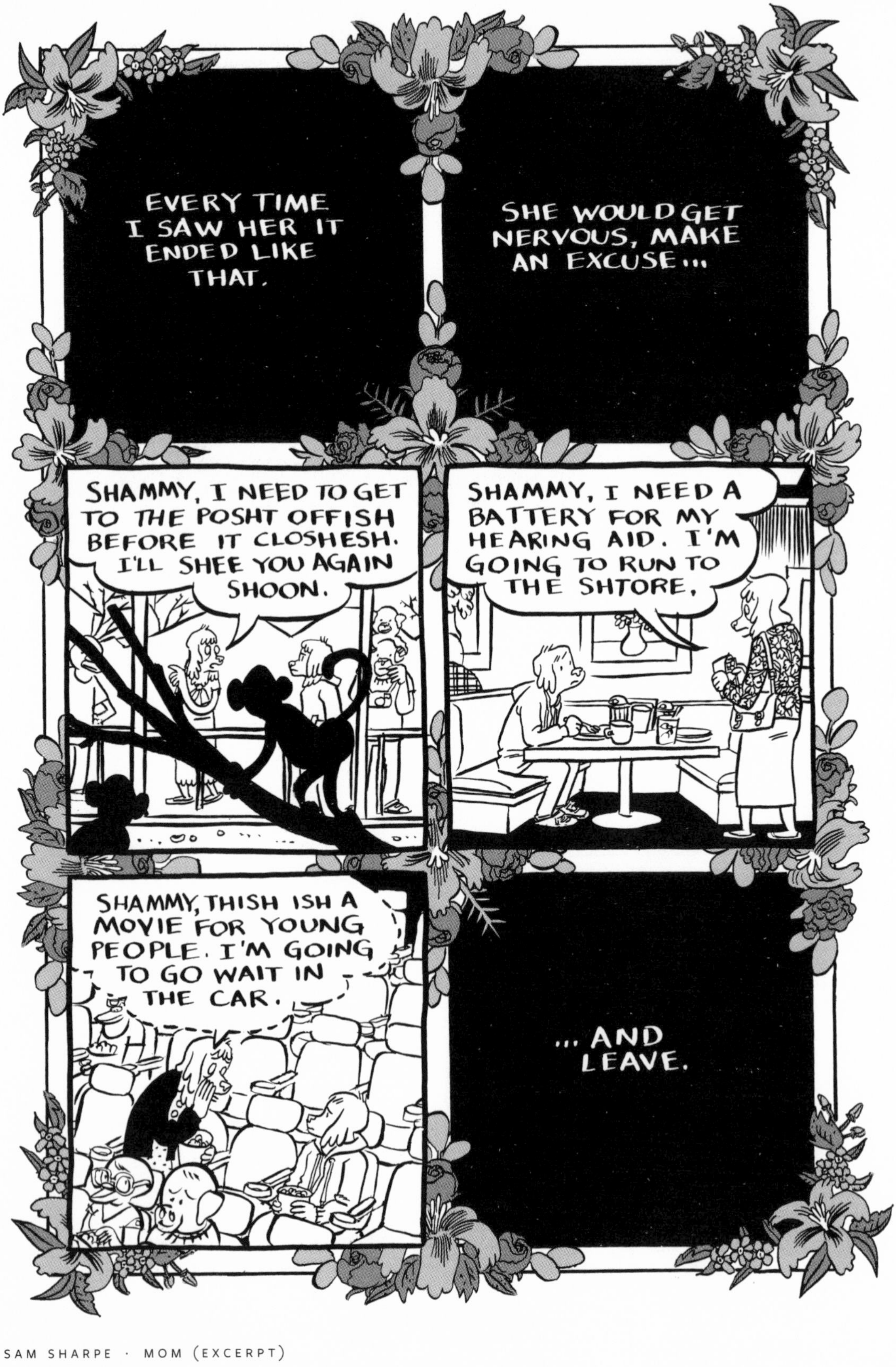
EVERY TIME I SAW HER IT ENDED LIKE THAT.
SHE WOULD GET NERVOUS, MAKE AN EXCUSE...
SHAMMY, I NEED TO GET TO THE POSHT OFFISH BEFORE IT CLOSHESH. I'LL SHEE YOU AGAIN SHOON.
SHAMMY, I NEED A BATTERY FOR MY HEARING AID. I'M GOING TO RUN TO THE SHTORE.
SHAMMY, THISH ISH A MOVIE FOR YOUNG PEOPLE. I'M GOING TO GO WAIT IN THE CAR.
...AND LEAVE.

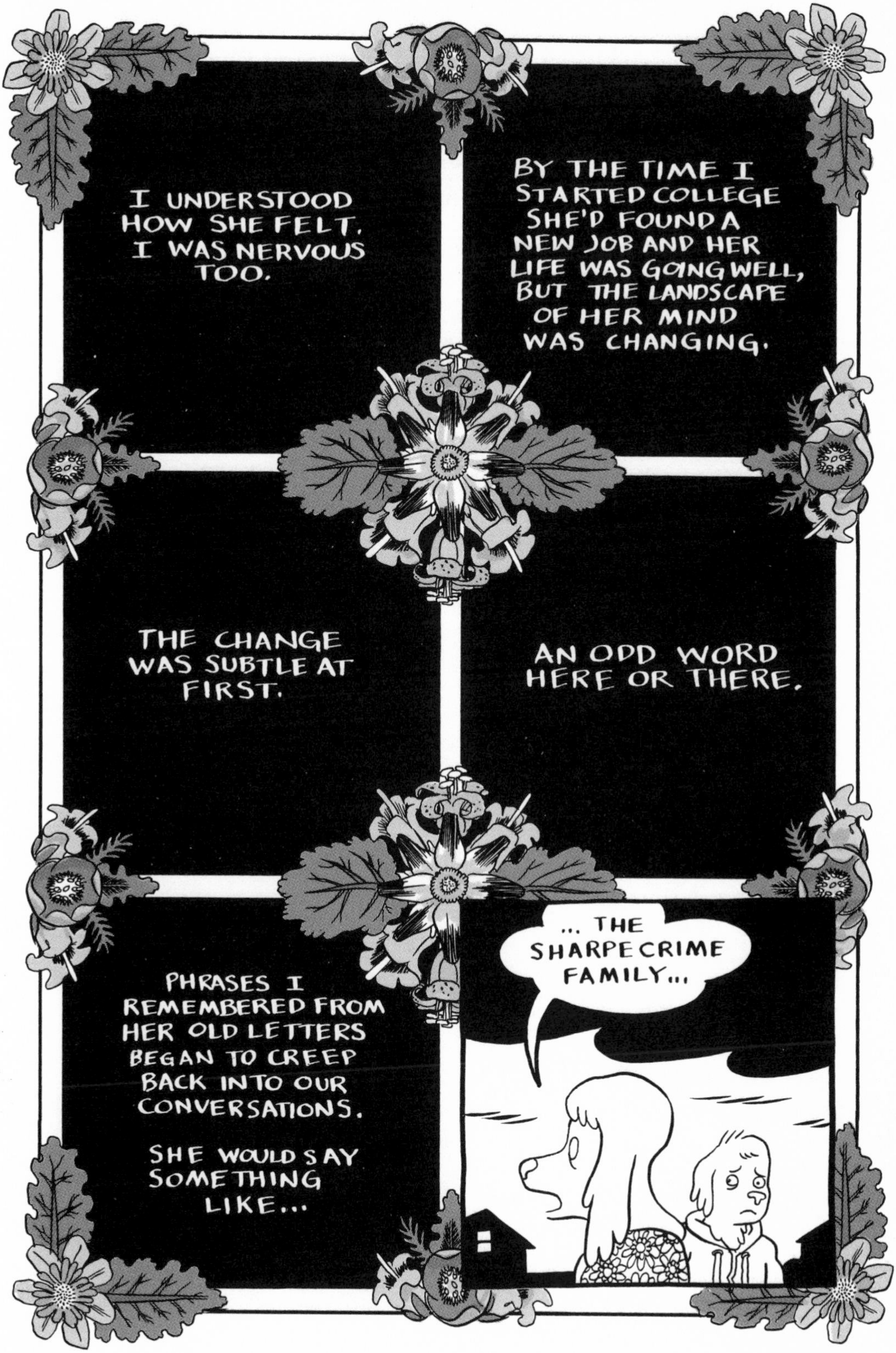
I UNDERSTOOD HOW SHE FELT. I WAS NERVOUS TOO.
BY THE TIME I STARTED COLLEGE SHE'D FOUND A NEW JOB AND HER LIFE WAS GOING WELL, BUT THE LANDSCAPE OF HER MIND WAS CHANGING.
THE CHANGE WAS SUBTLE AT FIRST.
AN ODD WORD HERE OR THERE.
PHRASES I REMEMBERED FROM HER OLD LETTERS BEGAN TO CREEP BACK INTO OUR CONVERSATIONS.
SHE WOULD SAY SOMETHING LIKE...
... THE SHARPE CRIME FAMILY...

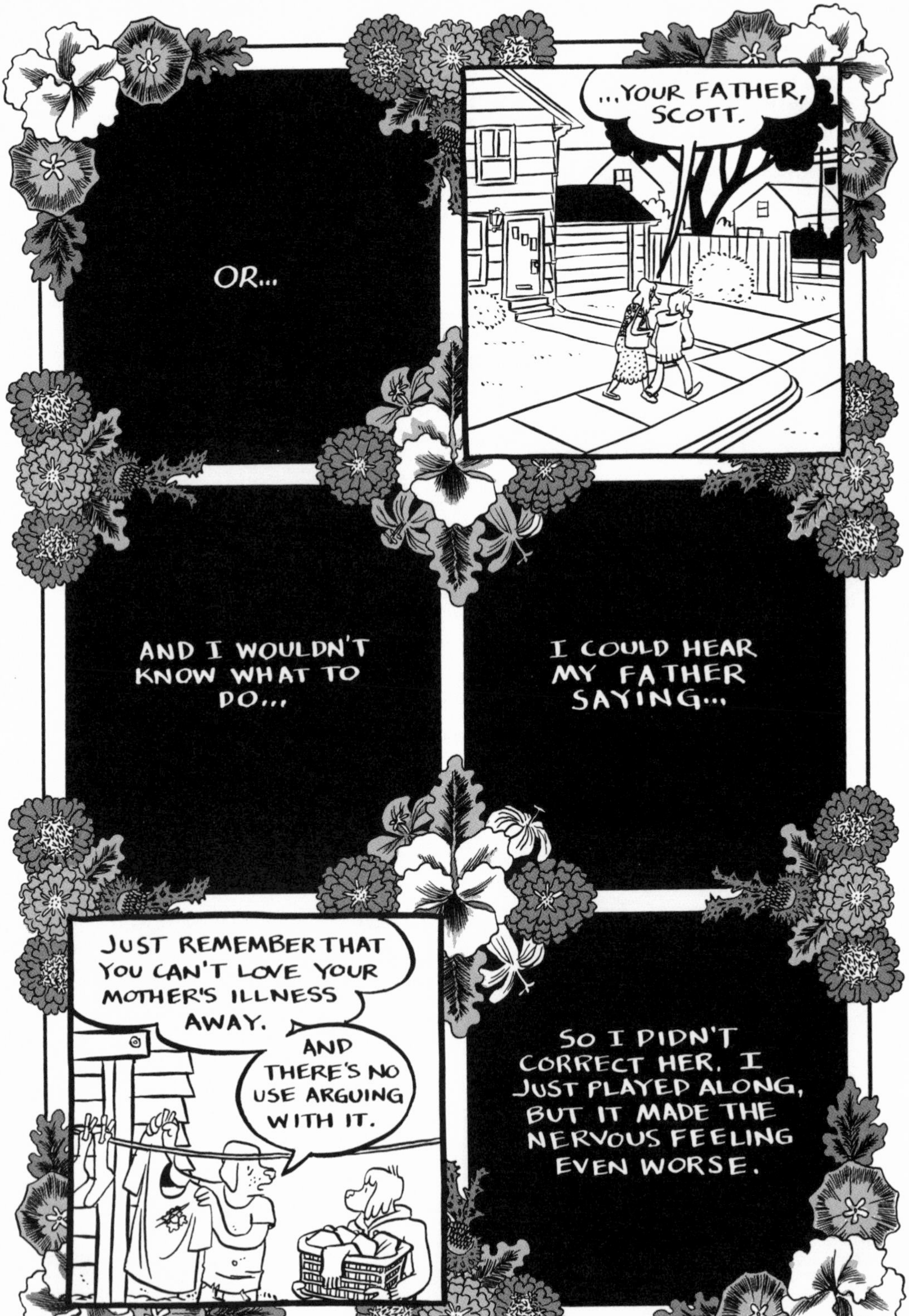
OR...
...YOUR FATHER, SCOTT.
AND I WOULDN'T KNOW WHAT TO DO...
I COULD HEAR MY FATHER SAYING...
JUST REMEMBER THAT YOU CAN'T LOVE YOUR MOTHER'S ILLNESS AWAY.
AND THERE'S NO USE ARGUING WITH IT.
SO I DIDN'T CORRECT HER. I JUST PLAYED ALONG, BUT IT MADE THE NERVOUS FEELING EVEN WORSE.

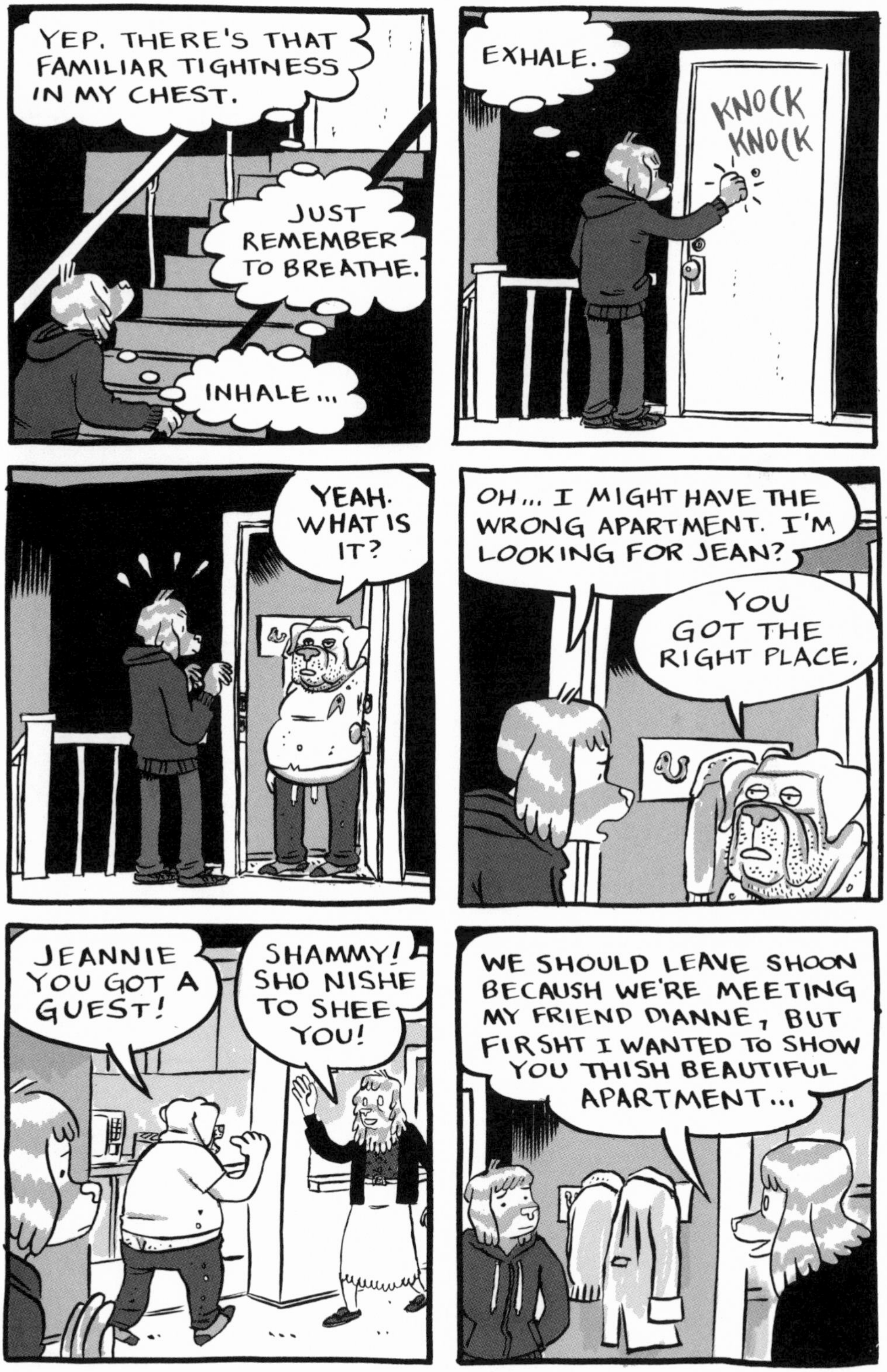
YEP. THERE'S THAT FAMILIAR TIGHTNESS IN MY CHEST.
JUST REMEMBER TO BREATHE.
INHALE...
EXHALE.
KNOCK KNOCK
YEAH. WHAT IS IT?
OH... I MIGHT HAVE THE WRONG APARTMENT. I'M LOOKING FOR JEAN?
YOU GOT THE RIGHT PLACE.
JEANNIE YOU GOT A GUEST!
SHAMMY! SHO NISHE TO SHEE YOU!
WE SHOULD LEAVE SHOON BECAUSH WE'RE MEETING MY FRIEND DIANNE, BUT FIRSHT I WANTED TO SHOW YOU THISH BEAUTIFUL APARTMENT...

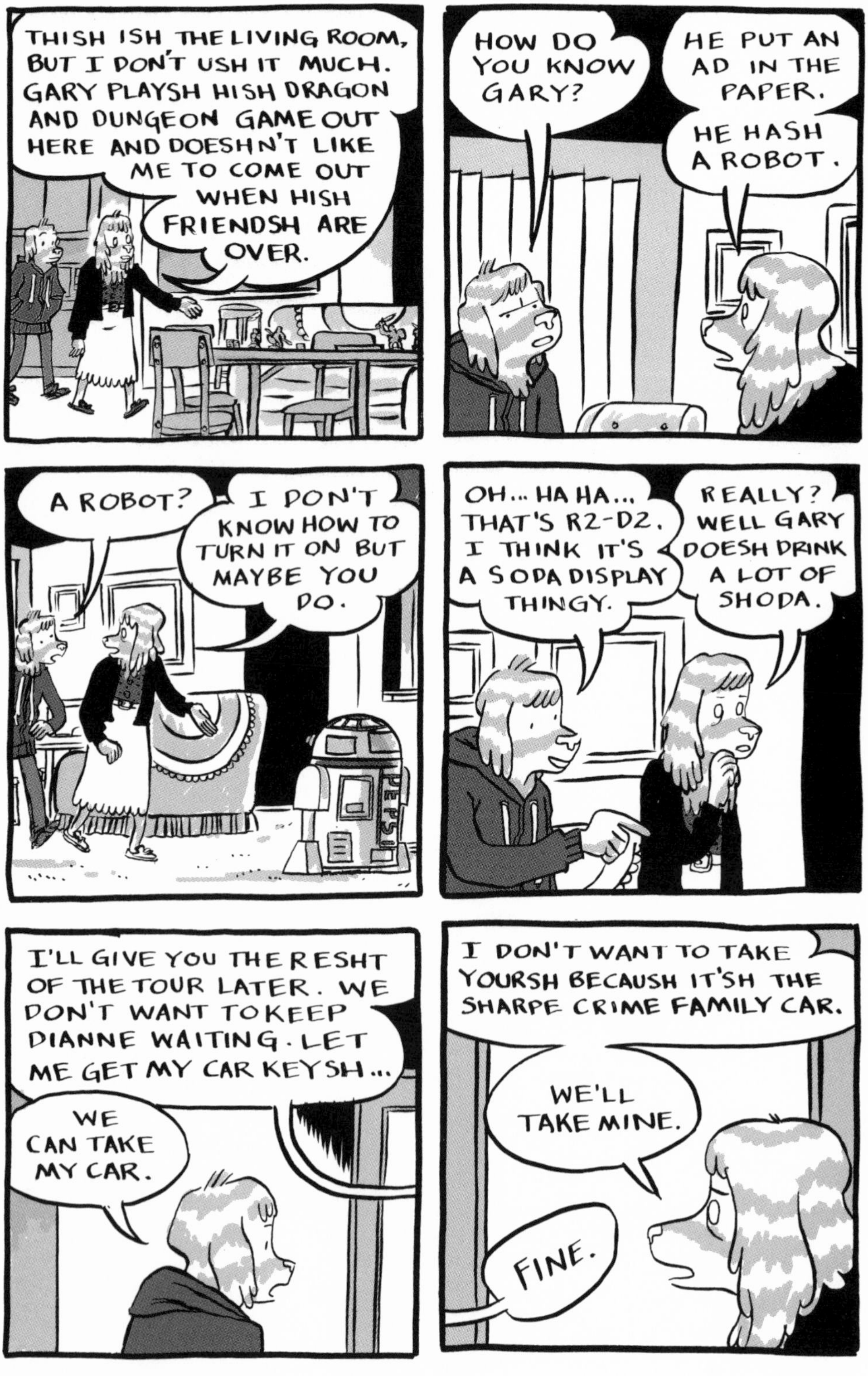
THISH ISH THE LIVING ROOM, BUT I DON'T USH IT MUCH. GARY PLAYSH HISH DRAGON AND DUNGEON GAME OUT HERE AND DOESHN'T LIKE ME TO COME OUT WHEN HISH FRIENDSH ARE OVER.
HOW DO YOU KNOW GARY?
HE PUT AN AD IN THE PAPER.
HE HASH A ROBOT.
A ROBOT?
I DON'T KNOW HOW TO TURN IT ON BUT MAYBE YOU DO.
PEPSI
OH... HA HA... THAT'S R2-D2. I THINK IT'S A SODA DISPLAY THINGY.
REALLY? WELL GARY DOESH DRINK A LOT OF SHODA.
I'LL GIVE YOU THE RESHT OF THE TOUR LATER. WE DON'T WANT TO KEEP DIANNE WAITING. LET ME GET MY CAR KEYSH...
WE CAN TAKE MY CAR.
I DON'T WANT TO TAKE YOURSH BECAUSH IT'SH THE SHARPE CRIME FAMILY CAR.
WE'LL TAKE MINE.
FINE.

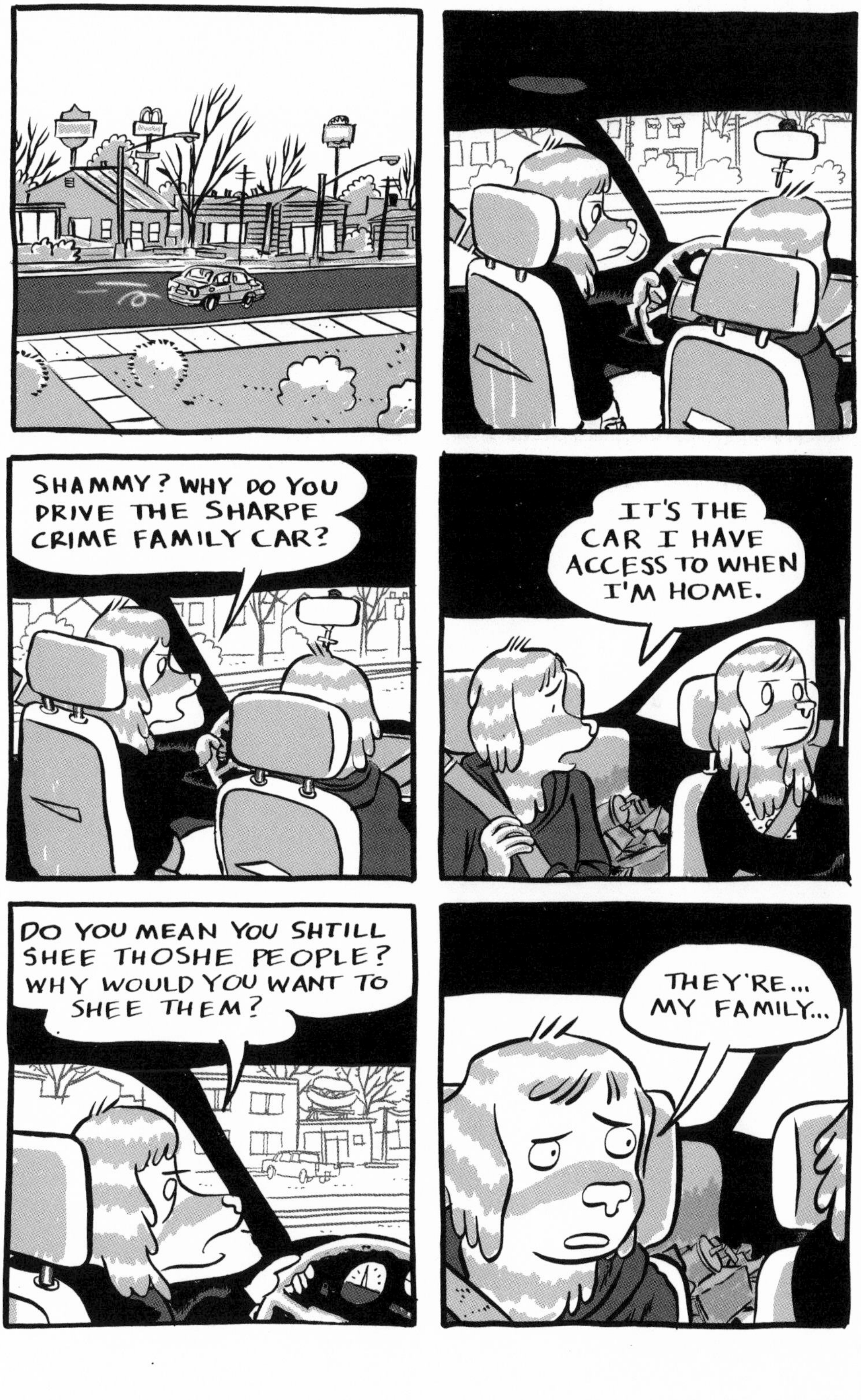
SHAMMY? WHY DO YOU DRIVE THE SHARPE CRIME FAMILY CAR?
IT'S THE CAR I HAVE ACCESS TO WHEN I'M HOME.
DO YOU MEAN YOU SHTILL SHEE THOSHE PEOPLE? WHY WOULD YOU WANT TO SHEE THEM?
THEY'RE... MY FAMILY...

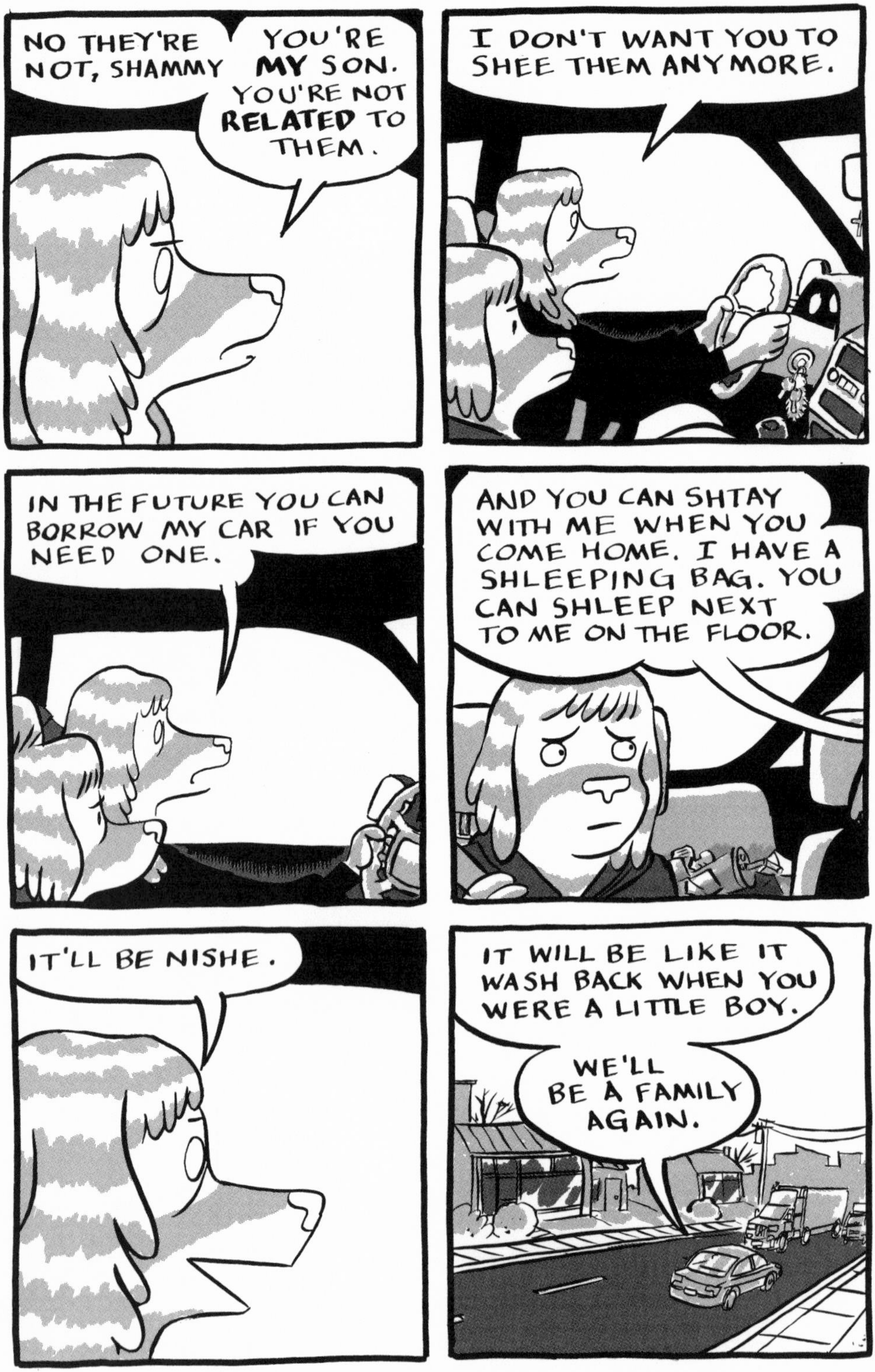
NO THEY'RE NOT, SHAMMY
YOU'RE MY SON. YOU'RE NOT RELATED TO THEM.
I DON'T WANT YOU TO SHEE THEM ANYMORE.
IN THE FUTURE YOU CAN BORROW MY CAR IF YOU NEED ONE.
AND YOU CAN SHTAY WITH ME WHEN YOU COME HOME. I HAVE A SHLEEPING BAG. YOU CAN SHLEEP NEXT TO ME ON THE FLOOR.
IT'LL BE NISHE.
IT WILL BE LIKE IT WASH BACK WHEN YOU WERE A LITTLE BOY.
WE'LL BE A FAMILY AGAIN.

August 1977

Nina Bunjevac

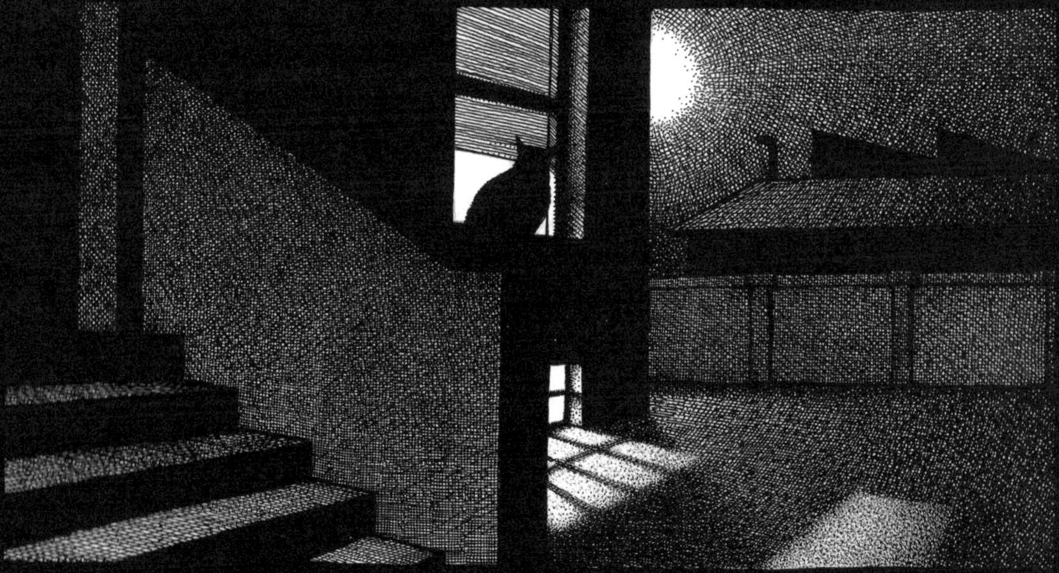

Dear husband, I have received the money you sent, it arrived just in time. The shipment of clothes arrived as well, though I was charged customs...

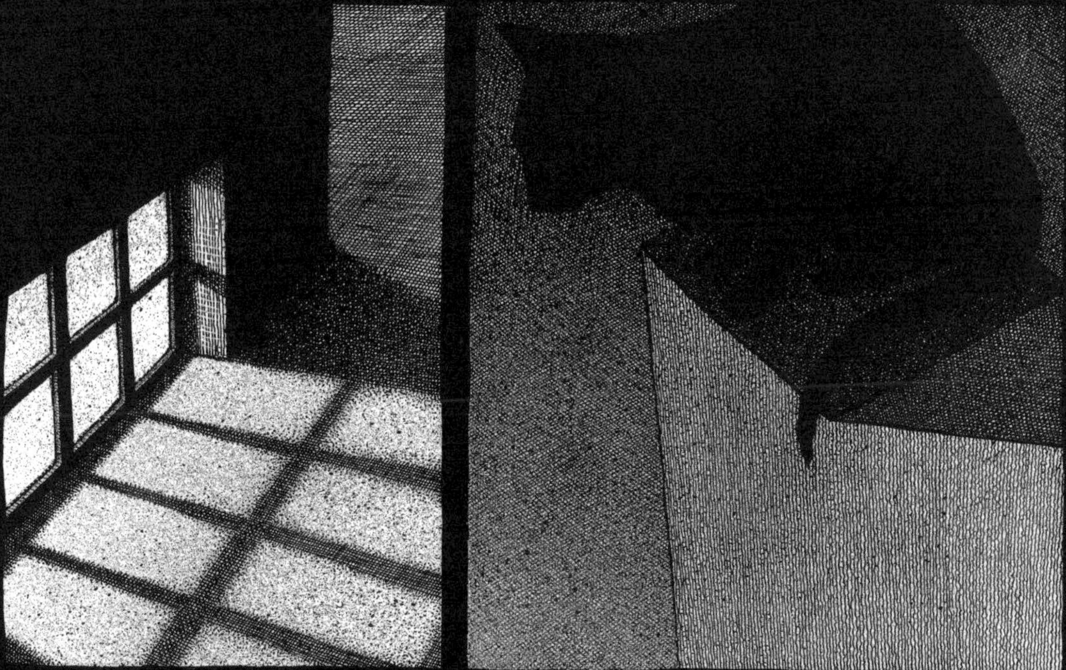

I can only imagine what will happen once the winter coats get here.

The little one is not in the best of health, neither am I.

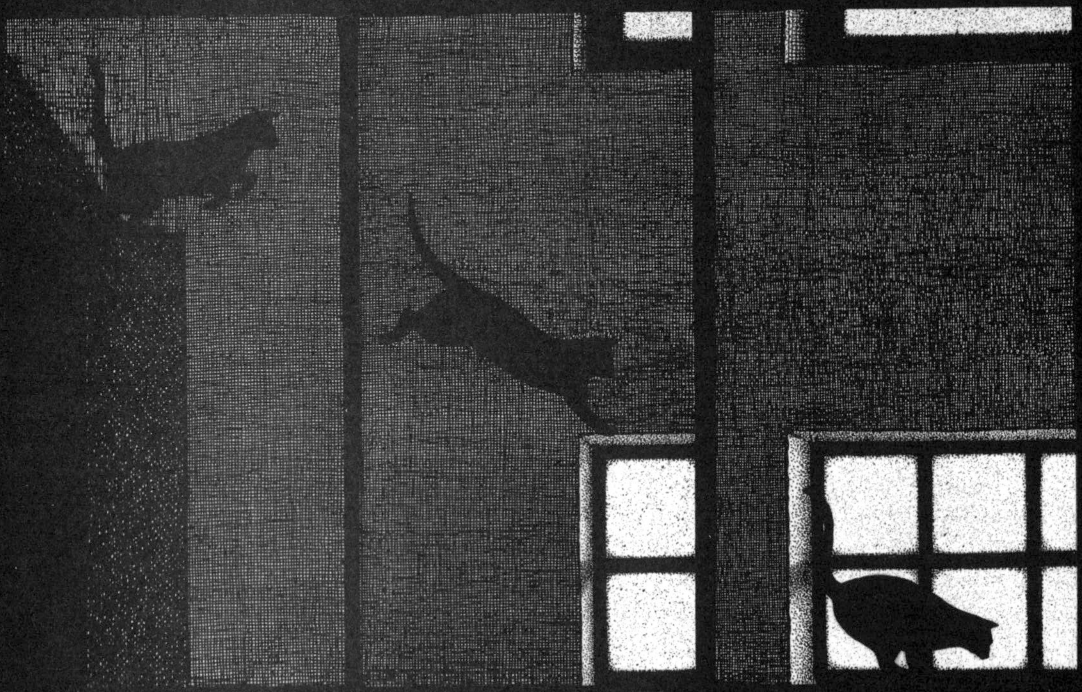

Doctor says it's due to the change of climate.

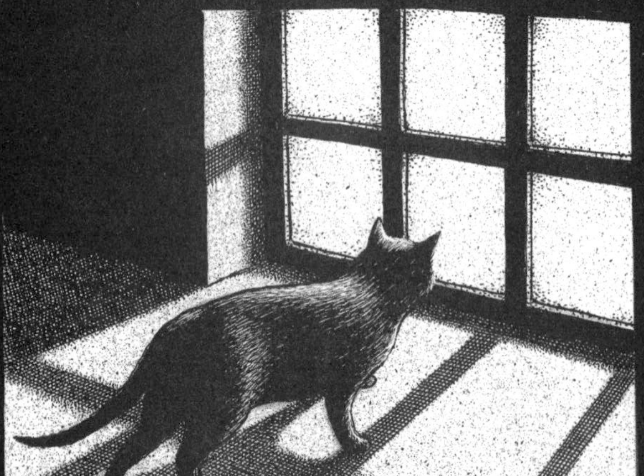

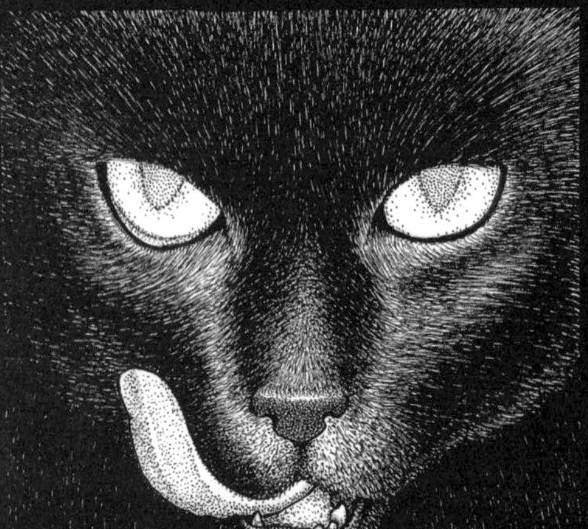

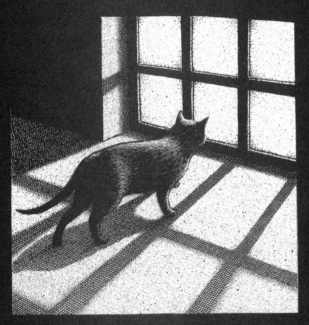

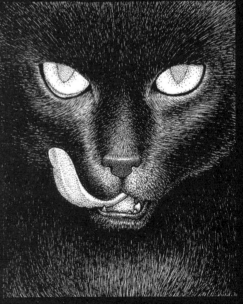

I took her to the doctor yesterday wrapped in blankets - she doesn't have a winter coat.

Did the boy get over his cold?

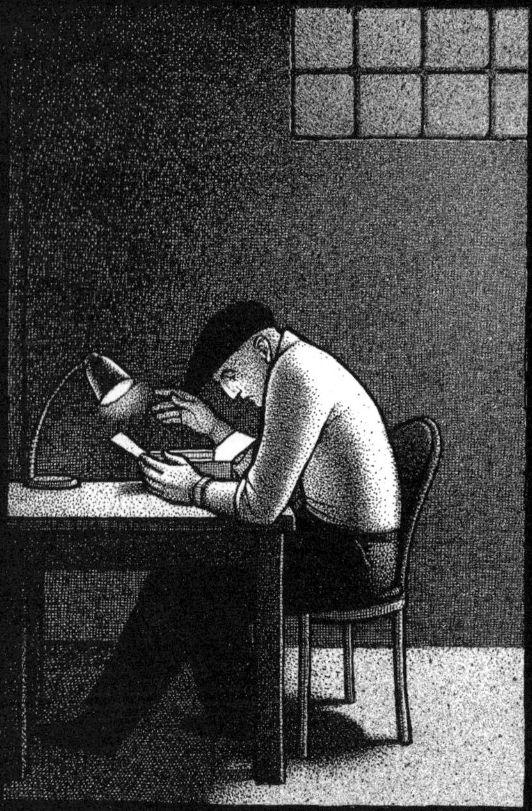

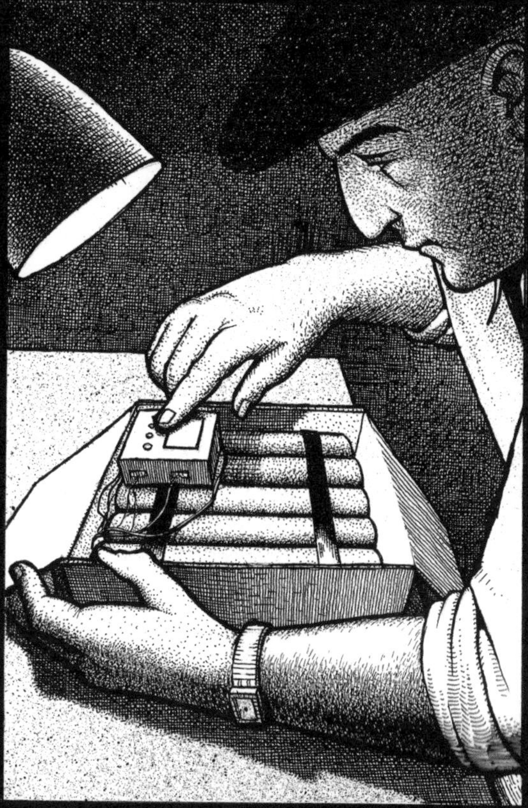

I got your last letter, and the one before that; the answer is still the same. I have had enough of your insults, have gotten sick of your attacks.

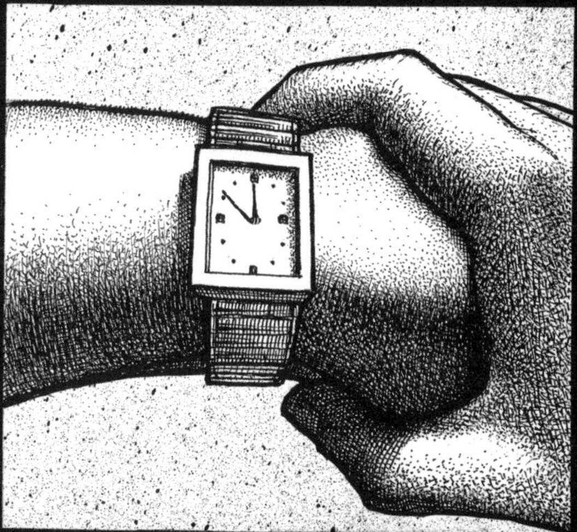

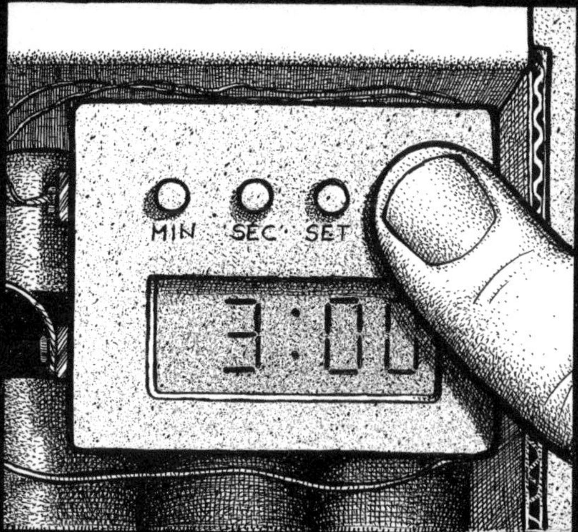
MIN
SEC
SET
3:00

Please try to understand, I need to be away from it all.

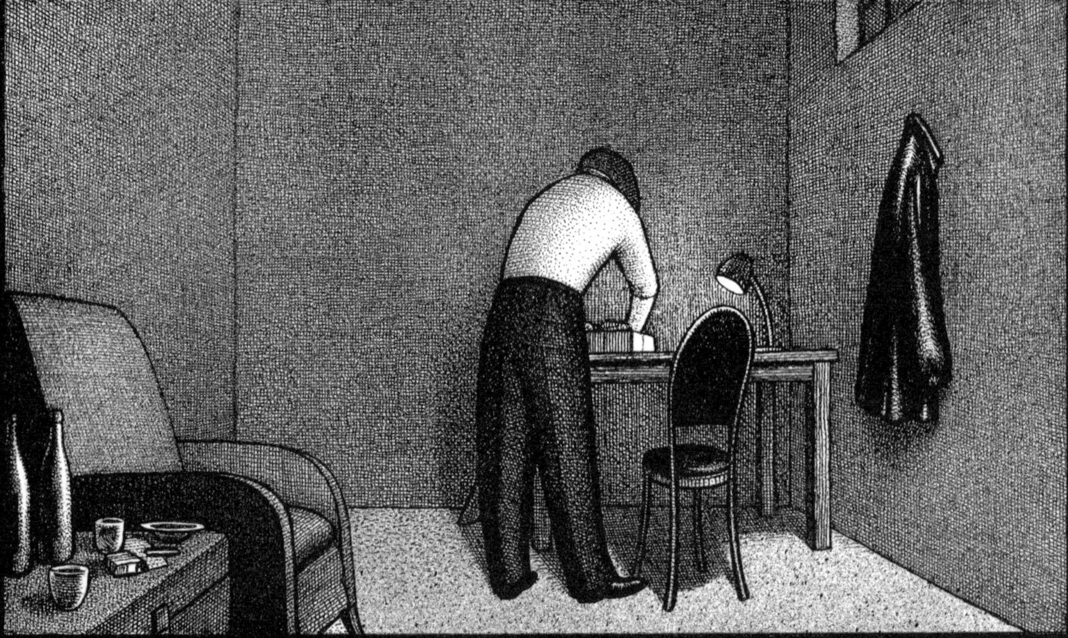

You know that I am an honourable woman, and that I will raise our daughter in the same way; whether or not you wish to make our life difficult is up to you.

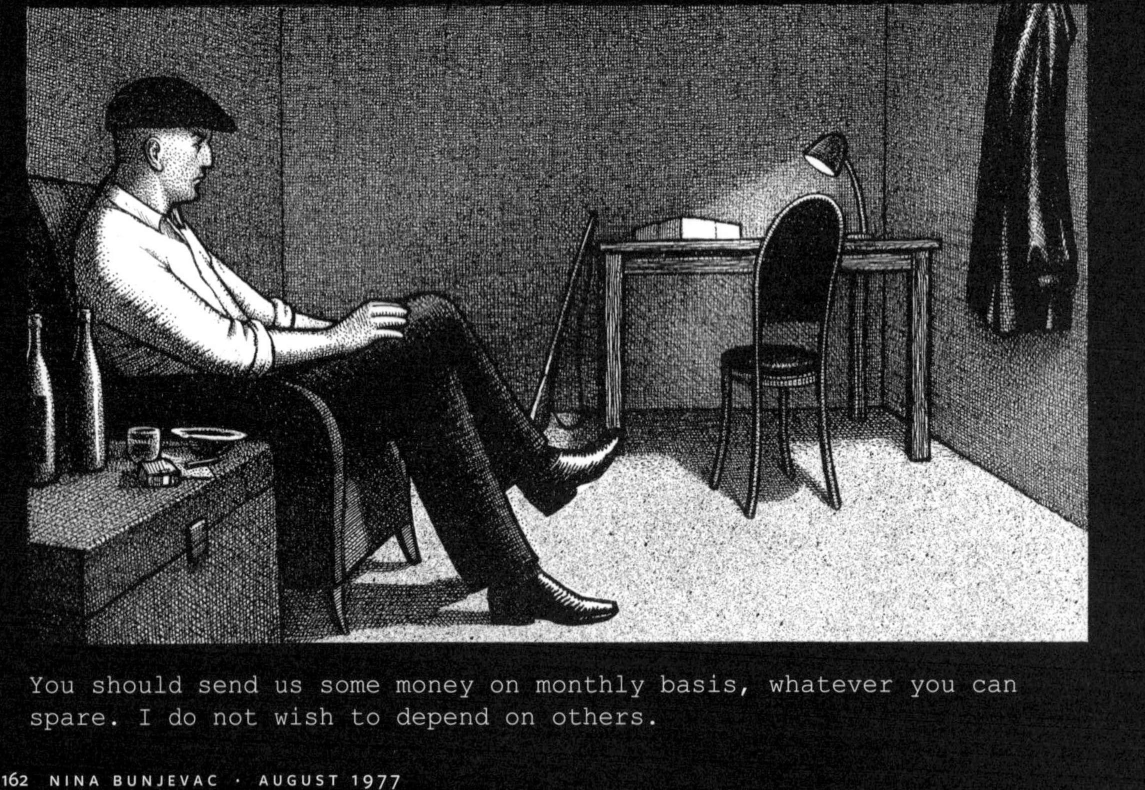

You should send us some money on monthly basis, whatever you can spare. I do not wish to depend on others.

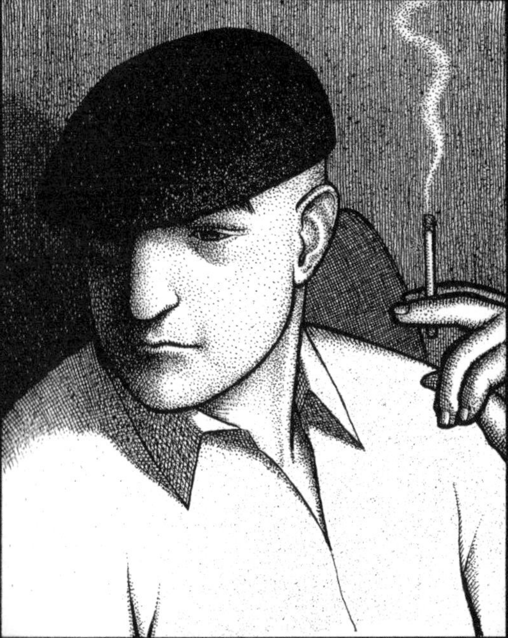

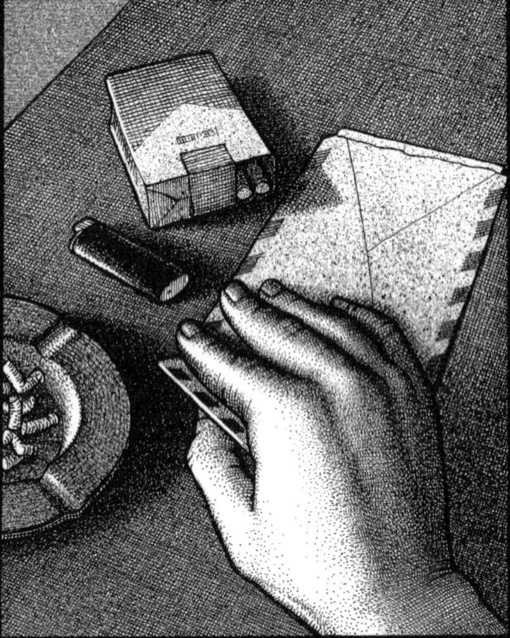

I swear on my life and lives of our children, the answer will not change. Do not hope in vain.
Kiss the boy and tell him that his mother loves him.

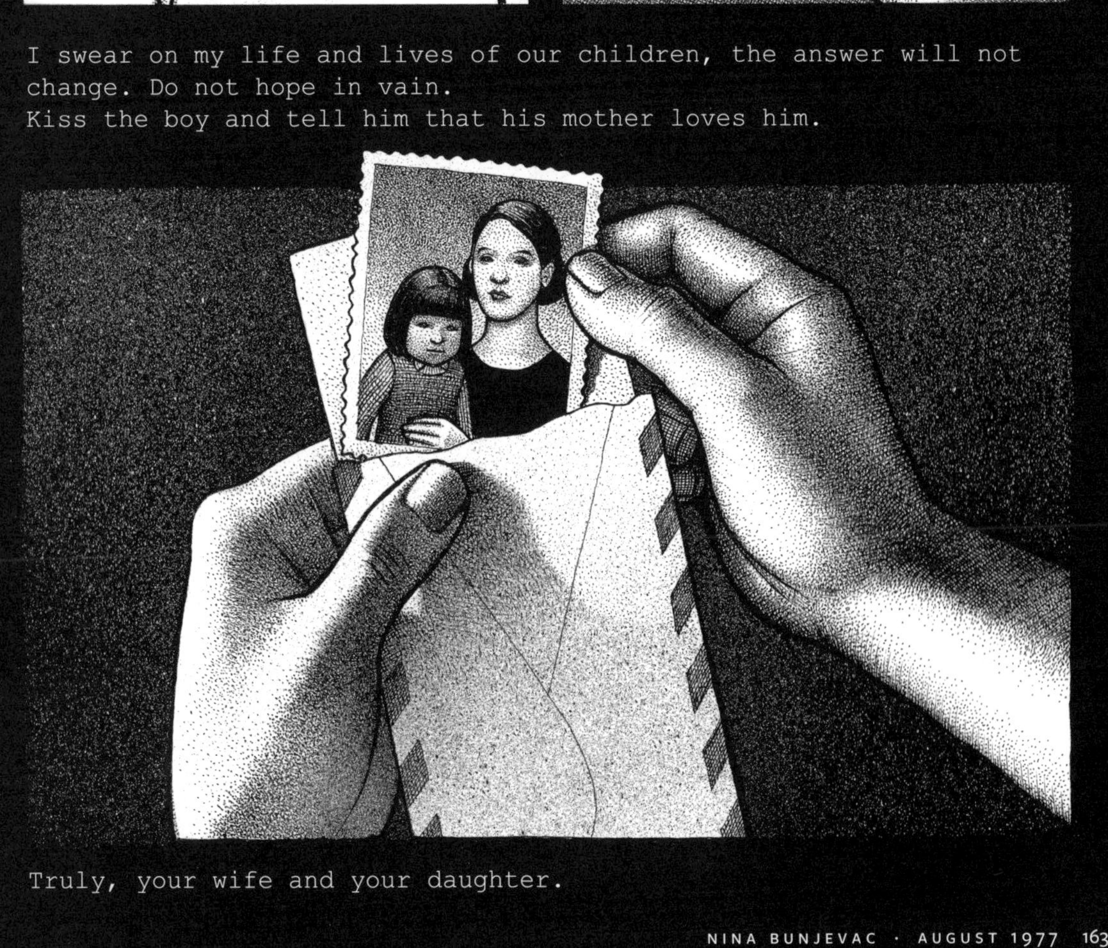

Truly, your wife and your daughter.

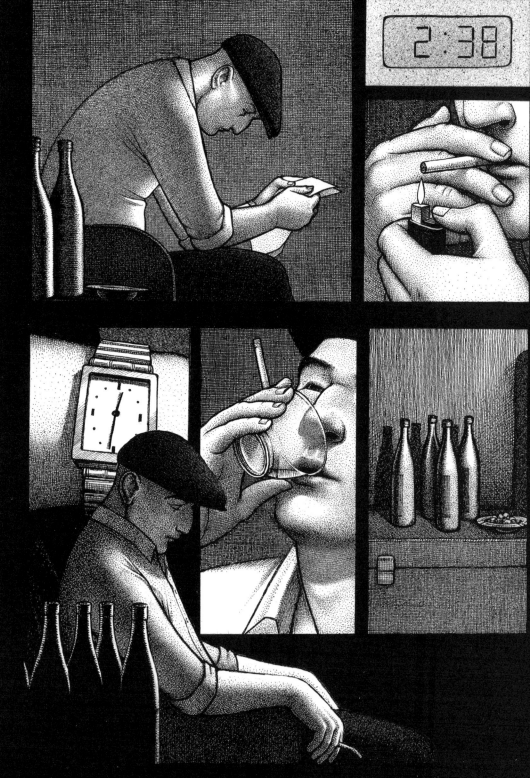

NINA BUNJEVAC · AUGUST 1977

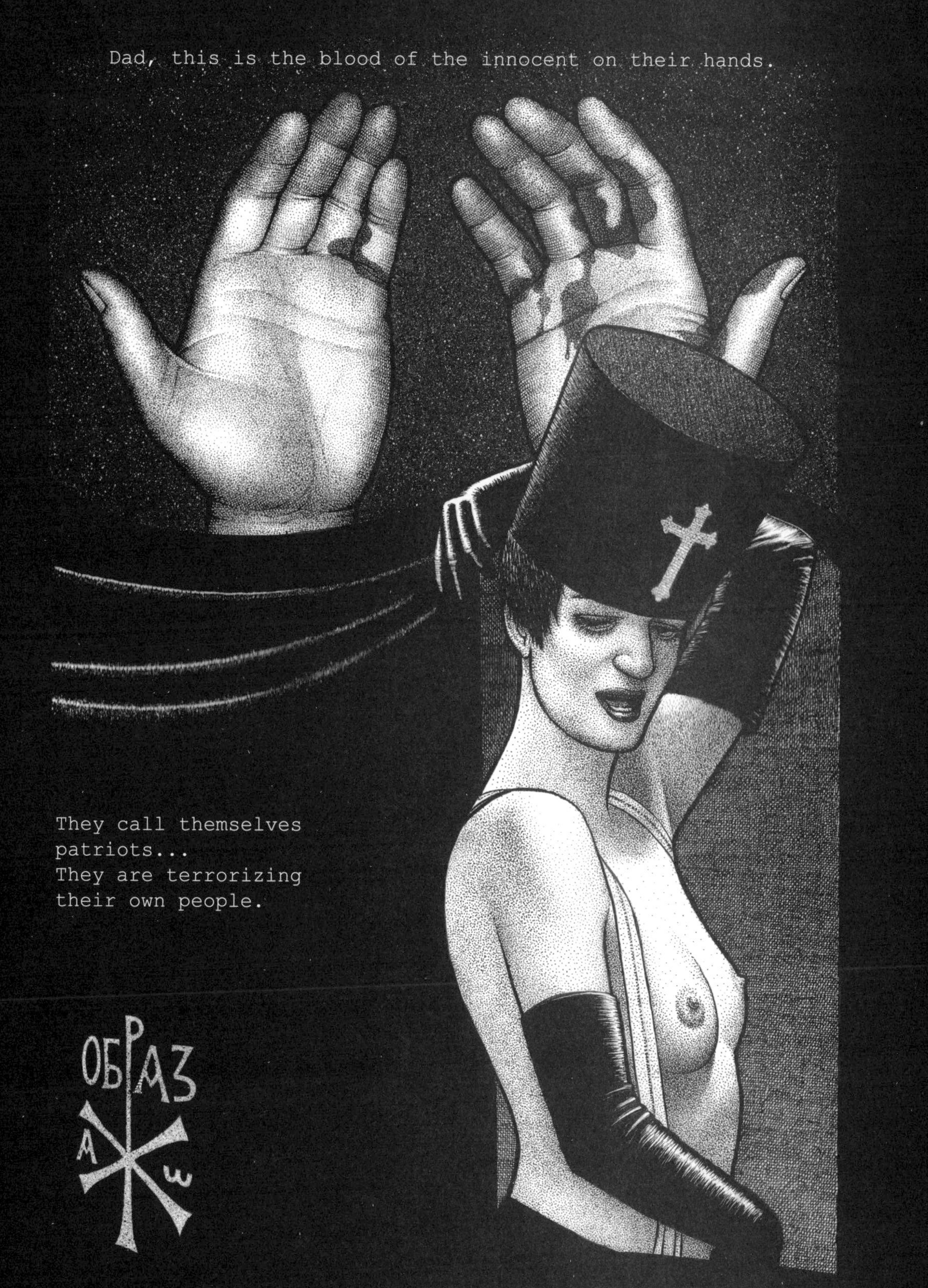
Dad, this is the blood of the innocent on their hands.
They call themselves patriots...
They are terrorizing their own people.
ОБРАЗ
А
ω

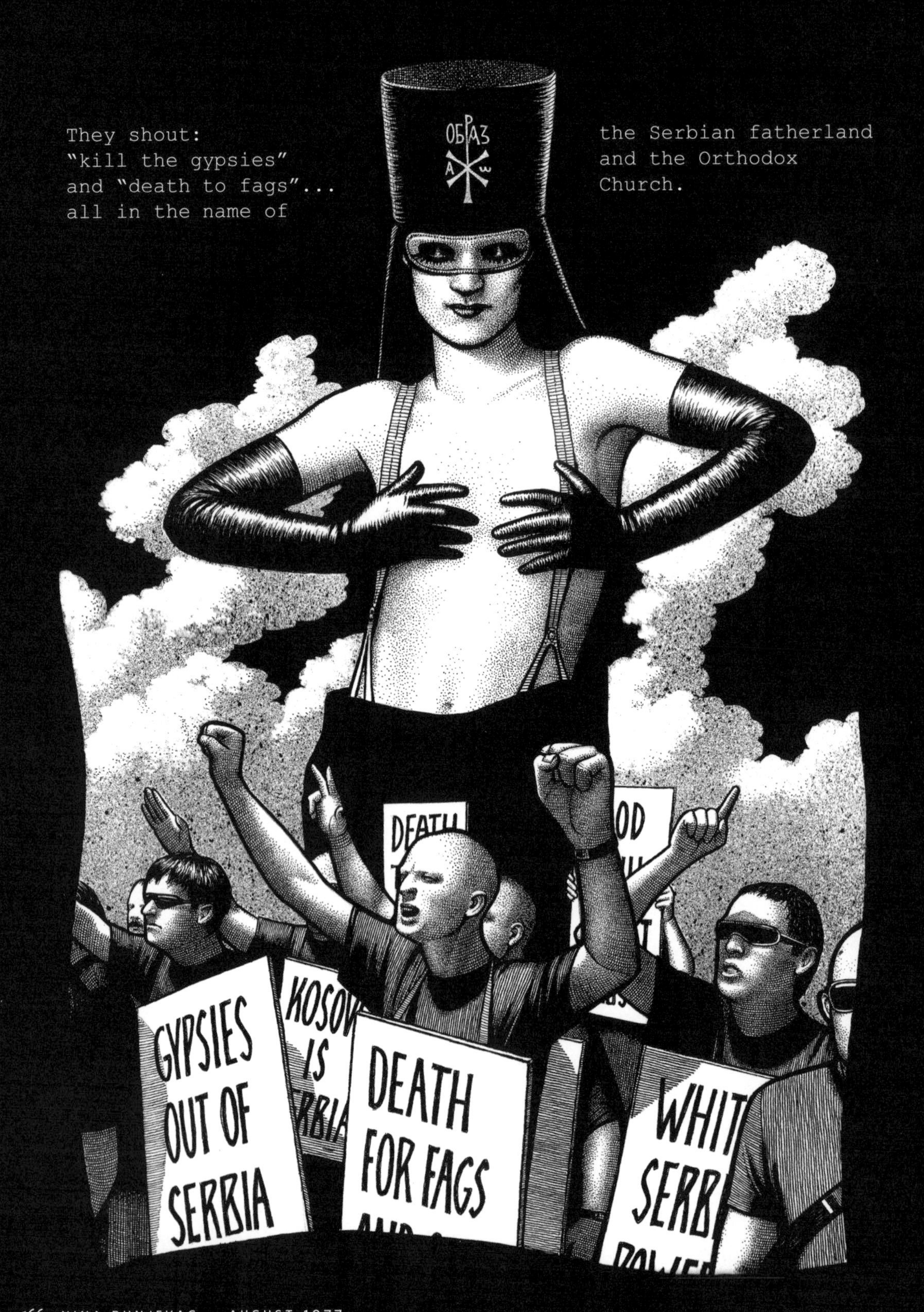
They shout:
"kill the gypsies"
and "death to fags"...
all in the name of
ОБРАЗ
the Serbian fatherland
and the Orthodox
Church.
GYPSIES OUT OF SERBIA
KOSOV
IS
RBIA
DEATH FOR FAGS
WHIT
SERB

The government is either helpless or chooses to stand aside;
the church preaches intolerance...

It keeps its people deaf, mute and blind.
Is this the future you fought and died for?

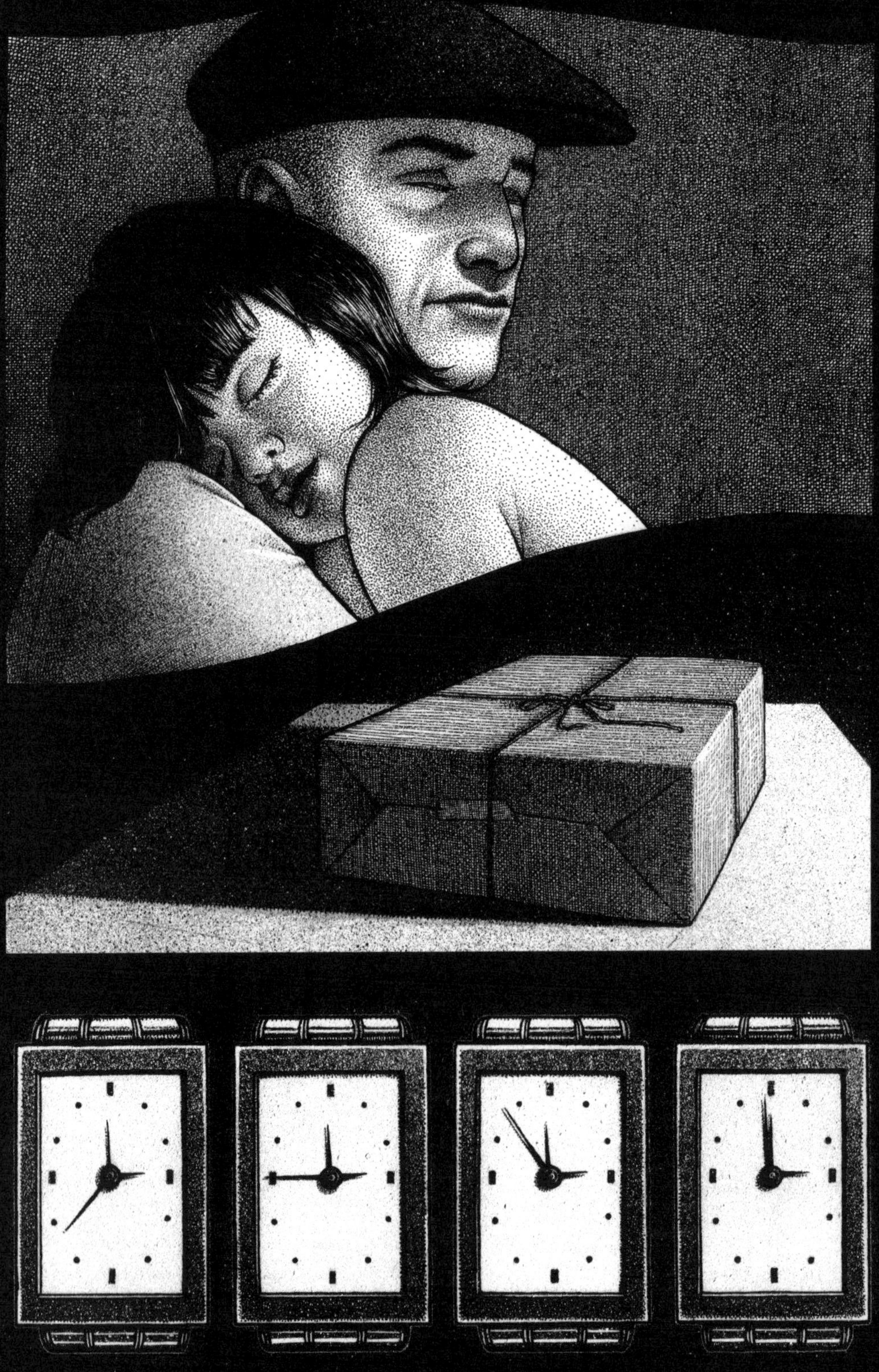

I have rejected your beliefs,
suppressed your rebellious spirit
and I found peace.
Your battles are not my battles
the chain stops here.

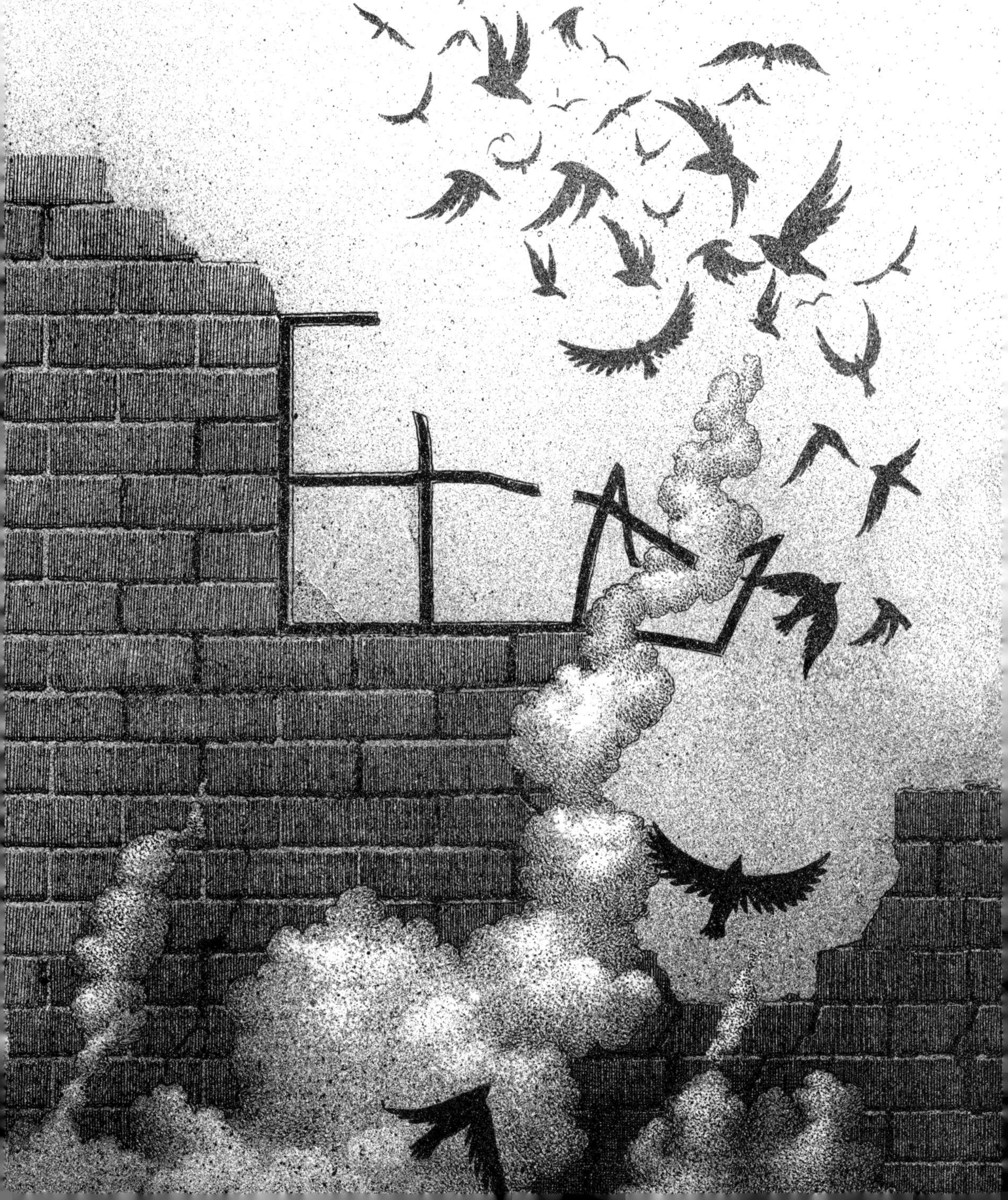

Strange Adventures

Many lifelong comics lovers in North America loved superhero comics as children, but became snooty and dismissive of them as they grew older. Not me. I was a different kind of fan. I was snooty and dismissive of superhero comics by the age of ten.

I read science fiction and fantasy novels. I read short stories. I read about the lives of microbiologists. Superhero comic books (the only species of comic I thought I knew, *Mad* magazine, somehow didn't count) were beneath me.

And it wasn't just the writing. I was also snooty about the artwork. By late in elementary school, I'd become obsessed with Surrealism. I loved Max Ernst and (of course) Salvador Dali. I used to make stilt-legged elephants out of modeling clay like the ones Dali painted, and decorate my bedroom with them. The crowded, boxed-off, crudely printed drawings in my friend Martin Manley's *Batman* comics just did not do it for me (although I was intrigued by the diagram on the back of one showing versions of popular superheroes from Earth One, Earth Two, and so forth; that seemed kinda cool).

Everything changed in middle school when I met a kid with thick brown glasses named Kurt Busiek. I don't know if we ever once had a class together, but we always met for lunch and quoted nerdy things at each other, mostly Monty Python routines and, later, bits from *The Goon Show*, which Kurt's family had episodes of on big reels of magnetic tape.

Most importantly for my purposes, Kurt played chess, which had become a full-time obsession for me by then. After school, Kurt would sometimes come over to my house and we'd play a game of chess on the back porch and a game of pool on our basement pool table. And it was during this time that Kurt shared his new obsession, comic books.

I can't stress this next part enough. Getting me into comic books was hard, really hard. Kurt had to practically force-feed me his favorite titles (*Daredevil* and *X-Men* for starters). I did not want to waste my time on those stupid comic books. This isn't one of those life-changing events that was bound to happen sooner or later, or that could've happened any number of ways. Almost any other kid would've given up, but Kurt didn't. In time, I started loving what I was reading, and here we are today; both of us have been making comics professionally now for over thirty years.

But despite loving them to death through most of high school, superheroes as a genre had lost a lot of its appeal for me by college in favor of other, more exotic flavors. Independent comics, small-press comics, European and Japanese comics, classic reprints, undergrounds, and the new American avant-garde movement spearheaded by Spiegelman and Mouly's groundbreaking *RAW* magazine—all seem to point to an art form rife with revolutionary new possibilities, far beyond that month's issue of *Sensational She-Hulk*.

Still, having learned my lesson the first time around, I didn't want to become snooty and dismissive all over again. I got that superhero comics were a legitimate genre, capable of accommodating great work, as a new generation, including Alan Moore and Kurt himself, would continue to demonstrate in the coming years. There weren't a lot of them that floated my boat, but that didn't mean I couldn't fall in love again.

One of the most lovable superhero comics in a long time has to be Marvel Comics' *Hawkeye*, featuring the long-running second-string Avenger, recently given a boost by some movie you and I might have seen once or twice. *Hawkeye* stands out as first rate, even in the broadening field of contemporary adventure comics. The title's fantastic artist David Aja is up to something both grounded and agile; I don't know if I've seen anything quite like it. And Matt Fraction's scripts crackle with nervous energy, but always seem to land in a place of warmth and vulnerability. We weren't able to include a selection from *Hawkeye* here for reasons beyond our control, but it's the Best American Superhero Comic of 2014 and leaves me hopeful for the genre. Track down an issue and tuck it between pages 172 and 173 of this volume for best results.

Some notes on the entries in this section:

There's a refreshingly humanist tone running through a lot of modern adventure-oriented comics, and there's no better poster boy for the trend than Brian K. Vaughan, the creator, along with artist Fiona Staples, of *Saga*. For all its fantasy and science fiction trappings, this one's all about the characters. Even the title's most bizarre and terrifying creatures (Staples has a wicked imagination!) still have to drag themselves out of bed in the morning and brush their teeth.

Sailor Twain was one of my top-five favorite books last year, but beyond that I can't say much because Mark Siegel is my editor on a 484-page graphic novel we're wrapping up and I'll only be accused of brown-nosing. But really, seriously—loved it like a baby koala.

If there's one artist who best captures the North American comics zeitgeist here in 2014, it would have to be Brandon Graham. Take every comic book, graphic novel, kids' comic, porno comic, translated *manga*, minicomic, and airline safety card in North America, put them in a gigantic blender and run it for ten days straight. The resulting smoothie—glistening pink and silver in its enormous molded glass cup, like a colossal Erté squid sculpture—would be Brandon Graham.

Finally, props to Ted May, whose little black-and-white vignette "Dimensions" from his comic book *Men's Feelings* made me laugh out loud. I had no idea where else to put it, so here it is. Even here on the Island of Misfit Toys, the thing is beyond categorization, although it is "strange," at least, so I guess that'll have to do.

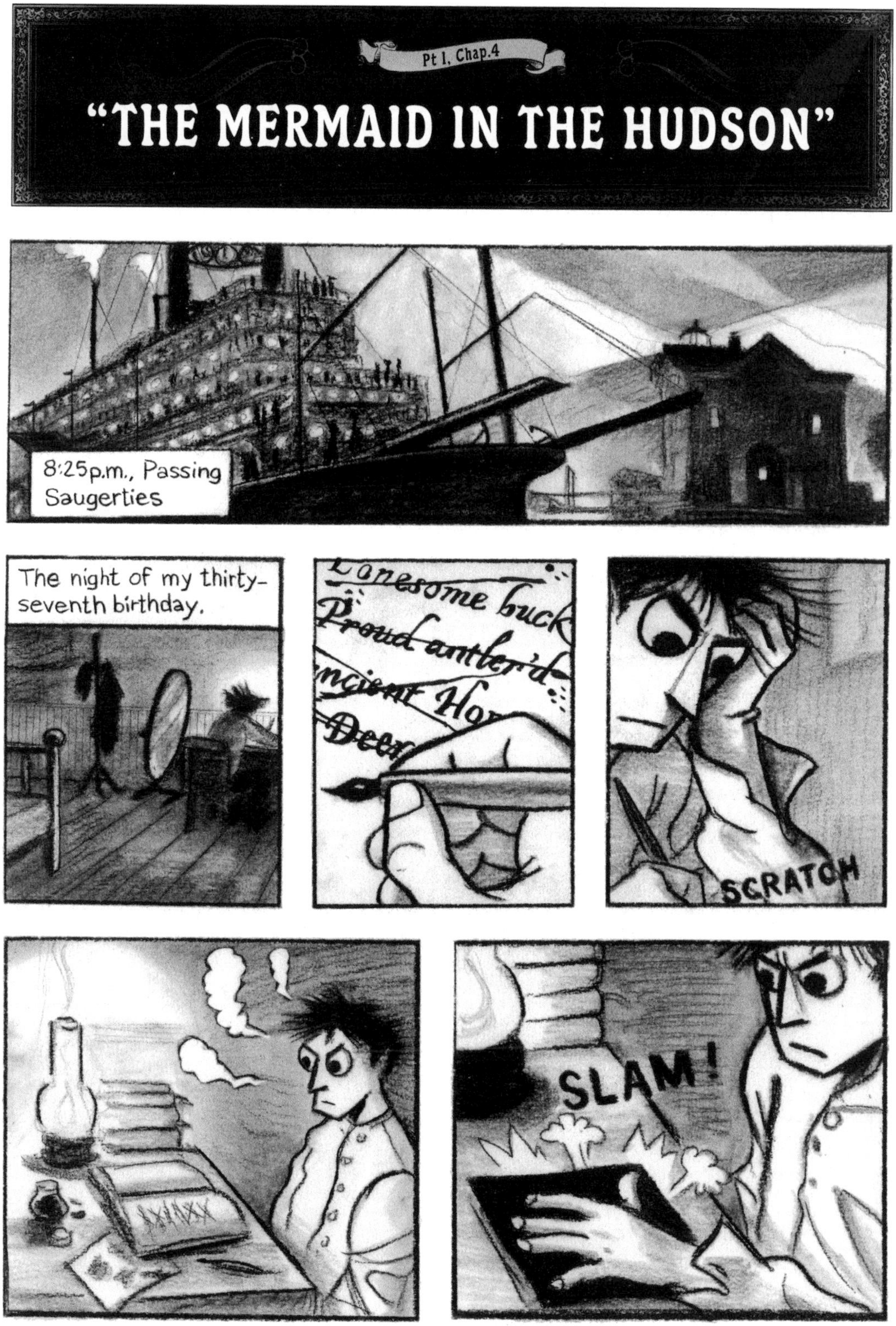
Pt I, Chap.4
"THE MERMAID IN THE HUDSON"
8:25p.m., Passing Saugerties
The night of my thirty-seventh birthday.
Lonesome buck
Proud antler'd
SCRATCH
SLAM!

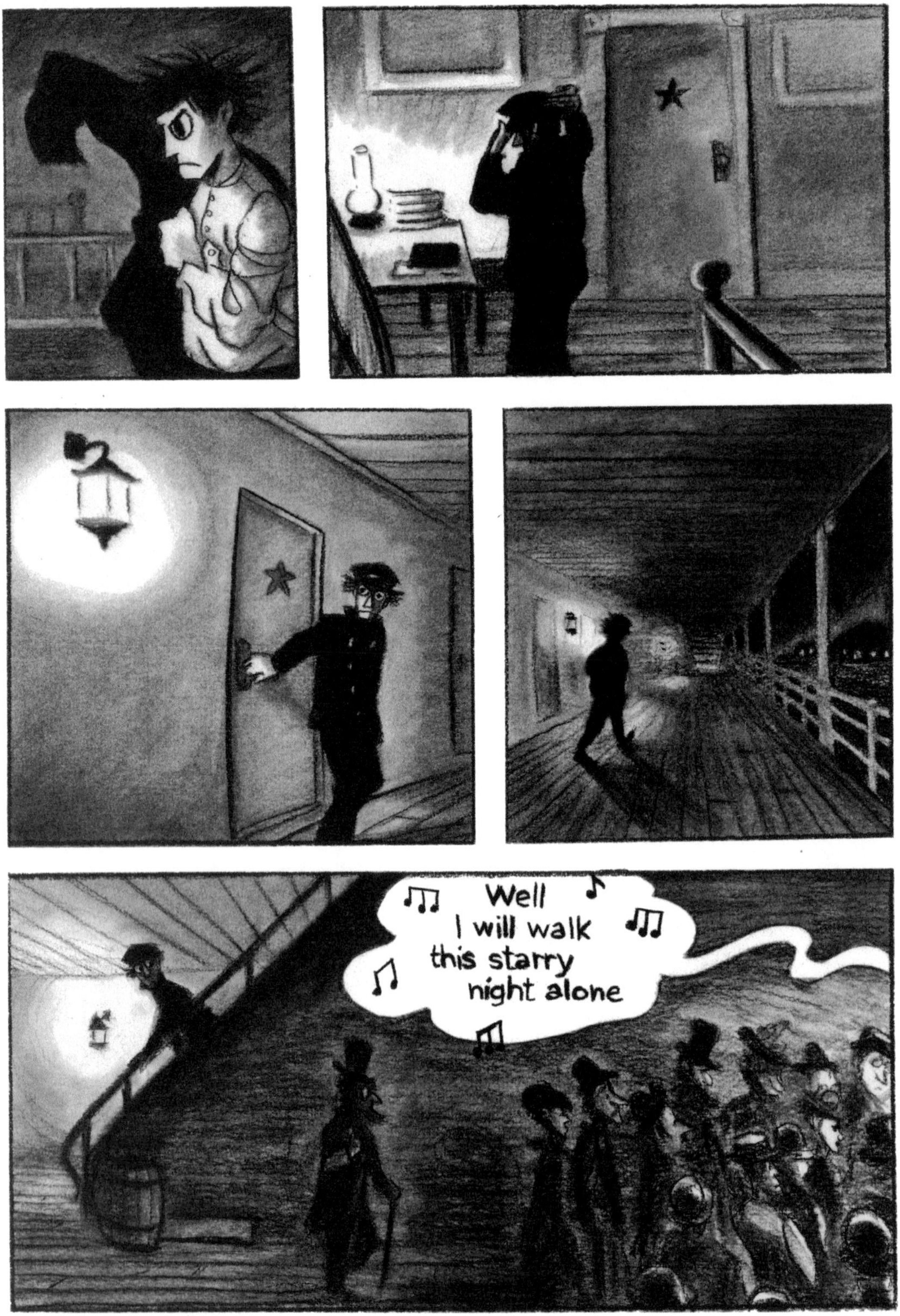
Well I will walk this starry night alone

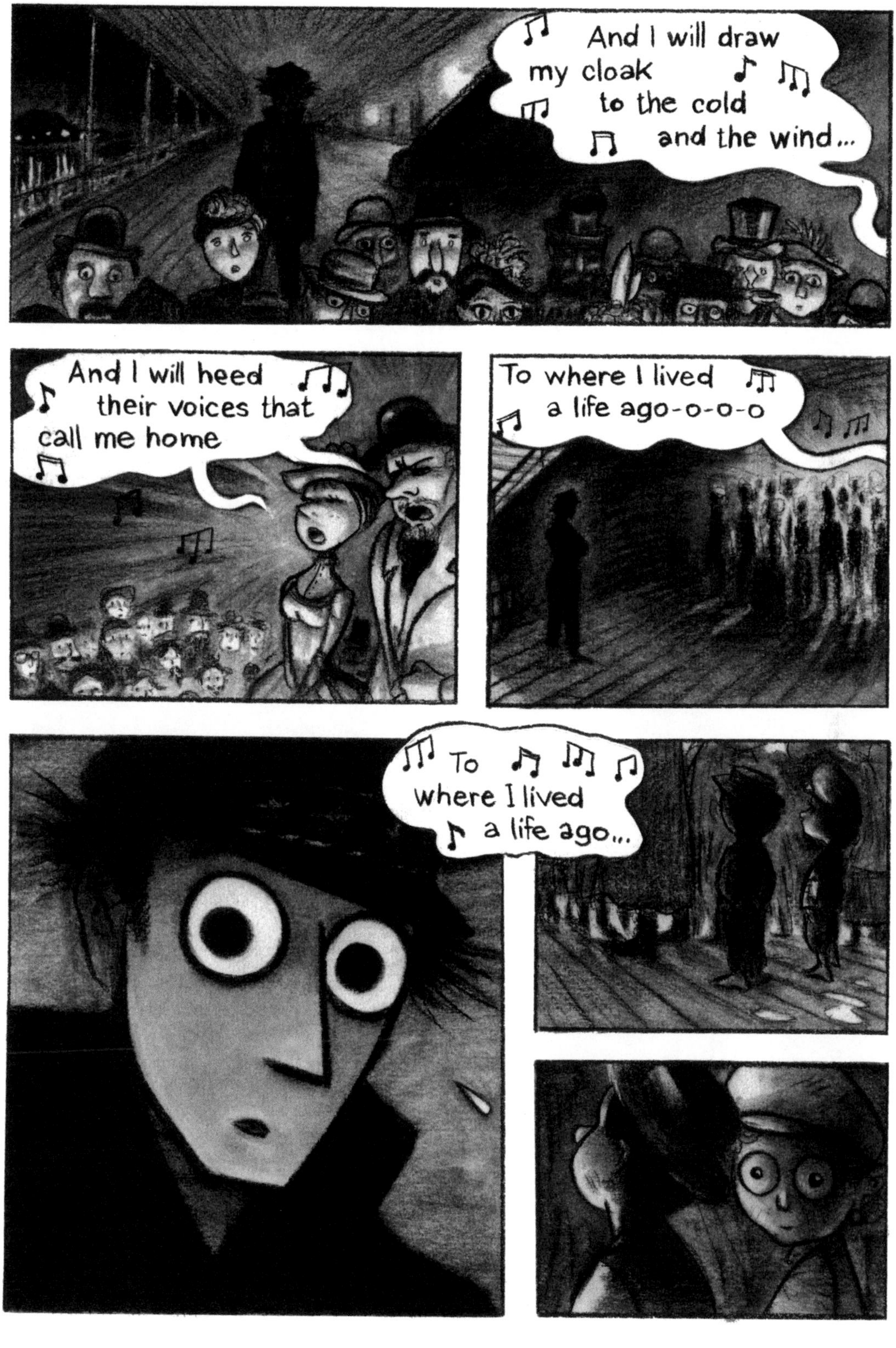

And I will draw my cloak to the cold and the wind...
And I will heed their voices that call me home
To where I lived a life ago-o-o-o
To where I lived a life ago...

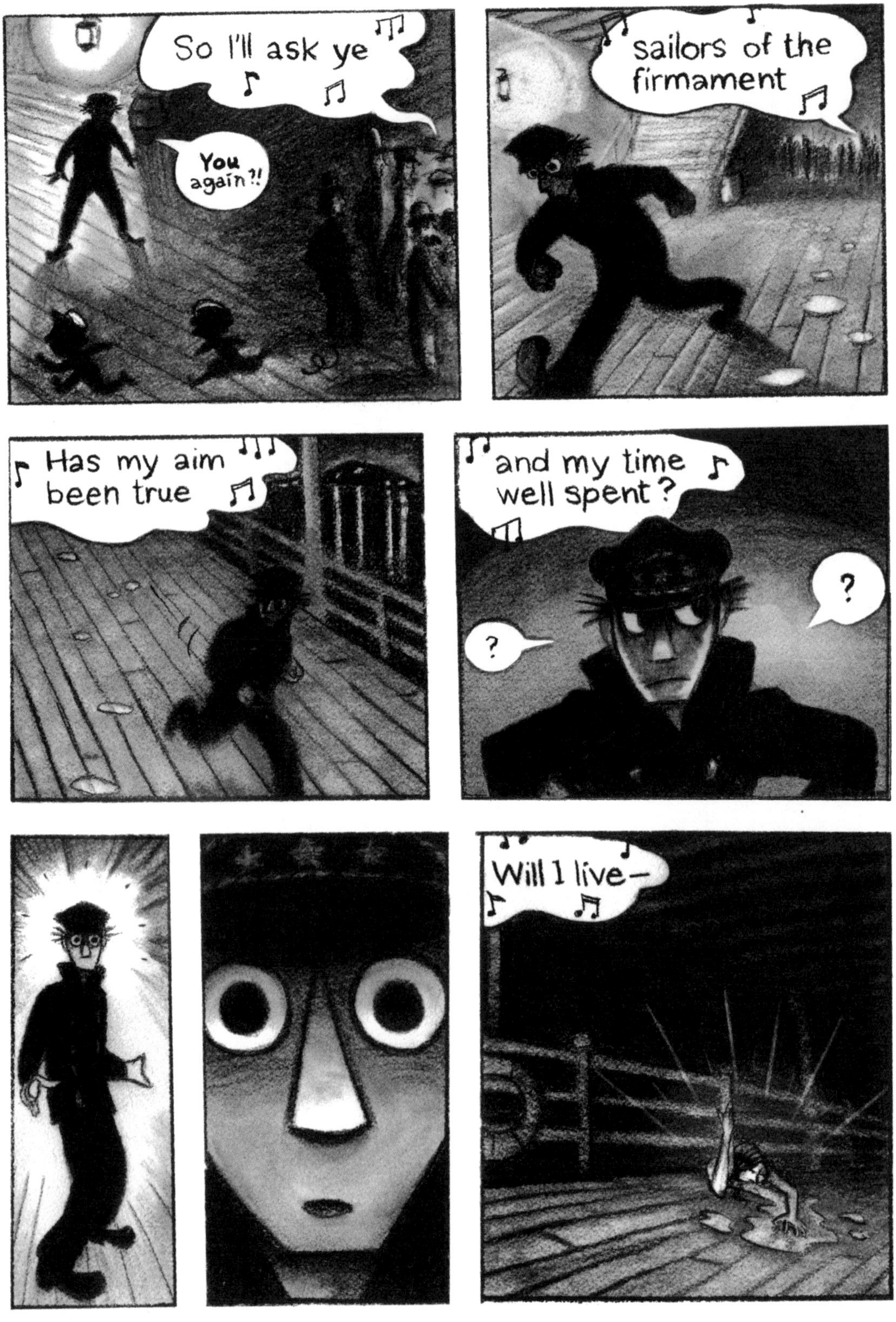
So I'll ask ye
You again?!
sailors of the firmament
Has my aim been true
and my time well spent?
?
?
Will I live–

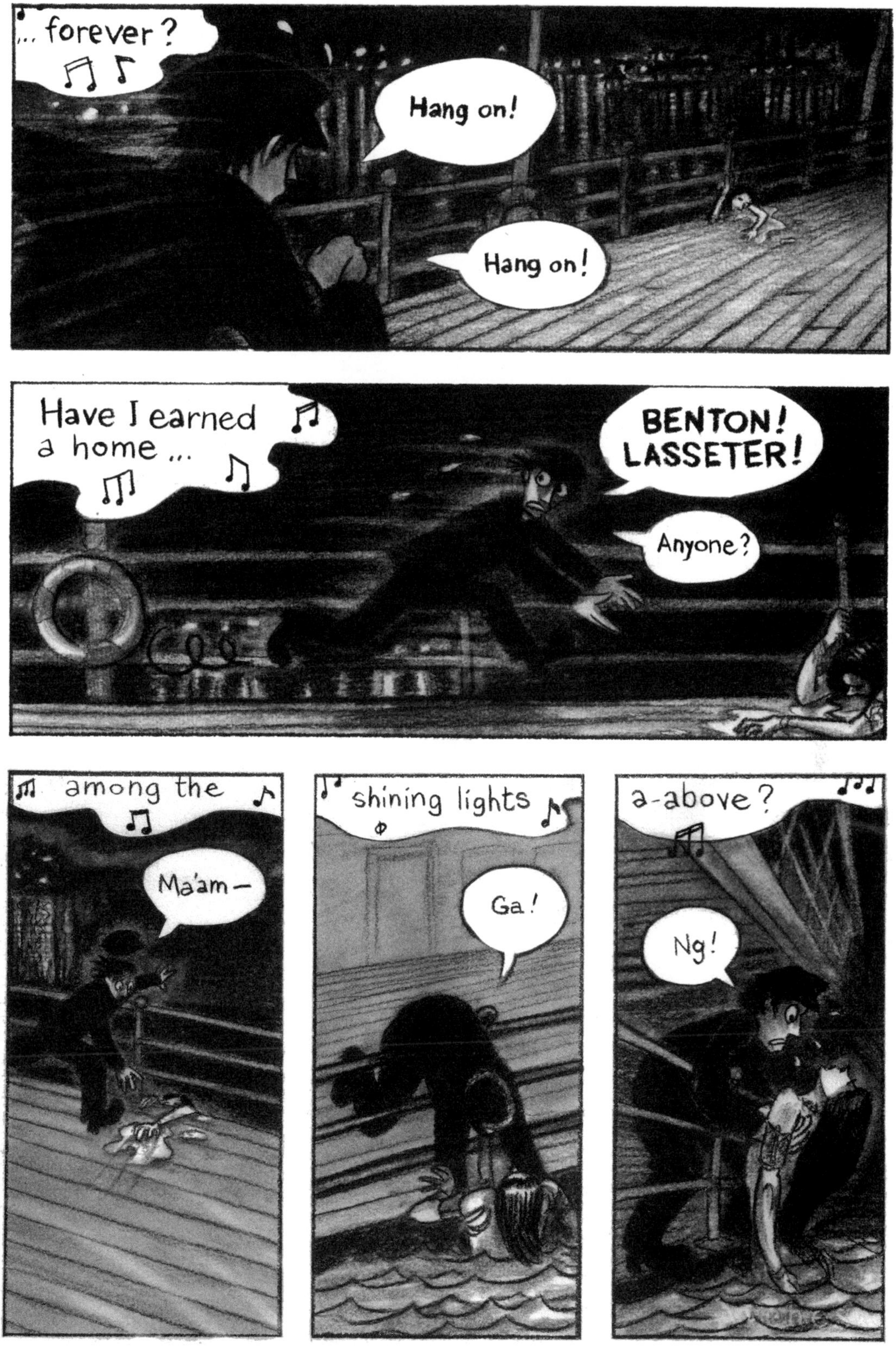
... forever?
Hang on!
Hang on!
Have I earned a home ...
BENTON! LASSETER!
Anyone?
among the
Ma'am—
shining lights
Ga!
a-above?
Ng!

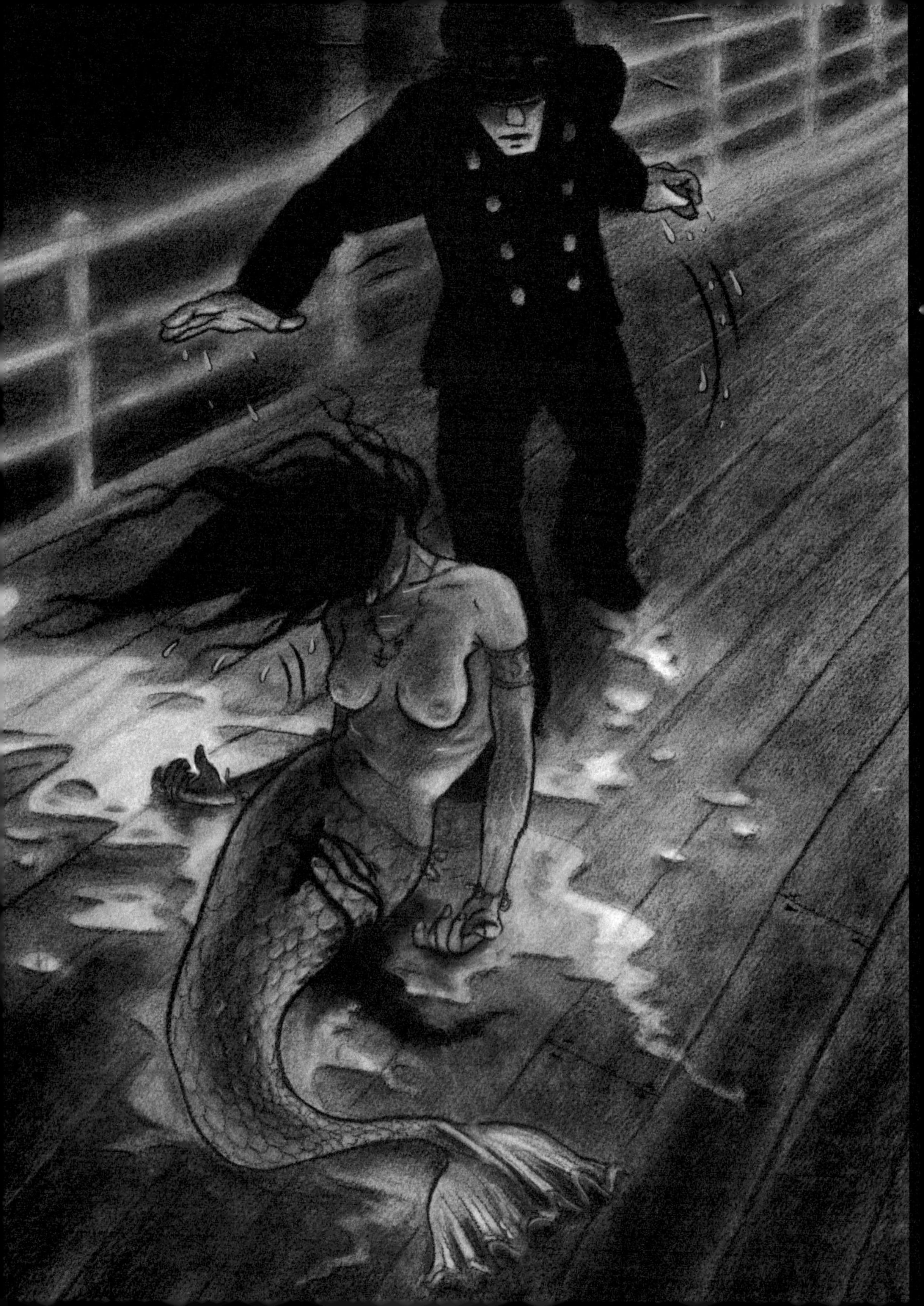

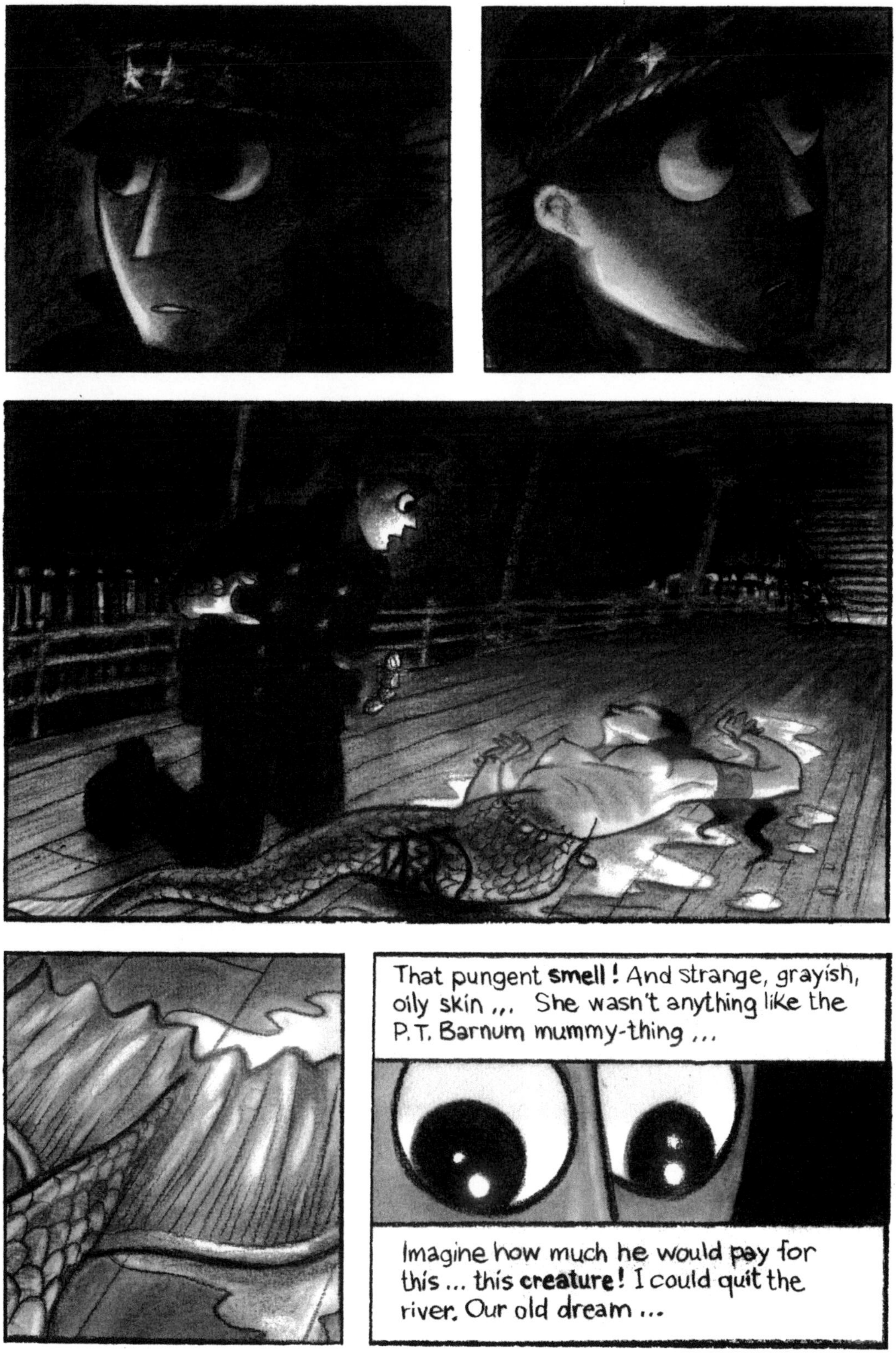
That pungent **smell**! And strange, grayish, oily skin ,,. She wasn't anything like the P. T. Barnum mummy-thing ...
Imagine how much he would pay for this ... this **creature**! I could quit the river. Our old dream ...

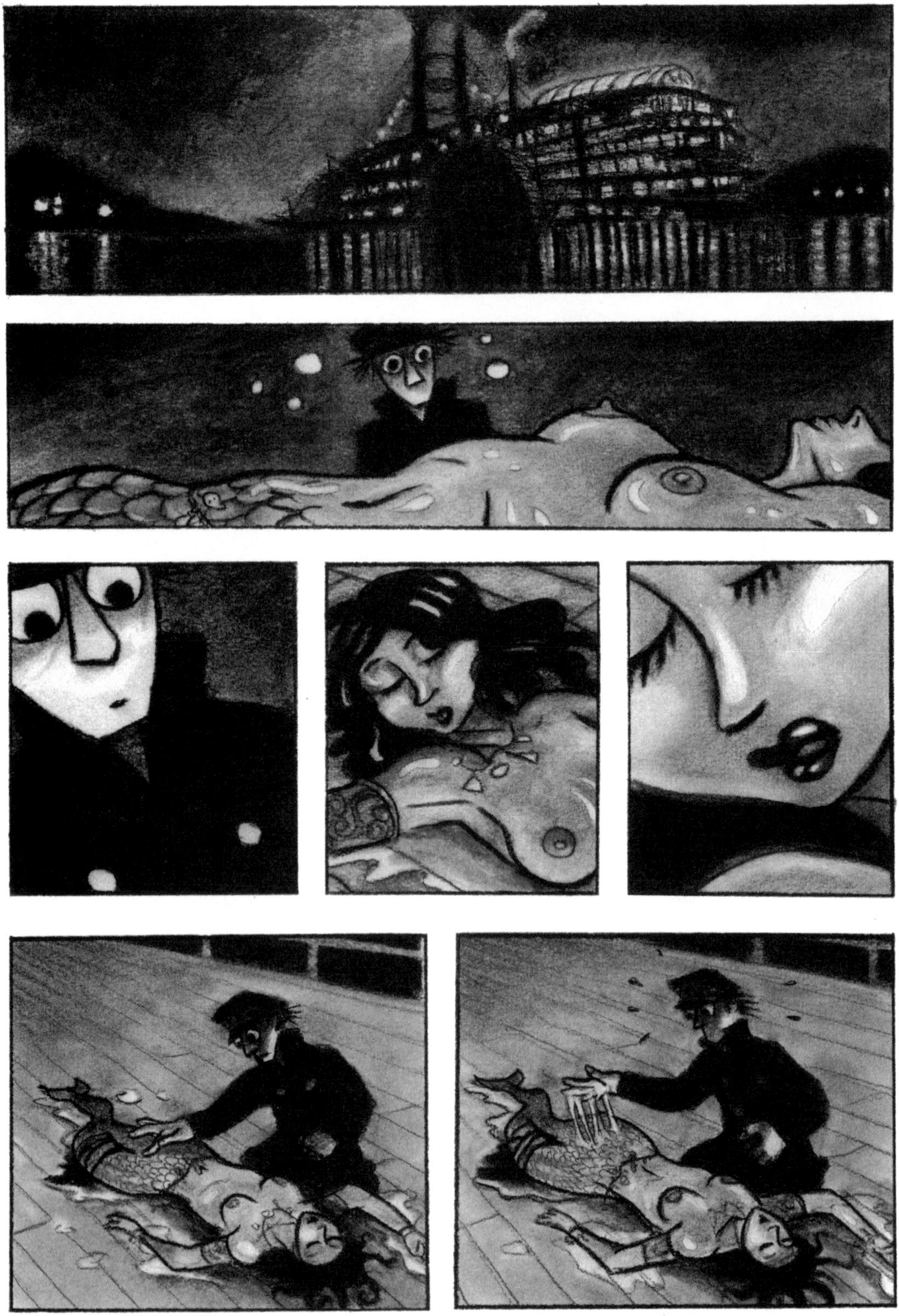

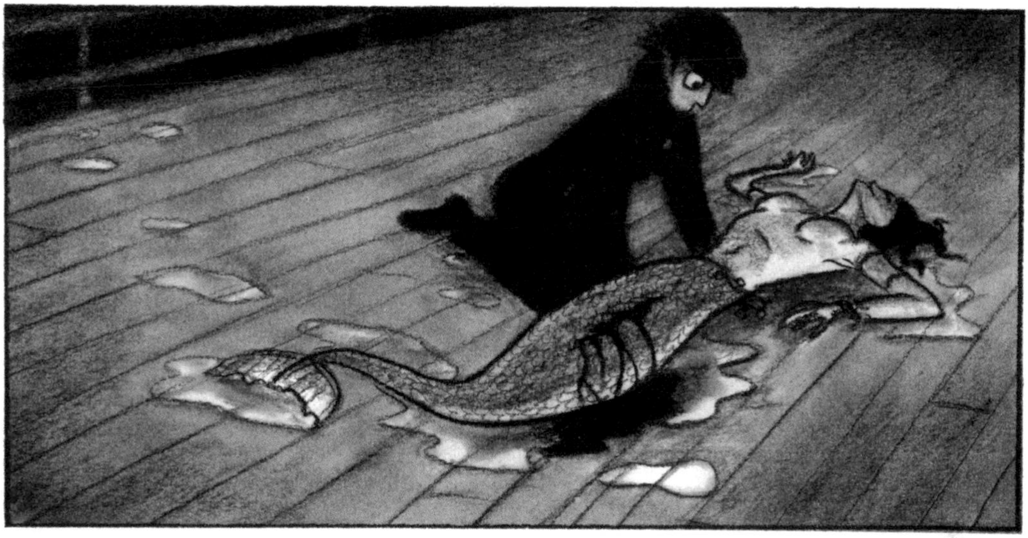

It was hurt. Maybe dying. Get the officers. Lafayette. And Doc Sycamore.

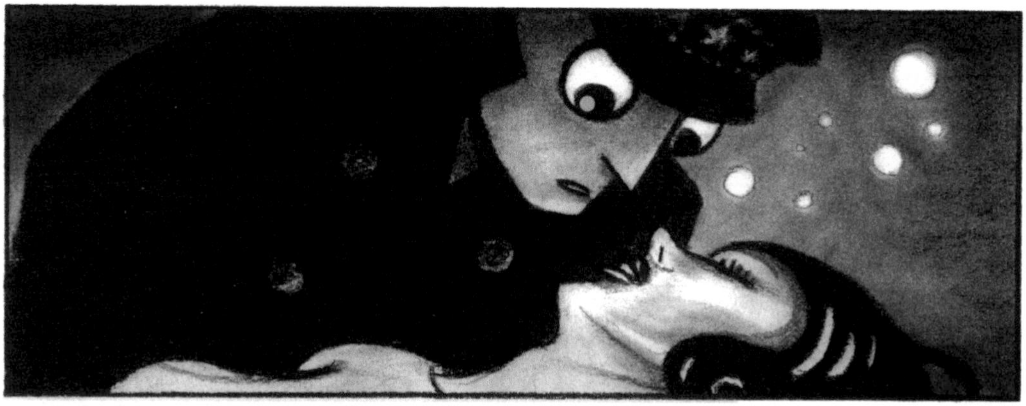

I felt dizzy and strange and a little sick. I wanted to throw the wounded thing back in the water, when suddenly—

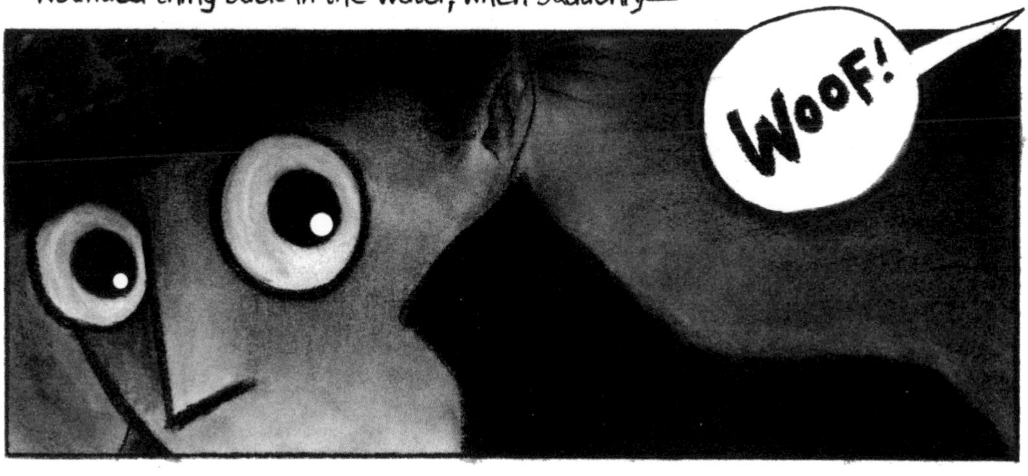
WOOF!

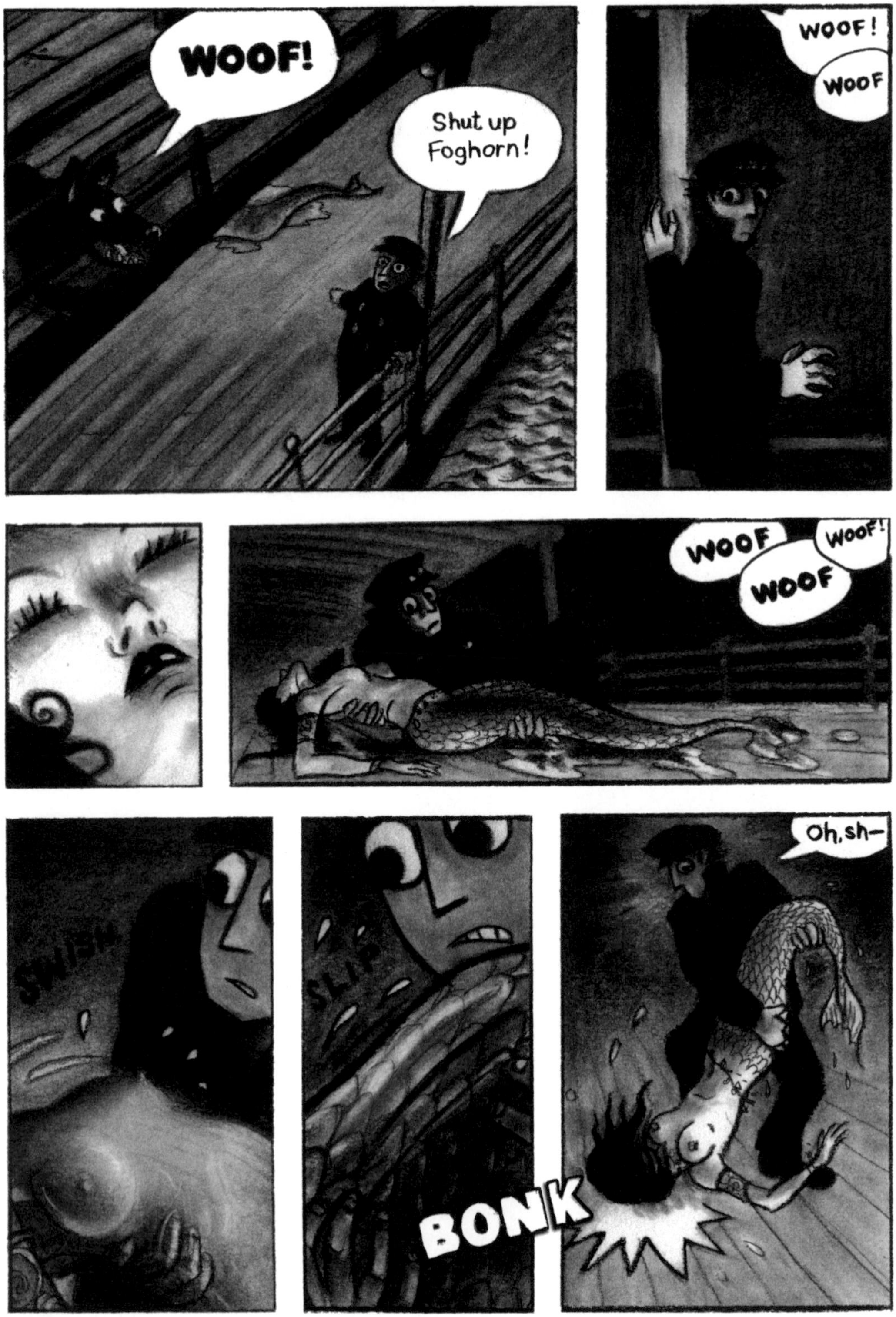
WOOF!
Shut up Foghorn!
WOOF!
WOOF
WOOF
WOOF!
WOOF
SWISH
SLIP
Oh, sh—
BONK

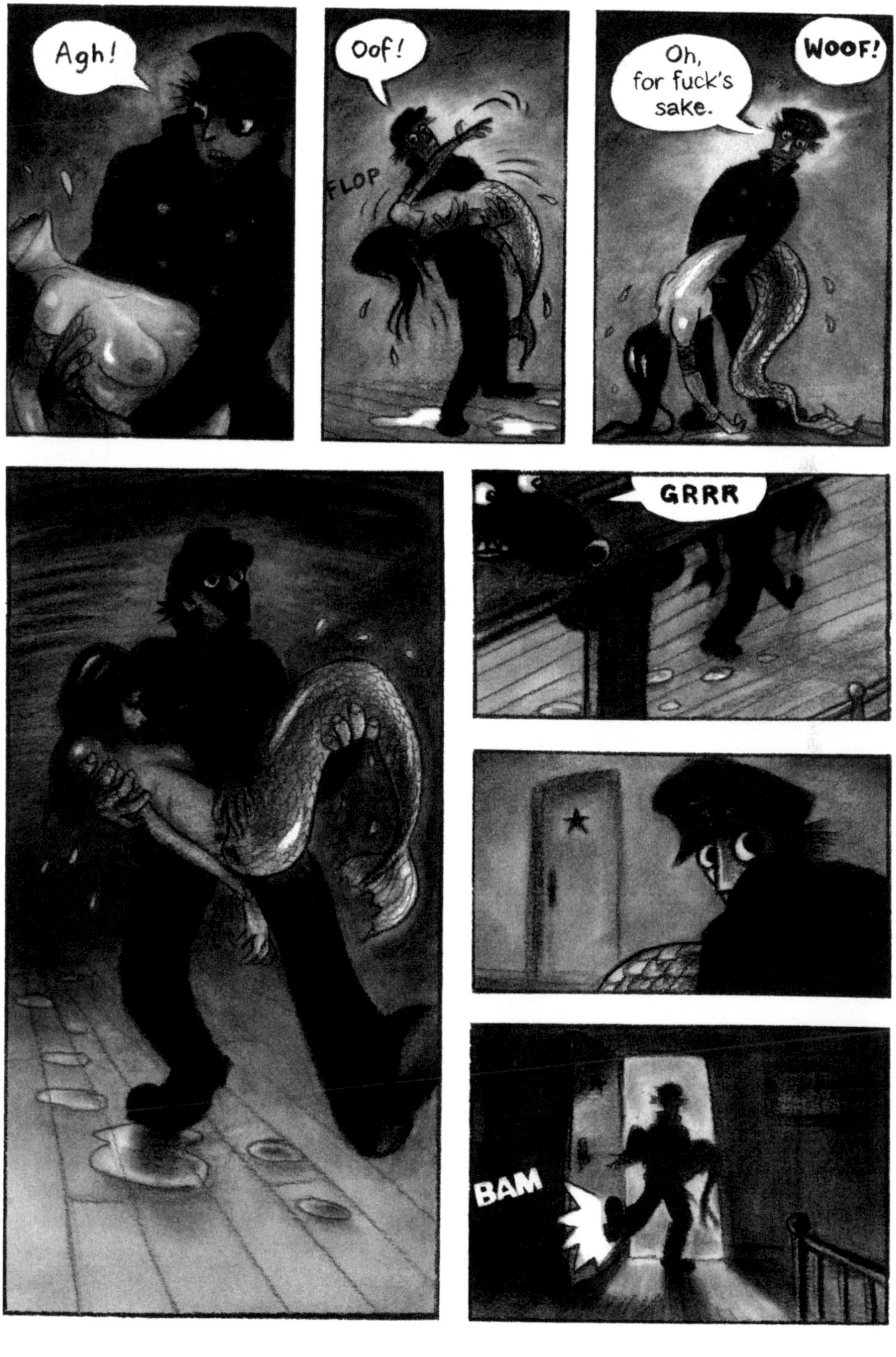
Agh!
Oof!
FLOP
Oh, for fuck's sake.
WOOF!
GRRR
BAM

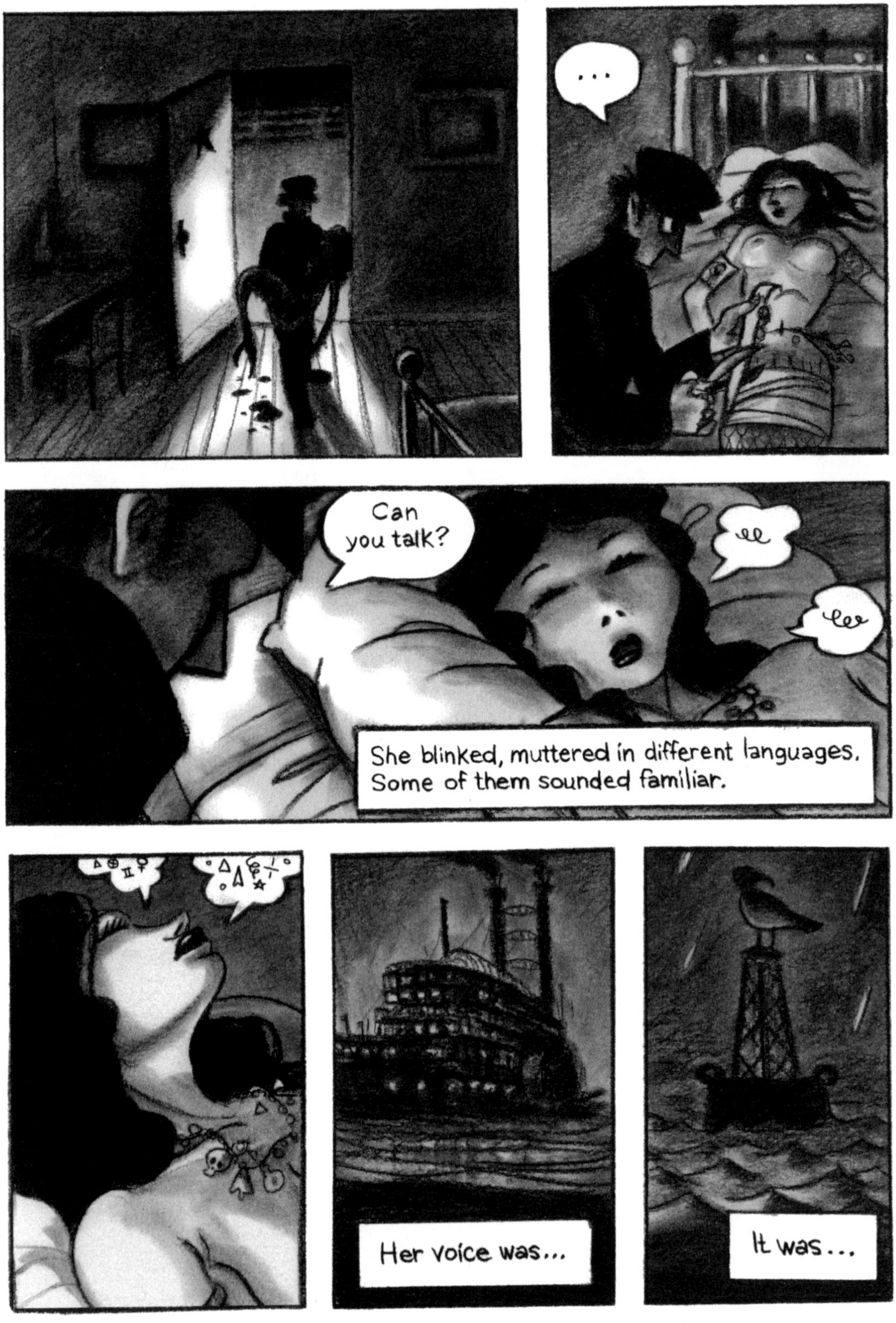
...
Can you talk?
She blinked, muttered in different languages. Some of them sounded familiar.
Her voice was...
It was...

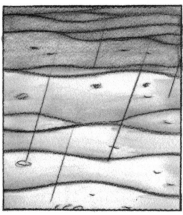

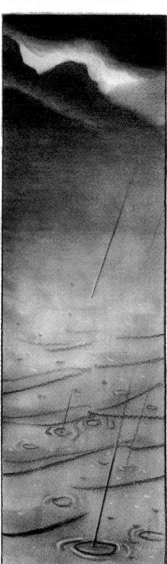
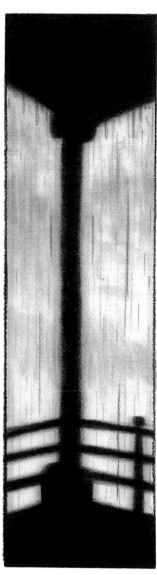

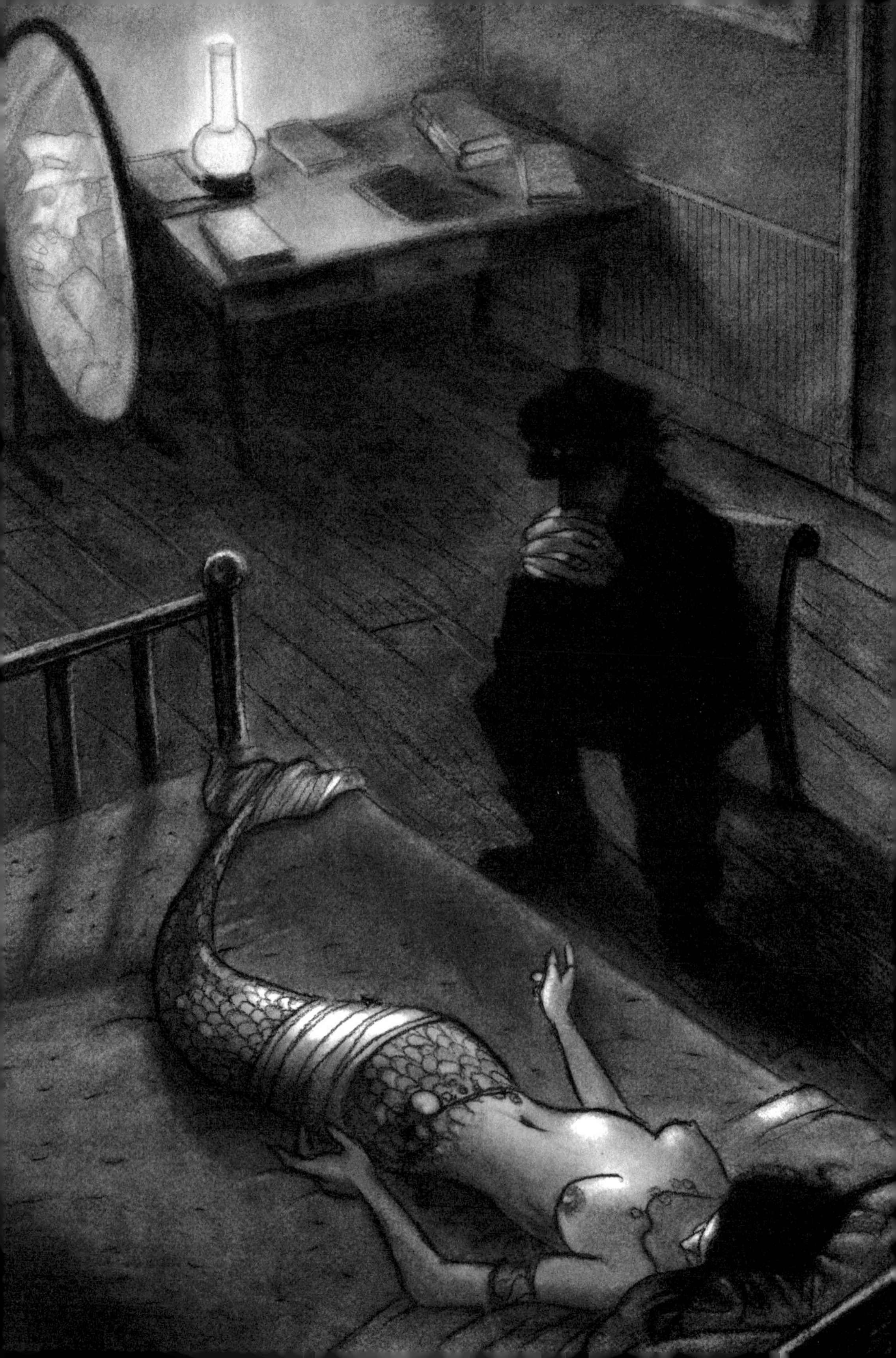

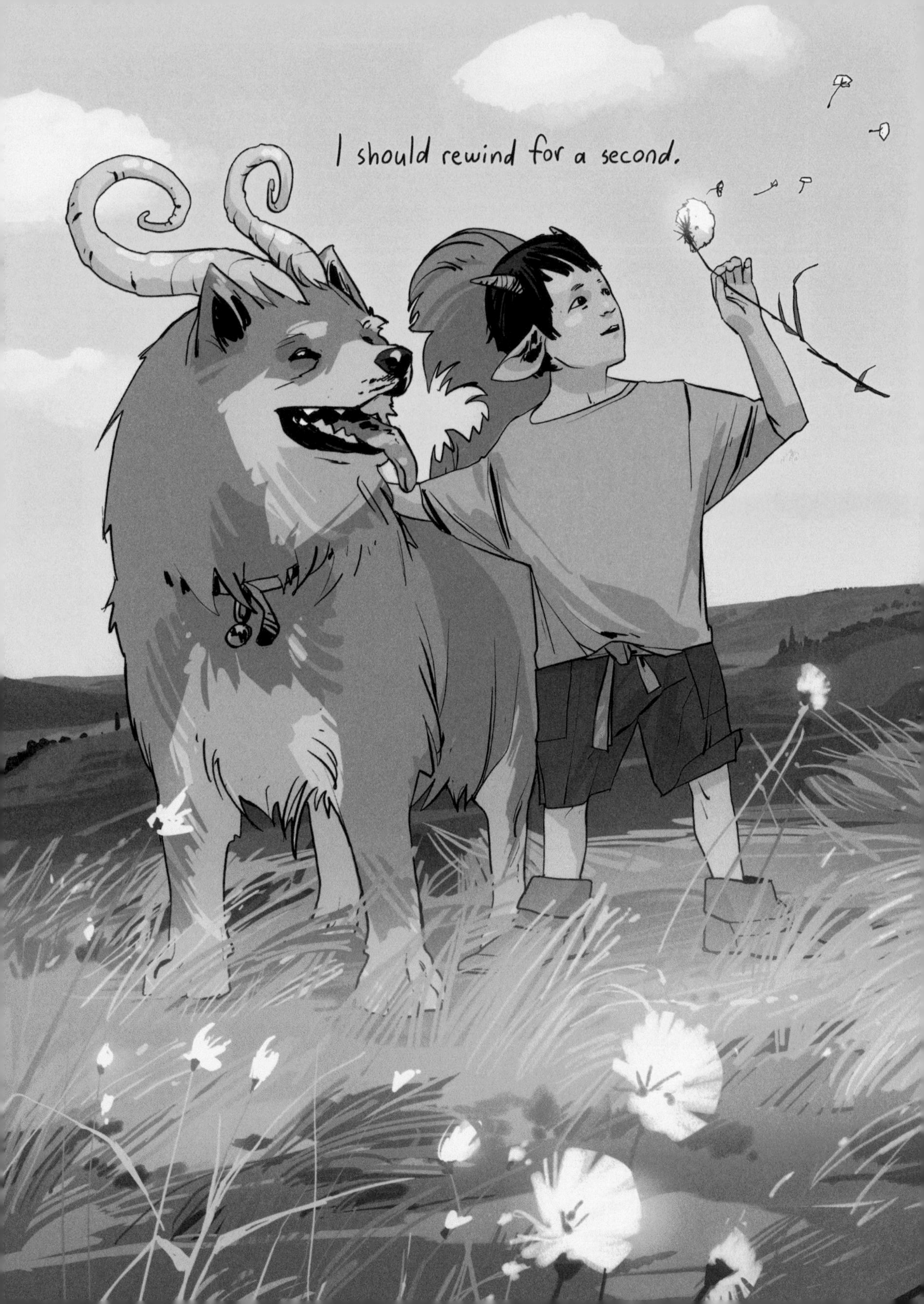
I should rewind for a second.

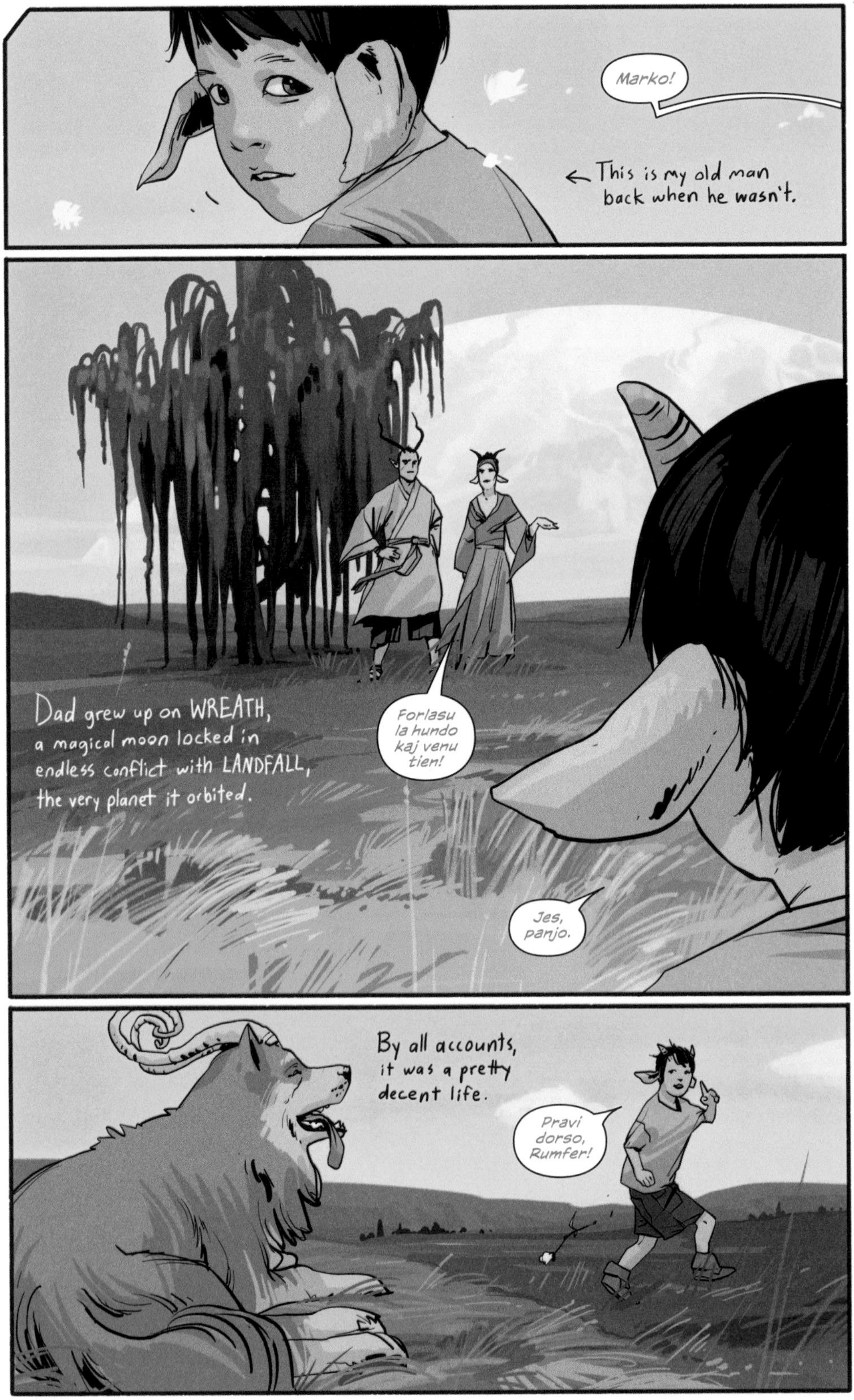
Marko!
← This is my old man back when he wasn't.
Dad grew up on WREATH, a magical moon locked in endless conflict with LANDFALL, the very planet it orbited.
Forlasu la hundo kaj venu tien!
Jes, panjo.
By all accounts, it was a pretty decent life.
Pravi dorso, Rumfer!

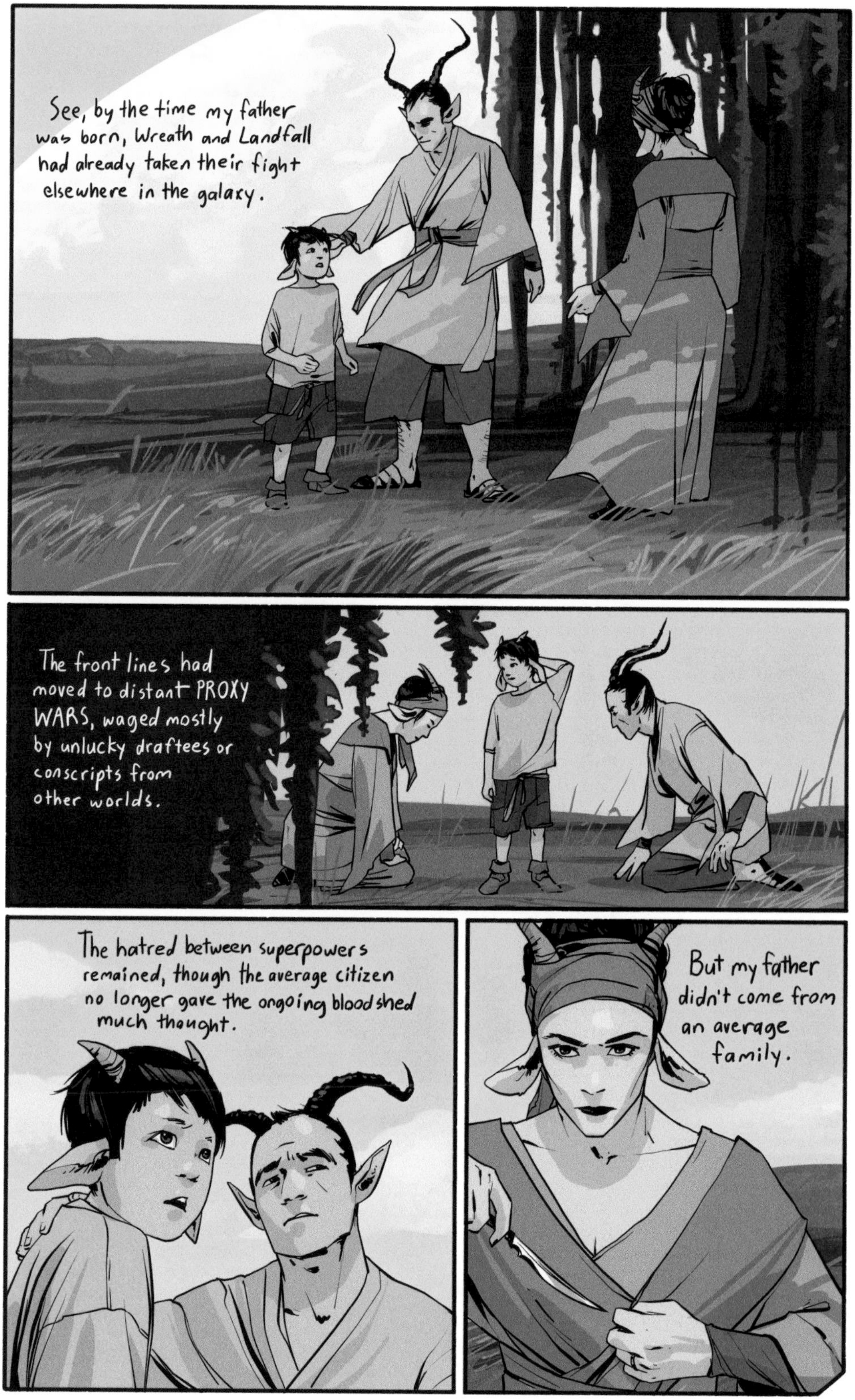
See, by the time my father was born, Wreath and Landfall had already taken their fight elsewhere in the galaxy.
The front lines had moved to distant PROXY WARS, waged mostly by unlucky draftees or conscripts from other worlds.
The hatred between superpowers remained, though the average citizen no longer gave the ongoing bloodshed much thought.
But my father didn't come from an average family.

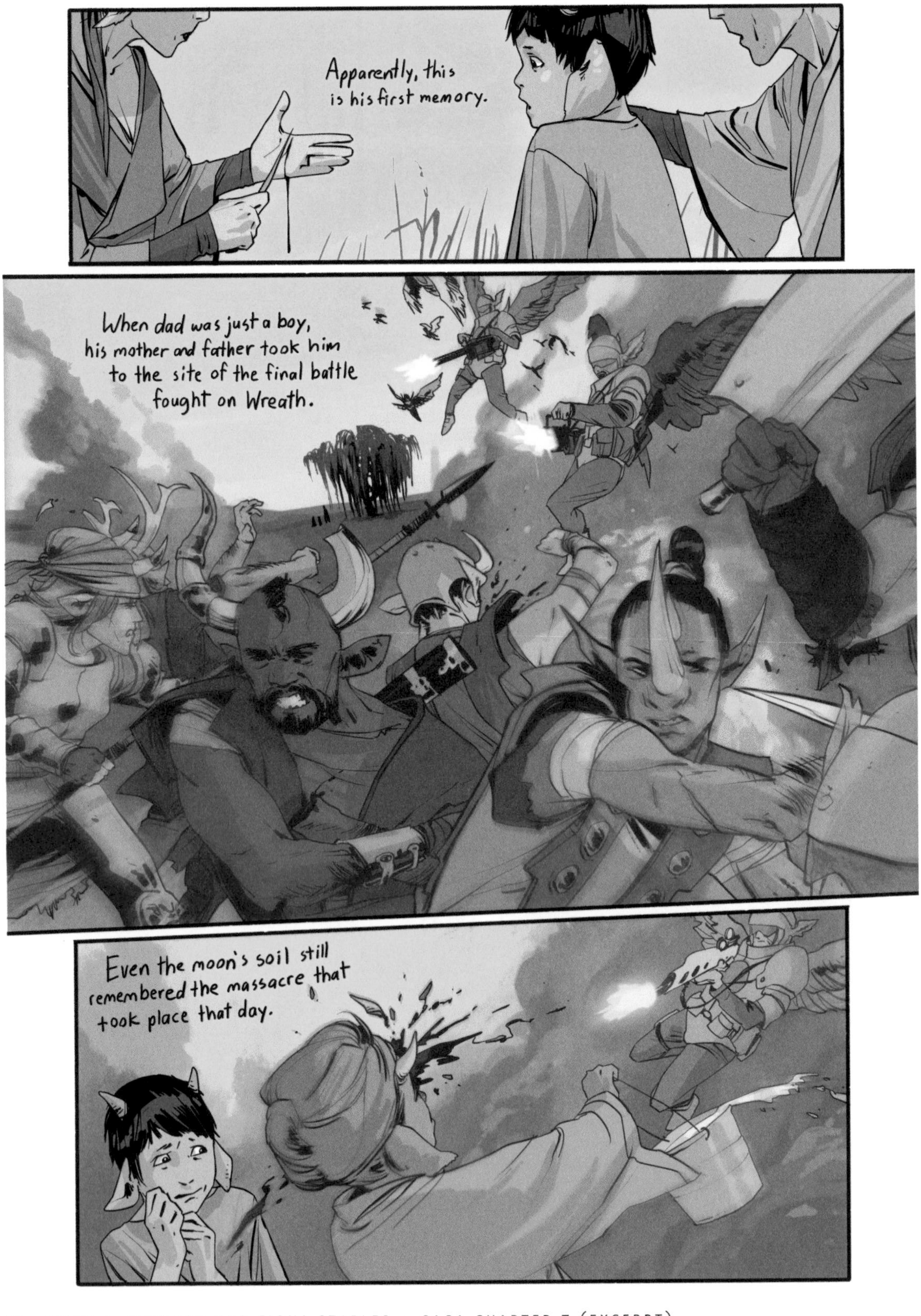
Apparently, this is his first memory.
When dad was just a boy, his mother and father took him to the site of the final battle fought on Wreath.
Even the moon's soil still remembered the massacre that took place that day.

His parents didn't say a word, but the point of their lesson was clear.

Never forget.

Never forget the countless heroes who sacrificed so much.

And more importantly, never forget those evil fucks with the wings.

So yeah, that was then.
Guys, I'd like you to meet Alana.
My wife.
Sankta fek.
I just wanted to make sure everyone was on the same page before this next part.

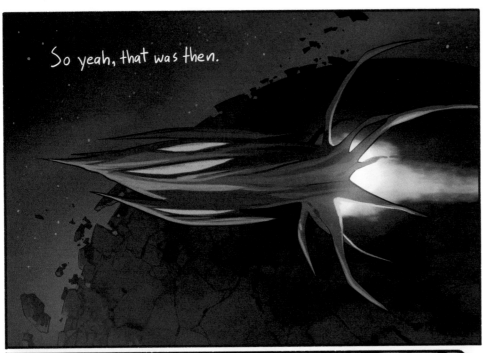

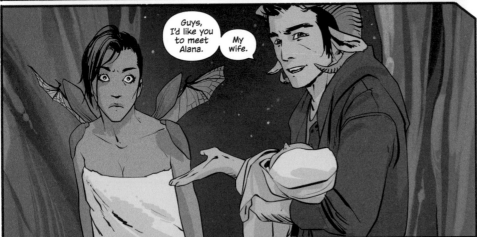

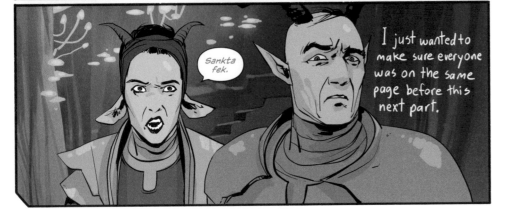

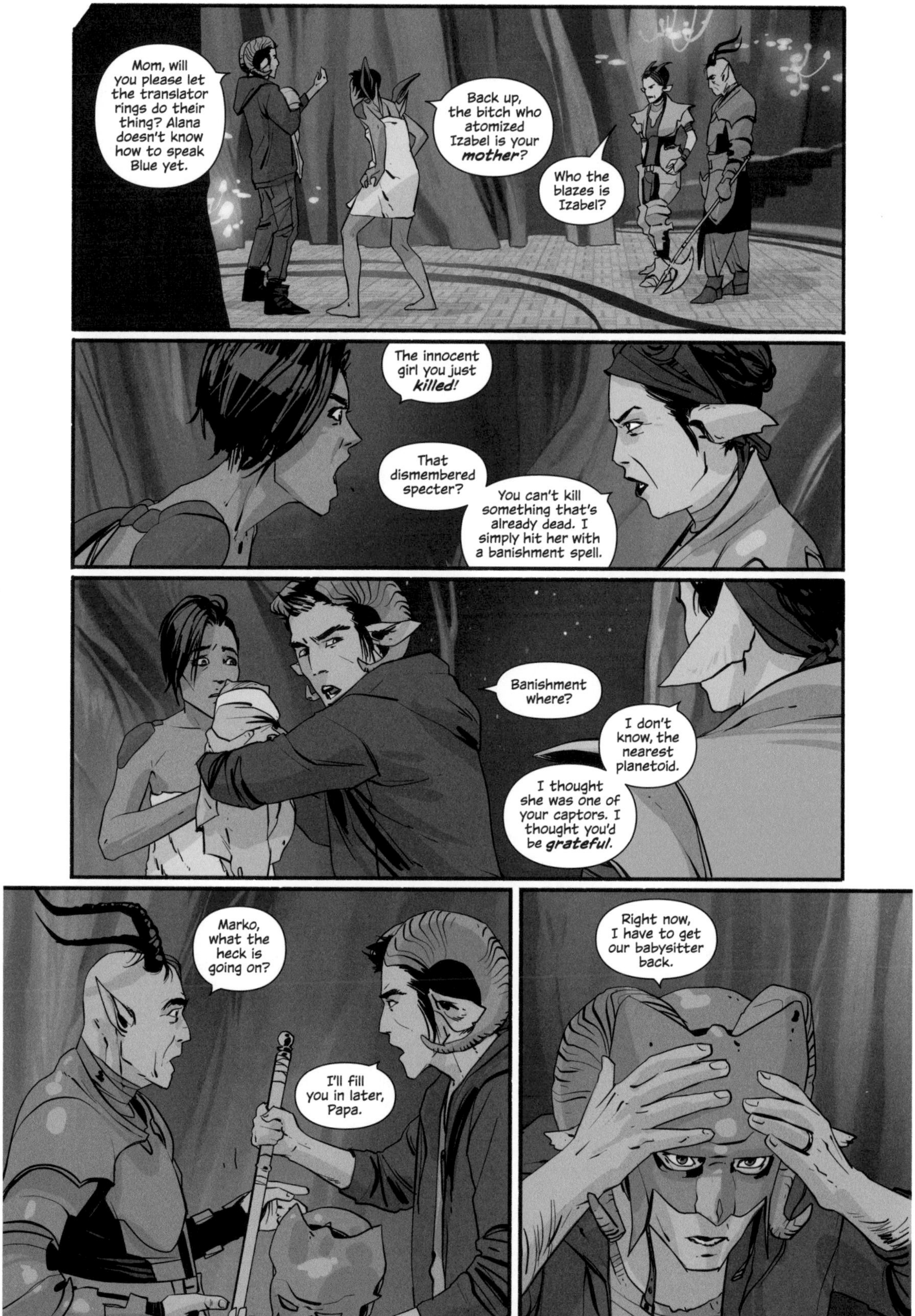
Mom, will you please let the translator rings do their thing? Alana doesn't know how to speak Blue yet.
Back up, the bitch who atomized Izabel is your *mother*?
Who the blazes is Izabel?
The innocent girl you just *killed!*
That dismembered specter?
You can't kill something that's already dead. I simply hit her with a banishment spell.
Banishment where?
I don't know, the nearest planetoid.
I thought she was one of your captors. I thought you'd be *grateful*.
Marko, what the heck is going on?
I'll fill you in later, Papa.
Right now, I have to get our babysitter back.

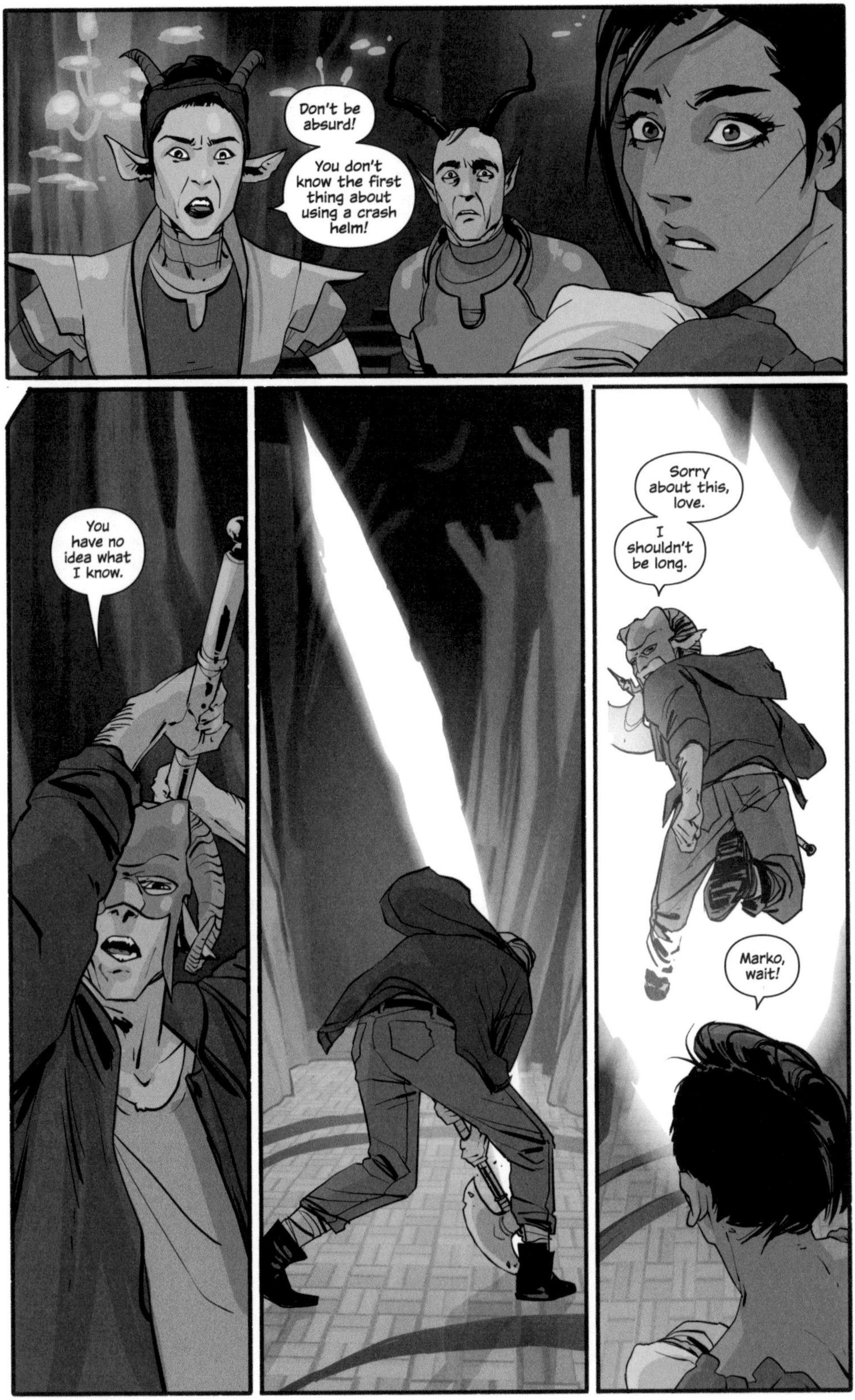
Don't be absurd!
You don't know the first thing about using a crash helm!
You have no idea what I know.
Sorry about this, love.
I shouldn't be long.
Marko, wait!

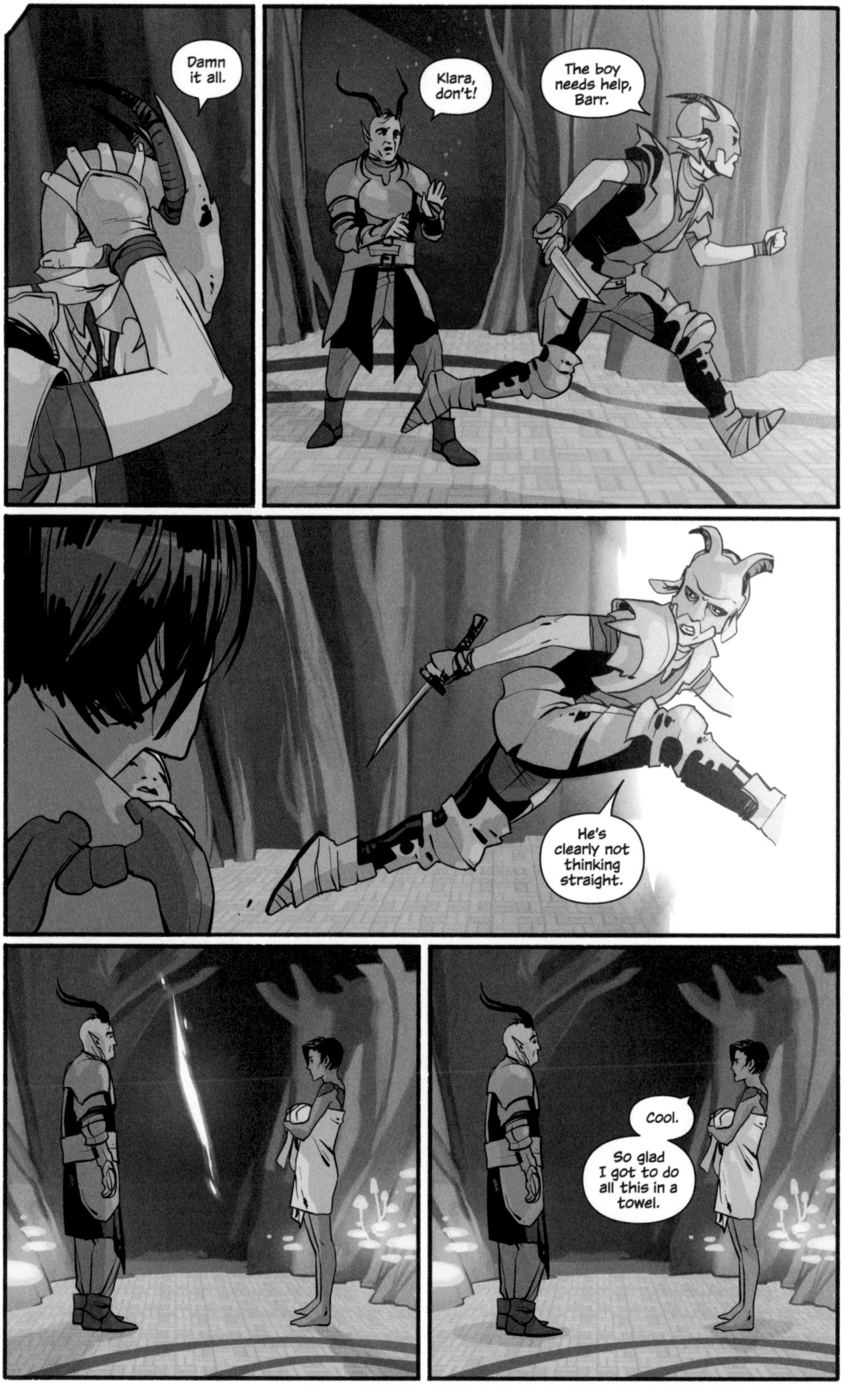
Damn it all.
Klara, don't!
The boy needs help, Barr.
He's clearly not thinking straight.
Cool.
So glad I got to do all this in a towel.

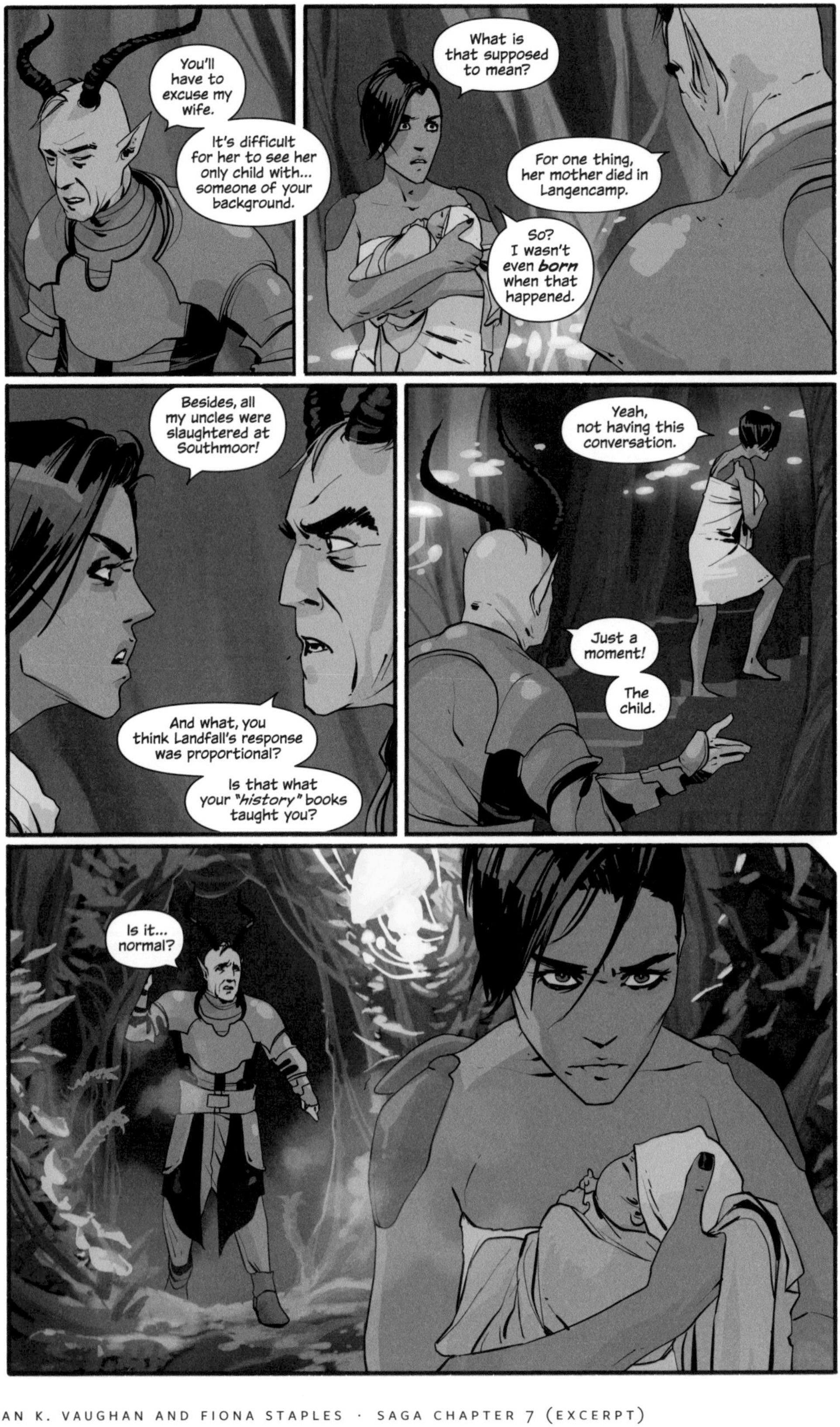
You'll have to excuse my wife.
It's difficult for her to see her only child with... someone of your background.
What is that supposed to mean?
For one thing, her mother died in Langencamp.
So? I wasn't even ***born*** when that happened.
Besides, all my uncles were slaughtered at Southmoor!
And what, you think Landfall's response was proportional?
Is that what your "*history*" books taught you?
Yeah, not having this conversation.
Just a moment!
The child.
Is it... normal?

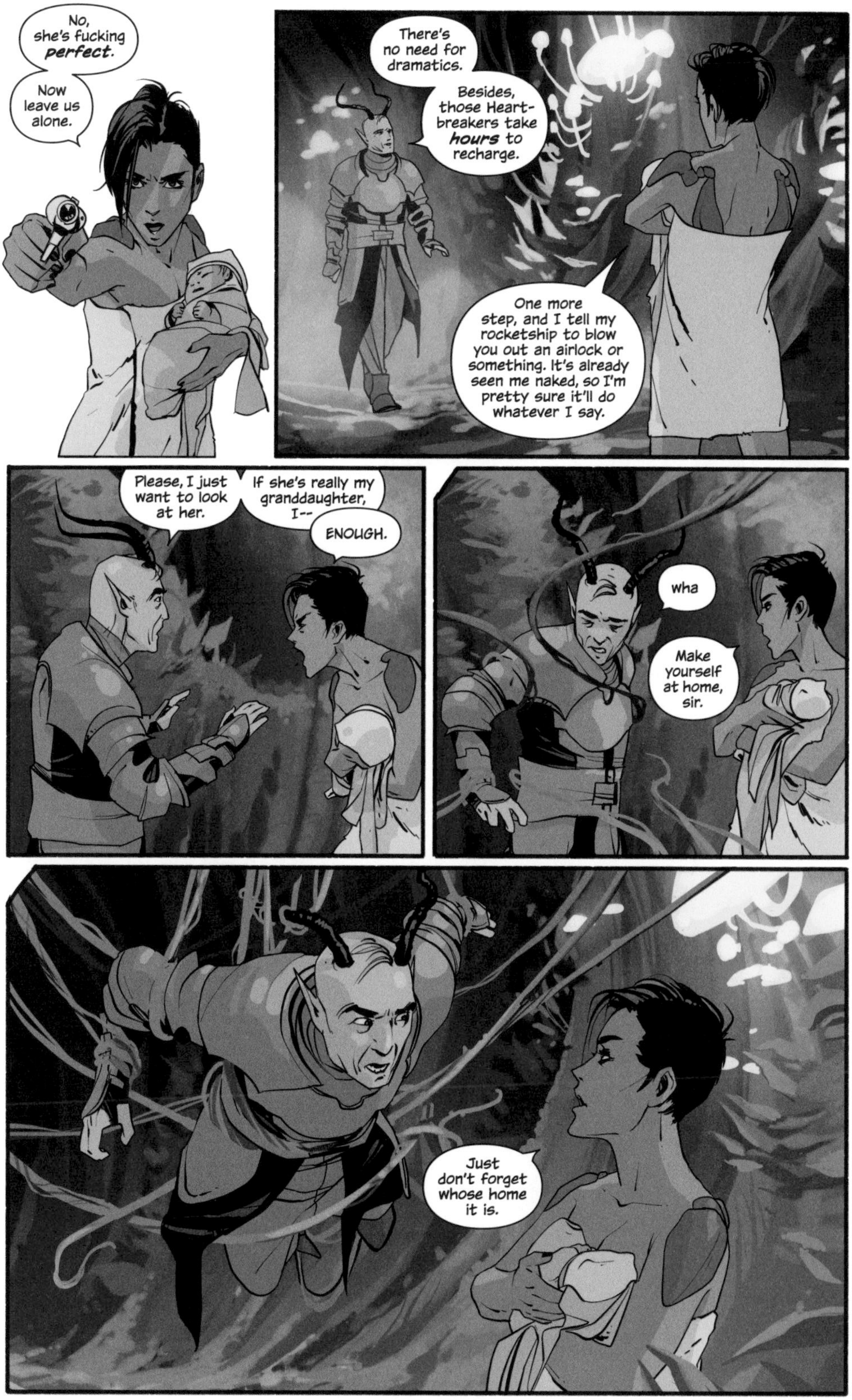

No, she's fucking **perfect**.
Now leave us alone.
There's no need for dramatics.
Besides, those Heart-breakers take **hours** to recharge.
One more step, and I tell my rocketship to blow you out an airlock or something. It's already seen me naked, so I'm pretty sure it'll do whatever I say.
Please, I just want to look at her.
If she's really my granddaughter, I--
ENOUGH.
wha
Make yourself at home, sir.
Just don't forget whose home it is.

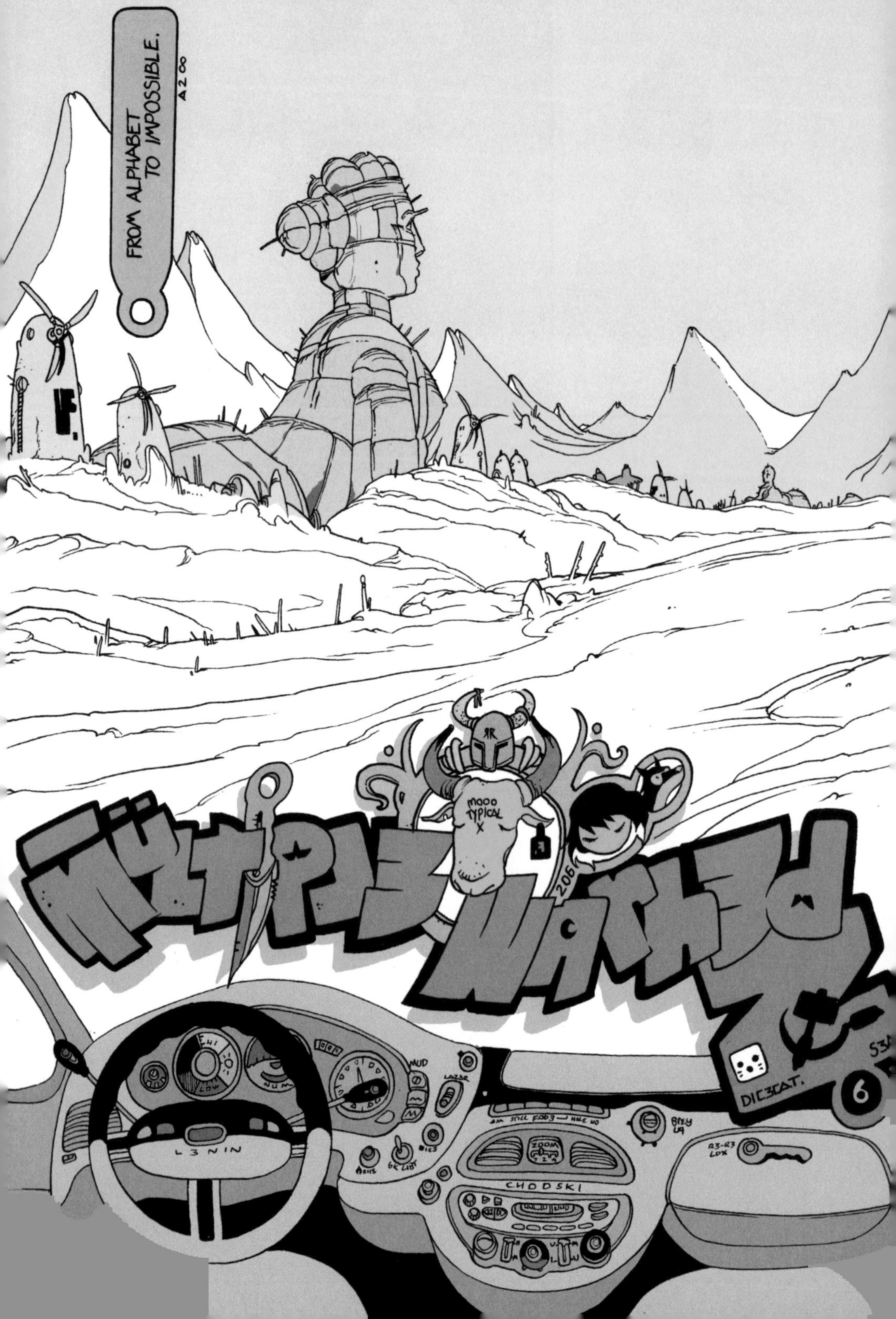
FROM ALPHABET
TO IMPOSSIBLE.
mooo
TYPICAL
X
MUD
L3NIN
ZOOM
CHODSKI
DIC3CAT.
6

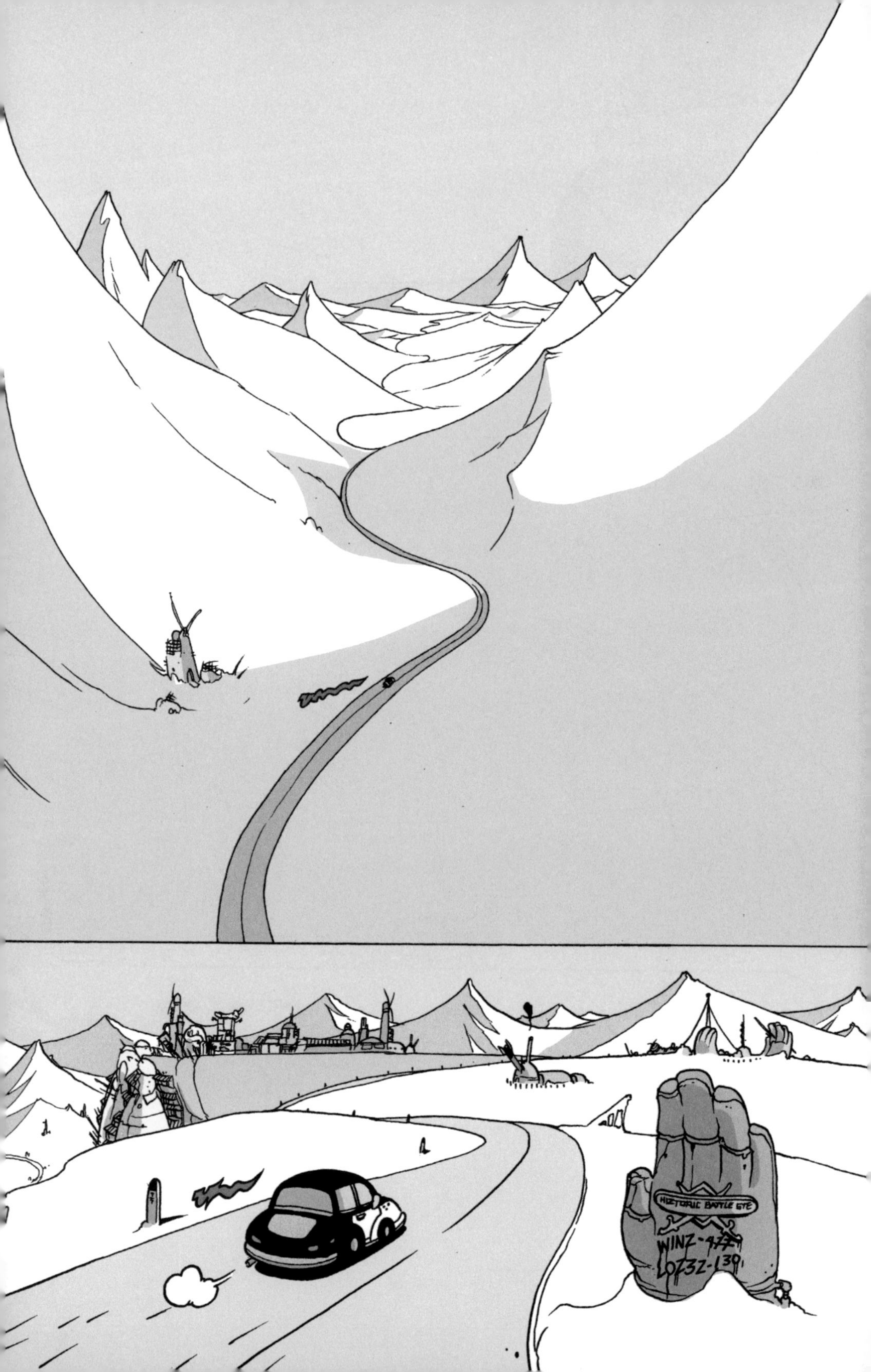

HISTORIC BATTLE SITE
WINZ-477
LOZ32-139

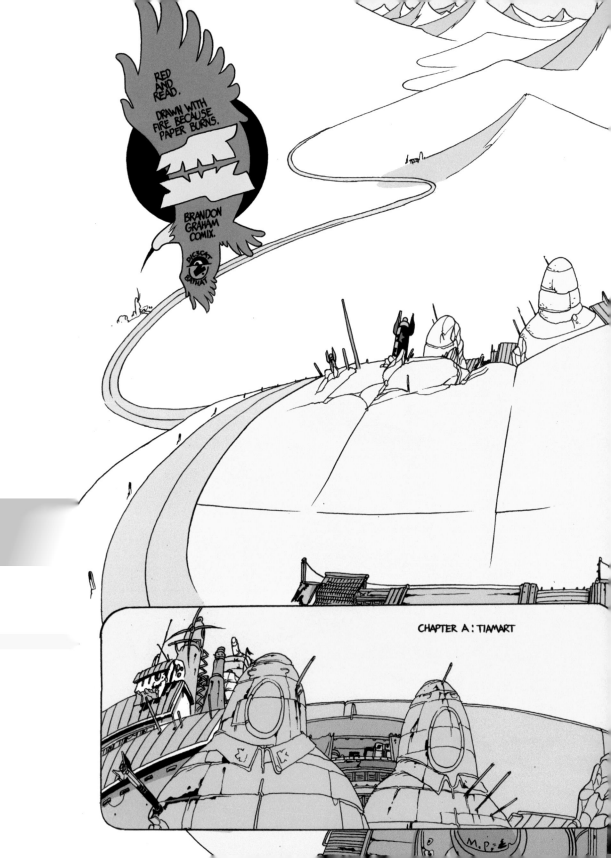

RED
AND
READ.

DRAWN WITH
FIRE BECAUSE
PAPER BURNS.

BRANDON
GRAHAM
COMIX.

CHAPTER A: TIAMART

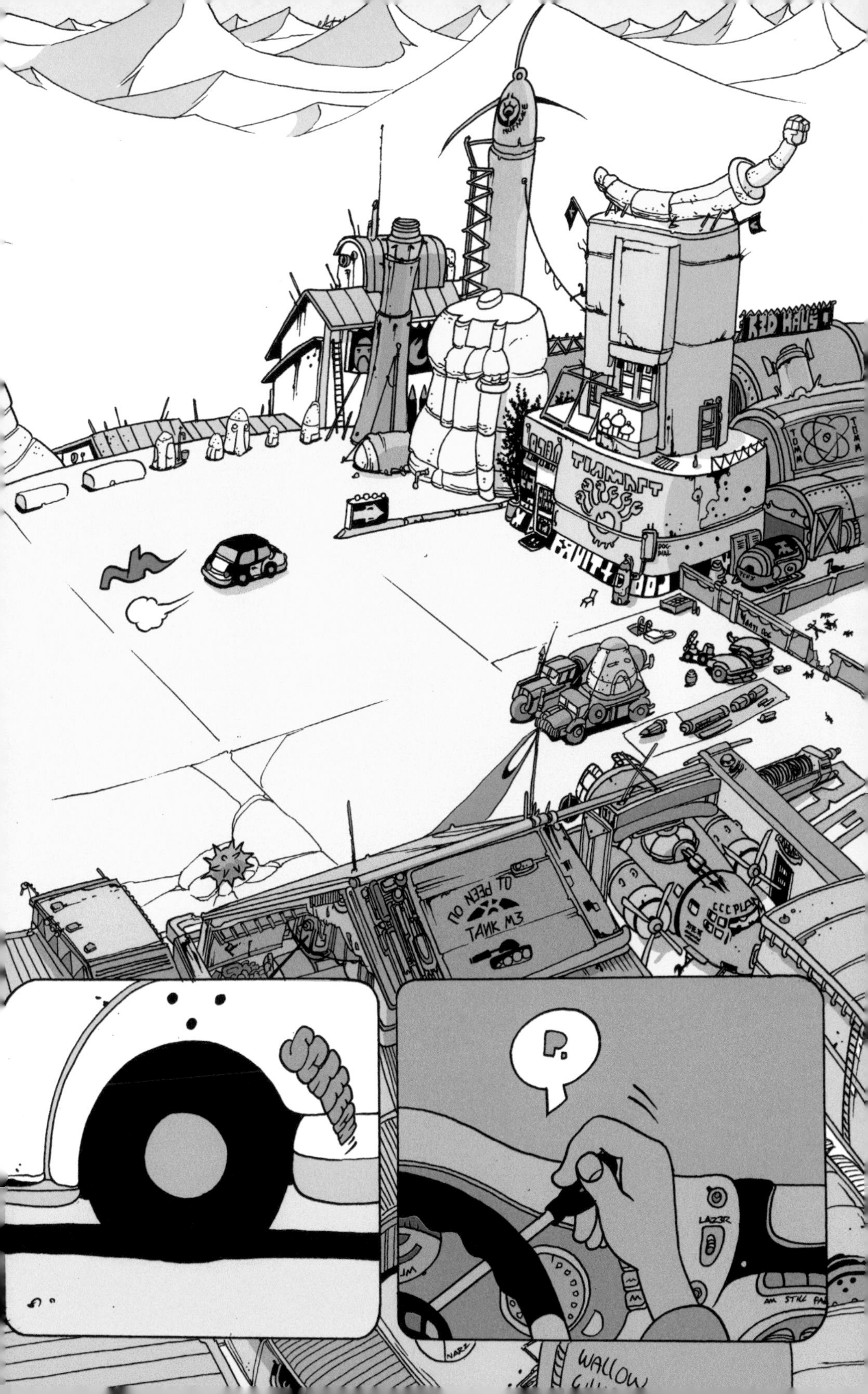
NO NEED TO
TANK M3
P.
WALLOW

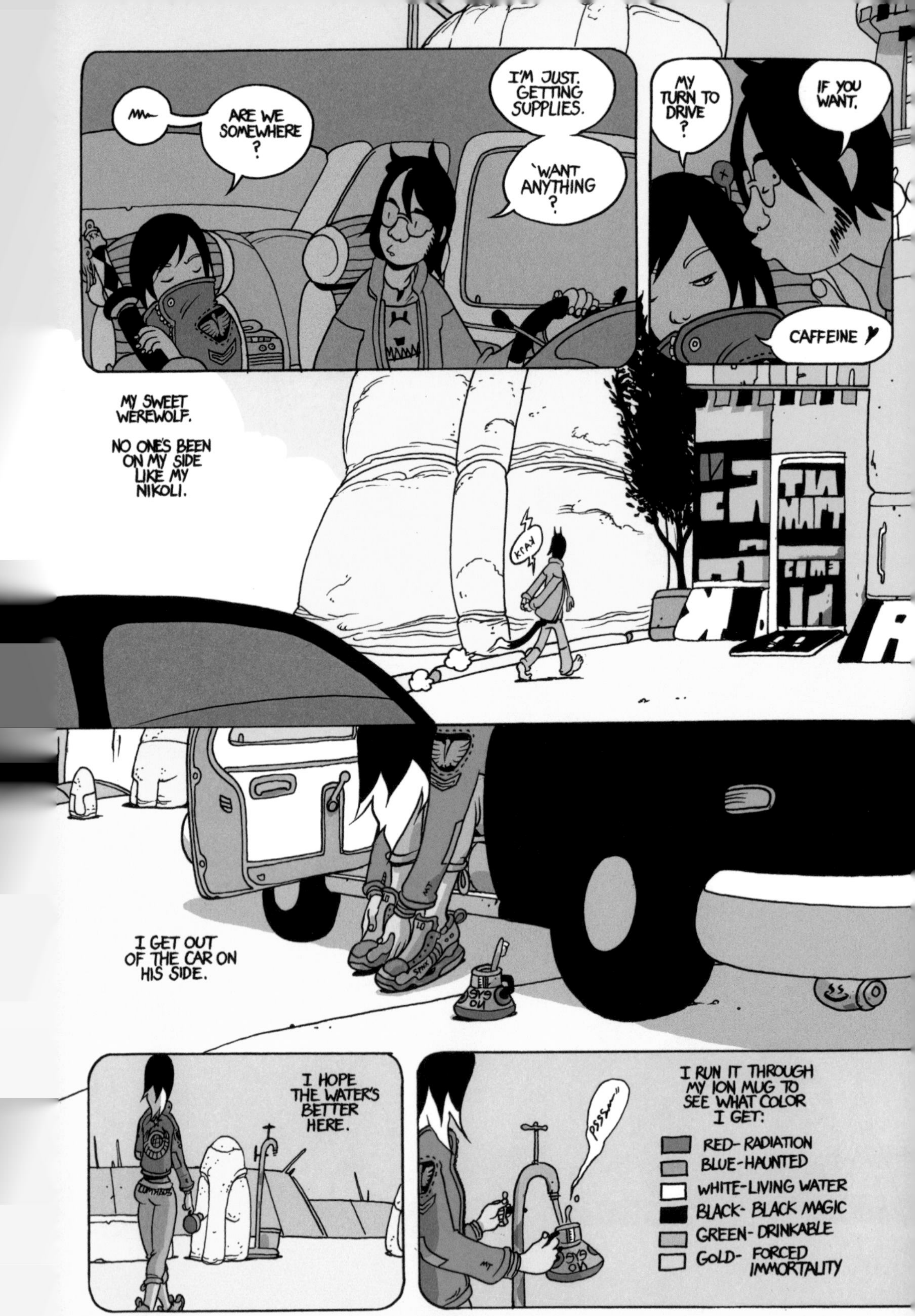
MM
ARE WE SOMEWHERE?
I'M JUST. GETTING SUPPLIES.
`WANT ANYTHING?
MY TURN TO DRIVE?
IF YOU WANT.
CAFFEINE
MY SWEET WEREWOLF.
NO ONE'S BEEN ON MY SIDE LIKE MY NIKOLI.
I GET OUT OF THE CAR ON HIS SIDE.
I HOPE THE WATER'S BETTER HERE.
I RUN IT THROUGH MY ION MUG TO SEE WHAT COLOR I GET:
RED- RADIATION
BLUE-HAUNTED
WHITE-LIVING WATER
BLACK- BLACK MAGIC
GREEN- DRINKABLE
GOLD- FORCED IMMORTALITY

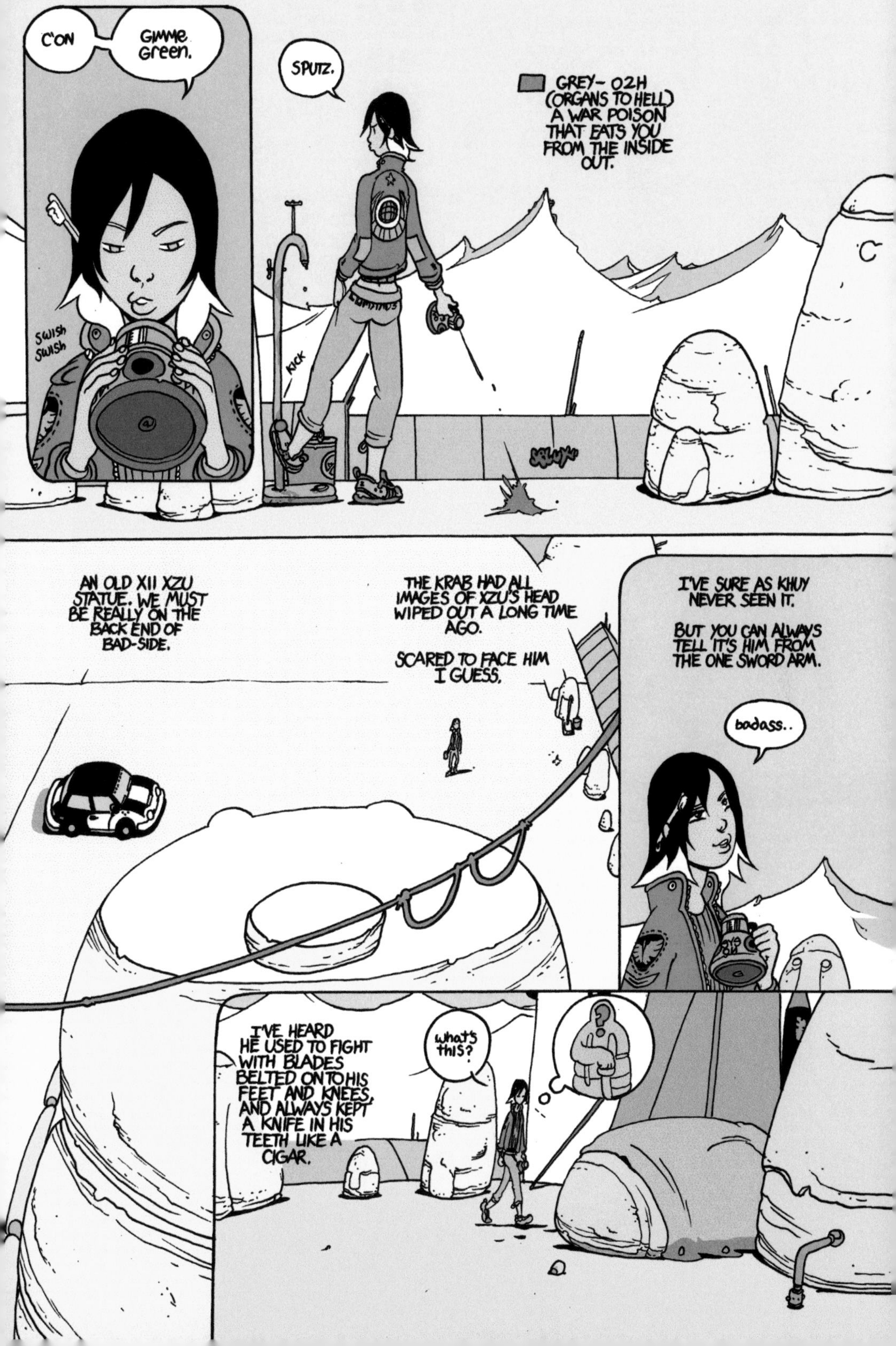
C'ON
GIMME Green.
SWISH SWISH
SPUTZ.
KICK
GREY- O2H (ORGANS TO HELL) A WAR POISON THAT EATS YOU FROM THE INSIDE OUT.
AN OLD XII XZU STATUE. WE MUST BE REALLY ON THE BACK END OF BAD-SIDE.
THE KRAB HAD ALL IMAGES OF XZU'S HEAD WIPED OUT A LONG TIME AGO.
SCARED TO FACE HIM I GUESS.
I'VE SURE AS KHUY NEVER SEEN IT.
BUT YOU CAN ALWAYS TELL IT'S HIM FROM THE ONE SWORD ARM.
badass..
I'VE HEARD HE USED TO FIGHT WITH BLADES BELTED ON TO HIS FEET AND KNEES, AND ALWAYS KEPT A KNIFE IN HIS TEETH LIKE A CIGAR.
what's this?

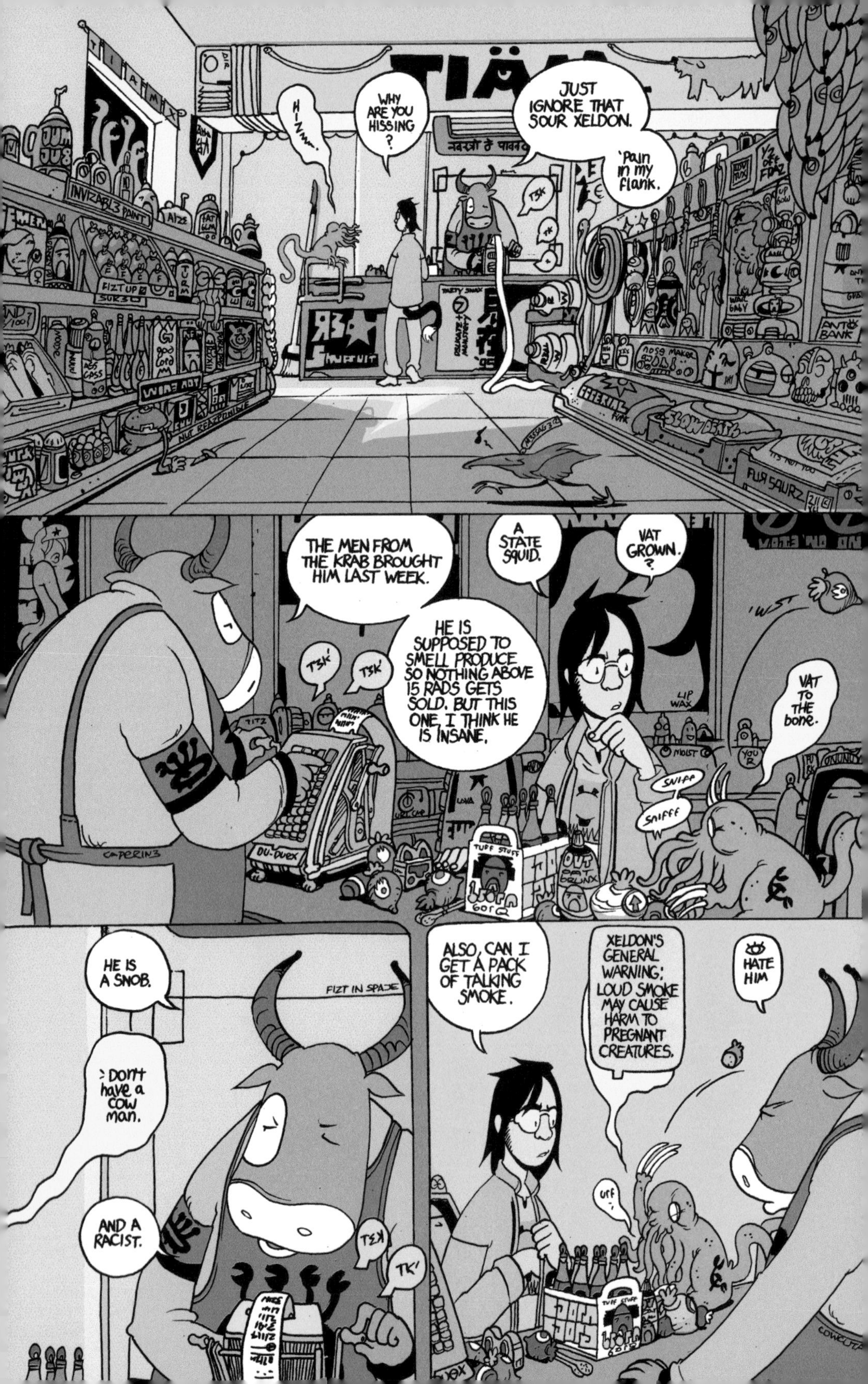

H-I-Z-Z-Z...
WHY ARE YOU HISSING ?
JUST IGNORE THAT SOUR XELDON.
'Pain in my flank.
TSK
TK
THE MEN FROM THE KRAB BROUGHT HIM LAST WEEK.
HE IS SUPPOSED TO SMELL PRODUCE SO NOTHING ABOVE 15 RADS GETS SOLD. BUT THIS ONE, I THINK HE IS INSANE.
TSK'
TSK'
A STATE SQUID.
VAT GROWN. ?
VAT TO THE bone.
SNIFF
SNIFFF
HE IS A SNOB.
>Don't have a cow man.
AND A RACIST.
TSK
TK'
ALSO, CAN I GET A PACK OF TALKING SMOKE.
XELDON'S GENERAL WARNING; LOUD SMOKE MAY CAUSE HARM TO PREGNANT CREATURES.
HATE HIM
urf

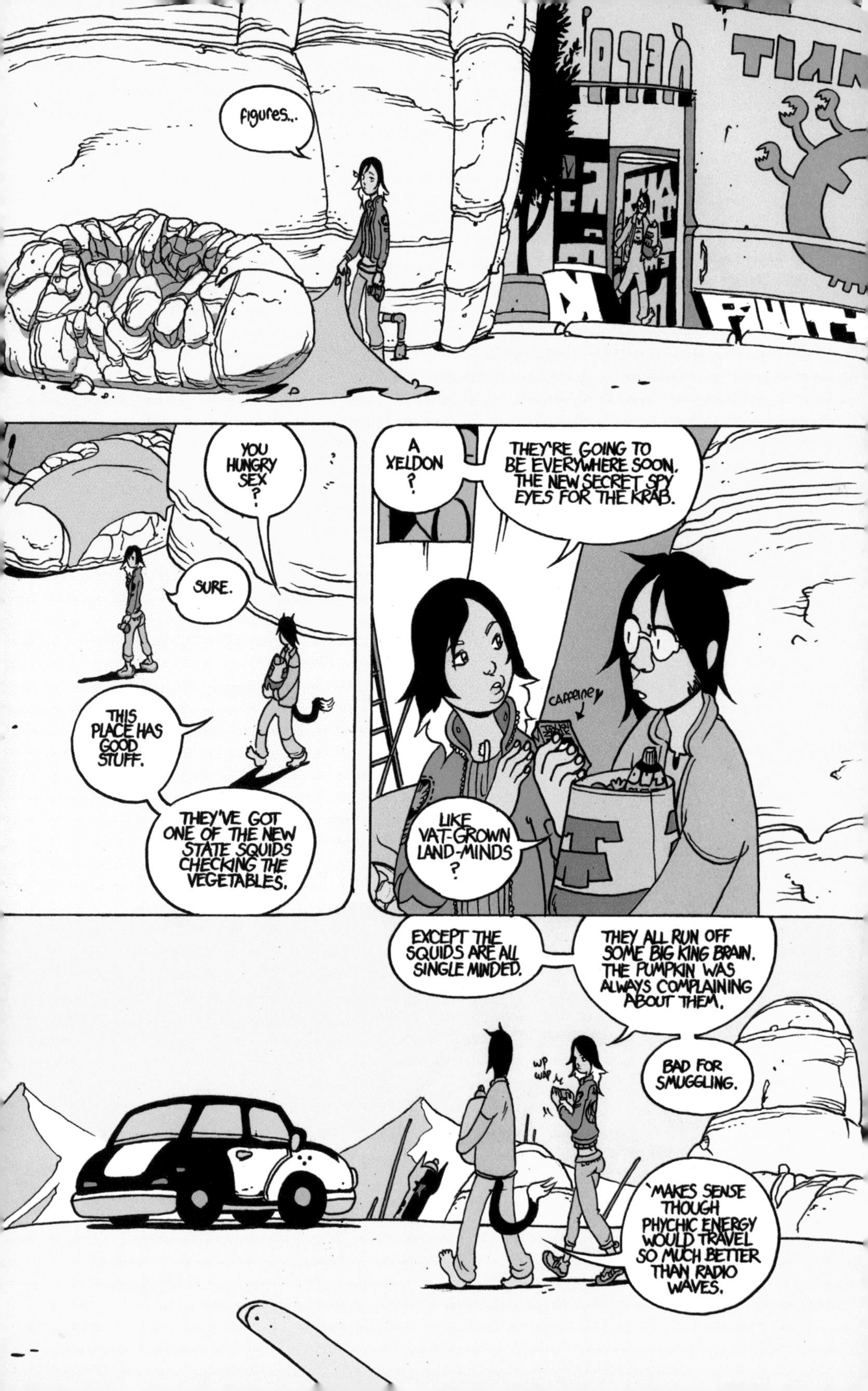
figures...
YOU HUNGRY SEX ?
SURE.
THIS PLACE HAS GOOD STUFF.
THEY'VE GOT ONE OF THE NEW STATE SQUIDS CHECKING THE VEGETABLES.
A XELDON ?
THEY'RE GOING TO BE EVERYWHERE SOON. THE NEW SECRET SPY EYES FOR THE KRAB.
caffeine
LIKE VAT-GROWN LAND-MINDS ?
EXCEPT THE SQUIDS ARE ALL SINGLE MINDED.
THEY ALL RUN OFF SOME BIG KING BRAIN. THE PUMPKIN WAS ALWAYS COMPLAINING ABOUT THEM.
BAD FOR SMUGGLING.
`MAKES SENSE THOUGH PHYCHIC ENERGY WOULD TRAVEL SO MUCH BETTER THAN RADIO WAVES.

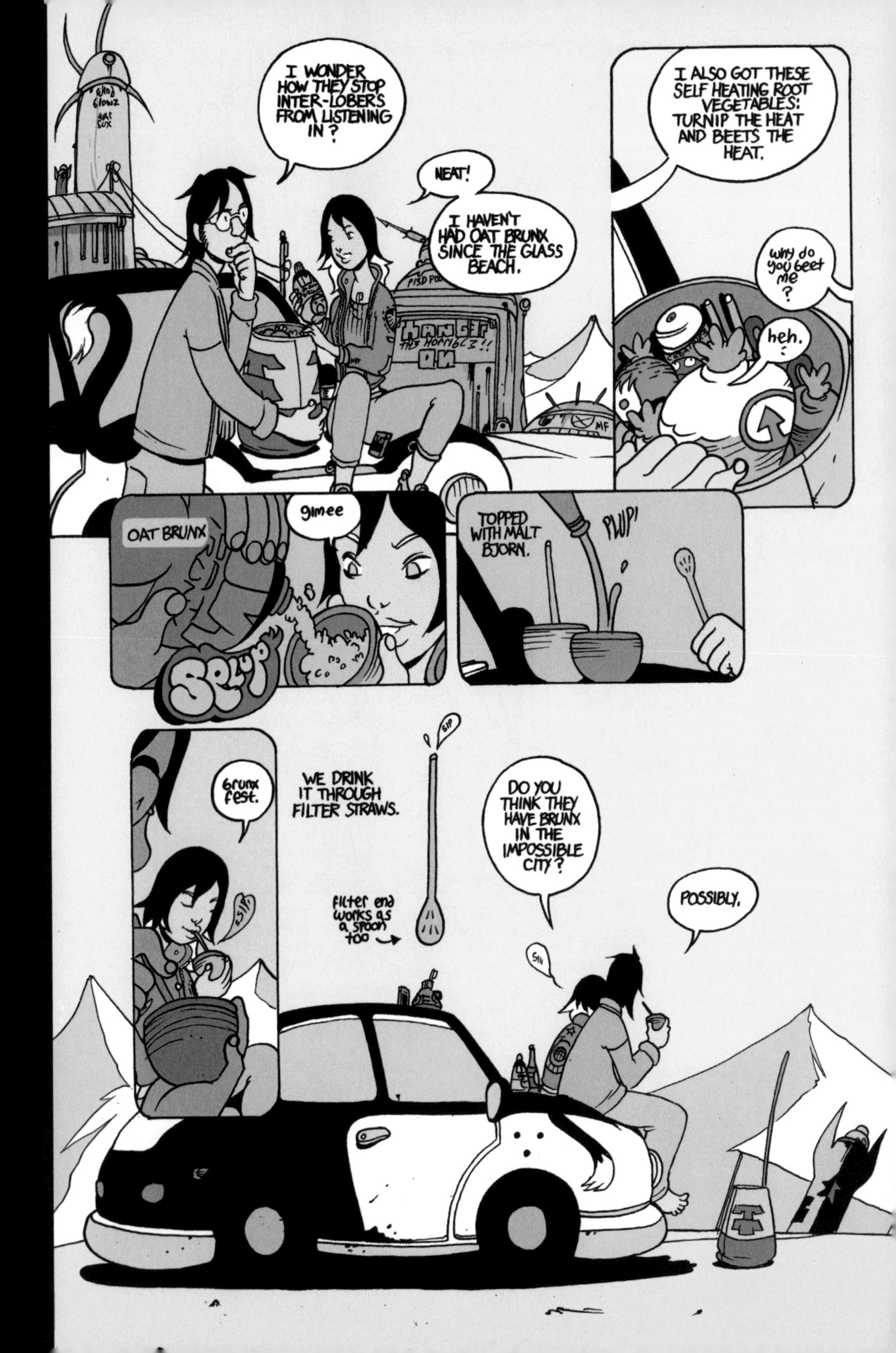

I WONDER HOW THEY STOP INTER-LOBERS FROM LISTENING IN?
NEAT!
I HAVEN'T HAD OAT BRUNX SINCE THE GLASS BEACH.
I ALSO GOT THESE SELF HEATING ROOT VEGETABLES: TURNIP THE HEAT AND BEETS THE HEAT.
why do you beet me?
heh.
OAT BRUNX
gimee
TOPPED WITH MALT BJORN.
PLUP!
Brunx fest.
sip
WE DRINK IT THROUGH FILTER STRAWS.
SIP
filter end works as a spoon too
DO YOU THINK THEY HAVE BRUNX IN THE IMPOSSIBLE CITY?
Sip
POSSIBLY.

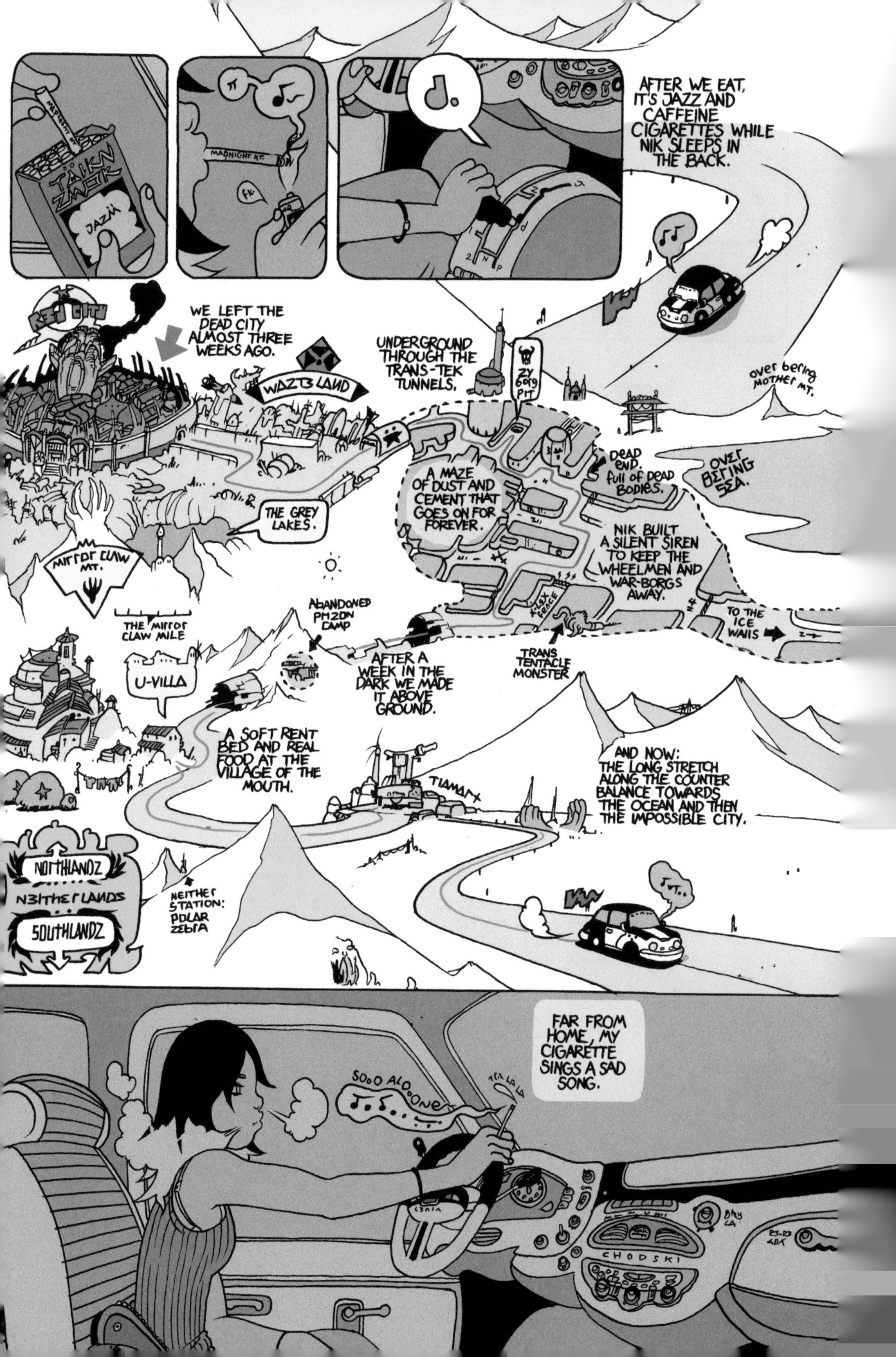

MADNIGHT KT.
JAZÄ
FK.
AFTER WE EAT, IT'S JAZZ AND CAFFEINE CIGARETTES WHILE NIK SLEEPS IN THE BACK.
WE LEFT THE DEAD CITY ALMOST THREE WEEKS AGO.
UNDERGROUND THROUGH THE TRANS-TEK TUNNELS.
ZY 6org PIT
over bering MOTHER MT.
A MAZE OF DUST AND CEMENT THAT GOES ON FOR FOREVER.
DEAD END. full of DEAD BODIES.
OVER BERING SEA.
THE GREY LAKES.
NIK BUILT A SILENT SIREN TO KEEP THE WHEELMEN AND WAR-BORGS AWAY.
MIRROR CLAW MT.
THE MIRROR CLAW MILE
ABANDONED PHZON CAMP
TO THE ICE WALLS
U-VILLA
TRANS TENTACLE MONSTER
AFTER A WEEK IN THE DARK WE MADE IT ABOVE GROUND.
A SOFT RENT BED AND REAL FOOD AT THE VILLAGE OF THE MOUTH.
AND NOW: THE LONG STRETCH ALONG THE COUNTER BALANCE TOWARDS THE OCEAN AND THEN THE IMPOSSIBLE CITY.
NORTHLANDZ
NEITHERLANDS
SOUTHLANDZ
NEITHER STATION: POLAR ZEBRA
FAR FROM HOME, MY CIGARETTE SINGS A SAD SONG.
SOoO ALOoONE
TRA LA LA
CHODSKI

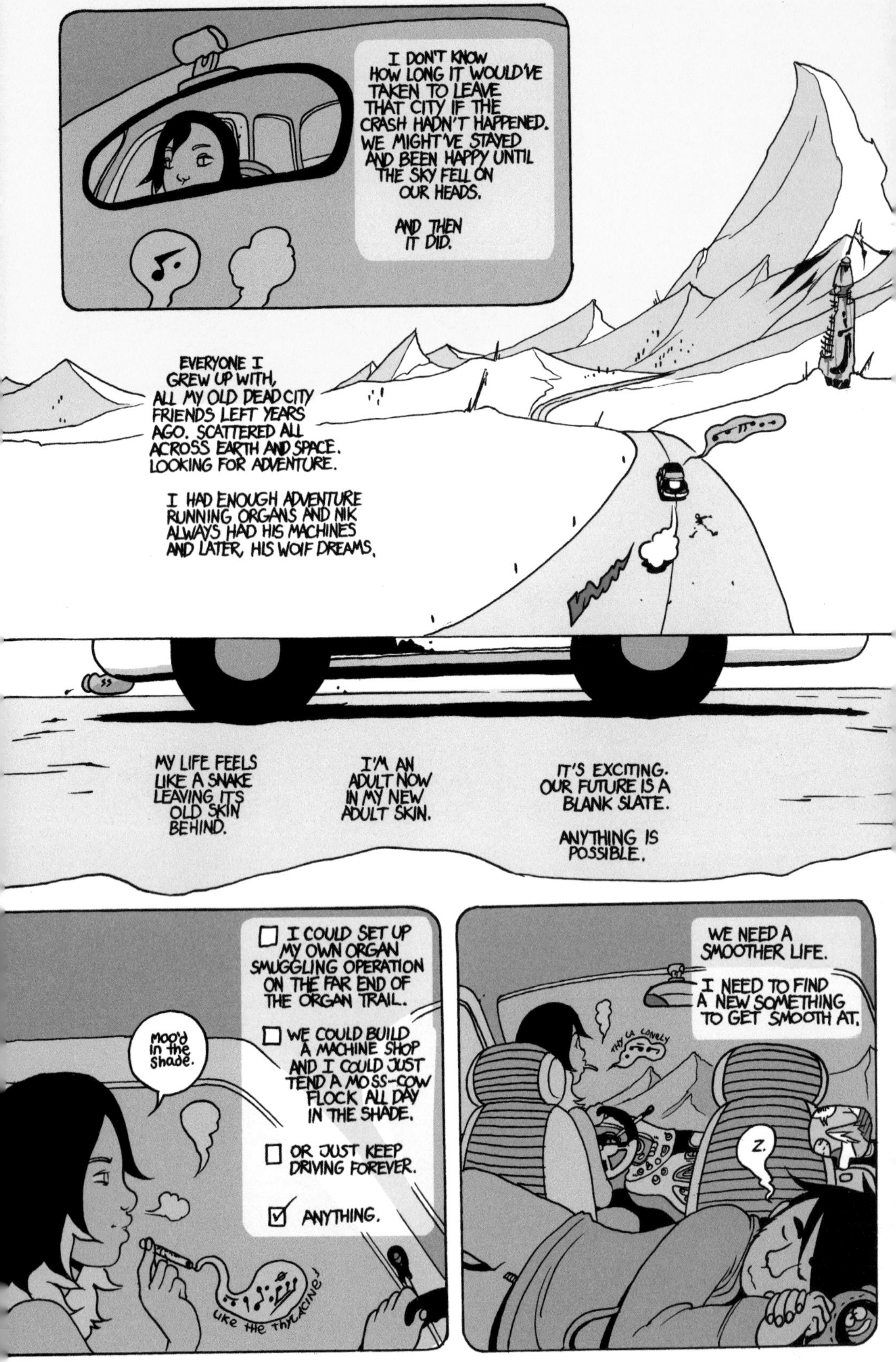

I DON'T KNOW HOW LONG IT WOULD'VE TAKEN TO LEAVE THAT CITY IF THE CRASH HADN'T HAPPENED. WE MIGHT'VE STAYED AND BEEN HAPPY UNTIL THE SKY FELL ON OUR HEADS.
AND THEN IT DID.
EVERYONE I GREW UP WITH, ALL MY OLD DEAD CITY FRIENDS LEFT YEARS AGO. SCATTERED ALL ACROSS EARTH AND SPACE. LOOKING FOR ADVENTURE.
I HAD ENOUGH ADVENTURE RUNNING ORGANS AND NIK ALWAYS HAD HIS MACHINES AND LATER, HIS WOIF DREAMS.
MY LIFE FEELS LIKE A SNAKE LEAVING ITS OLD SKIN BEHIND.
I'M AN ADULT NOW IN MY NEW ADULT SKIN.
IT'S EXCITING. OUR FUTURE IS A BLANK SLATE.
ANYTHING IS POSSIBLE.
Moo'd in the shade.
☐ I COULD SET UP MY OWN ORGAN SMUGGLING OPERATION ON THE FAR END OF THE ORGAN TRAIL.
☐ WE COULD BUILD A MACHINE SHOP AND I COULD JUST TEND A MOSS-COW FLOCK ALL DAY IN THE SHADE.
☐ OR JUST KEEP DRIVING FOREVER.
☑ ANYTHING.
like the thylacine
WE NEED A SMOOTHER LIFE.
I NEED TO FIND A NEW SOMETHING TO GET SMOOTH AT.
THYLACA LONELY
Z.

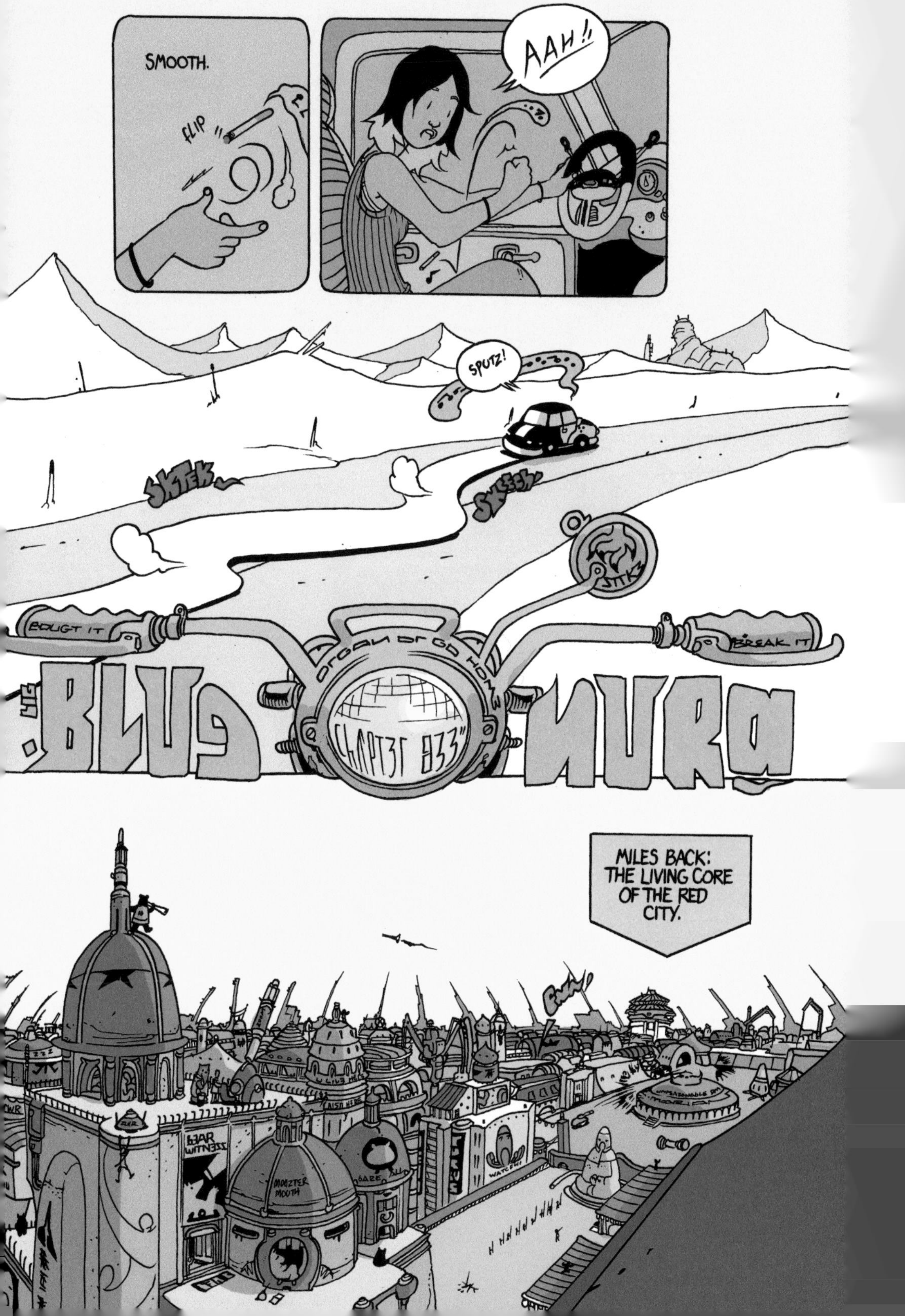
SMOOTH.
FLIP
AAH!!
SPUTZ!
BREAK IT
MILES BACK:
THE LIVING CORE
OF THE RED
CITY.

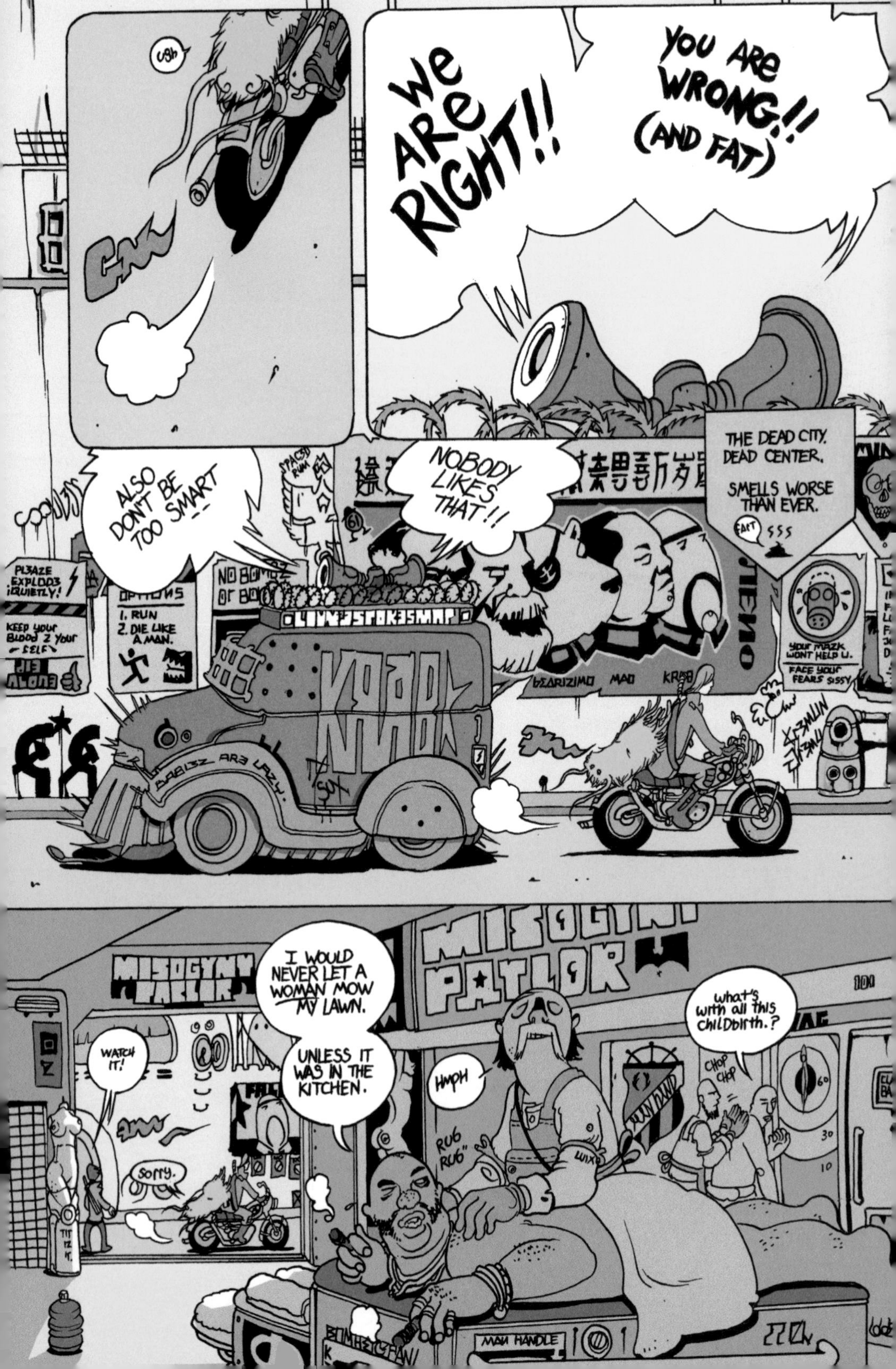

ugh
We ARE RIGHT!!
YOU ARE WRONG!! (AND FAT)
ALSO DON'T BE TOO SMART
NOBODY LIKES THAT!!
THE DEAD CITY. DEAD CENTER.
SMELLS WORSE THAN EVER.
FART
PL3AZE EXPLOD3 QUIETLY!
KEEP YOUR BLOOD 2 YOUR SELF
OPTIONS
1. RUN
2. DIE LIKE A MAN.
YOUR MAZK WONT HELP U.
FACE YOUR FEARS SISSY
BABI3Z ARE LAZY
MISOGYNY PARLOR
I WOULD NEVER LET A WOMAN MOW MY LAWN.
UNLESS IT WAS IN THE KITCHEN.
WATCH IT!
sorry.
HMPH
what's with all this childbirth.?
CHOP CHOP
RUG RUG
MAN HANDLE

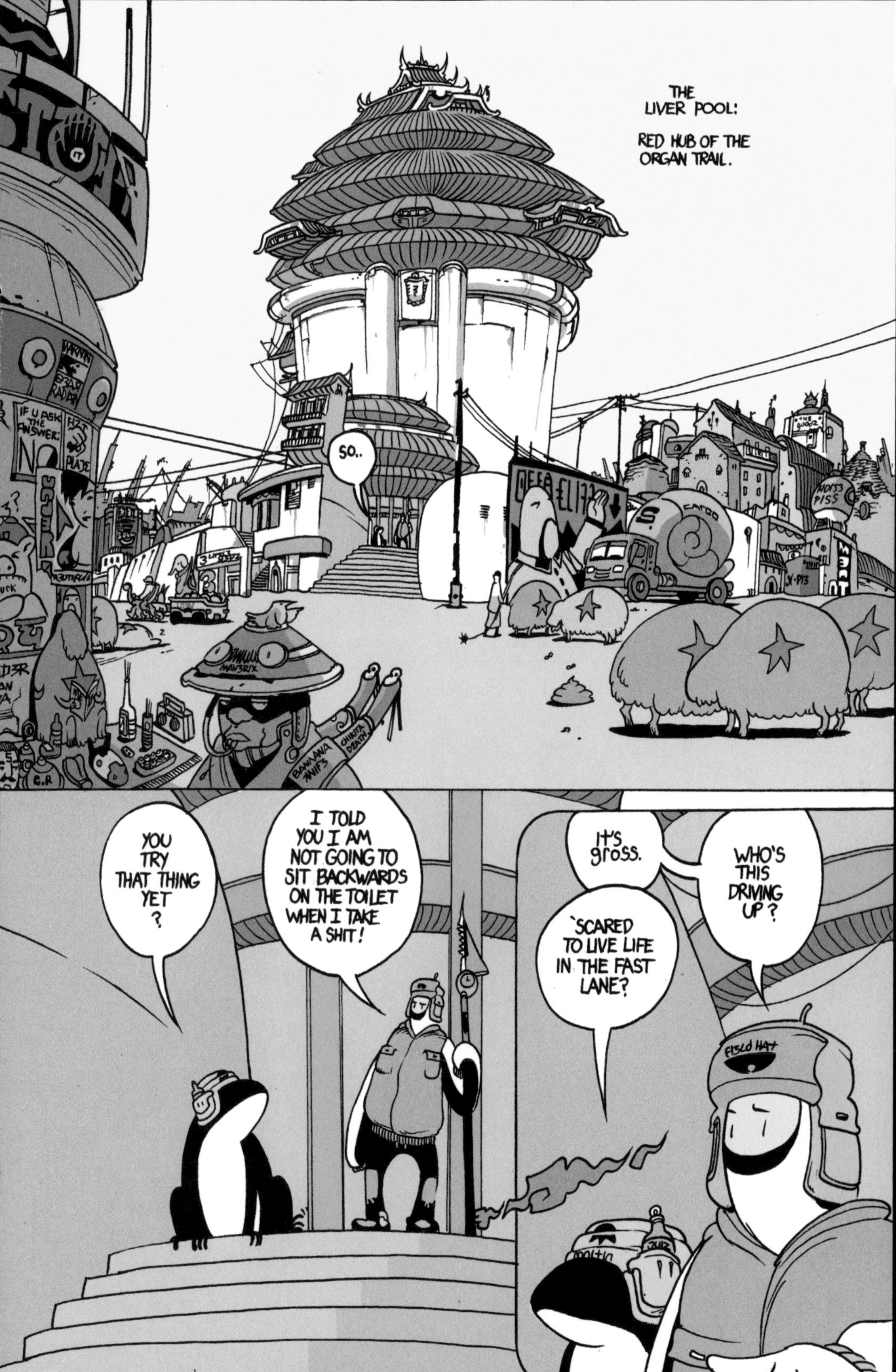
THE LIVER POOL:
RED HUB OF THE ORGAN TRAIL.
SO..
YOU TRY THAT THING YET ?
I TOLD YOU I AM NOT GOING TO SIT BACKWARDS ON THE TOILET WHEN I TAKE A SHIT!
IT'S gross.
WHO'S THIS DRIVING UP ?
'SCARED TO LIVE LIFE IN THE FAST LANE?

DIMENSIONS

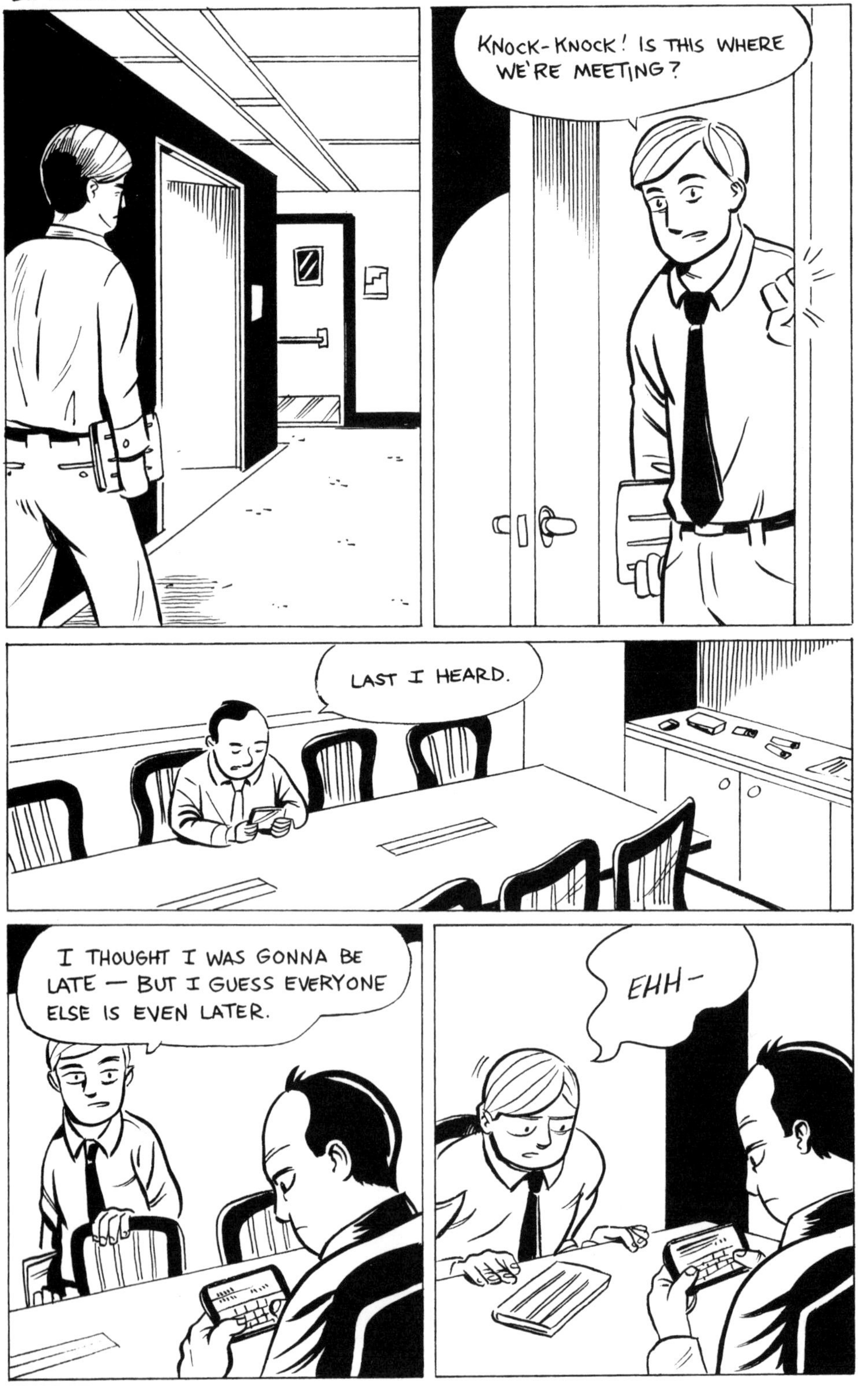

KNOCK-KNOCK! IS THIS WHERE WE'RE MEETING?
LAST I HEARD.
I THOUGHT I WAS GONNA BE LATE — BUT I GUESS EVERYONE ELSE IS EVEN LATER.
EHH-

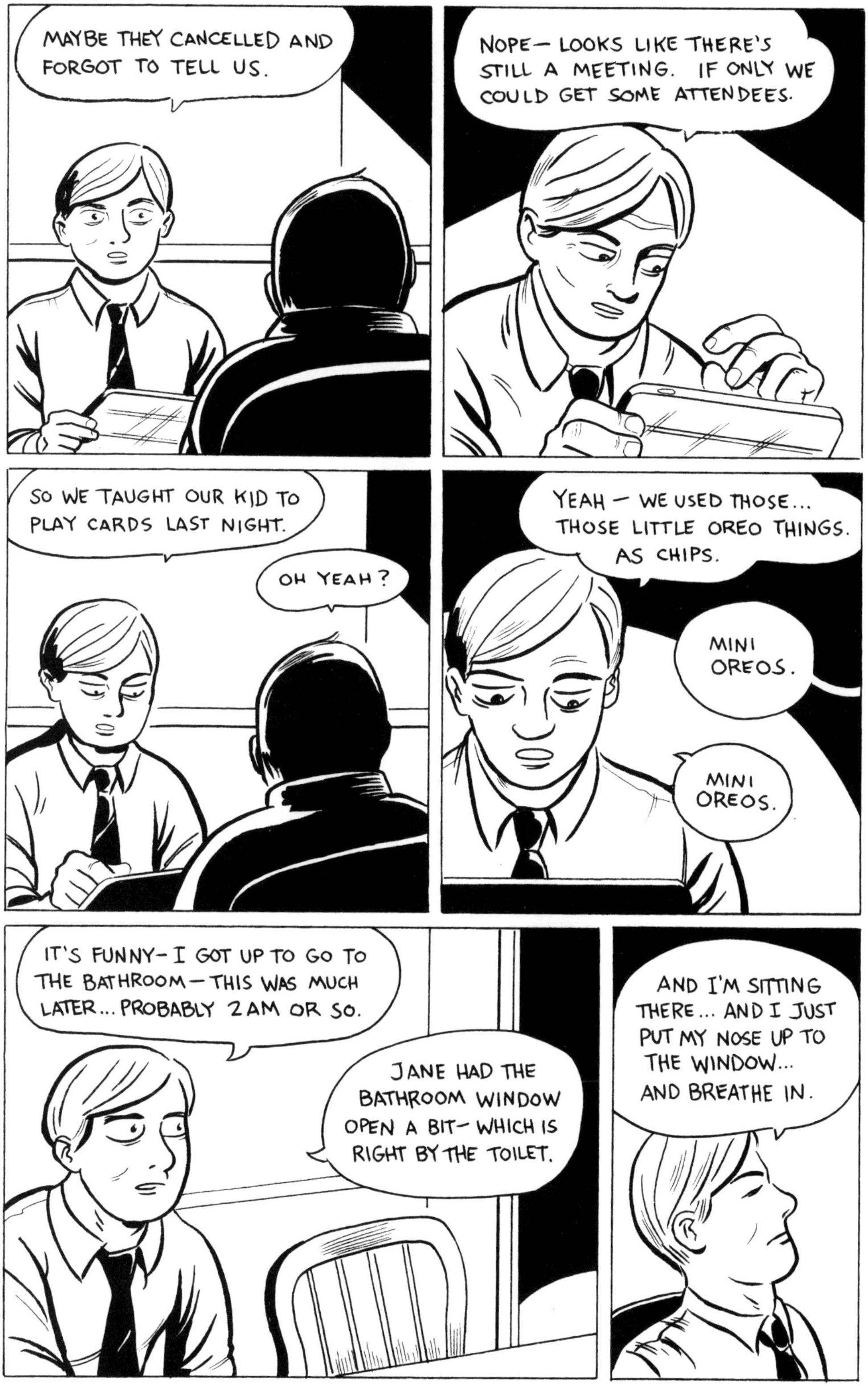
MAYBE THEY CANCELLED AND FORGOT TO TELL US.
NOPE— LOOKS LIKE THERE'S STILL A MEETING. IF ONLY WE COULD GET SOME ATTENDEES.
SO WE TAUGHT OUR KID TO PLAY CARDS LAST NIGHT.
OH YEAH?
YEAH — WE USED THOSE... THOSE LITTLE OREO THINGS. AS CHIPS.
MINI OREOS.
MINI OREOS.
IT'S FUNNY— I GOT UP TO GO TO THE BATHROOM — THIS WAS MUCH LATER... PROBABLY 2 AM OR SO.
JANE HAD THE BATHROOM WINDOW OPEN A BIT— WHICH IS RIGHT BY THE TOILET.
AND I'M SITTING THERE... AND I JUST PUT MY NOSE UP TO THE WINDOW... AND BREATHE IN.

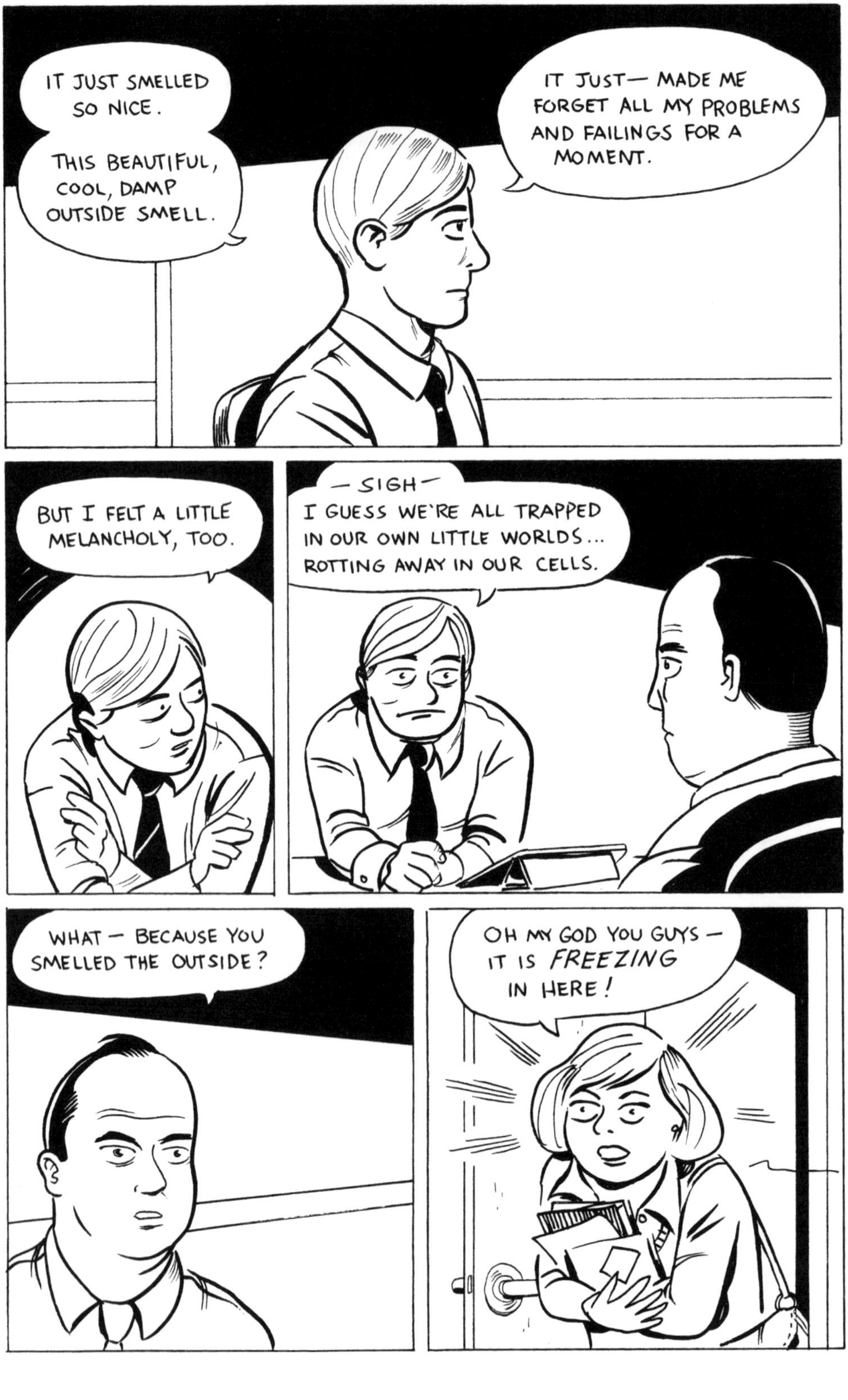
IT JUST SMELLED SO NICE.
THIS BEAUTIFUL, COOL, DAMP OUTSIDE SMELL.
IT JUST— MADE ME FORGET ALL MY PROBLEMS AND FAILINGS FOR A MOMENT.
BUT I FELT A LITTLE MELANCHOLY, TOO.
—SIGH—
I GUESS WE'RE ALL TRAPPED IN OUR OWN LITTLE WORLDS... ROTTING AWAY IN OUR CELLS.
WHAT — BECAUSE YOU SMELLED THE OUTSIDE?
OH MY GOD YOU GUYS — IT IS *FREEZING* IN HERE!

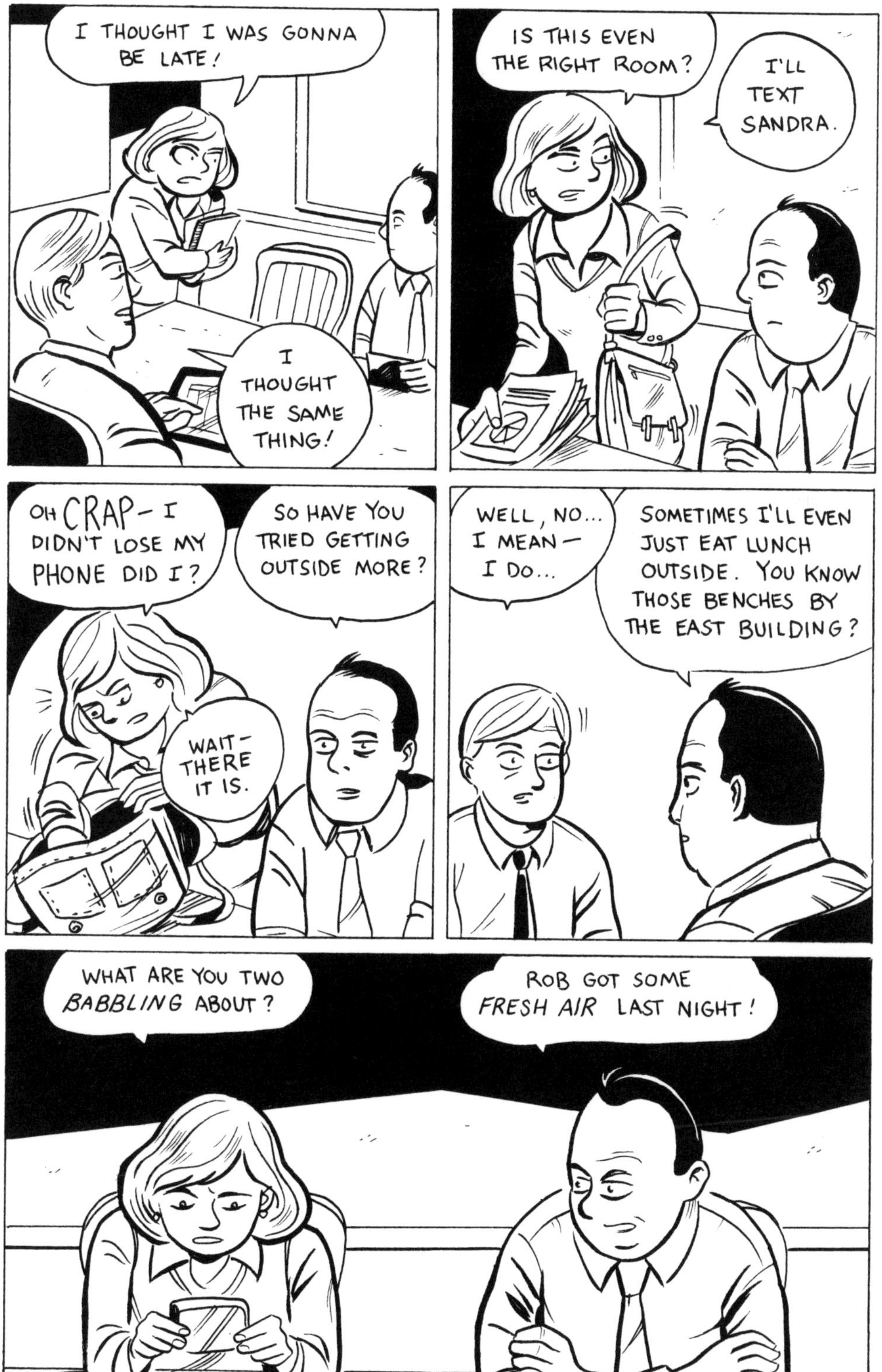
I THOUGHT I WAS GONNA BE LATE!
I THOUGHT THE SAME THING!
IS THIS EVEN THE RIGHT ROOM?
I'LL TEXT SANDRA.
OH CRAP– I DIDN'T LOSE MY PHONE DID I?
SO HAVE YOU TRIED GETTING OUTSIDE MORE?
WAIT– THERE IT IS.
WELL, NO... I MEAN– I DO...
SOMETIMES I'LL EVEN JUST EAT LUNCH OUTSIDE. YOU KNOW THOSE BENCHES BY THE EAST BUILDING?
WHAT ARE YOU TWO *BABBLING* ABOUT?
ROB GOT SOME *FRESH AIR* LAST NIGHT!

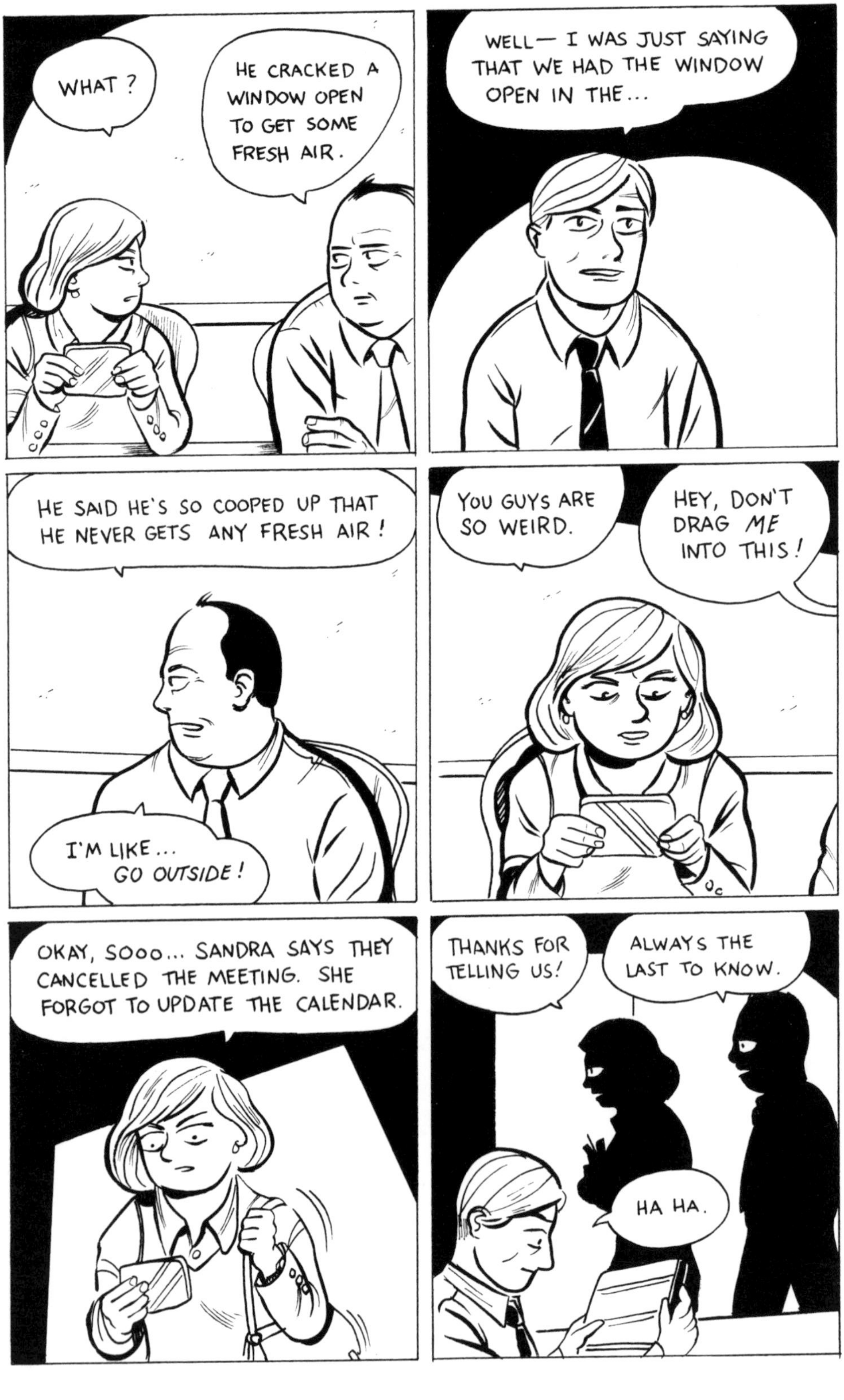
WHAT ?
HE CRACKED A WINDOW OPEN TO GET SOME FRESH AIR.
WELL— I WAS JUST SAYING THAT WE HAD THE WINDOW OPEN IN THE...
HE SAID HE'S SO COOPED UP THAT HE NEVER GETS ANY FRESH AIR!
I'M LIKE... GO OUTSIDE!
YOU GUYS ARE SO WEIRD.
HEY, DON'T DRAG ME INTO THIS!
OKAY, SOoo... SANDRA SAYS THEY CANCELLED THE MEETING. SHE FORGOT TO UPDATE THE CALENDAR.
THANKS FOR TELLING US!
ALWAYS THE LAST TO KNOW.
HA HA.

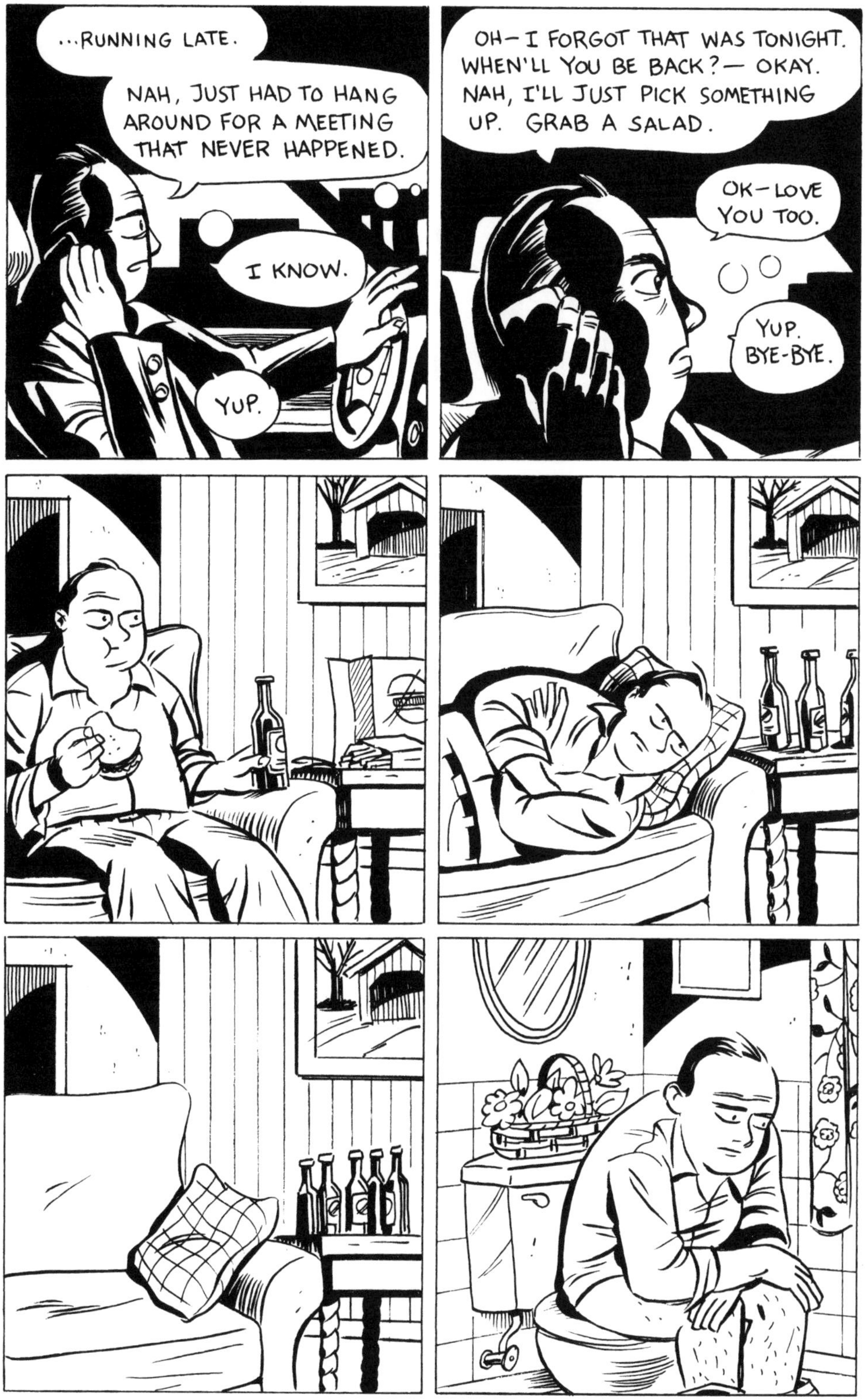
...RUNNING LATE.
NAH, JUST HAD TO HANG AROUND FOR A MEETING THAT NEVER HAPPENED.
I KNOW.
YUP.
OH— I FORGOT THAT WAS TONIGHT. WHEN'LL YOU BE BACK?— OKAY. NAH, I'LL JUST PICK SOMETHING UP. GRAB A SALAD.
OK— LOVE YOU TOO.
YUP. BYE-BYE.

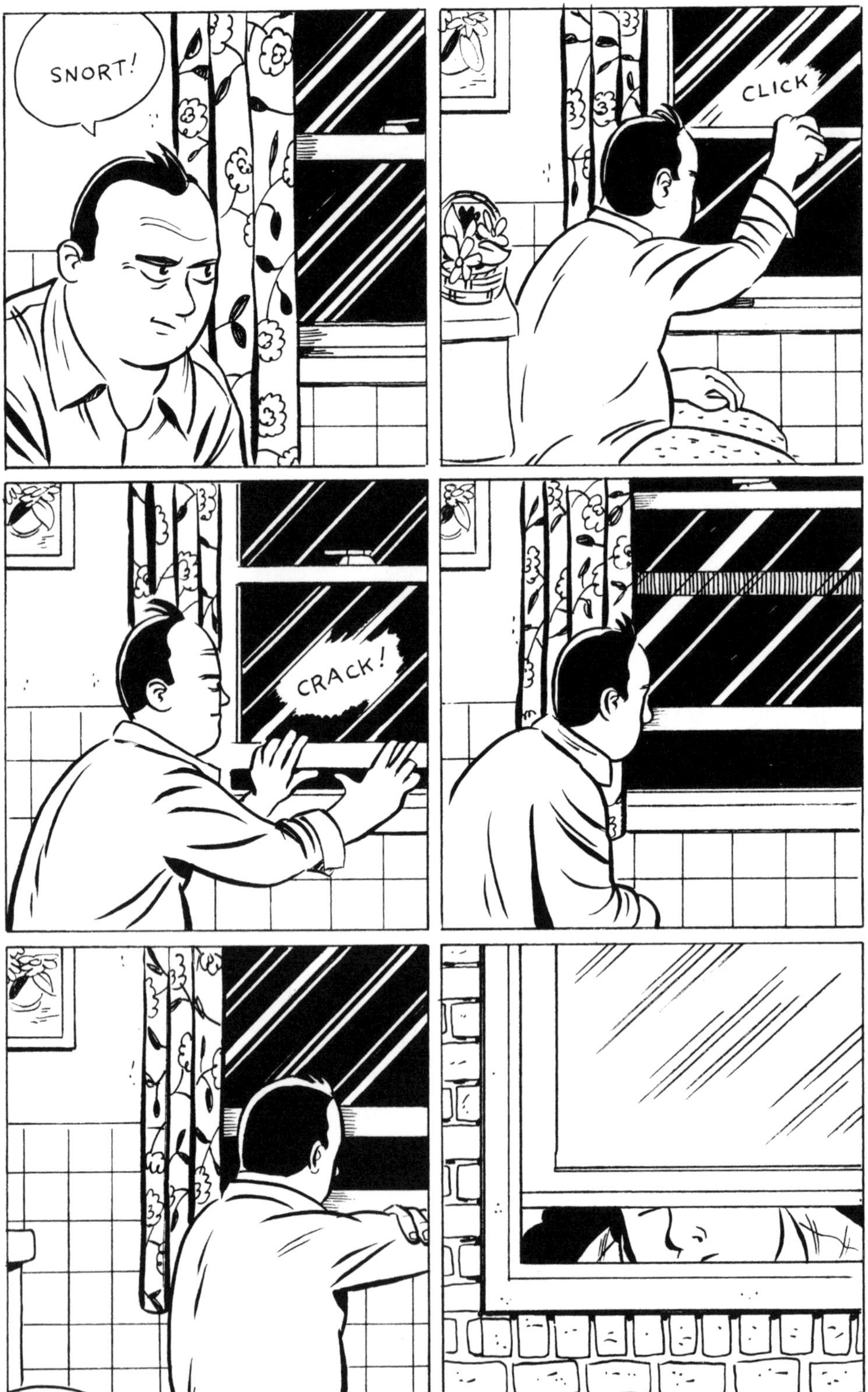
SNORT!
CLICK
CRACK!

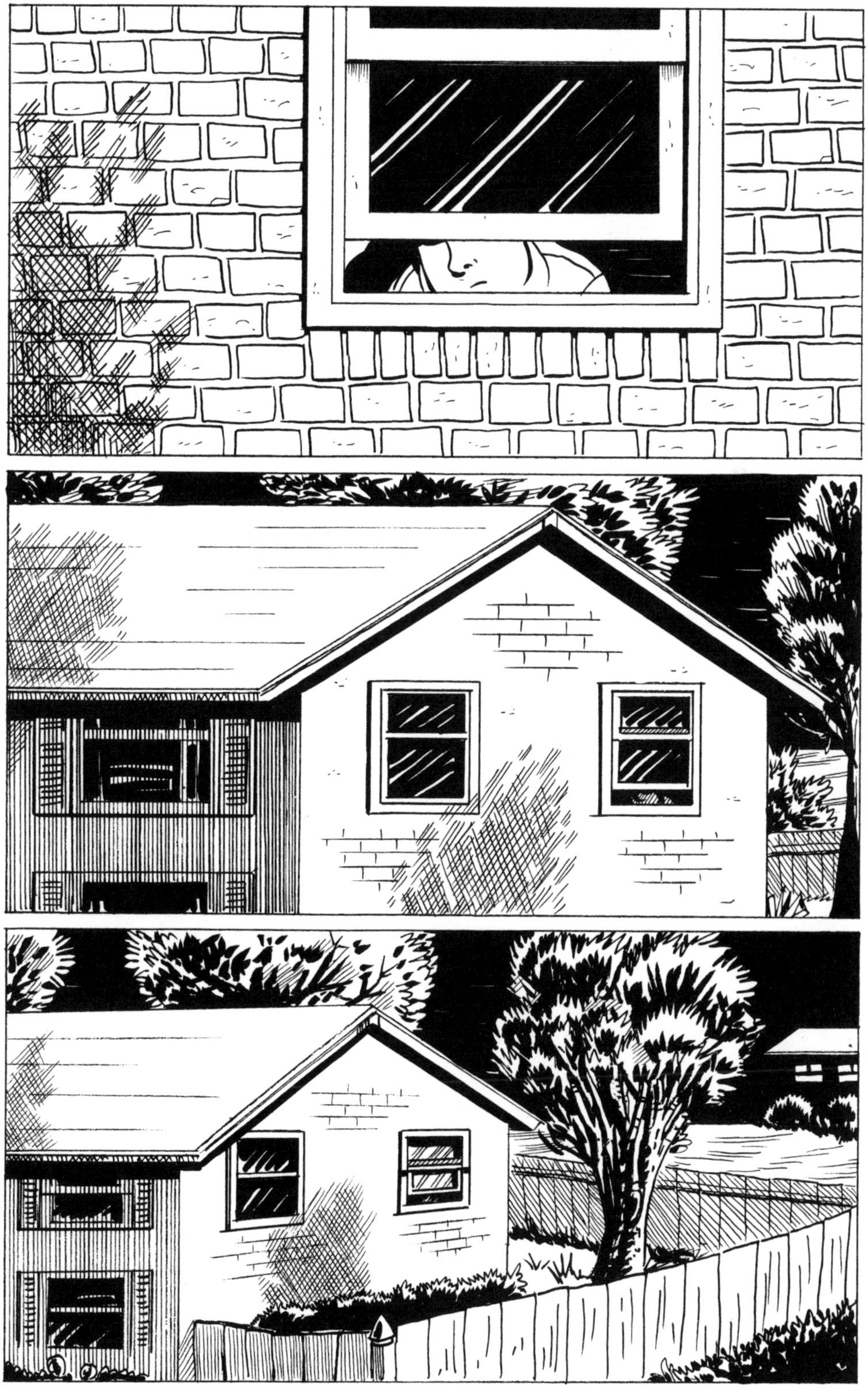

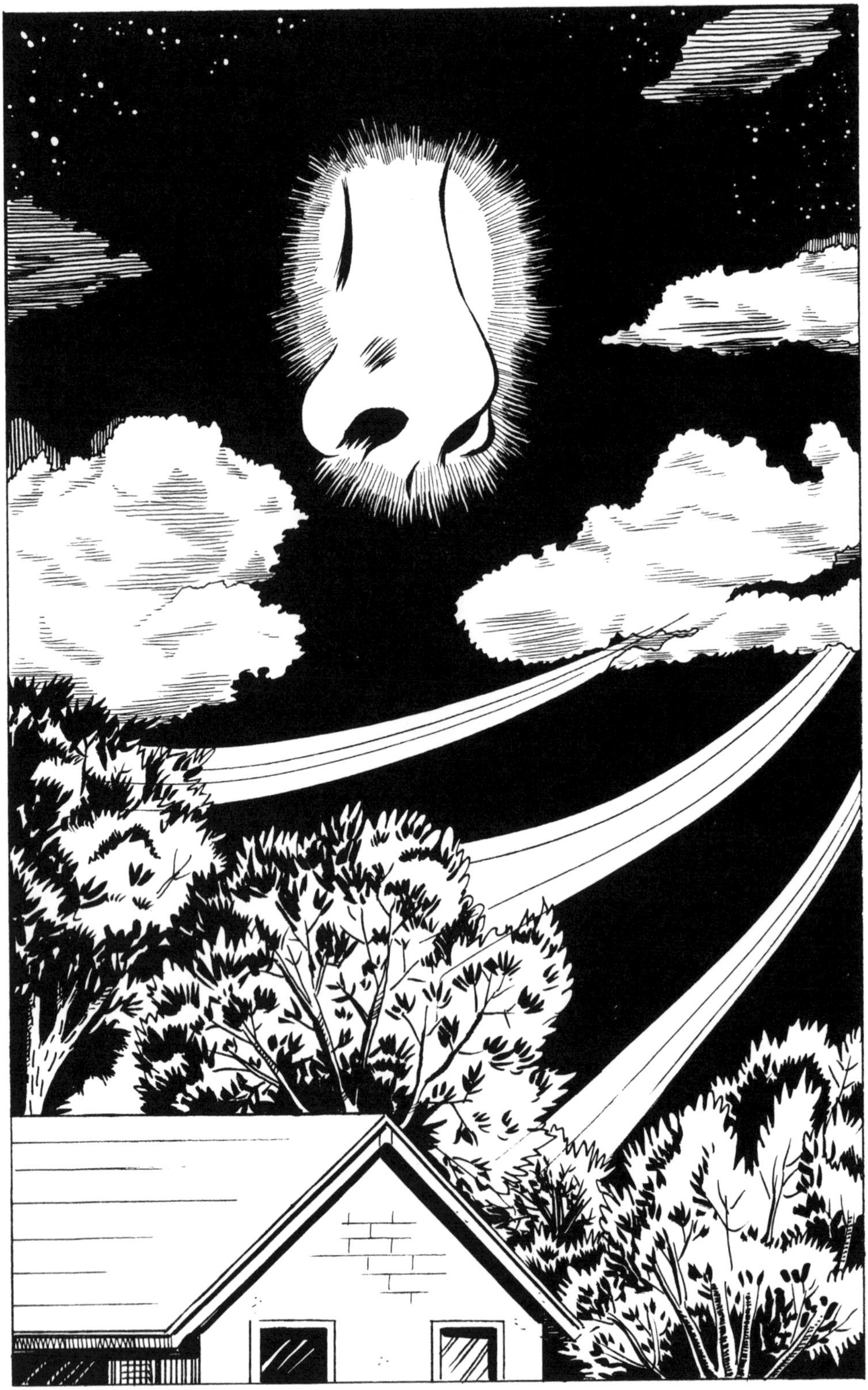

The Book of the Year

Is Not a Book

On almost any critic's list of North American cartoonists, Chris Ware's name is bound to land at or near the top. I know he's atop mine, along with precious few others. "Art is not a competition," I hear Ware's gentle, reedy voice in my head. Yeah, yeah. Easy for you to say, buddy.

Cartoonists joke about the "Chris Ware effect." No matter how puffed up we get, no matter how pleased we may be with ourselves from time to time, one look at the latest efforts from the House of Ware and we all slink off into our inky sunsets, under gloomy thought balloons reading: "I suck."

There are dissenters: readers who find Ware's comics too cold and depressing. "Depressing" I get, but if his work strikes you as "cold," I hope you'll consider spending a bit more time with it, discovering the compassion Ware has for his characters' struggles. If anything, the mercury in that particular thermometer has only risen lately.

Booksellers historically have had a more intractable gripe with Ware, tearing their hair out while trying to shelve each new Acme Novelty Library publication, with its ever-changing sizes and shapes.

Format has always been an important consideration for Ware. Everything from binding to paper stock to ink density clearly matters in a Chris Ware book; it's

a crucial aspect of the reading experience. At a time when more cartoonists than ever are turning to the nontangible Internet for distribution of their stories, Ware has planted his flag firmly in the tangible world, making beautiful, indispensable objects no one would ever think to describe as "ephemeral."

Ware's penchant for exotic print sizes has finally spiraled out of control in his latest project *Building Stories*, a boxed collection of fourteen interrelated narrative artifacts. Some look like a child's Golden Book, some are pamphlets, some broadsheets; there's even a giant narrative diagram in the form of a game board. Every part is beautiful and the whole is much, much more than the sum of its parts.

"At least he put it all in one box this time," I imagine relieved booksellers saying.

Any attempt to reprint all or part of this masterpiece is doomed to be a pale reflection of the original, but to not do so in a book that dares to put "Best" in the title would be worse. So, in the spirit of the Hippocratic oath, we chose a silent story that appeared as a small booklet and could be reprinted with only minimal resizing.

Special thanks to Ware himself, who graciously allowed us to print these strips two-to-a-page for space considerations.

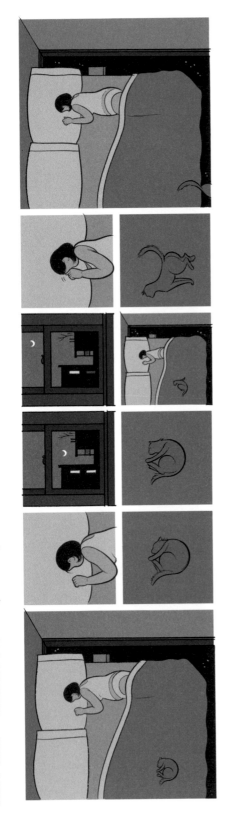

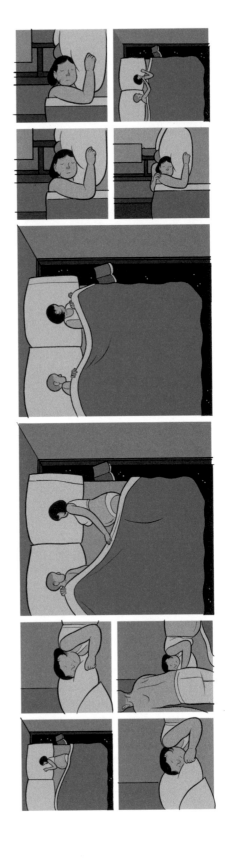

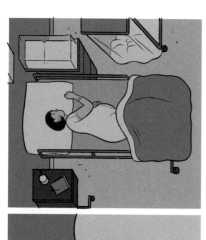

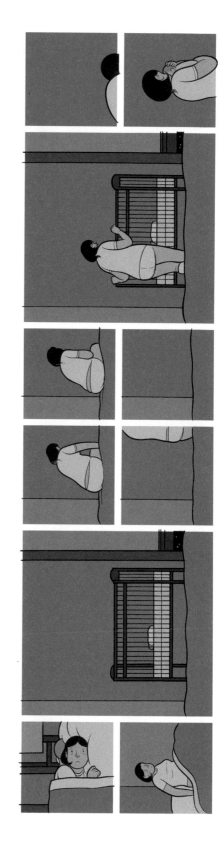

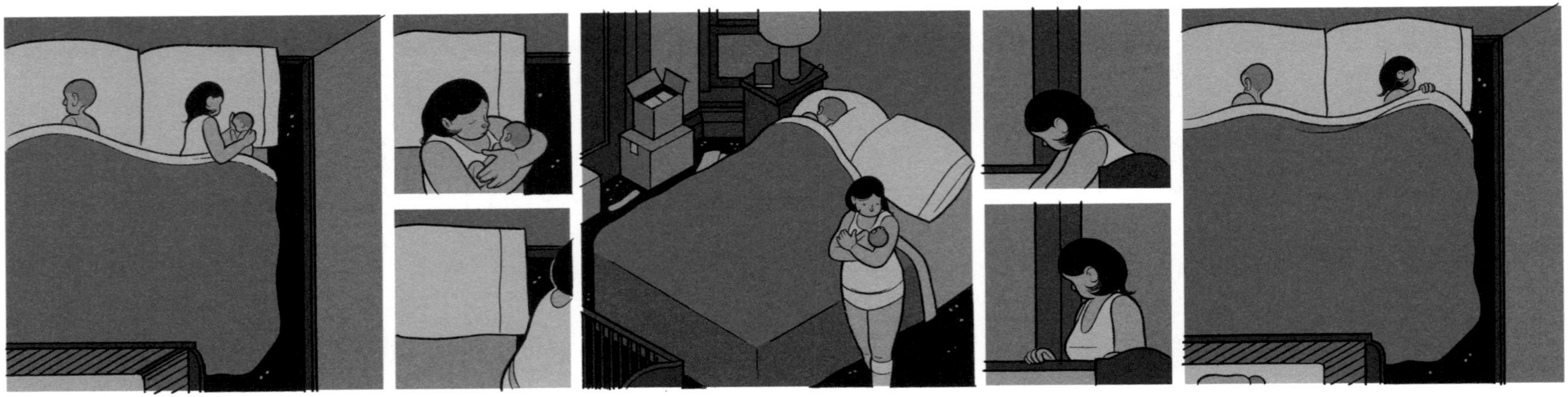

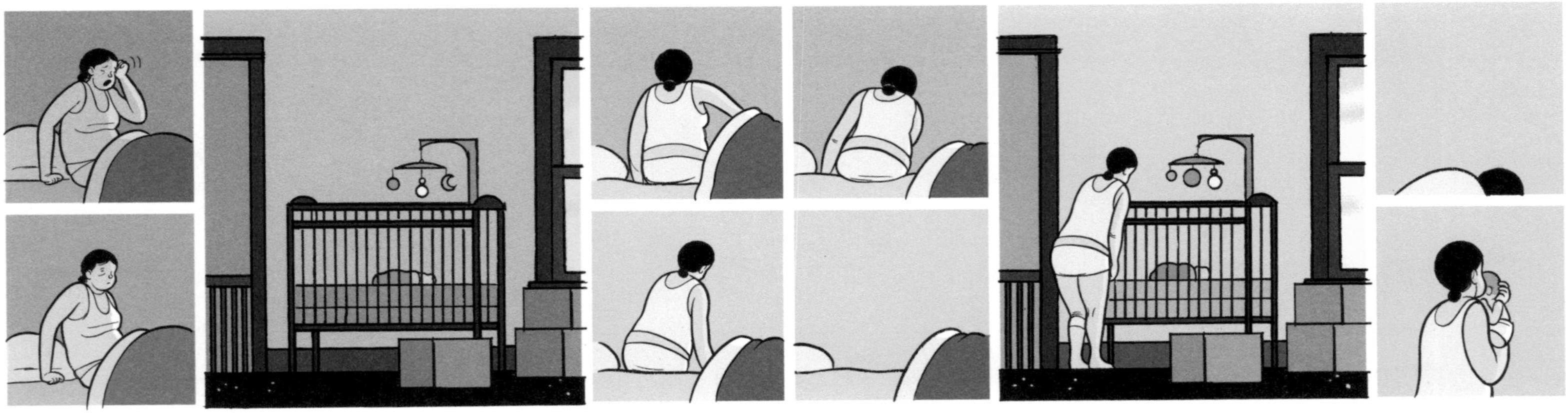

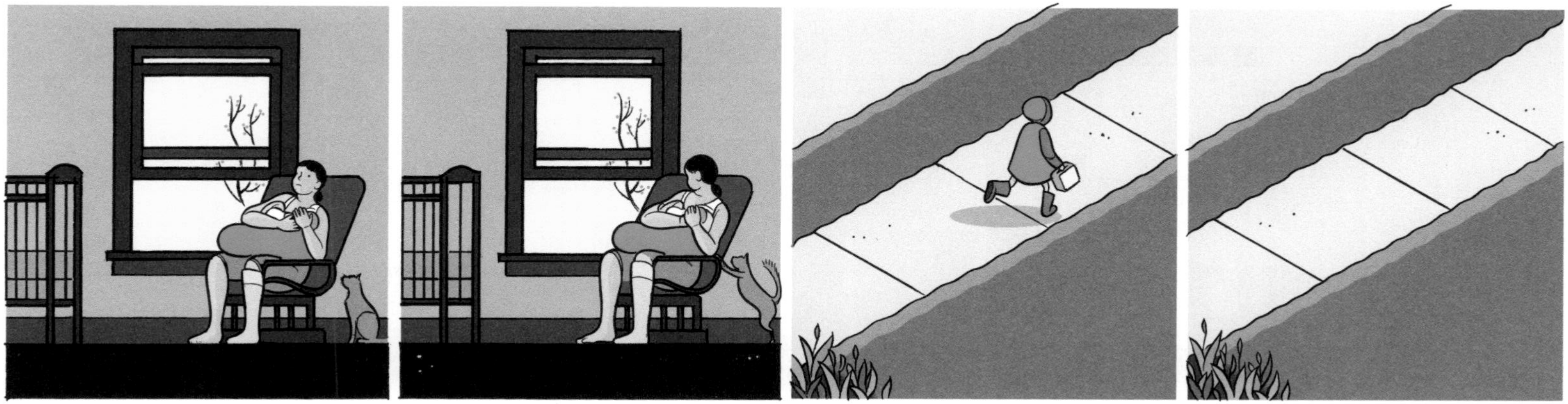

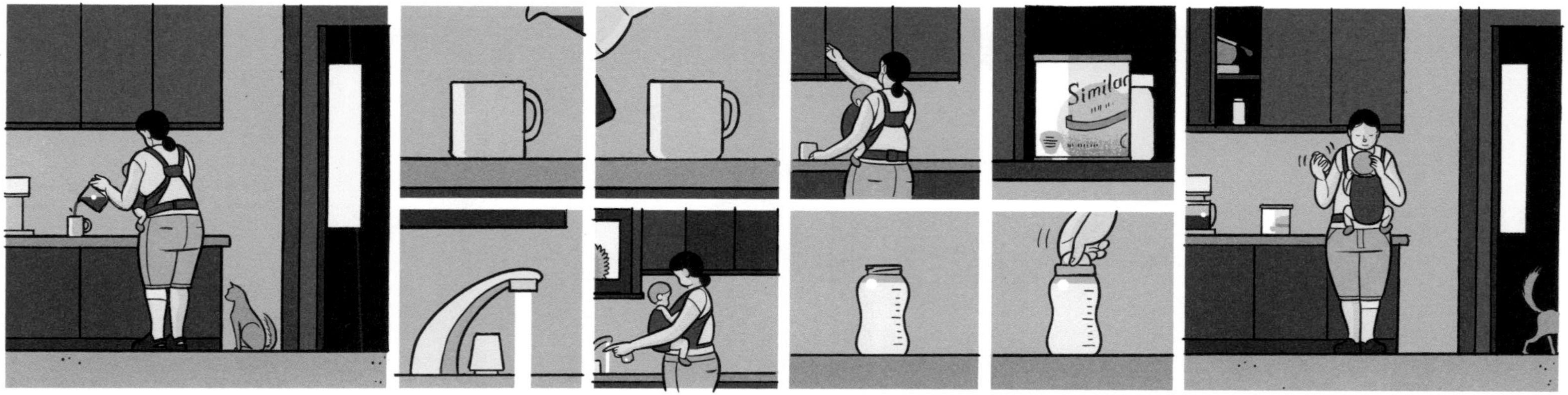

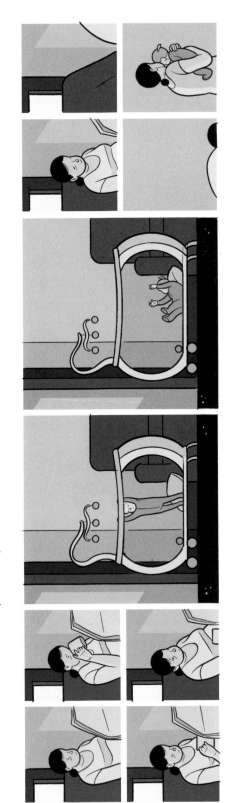

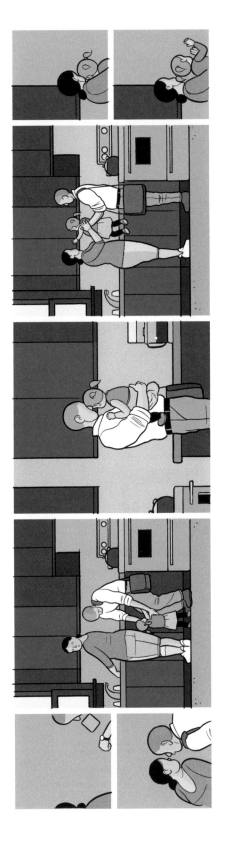

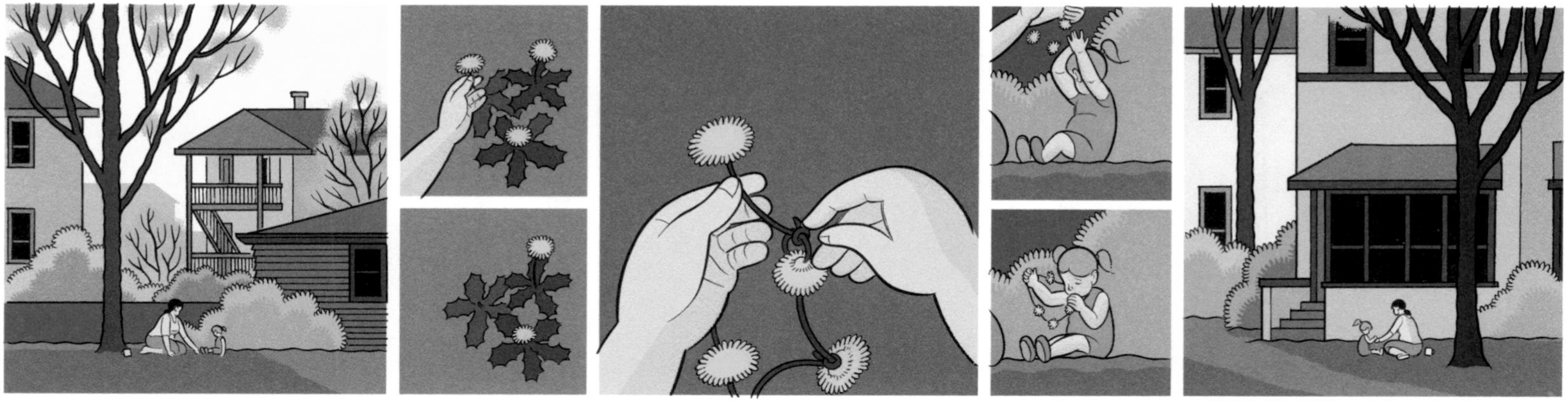

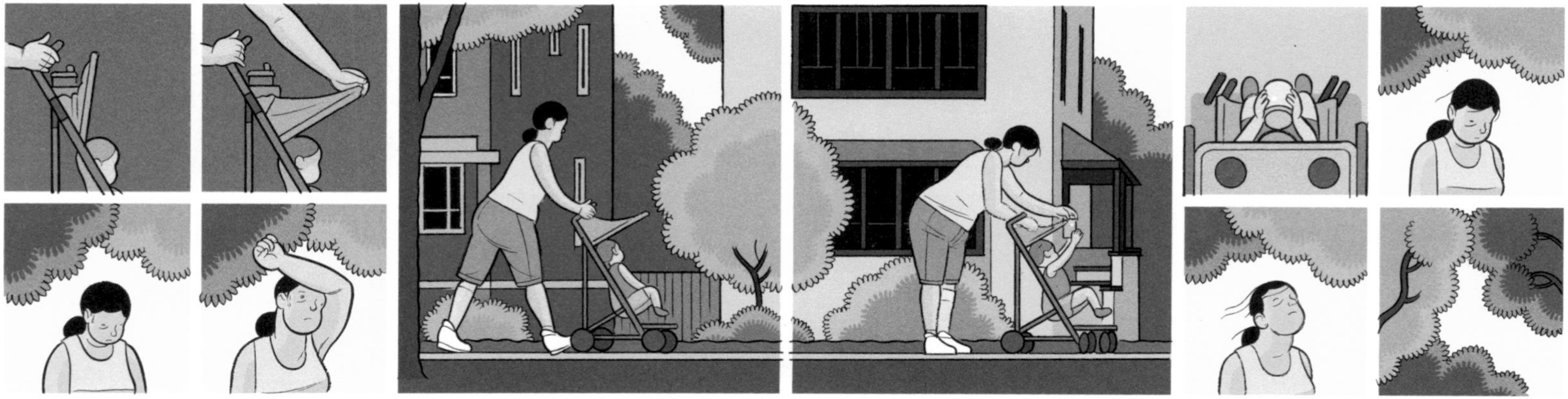

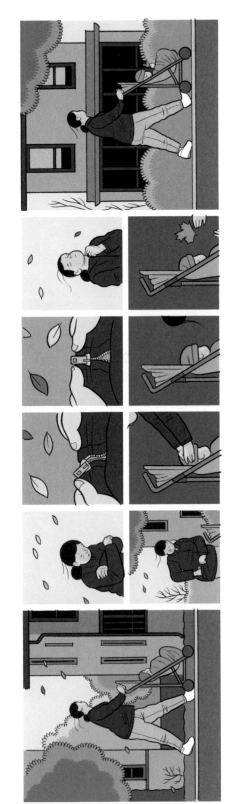

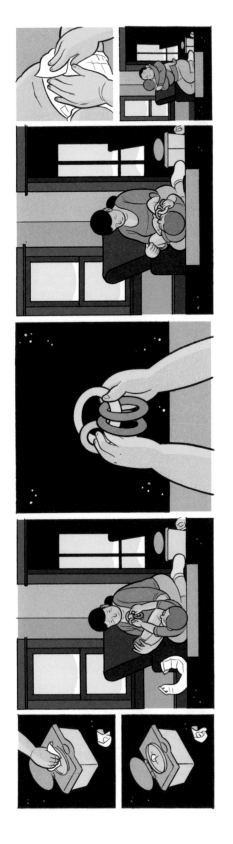

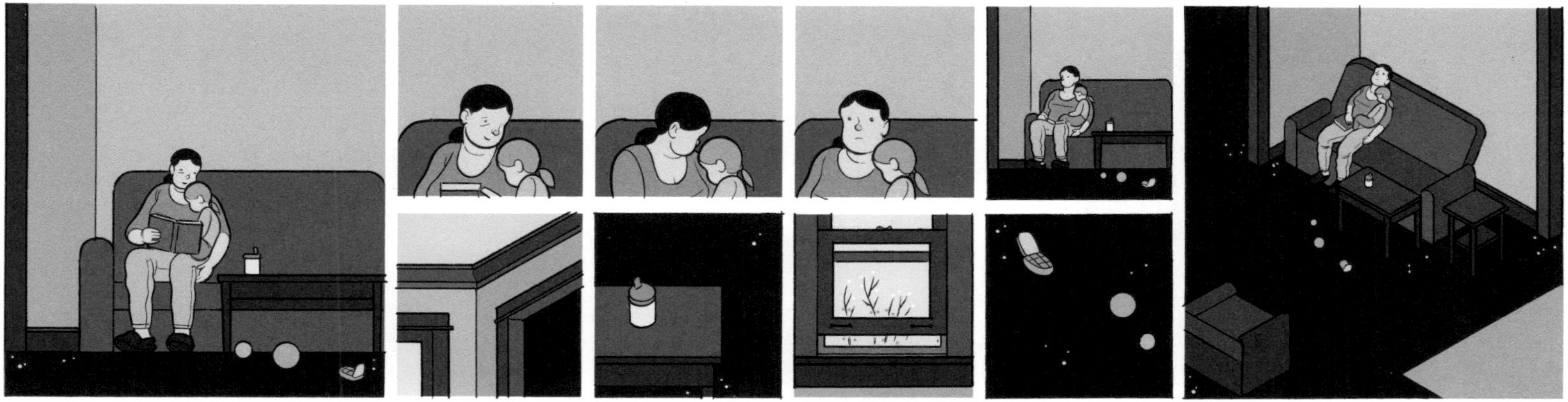

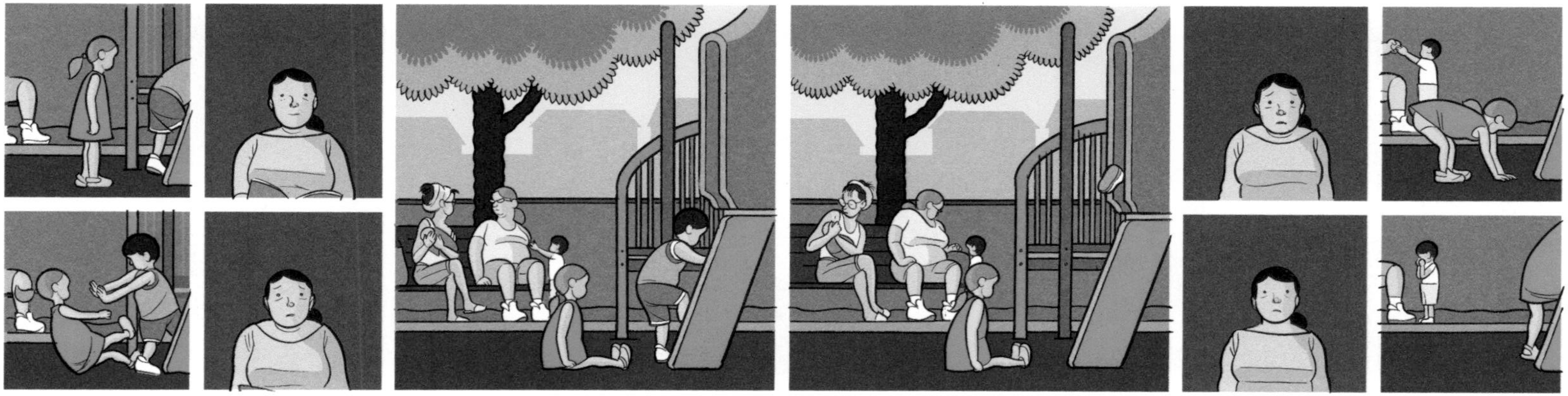

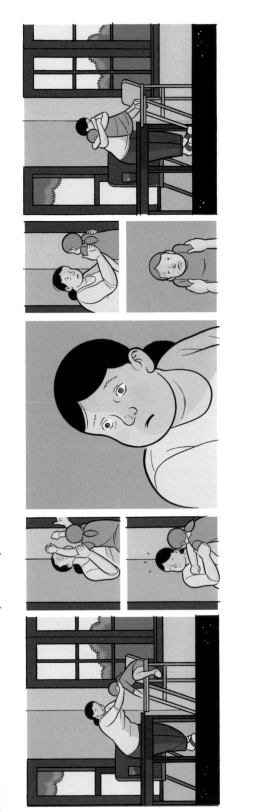

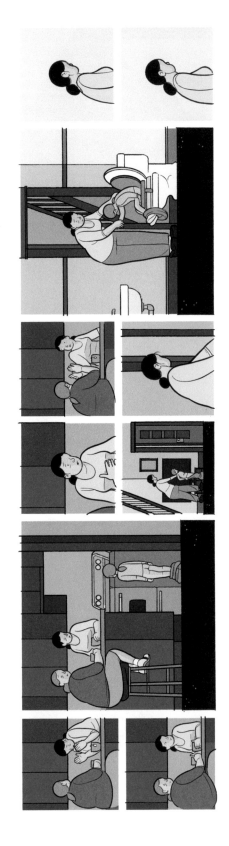

CHRIS WARE · BUILDING STORIES (EXCERPT) FROM BUILDING STORIES

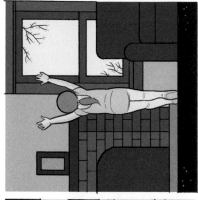

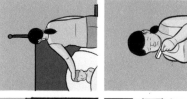
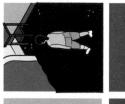

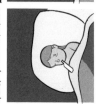

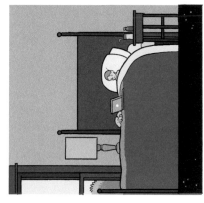

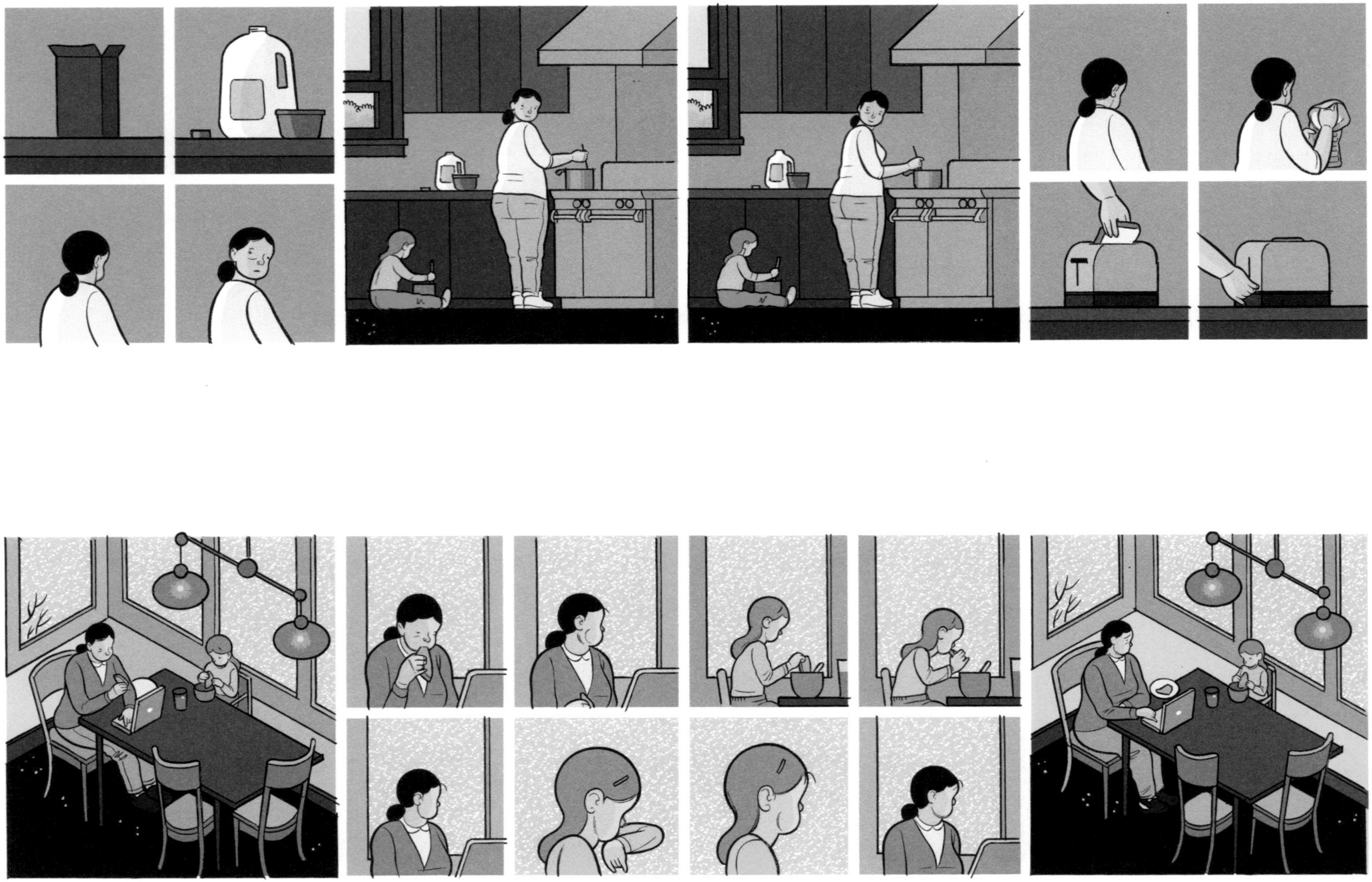

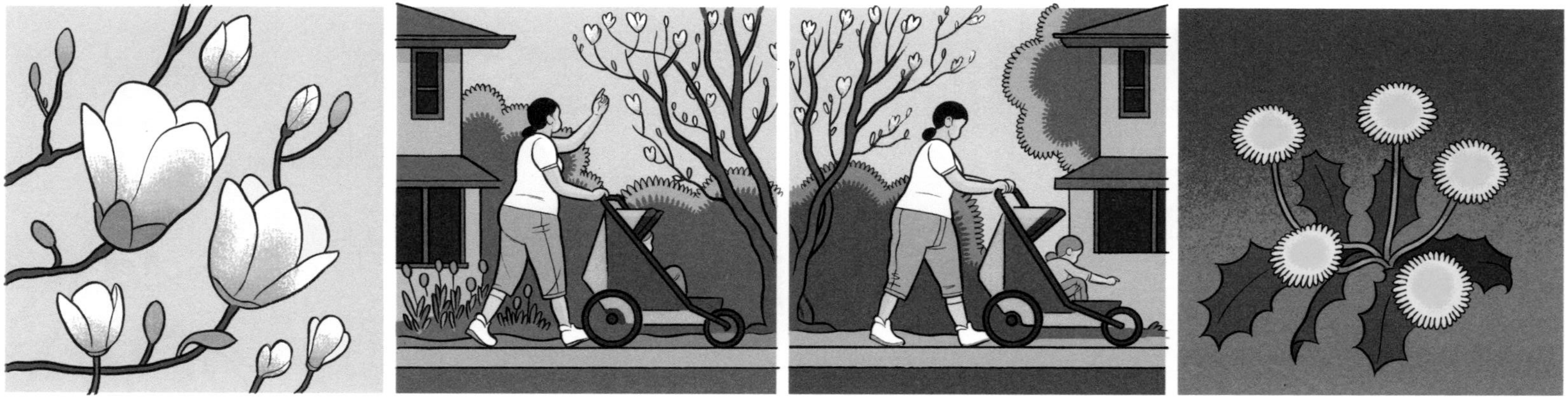

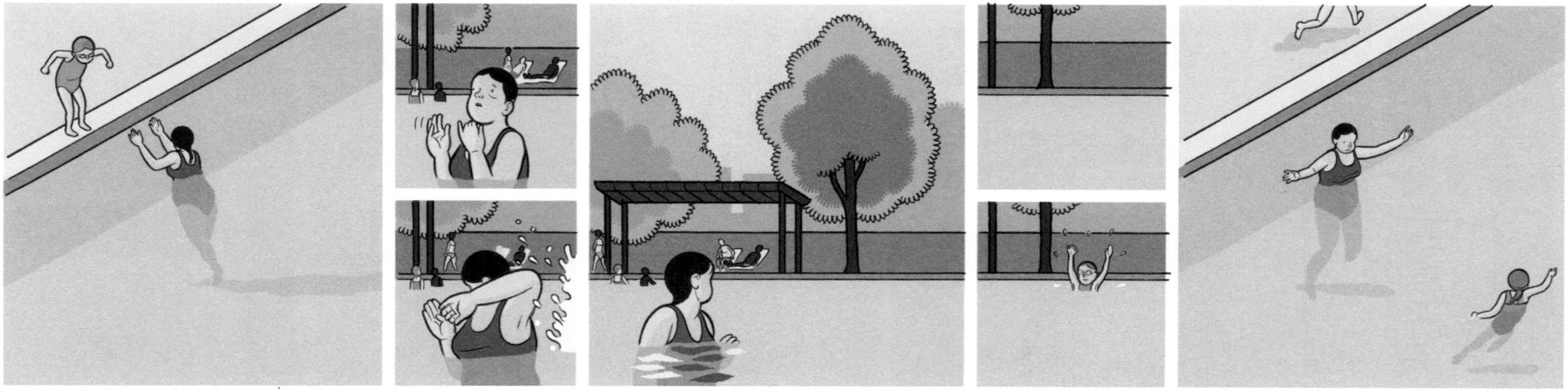

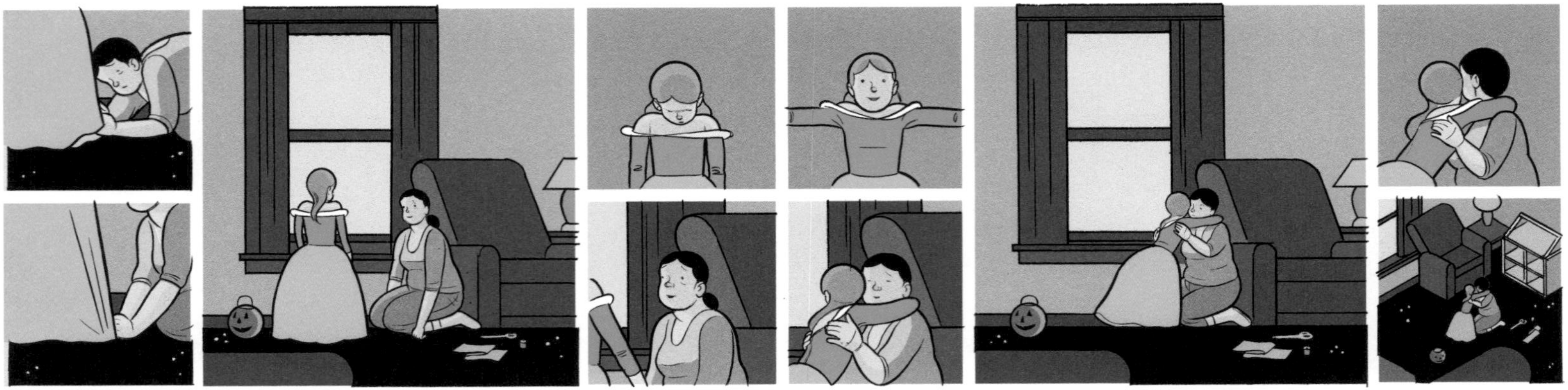

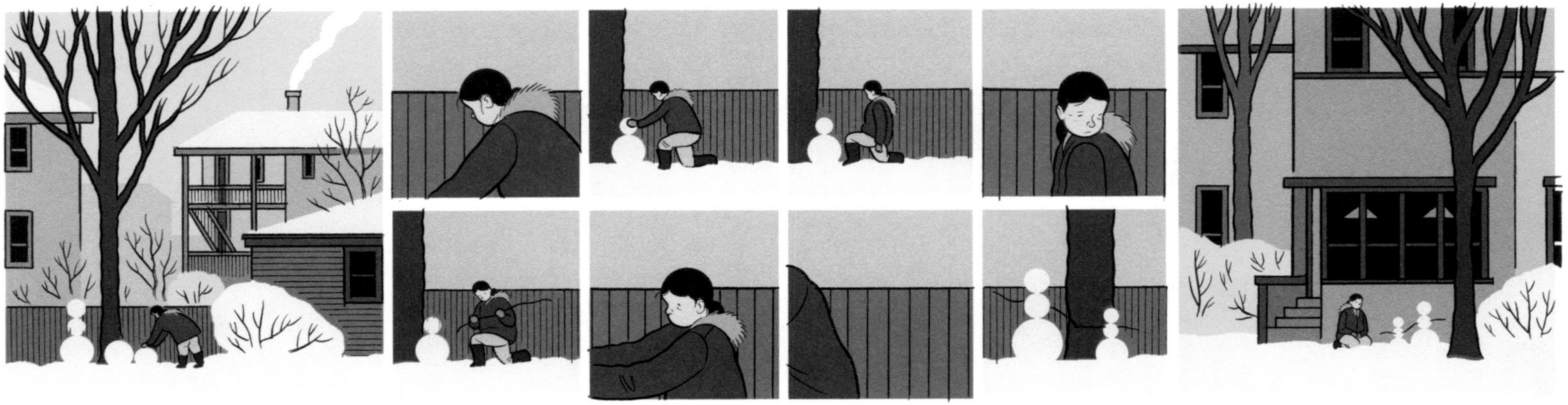

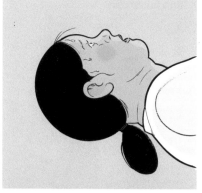

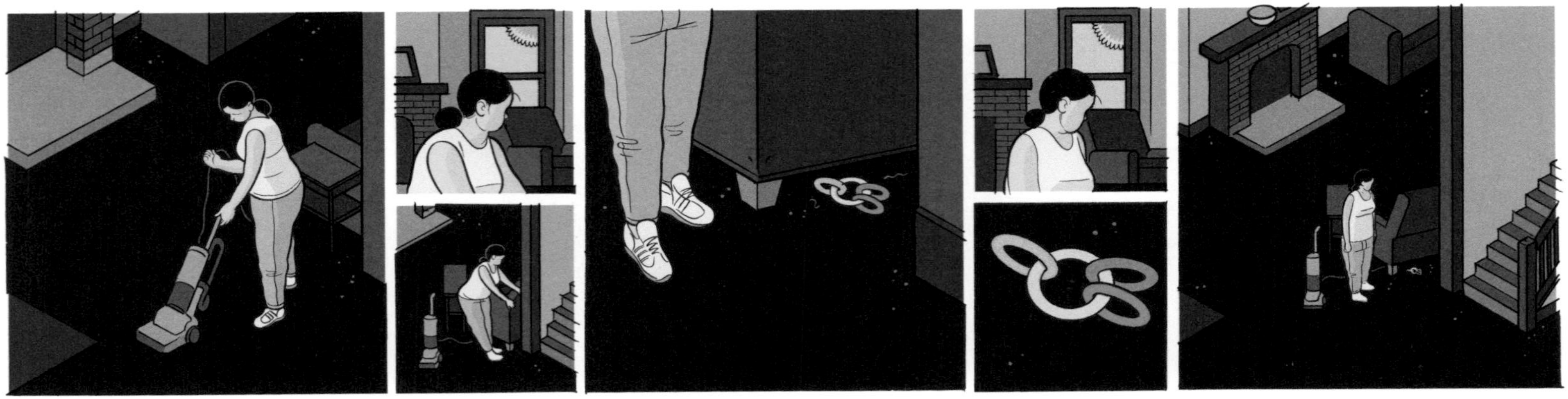

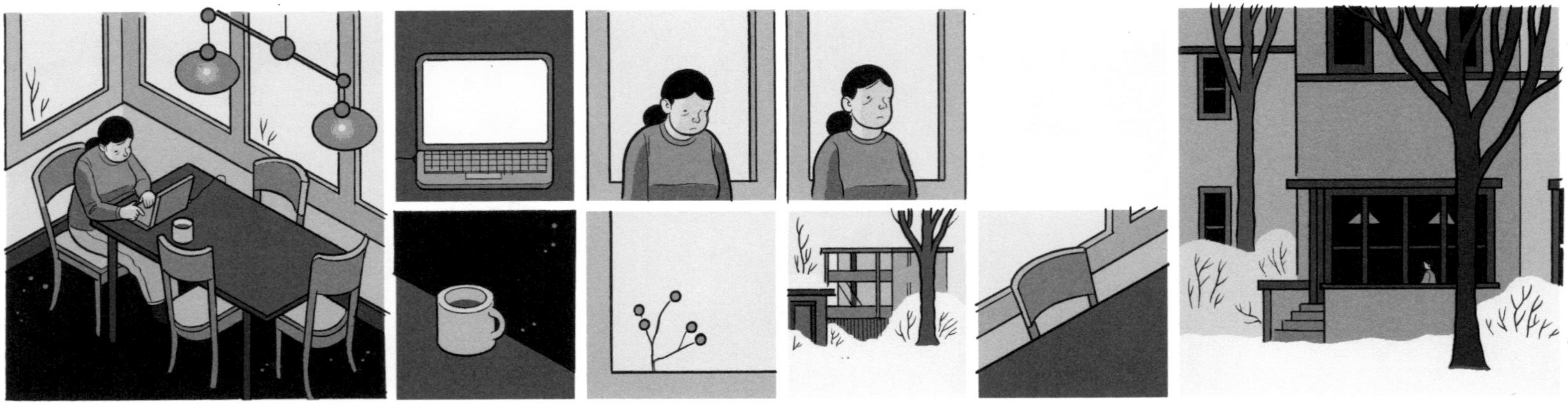

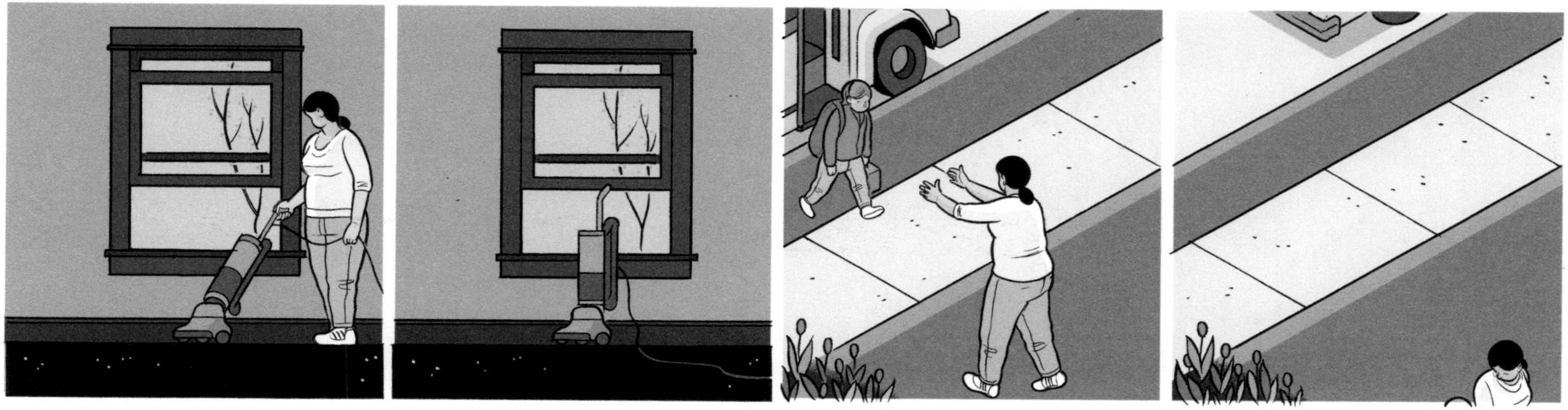

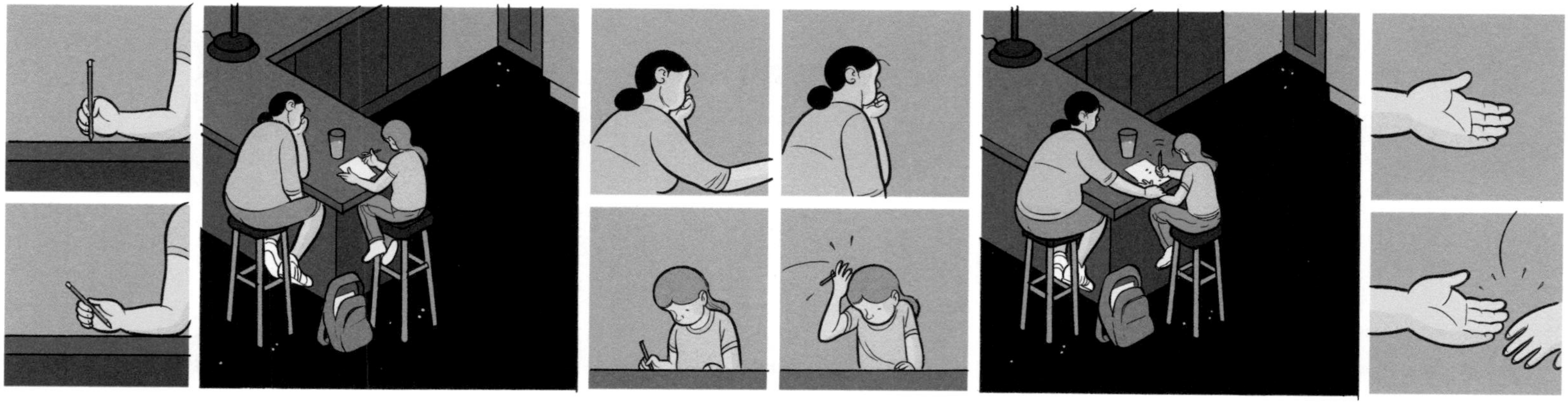

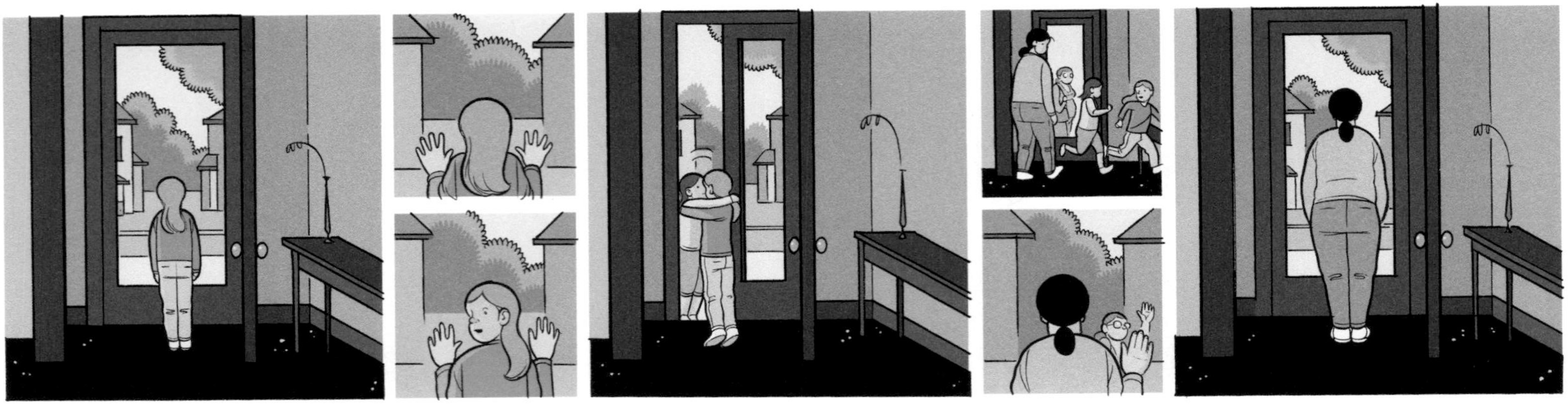

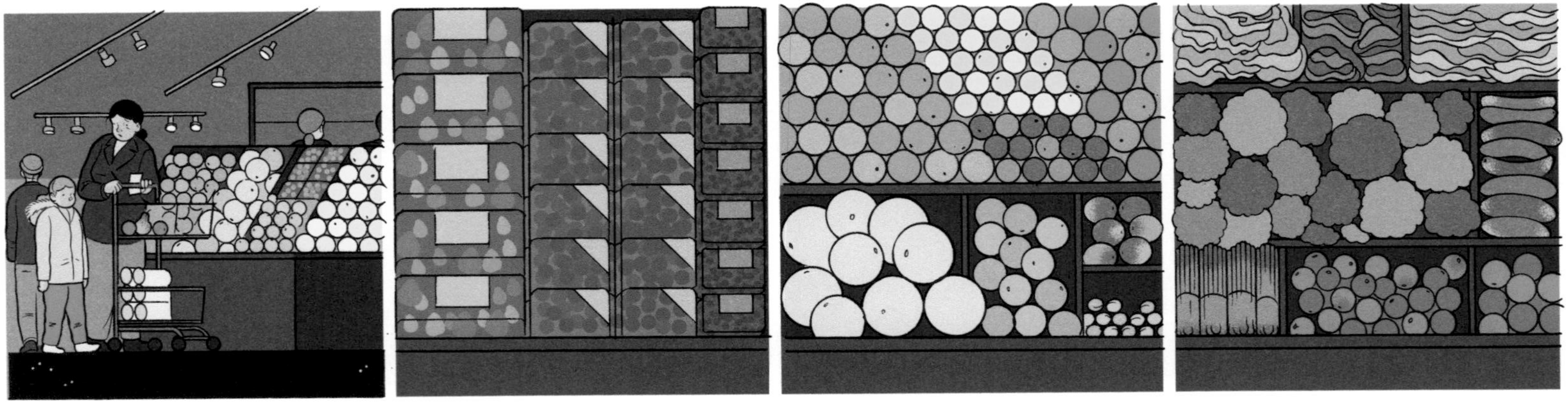

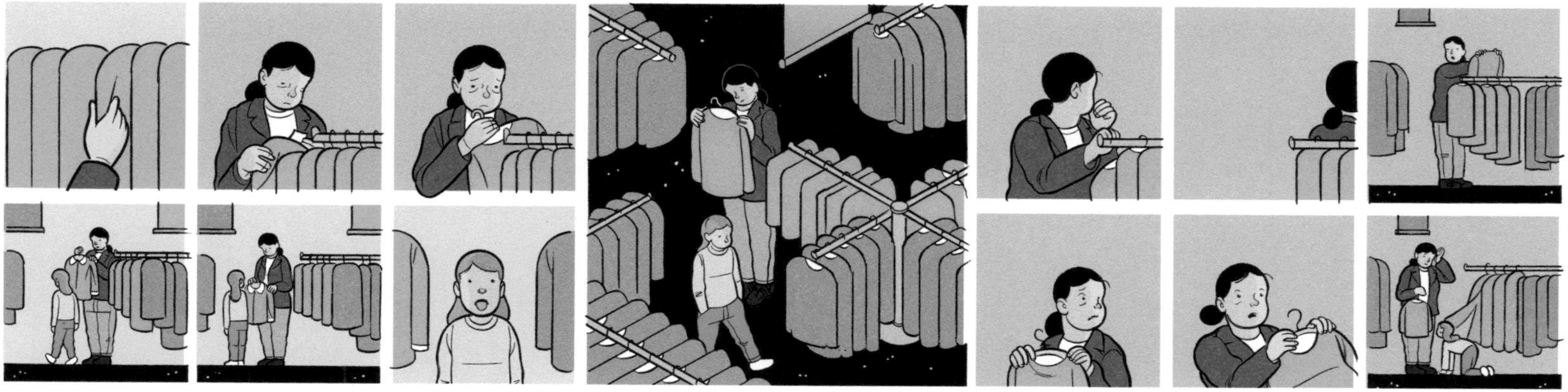

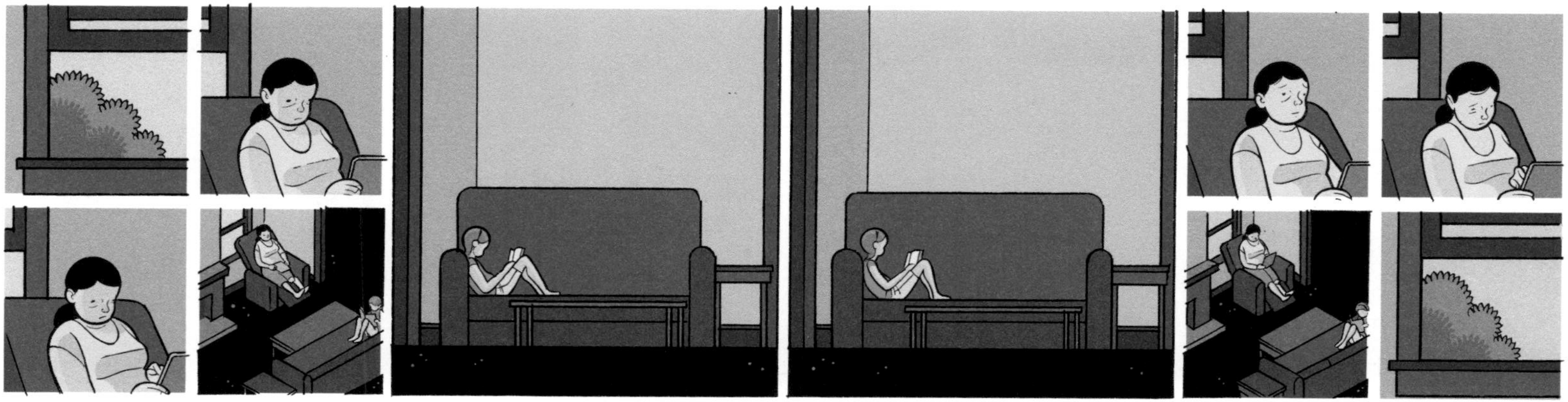

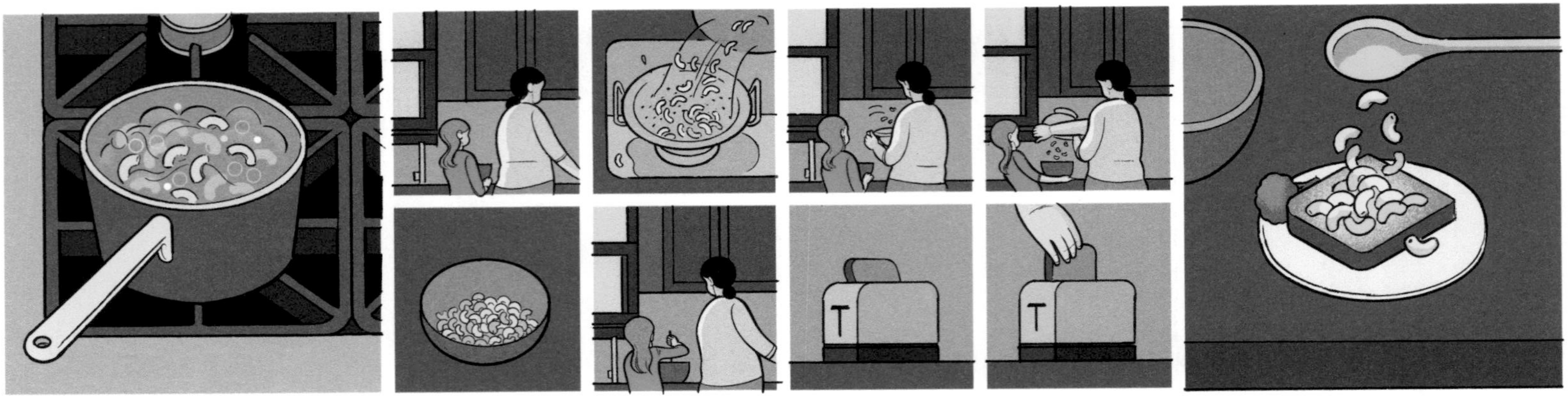

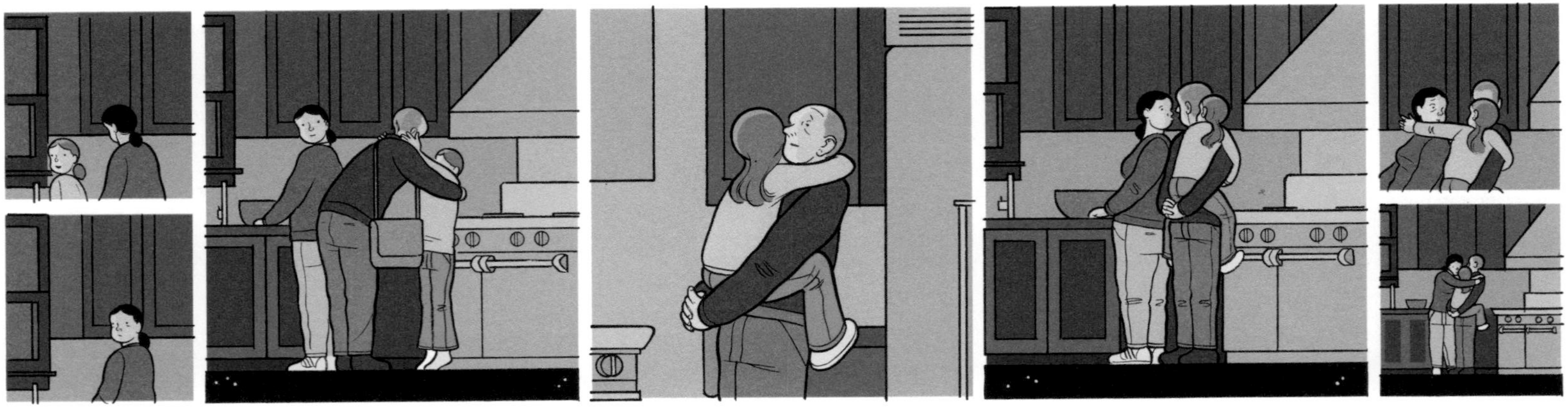

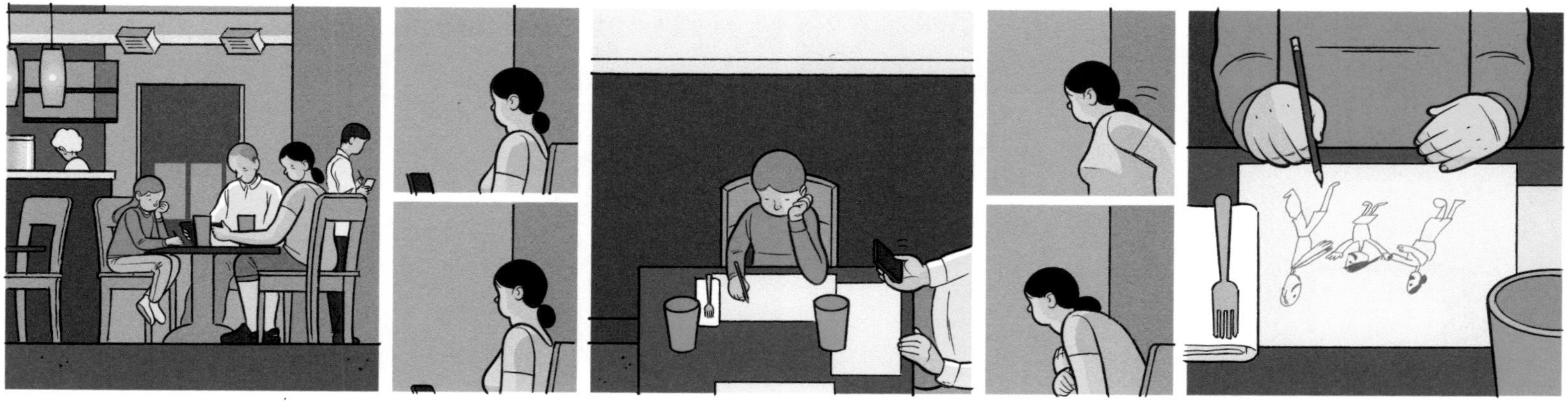

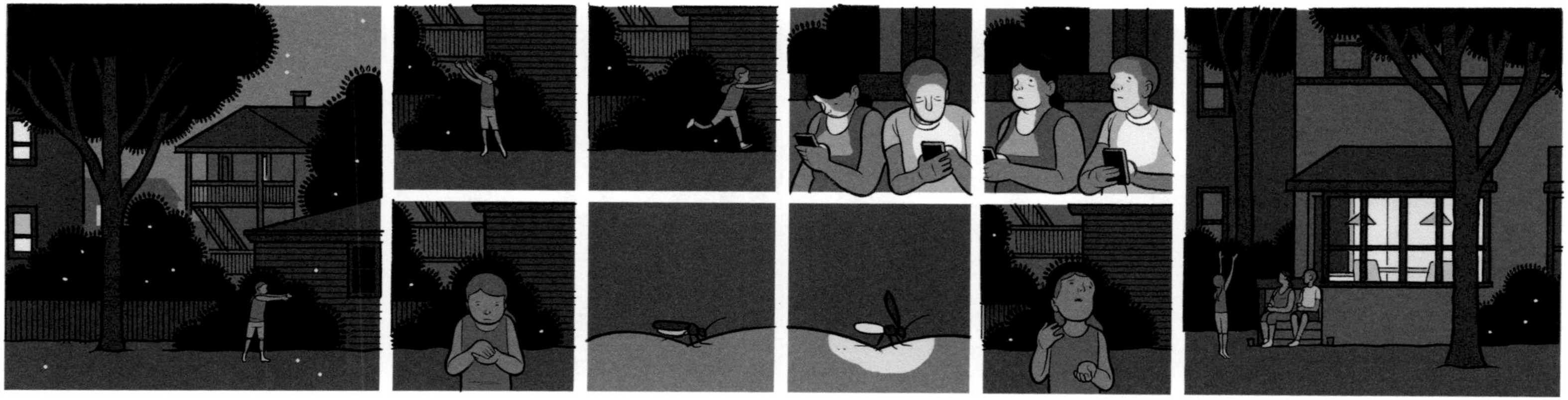

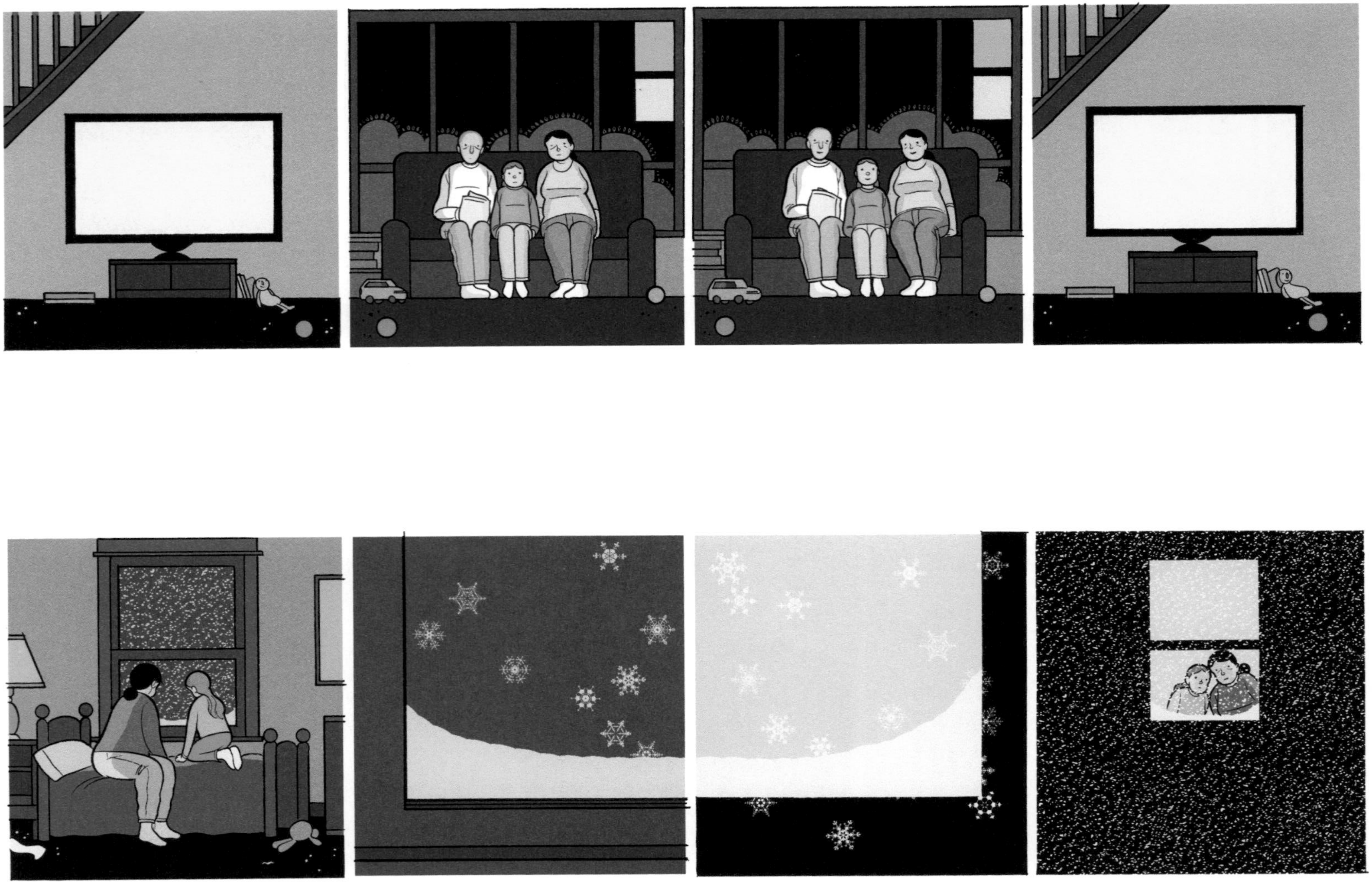

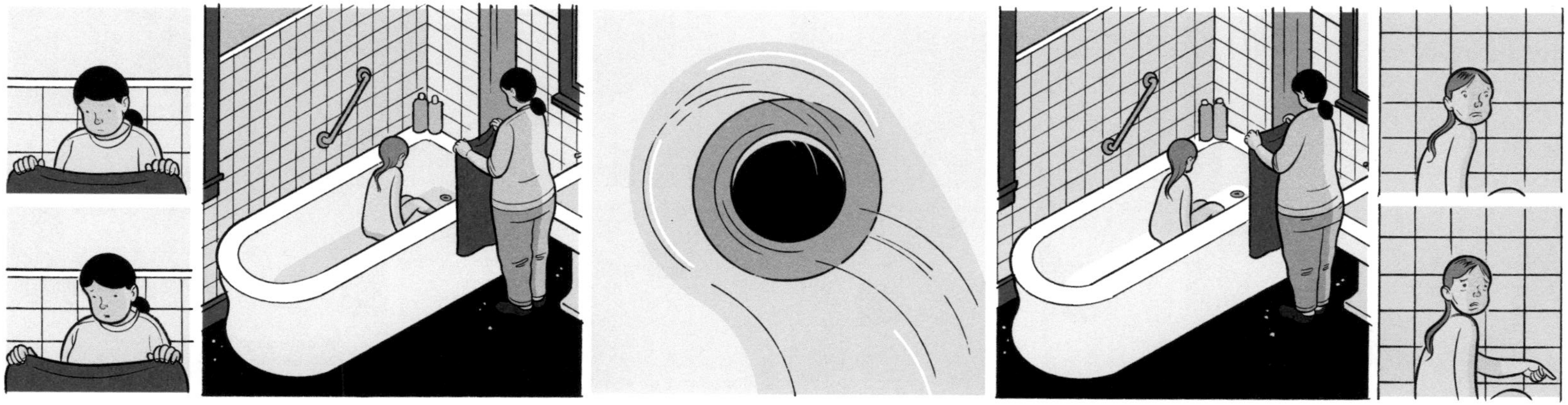

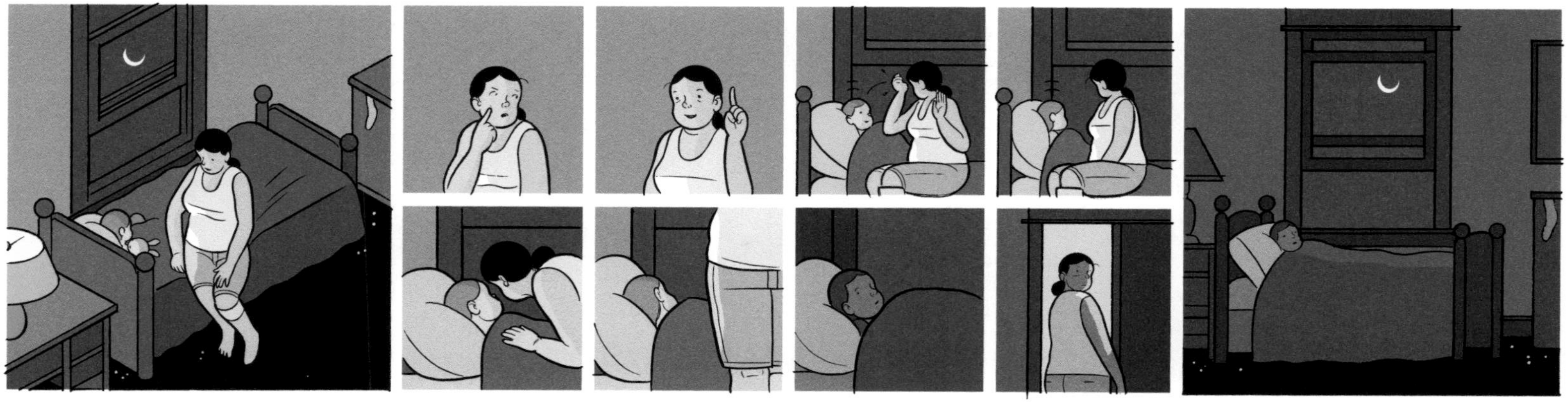

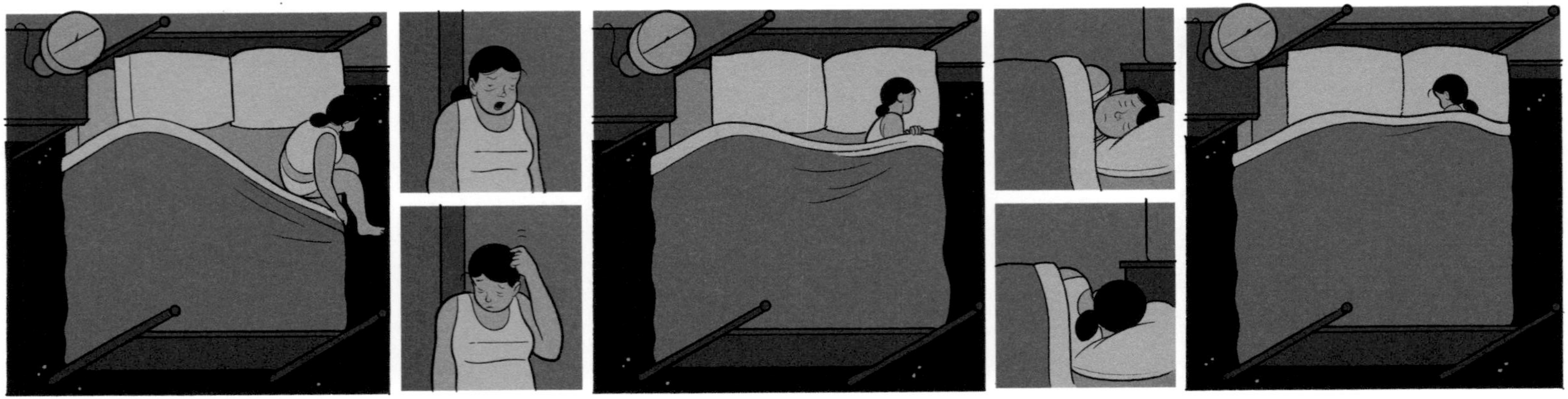

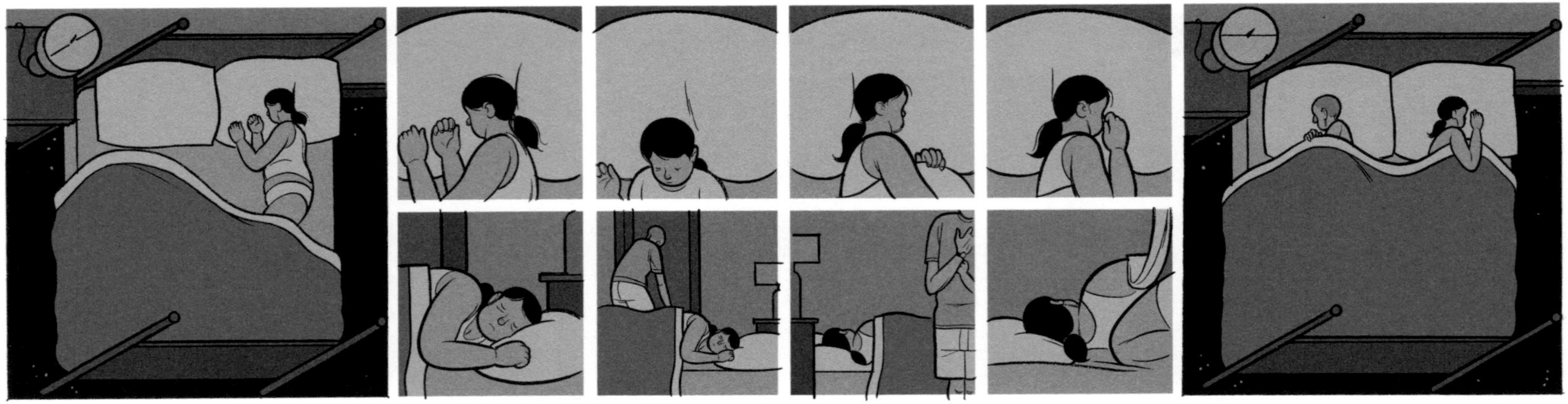

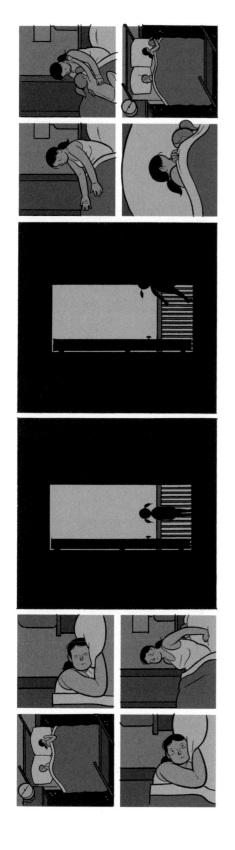

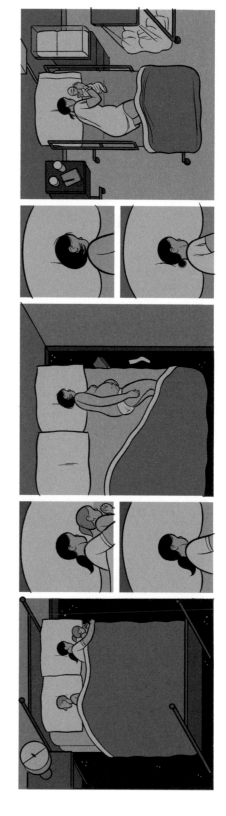

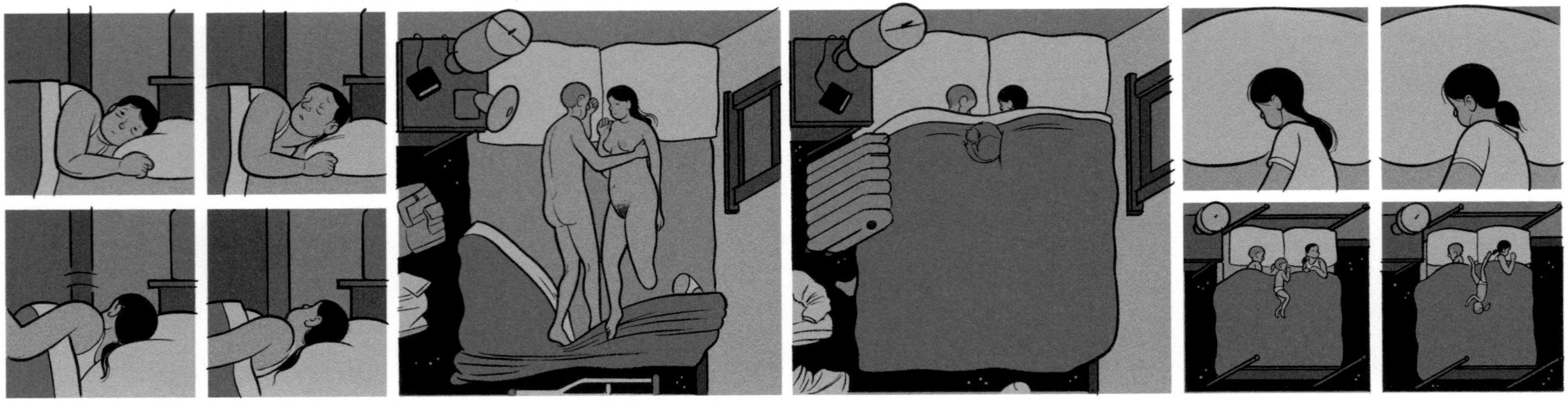

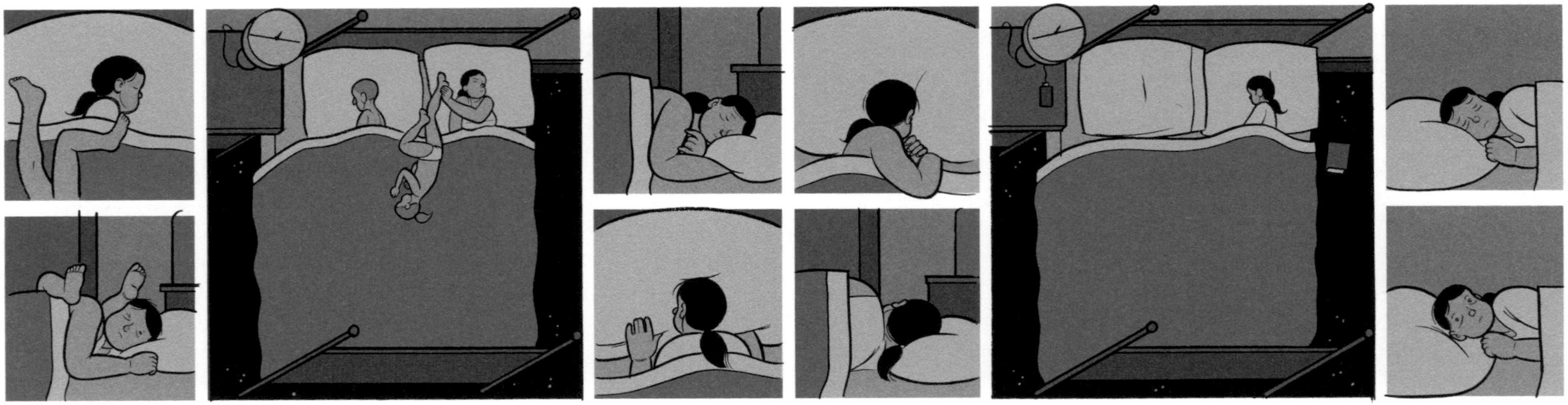

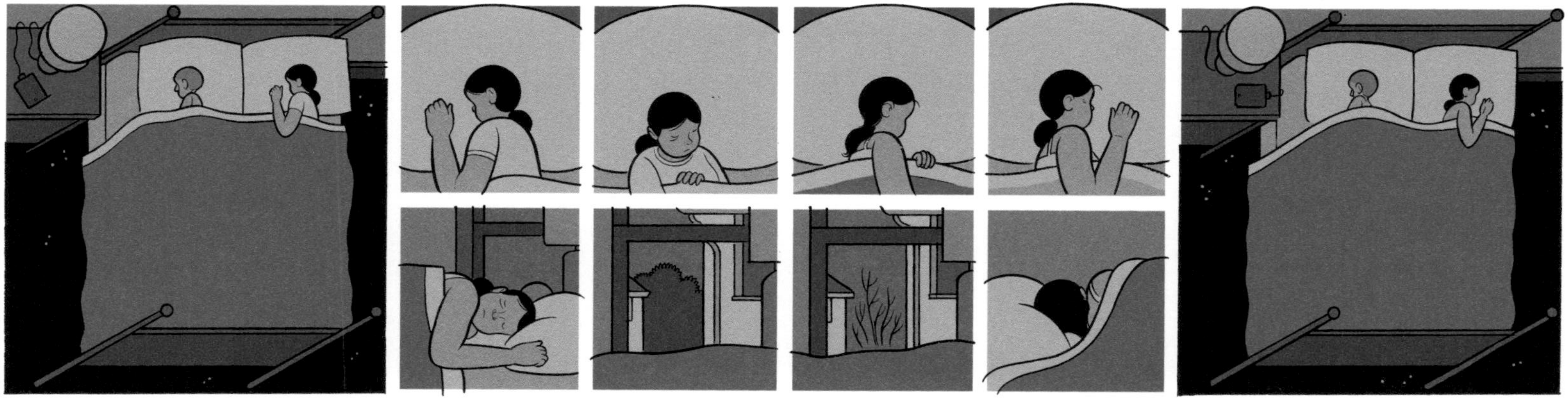

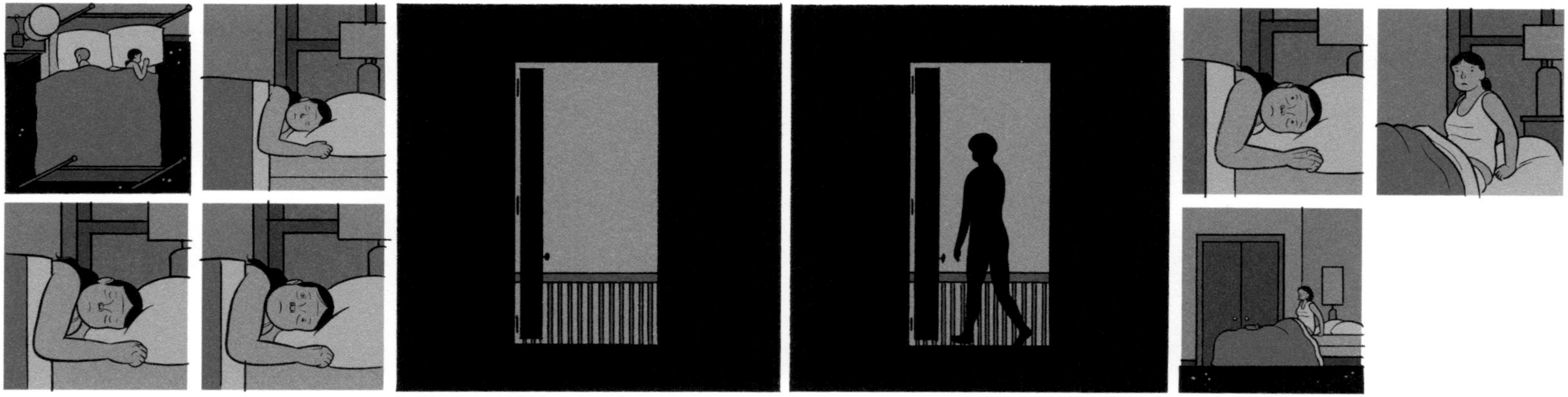

Testimonials

We like to tell ourselves that comics have come a long way, that when we were kids, they were a limited, cheap form of shallow entertainment, and today they can examine any issue, no matter how grave, and tell life-changing stories for adults. Our first excerpt in this section, *March: Book One* by John Lewis, Andrew Aydin, and Nate Powell, lends weight to this idea, although it also offers a small ironic counterweight.

March: Book One tells the story of Congressman John Lewis's early years and his crucial role in pivotal American civil rights events. It's a stirring story, well adapted by Aydin, and robustly visualized by Powell, and it's exactly the kind of substantial adult topic we in Team Comics like to encourage and celebrate.

Funny thing though: one of Lewis's own inspirations as a young man, as depicted elsewhere in *March: Book One*, was a civil rights–themed comic book published almost fifty years ago! *March* is a great introduction to history, to be sure, but let's give props to the original comic (*Martin Luther King and the Montgomery Story*) that, in retrospect, literally changed history for the better by spurring Lewis to action.

The other two comics in this section have a lot in common, at least superficially. Both tell stories of real musicians and the ways they changed the musical landscape around them, both deliberately imitate an earlier style of comic, and both are earnest and adorable.

The Carter Family: Don't Forget This Song by Frank M. Young and David Lasky tells the generations-spanning story of a family who would become country music legends. Lasky's art is a pitch-perfect re-creation of early twentieth-century comic strip sensibilities and it fits its subject matter like a glove. Lasky and Young's steadfast refusal to ramp up the drama, to include any of modern comics's hysterical flourishes, is refreshing. These were polite, God-fearin', quiet folk, and this is exactly the kind of unpretentious entertainment you can imagine them enjoying over pancakes and coffee in the morning.

Ed Piskor's *Hip Hop Family Tree* takes on a much broader subject, a comprehensive dramatization of the birth, rise, and evolution of hip hop and its hundreds of leading players and related scenes, drawn in the style of an '80s mainstream comic book. Like the Carter Family book, Piskor opts for short, bite-sized stories, many just a page or two long. It's gloriously dense, almost gasping for air as it frantically tries to include every last singer or musician who might legitimately stake a claim to this makeshift newsprint Hall of Fame.

It's a big, exhausting, crazy book, but also a handy, comprehensive guide to an important art movement that was about much more than just money or fashion.

All of these excerpts, on some level, are about respect. Respect for a people, respect for creative endeavor, respect for the struggles of ordinary working families. Hope you respect their missions and seek out the much longer works we clipped them from.

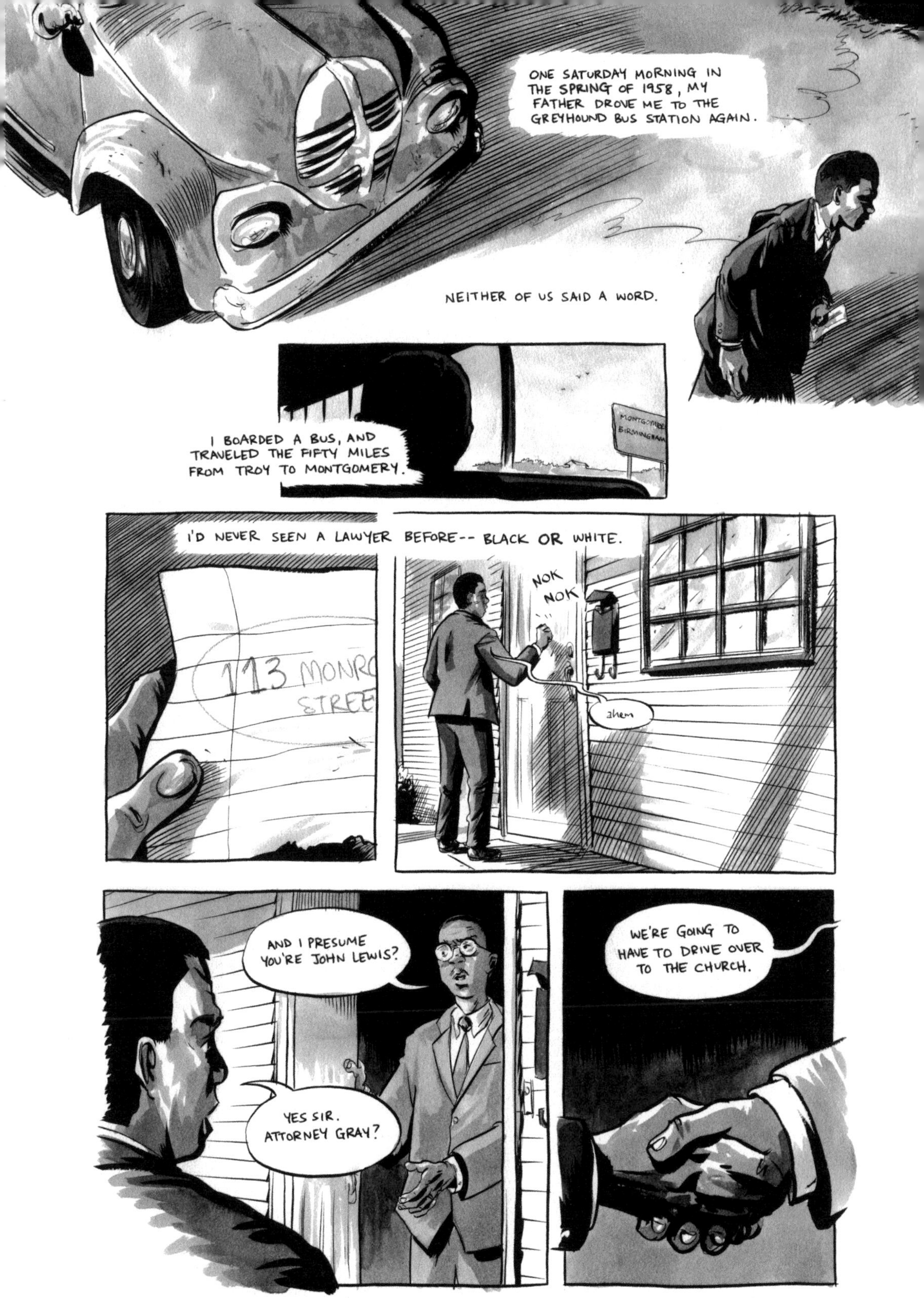
ONE SATURDAY MORNING IN THE SPRING OF 1958, MY FATHER DROVE ME TO THE GREYHOUND BUS STATION AGAIN.
NEITHER OF US SAID A WORD.
I BOARDED A BUS, AND TRAVELED THE FIFTY MILES FROM TROY TO MONTGOMERY.
I'D NEVER SEEN A LAWYER BEFORE-- BLACK OR WHITE.
NOK
NOK
ahem
AND I PRESUME YOU'RE JOHN LEWIS?
YES SIR. ATTORNEY GRAY?
WE'RE GOING TO HAVE TO DRIVE OVER TO THE CHURCH.

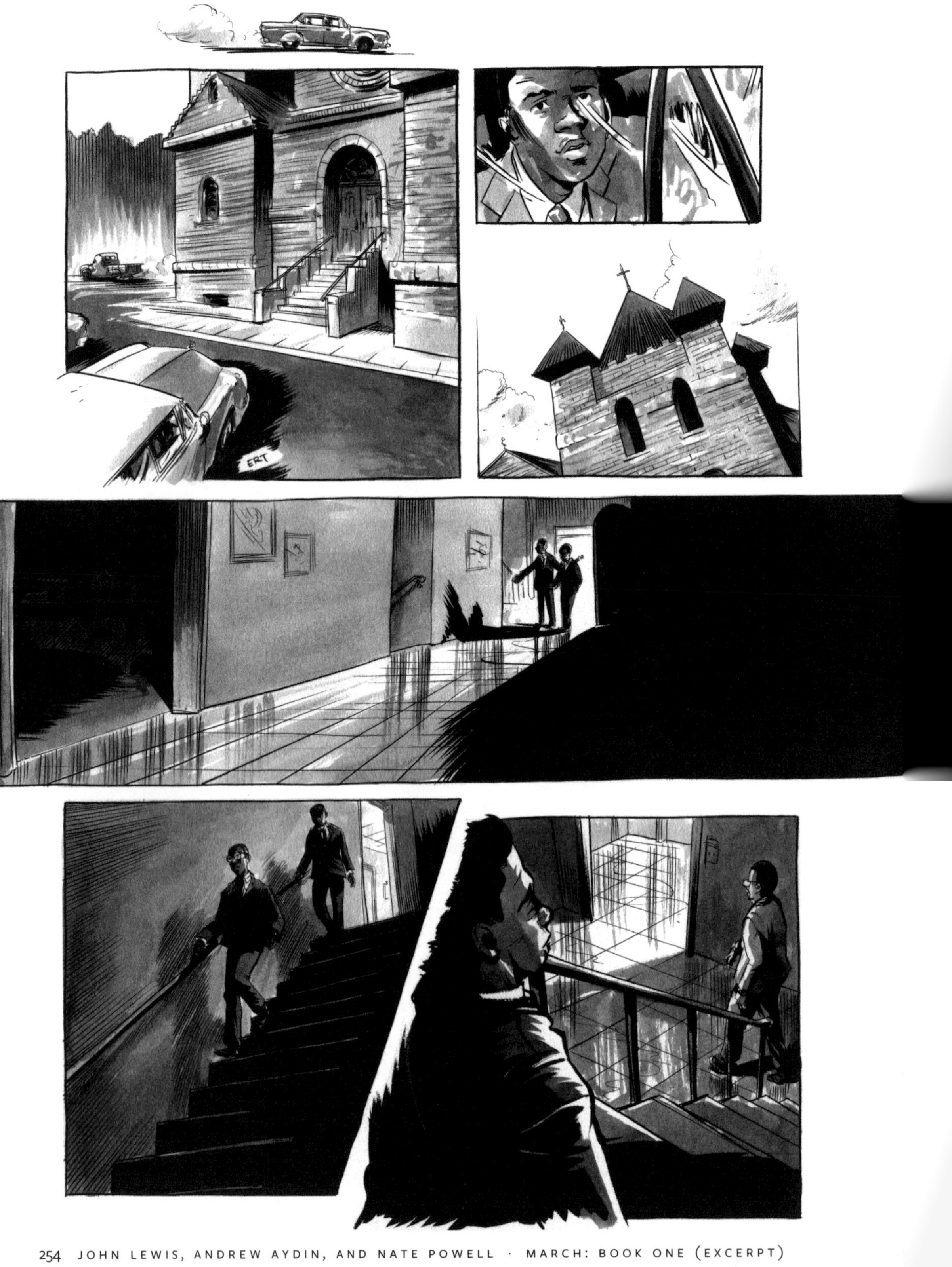

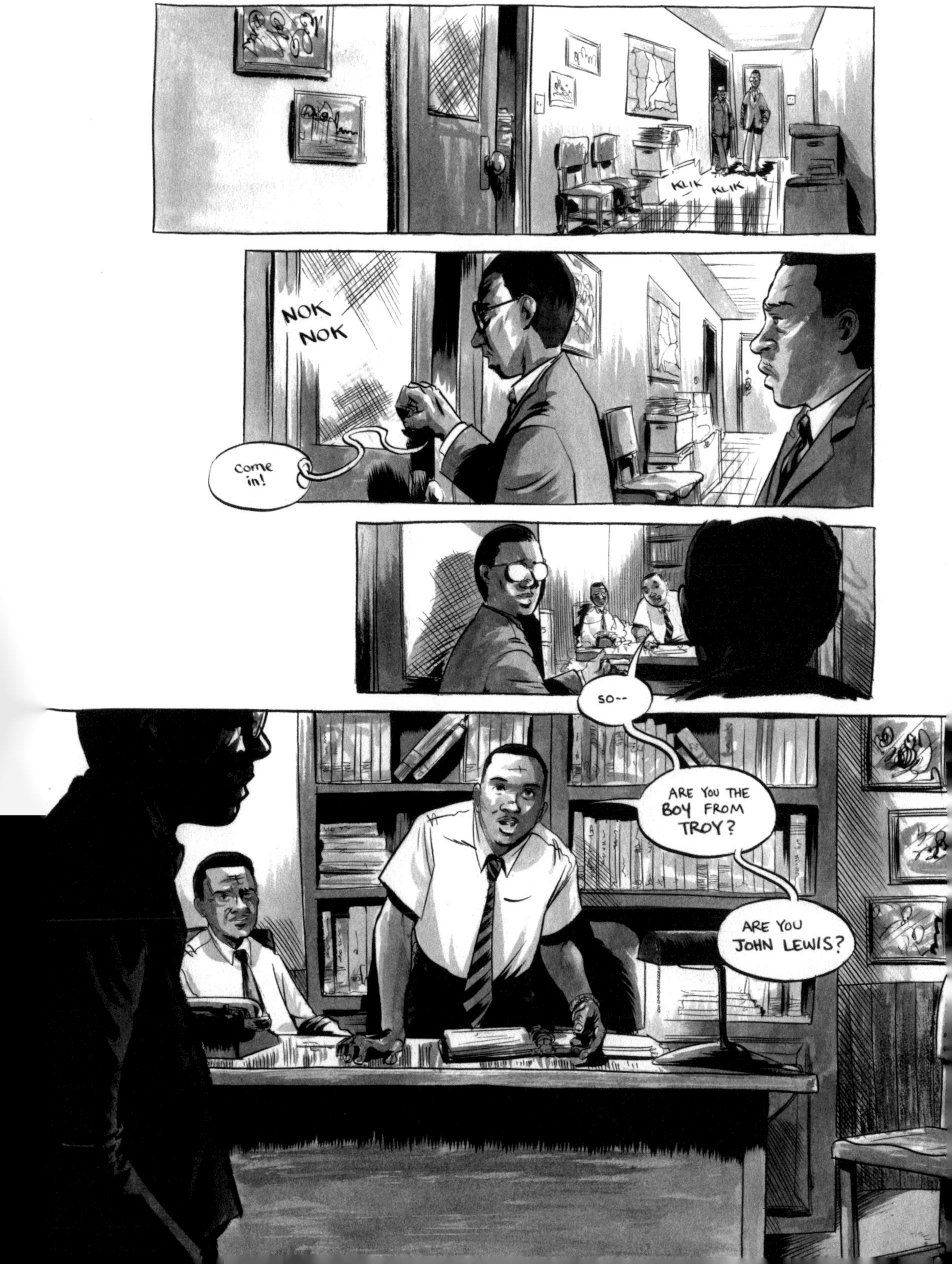
KLIK KLIK
NOK NOK
come in!
SO--
ARE YOU THE BOY FROM TROY?
ARE YOU JOHN LEWIS?

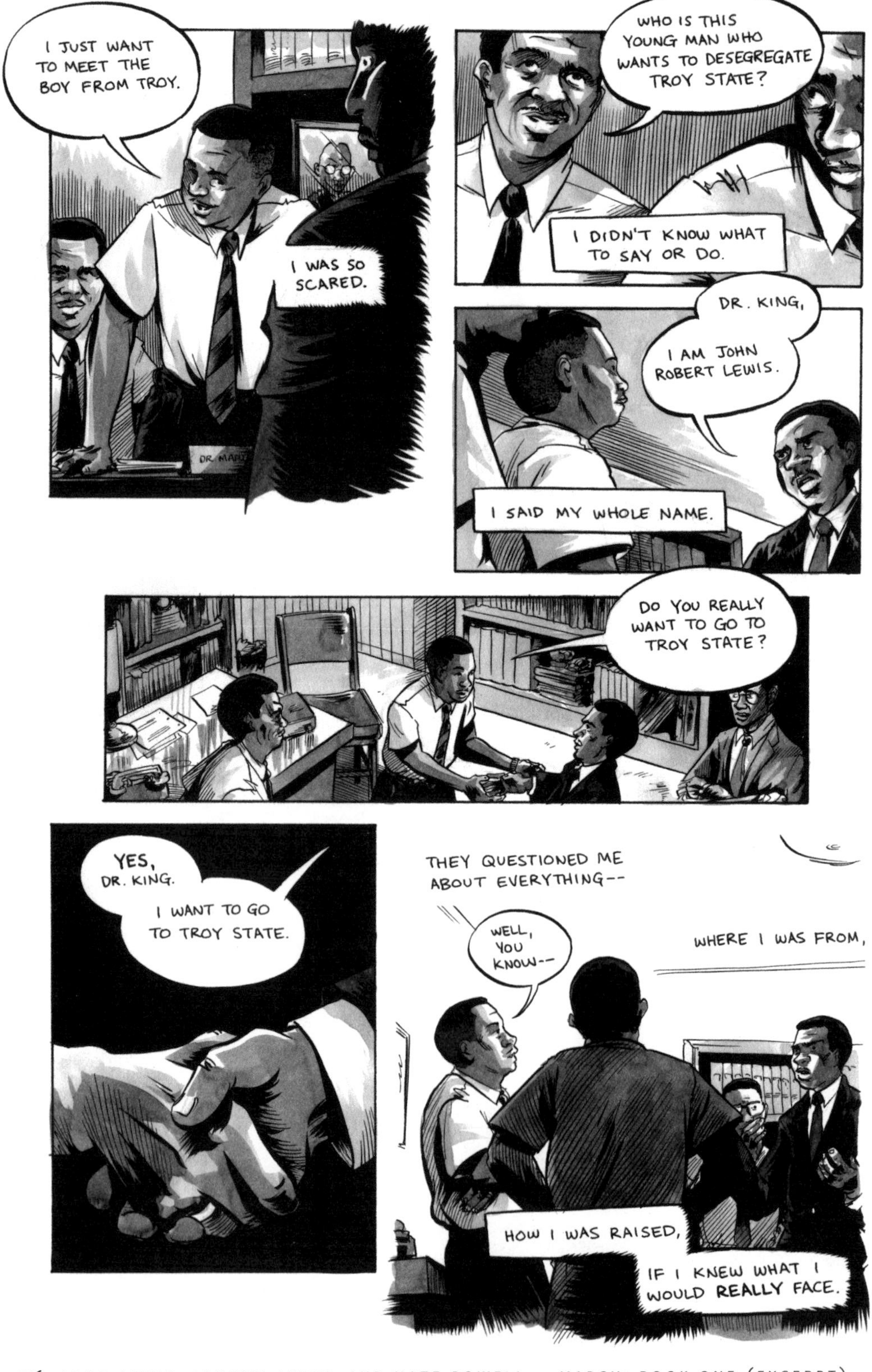
I JUST WANT TO MEET THE BOY FROM TROY.
I WAS SO SCARED.
WHO IS THIS YOUNG MAN WHO WANTS TO DESEGREGATE TROY STATE?
I DIDN'T KNOW WHAT TO SAY OR DO.
DR. KING,
I AM JOHN ROBERT LEWIS.
I SAID MY WHOLE NAME.
DO YOU REALLY WANT TO GO TO TROY STATE?
YES, DR. KING.
I WANT TO GO TO TROY STATE.
THEY QUESTIONED ME ABOUT EVERYTHING--
WELL, YOU KNOW--
WHERE I WAS FROM,
HOW I WAS RAISED,
IF I KNEW WHAT I WOULD **REALLY** FACE.

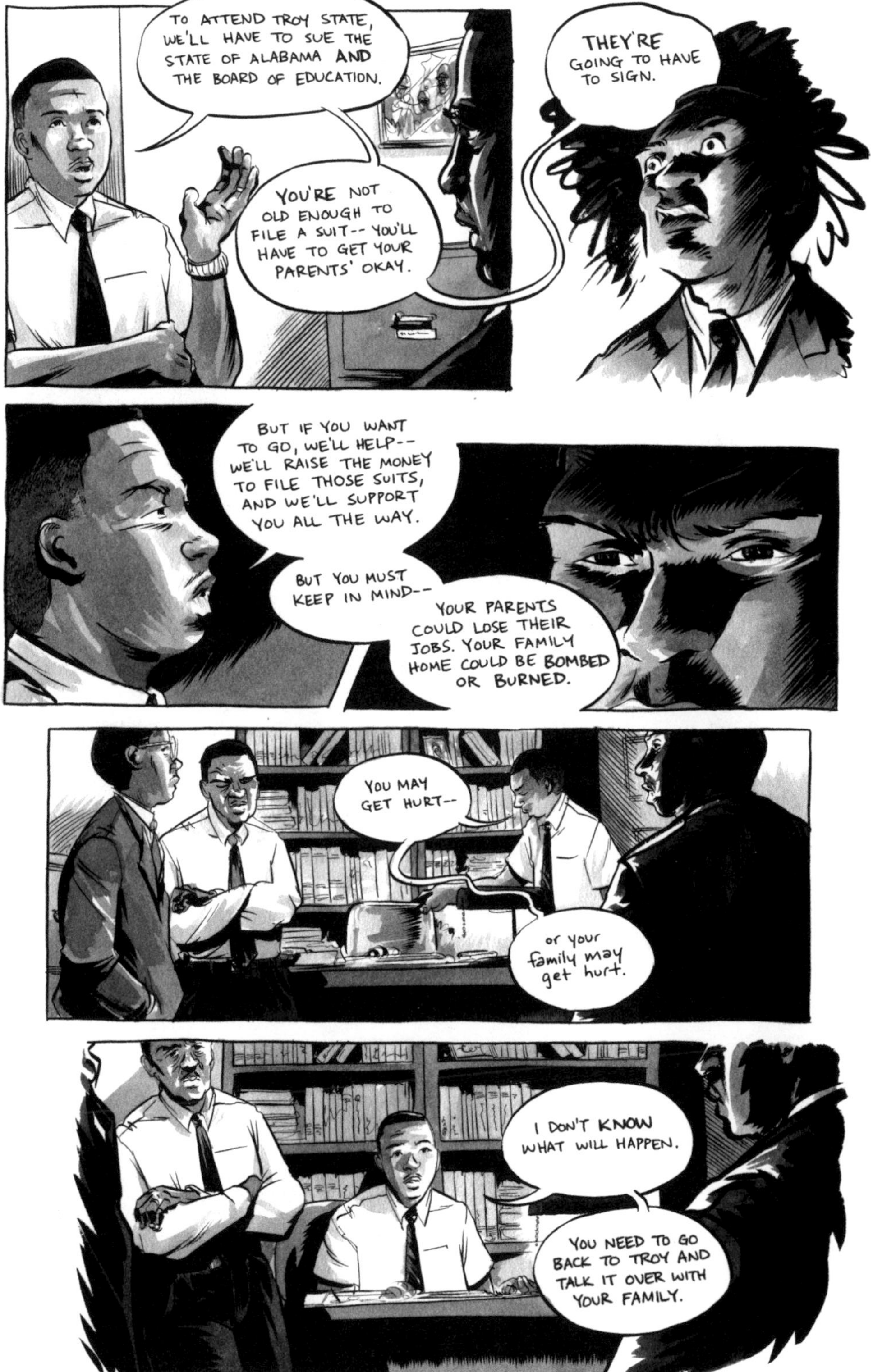
TO ATTEND TROY STATE, WE'LL HAVE TO SUE THE STATE OF ALABAMA AND THE BOARD OF EDUCATION.
YOU'RE NOT OLD ENOUGH TO FILE A SUIT-- YOU'LL HAVE TO GET YOUR PARENTS' OKAY.
THEY'RE GOING TO HAVE TO SIGN.
BUT IF YOU WANT TO GO, WE'LL HELP-- WE'LL RAISE THE MONEY TO FILE THOSE SUITS, AND WE'LL SUPPORT YOU ALL THE WAY.
BUT YOU MUST KEEP IN MIND--
YOUR PARENTS COULD LOSE THEIR JOBS. YOUR FAMILY HOME COULD BE BOMBED OR BURNED.
YOU MAY GET HURT--
or your family may get hurt.
I DON'T KNOW WHAT WILL HAPPEN.
YOU NEED TO GO BACK TO TROY AND TALK IT OVER WITH YOUR FAMILY.

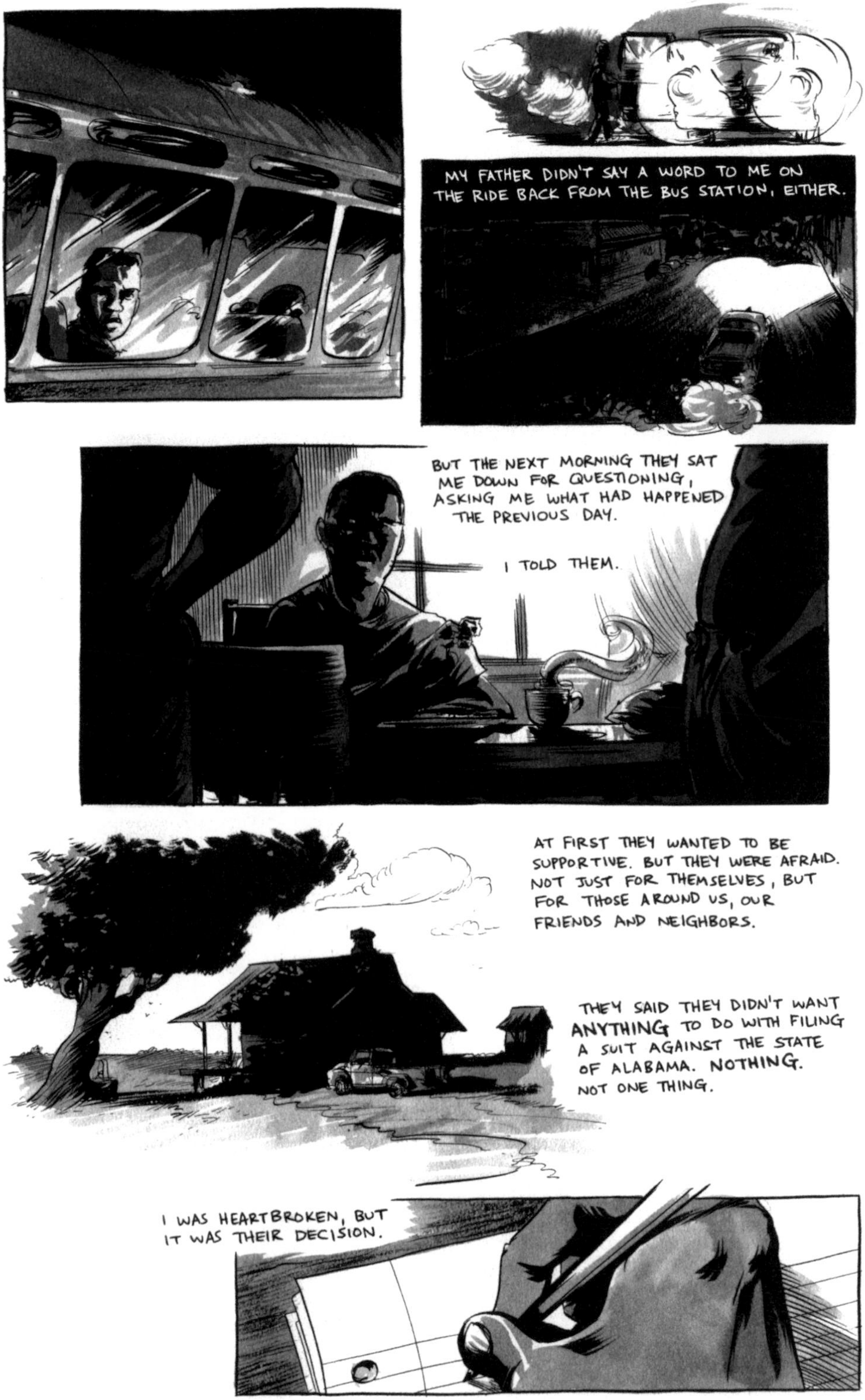

MY FATHER DIDN'T SAY A WORD TO ME ON THE RIDE BACK FROM THE BUS STATION, EITHER.
BUT THE NEXT MORNING THEY SAT ME DOWN FOR QUESTIONING, ASKING ME WHAT HAD HAPPENED THE PREVIOUS DAY.
I TOLD THEM.
AT FIRST THEY WANTED TO BE SUPPORTIVE. BUT THEY WERE AFRAID. NOT JUST FOR THEMSELVES, BUT FOR THOSE AROUND US, OUR FRIENDS AND NEIGHBORS.
THEY SAID THEY DIDN'T WANT ANYTHING TO DO WITH FILING A SUIT AGAINST THE STATE OF ALABAMA. NOTHING. NOT ONE THING.
I WAS HEARTBROKEN, BUT IT WAS THEIR DECISION.

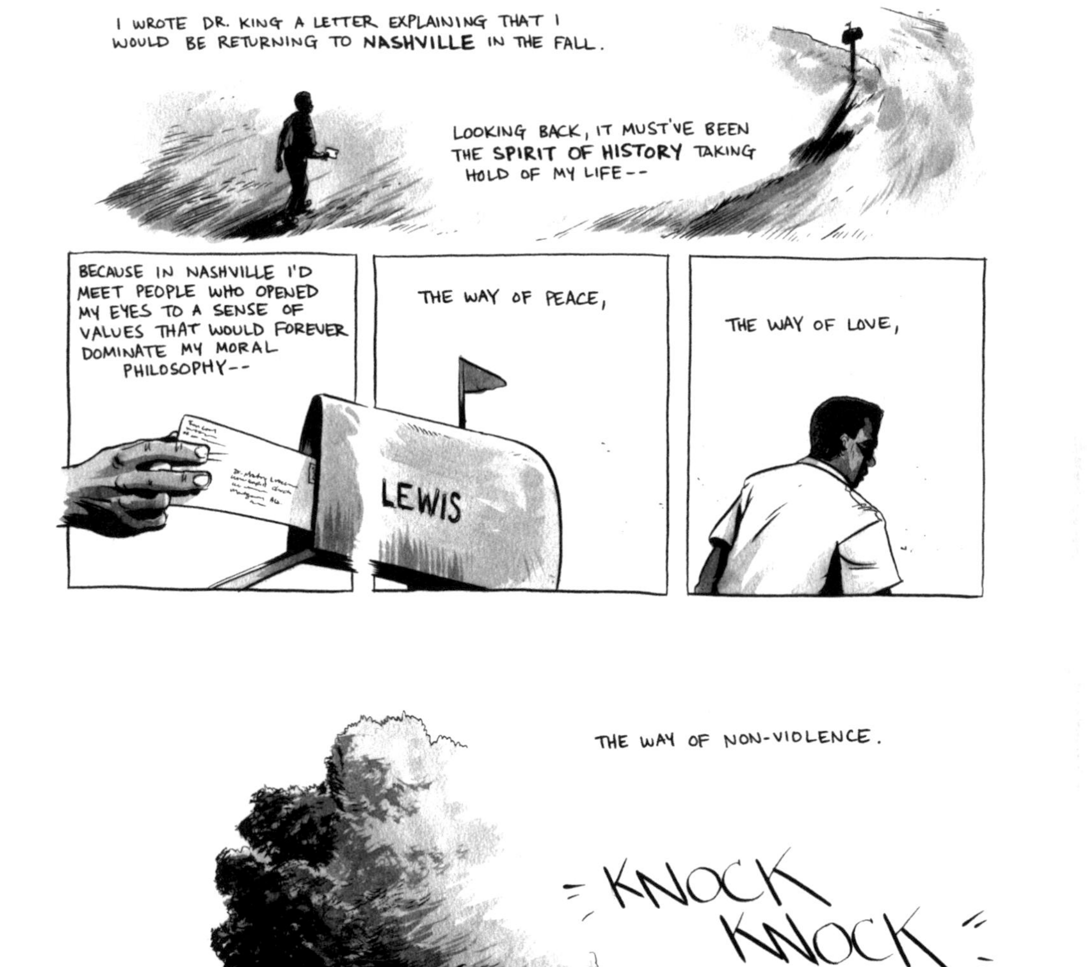
I WROTE DR. KING A LETTER EXPLAINING THAT I WOULD BE RETURNING TO NASHVILLE IN THE FALL.
LOOKING BACK, IT MUST'VE BEEN THE SPIRIT OF HISTORY TAKING HOLD OF MY LIFE--
BECAUSE IN NASHVILLE I'D MEET PEOPLE WHO OPENED MY EYES TO A SENSE OF VALUES THAT WOULD FOREVER DOMINATE MY MORAL PHILOSOPHY--
LEWIS
THE WAY OF PEACE,
THE WAY OF LOVE,
THE WAY OF NON-VIOLENCE.
KNOCK KNOCK
COME IN?

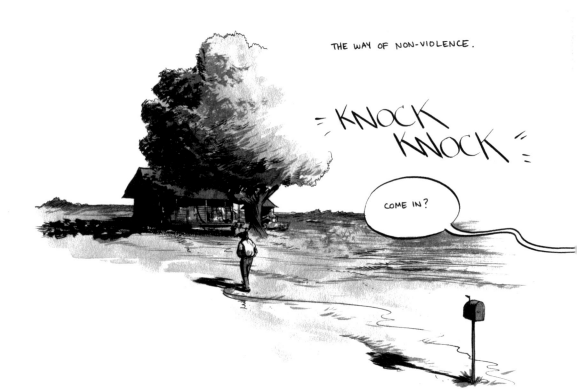

Oh! Almost forgot to mention this:

I actually got to meet Representative John Lewis last year and shake his hand. The civil rights legend was signing at the Top Shelf booth at Comic-Con.

Yeah, just go ahead reread that sentence as many times as you need to.

Chapter 20
The Program Is Morally Good
Beg pardon, mister... c'd you put this paper in y'r winder?
S'pose so... what's it fer?
"Look... Victor... artist..."
Thank y' kindly!
LOOK!
Victor Artist
P. CARTER
and the
Family
give a
Morally Good
Law, it's th' Carter Fam'ly!

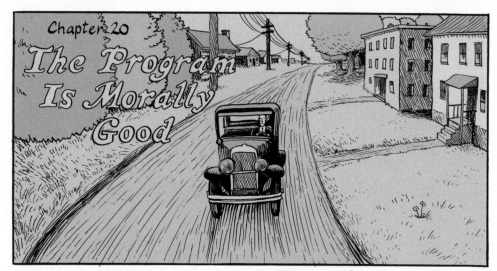

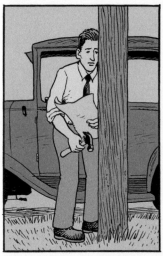

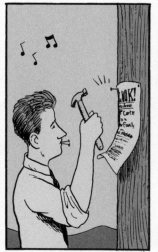

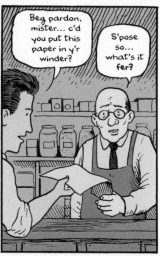

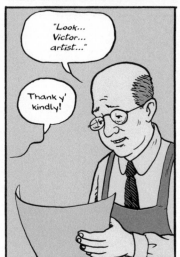

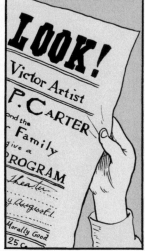

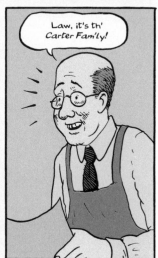

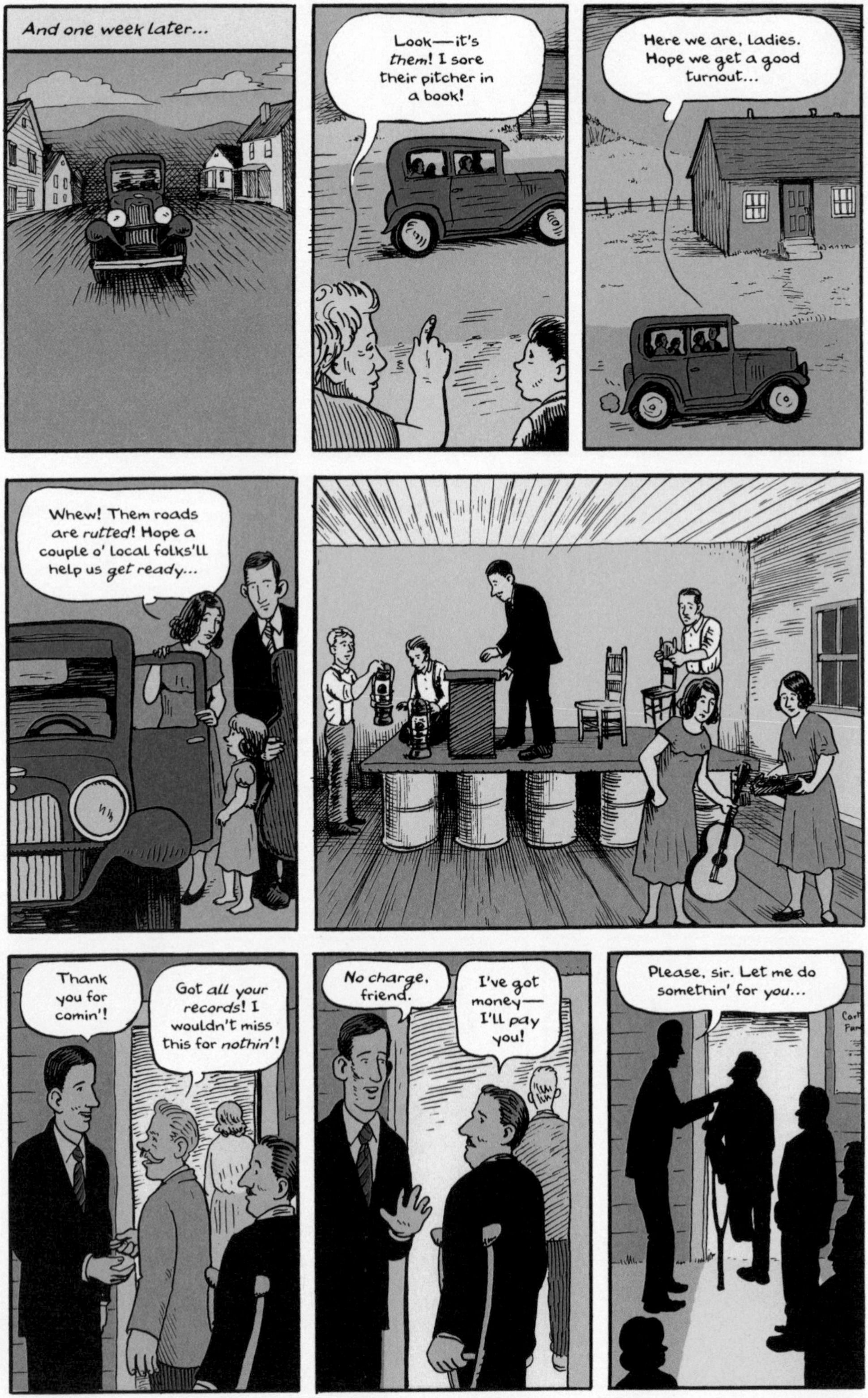
And one week later...
Look—it's them! I sore their pitcher in a book!
Here we are, ladies. Hope we get a good turnout...
Whew! Them roads are rutted! Hope a couple o' local folks'll help us get ready...
Thank you for comin'!
Got all your records! I wouldn't miss this for nothin'!
No charge, friend.
I've got money—I'll pay you!
Please, sir. Let me do somethin' for you...

plink, plink
Good evenin' to all you fine people... how do you *do?*
How do you do?
On behalf of Sara, Maybelle, an' myself... **thank you all** for comin' to spend th' evenin' with us! We hope you **enjoy it!**
We play an' sing *all kinds o' songs.* But the old *spirituals* are closest to our hearts. Songs such as—
Diamonds in the Rough
Anchored in Love
River of Jordan
God Gave Noah the Rainbow Sign

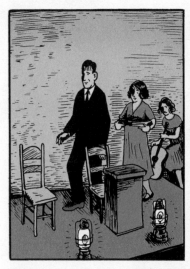

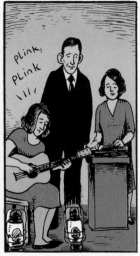

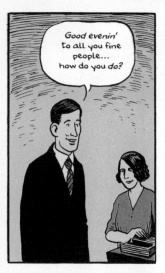

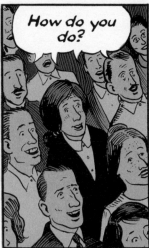

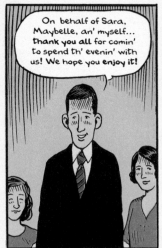

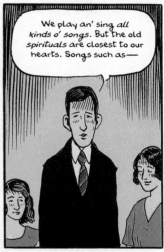

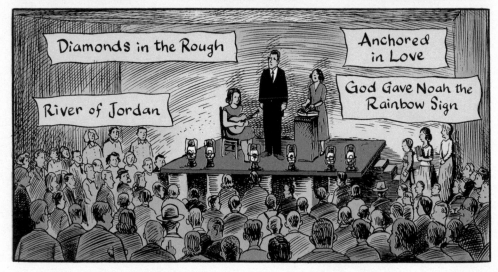

An' now, here's somethin' you'll **never** hear us do on our **records**!
We hope you liked that little breakdown...
Say, I think I'll sing one all by **myself**!
CLAP CLAP CLAP CLAP CLAP
Folks, Maybelle needs t' tune her gittar! *Please*—give her a *big hand*!
CLAP CLAP
While y' wait, here's my daughter *Gladys*! She's got a book f'r sale that might be to your likin'!
It has the words t' many of our songs! It only costs a dime. We *love* our children. We'd like t' sing a song *just for them!*
Chawin' chewin' gu-um... Chewin' chawin' gum...
CLAP CLAP CLAP CLAP

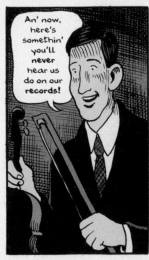

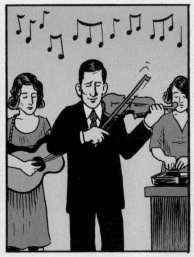

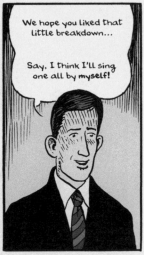

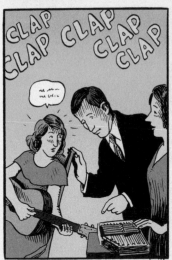

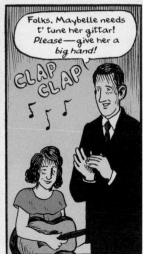

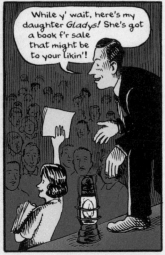

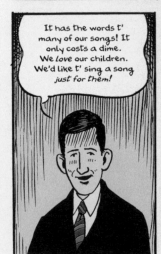

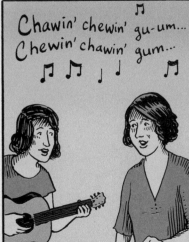

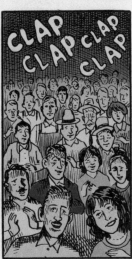

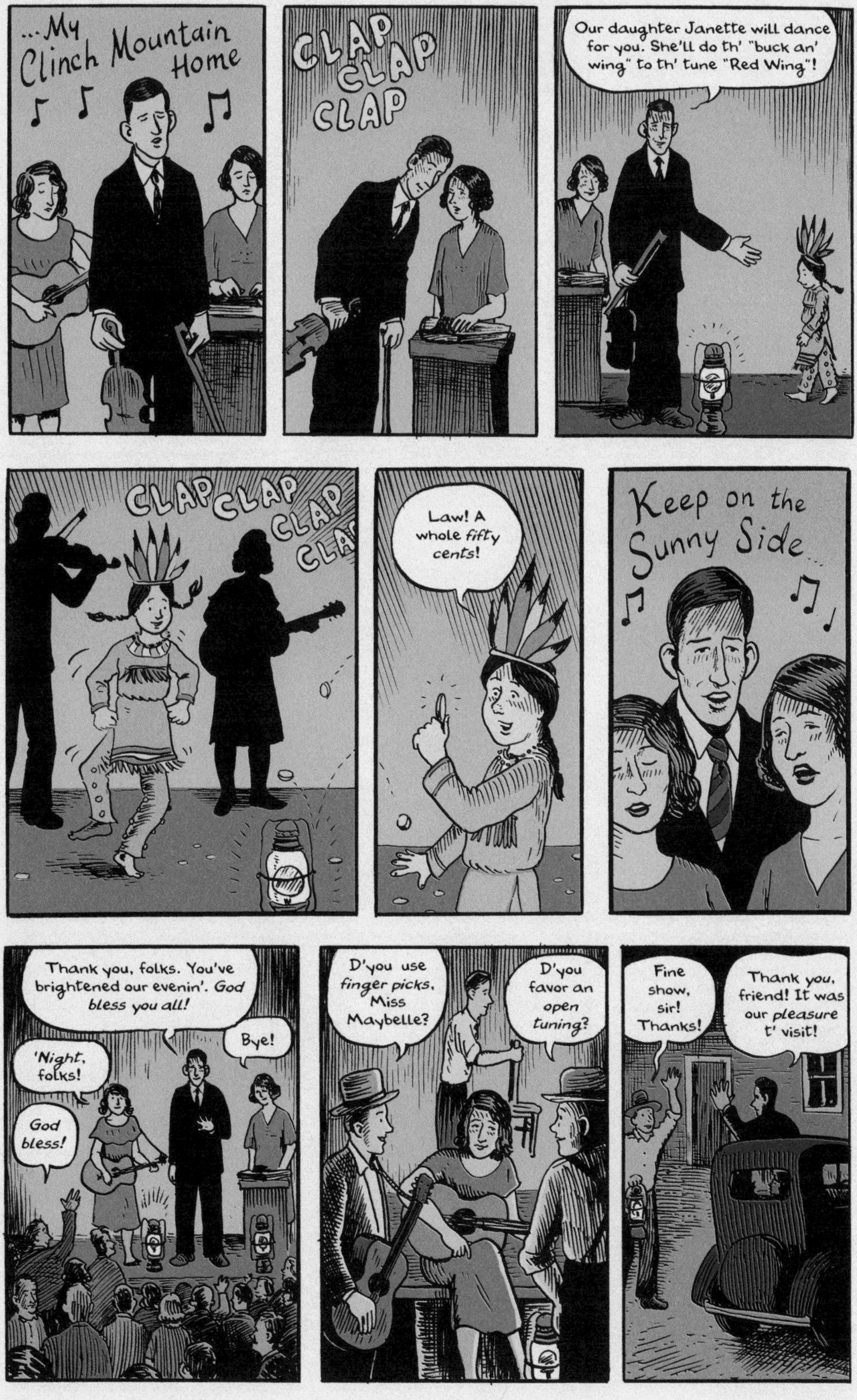

...My Clinch Mountain Home
CLAP CLAP CLAP
Our daughter Janette will dance for you. She'll do th' "buck an' wing" to th' tune "Red Wing"!
CLAP CLAP CLAP CLA
Law! A whole fifty cents!
Keep on the Sunny Side...
Thank you, folks. You've brightened our evenin'. God bless you all!
Bye!
'Night, folks!
God bless!
D'you use finger picks, Miss Maybelle?
D'you favor an open tuning?
Fine show, sir! Thanks!
Thank you, friend! It was our pleasure t' visit!

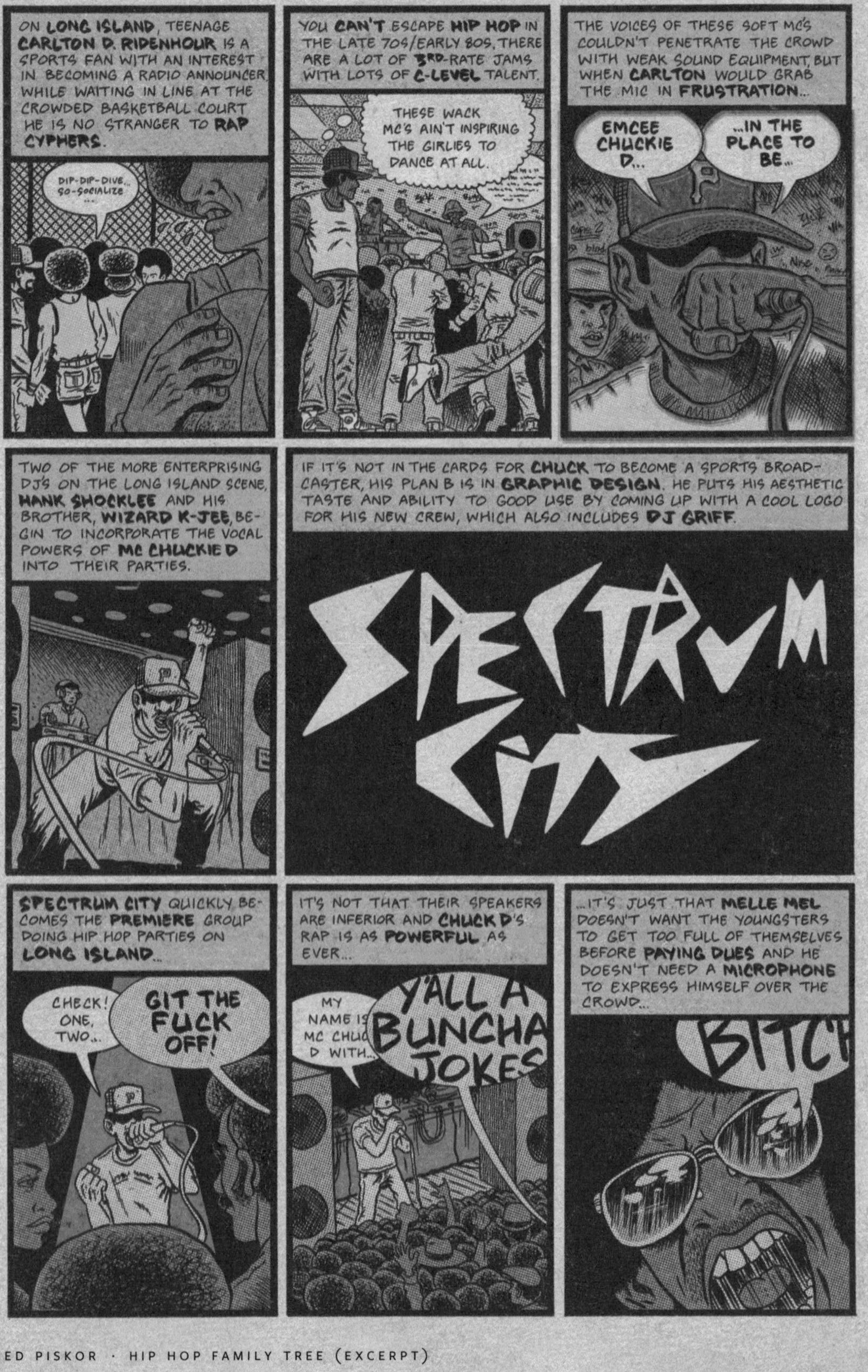
ON LONG ISLAND, TEENAGE CARLTON D. RIDENHOUR IS A SPORTS FAN WITH AN INTEREST IN BECOMING A RADIO ANNOUNCER. WHILE WAITING IN LINE AT THE CROWDED BASKETBALL COURT HE IS NO STRANGER TO RAP CYPHERS.
DIP-DIP-DIVE... SO-SOCIALIZE ...
YOU CAN'T ESCAPE HIP HOP IN THE LATE 70S/EARLY 80S. THERE ARE A LOT OF 3RD-RATE JAMS WITH LOTS OF C-LEVEL TALENT.
THESE WACK MC'S AIN'T INSPIRING THE GIRLIES TO DANCE AT ALL.
THE VOICES OF THESE SOFT MC'S COULDN'T PENETRATE THE CROWD WITH WEAK SOUND EQUIPMENT, BUT WHEN CARLTON WOULD GRAB THE MIC IN FRUSTRATION...
EMCEE CHUCKIE D...
...IN THE PLACE TO BE...
TWO OF THE MORE ENTERPRISING DJ'S ON THE LONG ISLAND SCENE, HANK SHOCKLEE AND HIS BROTHER, WIZARD K-JEE, BEGIN TO INCORPORATE THE VOCAL POWERS OF MC CHUCKIE D INTO THEIR PARTIES.
IF IT'S NOT IN THE CARDS FOR CHUCK TO BECOME A SPORTS BROADCASTER, HIS PLAN B IS IN GRAPHIC DESIGN. HE PUTS HIS AESTHETIC TASTE AND ABILITY TO GOOD USE BY COMING UP WITH A COOL LOGO FOR HIS NEW CREW, WHICH ALSO INCLUDES DJ GRIFF.
SPECTRUM CITY
SPECTRUM CITY QUICKLY BECOMES THE PREMIERE GROUP DOING HIP HOP PARTIES ON LONG ISLAND...
CHECK! ONE, TWO...
GIT THE FUCK OFF!
IT'S NOT THAT THEIR SPEAKERS ARE INFERIOR AND CHUCK D'S RAP IS AS POWERFUL AS EVER...
MY NAME IS MC CHUCK D WITH...
Y'ALL A BUNCHA JOKES
...IT'S JUST THAT MELLE MEL DOESN'T WANT THE YOUNGSTERS TO GET TOO FULL OF THEMSELVES BEFORE PAYING DUES AND HE DOESN'T NEED A MICROPHONE TO EXPRESS HIMSELF OVER THE CROWD...
BITCH

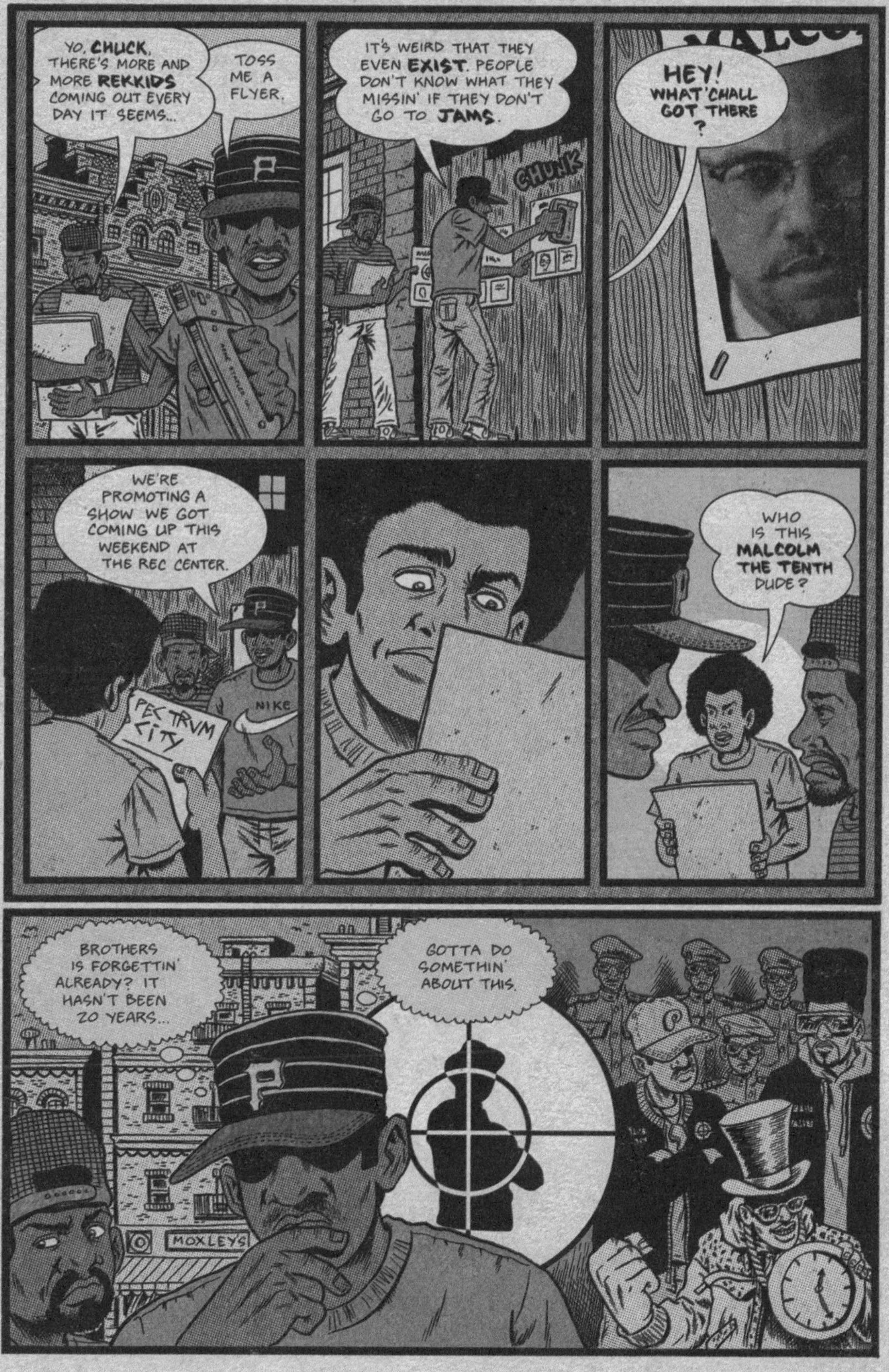
YO, CHUCK, THERE'S MORE AND MORE REKKIDS COMING OUT EVERY DAY IT SEEMS...
TOSS ME A FLYER.
IT'S WEIRD THAT THEY EVEN EXIST. PEOPLE DON'T KNOW WHAT THEY MISSIN' IF THEY DON'T GO TO JAMS.
CHUNK
HEY! WHAT'CHALL GOT THERE ?
WE'RE PROMOTING A SHOW WE GOT COMING UP THIS WEEKEND AT THE REC CENTER.
PEC TRUM CITY
NIKE
WHO IS THIS MALCOLM THE TENTH DUDE?
BROTHERS IS FORGETTIN' ALREADY? IT HASN'T BEEN 20 YEARS...
GOTTA DO SOMETHIN' ABOUT THIS.
MOXLEYS

ALLIE BROSH

Depression Part Two (*Excerpt*) **274**

from *Hypberbole and a Half*

WWW.HYPERBOLEANDAHALF.BLOGSPOT.COM

Oh, Crap—
Webcomics!

The Best American Comics series traditionally focuses on the world of paper and ink, but I'd have to commit seppuku with a Wacom stylus if I didn't at least try to put the role of today's webcomics into some kind of perspective. I've drifted from the scene in recent years while working on books geared more for print, but I could barely think about anything else in the early days, and even now, webcomics and their possibilities are never far from my mind.

I had grandiose dreams for digital comics in the Web's first decade (dating from the release of the first popular graphical Web browser, Mosaic, in late 1993, although, technically speaking, the Web itself was—oh, never mind). I promoted an idea in talks, and later on a site of my own, that we didn't have to break our comics into pages anymore, that we could treat the screen as a window and navigate through a whole graphic novel's worth of panels on a single plane. I used the term "infinite canvas" and soon people were calling anything you had to scroll through "infinite canvas comics."

A small battalion of nutty professors from around the world ran with the idea (especially after the 2000 publication of my technology-obsessed *Reinventing Comics*) and made some genuinely cool experiments that I'm still proud to be associated with. But since nobody was making a living from long-form experimental comics like ours (we tried to solve that problem too and failed), most cartoonists went back to making daily comic strips closer to the traditional newspaper style—a model that, by the late '90s, had yielded some genuine success stories online.

The boundaries between print and Web were important to my tribe of inventors, but today those boundaries have blurred beyond recognition. Artists and audiences connect any way they can: webcomics offer print collections, print comics can be read online or on tablets. Purists like me tear their hair out at the idea that we can just shove content from one platform to the next without redesigning it, but no one lets that slow them down. Grass grows through sidewalk cracks; vines crawl up every available wall; the city of information is covered in a hundred thousand green, growing new species, all reaching for sunlight.

Many of the most interesting mutations in the last two years have been in the community and economy of webcomics and the crucial role of the former as an engine of the latter. Crowdfunding sites like Kickstarter poured hundreds of millions of dollars into the creative economy in recent years and defied skeptics (like me) who thought the phenomenon would've collapsed by now. Joey Manley, the late, much-missed Web entrepreneur, liked to remind us that "Begging is not a business model," but today's entrepreneurs play in a strange new middle ground: a form of reader support with philanthropy at its heart, which still takes the outward form of fees for goods and services. "Begging" it isn't, but neither is it like anything else we've seen before. More recently, a site called Patreon is attempting to do for ongoing work (like regularly updating comics) what Kickstarter did for one-off projects. Time will tell if readers nod, laugh, or just scratch their heads when they stumble across these words in five or ten years.

The most vivid demonstration of how far down the rabbit hole we've traveled had to be 2013's online reality show *Strip Search,* which followed twelve aspiring webcomics artists competing for a cash prize and a chance to spend a year embedded in the offices of *Penny Arcade,* home to the massively popular video game–themed webcomic and its ancillary ventures. *Strip Search* was hands-down adorable. The artists themselves were so earnest and talented—and weirdly free of malice or envy—that I didn't want *any* of them to lose. My wife and I, and eventually our kids, waited with bated breath for each new episode. Watching it on our big flatscreen TV instead of the laptop reminded me too of how thoroughly a Web series could merge in my mind with the supposedly "real" world of broadcast and cable. It was as if being a Web cartoonist was every bit as legitimate, established, and lucrative a career as any other. Part fantasy maybe, but a few early pioneers—including the *Penny Arcade* guys themselves—had proven it was at least possible for some.

Standards of excellence in cartooning—the standards a series like this one rests upon—may be violently rewritten from time to time, and a long list of artistic prerequisites ripped to pieces. But then new sets of standards emerge and a new audience enthusiastically makes them their own. We're in a period of such creative destruction on the Web now. Some of the most popular new webcomics of the last decade are also some of the most radically stripped down or dissonant in appearance and style.

Andrew Hussie, creator of mspaintadventures.com, featuring the 5000-plus-page (panel? frame?) story *Homestuck,* is webcomics's most interesting and successful plunderer of cyber/pop culture's dubious pasts. *Homestuck* has a low-rent, choose-your-own-adventure theme (taking actual reader-chosen paths at the outset) and includes repeated references to bargain-bin movies and other cultural discards. *Homestuck* is so tangled in its references, internal continuity, and ironic feedback loops, it's hard to imagine how so many readers ever found a front door. But it also has a strange, melancholy background hum that's almost transcendent and—bad news for us—impossible to reprint in collections like this. The qualities that make *Homestuck* aesthetically interesting are exactly why we can't do more than point to it here.

From Homestuck *by Andrew Hussie. Note the use of animated gifs to, uh . . .*

Like *Homestuck*, Randall Munroe's long-running *xkcd* offers a deceptively simple, even crude, outer appearance. Stick figures without faces telling esoteric geek jokes—no matter how funny they are—don't move the needle much for readers looking for the next Craig Thompson or Jeff Smith. But, in recent years, Munroe has proven himself a thoughtful, inventive, and even hard-working cartoonist with a lot to say about space, time, and mortality. And, like Hussie, some of Munroe's most ambitious experiments are his least printable (links on pages 272-273).

Allie Brosh's *Hyperbole and a Half* may be the most jarring to traditional sensibilities, with its sloppy, scribbly style, but it's also proven tremendously accessible and wildly popular both inside and outside comics fandom. Funny, sad, and startlingly close to home, *Hyperbole and a Half* connects with readers strongly enough to rewire a million ideas of what "good" comics look like. I first caught up with Brosh's work in 2010. I'd linked to a strip of hers called "Dogs Don't Understand Basic Concepts Like Moving." I put one of her ridiculous dog faces on my blog and titled it "Someday, All Comics Will Look Like This." Most of the readers who commented sounded like they wouldn't necessarily mind if my prediction came true. I wasn't sure I would've minded myself.

Brosh's style grew out of the "rage comics" meme, which grew out of 4chan, the message board where all attempts at explanation trail off to nothing, like light near a black hole. Brosh used the rage comics baseline—crude but expressive faces drawn with primitive digital drawing tools—to hilarious effect, throwing her more observational drawings into the mix for a delightful graphic pileup, using it to illustrate her musings on life, the universe, and everything. When Brosh used the series to explore her struggles with depression, the moving and funny results made her one of the most widely read cartoonists on the planet. This story in particular struck Bill Kartalopoulos and me as emblematic of this moment in webcomics history, so we've included a small piece of "Depression Part Two" in this volume.

Fun Fact: A lot of work by both Brosh and Hussie doesn't technically fit my definition of comics. Nobody cares, least of all me. They're cool, funny, interesting, and worth your time.

The shape of comics on the Web also continues to change. Looped animation, parallax scrolling, and various methods of delivering panels and other storytelling components one at a time have started to catch on in some sectors. Even the humble animated gif has found new life in the clever hands of Hussie, Zac Gorman, Jen Lee, and Vincent Giard. Creativity is backwards compatible, and the Web's oldest artifacts are now being plundered in a retro spirit by artists who were barely in grade school when Mosaic slipped into our world. Everything old is new again. Even my old beloved infinite canvas has shown renewed life here in North America lately, thanks to talented new artists like Emily Carroll and pioneering stalwarts like my old pal Patrick Farley.

As always, some of the most talented writers and artists in comics distribute their work primarily on the Web just because that's where the readers are. In fact, several of the comics in this book were probably seen mostly by readers on the Web, even if formatted for print. Does that make them webcomics? Does it matter? I used to answer with a resounding YES, but these days I'm not so sure.

Meanwhile, it's hard to take the "world" out of the World Wide Web. France, Australia, South Korea, Norway . . . great, innovative, and moving webcomics are springing up all over the globe. In keeping with our series title, I've restricted this article to North American cartoonists, but webcomics in 2014 is increasingly a movement without boundaries of any kind: a massive, fast-changing marketplace of ideas, passions, hallucinations, and creative mutation. See the links below for a sampling of some of the work discussed here; then jump in and decide for yourself which is "Best."

Whatever that means.

Mentioned in This Article

Crowdfunding sites:

www.kickstarter.com and www.patreon.com

Joey Manley:

Wikipedia article en.wikipedia.org/wiki/Joey_Manley has basic info on the late Web entrepreneur. Also recommended: www.tcj.com/joey-manley-1965-2013

***Penny Arcade*'s online reality show *Strip Search*:**

www.penny-arcade.com/strip-search

More on my "infinite canvas" ideas:

www.scottmccloud.com/4-inventions/canvas/index.html

Andrew Hussie's site:

www.mspaintadventures.com

Two recent experimental examples from Randall Munroe's *xkcd*, and an older but more typical strip I like:

www.xkcd.com/1190

www.xkcd.com/1110

www.xkcd.com/552

Allie Brosh's blog:

www.hyperboleandahalf.blogspot.com

Rage comics:

www.knowyourmeme.com/memes/rage-comics

Looped animation/animated gif examples:

www.thunderpaw.co by Jen Lee

www.magicalgametime.com by Zac Gorman

www.aencre.org/blog/2010/bol-directors-cut/?lang=en by Montreal-based Vincent Giard

Parallax scrolling examples:

www.hobolobo.net

www.jessandruss.us

Infinite canvas examples by Emily Carroll and Patrick Farley:

www.emcarroll.com/comics/faceallred/01.html

www.electricsheepcomix.com/delta/firstword

A couple of comics I want you to read even though they're not North American (Shh! Don't tell!):

english.bouletcorp.com/2013/10/08/our-toyota-was-fantastic

www.jellyvampire.deviantart.com/art/Like-an-artist-197147822 (click to enlarge)

A site favoring an increasingly popular, as yet unnamed, form of page-building, popularized by cartoonist Yves Bigerel:

www.thrillbent.com

Depression Part Two

I remember being endlessly entertained by the adventures of my toys. Some days they died repeated, violent deaths; other days they traveled to space or discussed my swim lessons and how I absolutely should be allowed in the deep end of the pool, especially since I was such a talented doggy-paddler.

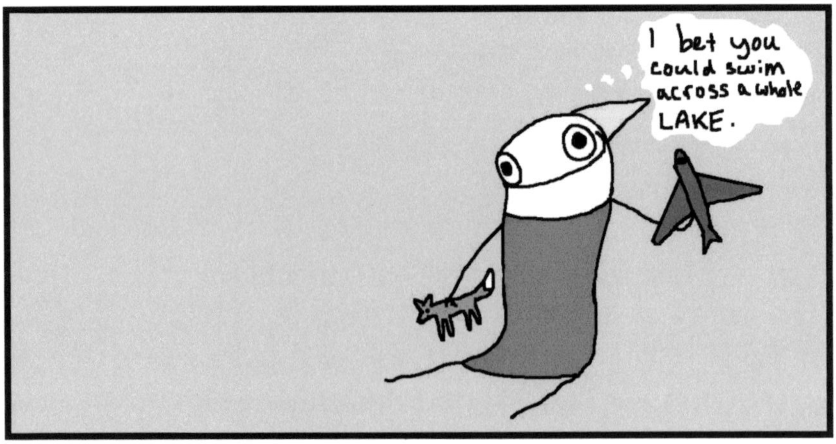
I bet you could swim across a whole LAKE.

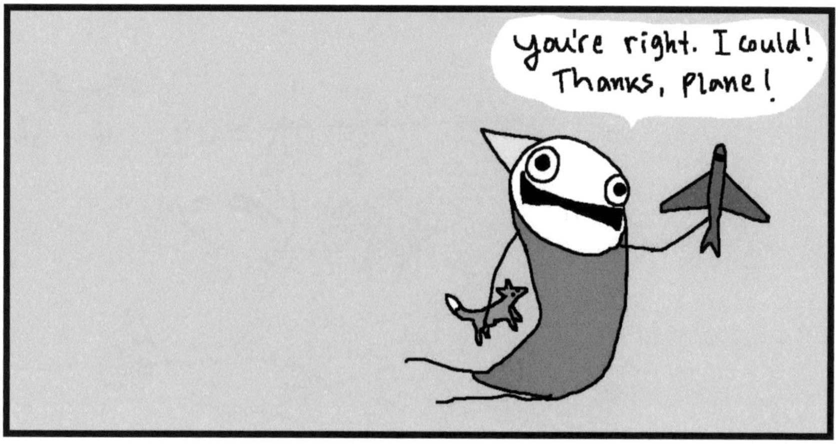
You're right. I could!
Thanks, Plane!

I didn't understand why it was fun for me, it just was.

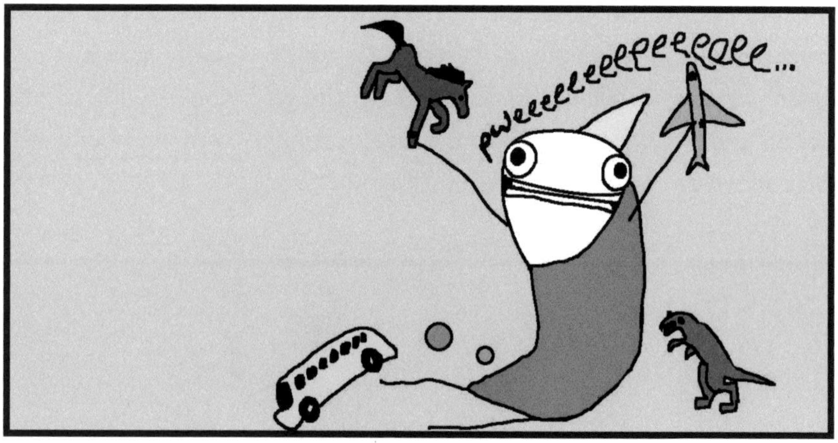
pweeeeeeeeeeeeeeee...

But as I grew older, it became harder and harder to access that expansive imaginary space that made my toys fun. I remember looking at them and feeling sort of frustrated and confused that things weren't the same.

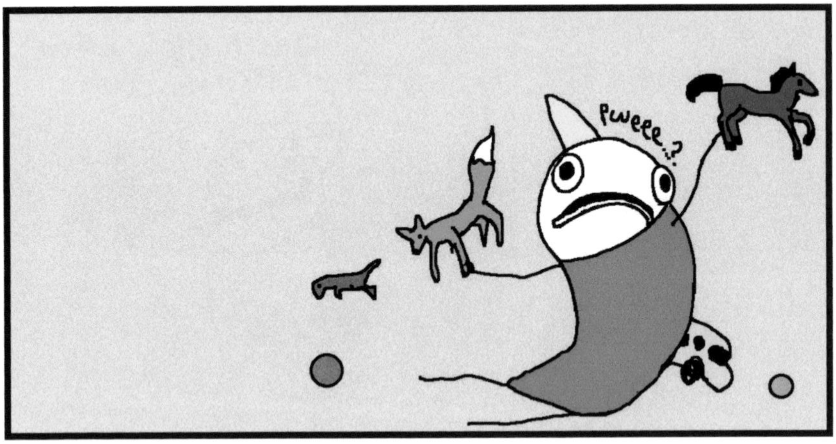
Pweee..?

I played out all the same story lines that had been fun before, but the meaning had disappeared. Horse's Big Space Adventure transformed into holding a plastic horse in the air, hoping it would somehow be enjoyable for me. Prehistoric Crazy-Bus Death Ride was just smashing a toy bus full of dinosaurs into the wall while feeling sort of bored and unfulfilled. I could no longer connect to my toys in a way that allowed me to participate in the experience.

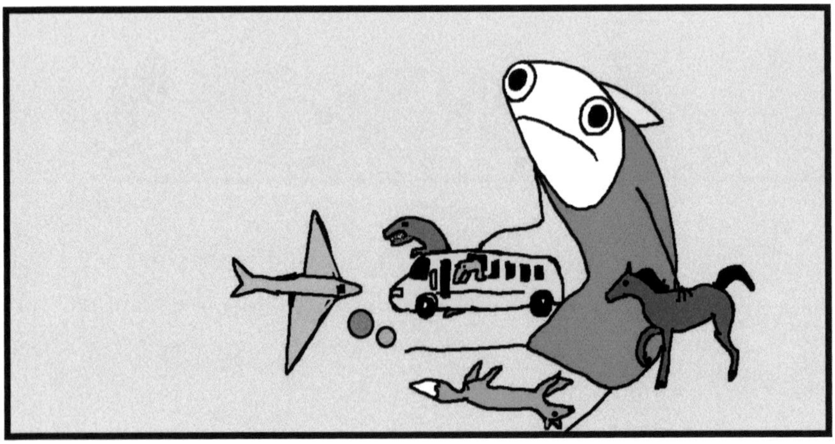

The second half of my depression felt almost exactly like that, except about everything.

At first, though, the invulnerability that accompanied the detachment was exhilarating. At least as exhilarating as something can be without involving real emotions.

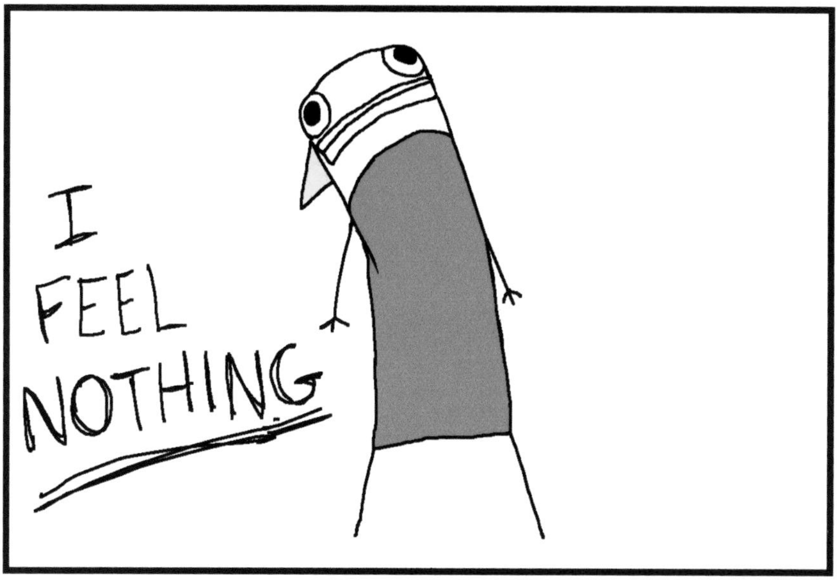
I FEEL NOTHING

The beginning of my depression had been nothing *but* feelings, so the emotional deadening that followed was a welcome relief. I had always viewed feelings as a weakness—annoying obstacles on my quest for total power over myself. And I finally didn't have to feel them anymore.

But my experiences slowly flattened and blended together until it became obvious that there's a huge difference between not giving a fuck and not being *able* to give a fuck. Cognitively, you might know that different things are happening to you, but they don't feel very different.

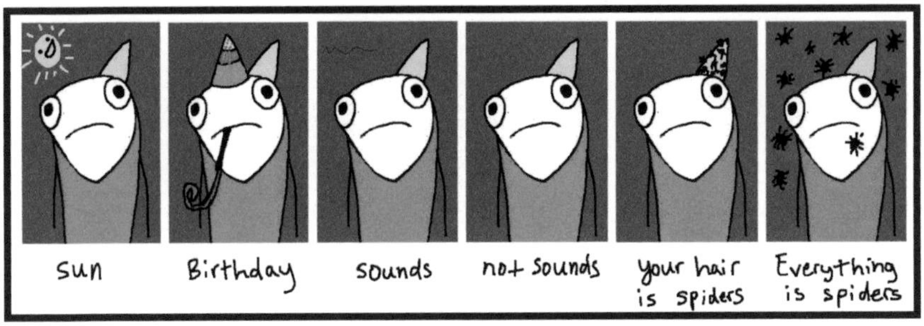
sun
Birthday
sounds
not sounds
your hair is spiders
Everything is spiders

Which leads to horrible, soul-decaying boredom.

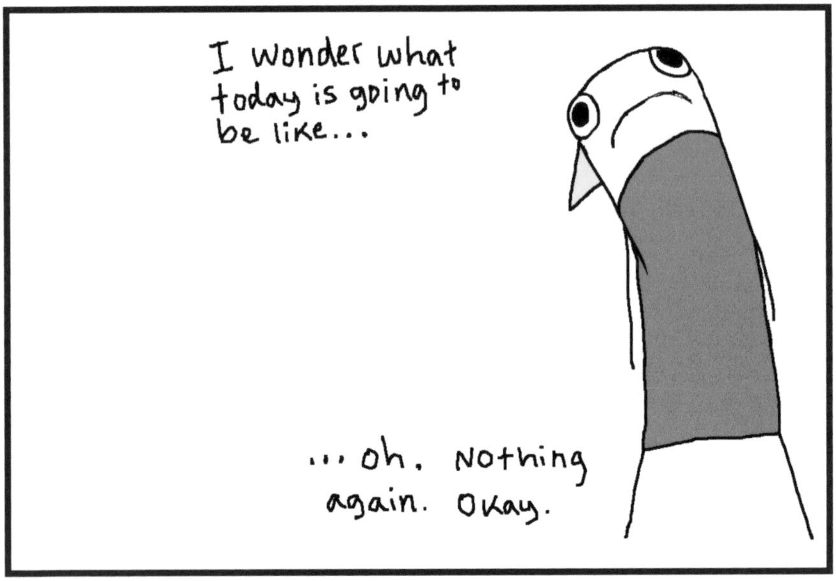
I wonder what today is going to be like...
...oh. Nothing again. Okay.

I tried to get out more, but most fun activities just left me existentially confused or frustrated with my inability to enjoy them.

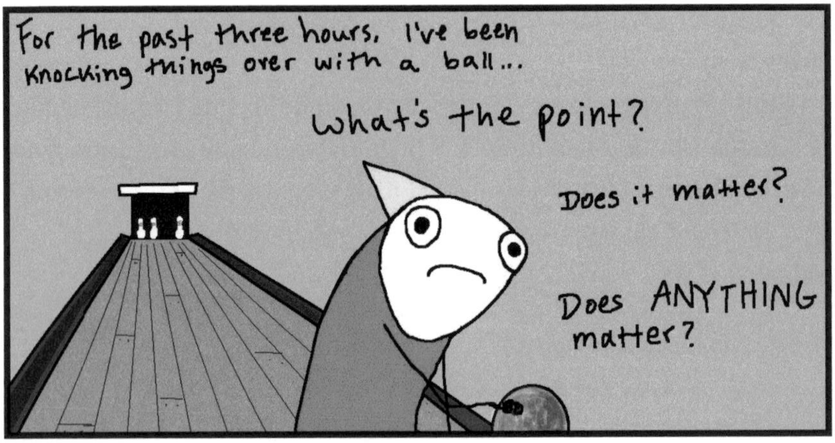
For the past three hours, I've been knocking things over with a ball...
What's the point?
Does it matter?
Does ANYTHING matter?

Months oozed by, and I gradually came to accept that maybe enjoyment was not a thing I got to feel anymore. I didn't want anyone to know, though. I was still sort of uncomfortable about how bored and detached I felt around other people, and I was still holding out hope that the whole thing would spontaneously work itself out. As long as I could manage to not alienate anyone, everything might be okay!

However, I could no longer rely on genuine emotion to generate facial expressions, and when you have to spend every social interaction consciously manipulating your face into shapes that are only approximately the right ones, alienating people is inevitable.

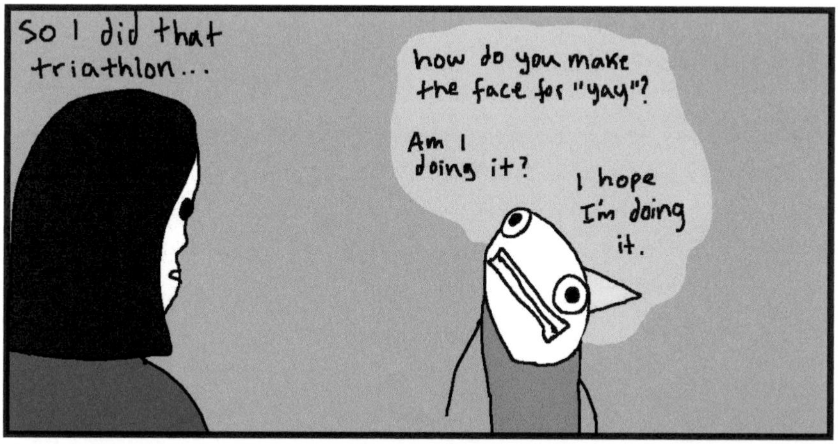
So I did that triathlon...
how do you make the face for "yay"?
Am I doing it?
I hope I'm doing it.

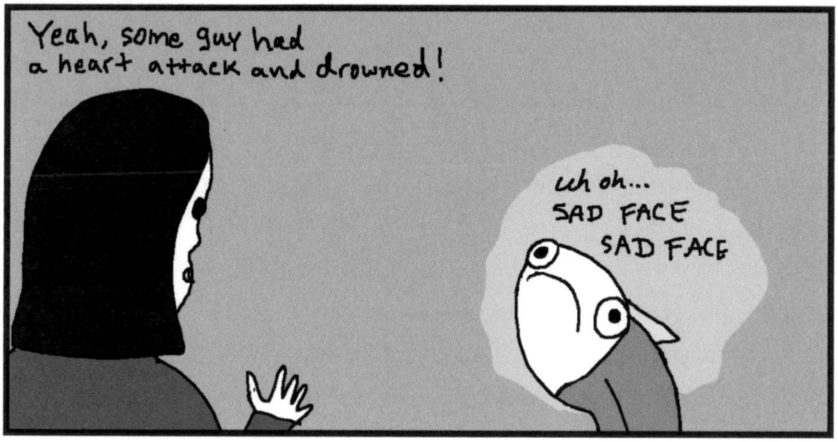
Yeah, some guy had a heart attack and drowned!
uh oh... SAD FACE SAD FACE

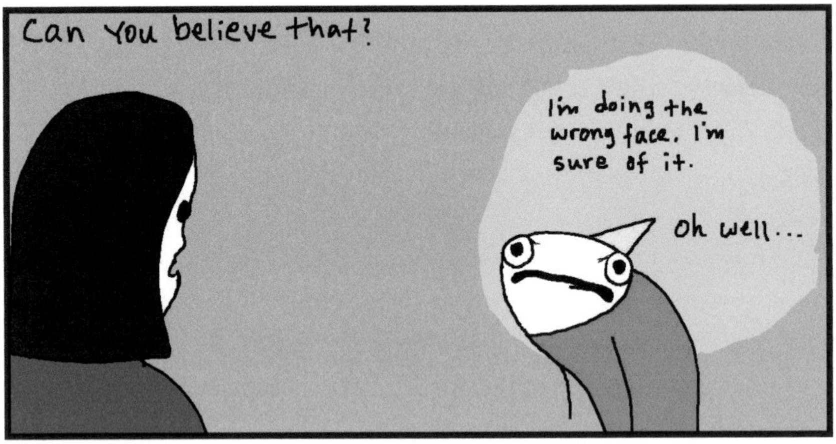
Can You believe that?
I'm doing the wrong face. I'm sure of it.
Oh well...

Everyone noticed.

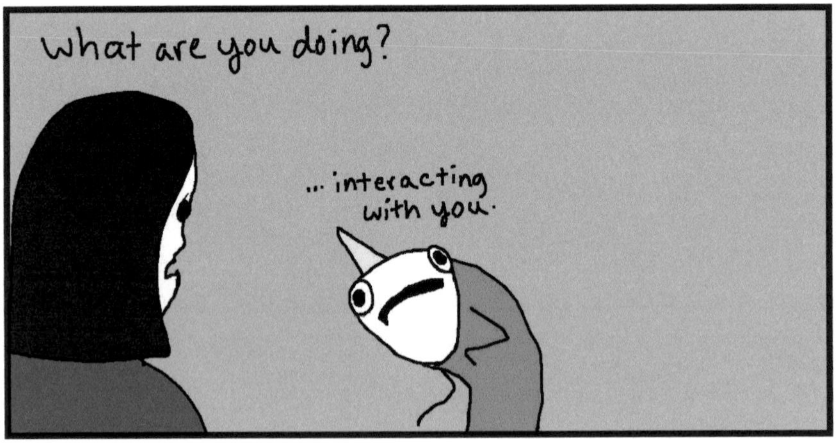
What are you doing?
...interacting with you.

It's weird for people who still have feelings to be around depressed people. They try to help you have feelings again so things can go back to normal, and it's frustrating for them when that doesn't happen. From their perspective, it seems like there has *got* to be some untapped source of happiness within you that you've simply lost track of, and if you could just see how beautiful things are . . .

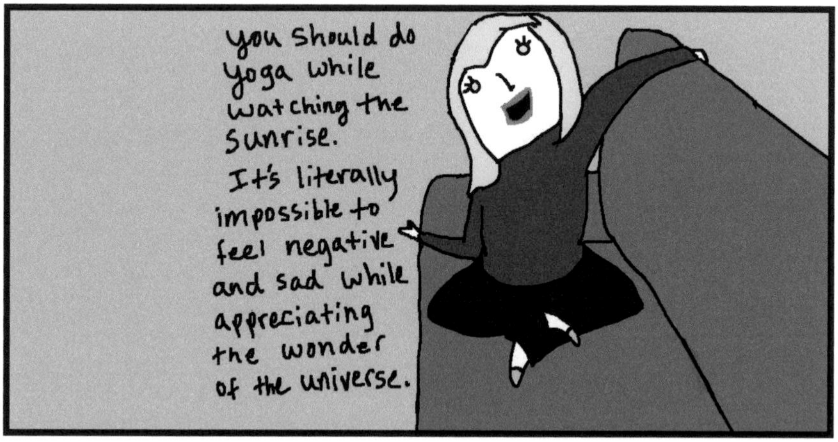
you should do yoga while watching the sunrise. It's literally impossible to feel negative and sad while appreciating the wonder of the universe.

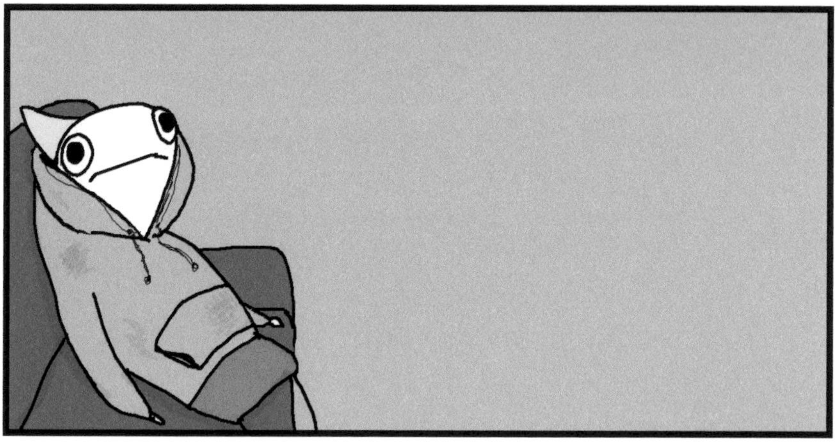

At first, I'd try to explain that it's not really negativity or sadness anymore, it's more just this detached, meaningless fog where you can't feel anything about anything—even the things you love, even fun things—and you're horribly bored and lonely, but since you've lost your ability to connect with any of the things that would normally make you feel less bored and lonely, you're stuck in the boring, lonely, meaningless void without anything to distract you from how boring, lonely, and meaningless it is.

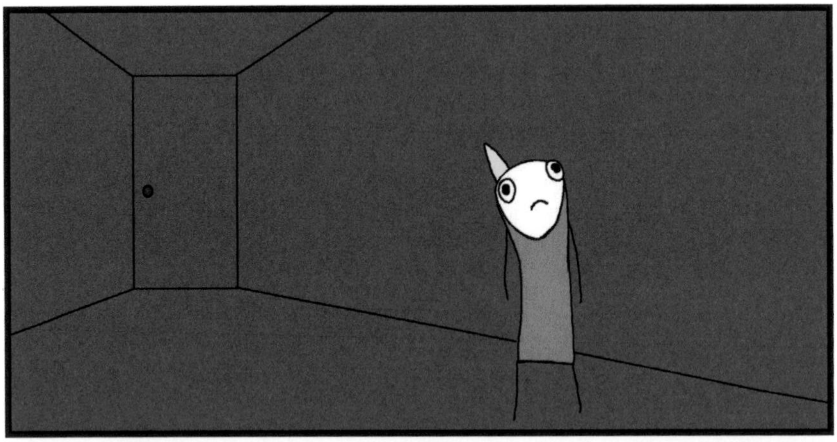

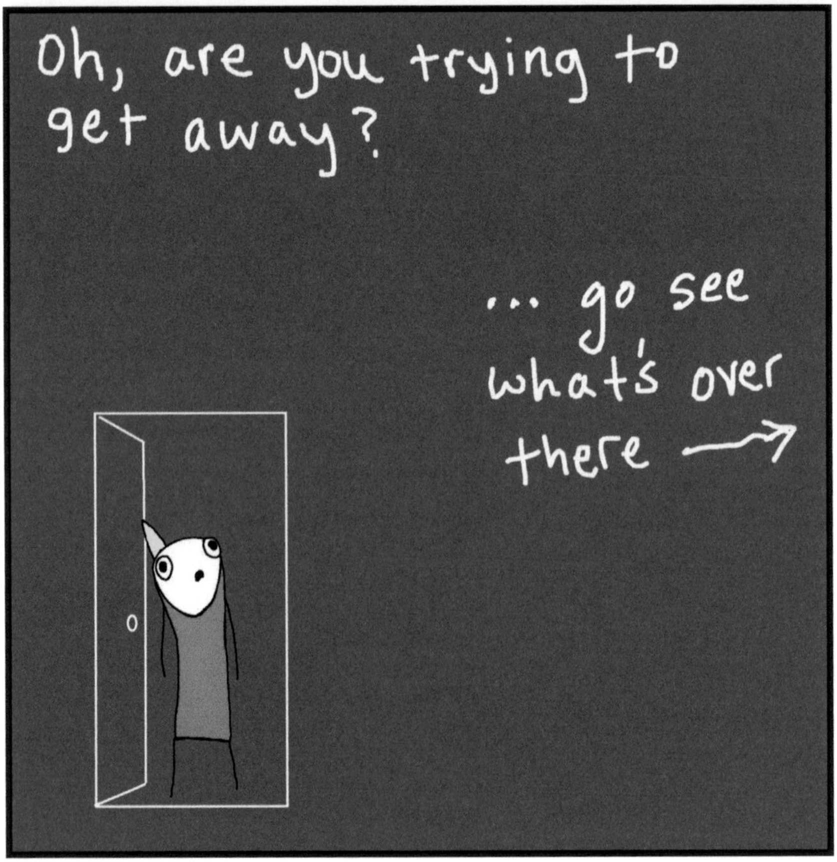
Oh, are you trying to get away?
... go see what's over there

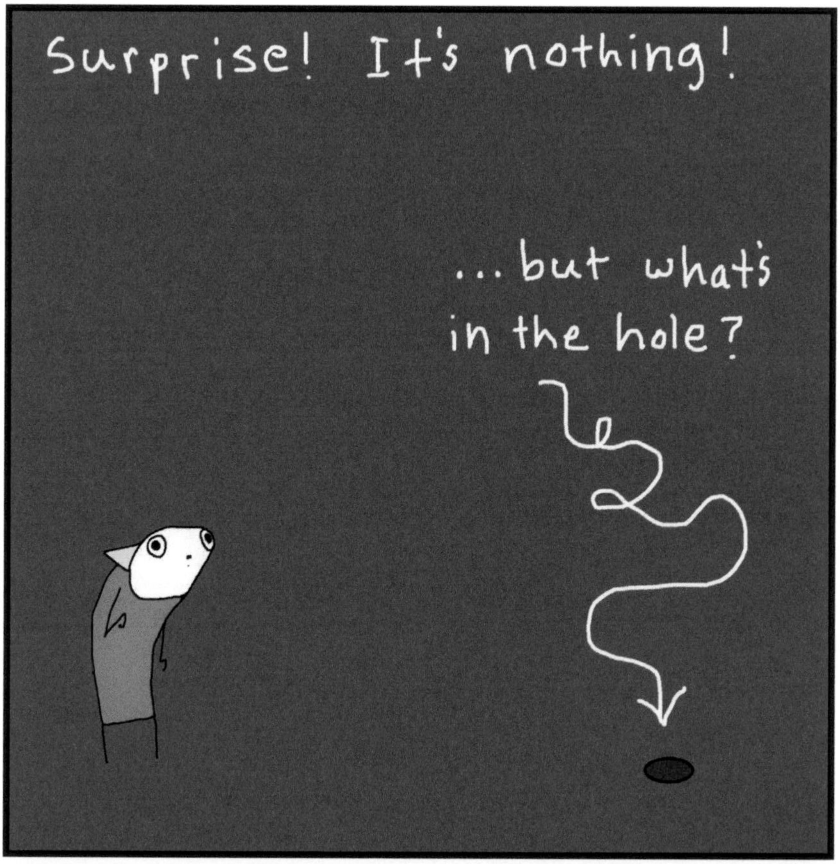
Surprise! It's nothing!
...but what's in the hole?

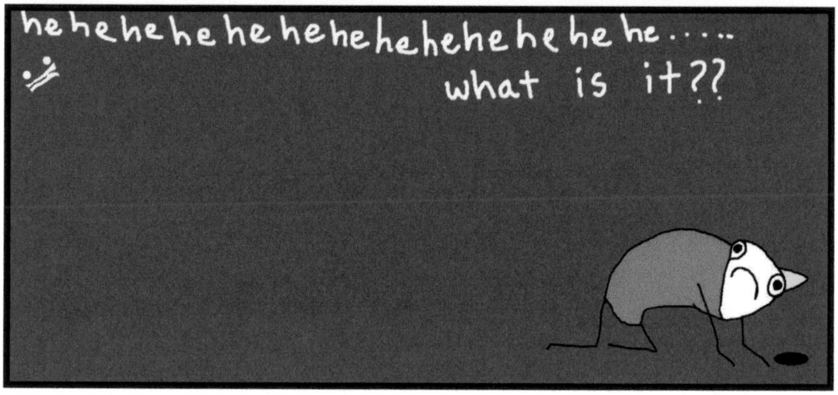
hehehehehehehehehehehehehehe.....
what is it??

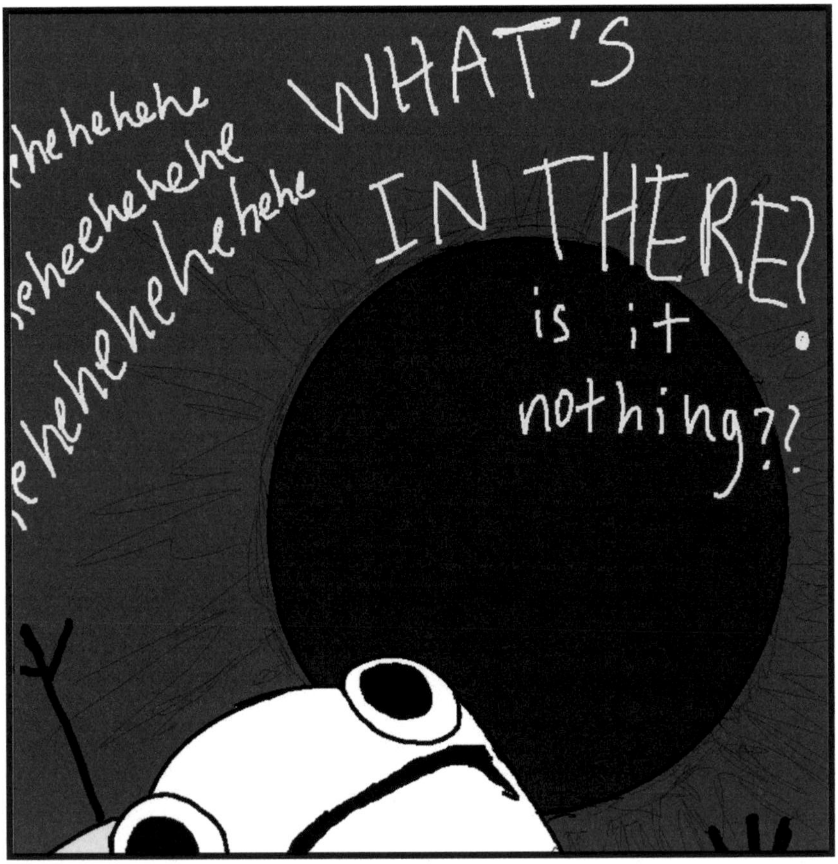
hehehehe
hehehehe
hehehehehe
hehehehe
WHAT'S IN THERE?
is it nothing??

But people want to help. So they try harder to make you feel hopeful and positive about the situation. You explain it again, hoping they'll try a less hope-centric approach, but re-explaining your total inability to experience joy inevitably sounds kind of negative, like maybe you WANT to be depressed. So the positivity starts coming out in a spray—a giant, desperate happiness sprinkler pointed directly at your face. And it keeps going like that until you're having this weird argument where you're trying to convince the person that you are far too hopeless for hope so that they'll give up on their optimism crusade and let you go back to feeling bored and lonely by yourself.

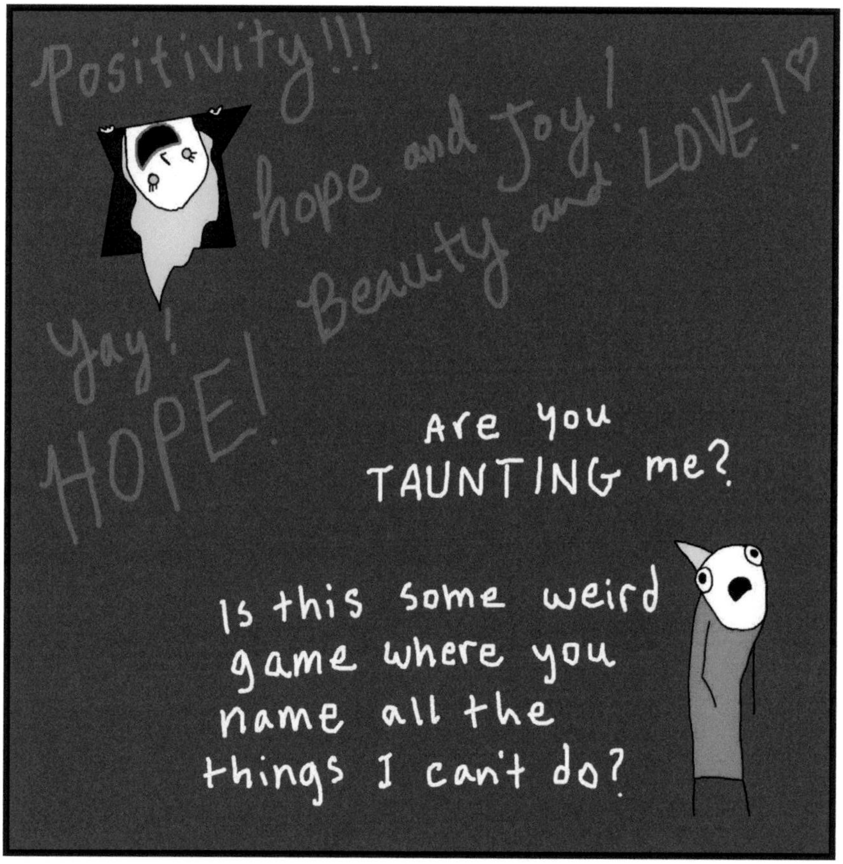
Positivity!!!
hope and Joy!
Beauty and LOVE!
Yay!
HOPE!
Are you TAUNTING me?
Is this some weird game where you name all the things I can't do?

And that's the most frustrating thing about depression. It isn't always something you can fight back against with hope. It isn't even something—it's nothing. And you can't combat nothing. You can't fill it up. You can't cover it. It's just there, pulling the meaning out of everything. That being the case, all the hopeful, proactive solutions start to sound completely insane in contrast to the scope of the problem.

It would be like having a bunch of dead fish, but no one around you will acknowledge that the fish are dead. Instead, they offer to help you look for the fish or try to help you figure out why they disappeared.

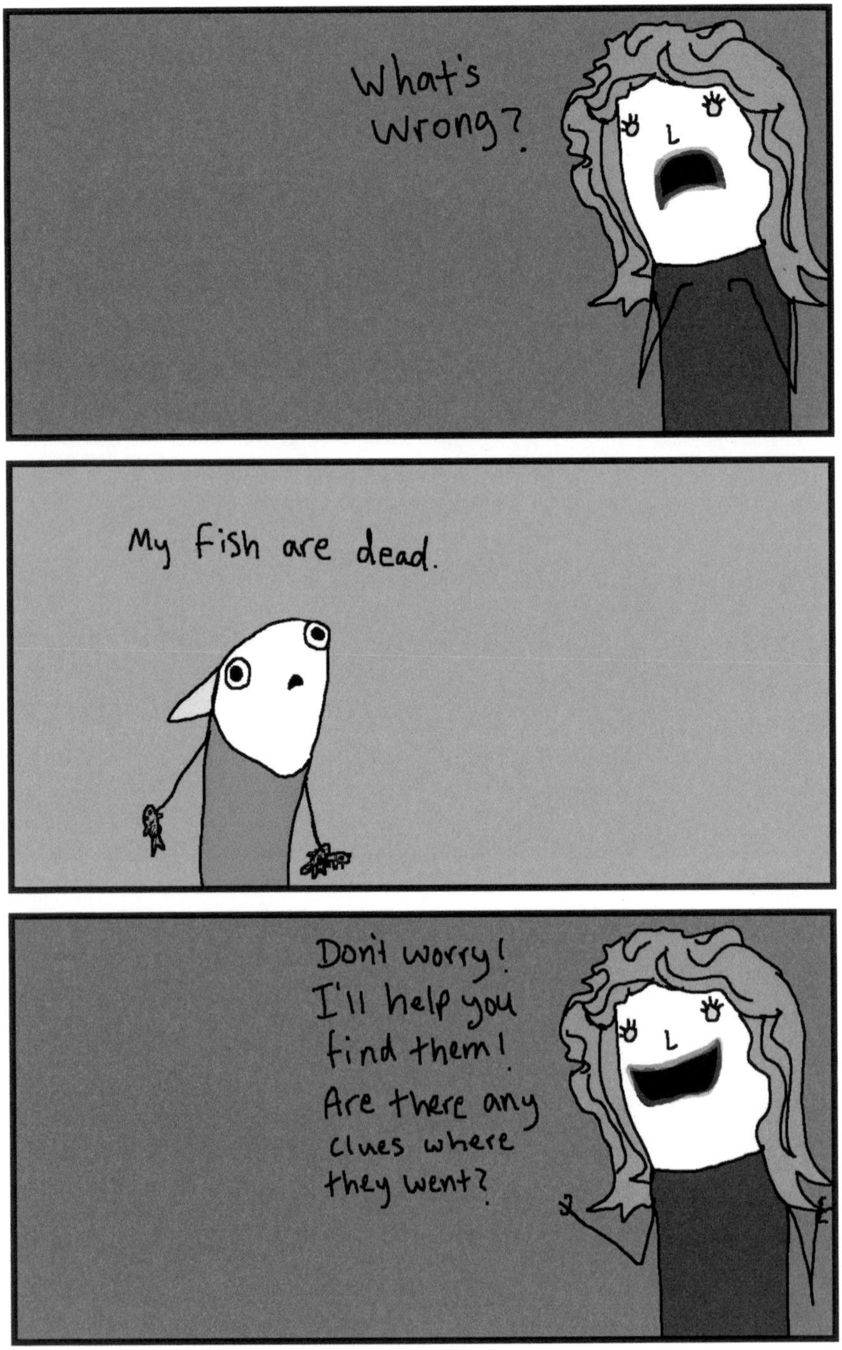
What's wrong?
My fish are dead.
Don't worry! I'll help you find them! Are there any clues where they went?

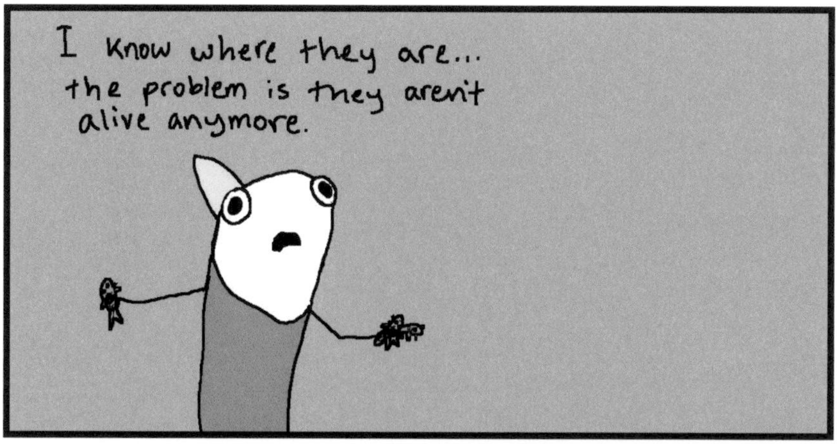
I know where they are...
the problem is they aren't
alive anymore.
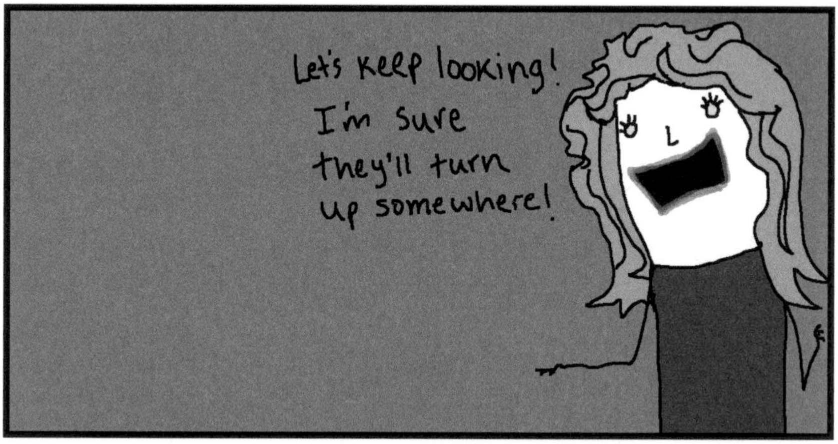
Let's keep looking!
I'm sure
they'll turn
up somewhere!
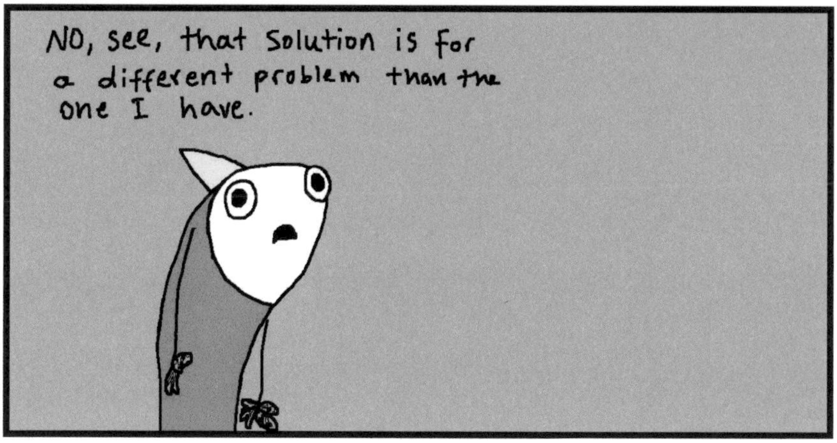
NO, see, that solution is for
a different problem than the
one I have.

Even Stranger Adventures

This portion of our journey takes us ever outward, past the rings of Saturn, toward the gas giants Uranus and Neptune. We only have two selections this time, although if Jesse Jacobs's *By This You Shall Know Him* hadn't launched quite so early (swerving into the orbit of our last guest editor, the inimitable Jeff Smith), I can imagine it floating comfortably alongside these two, as would Jim Woodring, the mad emperor of this realm, if his recent books had fallen within our time frame.

Not to suggest that the two artists presented in this section are even quite the same *kind* of artist. I think we can all agree that Michael DeForge is sui generis. No other cartoonist is "like" DeForge. Toss him into a game of Twenty Questions, and you'd be lucky to get past "Animal, Vegetable, or Mineral?"

But both DeForge and Theo Ellsworth surely have one thing in common: they're both surrealists in the classic sense of the word, deliberately journeying into realms of the subconscious as far as their delirious imaginations will take them. I mentioned my childhood love of surrealism earlier in the book—aw, you remembered this time! Thank you for reading in order—and sure enough, the kid in me really flips out for this stuff.

It's comforting for weirdos like me to know that mainstream culture has been gradually embracing the stranger sides of our imaginations. From *Pee-Wee's Playhouse* and *Teletubbies* on down, some of our most subversive, gloriously weird artists have infiltrated pop culture in startling ways. Google the phrase "Rozz Tox Manifesto" if you want to believe it's all a big conspiracy (I know I want to). Pendleton Ward's *Adventure Time* is the latest gathering place for these pop-culture double agents, and sure enough, there you'll find DeForge, and maybe Ellsworth too by the time you read this.

Check the back of this collection for more information on both cartoonists and for all the contributors to this anthology. You're just looking at the tip of a very big, very weird iceberg.

On a side note: I finally met Michael DeForge in Oslo last year. Gabrielle Bell (a frequent Best American cartoonist herself) was also at the show and did a great comic about a conversation the three of us had regarding Pop-Tarts, feces, Oscar Mayer meat products, and cannibalism. You can read the comic, and lots of others, at www.gabriellebell.com.

Canadian Royalty

THEIR LIFESTYLES AND FASHIONS

CHILDREN OF ROYAL OFFSPRING HAVE THEIR FEATURES SHAVED DOWN IMMEDIATELY AFTER BIRTH. SCABS OR GROWTHS THAT FORM ARE SANDED AT REGULAR INTERVALS UNTIL THEIR ADOLESCENCE

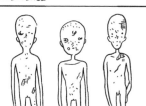

WHEN THEIR SMOOTH SKIN FINALLY SETS

A TYPICAL ROYAL HOUSEHOLD - DUKE AND DUCHESS CARAMEL WITH THEIR FIVE OFFSPRING. HOLDING THEIR YOUNGEST CHILD IS AN AU PAIR

A FLAP OF SKIN IS SURGICALLY ATTACHED TO COVER THEIR GENITALS

IT IS TRADITIONAL THAT ANY CHILD WITH ROYAL BLOOD BE COMPLETELY FEATURELESS. ONLY UPON INHERITING OR MARRYING INTO A NOBLE OR ARISTOCRATIC TITLE CAN THEY BE OUTFITTED IN ROYAL GARMENT

EACH OUTFIT IS UNIQUE TO ITS WEARER AND CAN ONLY BE REMOVED UPON DEATH. THEY ARE WATERPROOF

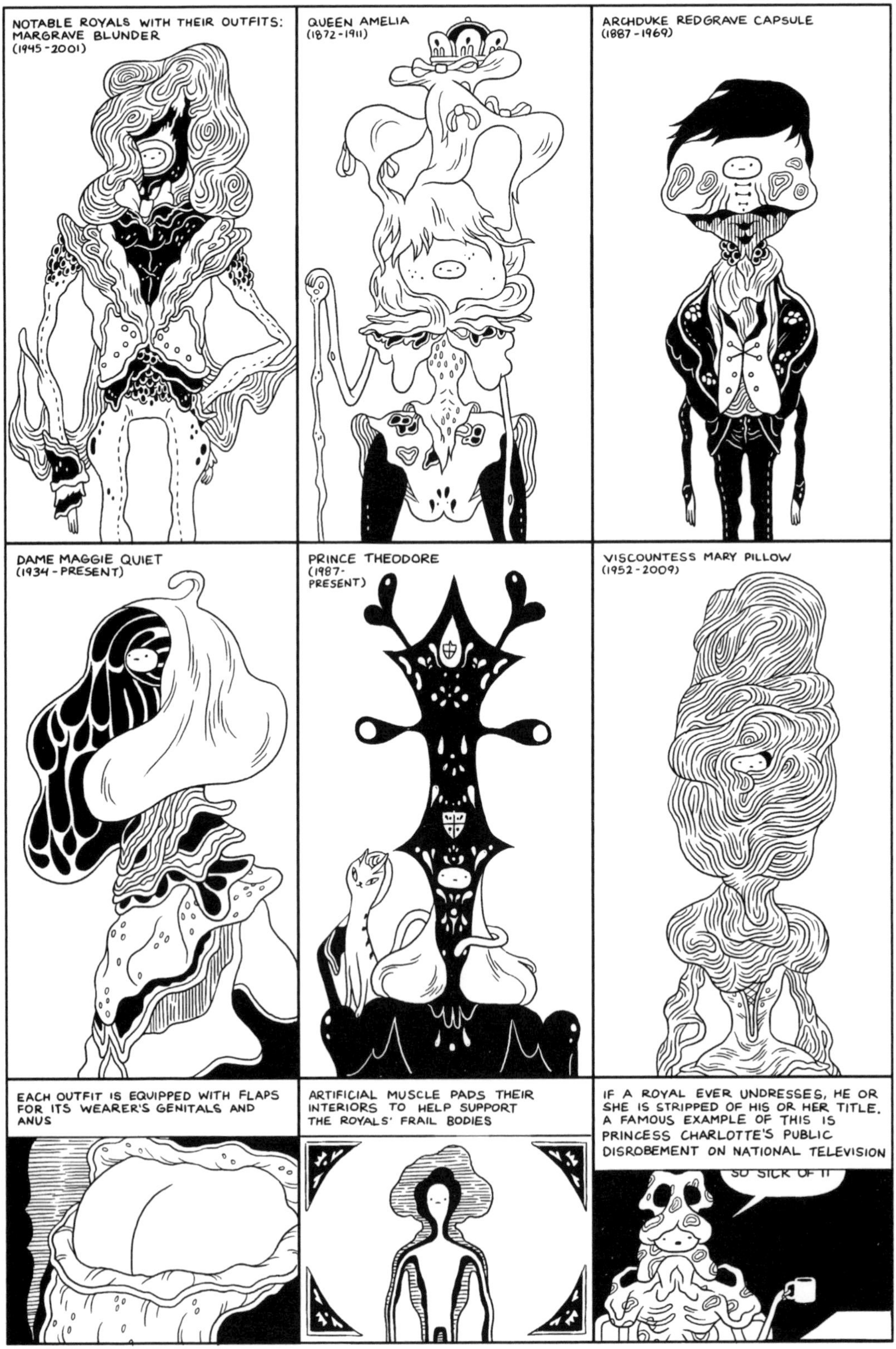
NOTABLE ROYALS WITH THEIR OUTFITS:
MARGRAVE BLUNDER
(1945-2001)
QUEEN AMELIA
(1872-1911)
ARCHDUKE REDGRAVE CAPSULE
(1887-1969)
DAME MAGGIE QUIET
(1934-PRESENT)
PRINCE THEODORE
(1987-PRESENT)
VISCOUNTESS MARY PILLOW
(1952-2009)
EACH OUTFIT IS EQUIPPED WITH FLAPS FOR ITS WEARER'S GENITALS AND ANUS
ARTIFICIAL MUSCLE PADS THEIR INTERIORS TO HELP SUPPORT THE ROYALS' FRAIL BODIES
IF A ROYAL EVER UNDRESSES, HE OR SHE IS STRIPPED OF HIS OR HER TITLE. A FAMOUS EXAMPLE OF THIS IS PRINCESS CHARLOTTE'S PUBLIC DISROBEMENT ON NATIONAL TELEVISION
SO SICK OF IT

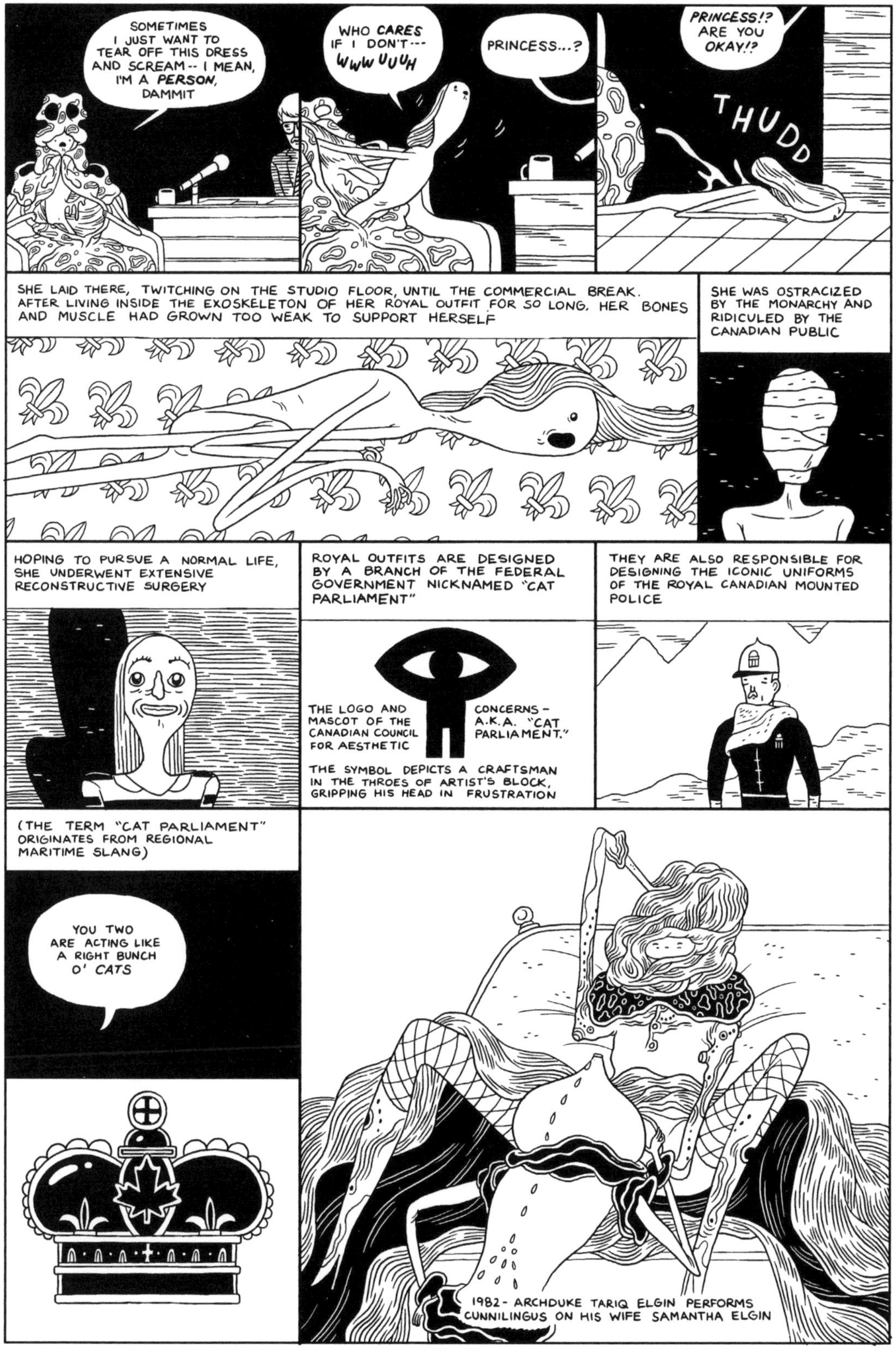
SOMETIMES I JUST WANT TO TEAR OFF THIS DRESS AND SCREAM -- I MEAN, I'M A *PERSON*, DAMMIT
WHO *CARES* IF I DON'T---
WWWUUUH
PRINCESS...?
PRINCESS!? ARE YOU *OKAY!?*
THUDD
SHE LAID THERE, TWITCHING ON THE STUDIO FLOOR, UNTIL THE COMMERCIAL BREAK. AFTER LIVING INSIDE THE EXOSKELETON OF HER ROYAL OUTFIT FOR SO LONG, HER BONES AND MUSCLE HAD GROWN TOO WEAK TO SUPPORT HERSELF
SHE WAS OSTRACIZED BY THE MONARCHY AND RIDICULED BY THE CANADIAN PUBLIC
HOPING TO PURSUE A NORMAL LIFE, SHE UNDERWENT EXTENSIVE RECONSTRUCTIVE SURGERY
ROYAL OUTFITS ARE DESIGNED BY A BRANCH OF THE FEDERAL GOVERNMENT NICKNAMED "CAT PARLIAMENT"
THE LOGO AND MASCOT OF THE CANADIAN COUNCIL FOR AESTHETIC CONCERNS - A.K.A. "CAT PARLIAMENT."
THE SYMBOL DEPICTS A CRAFTSMAN IN THE THROES OF ARTIST'S BLOCK, GRIPPING HIS HEAD IN FRUSTRATION
THEY ARE ALSO RESPONSIBLE FOR DESIGNING THE ICONIC UNIFORMS OF THE ROYAL CANADIAN MOUNTED POLICE
(THE TERM "CAT PARLIAMENT" ORIGINATES FROM REGIONAL MARITIME SLANG)
YOU TWO ARE ACTING LIKE A RIGHT BUNCH O' *CATS*
1982- ARCHDUKE TARIQ ELGIN PERFORMS CUNNILINGUS ON HIS WIFE SAMANTHA ELGIN

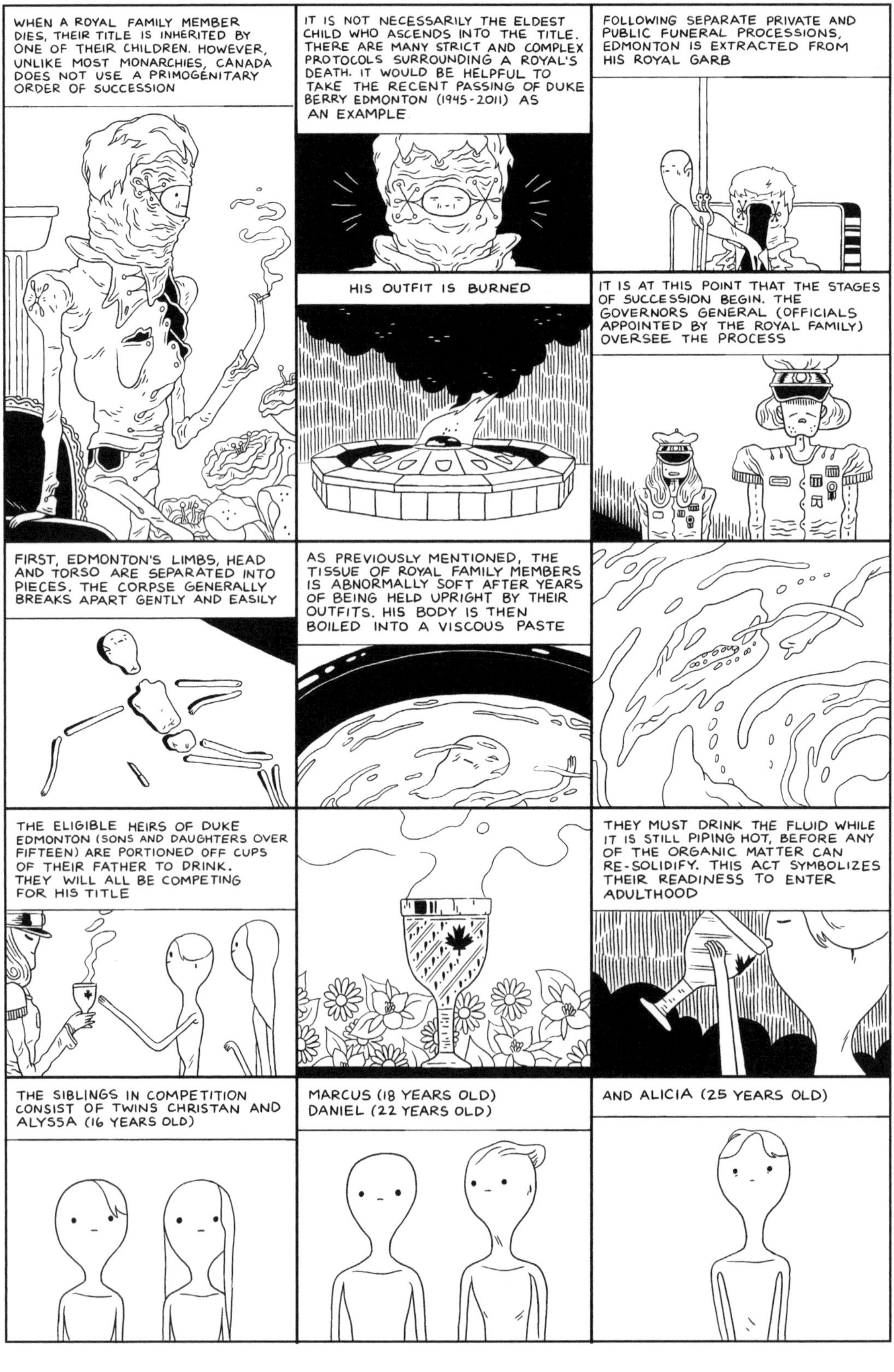

WHEN A ROYAL FAMILY MEMBER DIES, THEIR TITLE IS INHERITED BY ONE OF THEIR CHILDREN. HOWEVER, UNLIKE MOST MONARCHIES, CANADA DOES NOT USE A PRIMOGENITARY ORDER OF SUCCESSION
IT IS NOT NECESSARILY THE ELDEST CHILD WHO ASCENDS INTO THE TITLE. THERE ARE MANY STRICT AND COMPLEX PROTOCOLS SURROUNDING A ROYAL'S DEATH. IT WOULD BE HELPFUL TO TAKE THE RECENT PASSING OF DUKE BERRY EDMONTON (1945-2011) AS AN EXAMPLE
HIS OUTFIT IS BURNED
FOLLOWING SEPARATE PRIVATE AND PUBLIC FUNERAL PROCESSIONS, EDMONTON IS EXTRACTED FROM HIS ROYAL GARB
IT IS AT THIS POINT THAT THE STAGES OF SUCCESSION BEGIN. THE GOVERNORS GENERAL (OFFICIALS APPOINTED BY THE ROYAL FAMILY) OVERSEE THE PROCESS
FIRST, EDMONTON'S LIMBS, HEAD AND TORSO ARE SEPARATED INTO PIECES. THE CORPSE GENERALLY BREAKS APART GENTLY AND EASILY
AS PREVIOUSLY MENTIONED, THE TISSUE OF ROYAL FAMILY MEMBERS IS ABNORMALLY SOFT AFTER YEARS OF BEING HELD UPRIGHT BY THEIR OUTFITS. HIS BODY IS THEN BOILED INTO A VISCOUS PASTE
THE ELIGIBLE HEIRS OF DUKE EDMONTON (SONS AND DAUGHTERS OVER FIFTEEN) ARE PORTIONED OFF CUPS OF THEIR FATHER TO DRINK. THEY WILL ALL BE COMPETING FOR HIS TITLE
THEY MUST DRINK THE FLUID WHILE IT IS STILL PIPING HOT, BEFORE ANY OF THE ORGANIC MATTER CAN RE-SOLIDIFY. THIS ACT SYMBOLIZES THEIR READINESS TO ENTER ADULTHOOD
THE SIBLINGS IN COMPETITION CONSIST OF TWINS CHRISTAN AND ALYSSA (16 YEARS OLD)
MARCUS (18 YEARS OLD)
DANIEL (22 YEARS OLD)
AND ALICIA (25 YEARS OLD)

THE SIBLINGS UNDERGO SEVERAL ROUNDS OF PSYCHIATRIC SCREENING

THE GOVERNORS GENERAL MUST FIRST DEEM THEM MENTALLY "FIT" TO ASSUME THE RESPONSIBILITIES OF ROYAL LIFE

MARCUS IS QUICKLY DIAGNOSED WITH AVOIDANT PERSONALITY DISORDER. HE IS BARRED FROM COMPETITION AND STRIPPED OF HIS FAMILY NAME

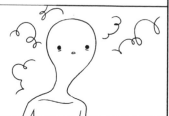

SEAL OF ROYAL ASCENSION

THE GOVERNORS GENERAL NOW SCORE THE REMAINING OFFSPRING ON THEIR PERFORMANCE IN THREE SEPARATE CATEGORIES

SEAL OF THE GOVERNORS GENERAL

MINISTRY OF ROYAL AFFAIRS

CATEGORY ONE: PHYSICAL ABILITY
WHERE COMPETITORS CAN SCORE UP TO 20 POINTS

CATEGORY TWO: MENTAL ACUITY
WHERE COMPETITORS CAN SCORE UP TO 35 POINTS

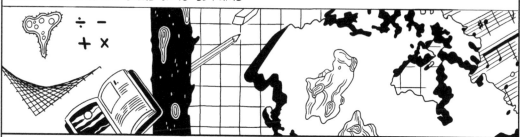

CATEGORY THREE: THE "TALENT SHOW" PORTION, A PUBLIC PERFORMANCE ON PARLIAMENT HILL
WHERE COMPETITORS CAN SCORE UP TO 5 POINTS

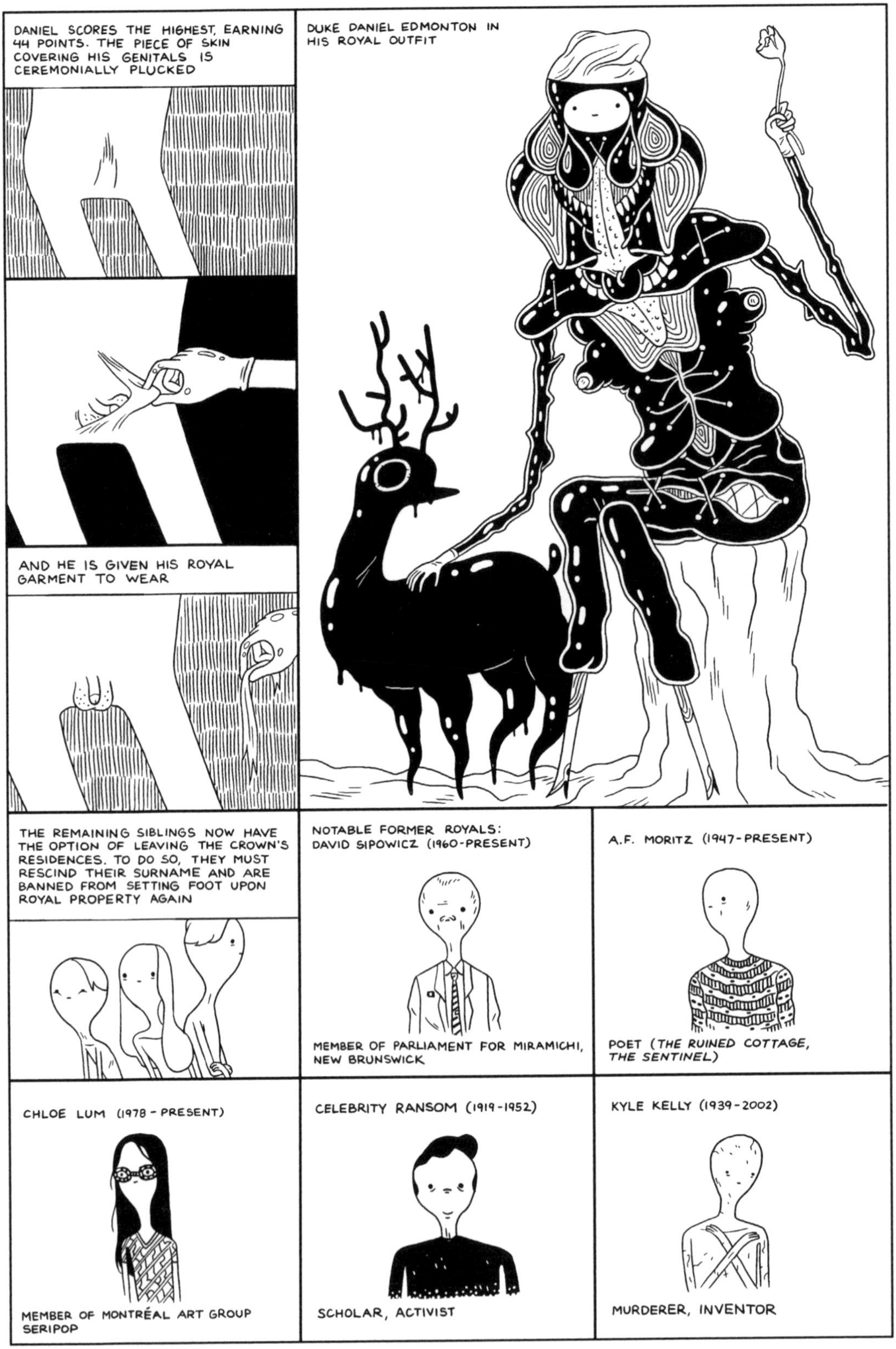
DANIEL SCORES THE HIGHEST, EARNING 44 POINTS. THE PIECE OF SKIN COVERING HIS GENITALS IS CEREMONIALLY PLUCKED
AND HE IS GIVEN HIS ROYAL GARMENT TO WEAR
DUKE DANIEL EDMONTON IN HIS ROYAL OUTFIT
THE REMAINING SIBLINGS NOW HAVE THE OPTION OF LEAVING THE CROWN'S RESIDENCES. TO DO SO, THEY MUST RESCIND THEIR SURNAME AND ARE BANNED FROM SETTING FOOT UPON ROYAL PROPERTY AGAIN
NOTABLE FORMER ROYALS: DAVID SIPOWICZ (1960-PRESENT)
MEMBER OF PARLIAMENT FOR MIRAMICHI, NEW BRUNSWICK
A.F. MORITZ (1947-PRESENT)
POET (*THE RUINED COTTAGE, THE SENTINEL*)
CHLOE LUM (1978 - PRESENT)
MEMBER OF MONTRÉAL ART GROUP SERIPOP
CELEBRITY RANSOM (1919-1952)
SCHOLAR, ACTIVIST
KYLE KELLY (1939-2002)
MURDERER, INVENTOR

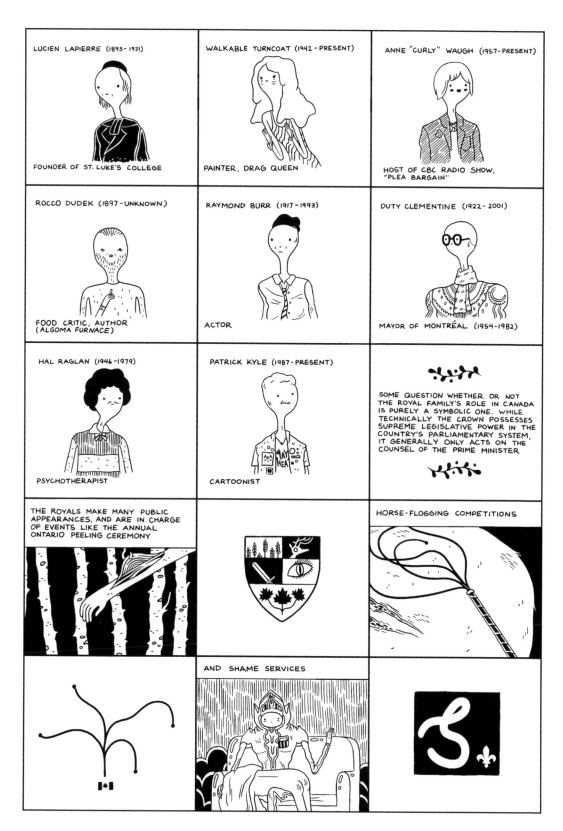

LUCIEN LAPIERRE (1893-1931)

FOUNDER OF ST. LUKE'S COLLEGE

WALKABLE TURNCOAT (1942-PRESENT)

PAINTER, DRAG QUEEN

ANNE "CURLY" WAUGH (1957-PRESENT)

HOST OF CBC RADIO SHOW, "PLEA BARGAIN"

ROCCO DUDEK (1897-UNKNOWN)

FOOD CRITIC, AUTHOR (ALGOMA FURNACE)

RAYMOND BURR (1917-1993)

ACTOR

DUTY CLEMENTINE (1922-2001)

MAYOR OF MONTRÉAL (1954-1982)

HAL RAGLAN (1946-1979)

PSYCHOTHERAPIST

PATRICK KYLE (1987-PRESENT)

CARTOONIST

SOME QUESTION WHETHER OR NOT THE ROYAL FAMILY'S ROLE IN CANADA IS PURELY A SYMBOLIC ONE. WHILE TECHNICALLY THE CROWN POSSESSES SUPREME LEGISLATIVE POWER IN THE COUNTRY'S PARLIAMENTARY SYSTEM, IT GENERALLY ONLY ACTS ON THE COUNSEL OF THE PRIME MINISTER

THE ROYALS MAKE MANY PUBLIC APPEARANCES, AND ARE IN CHARGE OF EVENTS LIKE THE ANNUAL ONTARIO PEELING CEREMONY

HORSE-FLOGGING COMPETITIONS

AND SHAME SERVICES

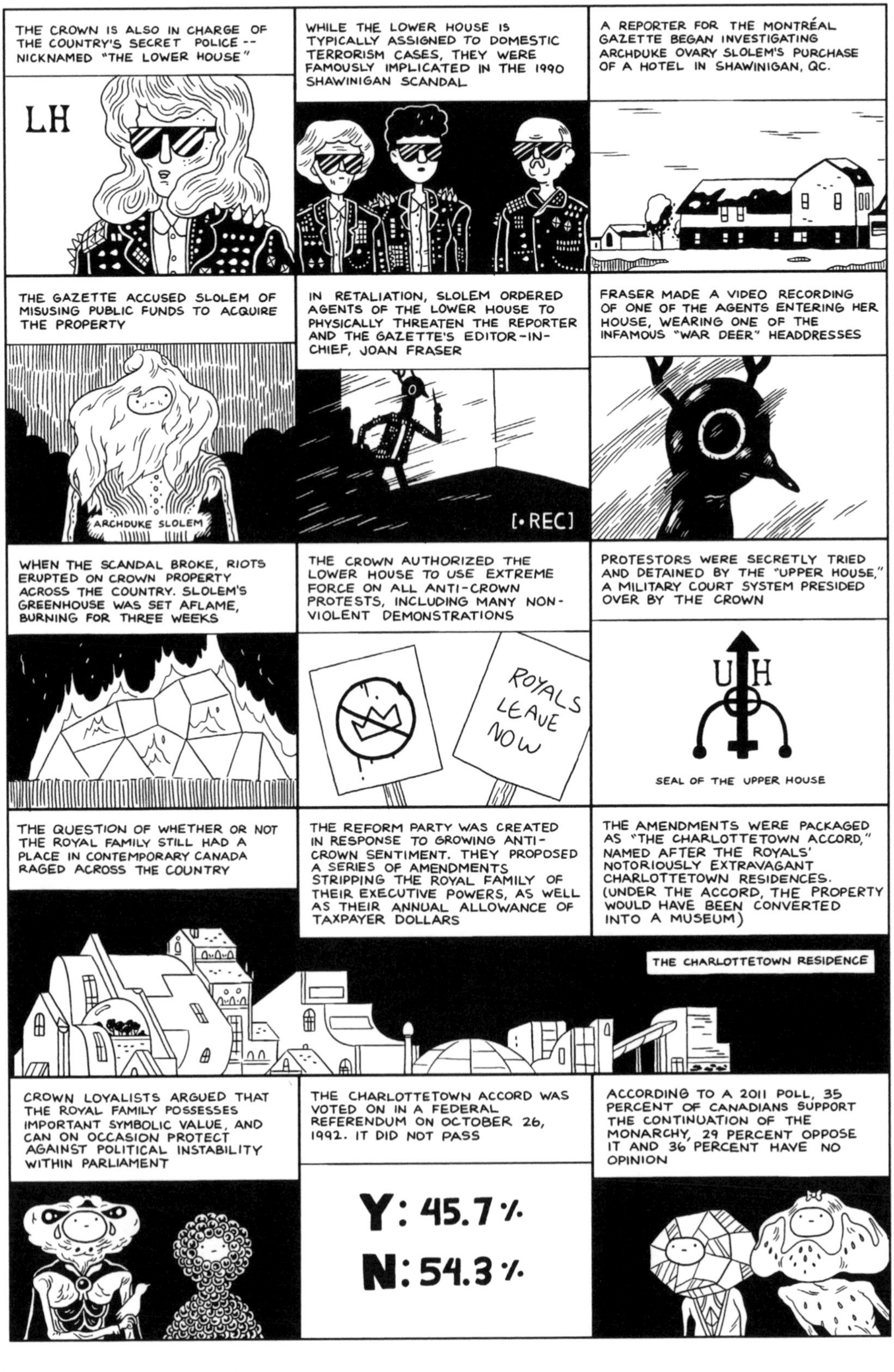

THE CROWN IS ALSO IN CHARGE OF THE COUNTRY'S SECRET POLICE -- NICKNAMED "THE LOWER HOUSE"

WHILE THE LOWER HOUSE IS TYPICALLY ASSIGNED TO DOMESTIC TERRORISM CASES, THEY WERE FAMOUSLY IMPLICATED IN THE 1990 SHAWINIGAN SCANDAL

A REPORTER FOR THE MONTRÉAL GAZETTE BEGAN INVESTIGATING ARCHDUKE OVARY SLOLEM'S PURCHASE OF A HOTEL IN SHAWINIGAN, QC.

THE GAZETTE ACCUSED SLOLEM OF MISUSING PUBLIC FUNDS TO ACQUIRE THE PROPERTY

ARCHDUKE SLOLEM

IN RETALIATION, SLOLEM ORDERED AGENTS OF THE LOWER HOUSE TO PHYSICALLY THREATEN THE REPORTER AND THE GAZETTE'S EDITOR-IN-CHIEF, JOAN FRASER

[·REC]

FRASER MADE A VIDEO RECORDING OF ONE OF THE AGENTS ENTERING HER HOUSE, WEARING ONE OF THE INFAMOUS "WAR DEER" HEADDRESSES

WHEN THE SCANDAL BROKE, RIOTS ERUPTED ON CROWN PROPERTY ACROSS THE COUNTRY. SLOLEM'S GREENHOUSE WAS SET AFLAME, BURNING FOR THREE WEEKS

THE CROWN AUTHORIZED THE LOWER HOUSE TO USE EXTREME FORCE ON ALL ANTI-CROWN PROTESTS, INCLUDING MANY NON-VIOLENT DEMONSTRATIONS

ROYALS LEAVE NOW

PROTESTORS WERE SECRETLY TRIED AND DETAINED BY THE "UPPER HOUSE," A MILITARY COURT SYSTEM PRESIDED OVER BY THE CROWN

SEAL OF THE UPPER HOUSE

THE QUESTION OF WHETHER OR NOT THE ROYAL FAMILY STILL HAD A PLACE IN CONTEMPORARY CANADA RAGED ACROSS THE COUNTRY

THE REFORM PARTY WAS CREATED IN RESPONSE TO GROWING ANTI-CROWN SENTIMENT. THEY PROPOSED A SERIES OF AMENDMENTS STRIPPING THE ROYAL FAMILY OF THEIR EXECUTIVE POWERS, AS WELL AS THEIR ANNUAL ALLOWANCE OF TAXPAYER DOLLARS

THE AMENDMENTS WERE PACKAGED AS "THE CHARLOTTETOWN ACCORD," NAMED AFTER THE ROYALS' NOTORIOUSLY EXTRAVAGANT CHARLOTTETOWN RESIDENCES. (UNDER THE ACCORD, THE PROPERTY WOULD HAVE BEEN CONVERTED INTO A MUSEUM)

THE CHARLOTTETOWN RESIDENCE

CROWN LOYALISTS ARGUED THAT THE ROYAL FAMILY POSSESSES IMPORTANT SYMBOLIC VALUE, AND CAN ON OCCASION PROTECT AGAINST POLITICAL INSTABILITY WITHIN PARLIAMENT

THE CHARLOTTETOWN ACCORD WAS VOTED ON IN A FEDERAL REFERENDUM ON OCTOBER 26, 1992. IT DID NOT PASS

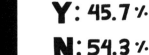

Y: 45.7%
N: 54.3%

ACCORDING TO A 2011 POLL, 35 PERCENT OF CANADIANS SUPPORT THE CONTINUATION OF THE MONARCHY, 29 PERCENT OPPOSE IT AND 36 PERCENT HAVE NO OPINION

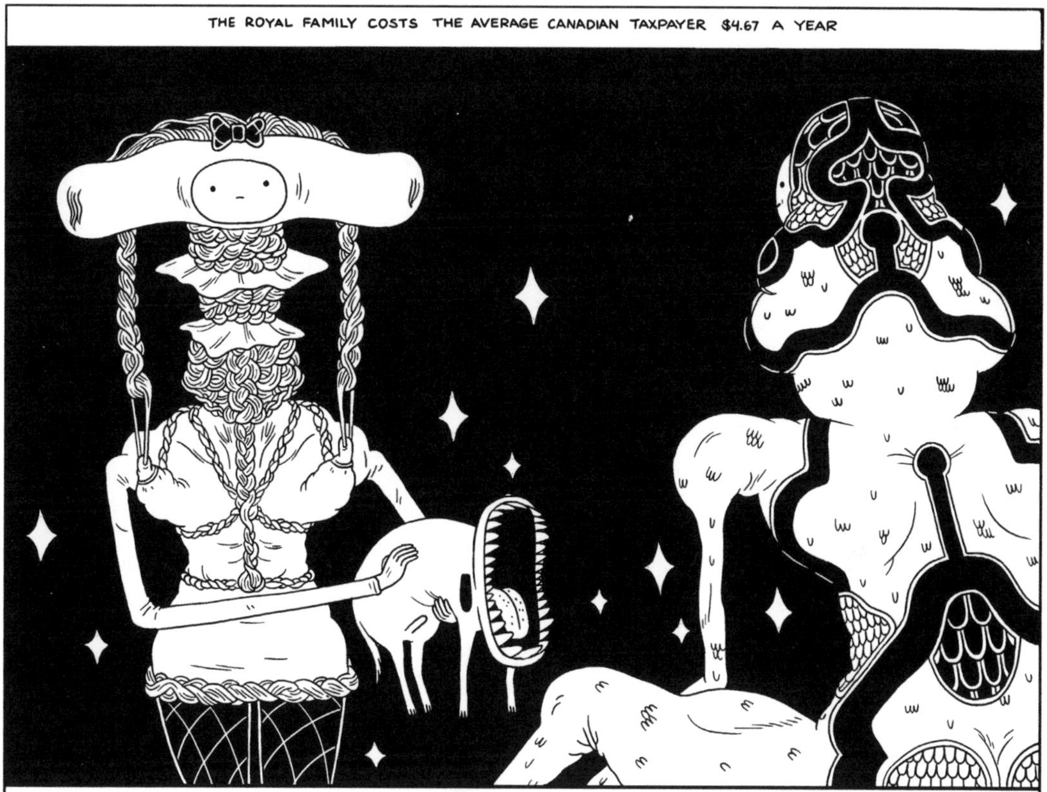
THE ROYAL FAMILY COSTS THE AVERAGE CANADIAN TAXPAYER $4.67 A YEAR

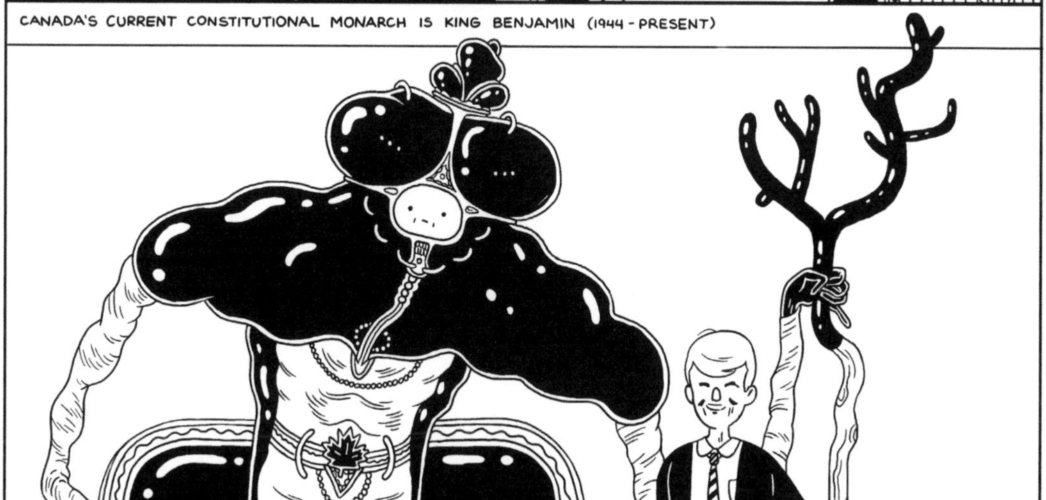
CANADA'S CURRENT CONSTITUTIONAL MONARCH IS KING BENJAMIN (1944 - PRESENT)
KING BENJAMIN PHOTOGRAPHED WITH CURRENT PRIME MINISTER CLAUDE MOVENPICK ON THE NIGHT OF THE 2008 ELECTION

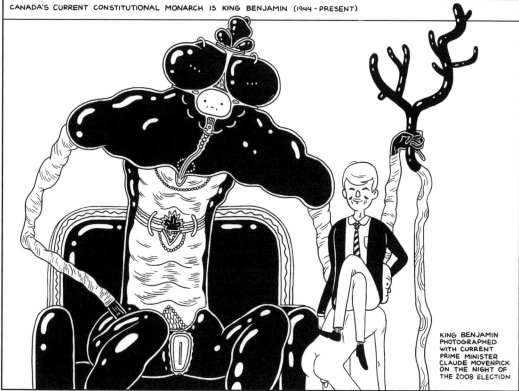

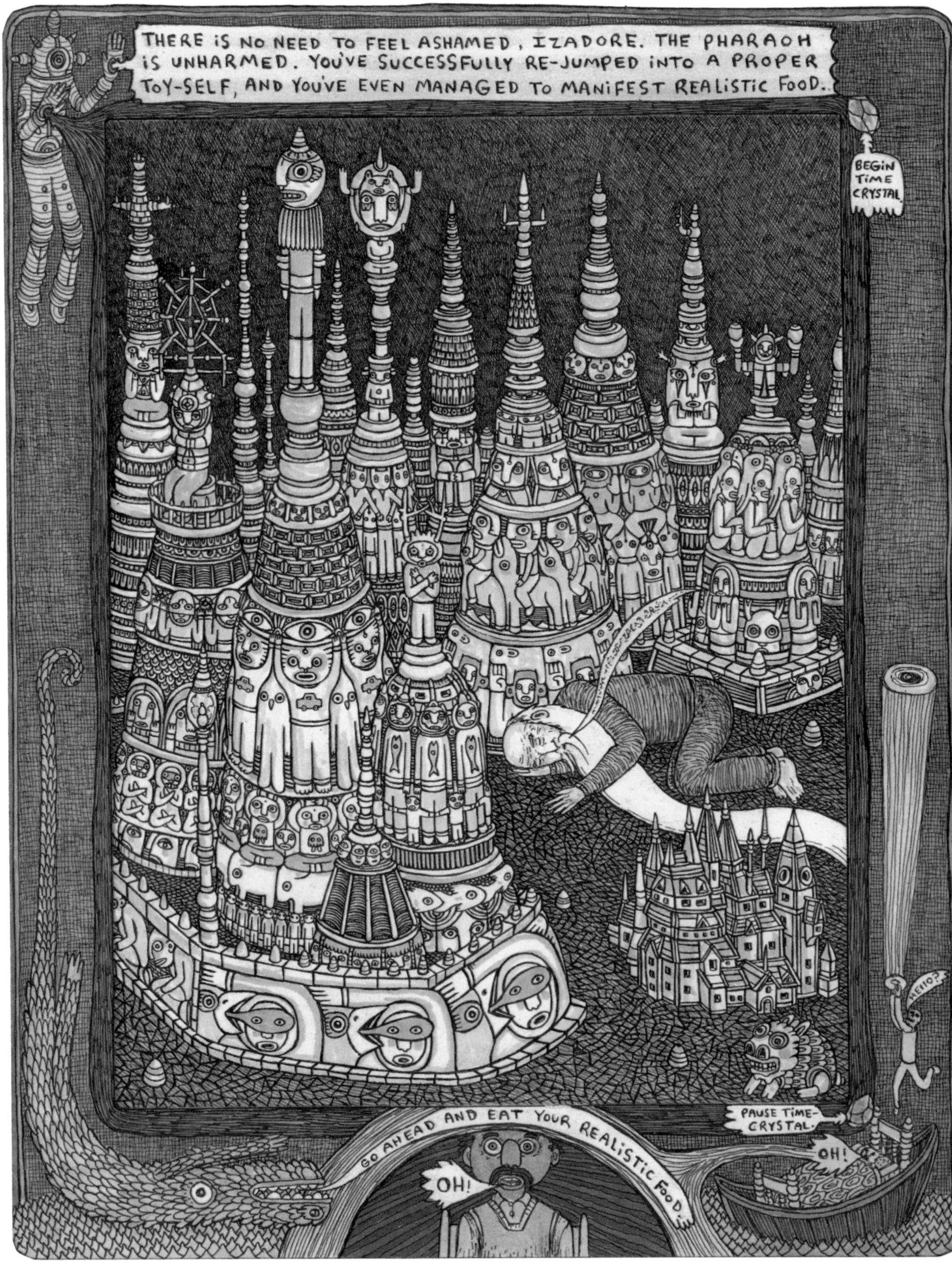
THERE IS NO NEED TO FEEL ASHAMED, IZADORE. THE PHARAOH IS UNHARMED. YOU'VE SUCCESSFULLY RE-JUMPED INTO A PROPER TOY-SELF, AND YOU'VE EVEN MANAGED TO MANIFEST REALISTIC FOOD.
BEGIN TIME CRYSTAL
HELLO?
PAUSE TIME-CRYSTAL.
GO AHEAD AND EAT YOUR REALISTIC FOOD.
OH!
OH!

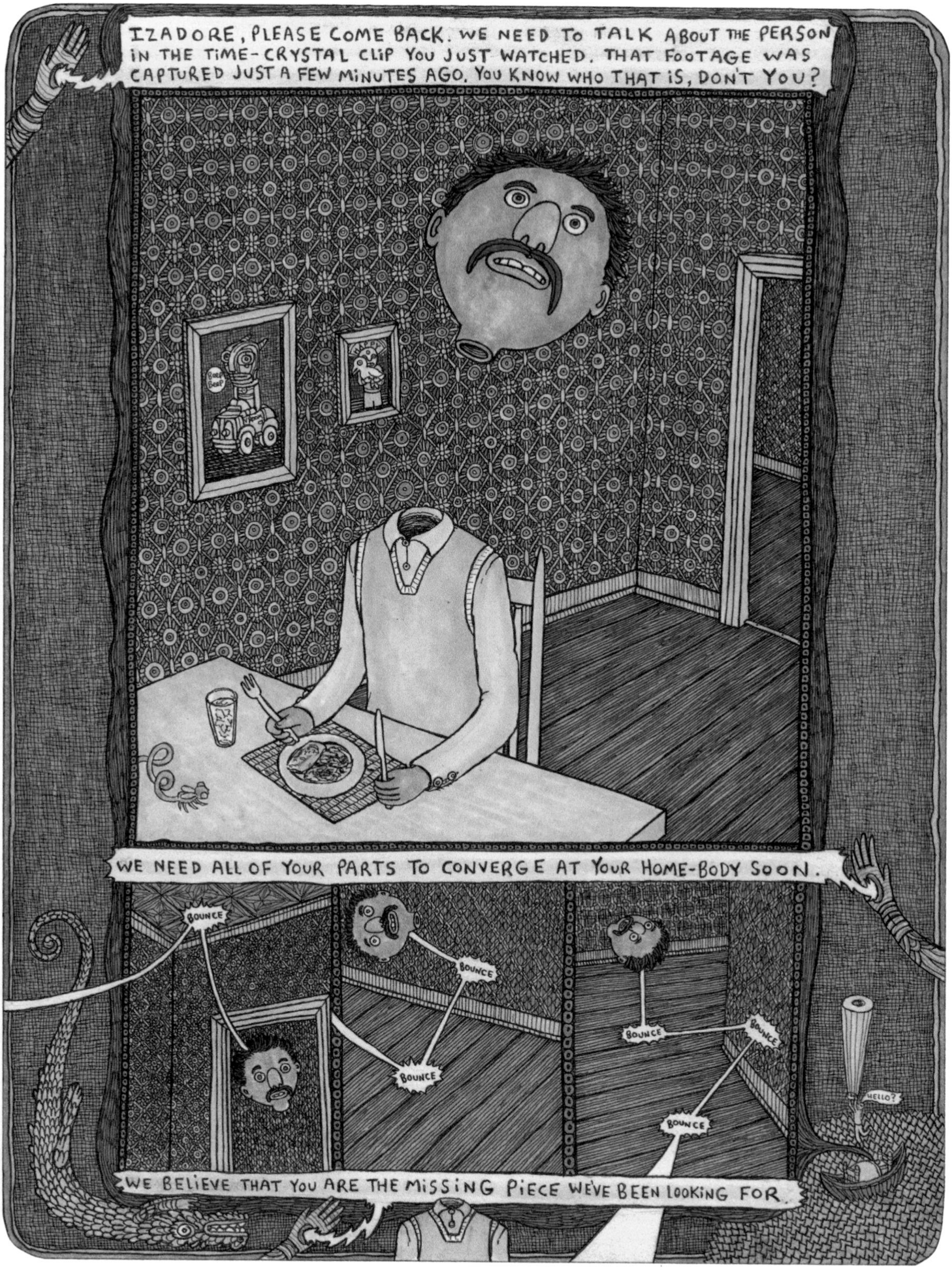
IZADORE, PLEASE COME BACK. WE NEED TO TALK ABOUT THE PERSON IN THE TIME-CRYSTAL CLIP YOU JUST WATCHED. THAT FOOTAGE WAS CAPTURED JUST A FEW MINUTES AGO. YOU KNOW WHO THAT IS, DON'T YOU?
BEEP BEEP
WE NEED ALL OF YOUR PARTS TO CONVERGE AT YOUR HOME-BODY SOON.
BOUNCE
BOUNCE
BOUNCE
BOUNCE
BOUNCE
BOUNCE
HELLO?
WE BELIEVE THAT YOU ARE THE MISSING PIECE WE'VE BEEN LOOKING FOR.

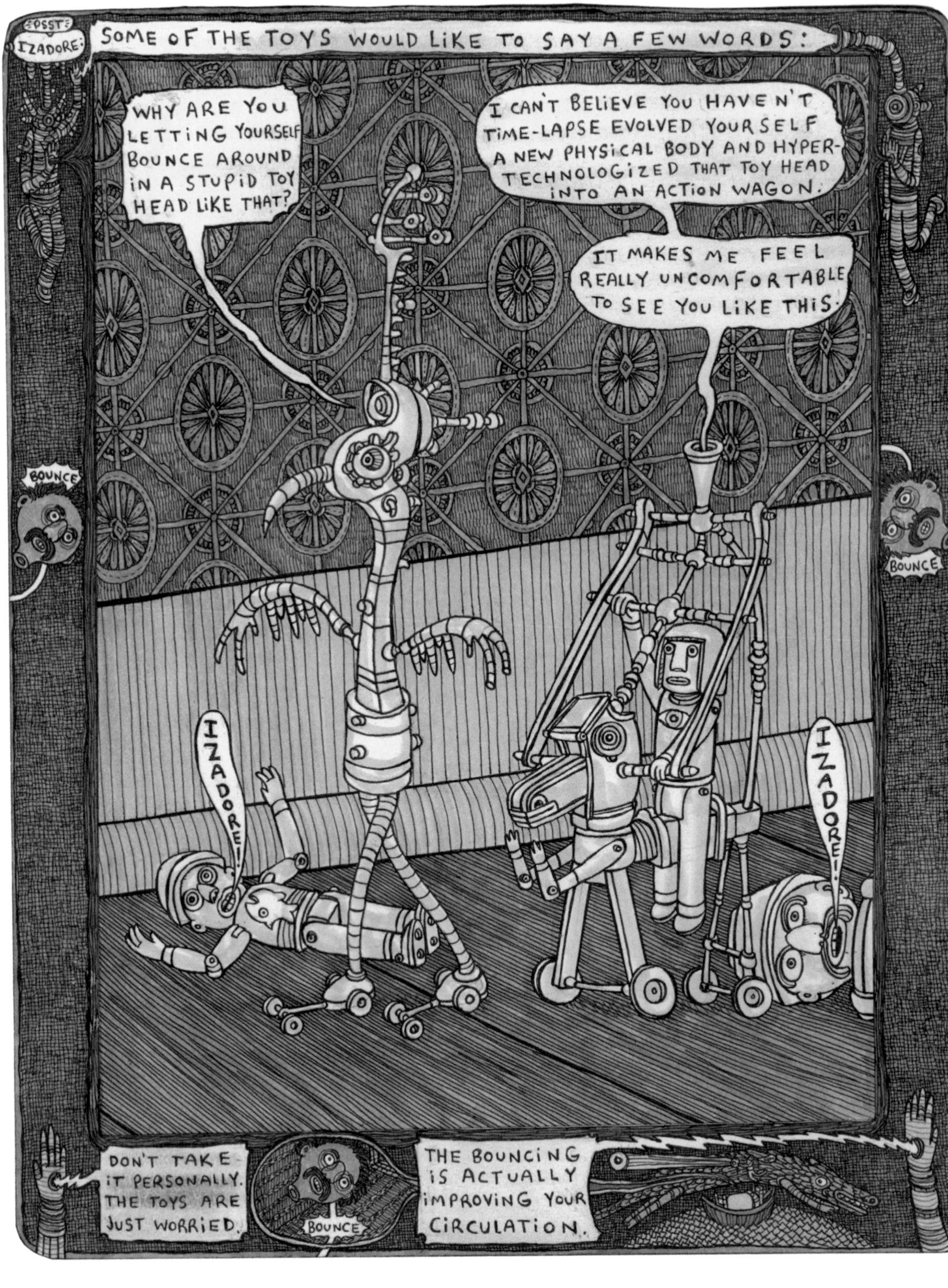
PSSST
IZADORE:
SOME OF THE TOYS WOULD LIKE TO SAY A FEW WORDS:
WHY ARE YOU LETTING YOURSELF BOUNCE AROUND IN A STUPID TOY HEAD LIKE THAT?
I CAN'T BELIEVE YOU HAVEN'T TIME-LAPSE EVOLVED YOURSELF A NEW PHYSICAL BODY AND HYPER-TECHNOLOGIZED THAT TOY HEAD INTO AN ACTION WAGON.
IT MAKES ME FEEL REALLY UNCOMFORTABLE TO SEE YOU LIKE THIS.
BOUNCE
BOUNCE
IZADORE!
IZADORE!
DON'T TAKE IT PERSONALLY. THE TOYS ARE JUST WORRIED.
BOUNCE
THE BOUNCING IS ACTUALLY IMPROVING YOUR CIRCULATION.

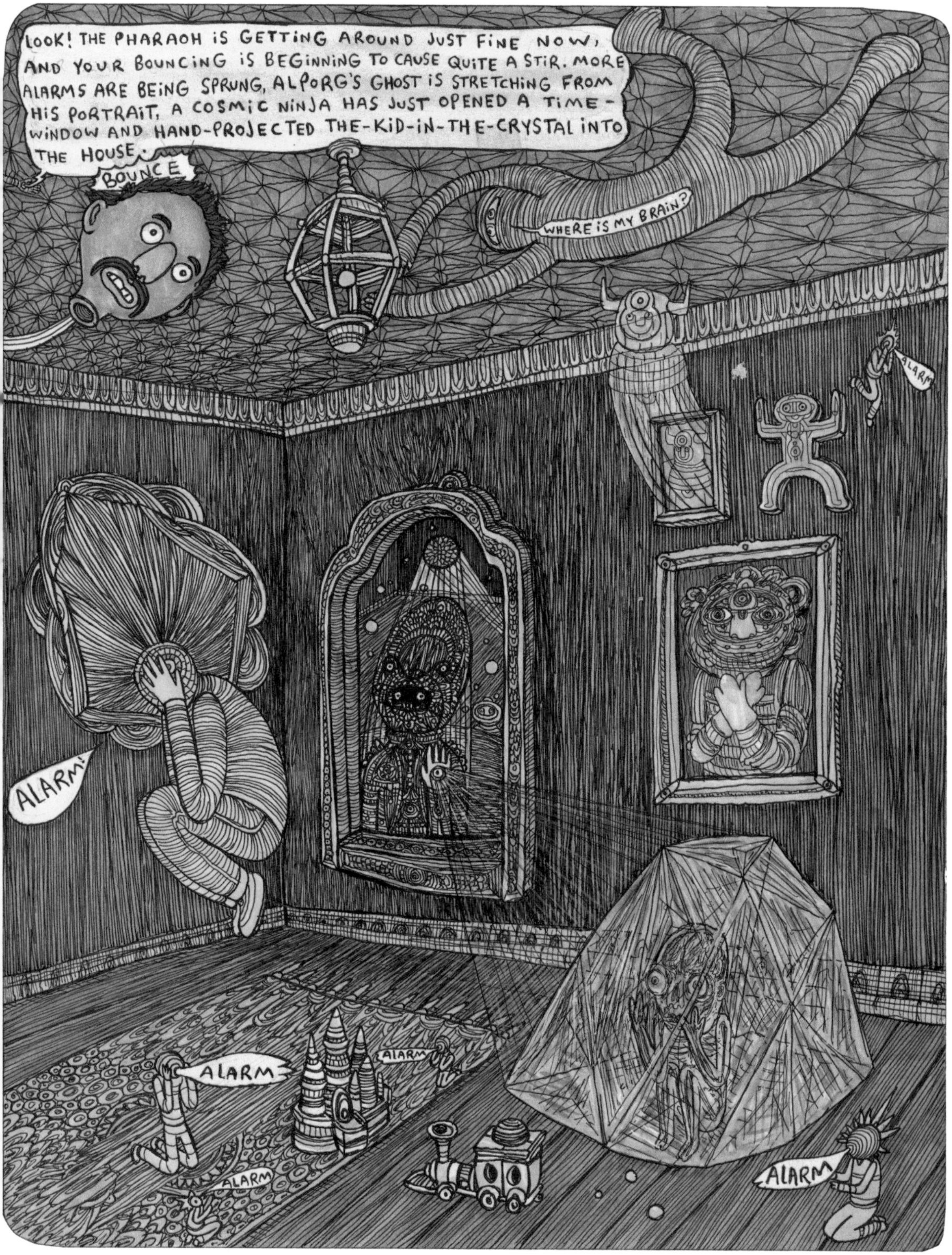
LOOK! THE PHARAOH IS GETTING AROUND JUST FINE NOW, AND YOUR BOUNCING IS BEGINNING TO CAUSE QUITE A STIR. MORE ALARMS ARE BEING SPRUNG, ALPORG'S GHOST IS STRETCHING FROM HIS PORTRAIT, A COSMIC NINJA HAS JUST OPENED A TIME-WINDOW AND HAND-PROJECTED THE-KID-IN-THE-CRYSTAL INTO THE HOUSE.
BOUNCE
WHERE IS MY BRAIN?
ALARM
ALARM!
ALARM
ALARM
ALARM
ALARM

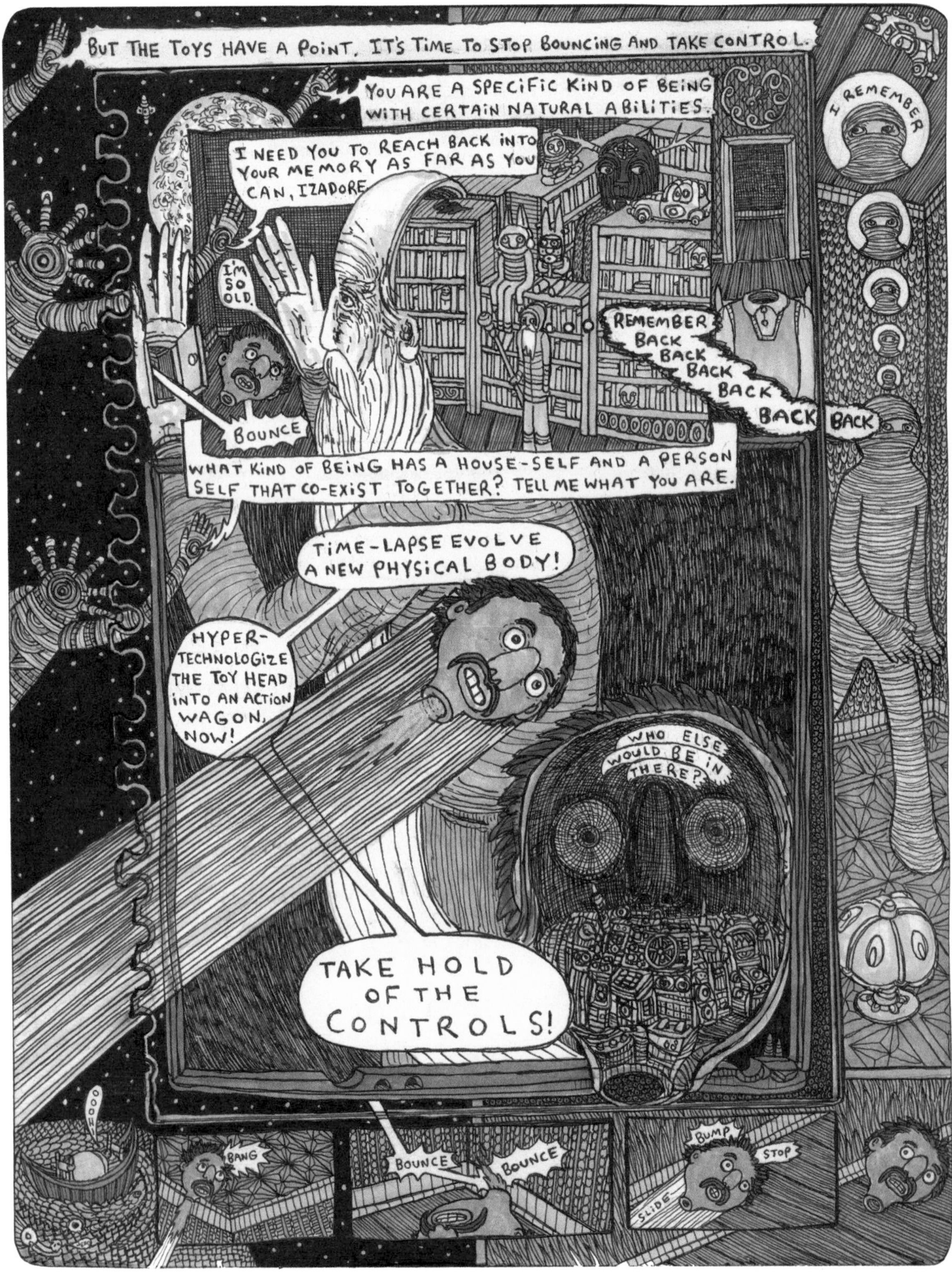

BUT THE TOYS HAVE A POINT. IT'S TIME TO STOP BOUNCING AND TAKE CONTROL.
YOU ARE A SPECIFIC KIND OF BEING WITH CERTAIN NATURAL ABILITIES.
I REMEMBER
I NEED YOU TO REACH BACK INTO YOUR MEMORY AS FAR AS YOU CAN, IZADORE.
I'M SO OLD.
REMEMBER BACK BACK BACK BACK BACK
BACK
BOUNCE
WHAT KIND OF BEING HAS A HOUSE-SELF AND A PERSON SELF THAT CO-EXIST TOGETHER? TELL ME WHAT YOU ARE.
TIME-LAPSE EVOLVE A NEW PHYSICAL BODY!
HYPER-TECHNOLOGIZE THE TOY HEAD INTO AN ACTION WAGON, NOW!
WHO ELSE WOULD BE IN THERE?
TAKE HOLD OF THE CONTROLS!
OOOH!
BANG
BOUNCE
BOUNCE
BUMP
STOP
SLIDE

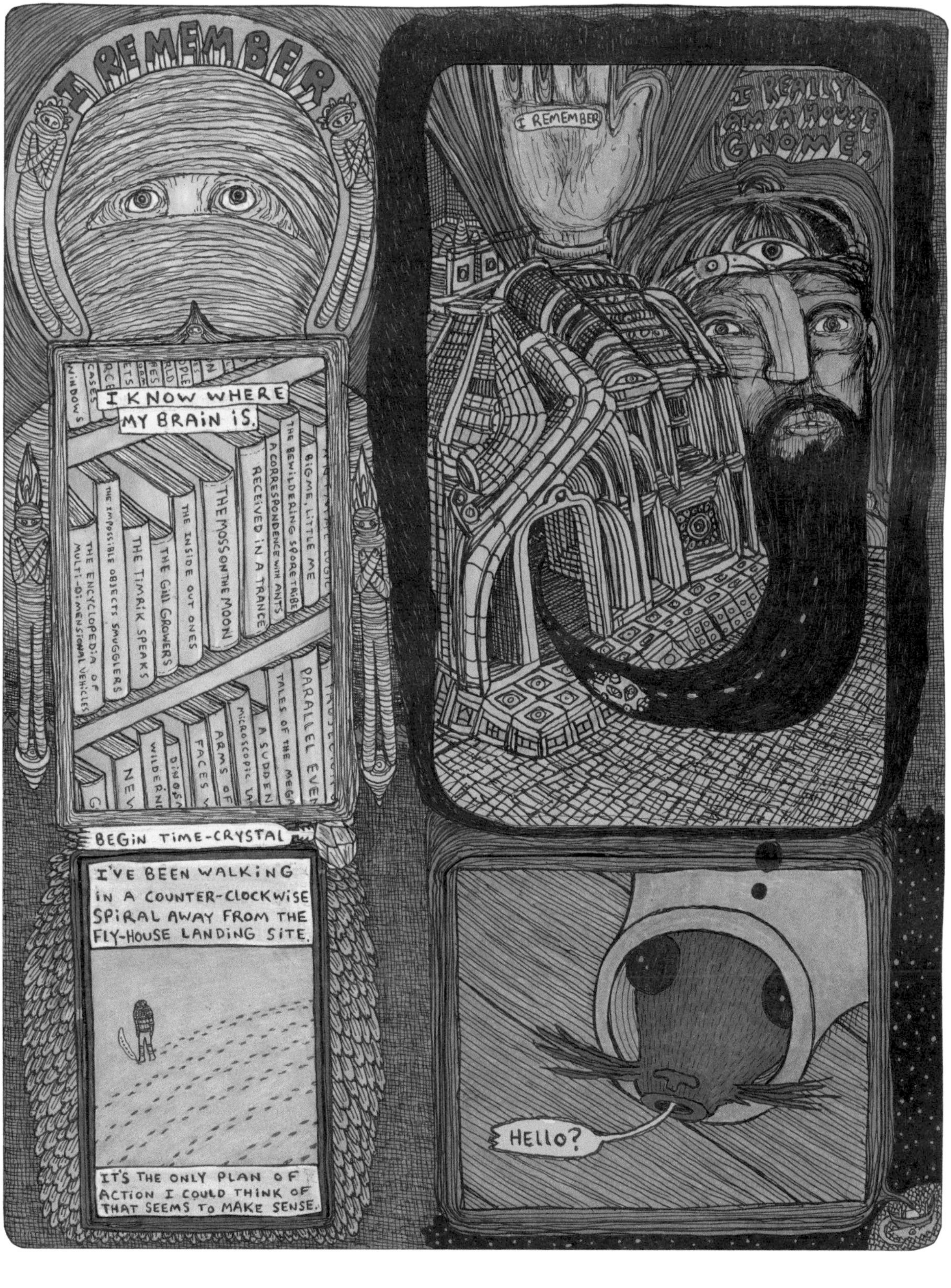
I REMEMBER
I KNOW WHERE MY BRAIN IS.
WINDOWS
CASES
BIGME, LITTLE ME
THE BEWILDERING SPORETRIBE
A CORRESPONDENCE WITH ANTS
RECEIVED IN A TRANCE
THE MOSS ON THE MOON
THE INSIDE OUT ONES
THE GILL GROWERS
THE TIMRIK SPEAKS
THE IMPOSSIBLE OBJECTS SMUGGLERS
THE ENCYCLOPEDIA OF MULTI-DIMENSIONAL VEHICLES
PARALLEL EVEN
TALES OF THE MEGA
A SUDDEN
MICROSCOPIC LA
ARMS OF
FACES
I REMEMBER
I REALLY AM A HOUSE GNOME.
BEGIN TIME-CRYSTAL
I'VE BEEN WALKING IN A COUNTER-CLOCKWISE SPIRAL AWAY FROM THE FLY-HOUSE LANDING SITE.
IT'S THE ONLY PLAN OF ACTION I COULD THINK OF THAT SEEMS TO MAKE SENSE.
HELLO?

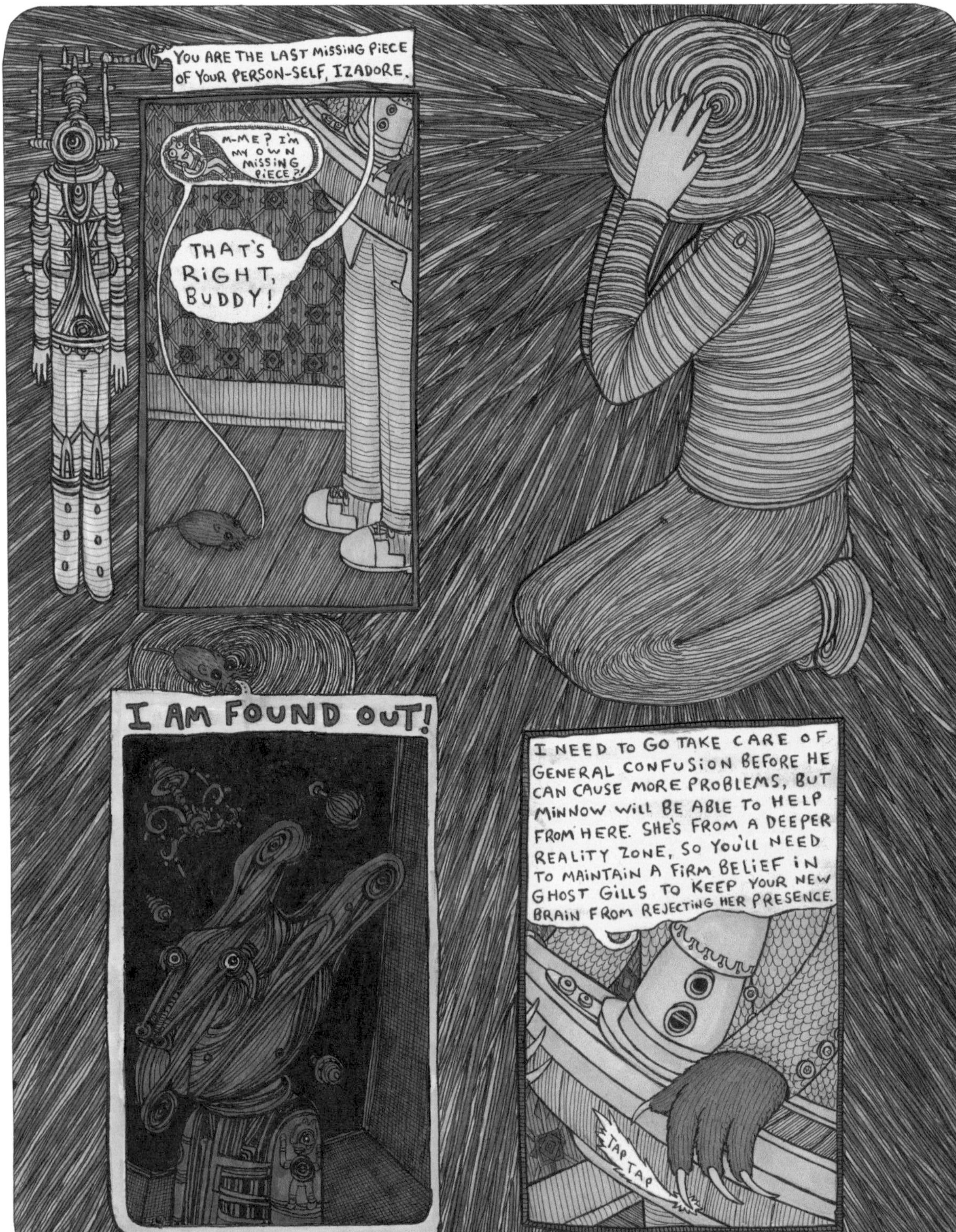
YOU ARE THE LAST MISSING PIECE OF YOUR PERSON-SELF, IZADORE.
M-ME? I'M MY OWN MISSING PIECE?!
THAT'S RIGHT, BUDDY!
I AM FOUND OUT!
I NEED TO GO TAKE CARE OF GENERAL CONFUSION BEFORE HE CAN CAUSE MORE PROBLEMS, BUT MINNOW WILL BE ABLE TO HELP FROM HERE. SHE'S FROM A DEEPER REALITY ZONE, SO YOU'LL NEED TO MAINTAIN A FIRM BELIEF IN GHOST GILLS TO KEEP YOUR NEW BRAIN FROM REJECTING HER PRESENCE.
TAP TAP

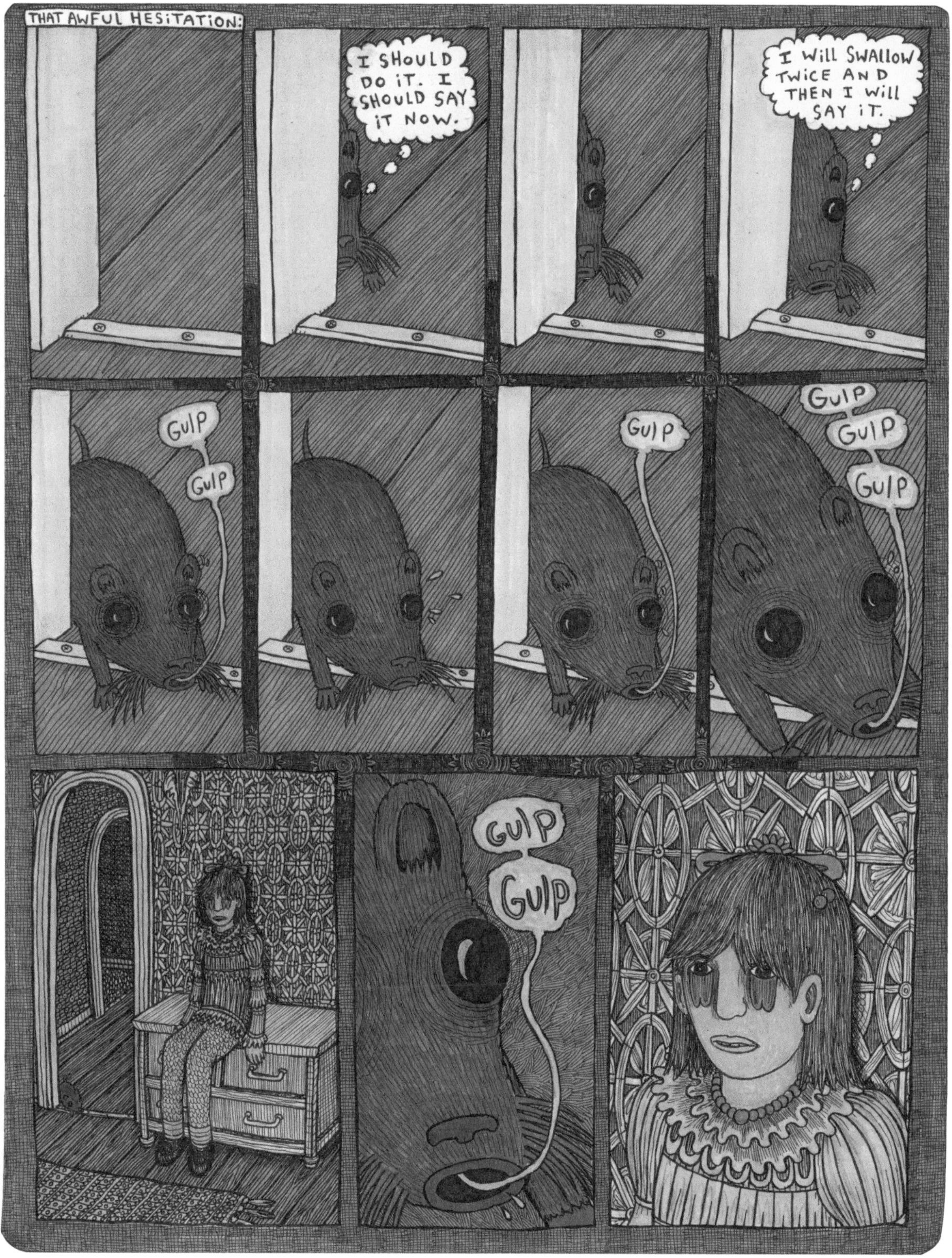
THAT AWFUL HESITATION:
I SHOULD DO IT. I SHOULD SAY IT NOW.
I WILL SWALLOW TWICE AND THEN I WILL SAY IT.
GULP
GULP
GULP
GULP
GULP
GULP
GULP
GULP

The Kuiper Belt

Remember this Internet meme from about ten years back?*

> *Aoccdrnig to rscheearch at an Elingsh uinervtisy, it deosn't mttaer in waht oredr the lt-teers in a wrod are, olny taht the frist and lsat ltteres are at the rghit pcleas. The rset can be a toatl mses and you can sitll raed it wouthit a porbelm. Tihs is bcuseae we do not raed ervey lteter by ilstef, but the wrod as a wlohe.*

Some of the richest art in the last century arose from an understanding that viewers will always try to find form and meaning in whatever they see, no matter how jumbled or incomplete. Art situated on the edge of form and meaning has the potential to pulse with a strange, seductive energy that more literal depictions lack.

Most of the artists in this section play in that far outer perimeter of meaning. Think of it as the North American comics equivalent to our solar system's Kuiper Belt, that huge, distant ring of crazy rocks we used to think comets came from. C.F., Lale Westvind, and Victor Cayro appropriate figures, gestures, and mannerisms from the pulpy action scenes of their youth and reconstitute them as alien, inscrutable, or just really, really loud. Ron Regé, Jr., and Onsmith attack the picture plane with hibachi knives and antipersonnel grenades—a dose of nuclear smelling salts for the eyes. Gerald Jablonski toils away, monklike, obsessively marking every nanometer of his territory. G. W. Duncanson doesn't so much draw as *breed* his fuzzy glyphs and avatars. Aidan Koch rearranges the horizon. Erin Curry rearranges our senses.

A note on the Erin Curry pages that end this section: reprinting those pages with conventional paper and ink doesn't do justice to the original, a series of translucent vellum overlays that are transformed by each page turn. Clearly the choice of materials mattered to Curry. I'm just being selfish here, hijacking it for my own purposes. I liked the way it echoed quietly, like an afterimage of everything that came before it, like the decomposing remnants of the last comic on earth.

Physicality—an awareness of the comic as an object—has been a big deal in the art comics movement for a long time. A lot dates back to Spiegelman and Mouly's *RAW* magazine in the '80s, with its carefully chosen paper stocks, process color tricks, custom tearing, and so on. Equally influential for some artists in the '90s was the collective called Fort

---

* Predictably enough, the phenomenon isn't quite that simple, but Graham Rawlinson—one of the likely originators of the meme—points to this phenomenon as evidence that "we have some powerful parallel processors at work."

Thunder, a bunch of cartoonists/musicians/provocateurs living in a house somewhere in Providence who did a lot of really cool hand-printed short-run comics.

You'll notice these are all short excerpts. Think of it as just a core sample of today's avant-garde comics scene.

If that doesn't screw up the whole outer space metaphor.

IS THERE SILENCE?

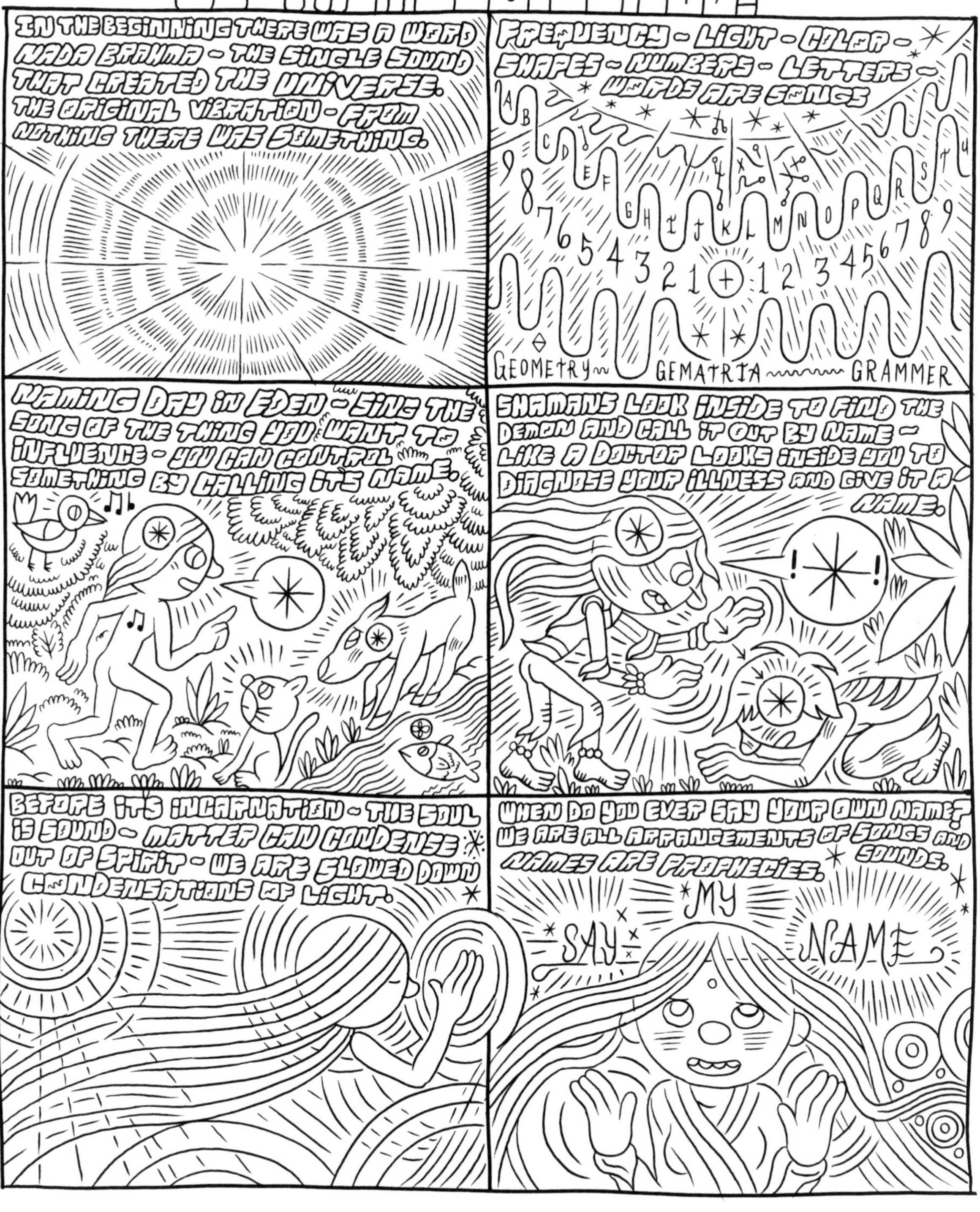
IN THE BEGINNING THERE WAS A WORD NADA BRAHMA ~ THE SINGLE SOUND THAT CREATED THE UNIVERSE. THE ORIGINAL VIBRATION ~ FROM NOTHING THERE WAS SOMETHING.
FREQUENCY ~ LIGHT ~ COLOR ~ SHAPES ~ NUMBERS ~ LETTERS ~ WORDS ARE SONGS
GEOMETRY
GEMATRIA
GRAMMER
NAMING DAY IN EDEN ~ SING THE SONG OF THE THING YOU WANT TO INFLUENCE ~ YOU CAN CONTROL SOMETHING BY CALLING IT'S NAME.
SHAMANS LOOK INSIDE TO FIND THE DEMON AND CALL IT OUT BY NAME ~ LIKE A DOCTOR LOOKS INSIDE YOU TO DIAGNOSE YOUR ILLNESS AND GIVE IT A NAME.
BEFORE ITS INCARNATION ~ THE SOUL IS SOUND ~ MATTER CAN CONDENSE OUT OF SPIRIT ~ WE ARE SLOWED DOWN CONDENSATIONS OF LIGHT.
WHEN DO YOU EVER SAY YOUR OWN NAME? WE ARE ALL ARRANGEMENTS OF SONGS AND SOUNDS. NAMES ARE PROPHECIES.
SAY MY NAME

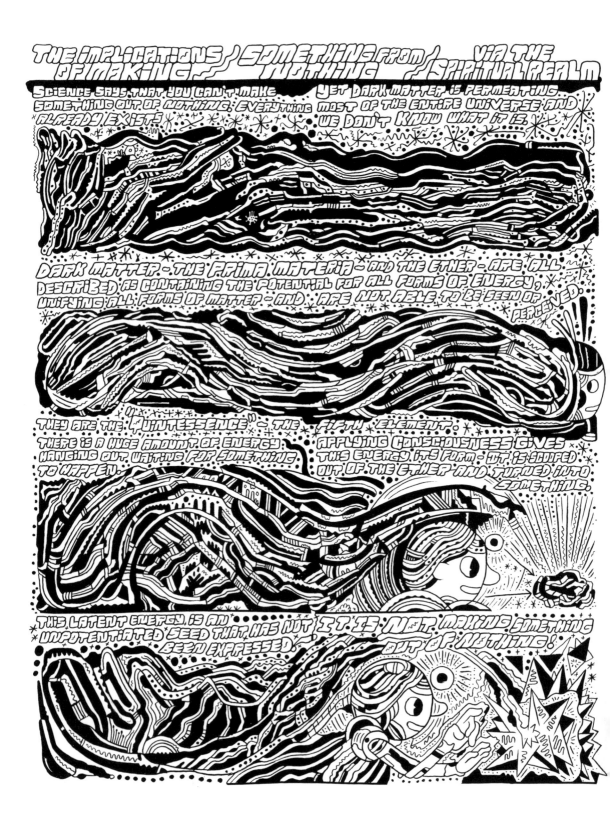

THE IMPLICATIONS OF MAKING / SOMETHING FROM NOTHING / VIA THE SPIRITUAL REALM

Science says that you can't make something out of nothing. Everything already exists?

Yet dark matter is permeating most of the entire universe and we don't know what it is.

Dark matter - the P.Rima materia - and the ether - are all described as containing the potential for all forms of energy, unifying all forms of matter - and are not able to be seen or perceived.

They are the "quintessence" - the fifth element.

There is a huge amount of energy hanging out waiting for something to happen.

Applying consciousness gives this energy its form - it is scooped out of the ether and turned into something.

This latent energy is an unpotentiated seed that has not been expressed

It is not making something out of nothing!

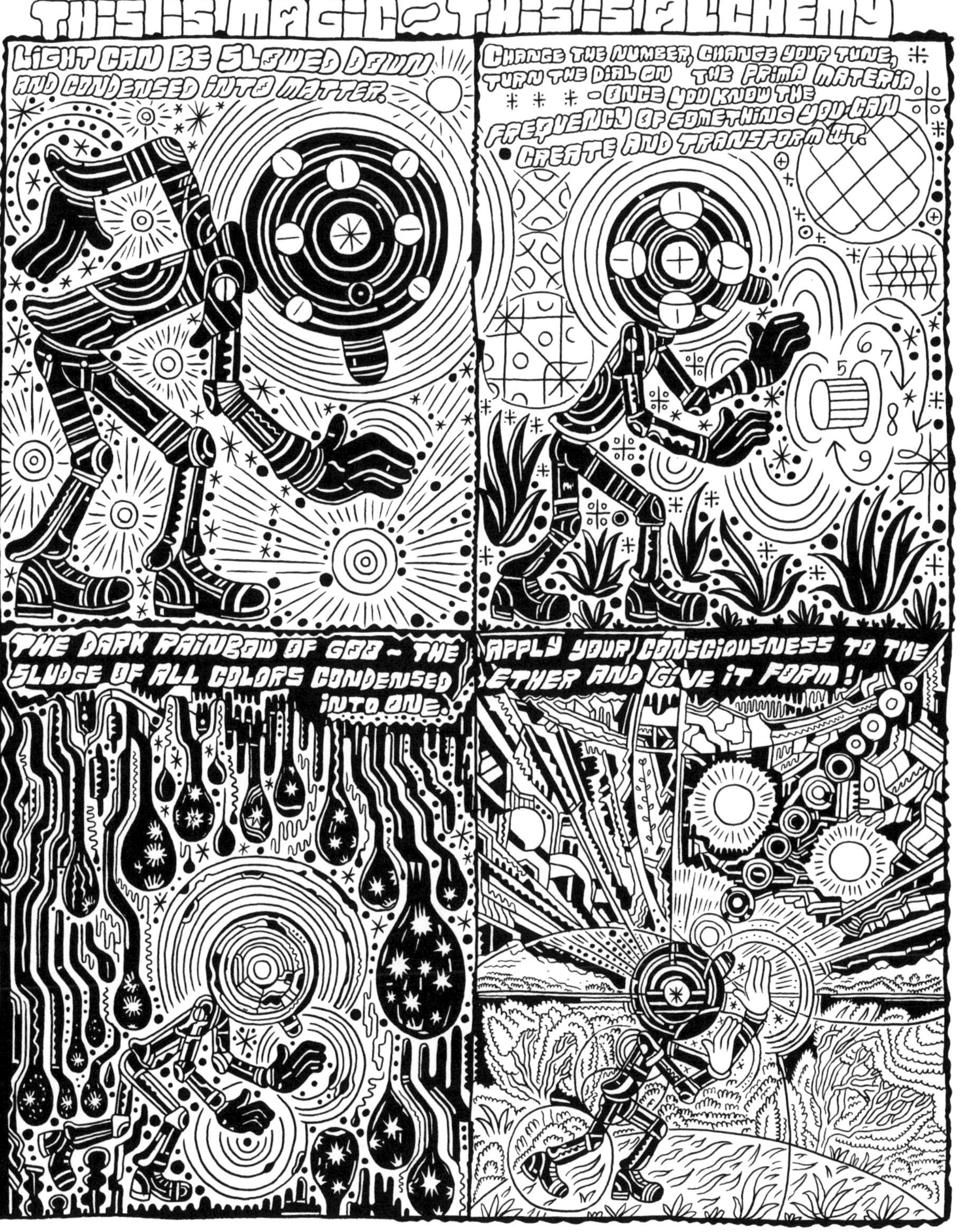
THIS IS MAGIC ~ THIS IS ALCHEMY
LIGHT CAN BE SLOWED DOWN AND CONDENSED INTO MATTER.
CHANGE THE NUMBER, CHANGE YOUR TUNE, TURN THE DIAL ON THE PRIMA MATERIA - ONCE YOU KNOW THE FREQUENCY OF SOMETHING YOU CAN CREATE AND TRANSFORM IT.
5
6
7
8
9
THE DARK RAINBOW OF GOD ~ THE SLUDGE OF ALL COLORS CONDENSED INTO ONE.
APPLY YOUR CONSCIOUSNESS TO THE ETHER AND GIVE IT FORM!

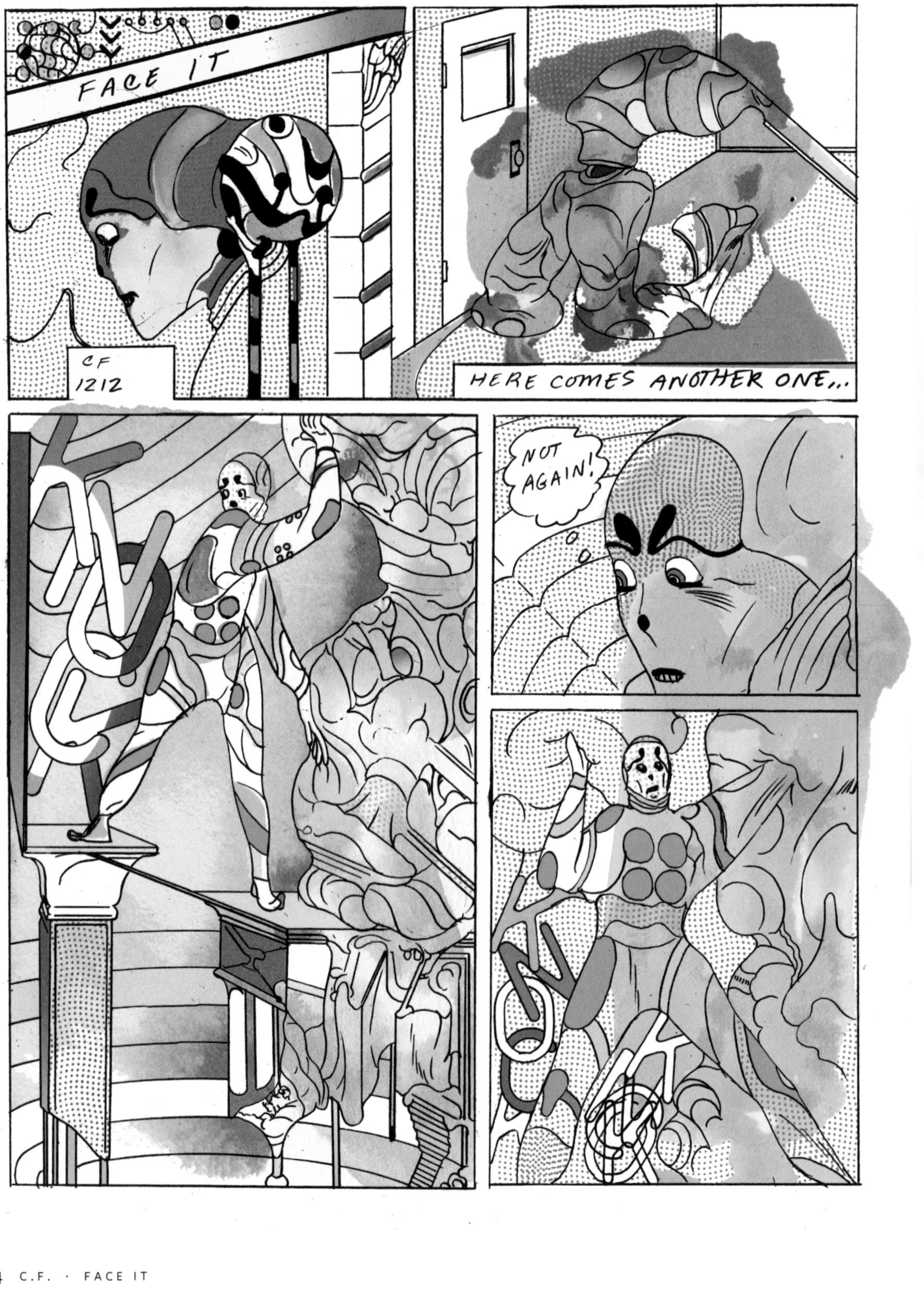

FACE IT
CF 1212
HERE COMES ANOTHER ONE...
NOT AGAIN!

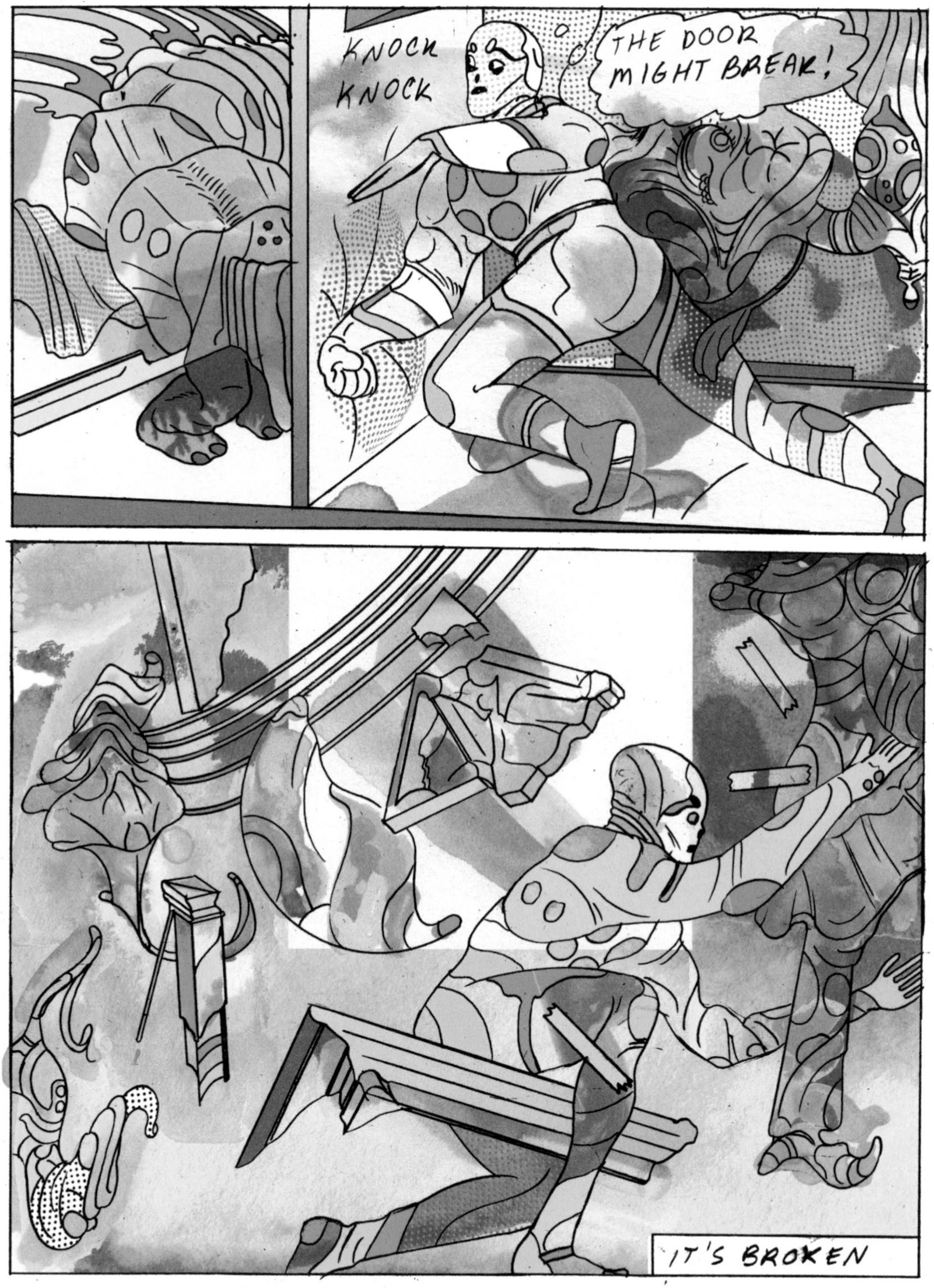
KNOCK KNOCK
THE DOOR MIGHT BREAK!
IT'S BROKEN

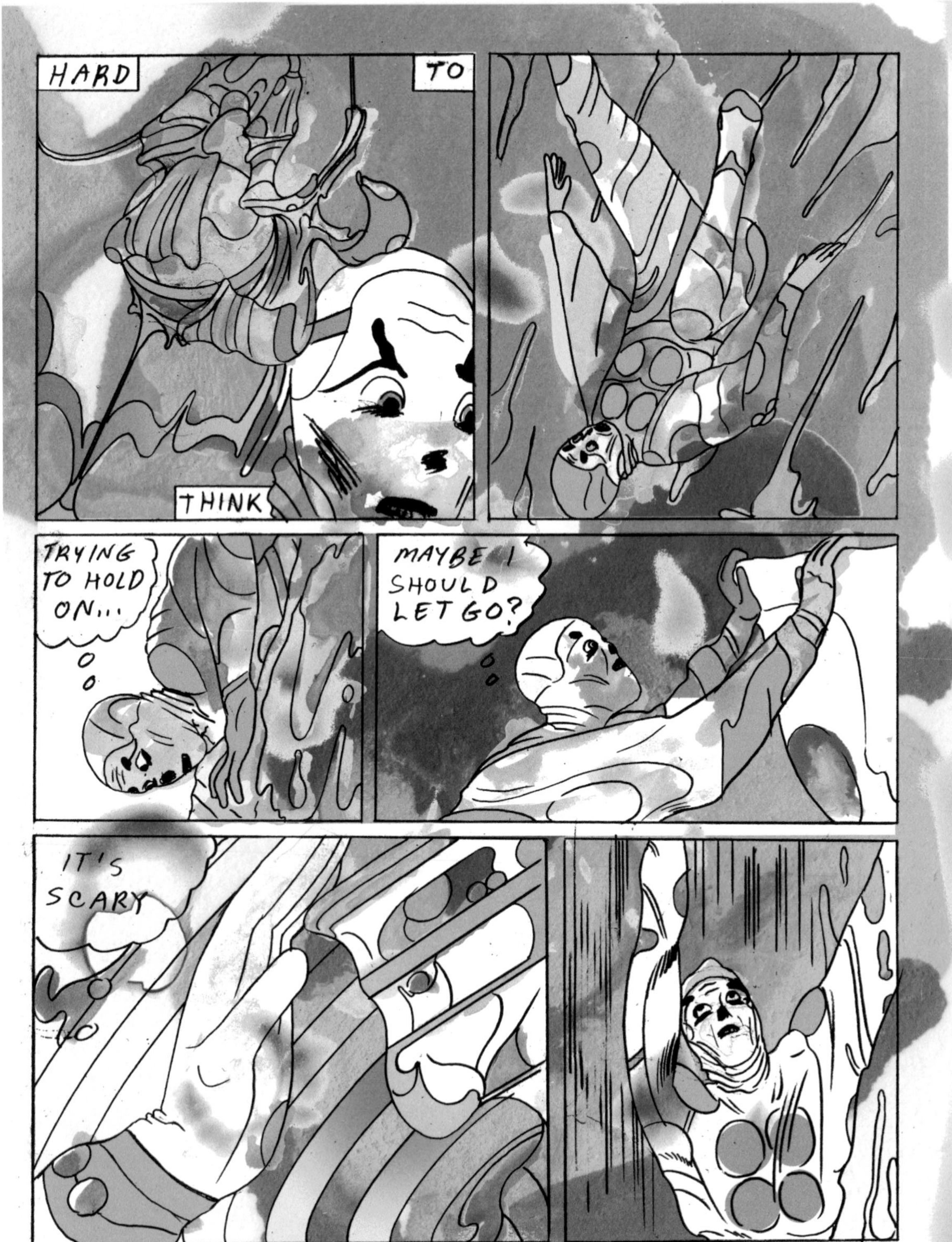
HARD
TO
THINK
TRYING TO HOLD ON...
MAYBE I SHOULD LET GO?
IT'S SCARY

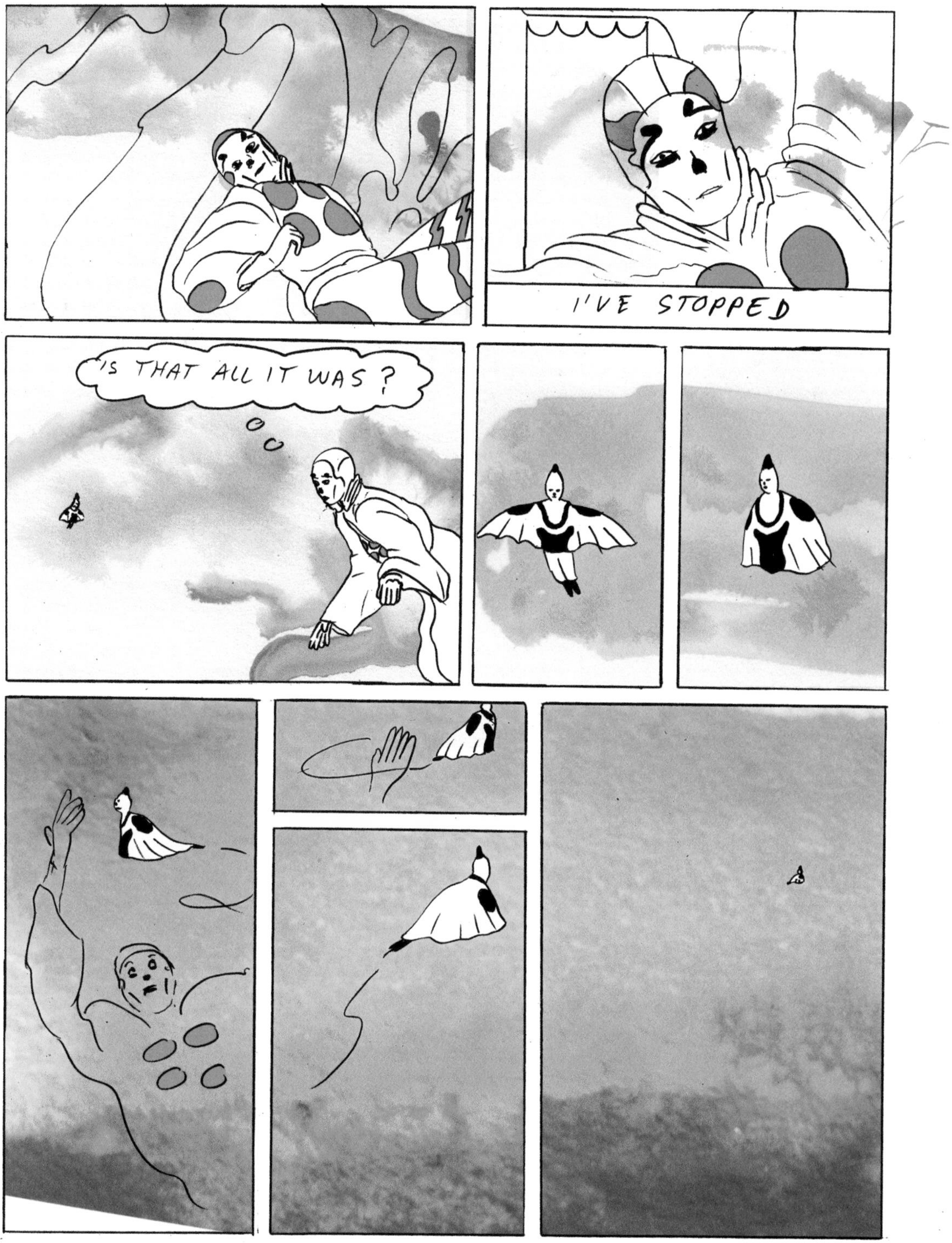
I'VE STOPPED
IS THAT ALL IT WAS?

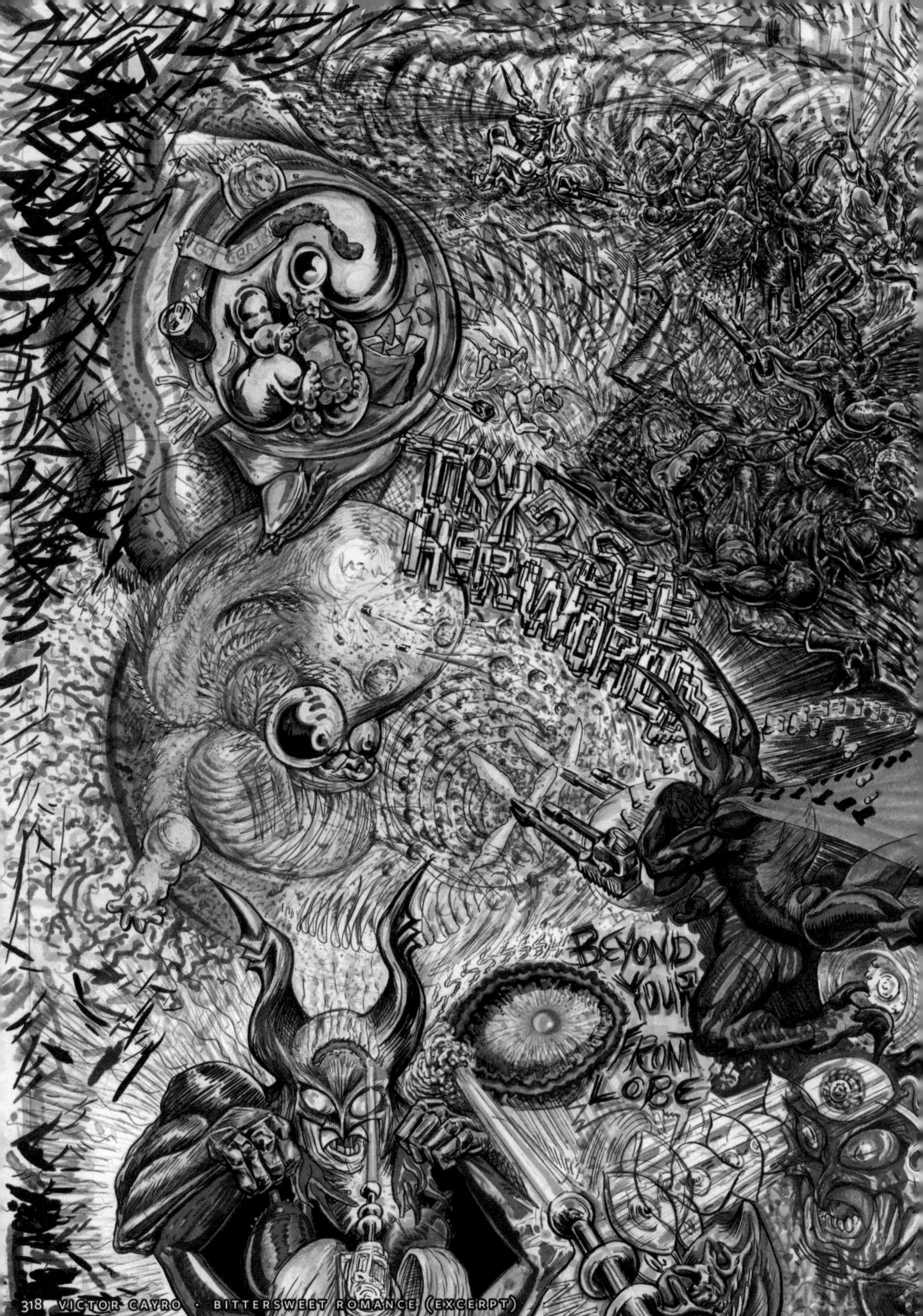
TRY 2 SEE
HER WORLD
BEYOND YOUR FRONT LOBE

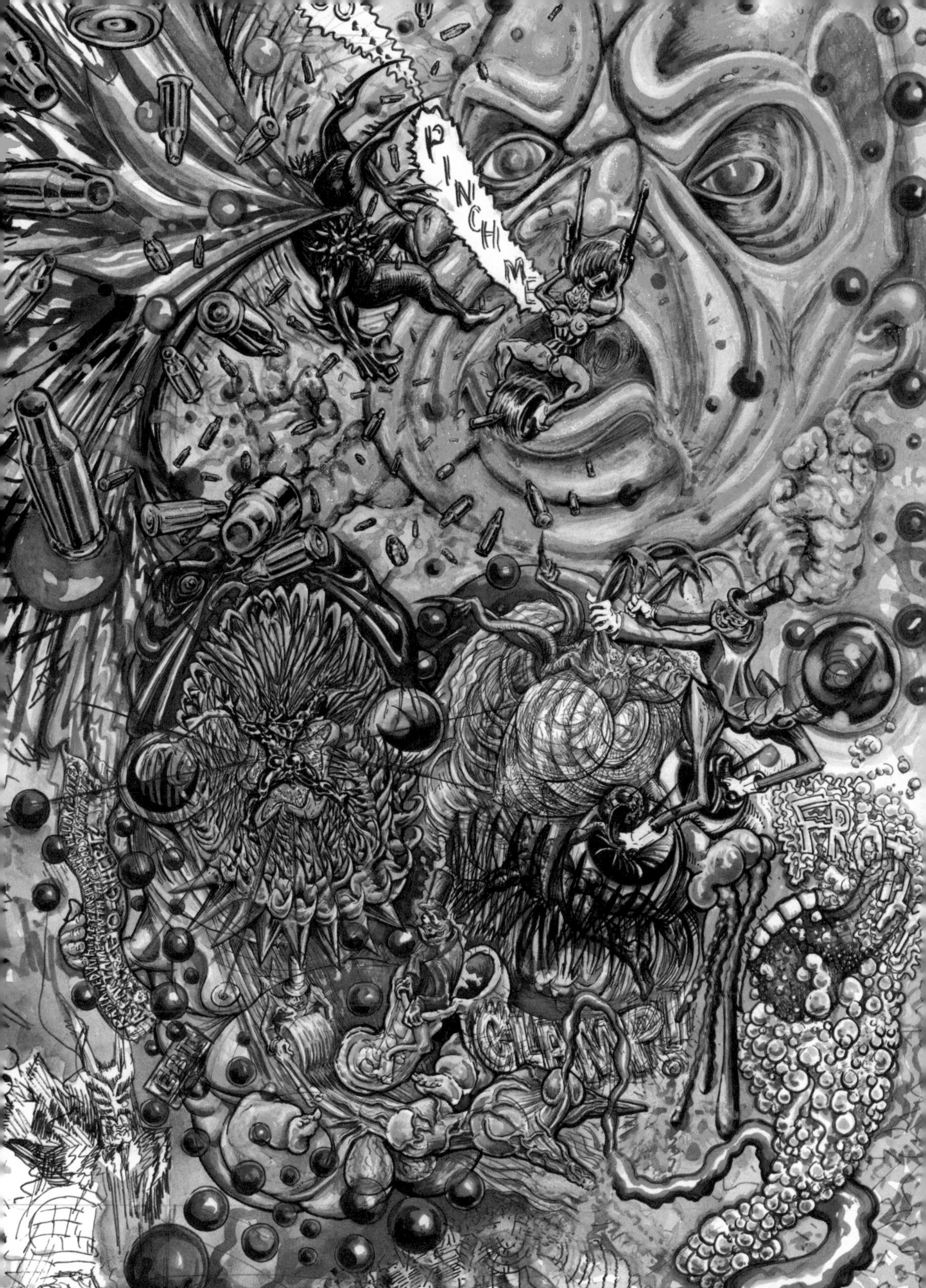
PIN'CHI ME
FROT
GLAMP!

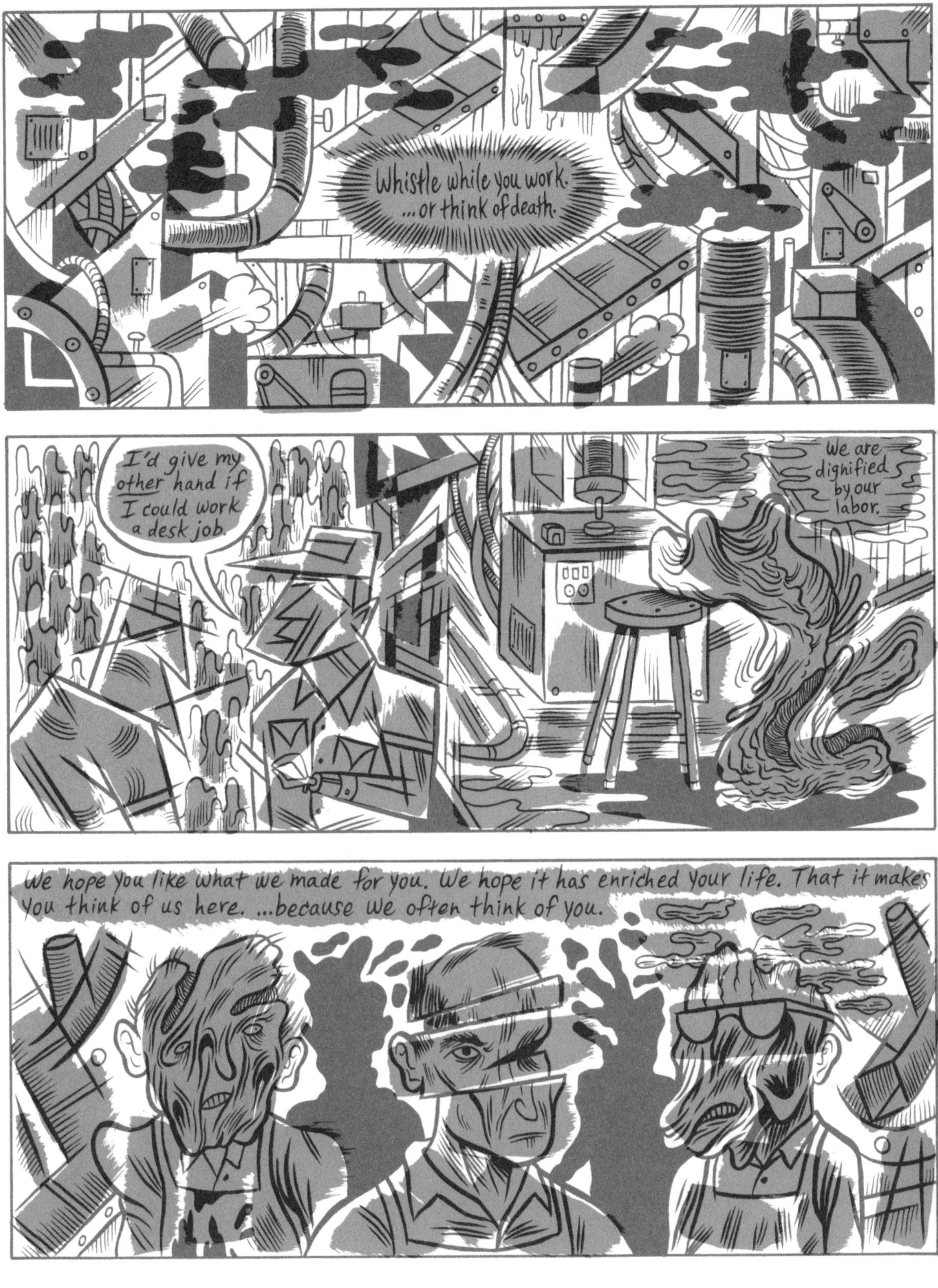
Whistle while you work. ...or think of death.
I'd give my other hand if I could work a desk job.
We are dignified by our labor.
We hope you like what we made for you. We hope it has enriched your life. That it makes you think of us here. ...because we often think of you.

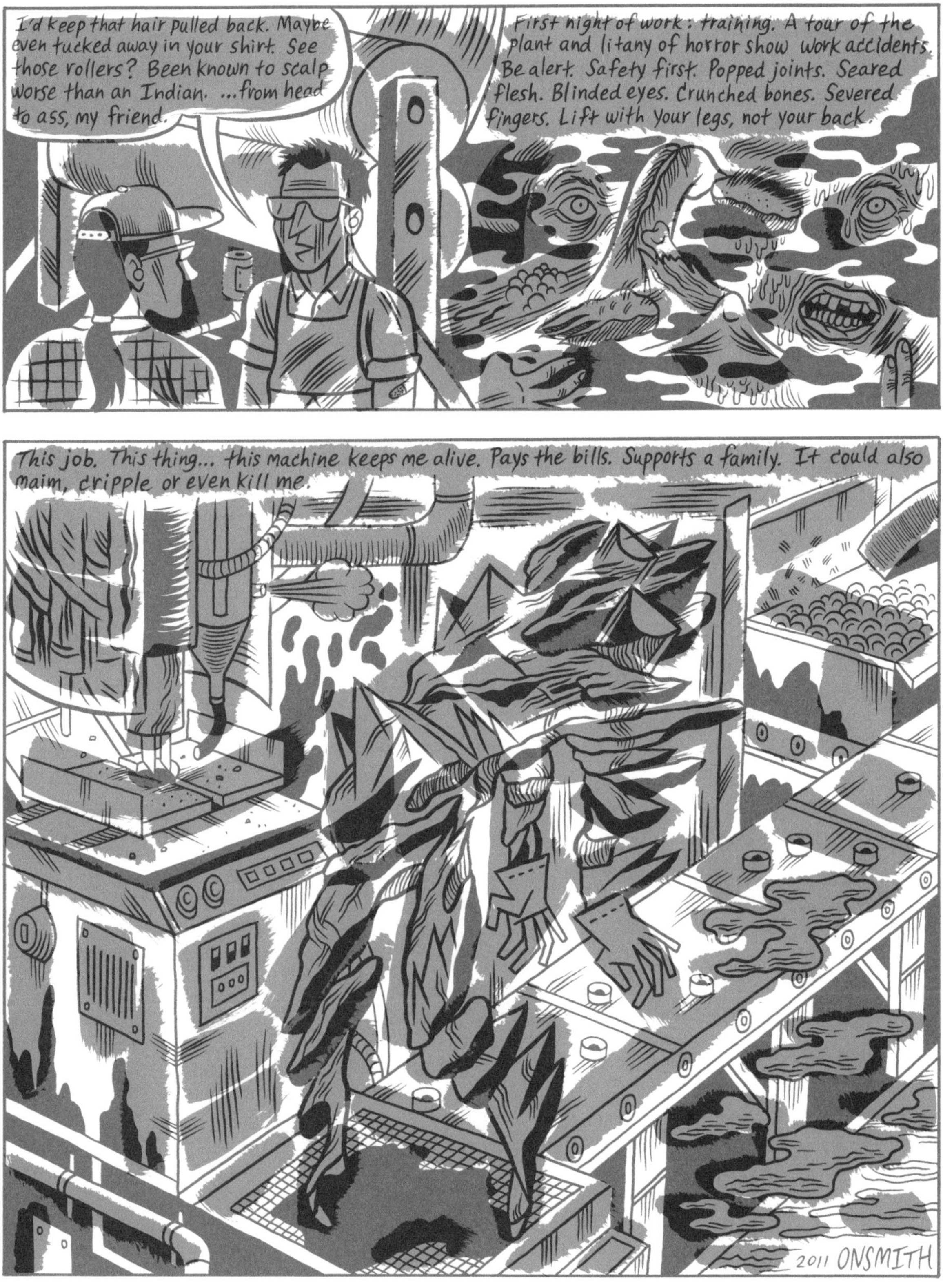
I'd keep that hair pulled back. Maybe even tucked away in your shirt. See those rollers? Been known to scalp worse than an Indian. ...from head to ass, my friend.
First night of work: training. A tour of the plant and litany of horror show work accidents. Be alert. Safety first. Popped joints. Seared flesh. Blinded eyes. Crunched bones. Severed fingers. Lift with your legs, not your back.
This job. This thing... this machine keeps me alive. Pays the bills. Supports a family. It could also maim, cripple or even kill me.
2011 ONSMITH

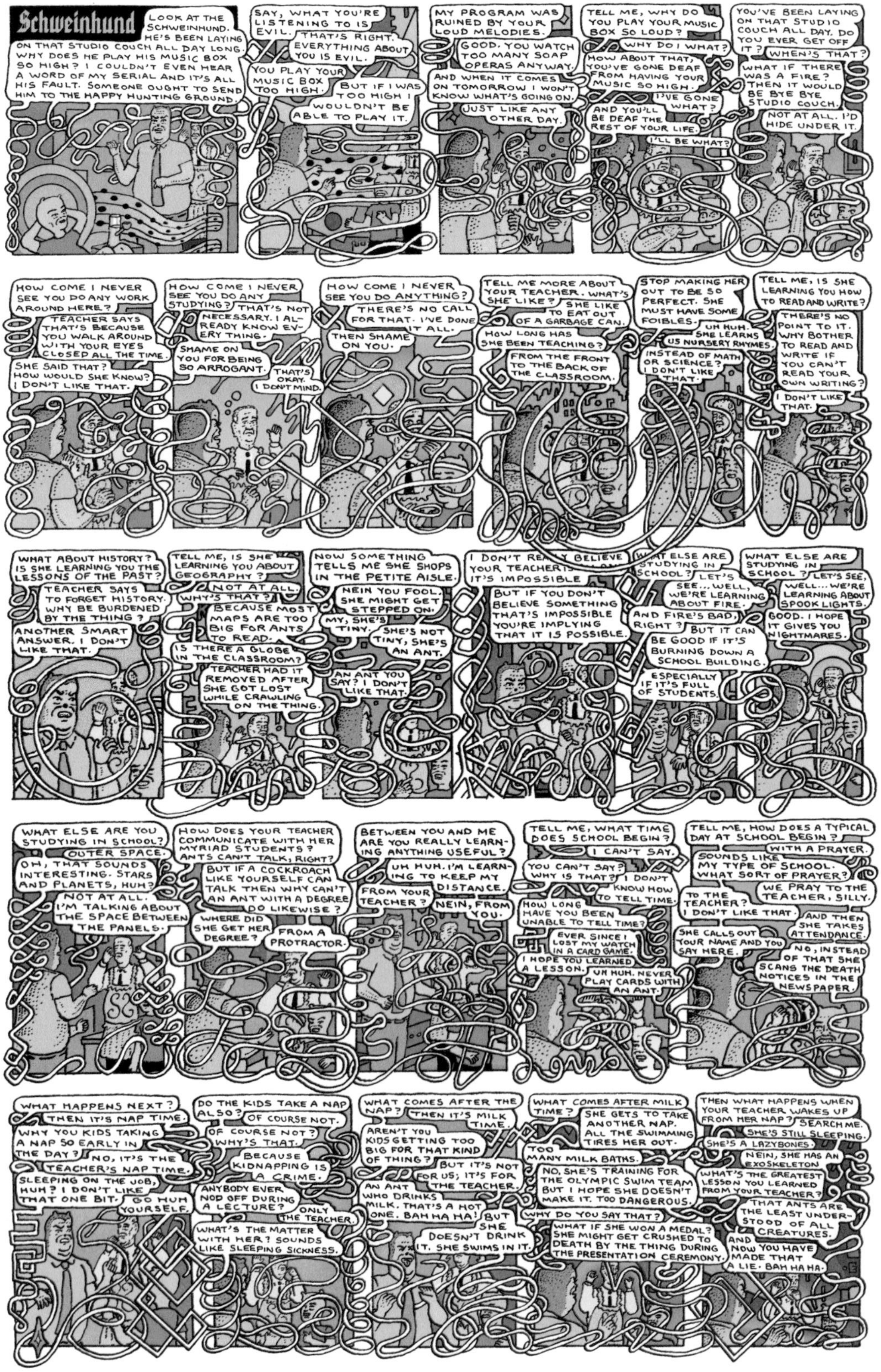
Schweinhund
LOOK AT THE SCHWEINHUND. HE'S BEEN LAYING ON THAT STUDIO COUCH ALL DAY LONG. WHY DOES HE PLAY HIS MUSIC BOX SO HIGH? I COULDN'T EVEN HEAR A WORD OF MY SERIAL AND IT'S ALL HIS FAULT. SOMEONE OUGHT TO SEND HIM TO THE HAPPY HUNTING GROUND.
SAY, WHAT YOU'RE LISTENING TO IS EVIL.
THAT'S RIGHT. EVERYTHING ABOUT YOU IS EVIL.
YOU PLAY YOUR MUSIC BOX TOO HIGH.
BUT IF I WAS TOO HIGH I WOULDN'T BE ABLE TO PLAY IT.
MY PROGRAM WAS RUINED BY YOUR LOUD MELODIES.
GOOD. YOU WATCH TOO MANY SOAP OPERAS ANYWAY.
AND WHEN IT COMES ON TOMORROW I WON'T KNOW WHAT'S GOING ON.
JUST LIKE ANY OTHER DAY.
TELL ME, WHY DO YOU PLAY YOUR MUSIC BOX SO LOUD?
WHY DO I WHAT?
HOW ABOUT THAT, YOU'VE GONE DEAF FROM HAVING YOUR MUSIC SO HIGH.
I'VE GONE WHAT?
AND YOU'LL BE DEAF THE REST OF YOUR LIFE.
I'LL BE WHAT?
YOU'VE BEEN LAYING ON THAT STUDIO COUCH ALL DAY. DO YOU EVER GET OFF IT?
WHEN'S THAT?
WHAT IF THERE WAS A FIRE? THEN IT WOULD BE BYE BYE STUDIO COUCH.
NOT AT ALL. I'D HIDE UNDER IT.
HOW COME I NEVER SEE YOU DO ANY WORK AROUND HERE?
TEACHER SAYS THAT'S BECAUSE YOU WALK AROUND WITH YOUR EYES CLOSED ALL THE TIME.
SHE SAID THAT? HOW WOULD SHE KNOW? I DON'T LIKE THAT.
HOW COME I NEVER SEE YOU DO ANY STUDYING?
THAT'S NOT NECESSARY. I ALREADY KNOW EVERY THING.
SHAME ON YOU FOR BEING SO ARROGANT.
THAT'S OKAY. I DON'T MIND.
HOW COME I NEVER SEE YOU DO ANYTHING?
THERE'S NO CALL FOR THAT. I'VE DONE IT ALL.
THEN SHAME ON YOU.
TELL ME MORE ABOUT YOUR TEACHER. WHAT'S SHE LIKE?
SHE LIKE TO EAT OUT OF A GARBAGE CAN.
HOW LONG HAS SHE BEEN TEACHING?
FROM THE FRONT TO THE BACK OF THE CLASSROOM.
STOP MAKING HER OUT TO BE SO PERFECT. SHE MUST HAVE SOME FOIBLES.
UH HUH. SHE LEARNS US NURSERY RHYMES.
INSTEAD OF MATH OR SCIENCE? I DON'T LIKE THAT.
TELL ME, IS SHE LEARNING YOU HOW TO READ AND WRITE?
THERE'S NO POINT TO IT. WHY BOTHER TO READ AND WRITE IF YOU CAN'T READ YOUR OWN WRITING?
I DON'T LIKE THAT.
WHAT ABOUT HISTORY? IS SHE LEARNING YOU THE LESSONS OF THE PAST?
TEACHER SAYS TO FORGET HISTORY. WHY BE BURDENED BY THE THING?
ANOTHER SMART ANSWER. I DON'T LIKE THAT.
TELL ME, IS SHE LEARNING YOU ABOUT GEOGRAPHY?
NOT AT ALL.
WHY'S THAT?
BECAUSE MOST MAPS ARE TOO BIG FOR ANTS TO READ.
IS THERE A GLOBE IN THE CLASSROOM?
TEACHER HAD IT REMOVED AFTER SHE GOT LOST WHILE CRAWLING ON THE THING.
NOW SOMETHING TELLS ME SHE SHOPS IN THE PETITE AISLE.
NEIN YOU FOOL. SHE MIGHT GET STEPPED ON.
MY, SHE'S TINY.
SHE'S NOT TINY, SHE'S AN ANT.
AN ANT YOU SAY? I DON'T LIKE THAT.
I DON'T REA Y BELIEVE YOUR TEACHER IS IT'S IMPOSSIBLE
BUT IF YOU DON'T BELIEVE SOMETHING THAT'S IMPOSSIBLE YOU'RE IMPLYING THAT IT IS POSSIBLE.
WHAT ELSE ARE STUDYING IN SCHOOL?
LET'S SEE... WELL, WE'RE LEARNING ABOUT FIRE.
AND FIRE'S BAD, RIGHT?
BUT IT CAN BE GOOD IF IT'S BURNING DOWN A SCHOOL BUILDING.
ESPECIALLY IF IT'S FULL OF STUDENTS.
WHAT ELSE ARE STUDYING IN SCHOOL?
LET'S SEE, WELL... WE'RE LEARNING ABOUT SPOOK LIGHTS.
GOOD. I HOPE IT GIVES YOU NIGHTMARES.
WHAT ELSE ARE YOU STUDYING IN SCHOOL?
OUTER SPACE.
OH, THAT SOUNDS INTERESTING. STARS AND PLANETS, HUH?
NOT AT ALL. I'M TALKING ABOUT THE SPACE BETWEEN THE PANELS.
HOW DOES YOUR TEACHER COMMUNICATE WITH HER MYRIAD STUDENTS? ANTS CAN'T TALK, RIGHT?
BUT IF A COCKROACH LIKE YOURSELF CAN TALK THEN WHY CAN'T AN ANT WITH A DEGREE DO LIKEWISE?
WHERE DID SHE GET HER DEGREE?
FROM A PROTRACTOR.
BETWEEN YOU AND ME ARE YOU REALLY LEARNING ANYTHING USEFUL?
UH HUH. I'M LEARNING TO KEEP MY DISTANCE.
FROM YOUR TEACHER?
NEIN, FROM YOU.
TELL ME, WHAT TIME DOES SCHOOL BEGIN?
I CAN'T SAY.
YOU CAN'T SAY? WHY IS THAT?
I DON'T KNOW HOW TO TELL TIME.
HOW LONG HAVE YOU BEEN UNABLE TO TELL TIME?
EVER SINCE I LOST MY WATCH IN A CARD GAME.
I HOPE YOU LEARNED A LESSON.
UH HUH. NEVER PLAY CARDS WITH AN ANT.
TELL ME, HOW DOES A TYPICAL DAY AT SCHOOL BEGIN?
WITH A PRAYER.
SOUNDS LIKE MY TYPE OF SCHOOL. WHAT SORT OF PRAYER?
WE PRAY TO THE TEACHER, SILLY.
TO THE TEACHER? I DON'T LIKE THAT.
AND THEN SHE TAKES ATTENDANCE.
SHE CALLS OUT YOUR NAME AND YOU SAY HERE.
NO, INSTEAD OF THAT SHE SCANS THE DEATH NOTICES IN THE NEWSPAPER.
WHAT HAPPENS NEXT?
THEN IT'S NAP TIME.
WHY YOU KIDS TAKING A NAP SO EARLY IN THE DAY?
NO, IT'S THE TEACHER'S NAP TIME.
SLEEPING ON THE JOB, HUH? I DON'T LIKE THAT ONE BIT.
GO HUM YOURSELF.
DO THE KIDS TAKE A NAP ALSO?
OF COURSE NOT.
OF COURSE NOT? WHY'S THAT.
BECAUSE KIDNAPPING IS A CRIME.
ANYBODY EVER NOD OFF DURING A LECTURE?
ONLY THE TEACHER.
WHAT'S THE MATTER WITH HER? SOUNDS LIKE SLEEPING SICKNESS.
WHAT COMES AFTER THE NAP?
THEN IT'S MILK TIME.
AREN'T YOU KIDS GETTING TOO BIG FOR THAT KIND OF THING?
BUT IT'S NOT FOR US; IT'S FOR THE TEACHER.
AN ANT WHO DRINKS MILK. THAT'S A HOT ONE. BAH HA HA!
BUT SHE DOESN'T DRINK IT. SHE SWIMS IN IT.
WHAT COMES AFTER MILK TIME?
SHE GETS TO TAKE ANOTHER NAP. ALL THE SWIMMING TIRES HER OUT.
TOO MANY MILK BATHS.
NO, SHE'S TRAINING FOR THE OLYMPIC SWIM TEAM BUT I HOPE SHE DOESN'T MAKE IT. TOO DANGEROUS.
WHY DO YOU SAY THAT?
WHAT IF SHE WON A MEDAL? SHE MIGHT GET CRUSHED TO DEATH BY THE THING DURING THE PRESENTATION CEREMONY.
THEN WHAT HAPPENS WHEN YOUR TEACHER WAKES UP FROM HER NAP?
SEARCH ME. SHE'S STILL SLEEPING.
SHE'S A LAZYBONES.
NEIN, SHE HAS AN EXOSKELETON.
WHAT'S THE GREATEST LESSON YOU LEARNED FROM YOUR TEACHER?
THAT ANTS ARE THE LEAST UNDERSTOOD OF ALL CREATURES.
AND NOW YOU HAVE MADE THAT A LIE. BAH HA HA.

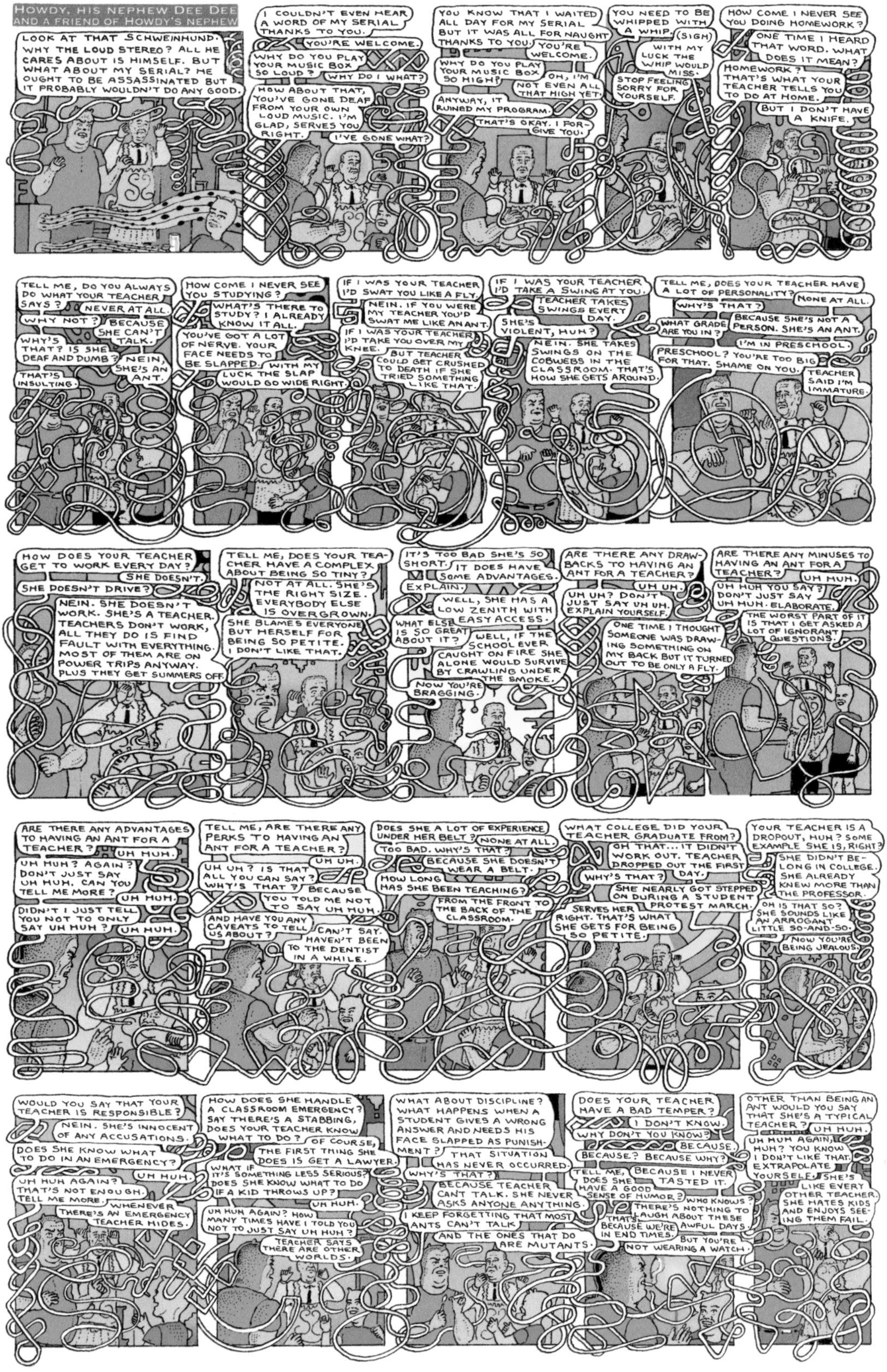
HOWDY, HIS NEPHEW DEE DEE AND A FRIEND OF HOWDY'S NEPHEW
LOOK AT THAT SCHWEINHUND. WHY THE LOUD STEREO? ALL HE CARES ABOUT IS HIMSELF. BUT WHAT ABOUT MY SERIAL? HE OUGHT TO BE ASSASSINATED BUT IT PROBABLY WOULDN'T DO ANY GOOD.
I COULDN'T EVEN HEAR A WORD OF MY SERIAL THANKS TO YOU.
YOU'RE WELCOME.
WHY DO YOU PLAY YOUR MUSIC BOX SO LOUD?
WHY DO I WHAT?
HOW ABOUT THAT, YOU'VE GONE DEAF FROM YOUR OWN LOUD MUSIC. I'M GLAD, SERVES YOU RIGHT.
I'VE GONE WHAT?
YOU KNOW THAT I WAITED ALL DAY FOR MY SERIAL BUT IT WAS ALL FOR NAUGHT THANKS TO YOU.
YOU'RE WELCOME.
WHY DO YOU PLAY YOUR MUSIC BOX SO HIGH?
OH, I'M NOT EVEN ALL THAT HIGH YET.
ANYWAY, IT RUINED MY PROGRAM.
THAT'S OKAY. I FORGIVE YOU.
YOU NEED TO BE WHIPPED WITH A WHIP.
(SIGH)
WITH MY LUCK THE WHIP WOULD MISS.
STOP FEELING SORRY FOR YOURSELF.
HOW COME I NEVER SEE YOU DOING HOMEWORK?
ONE TIME I HEARD THAT WORD. WHAT DOES IT MEAN?
HOMEWORK? THAT'S WHAT YOUR TEACHER TELLS YOU TO DO AT HOME.
BUT I DON'T HAVE A KNIFE.
TELL ME, DO YOU ALWAYS DO WHAT YOUR TEACHER SAYS?
NEVER AT ALL.
WHY NOT?
BECAUSE SHE CAN'T TALK.
WHY'S THAT? IS SHE DEAF AND DUMB?
NEIN, SHE'S AN ANT.
THAT'S INSULTING.
HOW COME I NEVER SEE YOU STUDYING?
WHAT'S THERE TO STUDY? I ALREADY KNOW IT ALL.
YOU'VE GOT A LOT OF NERVE. YOUR FACE NEEDS TO BE SLAPPED.
WITH MY LUCK THE SLAP WOULD GO WIDE RIGHT.
IF I WAS YOUR TEACHER I'D SWAT YOU LIKE A FLY.
NEIN. IF YOU WERE MY TEACHER YOU'D SWAT ME LIKE AN ANT.
IF I WAS YOUR TEACHER I'D TAKE YOU OVER MY KNEE.
BUT TEACHER COULD GET CRUSHED TO DEATH IF SHE TRIED SOMETHING LIKE THAT.
IF I WAS YOUR TEACHER I'D TAKE A SWING AT YOU.
TEACHER TAKES SWINGS EVERY DAY.
SHE'S VIOLENT, HUH?
NEIN. SHE TAKES SWINGS ON THE COBWEBS IN THE CLASSROOM. THAT'S HOW SHE GETS AROUND.
TELL ME, DOES YOUR TEACHER HAVE A LOT OF PERSONALITY?
NONE AT ALL.
WHY'S THAT?
BECAUSE SHE'S NOT A PERSON. SHE'S AN ANT.
WHAT GRADE ARE YOU IN?
I'M IN PRESCHOOL.
PRESCHOOL? YOU'RE TOO BIG FOR THAT. SHAME ON YOU.
TEACHER SAID I'M IMMATURE.
HOW DOES YOUR TEACHER GET TO WORK EVERY DAY?
SHE DOESN'T.
SHE DOESN'T DRIVE?
NEIN. SHE DOESN'T WORK. SHE'S A TEACHER. TEACHERS DON'T WORK, ALL THEY DO IS FIND FAULT WITH EVERYTHING. MOST OF THEM ARE ON POWER TRIPS ANYWAY. PLUS THEY GET SUMMERS OFF.
TELL ME, DOES YOUR TEACHER HAVE A COMPLEX ABOUT BEING SO TINY?
NOT AT ALL. SHE'S THE RIGHT SIZE. EVERYBODY ELSE IS OVERGROWN.
SHE BLAMES EVERYONE BUT HERSELF FOR BEING SO PETITE. I DON'T LIKE THAT.
IT'S TOO BAD SHE'S SO SHORT.
IT DOES HAVE SOME ADVANTAGES.
EXPLAIN.
WELL, SHE HAS A LOW ZENITH WITH EASY ACCESS.
WHAT ELSE IS SO GREAT ABOUT IT?
WELL, IF THE SCHOOL EVER CAUGHT ON FIRE SHE ALONE WOULD SURVIVE BY CRAWLING UNDER THE SMOKE.
NOW YOU'RE BRAGGING.
ARE THERE ANY DRAWBACKS TO HAVING AN ANT FOR A TEACHER?
UH UH.
UH UH? DON'T JUST SAY UH UH. EXPLAIN YOURSELF.
ONE TIME I THOUGHT SOMEONE WAS DRAWING SOMETHING ON MY BACK BUT IT TURNED OUT TO BE ONLY A FLY.
ARE THERE ANY MINUSES TO HAVING AN ANT FOR A TEACHER?
UH HUH.
UH HUH YOU SAY? DON'T JUST SAY UH HUH. ELABORATE.
THE WORST PART OF IT IS THAT I GET ASKED A LOT OF IGNORANT QUESTIONS.
ARE THERE ANY ADVANTAGES TO HAVING AN ANT FOR A TEACHER?
UH HUH.
UH HUH? AGAIN? DON'T JUST SAY UH HUH. CAN YOU TELL ME MORE?
UH HUH.
DIDN'T I JUST TELL YOU NOT TO ONLY SAY UH HUH?
UH HUH.
TELL ME, ARE THERE ANY PERKS TO HAVING AN ANT FOR A TEACHER?
UH UH.
UH UH? IS THAT ALL YOU CAN SAY? WHY'S THAT?
BECAUSE YOU TOLD ME NOT TO SAY UH HUH.
AND HAVE YOU ANY CAVEATS TO TELL US ABOUT?
CAN'T SAY. HAVEN'T BEEN TO THE DENTIST IN A WHILE.
DOES SHE A LOT OF EXPERIENCE UNDER HER BELT?
NONE AT ALL.
TOO BAD. WHY'S THAT?
BECAUSE SHE DOESN'T WEAR A BELT.
HOW LONG HAS SHE BEEN TEACHING?
FROM THE FRONT TO THE BACK OF THE CLASSROOM.
WHAT COLLEGE DID YOUR TEACHER GRADUATE FROM?
OH THAT... IT DIDN'T WORK OUT. TEACHER DROPPED OUT THE FIRST DAY.
WHY'S THAT?
SHE NEARLY GOT STEPPED ON DURING A STUDENT PROTEST MARCH.
SERVES HER RIGHT. THAT'S WHAT SHE GETS FOR BEING SO PETITE.
YOUR TEACHER IS A DROPOUT, HUH? SOME EXAMPLE SHE IS, RIGHT?
SHE DIDN'T BELONG IN COLLEGE. SHE ALREADY KNEW MORE THAN THE PROFESSOR.
OH IS THAT SO? SHE SOUNDS LIKE AN ARROGANT LITTLE SO-AND-SO.
NOW YOU'RE BEING JEALOUS.
WOULD YOU SAY THAT YOUR TEACHER IS RESPONSIBLE?
NEIN. SHE'S INNOCENT OF ANY ACCUSATIONS.
DOES SHE KNOW WHAT TO DO IN AN EMERGENCY?
UH HUH.
UH HUH AGAIN? THAT'S NOT ENOUGH. TELL ME MORE.
WHENEVER THERE'S AN EMERGENCY TEACHER HIDES.
HOW DOES SHE HANDLE A CLASSROOM EMERGENCY? SAY THERE'S A STABBING, DOES YOUR TEACHER KNOW WHAT TO DO?
OF COURSE, THE FIRST THING SHE DOES IS GET A LAWYER.
WHAT IF IT'S SOMETHING LESS SERIOUS? DOES SHE KNOW WHAT TO DO IF A KID THROWS UP?
UH HUH.
UH HUH AGAIN? HOW MANY TIMES HAVE I TOLD YOU NOT TO JUST SAY UH HUH?
TEACHER SAYS THERE ARE OTHER WORLDS.
WHAT ABOUT DISCIPLINE? WHAT HAPPENS WHEN A STUDENT GIVES A WRONG ANSWER AND NEEDS HIS FACE SLAPPED AS PUNISHMENT?
THAT SITUATION HAS NEVER OCCURRED.
WHY'S THAT?
BECAUSE TEACHER CAN'T TALK. SHE NEVER ASKS ANYONE ANYTHING.
I KEEP FORGETTING THAT MOST ANTS CAN'T TALK.
AND THE ONES THAT DO ARE MUTANTS.
DOES YOUR TEACHER HAVE A BAD TEMPER?
I DON'T KNOW.
WHY DON'T YOU KNOW?
BECAUSE.
BECAUSE? BECAUSE WHY?
BECAUSE I NEVER TASTED IT.
TELL ME, DOES SHE HAVE A GOOD SENSE OF HUMOR?
WHO KNOWS? THERE'S NOTHING TO LAUGH ABOUT THESE AWFUL DAYS.
THAT'S BECAUSE WE'RE IN END TIMES.
BUT YOU'RE NOT WEARING A WATCH.
OTHER THAN BEING AN ANT WOULD YOU SAY THAT SHE'S A TYPICAL TEACHER?
UH HUH.
UH HUH AGAIN, HUH? YOU KNOW I DON'T LIKE THAT. EXTRAPOLATE YOURSELF.
SHE'S LIKE EVERY OTHER TEACHER. SHE HATES KIDS AND ENJOYS SEEING THEM FAIL.

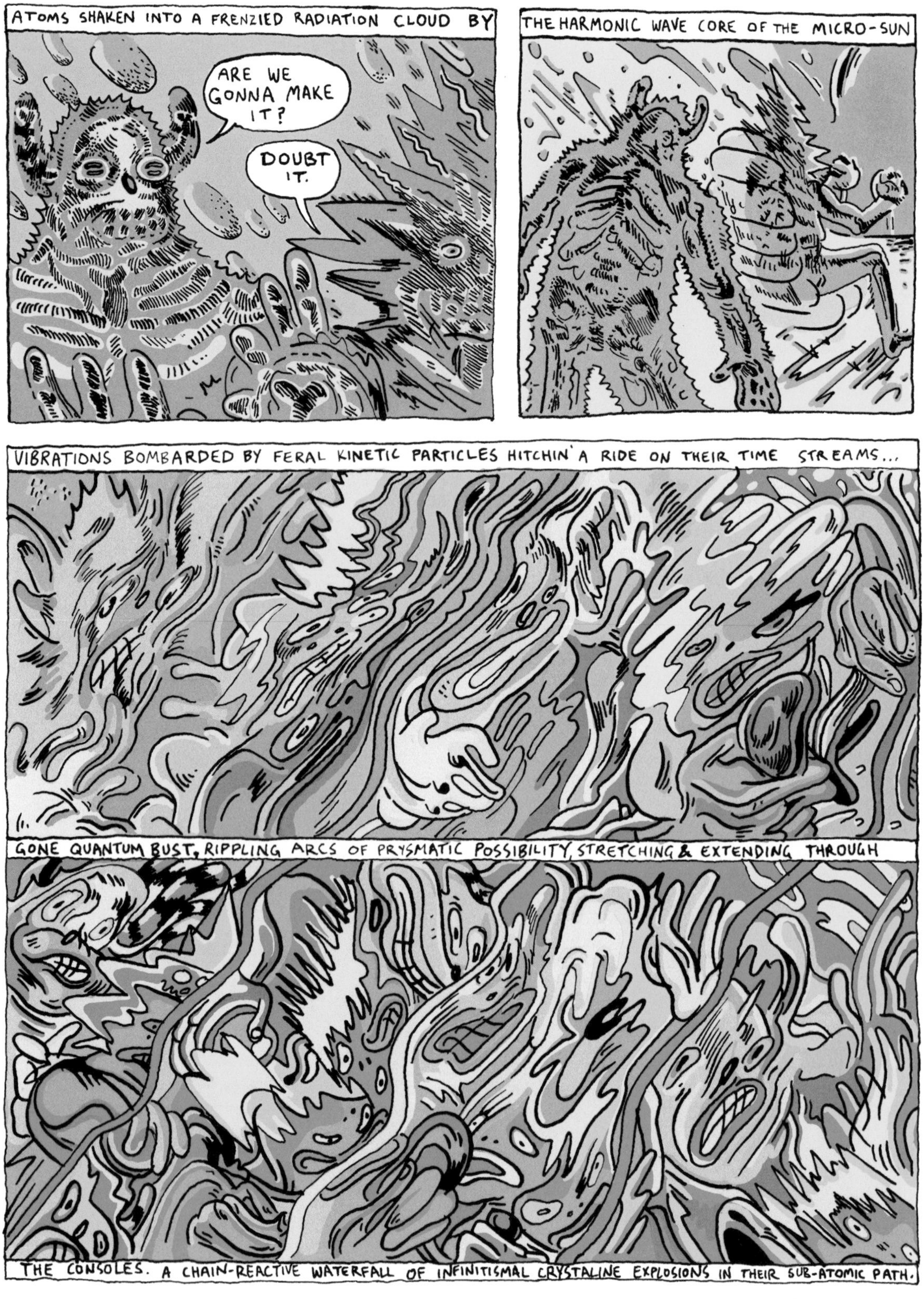
ATOMS SHAKEN INTO A FRENZIED RADIATION CLOUD BY
ARE WE GONNA MAKE IT?
DOUBT IT.
THE HARMONIC WAVE CORE OF THE MICRO-SUN
VIBRATIONS BOMBARDED BY FERAL KINETIC PARTICLES HITCHIN' A RIDE ON THEIR TIME STREAMS...
GONE QUANTUM BUST, RIPPLING ARCS OF PRYSMATIC POSSIBILITY, STRETCHING & EXTENDING THROUGH
THE CONSOLES. A CHAIN-REACTIVE WATERFALL OF INFINITISMAL CRYSTALINE EXPLOSIONS IN THEIR SUB-ATOMIC PATH.

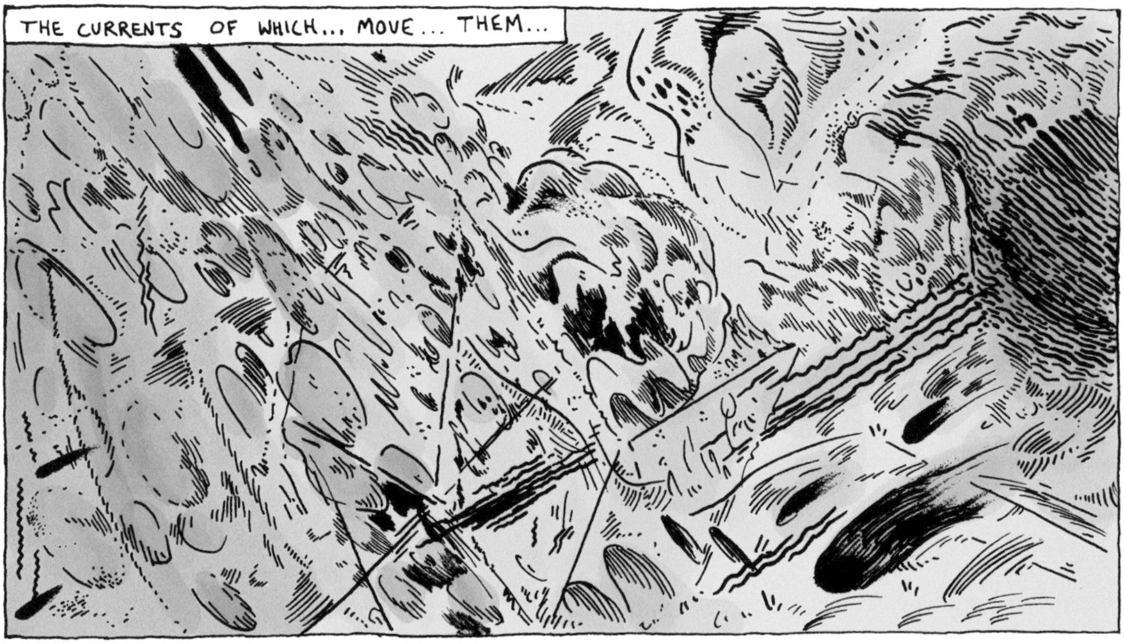
THE CURRENTS OF WHICH... MOVE... THEM...

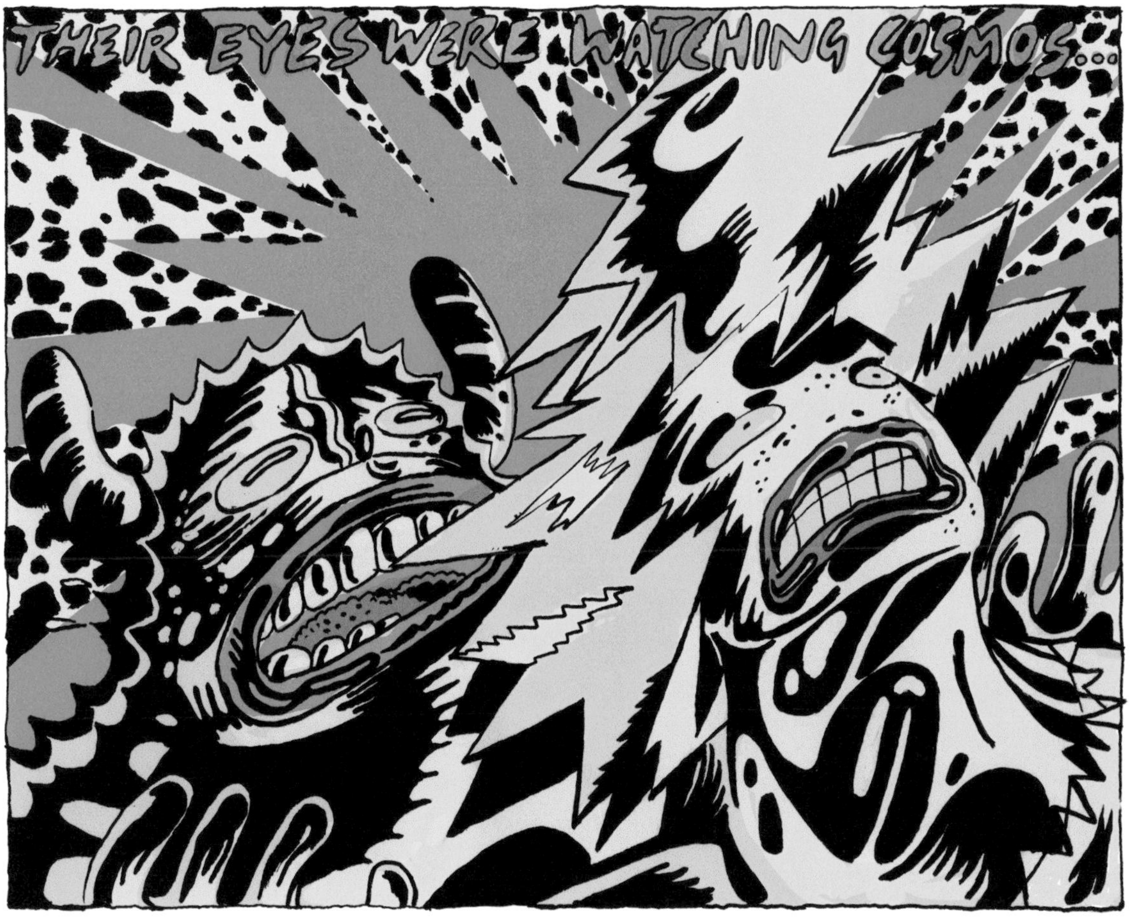
THEIR EYES WERE WATCHING COSMOS...

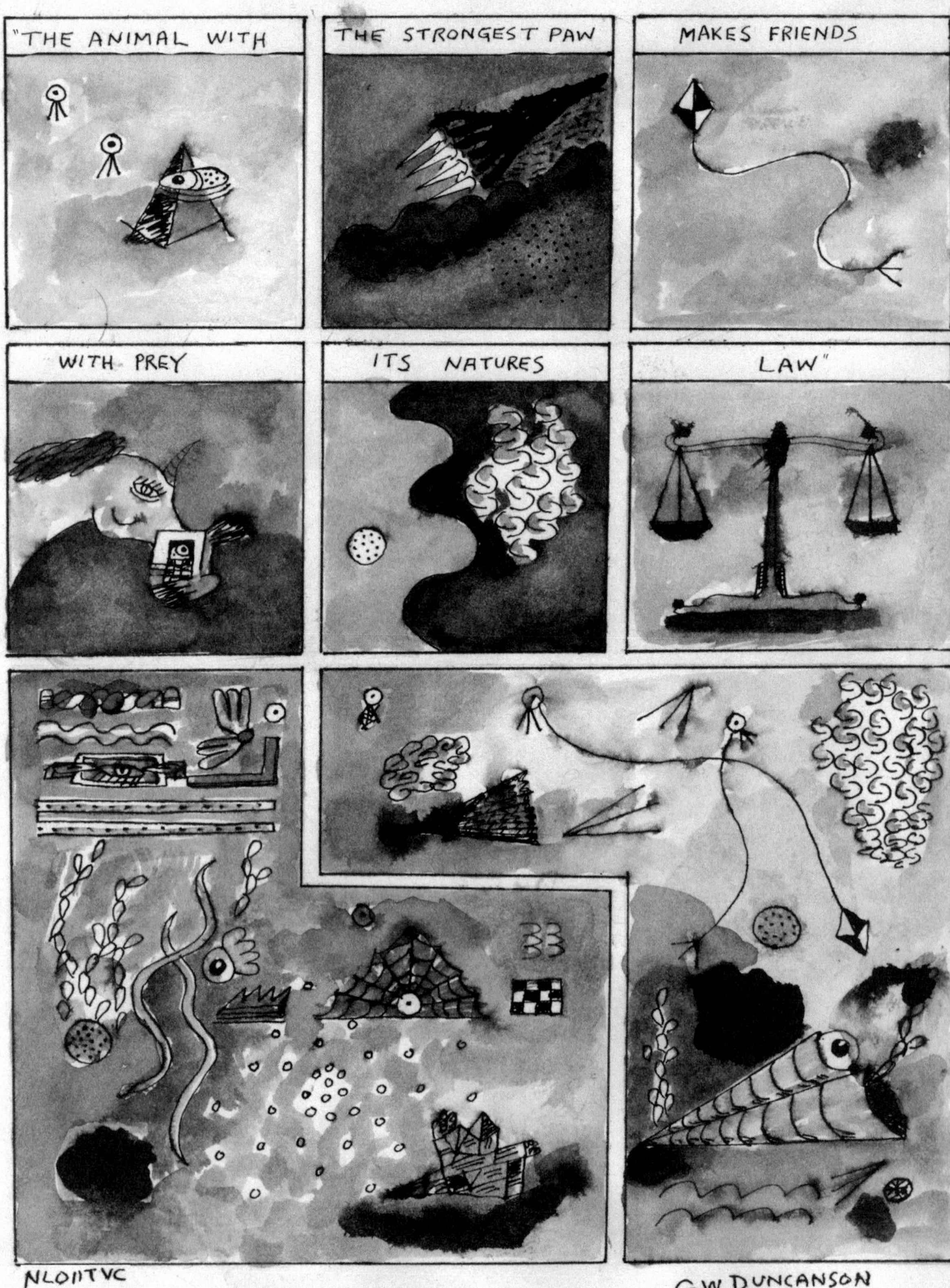
"THE ANIMAL WITH
THE STRONGEST PAW
MAKES FRIENDS
WITH PREY
ITS NATURES
LAW"
NLOIITVC
GW DUNCANSON

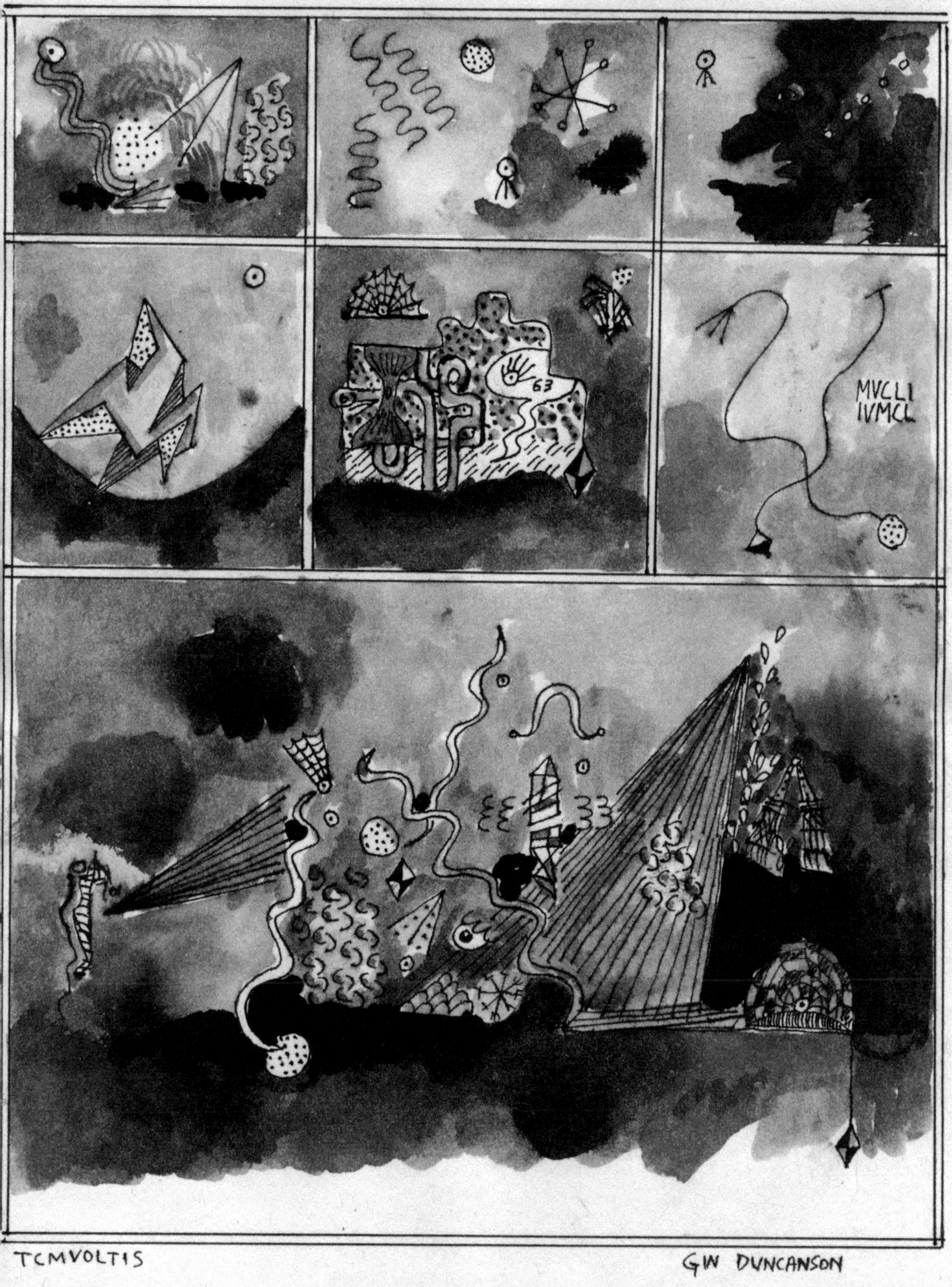
63
MVCLI
IVMCL
TCMVOLTIS
GW DUNCANSON

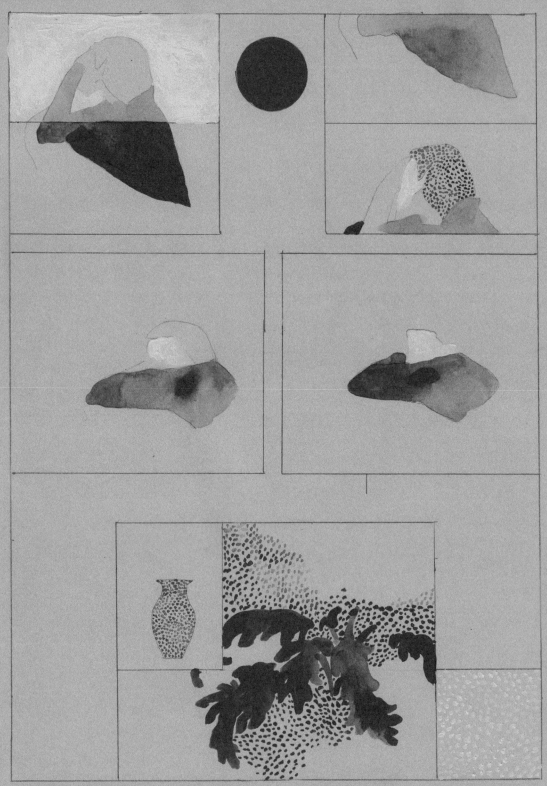

WHAT'S THE POINT YOU REACH WHERE EVERYTHING BECOMES BLUE?

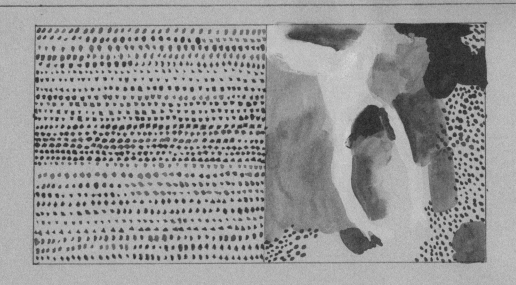

IS IT SADNESS, STRUGGLE? OR JUST A SHIFT IN VISION   A FILTER OVER YOUR EYES

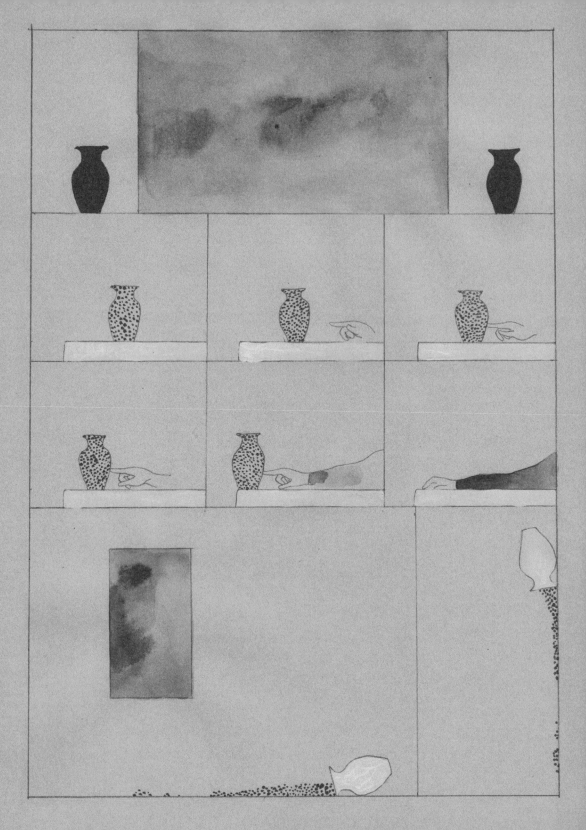

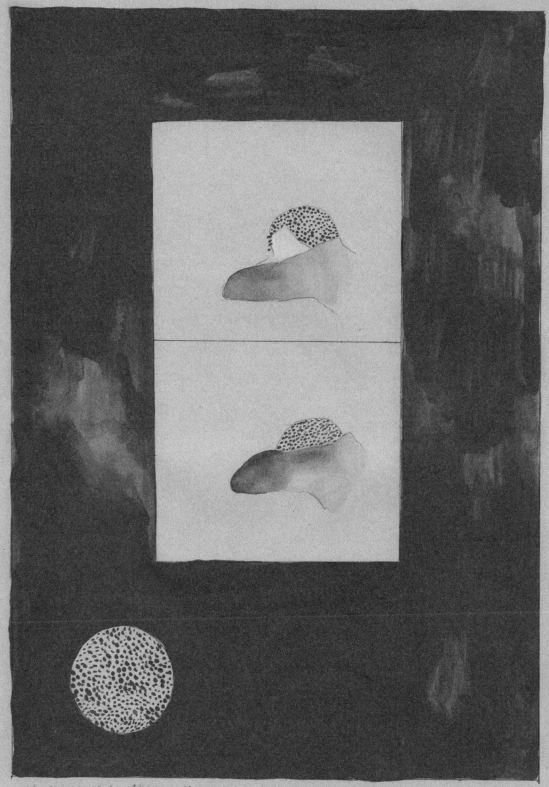

IN SOME WAYS DOESN'T IT MAKE EVERYTHING MORE BEAUTIFUL?

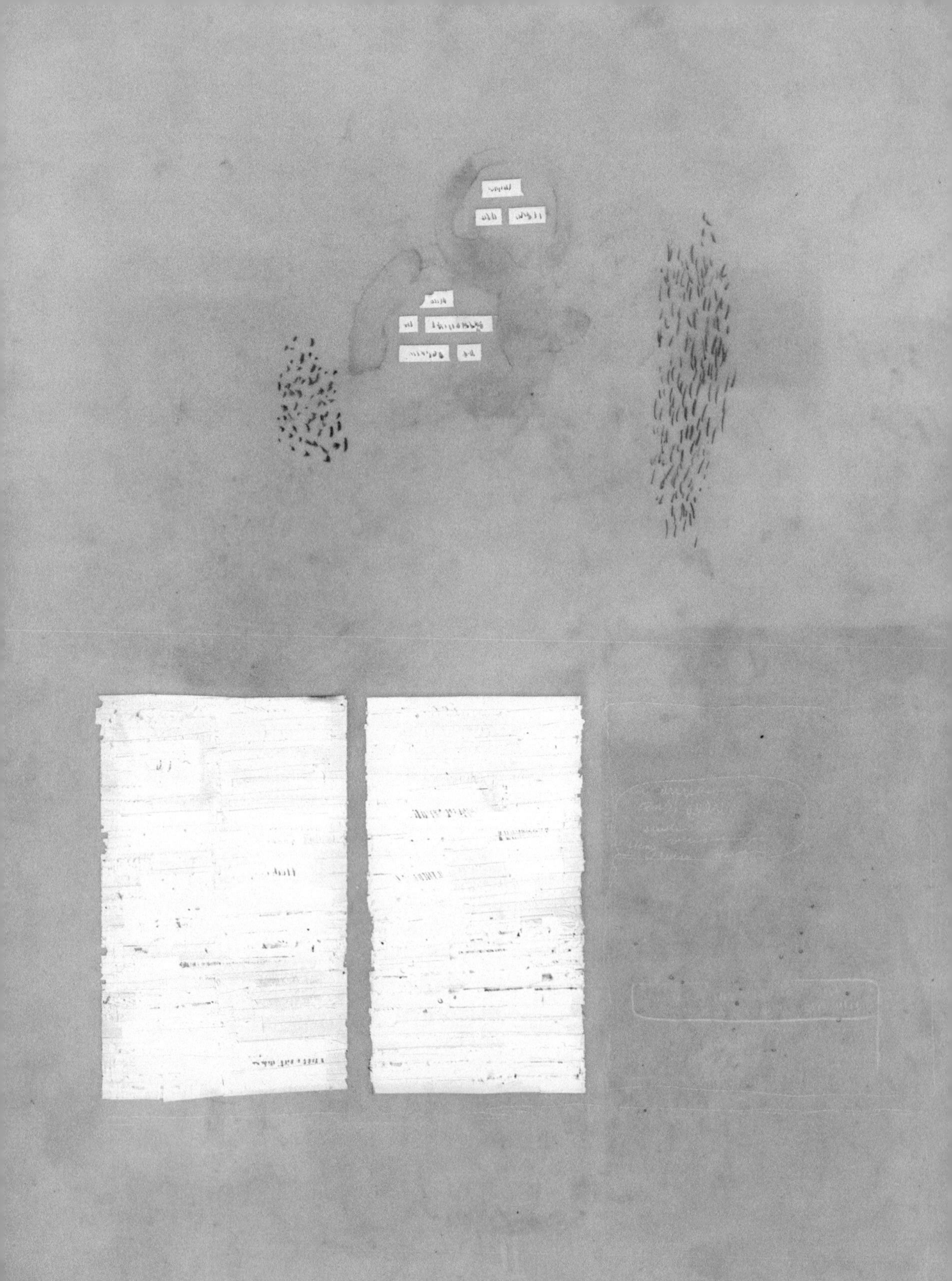

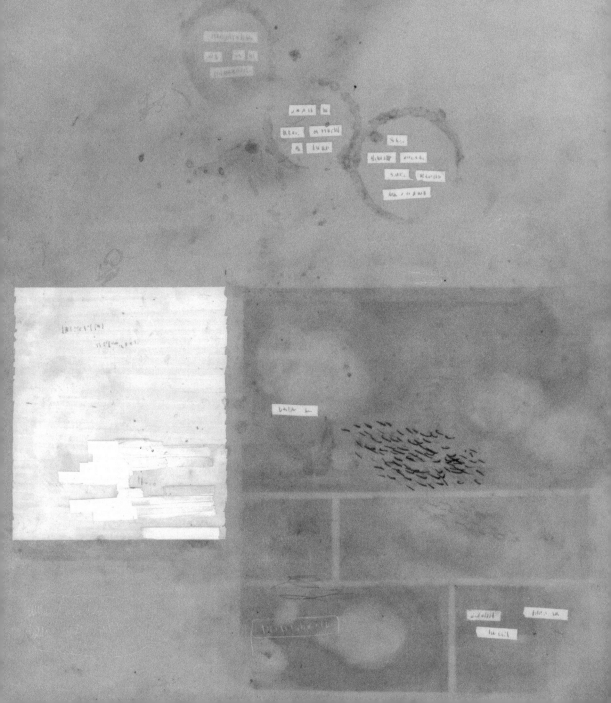

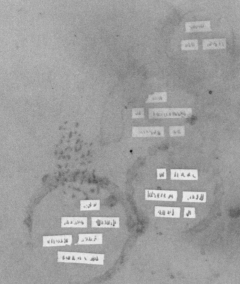

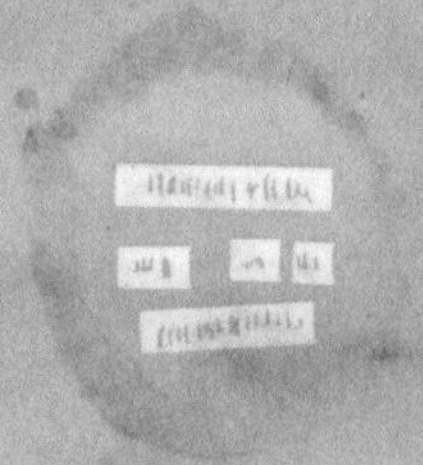

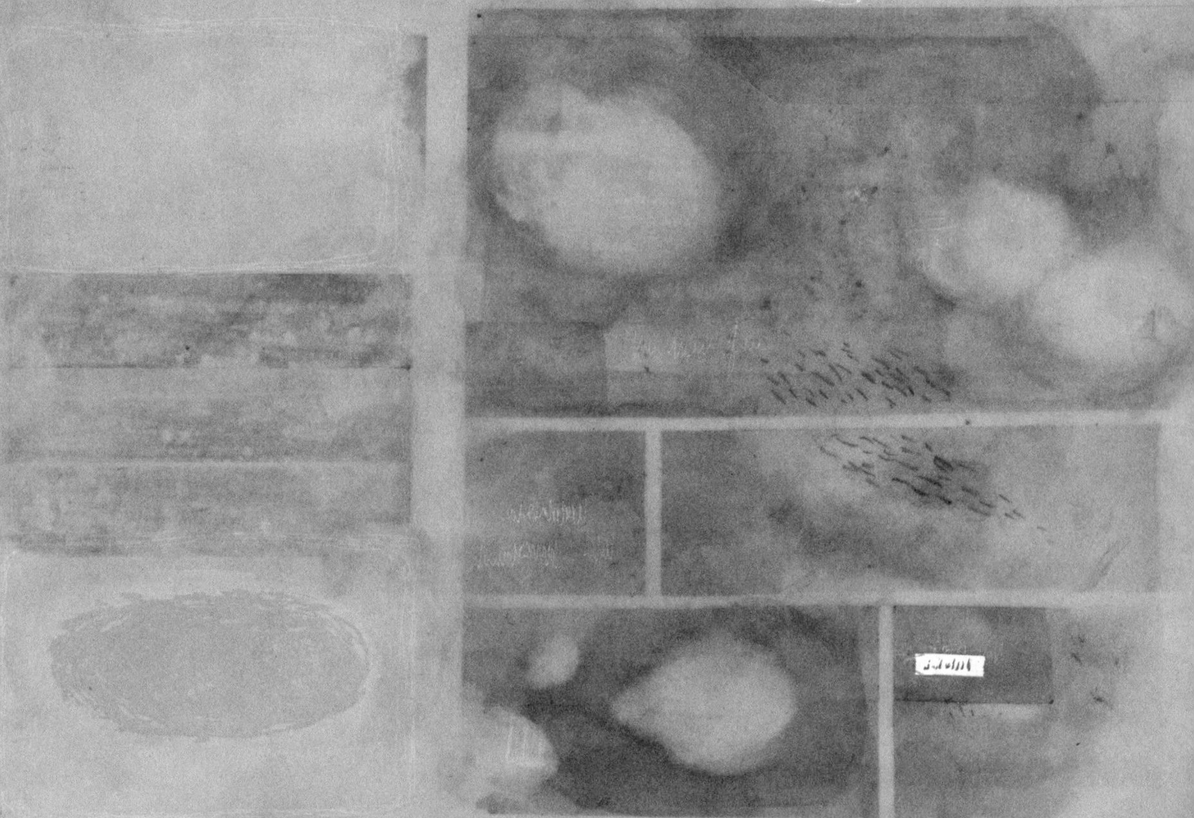

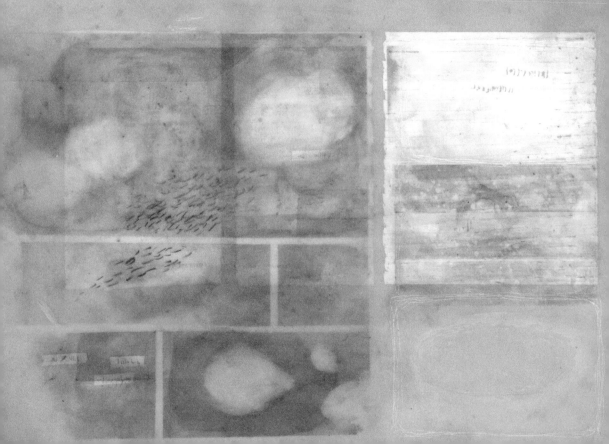

III.

Memory Boxes

In November 2001, only two months after the September 11 attacks, I was a guest at the Chicago Humanities Festival. They'd decided to shine a spotlight on comics that year and they took their mission seriously. One of the events was a panel featuring Will Eisner, Neil Gaiman, Chris Ware, Ben Katchor (who'd just won a MacArthur Foundation "genius grant"—boy, did we make fun of him at breakfast), and me. The moderator was Michael Chabon. One of the questions that made the rounds was about the role of nostalgia in our work. When it came to me, I had to admit that I was pretty indifferent to nostalgia. I'd done a retro-hero comic when I was starting out, but comics and nostalgia didn't really mix for me; I was far more interested in the future. I also suggested I'd never seen that much nostalgia in Will Eisner's work—even though he was probably twice the age of anyone else on the panel.

But Chris Ware? Yeah, he had the nostalgia thing going on in spades. Not the warm, sunny glow of bygone days, more a sense of the *burden* of memories, the haunting specter of childhood dreams gone wrong, beloved memories perverted, parental love denied . . . And it wasn't just Ware's stories giving off that "now is the golden hour of our discontent" vibe. Even their physical form and style seemed to speak of a melancholy obsolescence. Somehow, paradoxically, just as he was helping to invigorate the comics art form and usher in its future, he was also helping to foster the misconception that it was on its last legs.

I don't think it was deliberate on Ware's part, but this weird crosscurrent might have actually worked to our benefit. It kicked up an irony-laced reality distortion field that masked the bracing newness of modern comics and allied them instead with cherished traditions of a seemingly endangered species: print. The literary establishment shed a tear, gave comics a warm, hearty bear hug, and took it home for dinner, never noticing the barbarian hordes at the gate brandishing *xkcd*, *SuperF*ckers*, and *Fullmetal Alchemist*.

Like my mentor Eisner—gone at 87 just a few years after Chicago—I don't worry about the survival of the art form. The art form has never been healthier. The ever-resourceful Hive Mind might even find a way for young cartoonists to make a living soon. But that doesn't mean there haven't been casualties, and chief among them is the American newspaper comic strip.

The great Bill Watterson (fast becoming one of the most widely known and loved cartoonists in the world, despite permanently shutting off the spigot many years ago) once drew a cartoon panel showing the evolution of the American comic strip as a perverse reversal of the famous "Ascent of Man" sequence. In Watterson's version, comics starts off as a dapper gentleman, becomes an ape, then a . . . horny toad?—can't tell—then finally a barely sentient lump of goo with a stupid grin on its face.

Watterson was in awe of the invention, imagination, and boundless promise in those first decades of twentieth-century newspaper comics. And he had nothing but contempt for what he felt they'd gradually become: shrunken and degraded until it seemed there was nothing left worth saving.

Until *Cul de Sac* by Richard Thompson, that is. Watterson really loved that strip, and he wasn't alone. "I thought the best newspaper comic strips were long gone, and I've never been happier to be wrong," he wrote in 2008.

Cul de Sac captured everything funny and charming and true about the best American comic strips, from Segar to Johnston to Schulz. It was alive, it made you laugh, it popped off the page like a ladybug. But like Watterson did with *Calvin and Hobbes*, Thompson decided to call it quits in 2012 and run his last strip. He didn't do so in disgust or in protest or because the strip had run its course. He wasn't out of ideas. He hadn't lost interest. He just couldn't hold a pen steady anymore due to Parkinson's disease.

It's hard to imagine a shittier piece of luck befalling such a wonderful artist, but it's also sobering to consider that getting sick might've only been the *second*-worst misfortune to befall Thompson—second only to being born thirty years too late.

The last strips to run (included here) were technically reprints, but we felt it important to offer an acknowledgment of this wonderful strip's conclusion, and of Thompson's creative vision.

Are there other talented, dedicated newspaper strip artists out there? Of course. With all due respect to Watterson, I can still imagine an unexpected renaissance in newspaper strips even now. But when talk turns to "the future of comics," my mind turns elsewhere, and I know I'm not alone. Comic strips as a form are now primarily associated with the Web, as is the news itself. The art survives, even thrives, but not the way my parents knew it.

I'm an optimist—a card-carrying member of the Team Comics cheering section—but I'm also on record as believing that the story of comics in the twentieth century was marked by one squandered opportunity after another, a parade of inspired artists with compelling visions for their chosen art form who were eventually driven into obscurity and buried by an industry that had no use for them. That's our past, but I don't think it has to be our future.

Take Sam Alden, the artist of our final selection, "Hawaii 1997." There are plenty of starving artists out there, barely squeezing a dime out of their dreams yet, and I wouldn't be surprised to learn that Alden is one of them. But when a cartoonist like Alden comes around in this era—someone who might be rough around the edges but clearly has that spark, that understanding of what comics can do—we don't worry that he'll be buried or denied an audience. Nobody can bury artists like Alden any more. He might have to scramble for a while, but there isn't enough dirt in the world to prevent him from tunneling to daylight.

They say the "Golden Age of Comics" is whenever you were ten years old. I know what they mean, I get it, I do. Nostalgia is a powerful thing. But every time I hear someone say it, I want to call bullshit. I've read a metric ton of comics over four decades, and I can say without hesitation that compared to the era we're in right now, comics *sucked* when I was ten.

And that's when Kirby was still drawing *Fantastic Four*!

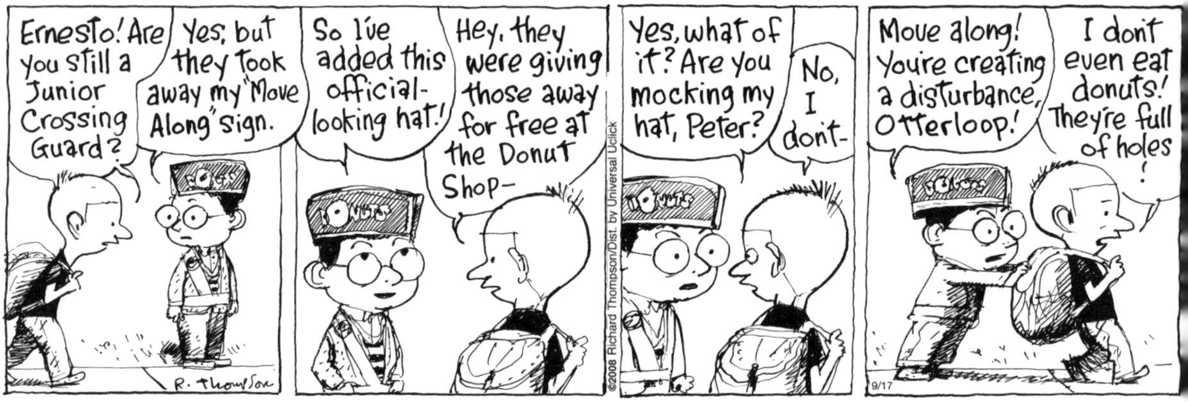
Ernesto! Are you still a Junior Crossing Guard?
Yes, but they took away my "Move Along" sign.
R. Thompson
So I've added this official-looking hat!
Hey, they were giving those away for free at the Donut Shop-
DONUTS
©2008 Richard Thompson/Dist. by Universal Uclick
Yes, what of it? Are you mocking my hat, Peter?
No, I don't-
Move along! You're creating a disturbance, Otterloop!
I don't even eat donuts! They're full of holes!
9/17

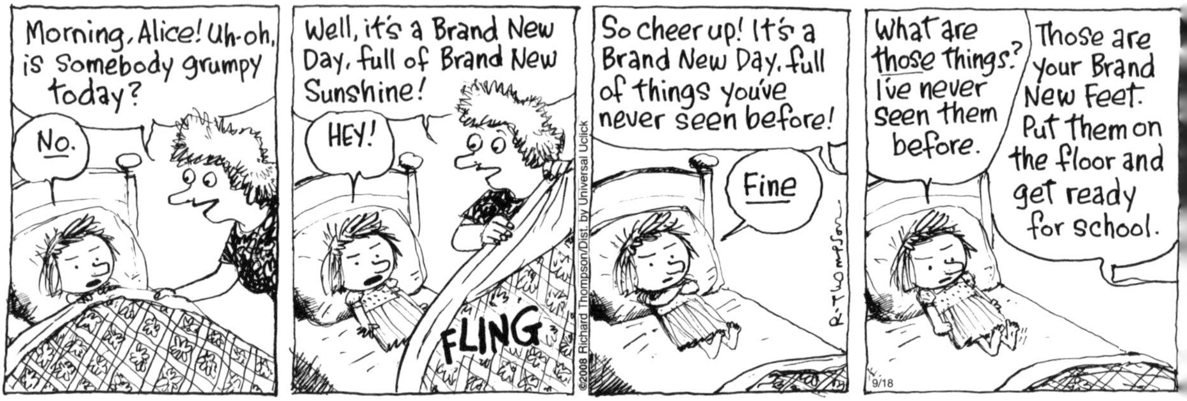
Morning, Alice! Uh-oh, is somebody grumpy today?
No.
Well, it's a Brand New Day, full of Brand New Sunshine!
HEY!
FLING
©2008 Richard Thompson/Dist. by Universal Uclick
So cheer up! It's a Brand New Day, full of things you've never seen before!
Fine
R-Thompson
What are those things? I've never seen them before.
Those are your Brand New Feet. Put them on the floor and get ready for school.
9/18

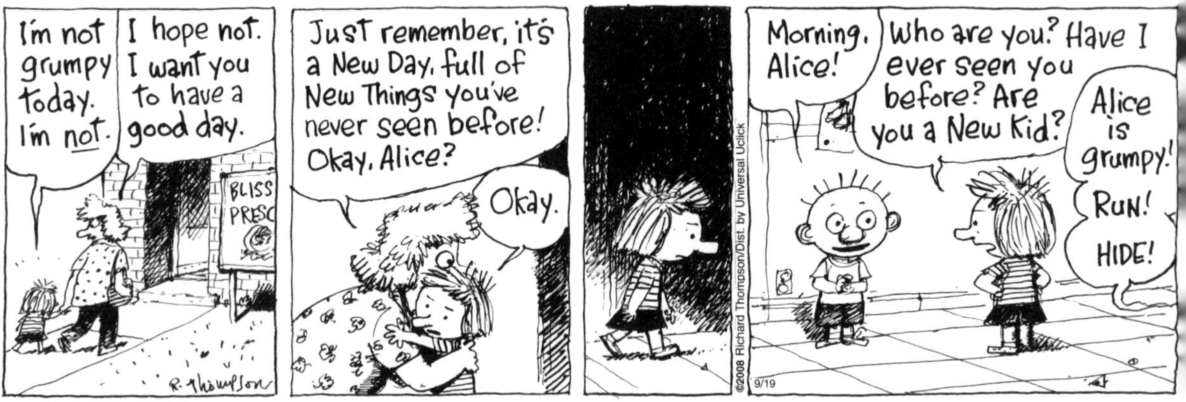
I'm not grumpy today. I'm not.
I hope not. I want you to have a good day.
BLISS PRESC
R. Thompson
Just remember, it's a New Day, full of New Things you've never seen before! Okay, Alice?
Okay.
©2008 Richard Thompson/Dist. by Universal Uclick
Morning, Alice!
Who are you? Have I ever seen you before? Are you a New Kid?
Alice is grumpy!
RUN!
HIDE!
9/19

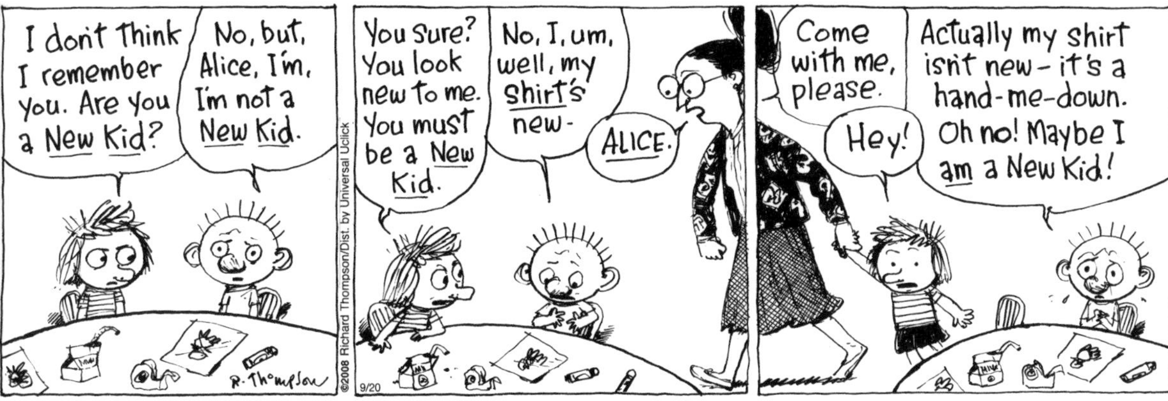
I don't Think I remember you. Are you a New Kid?
No, but, Alice, I'm, I'm not a New Kid.
©2008 Richard Thompson/Dist. by Universal Uclick
You sure? You look new to me. You must be a New Kid.
No, I, um, well, my shirt's new-
ALICE.
Come with me, please.
Hey!
Actually my shirt isn't new - it's a hand-me-down. Oh no! Maybe I am a New Kid!

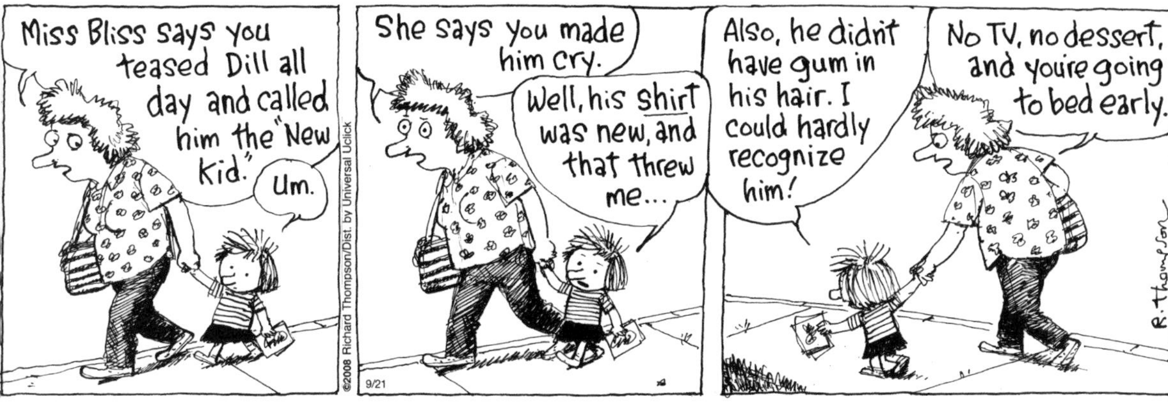
Miss Bliss says you teased Dill all day and called him the "New Kid."
Um.
©2008 Richard Thompson/Dist. by Universal Uclick
She says you made him cry.
Well, his shirt was new, and that threw me...
Also, he didn't have gum in his hair. I could hardly recognize him!
No TV, no dessert, and you're going to bed early.

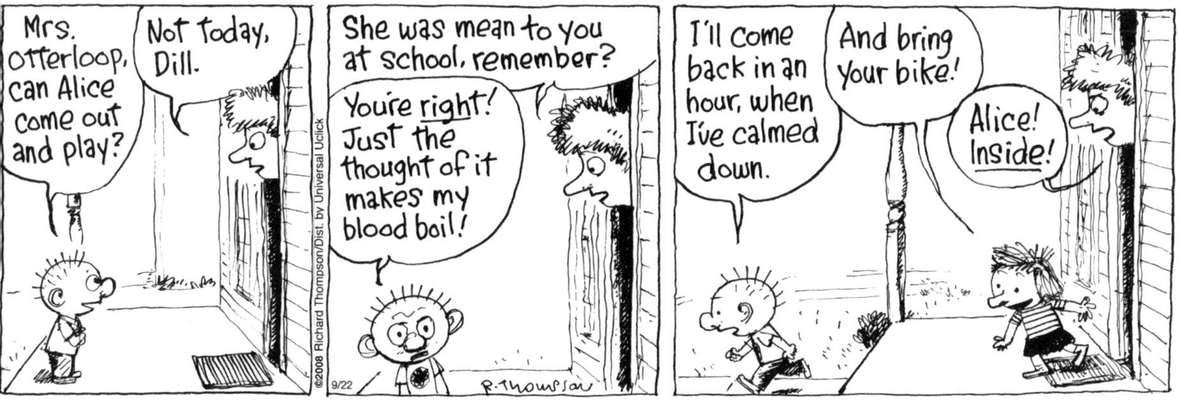
Mrs. Otterloop, can Alice come out and play?
Not today, Dill.
©2008 Richard Thompson/Dist. by Universal Uclick
She was mean to you at school, remember?
You're right! Just the thought of it makes my blood boil!
I'll come back in an hour, when I've calmed down.
And bring your bike!
Alice! Inside!

CUL DE SAC

BY RICHARD THOMPSON

Panel 1:
Petey, what're those?

They're "comic strips," examples of a mighty, yet dying art form.

Panel 2:
Read this one to me.

Well, see the cat says—

Panel 3:
Is he happy or sad?

I don't know yet.

Panel 4:
I think he's sad.

Okay. He says—

Panel 5:
He's sad because the last cat here is eating pie.

No! He—

Panel 6:
Yes he is! He hates the cat in the last box on the end! If he wasn't in a box too, he'd go beat up that cat and take his pie!

Panel 7:
ALICE! IT'S ALL THE SAME CAT! SEE? THEY'RE ALL HIM!

Panel 8:
Actually, I think he's a girl cat.

Maybe it's just as well comic strips are a dying art form.

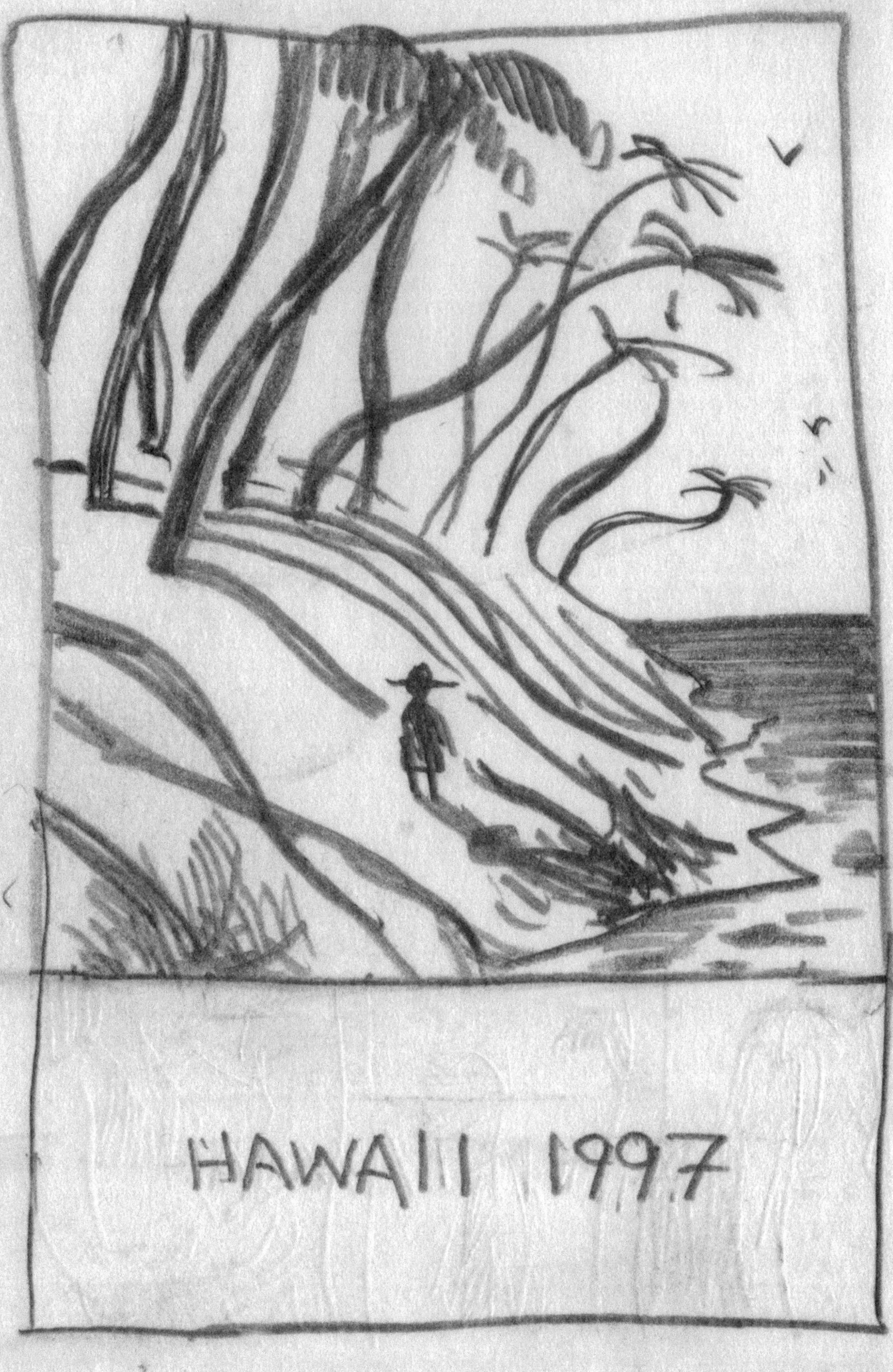
HAWAII 1997

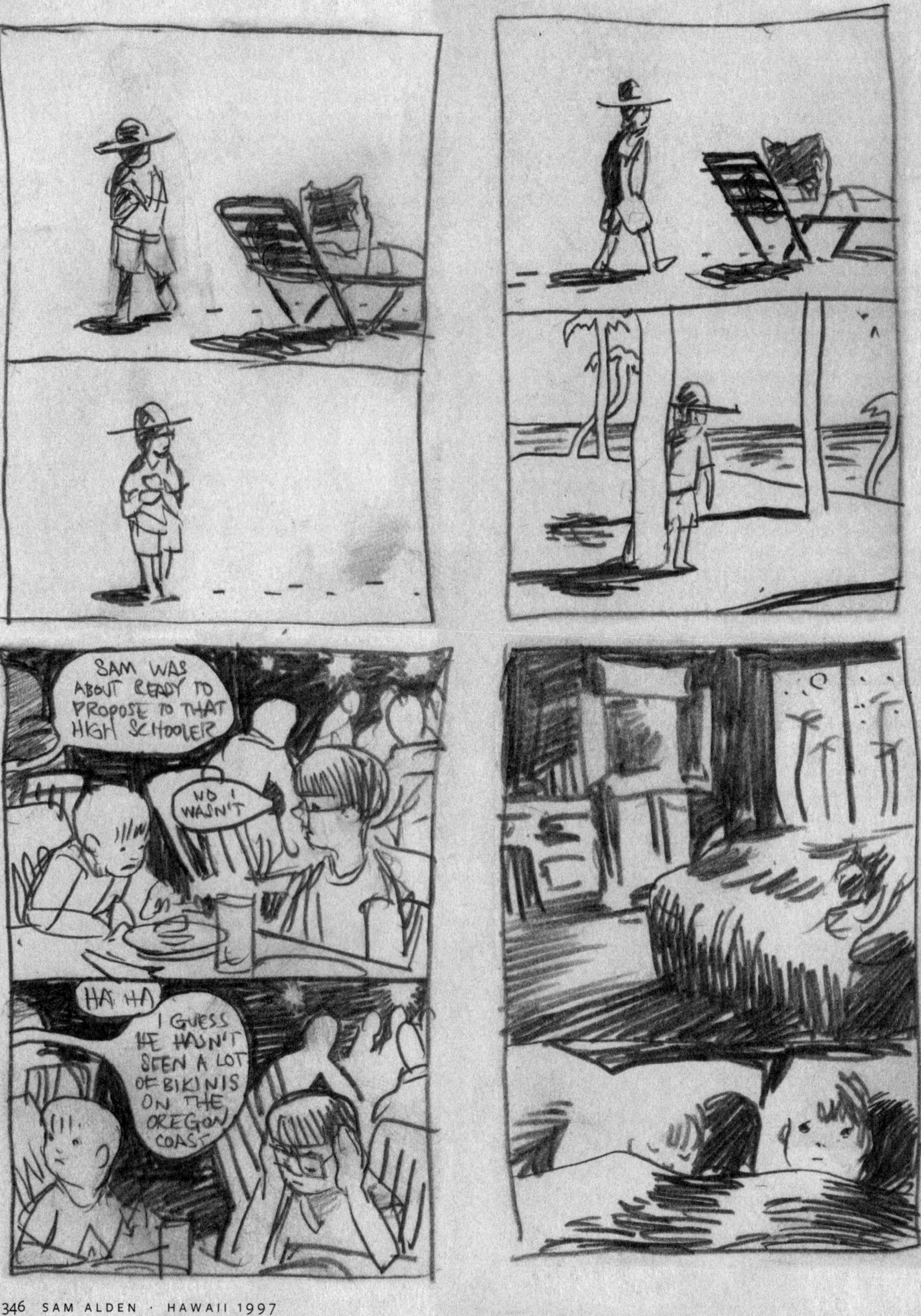
SAM WAS ABOUT READY TO PROPOSE TO THAT HIGH SCHOOLER
NO I WASN'T
HA HA
I GUESS HE HASN'T SEEN A LOT OF BIKINIS ON THE OREGON COAST

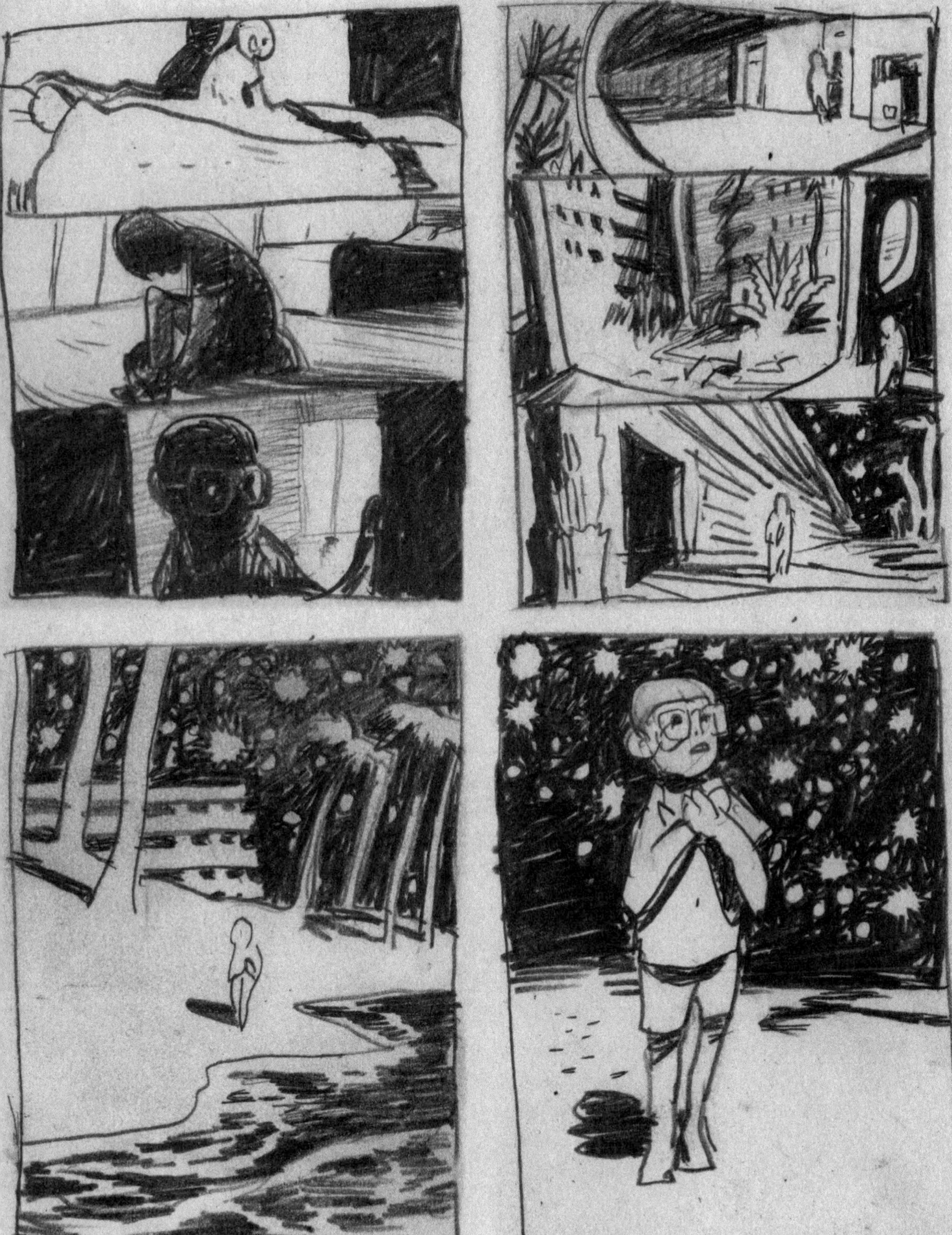

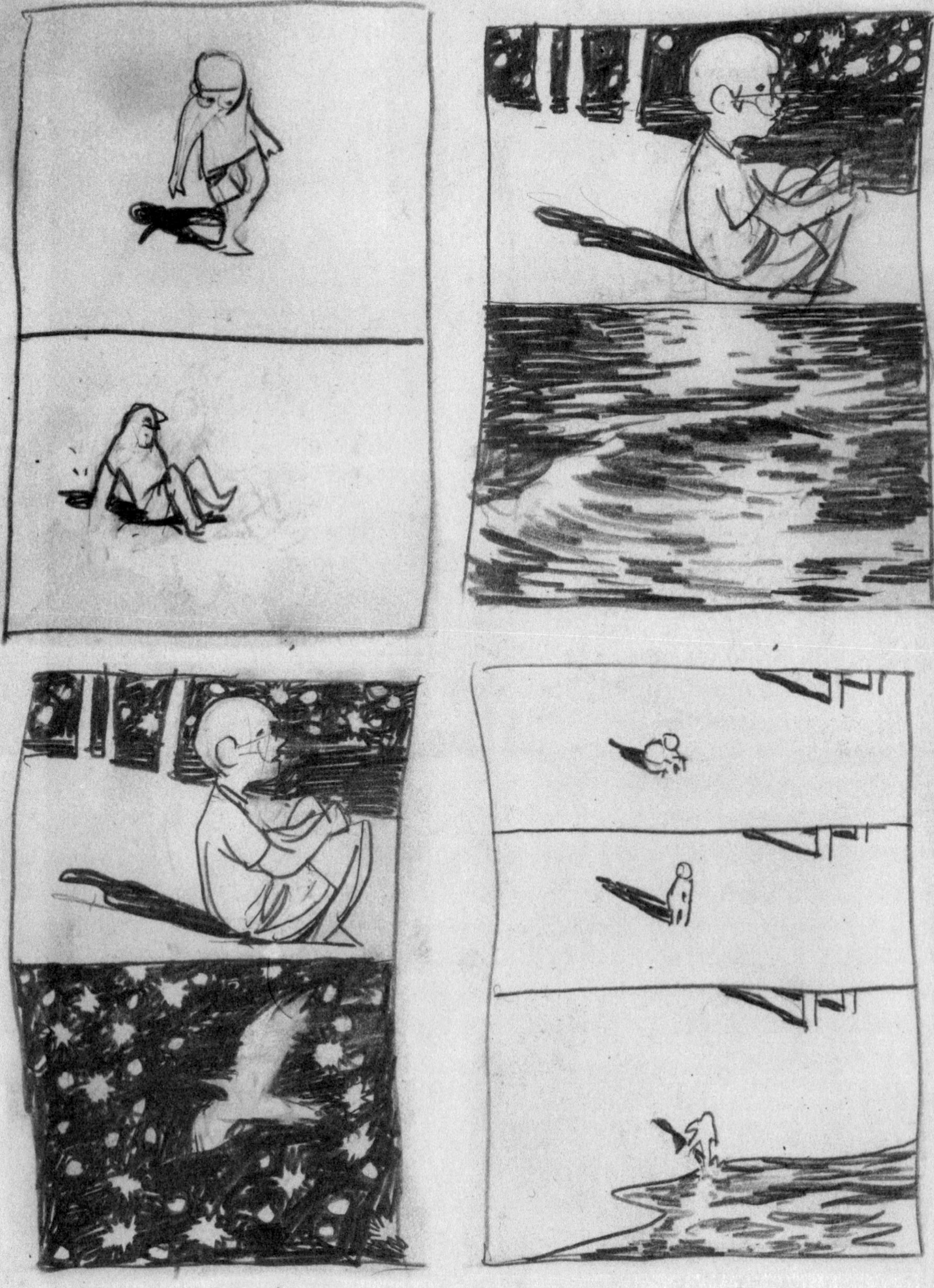

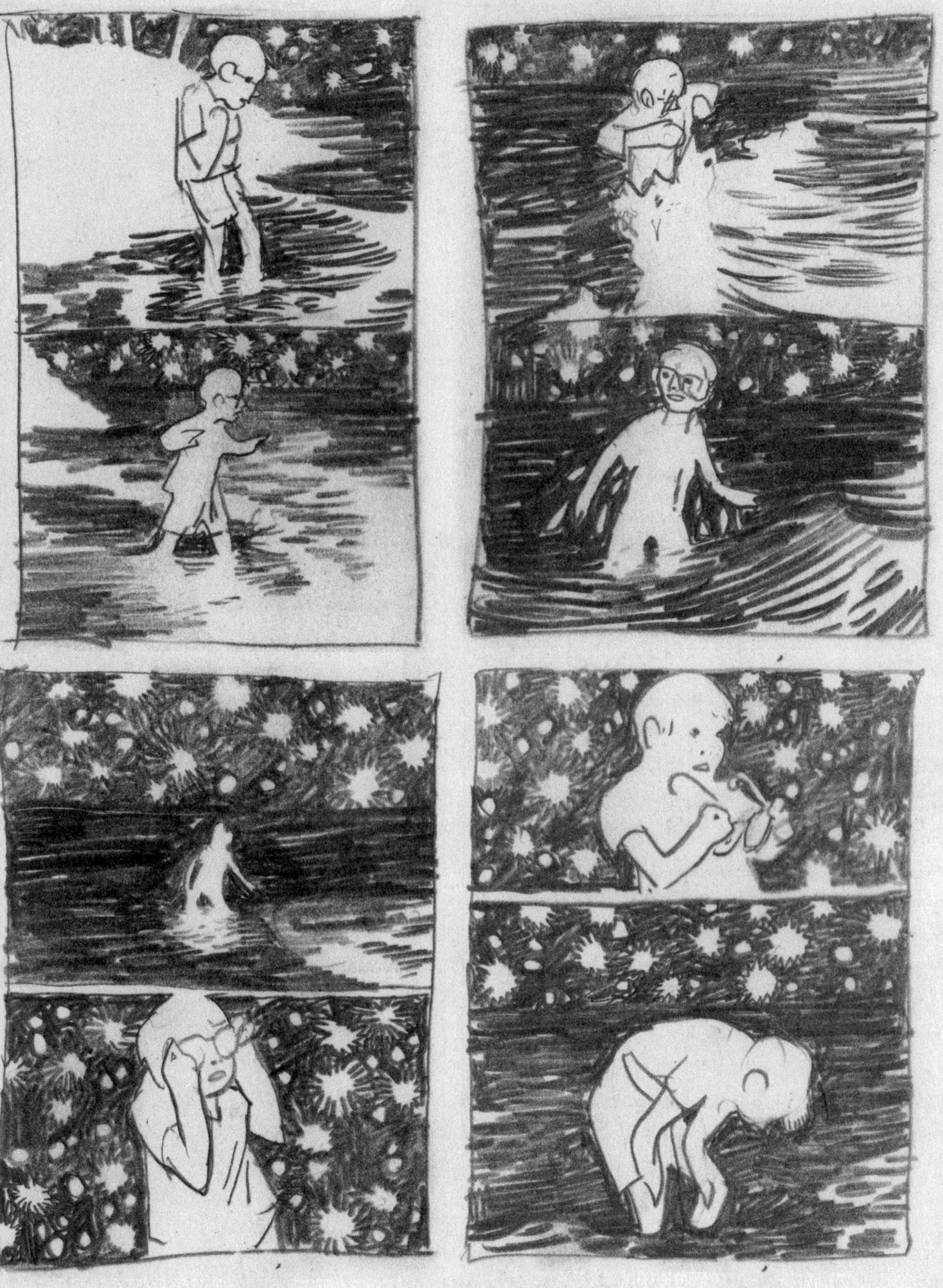

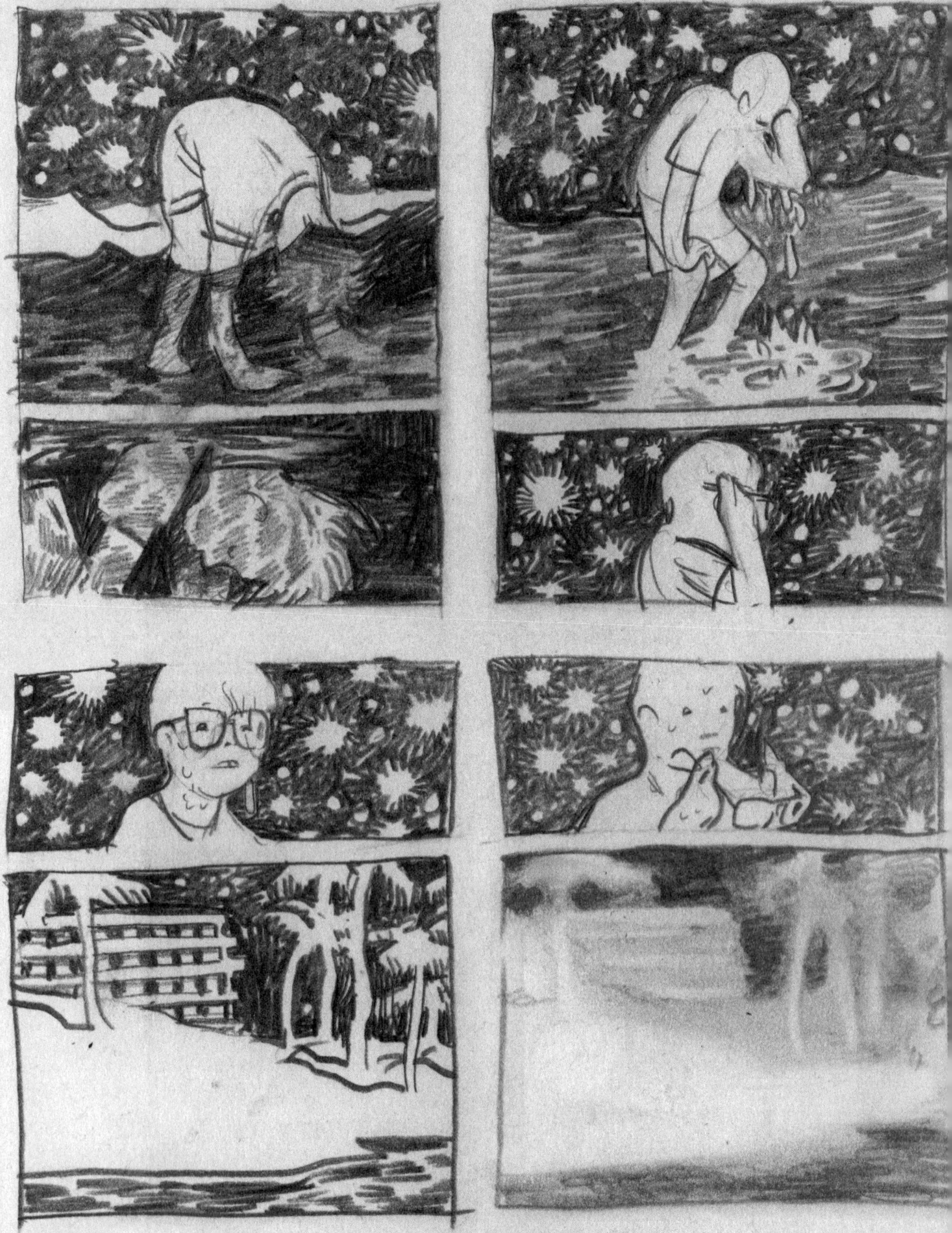

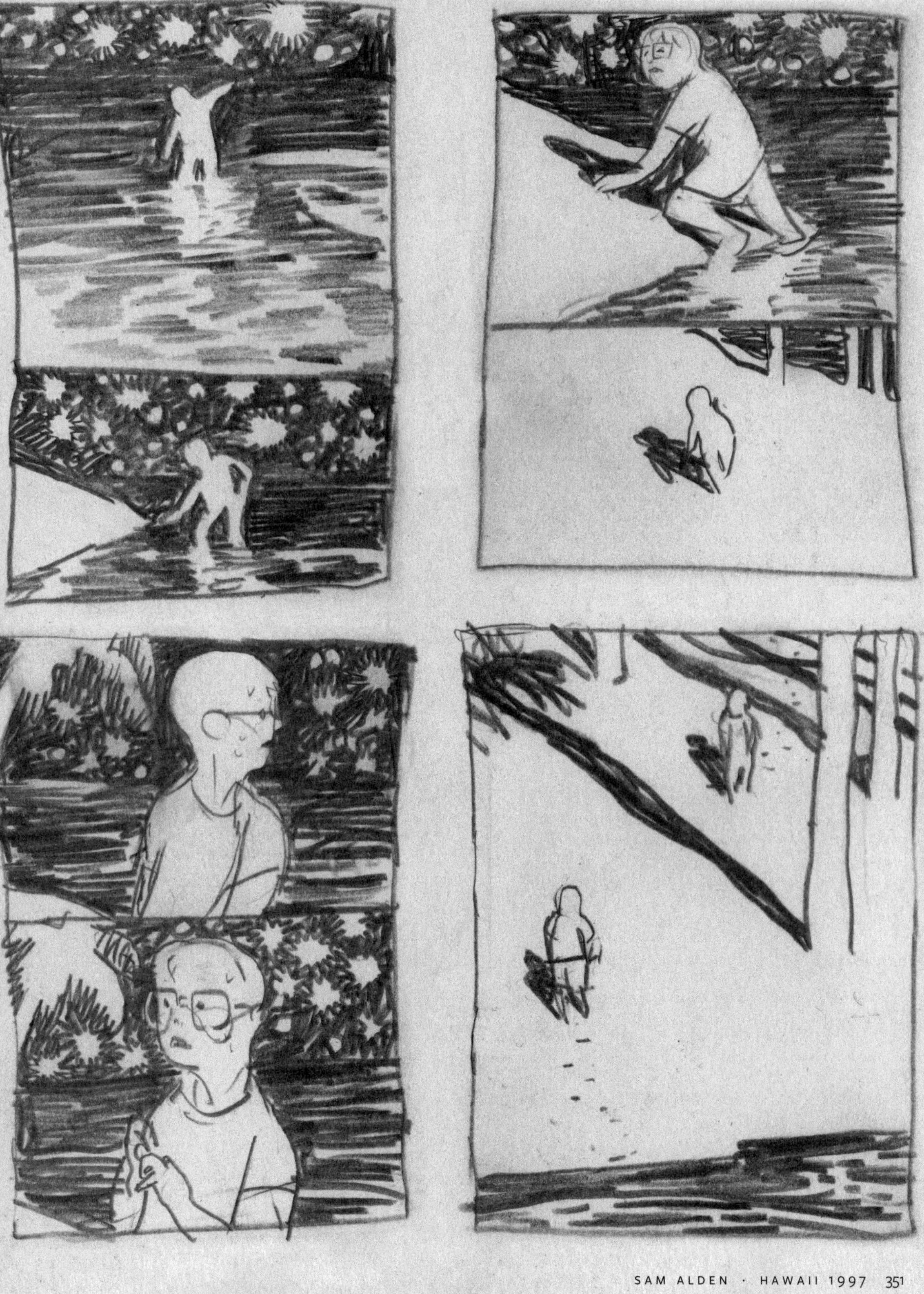

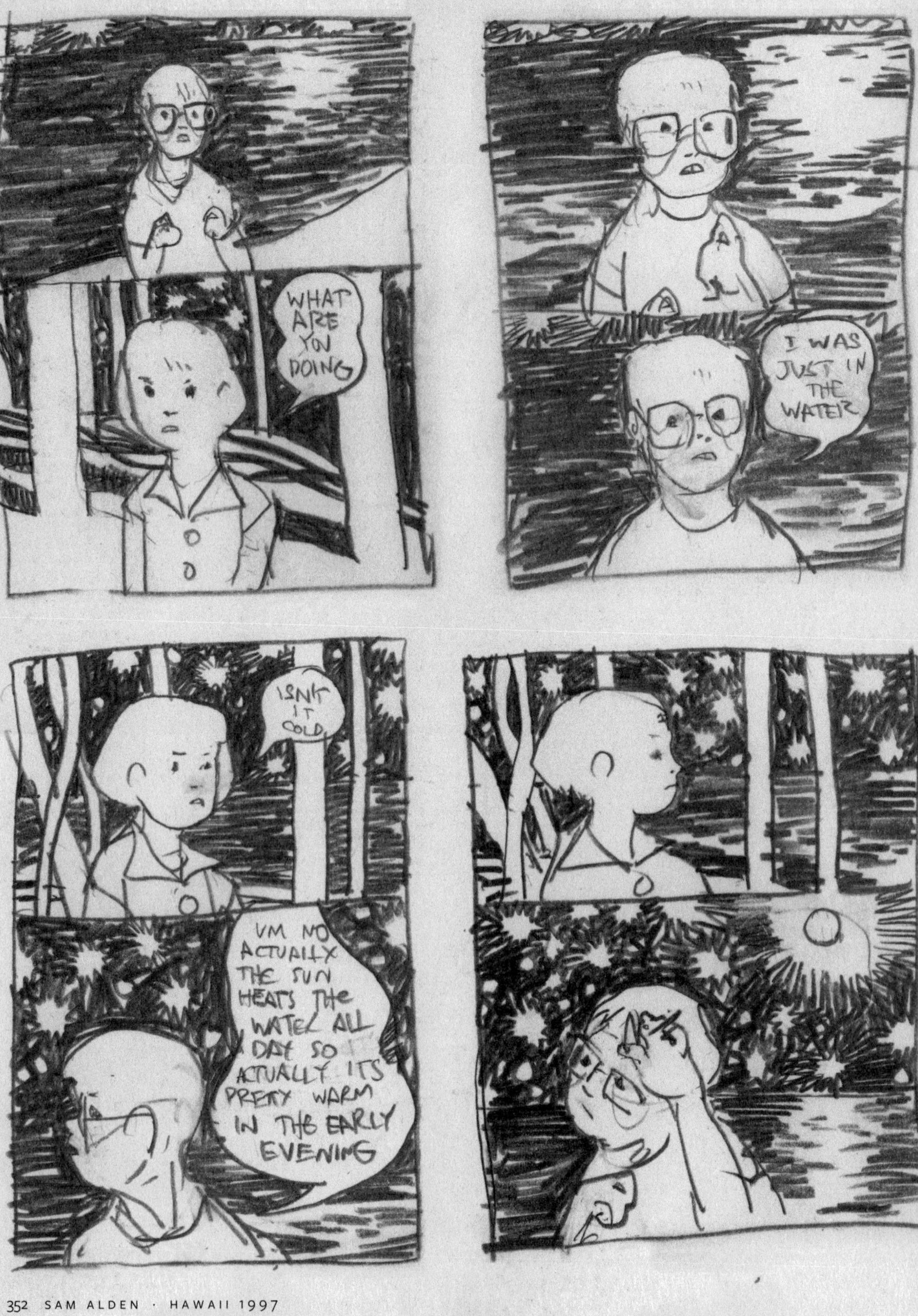
WHAT ARE YOU DOING
I WAS JUST IN THE WATER
ISNT IT COLD
UM NO ACTUALLY THE SUN HEATS THE WATER ALL DAY SO ACTUALLY ITS PRETTY WARM IN THE EARLY EVENING

STOMPED YOUR HEAD
YOU DID NOT
STILL STOMPING ON YOUR HEAD
HA
STOMPED
OW HA HA

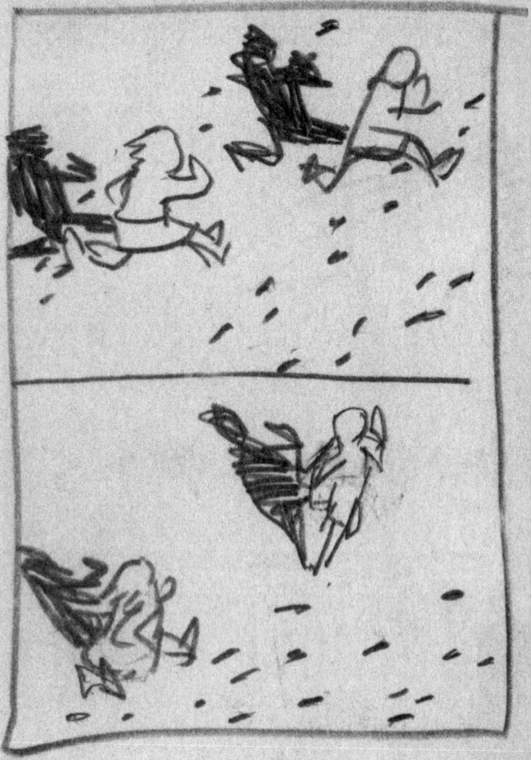

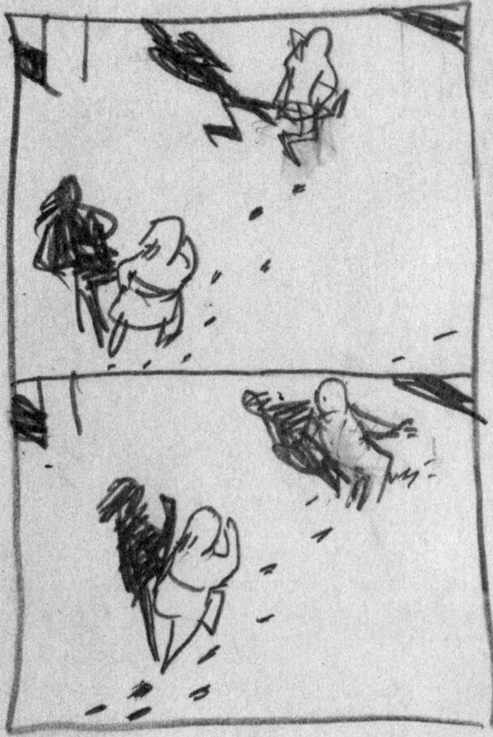

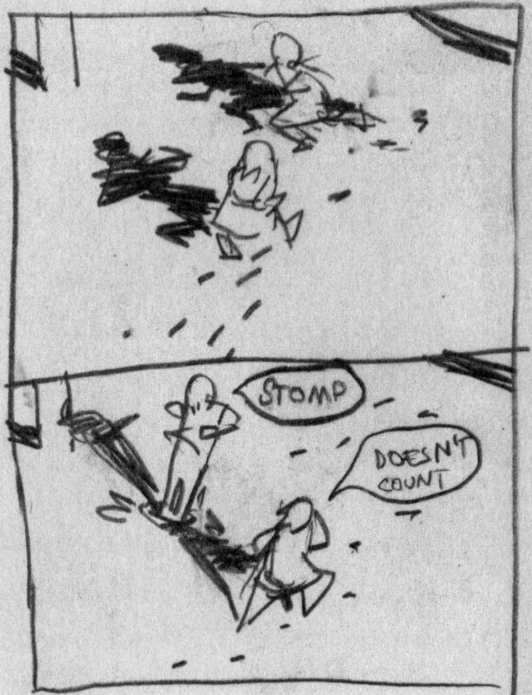
STOMP
DOESN'T COUNT

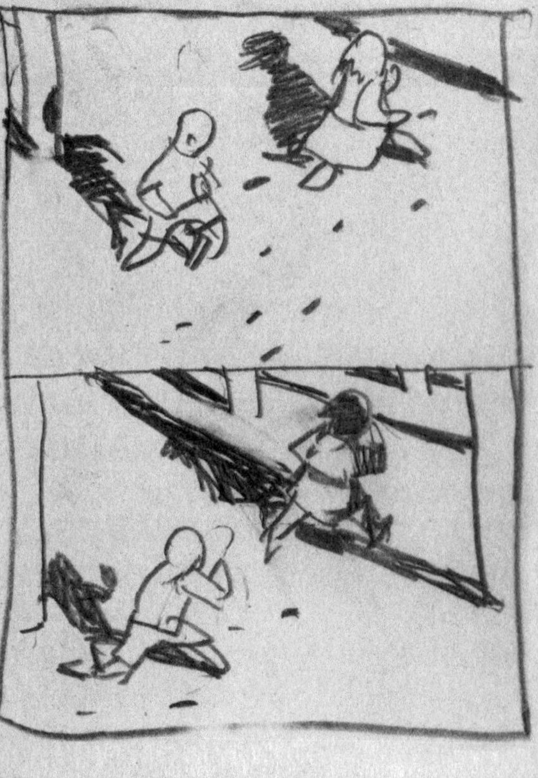

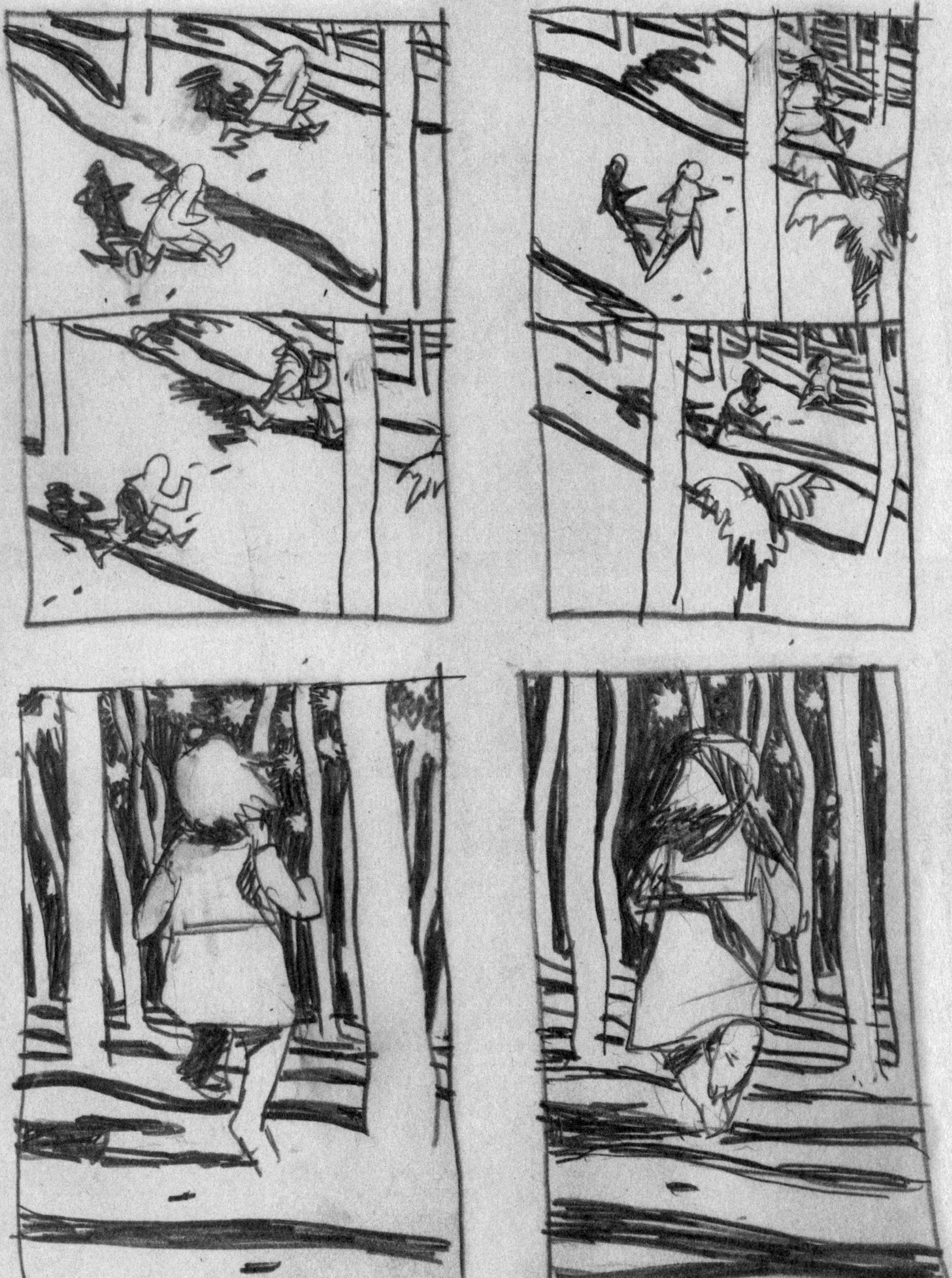

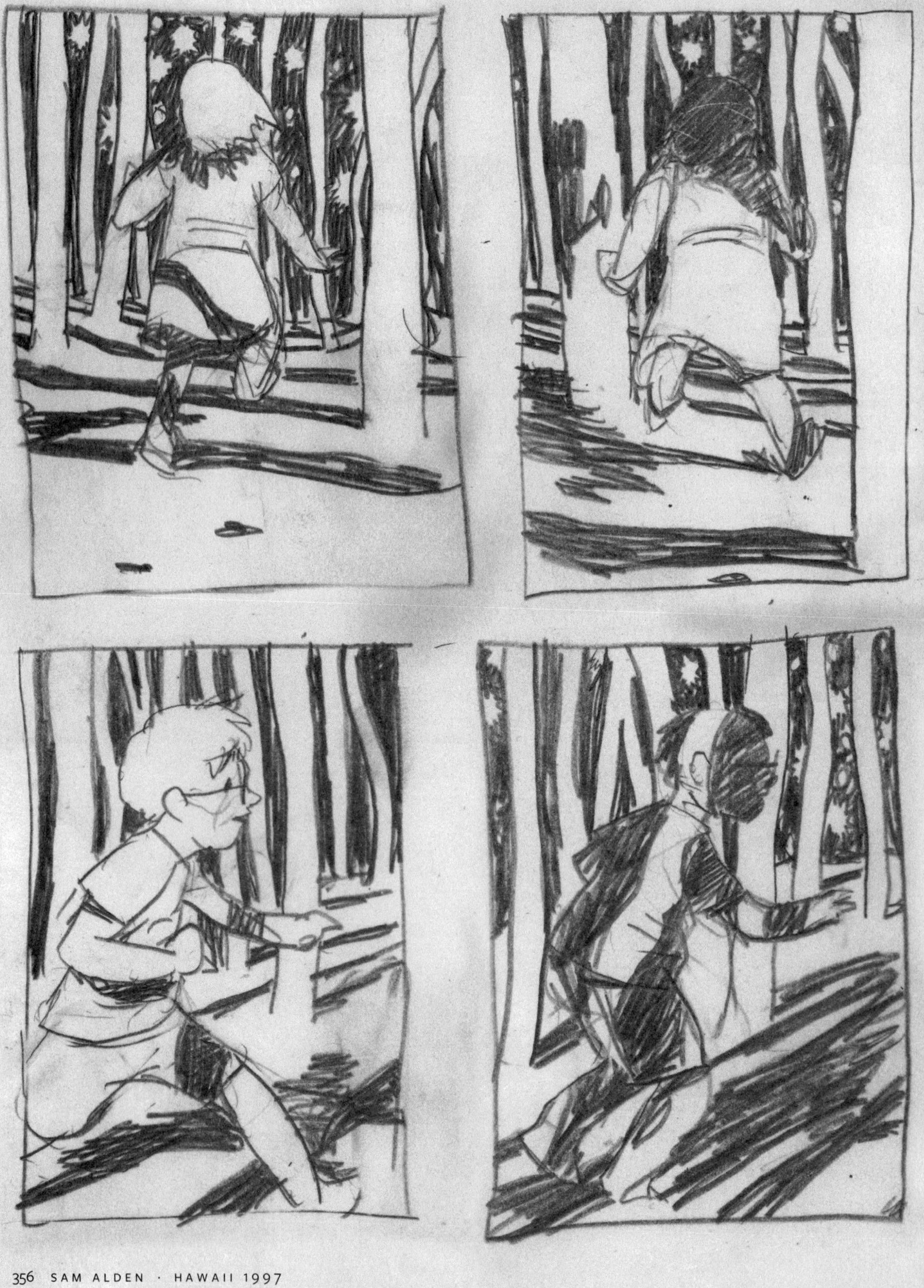

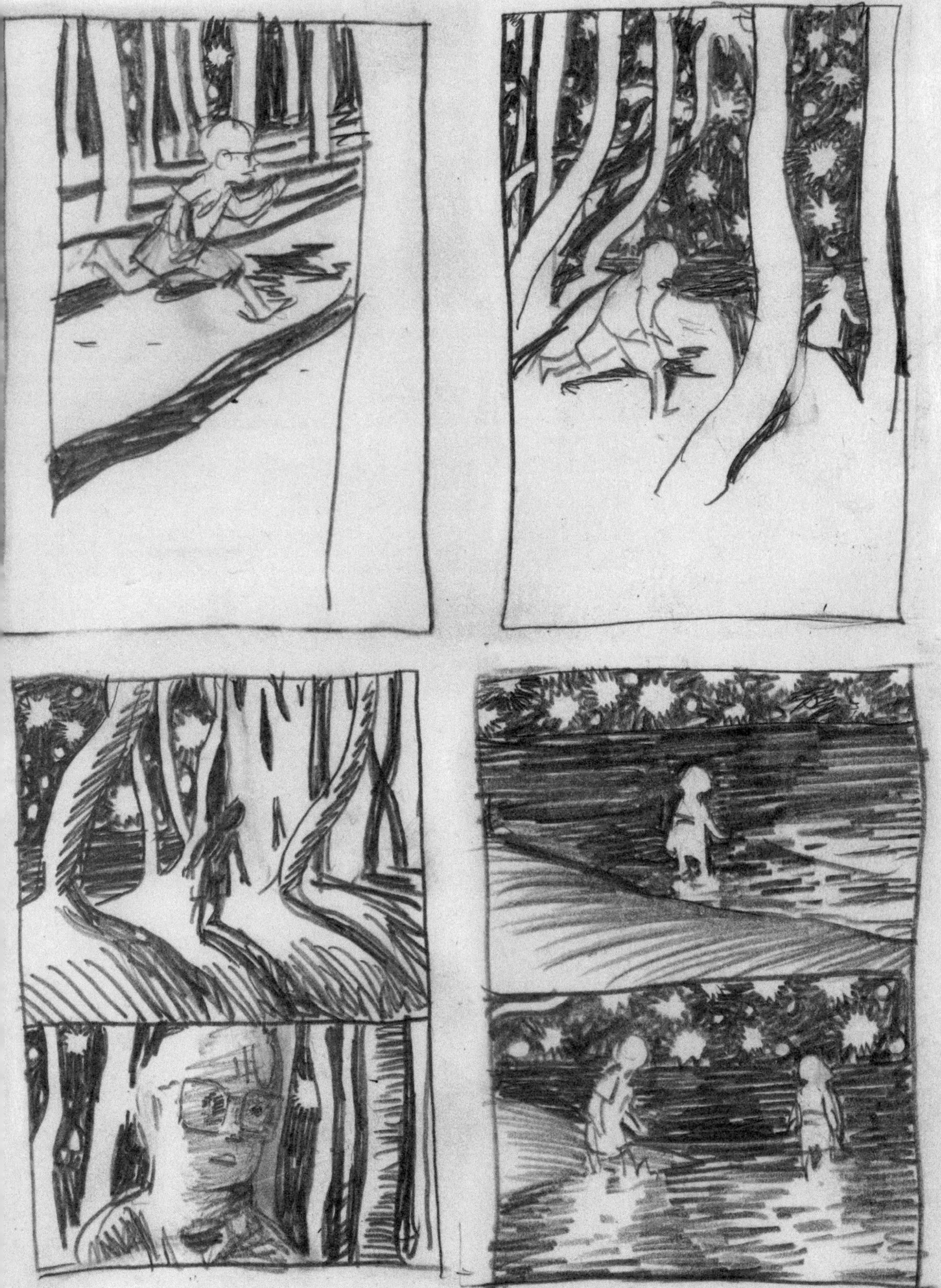

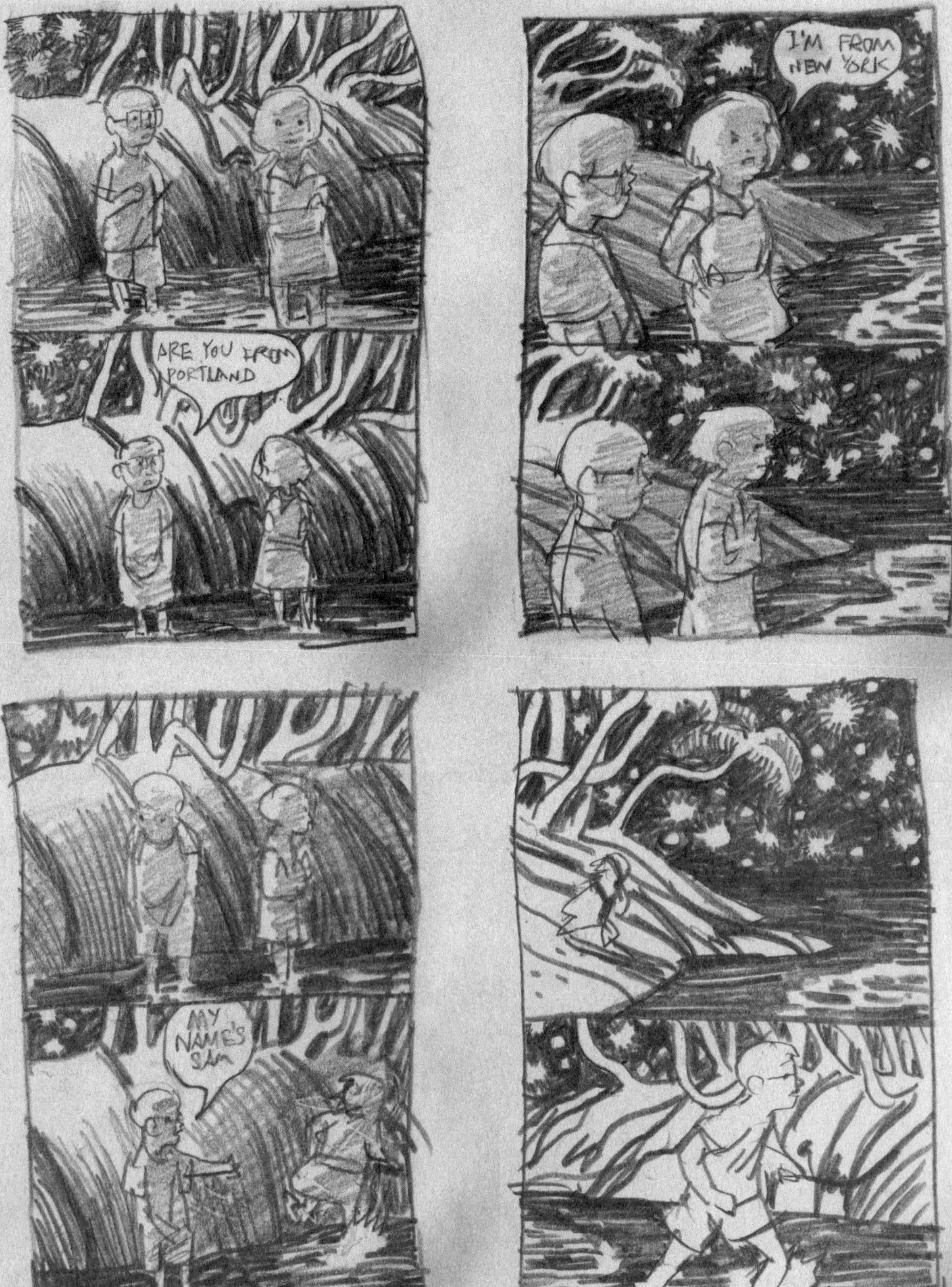
ARE YOU FROM PORTLAND
I'M FROM NEW YORK
MY NAME'S SAM

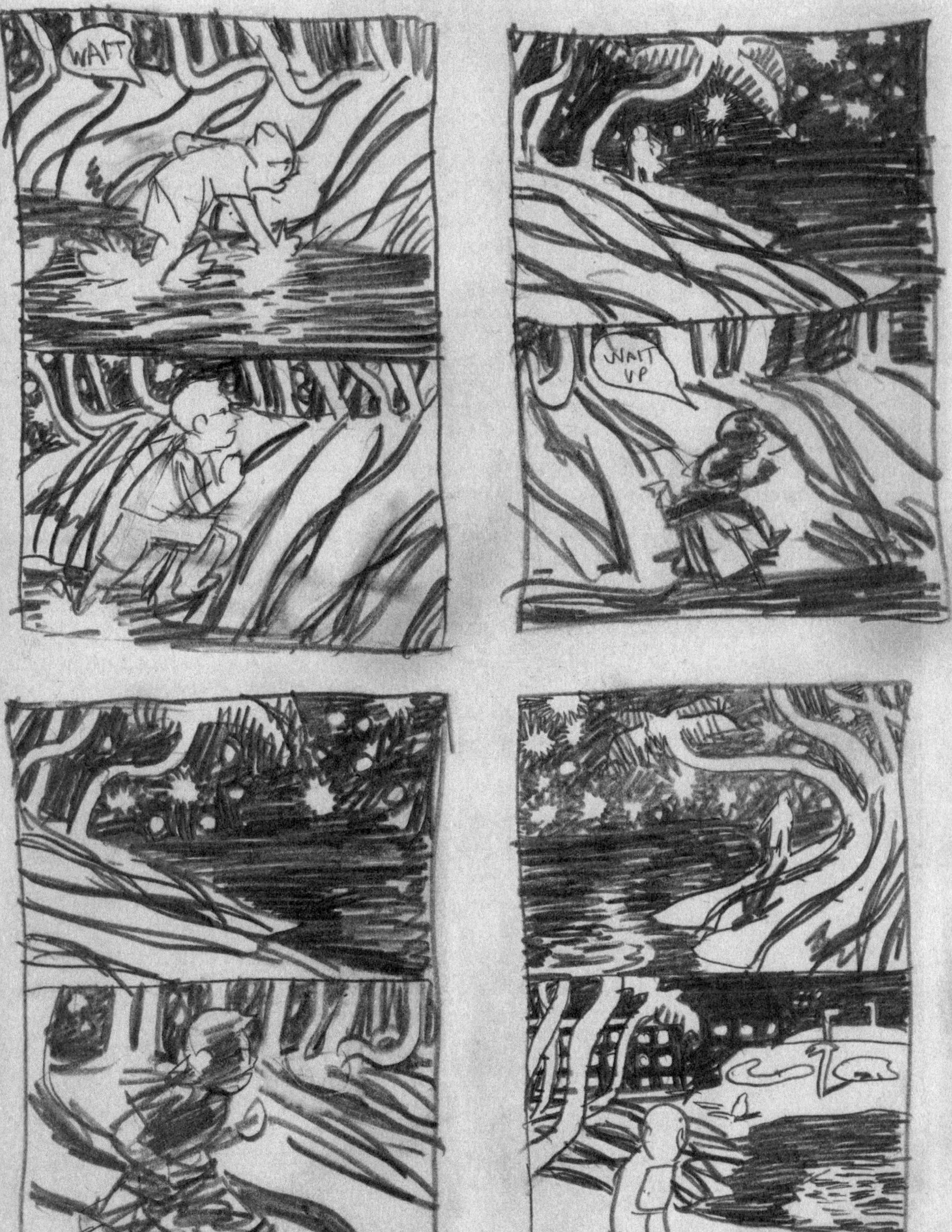
WAIT
WAIT UP

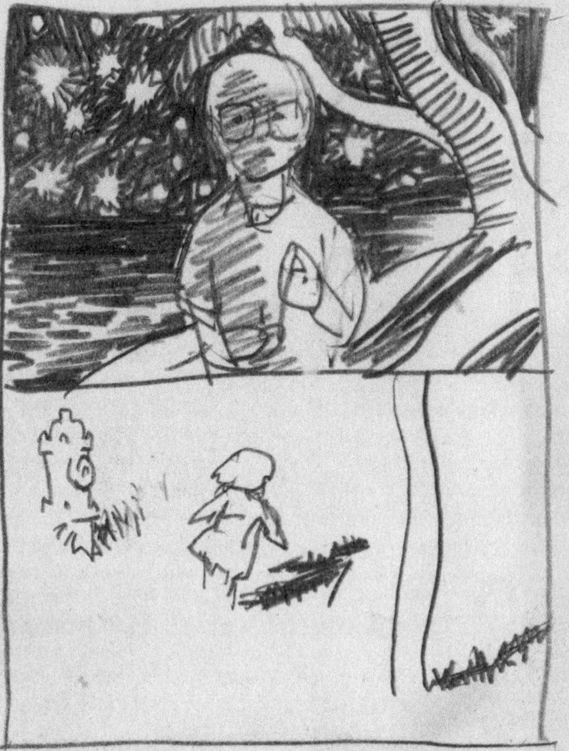

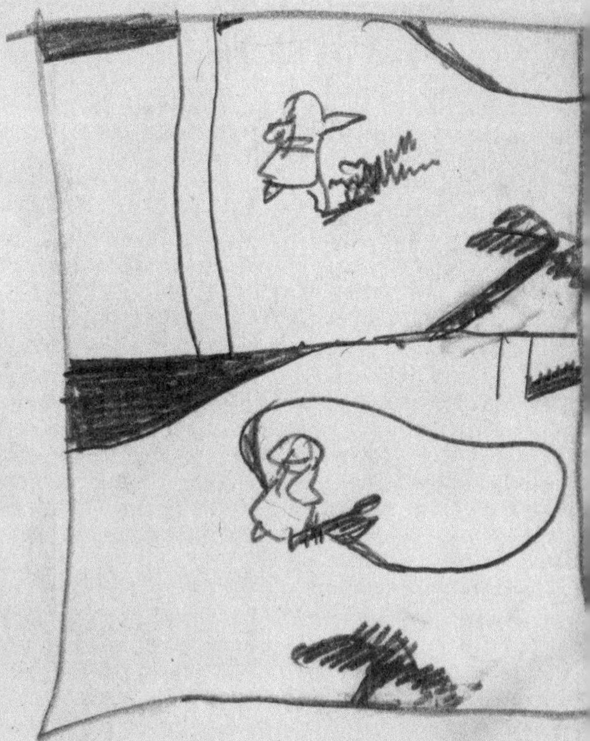

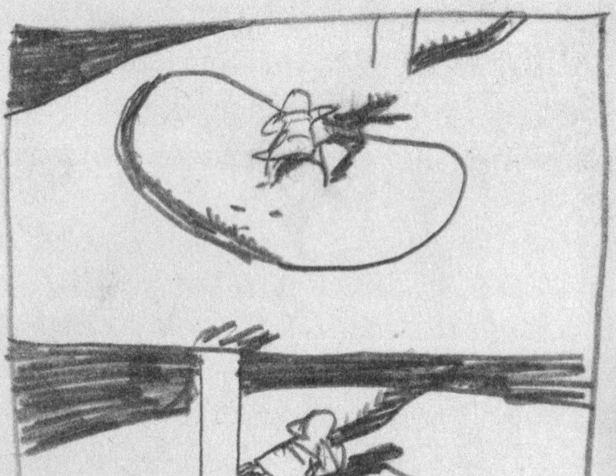

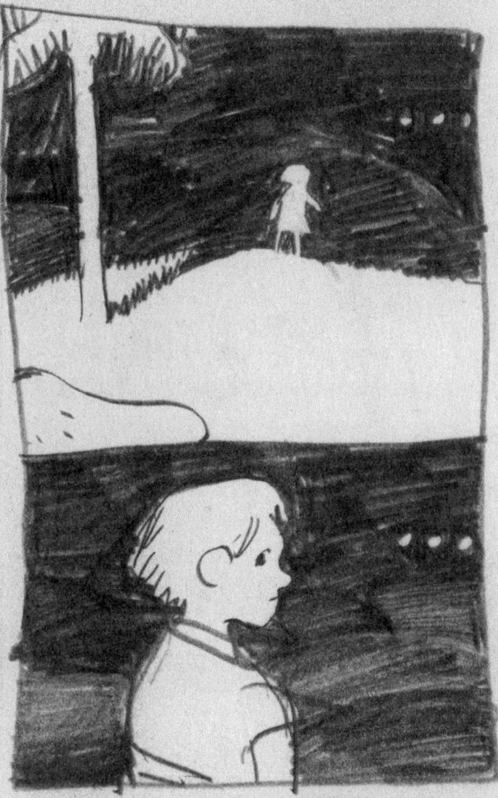

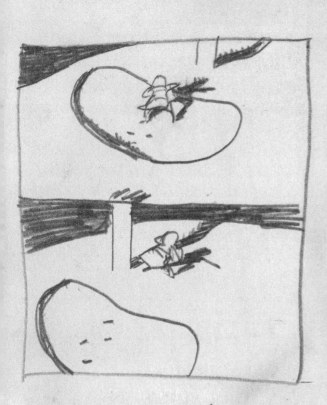

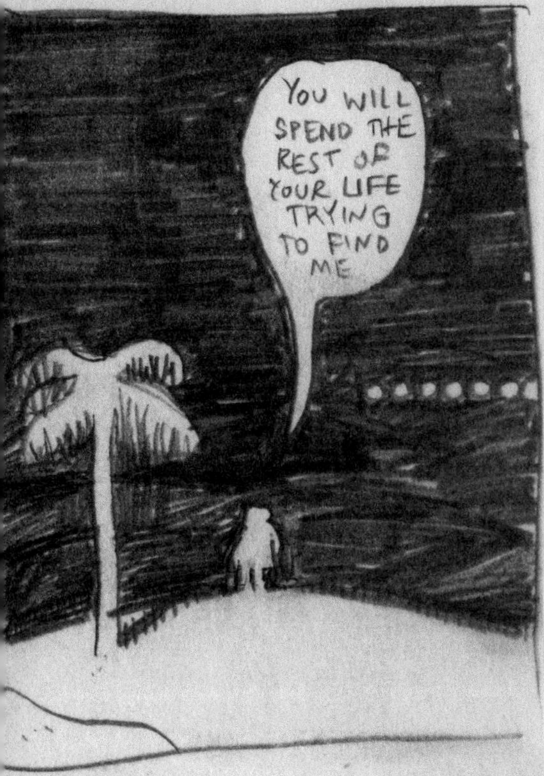
YOU WILL SPEND THE REST OF YOUR LIFE TRYING TO FIND ME

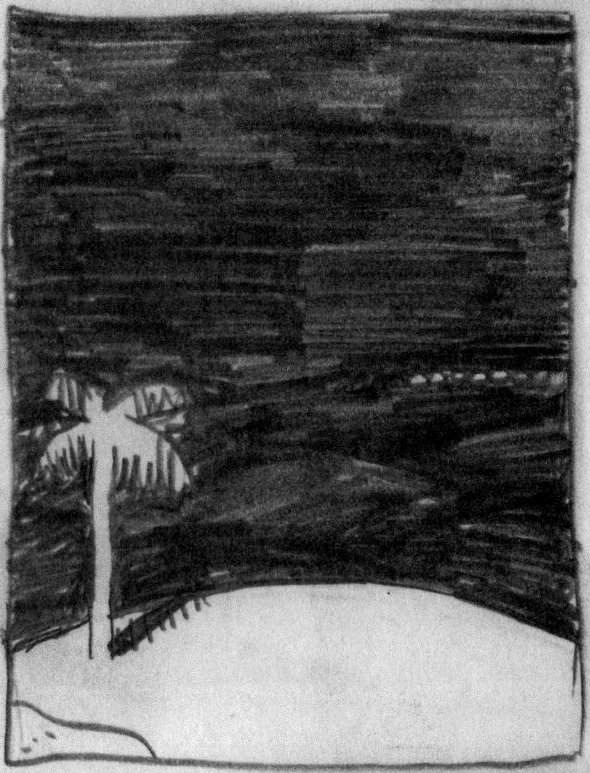

Contributors' Notes

Sam Alden was born in Portland, Oregon, in 1988. www.gingerlandcomics.com.

▪ "Hawaii 1997" was drawn almost entirely in transit, during a thirty-hour plane trip between Bologna, Italy, and my hometown of Portland. It was originally self-published as a minicomic and was later collected in *It Never Happened Again,* available from Uncivilized Books.

Isabelle Arsenault is a celebrated Canadian illustrator. Alternately working in pencil, watercolor, collage, and digital color, her sensitive style conveys a warmth and emotion that speaks equally to children and adults. She is especially well known for her children's book illustrations. Isabelle has won the prestigious Governor General's Literary Award three times, the latest being for *Jane, the Fox and Me* (Children's Literature, French—Illustration, 2013) and has twice been a finalist. The *New York Times* listed her book *Migrant* among the ten best-illustrated books of 2011, and her book *Jane, the Fox and Me* among the ten best-illustrated books of 2013. Isabelle lives in Montreal with her husband and their two sons.

▪ For this project I had total freedom from both Fanny Britt and my publisher. I decided to create a very gloomy look, using mainly gray tones for the "real" life of Hélène, the main character. When she escapes through her reading of *Jane Eyre,* I decided to use a more colorful approach, giving a dreamlike effect to these pages. This helped to create a contrast between the two worlds. Also, I decided to draw Hélène in a very "normal" way, not being necessarily chubby nor slim, just a very normal young girl. This way the reader is more drawn to her feelings and the magnificent and emotional text that Fanny wrote, creating a very subtle way to feel the bullying effects.

Andrew Aydin, an Atlanta native, currently serves in Rep. John Lewis's congressional office handling telecommunications and technology policy as well as new media. Previously, he served as communications director and press secretary during Rep. Lewis's 2008 and 2010 reelection campaigns, as district aide to Rep. John Larson (D-CT), and as special assistant to Connecticut Lt. Governor Kevin Sullivan. Andrew is a graduate of the Lovett School in Atlanta, Trinity College in Hartford, and Georgetown University in Washington, D.C., where his graduate thesis "The Comic Book That Changed the World" examined the history and global legacy of the 1957 comic book *Martin Luther King and the Montgomery Story.*

▪ I've been reading comic books since I was eight years old. John Lewis has been my congressman since I was three years old, and my boss since I was twenty-three. So when he told me about a comic book he had read during the civil rights movement, a comic that had inspired young people to stand up and speak out against segregation, I was captivated. I started learning everything I could about this little book, *Martin Luther King and the Montgomery Story*: how it was edited and approved by Dr. King himself, how it helped inspire the Greensboro sit-ins, how it found its way all across the globe and into several languages. When I suggested to Congressman Lewis that he should carry on that legacy with his own graphic novel, I was stunned that he agreed—and humbled that he asked me to write it with him. Five years later, the first book of our trilogy is real. I hope that our work can honor the legacy of those whose story we tell, and help empower a new generation to continue the struggle.

Fanny Britt is a Quebec playwright, author, and translator. Her work has been performed for the stage in Montreal, Quebec City, Ottawa, Lyon, Avignon, and Paris. Her most recent play, *Bienveillance*, earned her a Governor General's Award (one of the most prestigious literary awards in Canada) for drama in 2013. She is also a seasoned translator, having translated more than fifteen plays, mostly by contemporary playwrights, among them Martin McDonagh and Dennis Kelly. *Jane, le renard et moi* (with illustrator Isabelle Arsenault) has earned a dozen awards and prizes since its release in 2012, as well as making it to the prestigious *New York Times* Best Illustrated Children's Books list for 2013. She lives in Montreal with her family.

■ *Jane, the Fox and Me* started out as an autobiographical account of my childhood adventures. In writing the story, I wanted to revisit the feelings of isolation and sadness brought upon by bullying and social rejection, but I also wanted to tell the story of my own redemption through literature and friendship. By exploring the idea of a good book as a fantastic "it gets better" tool, I hope to have written a story of hope over despair, and of strength over fear.

Allie Brosh is a writer, illustrator, and author of the best-selling book *Hyperbole and a Half*. She began writing a blog of the same name in 2009, and currently lives in Bend, Oregon. **www. hyperboleandahalf.blogspot.com.**

■ The excerpt featured is from a piece called "Depression Part Two" that I posted on my blog in 2013, and which is a follow-up to a piece titled "Adventures in Depression" (from 2011). The full story of "Depression Part Two" is about my continued experience with depression and my attempts to cope with it and explain it to those around me, and it uses humor and illustration as a means to do so.

Nina Bunjevac is a Toronto-based comics artist and illustrator. Her comics have been published in a number of North American and European publications: *Komikaze* (Croatia), *Black* (Italy), *Stripburger* (Slovenia), *Stripolis* (Serbia), *Zone 5300* (Netherlands), *Asiatroma/Le Dernier Cri* (France), *Mineshaft* (USA), *ELQ*, *Taddle Creek*, and *Broken Pencil* (Canada). Nina's debut collection of comics, *Heartless,* came out in September 2012 with Conundrum Press (Nova Scotia, Canada). In 2013 *Heartless* won the Doug Wright Award in the Nipper category. Her second book, *Fatherland* is due to come out in the summer of 2014 with Cape Graphic/Random House. **www.ninabunjevac.com.**

■ My father was an active member of a secret Serbian nationalist and anticommunist terrorist organization, *Freedom for the Serbian Fatherland,* which operated in the USA and Canada between 1967 and 1978; he died in an explosion in August 1977 while planning an attack on the Yugoslavian consulate in Toronto's Spadina Village. "August 1977" is a metaphoric look at the last three hours of his life. The text featured in the first half of the comic comes from an actual letter written by my mother to my father; the second half from a letter written by me, twenty-four years later.

Charles Burns is a cartoonist and illustrator who was born in Washington, DC, in 1955. His first significant work appeared in *RAW* magazine in the early 1980s, and he has since gone on to work on a wide range of comics and projects. His illustrations have appeared in *The New Yorker*, *Rolling Stone*, the *New York Times Magazine,* and starting in 2003 he became the regular cover artist for

The Believer. His books include *Skin Deep* (2001, Fantagraphics Books), *Black Hole* (2005, Pantheon Books), *X'ed Out* (2010, Pantheon Books), and *The Hive* (2012, Pantheon Books).

▪ This is an excerpt from *The Hive.* *The Hive* is the second in a series of three books that begins with *X'ed Out* and concludes in *Sugar Skull.* This selection focuses on the early days of Doug and Sarah's bumpy, romantic relationship.

Victor Cayro is a self-taught subhuman that attempts to create art and comics. Void of mystique, he loves to cook and empathize with your pain and joys. He also loves to laugh. There is nothing more to this simple beast. Favorite podcast: the Duncan Trussel Family Hour. Favorite movies: still *Robocop*, *A Better Tomorrow* part 1 and 2, *Akira*, and Kurosawa's *Ikiru.* *special nod to T. Miike's *Graveyard of Honor** **www.bald-eagles.tumblr.com**.

▪ Our deplorable antihero plunges phallus first into the manufactured virtual reality provided by his beguiling omnisexual dark spiritual guide/hijacker, force-feeding equal parts truthful enlightenment and the keys to deeper lower-self imprisonment. The protagonist, at the behest of the Incu-Sucu'bus amalgam, must rally the inner strength to become everything he should hate. A complete deceiver entity is at work. Based on innumerable true stories, look into the mirror on mushrooms and knowingly concur, plze n' thnx.

R. Crumb was born in Philadelphia in 1943 and grew up reading and drawing comic books. **Aline Kominsky-Crumb** was born on Long Island, New York. She had an active interest in art and painting since childhood but didn't begin drawing comics until she discovered "underground" comics around 1970 and saw that this medium could be used to tell highly personal stories. R. Crumb began drawing "underground" comics in 1966–67 after a brief career in commercial art.

▪ Aline and Robert met in San Francisco in late 1971 and began drawing collaborative comics in the fall of 1972, all the while pursuing their individual work. They have continued to do collaborations off and on over the years, right up to the present. They completed two issues of *Dirty Laundry Comics* together, two issues of *Self Loathing Comics*, several stories for *Weirdo* and several strips for *The New Yorker*, as well as for a French women's magazine, *Causette.* Two books of their collaborations have been published, *The Complete Dirty Laundry* (1992), and *Drawn Together* (2012). They now live in the South of France, where old artists go to die.

Erin Curry grew up in a house her father built surrounded by art her mother made. Makers continue to signal a sense of home. Her artwork reflects her fascination (and frustration) with the inadequacies of language. She uses drawing, sculpture, and textiles with allusions to writing and storytelling to relay longing and lostness. Sails of traced newspapers, pools of smocked silk, and constellations of freckles emerge from her studio. The Sequential Artists Workshop and Tom Hart guided her foray into comics. Now she's a SAW board member and contributor to the *Abstract Comics* blog. Currently she's an MFA candidate at the University of Florida. For more work, visit **www.erincurry.com**.

▪ My comics tend toward nonnarrative abstraction, and I find the work through the process of creating it. In *Ambient Air*, whiteout tape, burst bubbles, and asemic writing imply fractured and vague dialogue, while the layers of translucent Mylar emphasize anticipation and memory. A moment of serendipity shaped this work—as I settled in to begin, a tiny bottle of bubbles tumbled out of a friend's bag. Bubbles and word balloons collided and I persuaded him to give them to me. The circles in this excerpt mark the result.

Michael DeForge was born in 1987 and works as a cartoonist in Toronto, Ontario. His comic *Lose* is serialized annually by Koyama Press and has been collected in book form as *A Body Beneath*. His graphic novel *Ant Colony* was published by Drawn and Quarterly. **www.kingtrash.com**.

- "Canadian Royalty" is part of an ongoing series of semirelated stories about Canadian life.

G. W. Duncanson is a native of Yonkers, New York. After studying filmmaking, he worked in local TV journalism and currently plows the fields as a cinematographer, video editor, and sound engineer. His auspicious debut as an artist happened to coincide with the aftermath of Hurricane Sandy when, without electricity for a week, he was inspired to try his hand at making comics. His prolific pace has resulted in over 2,250 panels of unique, painterly comics in 2013 alone. Not bad for a first year. **cash-money-cartoons.tumblr.com**.

- The pages featured here were originally published on my blog. They are improvised ink drawings and were the starting point for the self-published book *Microscope* I released last year in an edition of twenty copies.

Theo Ellsworth lives with his family in Montana. He is the author of *Capacity*, *Sleeper Car*, and *The Understanding Monster*, all published by Secret Acres in Brooklyn, New York. He's also self-published numerous art 'zines including *Imaginary Homework*, *Thought Cloud Shrines*, and *Logic Storm*. A story from *Sleeper Car* was included in *The Best American Comics 2010*. *The Understanding Monster—Book One* was a 2012 Lynd Ward Honor book, and he was awarded an Artist Innovation award from the Montana Arts Council in 2014. He is the house artist for the London-based record labels Space Cadets and Astral Industries. He shows his woodcut art pieces in galleries from time to time and he likes to read comics. **theoellsworth.blogspot.com**.

- Izadore is in the middle of an Extreme Identity Crisis, but he's receiving emergency assistance. The excerpt begins at a very important moment for Izadore. In the pages leading up to this, he accidentally jumps into the head of a mummy who has just been resurrected. He feels an odd, overwhelming sense of shame in having done this, but no harm is done. A Phantom Lizard and a Multi-Dimensional Robot help re-separate him from the Mummy's head fairly quickly, and the mummy runs off through the house. At the exact moment that Izadore experiences shame, his missing piece shows itself: a toy suddenly breaks into a nervous run while manifesting a plate of realistic food. The Phantom Lizard tries to encourage Izadore's missing piece to sit and eat, and the Multi-Dimensional Robot begins to show him live footage of an old man sleeping. Izadore is shocked at the sight of himself and his head gets away from him.

C.F. is a Providence-based artist and musician. He has exhibited in New York, Los Angeles, Providence, Athens, Tokyo, and Switzerland. His books include *Powr Mastrs*, vols. 1–3, *Sediment*, and *Mere*. **www.freecf.com**.

- This comic is about putting things in perspective and gaining presence of mind. It was made for the *New York Times* blog about anxiety.

Brandon Graham is an American living in Vancouver, British Columbia, with bad-dude Marian Churchland (who also writes and draws). His comics include *King City*, *Multiple Warheads*, *Escalator*, *Perverts of the Unknown*, *Pillow Fight*, *Prophet* (which he writes with art from some fantastic artists), and *8house*. He has sleeping pajamas and work pajamas. **royalboiler.wordpress.com**.

- I drew these pages while another book of mine, *King City*, was on hold while a deal was worked out between my old publisher and my newer publisher. So *Warheads* was a nice escape from that. I was trying to think about how color could work in the story. The way the mug reads water, I tried to give each vehicle its own color of sound effect—trying to use color the way the story of *Peter and the Wolf* uses a song for each character. I had a lot of fun thinking up backstories for everything the characters interact with. I imagine a lot of the ideas I had will never make it onto the pages, but it's so much fun to dig into that stuff.

Tom Hart is a cartoonist and teacher and executive director of the Sequential Artists Workshop, a school for comics and graphic novels in Gainesville, Florida. He has been publishing comics since the early '90s and has been nominated for the Eisner, the Ignatz, and the Harvey awards. He lives with his wife, the cartoonist Leela Corman, and their daughter, Molly Rose. **www.tomhart.net**.

▪ Printed as a photocopied minicomic during the development of a larger book about the loss of our daughter in 2011. The finished book, *Rosalie Lightning,* will be published by St. Martins Press. My many gracious thanks to everyone who helped us during this time.

Gilbert Hernandez grew up in Oxnard, California, in the 1960s, an avid reader of comics at an early age. All types of comics were enjoyed, from superheroes to kids' comics to horror comics to war comics to *Mad* magazine to sci-fi to . . . everything except romance comics. Gilbert, with younger brother Jaime, would fix that in creating *Love and Rockets,* romance comics for the reader who doesn't like romance comics. Gilbert is most known for his Palomar series in *Love and Rockets,* about the people of a small village in Latin America. *Love and Rockets* has continued going strong for over thirty years.

▪ "Marble Season" is an idea I've been cooking up for more than several years now. I've always wanted to do a valentine to childhood without exploiting the heavy trauma so many kids go through. I wanted a "childhood lite" story about (mostly) the fun part of being a kid. When we're ten years old and life is good, we're the rulers of the universe. Our only problem (outside of bullies and homework) is deciding what fun to have next and how to keep from getting bored. I'm happy with how the book came out.

Jaime Hernandez: I have been been making comics professionally for over thirty years, starting with *Love and Rockets*. I've done other comic and illustration work, but my work in *Love and Rockets* will always be the most personal to me, and therefore my best work. I can't think of a better job.

▪ In this story, teen-aged Tonta spends a weekend at her older sister Vivian's home and is exposed to the seedy underworld in which the fireballish Vivian dwells. Sometimes writing characters with little or no conscience is easier and more satisfying because they open up more story opportunity, but the real trick is to keep from turning it into bad genre fiction. Succeeding, of course, is a whole other animal.

Gerald Jablonski: Drawing comics has been a lifelong hobby. I enjoy thinking up crazy stories to illustrate. Coloring the comics is the most fun part of the process.

▪ *Cryptic Wit* 3 is a self-published print-on-demand comic book, available from Indyplanet.com.

Ben Katchor's latest book, *Hand-Drying in America and Other Stories* (Pantheon) is a collection of strips from his series in *Metropolis Magazine* on the subjects of design and architecture. He teaches at Parsons The New School for Design in New York City. **www.katchor.com**.

▪ Through these picture-stories, I aim to incite my readers to take direct action in dismantling the military-industrial complex and world banking system. For those readers who end up in prison, I hope my work will provide a moment of aesthetic pleasure during their allotted reading time.

Miriam Katin: I was born in Budapest in 1942. Among my earliest memories is a book my father brought home. A hardcover with empty white pages. I started to draw. It seems to me that it is that book I am still trying to fill. In 1957 we immigrated to Israel. The Army service was my true education as I never returned to school. Throughout years of marriage and raising children, I was always drawing with great passion. This led to work in background design at Jumbo Pictures, MTV, and Disney in New York. I discovered comics for myself at age 63. www.miriamkatin.com.

▪ Most of my comics are the stories my mother told me about the war, our family, and my memories after the war. At some point I felt that I had finished with those subjects until I had to face a great trauma. My son decided to live in Berlin. It was a shock for my Holocaust-centric existence. I started to draw and write and collect pictures and articles; I surrounded myself with these and decided to do a book. I needed this process to deal with the pain and fear. To face the Germany of today. The book is dedicated to the past, present, and the new Berlin.

Aidan Koch is an artist living and working in Sebastopol, California. She received her BFA in Illustration from the Pacific NW College of Art in Portland, Oregon, in 2009. She has released several books including Oregon Book Award nominee, *The Whale*, Xeric Award winner, *The Blonde Woman*, the anthology *Astral Talk*, and a small book of travel drawings, *Field Studies*. She has exhibited work in galleries in Antwerp, Austin, New York, and Portland. www.aidankoch.com.

▪ "Blue Period" is a meditation on color and consciousness. It explores perception through the abstraction of simple elements and actions to encompass the reader in contemplation; "What's the point you reach where everything becomes blue?" "Blue Period" originally appeared in the second issue of *Sonatina* edited by Scott Longo.

Seattle artist **David Lasky** has been writing and drawing comics for over twenty years. His earliest success was a nine-page mini-adaptation of James Joyce's *Ulysses* (self-published). In the '90s he was known for the solo comic *Boom Boom*, and then collaborated with Greg Stump on the Harvey-nominated *Urban Hipster*. His stories have appeared in countless anthologies over the years, including *Kramers Ergot* and The Best American Comics. With writer Frank M. Young, he cocreated two graphic novels: *Oregon Trail: The Road to Destiny* and *The Carter Family: Don't Forget This Song* (for which they won an Eisner Award in 2013). www.carterfamilycomix.blogspot.com.

▪ This chapter from the book is a re-creation of a Carter Family concert as remembered by June Carter Cash in her writings. Because the original Carter Family group was never captured on film, it was especially important to Frank and me to present a complete performance. They usually played in schoolhouses and were often lit by lamps from the local coal mines, as shown here. I referenced every visual detail I could, from the car to the clothing to the lamps. Sean Michael Robinson kindly assisted by inking the architecture and all that cross-hatching.

John Lewis has been an icon of the civil rights movement since his college days in Nashville, organizing sit-ins and participating in the first Freedom Rides. As chairman of the Student Nonviolent Coordinating Committee (SNCC), he was the youngest speaker at the 1963 March on Washington and a leader of the 1965 Selma-Montgomery March (known as "Bloody Sunday"), where police brutality spurred national outrage and hastened passage of the Voting Rights Act of 1965. He has represented Georgia in Congress for over twenty-five years and recently received the Presidential

Medal of Freedom. Following his previous award-winning books *Walking with the Wind* and *Across that Bridge*, he has joined cowriter Andrew Aydin and artist Nate Powell for the new graphic novel *March: Book One*, a #1 *New York Times* bestseller.

▪ It has been a tremendous joy to work with these two talented young men, Andrew Aydin and Nate Powell. Nate has taken our words and made them come alive on the page, made the story so real you can almost taste it. So I feel deeply grateful to Andrew for bringing this idea to me more than five years ago, and for not giving up or giving in. On this journey, the three of us have become like a band of brothers, a circle of trust. I'll never forget reading the comic book *Martin Luther King and the Montgomery Story* in Nashville in 1958. It is my hope that, with history as our guide, *March* will bring the lessons and the tools of the civil rights movement to a new generation and inspire them to carry on the struggle to create "the beloved community," a world community at peace with itself.

Ted May is a humor cartoonist living in St. Louis, Missouri. His work has appeared in *Kramers Ergot*, *Vice*, and *Bart Simpson Comics*, as well as his own *Injury Comics*. One of May's comics (in collaboration with writer Jeff Wilson) was nominated for an Eisner Award in 2013.

▪ "Dimensions" is a story from my most recent book, *Men's Feelings*. The book comprises short, unrelated strips. These are vignettes that I found compelling but that didn't fit into any larger narrative. "Dimensions" is probably the best example of what I was trying to accomplish with the book. I wrote it because I needed a closer for the volume that had a little heft to it. And to pad out my page count.

Onsmith is an artist and cartoonist living in Chicago. His comics, prints, and illustrations have appeared in numerous publications such as *Black Eye*, *Hotwire Comics*, *Study Group Magazine*, *The Graphic Canon*, *An Anthology of Graphic Fiction*, and many others. *Diminished Returns*, a collection of selected works, will be published by Yam Books. **www.onsmith.tumblr.com**.

▪ My father is a retired factory worker. I also worked in a factory for a while, machining metal pipe fittings. In the small town in Oklahoma where I grew up, you're lucky to get a job like that. I remember stories of people getting badly injured and even killed in these factories. Labor, tragedy, and marginalized people have been focal points in many of my comics and drawings. Physical degradation is shown here (in absurd ways), but I also wanted to imply the mental and emotional toll this type of work takes as well.

Ed Piskor cut his teeth drawing *American Splendor* strips for Harvey Pekar. They went on to create two graphic novels in collaboration, *Macedonia* (2005, Villard) and *The Beats* (2007, Hill and Wang). Piskor then went on to create his own comics, the first being *Wizzywig* (2012, Top Shelf). He now does *Hip Hop Family Tree* full-time, published by Fantagraphics. **www.edpiskor.com**.

▪ The *Hip Hop Family Tree* series is an exercise in reconstructing the culture. This strip features the humble origins of the rap group that goes on to become Public Enemy. Anecdotes pulled from interviews, books, and magazine articles were compiled to write the narrative.

Nate Powell (b. 1978, Little Rock, Arkansas) began self-publishing at age fourteen, and graduated from School of Visual Arts in New York in 2000. His work includes the *March* trilogy with Congressman John Lewis, Rick Riordan's *The Lost Hero*, *Any Empire*, the Eisner Award–winning graphic novel *Swallow Me Whole*, *The Silence of Our Friends*, and *The Year of the Beasts*. From 1999 to 2009, Powell worked full-time providing support for adults with developmental disabilities alongside his cartooning efforts. He managed the DIY punk record label Harlan Records and performed in the bands Soophie Nun Squad and Universe. He lives in Bloomington, Indiana. **www. seemybrotherdance.org**.

▪ This collaboration has introduced several unique narrative challenges on the visual end. The balance between accurate, responsible depiction of well-documented historical content, while finding space to maneuver freely within the script, focusing and expanding on powerful personal sequences, has helped give *March* a rich life of its own. I've learned to trust my own narrative instincts while respecting the sovereignty of a script rooted in Congressman Lewis's decades-long strength as an oral storyteller. The three of us have grown quite close throughout the process, both creatively and personally. It's a deep honor every day to be a part of it all.

After making xeroxed minicomics throughout the 1990s, **Ron Regé, Jr.**'s first book, the unconsciously channeled shaman's journey, *Skibber Bee~Bye,* was first published in 2000. In 2013 his comics and illustrations appeared in the *New York Times,* the *Pitchfork Review, Lucky Peach, Los Angeles Review of Books, Arthur,* and *Abraxas,* as well as on book covers for Bill Cotter's novel *The Parallel Apartments* and *The Treasury of Mini Comics.* **ronregejr.tumblr.com**.

▪ This selection from *The Cartoon Utopia* is adapted from lecture notes for one of the *Magic Classes* taught by Maja D'Aoust every second Sunday of the month at the Annie Besant Theosophical Hall in Beachwood Canyon, Los Angeles.

Sam Sharpe writes, draws, and self-publishes the comic series *Viewotron.* He grew up in Madison, Wisconsin, and studied film/animation/video at the Rhode Island School of Design. He lives in Chicago, where he works as an illustrator and teaching artist. **www.viewotron.com**.

▪ This is an excerpt from a forty-page story titled "Mom," which originally appeared in the second issue of my comic series *Viewotron.* I'm sixteen years old in the beginning of this excerpt. The events in this story are true and the dialogue is as close as I could recall to what was said. No dialogue was invented, but the conversations have been edited down significantly to make the storytelling as efficient as possible.

Mark Siegel has written and illustrated several award-winning picture books. *Sailor Twain* is his first adult graphic novel. Siegel is also the founder and editorial director of Macmillan's graphic novel imprint First Second. **www.sailortwain.com**.

▪ The full *Sailor Twain* is four hundred pages of intertwined love stories, set in 1887 in New York's Gilded Age, mostly aboard a giant steamboat called the *Lorelei.* I was immersed in Conrad, Melville, and Twain when I started; I was also riding a train along the Hudson River every day. Research unearthed all kinds of mysteries surrounding New York's great waterway. The mermaid theme was drawn from personal experience.

Canadian artist **Fiona Staples** has worked in comics since 2006. In 2010 she was nominated for the Best Penciller/Inker Eisner Award for her work on the DC horror series *North 40,* and in 2011 she won a Joe Shuster award for her cover work on titles such as *Mystery Society, Superman/Batman,* and *DV8.* She has also provided covers for books ranging from *Archie* and *Josie & the Pussycats* to *Red Sonja, Criminal Macabre,* and *Alien.*

▪ These pages open with a flashback within a flashback—we're taken to Marko's childhood, where his parents are showing him a magical re-creation of an ancient battle. We hop from planet to planet a lot in this series, so I often use color to help identify locations. Marko's home moon is the only setting with a yellow sky, for instance. From here we snap back to the present, where adult Marko and his family are on board their wooden rocket ship, orbiting a crumbling planet. I generally try to make their rocket tree look homey and safe, but here the red gas cloud outside is (hopefully) hinting at danger.

Raina Telgemeier is the #1 *New York Times* bestselling author of *Drama* and *Smile*, and the recipient of a Stonewall Book Award Honor, a Will Eisner Award for Best Publication for Teens, and a Boston Globe–Horn Book Honor. Raina also adapted and illustrated the Baby-sitters Club graphic novels. Her forthcoming graphic memoir, *Sisters*, a companion to *Smile*, will be published in 2014 by Scholastic/Graphix. She lives in Astoria, New York. **www.goraina.com.**

▪ *Drama* was inspired by my days in middle school and high school musical theater, although I was never part of stage crew—there's plenty of media that focuses on performers, but not enough about behind-the-scenes people! I had a lot of fun developing Callie and her middle school life and friends, but including gay characters in the mix seemed to really irk a few parents. I guess they've never spent time with a group of young theater enthusiasts! Lucky for me, plenty of other readers connected with the story, and I've gotten some very touching and wonderful emails, as well as a Stonewall Book Honor—the highest award in LGBTQ literature!

Richard Thompson's cartoons once roamed the land in great herds. Vast flocks of them darkened the skies, like graphic dodo birds (if dodo birds could fly). Today, however, sightings are rare and many believe Richard Thompson cartoons are extinct, or worse, imaginary. We can only hope the work included in the present collection boosts Thompson's reputation, let alone his corporeal reality.

For almost thirty years, Richard Thompson's drawings have appeared on slick paper in such magazines as *The New Yorker, National Geographic,* the *Atlantic, Mother Jones, U.S. News & World Report,* and *Yankee,* but his favorite stuff, the daily comic *Cul de Sac* and the weekly cartoon *Richard's Poor Almanac,* were printed on good old cheap newsprint. **richardspooralmanac.blogspot.com.**

▪ This selection of *Cul de Sac* dailies is from the final week, when we were running repeats because I was unable to draw. It's a normal week, nothing unusual. We get a glimpse of Petey dealing with his bête noire, Ernesto, and we see Alice not at her best. The Sunday strip, the last to run in papers as a "new" strip, is possibly my favorite strip of all. It has drama, pathos, comedy, misunderstanding, and cats, and if that don't say it all I don't know what does.

Adrian Tomine was born in 1974 in Sacramento, California. He is the writer/artist of the comic book series *Optic Nerve,* as well as the books *Shortcomings, Summer Blonde,* and *Scenes from an Impending Marriage.* He contributes comics, covers, and illustrations to *The New Yorker* with some regularity, and a comprehensive collection of that work was recently published in book form under the title *New York Drawings.* Tomine lives in Brooklyn, New York, with his wife and daughter. **www.adrian-tomine.com.**

▪ This story was originally published in issue 13 of *Optic Nerve,* published by Drawn & Quarterly.

Brian K. Vaughan is the writer of *Y: The Last Man, Ex Machina, Pride of Baghdad, Runaways, The Private Eye,* and the Hugo Award–winning Image Comics series *Saga,* cocreated with artist Fiona Staples. He lives with his family in Los Angeles, where he sometimes dabbles in television. Vaughn is indebted to the tireless work of *Saga* publisher Eric Stephenson, and the book's letterer, a man of mystery known only as Fonografiks. **www.panelsyndicate.com.**

▪ *Saga* is the story of Hazel, a baby born to parents from opposite sides of a never-ending galactic war. Now on the run from the two armies they deserted, the forbidden lovers must survive endless threats while trying to raise their daughter. In Chapter Seven, the young family faces one of its greatest challenges yet: a visit from Hazel's grandparents.

Chris Ware lives in Oak Park, Illinois, and is the author of *Jimmy Corrigan—the Smartest Kid on Earth*. His most recent graphic novel, *Building Stories*, was deemed a Top Ten Fiction Book by the *New York Times* and *Time,* and chosen as the Best Book of the Year by *Publishers Weekly*. His work has been exhibited at the MoCA Los Angeles, the MCA Chicago, and the Whitney Museum of American Art.

- These fifty-two tiers originally appeared, one per page, as one of the fourteen books in *Building Stories*, mirroring an analogous fifty-two tier passage fragmented elsewhere portraying the main character's daily life prior to her marriage and motherhood. Written to capture the perceived speed at which all children grow up ("it happens so fast!"), it layers the formula of one season/twenty minutes/three months per tier over the course of one day, accumulating isolated memories of her daughter's life from birth to the cusp of her own womanhood at age eleven.

Lale Westvind makes comics and animations in Harlem, New York City. Her self-published *Hot Dog Beach* won an Ignatz Award in 2012. She is currently working on a new animation and the next installments in three different self-published comics series. Her work has been published in anthologies and alternative papers such as *Arthur, Happiness, Monster,* and *Smoke Signal*. lalewestvind.blogspot.com.

- This is the beginning of *Hyperspeed to Nowhere* #2, a never-ending epic of interconnected sci-fi tales spanning many planets and species. Mop and Plumo are passing through a star. Their vehicle is powered by a Will Box. I traveled solo across the United States on a motorcycle for some months after college and found my thoughts seemed to affect the inner workings of the machine I depended on. The Will Box functions entirely in this way; the whole comic functions this way. That's the only take on science fiction I am capable of: far out enough that the hardware is near invisible and the interface is thought-based.

Frank M. Young is a writer, cartoonist, and musician who currently lives in western Washington State. He has two published graphic novels, *Oregon Trail: The Road to Destiny* (Sasquatch Press) and *The Carter Family: Don't Forget This Song* (Abrams ComicArts), both in collaboration with David Lasky. He provided graytone and color for Cindy Copeland's graphic novel *Good Riddance* (Abrams ComicArts). Young is also a comics historian and curator of the award-winning blog, *Stanley Stories* (stanleystories.blogspot.com). He is currently figuring out what in the world to do next.

- The first page of this chapter was among the earliest completed pages of the book. At the time, we envisioned this chapter as much longer. Lack of rights to use full song lyrics led us to compress this chapter—perhaps more than it merited. My favorite part of this chapter is its intimate, atmospheric color palette. I wanted the feeling of a warm, humid space with no electric lighting. I also liked the predawn feel of the chapter's first page. I enjoyed my role of colorist as much as I did writing the book's dialect-filled dialogue.

Notable Comics

from September 1, 2012, to August 31, 2013

Selected by Bill Kartalopoulos

CHRISTOPHER ADAMS
  Strong Eye Contact.

DERIK BADMAN
  Colletta Suite I–VI. *Comics as Poetry.*

PETER BAGGE
  "Mr. Unpopularity." *Dark Horse Presents* #27.

TAYLOR-RUTH BALDWIN
  the "doing nothing now"s turn into weeks
  turn into months turn into what am i
  doing with my life. *Hanging Rock Comics.*
  thisishangingrockcomics.tumblr.com

DEREK BALLARD
  Cartoonshow #2: Your Daughters Will Bear
  Our Children.

JOSH BAYER
  Raw Power #2.

DREW BECKMEYER
  Everything Unseen, Parts 6 & 7.

GABRIELLE BELL
  July Diary 2013. *gabriellebell.com.*

SAMAN BEMEL-BENRUD
  Abyss.

E. A. BETHEA
  Single-page comics from *Tusen Hjärten
  Stark* #1.

ELIJAH BRUBAKER
  Reich #9 & 10.

TESSA BRUNTON
  Second Banana.

ANDY BURKHOLDER
  Qviet. *qviet.tumblr.com.*

ADAM BUTTRICK
  Idol Worship.

LILLI CARRÉ
  Rainbow Moment. *Heads or Tails.*

GENEVIÈVE CASTRÉE
  Susceptible.

SHAWN CHENG
  The Suitor.

SEYMOUR CHWAST
  The Odyssey.

MAX CLOTFELDER
  Buster.

WARREN CRAGHEAD
  Gloucester Is a Colony. *Comics as Poetry.*

JORDAN CRANE
  Keeping Two, Part 5. *whatthingsdo.com.*

ANYA DAVIDSON
  The Whole Hole.

ANDY DOUGLAS DAY
  Chauncey.

ALEX DEGAN (A.D.)
  Soft X-Ray. *Chromazoid* #2.

KIM DEITCH
  The Amazing, Enlightening and Absolutely
  True Adventures of Katherine Whaley.

JULIE DELPORTE
  Journal.

JO DERY
  Metal Travels. *Cake 2013 Digest.*

STEVE DITKO
  #17 and Ate Tea N: 18.

J. T. DOCKERY
  The Black Riders and Other Lines. *Despair,*
  vol. 1.

NICK DRNASO
  Young, Dumb, & Full of Cum.

AUSTIN ENGLISH
  The Life Problem.

CHAR ESME
  The Secret of the Saucers.

EAMON ESPEY
  Songs of the Abyss.

INÉS ESTRADA
  Lapsos, I-I & I-II.

EDIE FAKE
Untitled. *Monster 2013*, vol. 1.

XELA FLACTEM
Bad Sex. *Spider's Pee-Paw* #1.

EROYN FRANKLIN
Making Tide and Other Stories.

NOEL FREIBERT
Single-page comics from *Weird* #3.

RENÉE FRENCH
Baby Bjornstrand, Parts 1–3. *studygroupcomics. com.*

MARNIE GALLOWAY
In the Sounds and Seas, vol. 1.

JULIA GFRÖRER
Unclean. *Black Eye* 2.

LEIF GOLDBERG
National Waste #8.

V. A. GRAHAM
Lode.

LISA HANAWALT
Moosefingers. *My Dumb Dirty Eyes.*

GEOFFREY HAYES
Patrick Eats His Peas and Other Stories.

LIZZ HICKEY
Jammers.

KEVIN HOOYMAN
Conditions on the Ground #1–4.

DUNJA JANKOVIC
Cicadas. *Sonatina* #2.

KEITH JONES
Morons #1.

AARON LANGE
Trim #1.

JASON LITTLE
Borb. *beecomix.com.*

MATT MADDEN
Pantoum for Hiram. *Columbia*, vol. 51.

MARDOU
Sky in Stereo #2.

JED MCGOWAN
Voyager. *jedmcgowan.com.*

RICHARD MCGUIRE
Untitled spot illustrations for *The New Yorker.*

MICHAEL MCMILLAN
The ZZZZZ Series and Other Stories.

MELISSA MENDES
Lou #7–15.

DREW MILLER
Poor Thing #1.

TALYA MODLIN
The Big Sweet.

JONNY NEGRON
Infinite Lover. *Studygroup Magazine* #2.

DAVID NYTRA
The Secret of the Stone Frog.

MARÉ ODOMO
Internet Comics.

JOE OLLMAN
Science Fiction.

RAYMOND PETTIBON, WITH TEXT BY JONATHAN LETHEM
Four Paintings by Raymond Pettibon: A New Collaboration. *The Believer*, vol. 11, #3.

ETHAN RILLY
Pope Hats #3.

KEILER ROBERTS
Powdered Milk #11.

ALEXANDER ROCINE
The Bloomer.

JAMES ROMBERGER
Post York.

ZAK SALLY
Sammy the Mouse, vol. 2.

SETH SCRIVER
Blob Top Magazine #1.

ROBERT SERGEL
Eschew #3.

SAR SHAHAR
Sequential Vacation #2.

DASH SHAW
New School.

R. SIKORYAK
The Expectations That Made a Man Out of Pip. *The Devastator*, August 2013.

JORDAN SPEER
Support Group. *Future Shock* #4.

OTTO SPLOTCH
Stink Helmet.

LESLIE STEIN
Eye of the Majestic Creature, vol. 2.

MIKE TAYLOR
Late Era Clash #25.

SETH TOBOCMAN WITH HAYLEY GOLD
The World's Most Criminal Defense Attorney. *worldwar3illustrated.tumblr.com.*

PETE TOMS
On Hiatus, Part 1. *studygroupcomics.com.*

CAROL TYLER
You'll Never Know, Book 3: Soldier's Heart.

TOM VAN DEUSEN
Scorched Earth, vol. 1.

OLGA VOLOZOVA
The Golem of Gabirol.

LANCE WARD
Kmart Shoes.

PETER WARTMAN
Over the Wall.

ESTHER PEARL WATSON
A Portrait Without a Face.

LESLIE WEIBELER
Dionysian Spirit. *Sonatina #2.*

LAUREN WEINSTEIN
If This Is All You Get. *The Big Feminist BUT.*

STEVEN WEISSMAN
Barack Hussein Obama. *whatthingsdo.com.*

JULIA WERTZ
The Infinite Wait.

DYLAN WILLIAMS
The Dead of Night. *The Big Feminist BUT.*

ERIC KOSTIUK WILLIAMS
Hungry Bottom Comics #2: 2 Fags 2 Furious.

RON WIMBERLY
Prince of Cats.

CHRIS WRIGHT
Blacklung.

SUA YOO
DJ Paintings. *vice.com.*

MICKEY ZACCHILLI
RAV #7 & 8.

.

CREDITS

"Hawaii 1997" by Sam Alden. First published in *It Never Happened Again*, April 14, 2013. Copyright © 2014 by Sam Alden. Reprinted by permission of Sam Alden.

"Jane, the Fox and Me" by Fanny Britt and Isabelle Arsenault from *Jane, the Fox and Me*. Copyright © 2012 by Fanny Britt and Isabelle Arsenault. Copyright © 2012 by Les Editions de la Pasteque. First published in French in 2012 as *Jane, le renard & moi* by Les Editions de la Pasteque, Montreal, Quebec. English translation copyright © 2013 by Christelle Morelli and Susan Ouriou. First published in English in Canada and the USA in 2013 by Groundwood Books.

"Depression Part Two" (excerpt) (pp. 121–34) from *Hyperbole and a Half: Unfortunate Situations, Flawed Coping Mechanisms, Mayhem, and Other Things that Happened* by Allie Brosh. Copyright © 2013 by Alexandra Brosh. Reprinted with permission of Scribner Publishing Group/Simon & Schuster, Inc. from the Touchstone Edition. All rights reserved.

"August 1977" by Nina Bunjevac. First published in *Heartless*, September 15, 2012. Copyright © 2012 by Nina Bunjevac. Reprinted by permission of Nina Bunjevac.

"The Hive" (excerpt) by Charles Burns. First published in *The Hive* by Charles Burns, copyright © 2012 by Charles Burns. Used by permission of Pantheon Books, an imprint of the Knopf Doubleday Publishing Group, a division of Random House LLC. All rights reserved.

"Bittersweet Romance" (excerpt) by Victor Cayro. First published in *Bittersweet Romance*. Copyright © 2013 by Victor Cayro. Reprinted by permission of Victor Cayro.

"High Road to the Shmuck Seat" by Aline Kominsky-Crumb and Robert Crumb. First published in *Drawn Together*, W.W. Norton. Copyright © 2012 by A. and R. Crumb. Reprinted by permission of A. and R. Crumb.

"Ambient Air (Part II)" by Erin Curry. First published at www.erincurry.com/ambient-air. Copyright © 2013 by Erin Curry. Reprinted by permission of Erin Curry.

"Canadian Royalty" by Michael DeForge. First published in *Lose #4*. Copyright © 2012 by Michael DeForge. Reprinted by permission of Koyama Press.

"Untitled" by G. W. Duncanson. First published at www.cash-money-cartoons.tumblr.com. Copyright © 2013 by G. W. Duncanson. Reprinted by permission of G. W. Duncanson.

Excerpt from "The Understanding Monster—Book One" (excerpt) by Theo Ellsworth. First published in *The Understanding Monster—Book One*. Copyright © 2012 by Theo Ellsworth. Reprinted by permission of Theo Ellsworth.

"Face It" by C. F. First published in *New York Times Opinionator Blog*, February 18, 2013. Copyright © 2014 by Christopher Forgues. Reprinted by permission of Christopher Forgues.

"Multiple Warheads: Alphabet to Infinity #1" by Brandon Graham. First published in *Multiple Warheads: Alphabet to Infinity #1*. Copyright © 2013 by Brandon Graham. Reprinted by permission of Brandon Graham.

"RL" (excerpt) by Tom Hart. From *Rosalie Lightning* © 2015 by Tom Hart. Reprinted by permission of St. Martin's Press. All Rights Reserved.

"All the Marbles" (excerpt) by Gilbert Hernandez. First published in *Marble Season* (*Drawn & Quarterly*), April 16, 2013. Reprinted by permission of *Drawn & Quarterly*.

"Crime Raiders International Mobsters and Executioners" by Jaime Hernandez. First published in *Love and Rockets: New Stories #5*. Copyright © 2012 by Jaime Hernandez. Reprinted by permission of Jaime Hernandez.

"Homestuck" by Andrew Hussie. First published in 2009. Copyright © 2014 by Andrew Hussie. Reprinted by permission of Andrew Hussie.

"Schweinhund" and "Howdy, His Nephew Dee Dee and a Friend of Howdy's Nephew" by Gerald Jablonski. First published in *Cryptic Wit 3*. Copyright © 2012 by Gerald Jablonski. Reprinted by permission of Gerald Jablonski.

"Picnic Now!," "Sickroom Reading," "The Hand Laundry," and "A 21st Century Still Life" by Ben Katchor. First published in *Metropolis Magazine*. Copyright © 2013 by Ben Katchor. Reprinted by permission of Ben Katchor.

"Letting It Go" (excerpt) by Miriam Katin. First published in *Letting It Go* (*Drawn & Quarterly*), March 19, 2013. Copyright © 2013 by Miriam Katin. Reprinted by permission of *Drawn & Quarterly*.

"Blue Period" from Aidan Koch. First published in *Sonatina #2*. Copyright © 2013 by Aidan Koch. Reprinted by permission of Aidan Koch.

"March: Book One" (excerpt) by John Lewis, Andrew Aydin, and Nate Powell. First published in *March* (Book One), pp. 67–73, Top Shelf Productions, Inc. Copyright © 2014 by John Lewis and Andrew Aydin. Reprinted by permission of Top Shelf Productions, Inc.

"Dimensions" by Ted May. First published in *Men's Feelings*, Revival House Press. Copyright © 2014 by Edward May. Reprinted by permission of Edward May.

"Whistle While You Work . . . Or Think of Death" by Onsmith. First published in *Study Group Magazine #2*. Copyright © 2013 by Onsmith. Reprinted by permission of Onsmith.

"Hip Hop Family Tree" (excerpt) by Ed Piskor. First published in *Hip Hop Family Tree*. Copyright © 2013 by Ed Piskor. Reprinted by permission of Ed Piskor.

"The Implications of Making Something from Nothing via the Spiritual Realm," "This is Magic—This is Alchemy," and "Is There Silence?" by Ron Regé, Jr. First published in *The Cartoon Utopia*. Copyright © 2012 by Ron Regé, Jr. Reprinted by permission of Ron Regé, Jr.

"Mom" (excerpt) by Sam Sharpe. First published in *Viewotron #2*. Copyright © 2013 by Samuel Sharpe. Reprinted by permission of Samuel Sharpe.

"The Mermaid in the Hudson" (excerpt) by Mark Siegel. First published in *Sailor Twain: Or: The Mermaid in the Hudson* © 2012 by Mark Siegel. Reprinted by permission of First Second, an imprint of Roaring Brook Press, a division of Holtzbrinck Publishing Holdings Limited Partnership. All Rights Reserved.

"Drama" (excerpt) by Raina Telgemeier. First published in *Drama*, Graphix/Scholastic, 2012. Copyright © 2014 by Raina Telgemeier. Reprinted by permission of Raina Telgemeier.

Cul de Sac © 2012 Richard Thompson. Distributed by Universal Uclick. Reprinted with permission. All rights reserved.

"Translated, from the Japanese," by Adrian Tomine. First published in *Optic Nerve #13* (*Drawn & Quarterly*). Copyright © 2013 by Adrian Tomine. Reprinted by permission of *Drawn & Quarterly*.

"Saga Chapter 7" (excerpt) by Brian K. Vaughan and Fiona Staples. First published in *Saga #7*. Copyright © 2014 by Brian K. Vaughan and Fiona Staples. Reprinted by permission of Brian K. Vaughan and Fiona Staples.

"Building Stories" (excerpt) from *Building Stories* by Chris Ware, copyright © 2012 by Chris Ware. Used by permission of Pantheon Books, an imprint of the Knopf Doubleday Publishing Group, a division of Random House LLC. All rights reserved.

"Hyperspeed to Nowhere, Return to Entropy" (excerpt) by Lale Westvind. First published in *Hyperspeed to Nowhere #2*. Copyright © 2012 by Lale Westvind. Reprinted by permission of Lale Westvind.

"The Program Is Morally Good" (excerpt) by Frank M. Young and David Lasky. First published in *The Carter Family: Don't Forget This Song* by Frank M. Young and David Lasky. Copyright © 2012 by Frank M. Young and David Lasky. Used by permission of Abrams ComicArts, an imprint of Abrams, New York. All rights reserved.

THE BEST AMERICAN SERIES®

FIRST, BEST, AND BEST-SELLING

The Best American series is the premier annual showcase for the country's finest short fiction and nonfiction. Each volume's series editor selects notable works from hundreds of magazines, journals, and websites. A special guest editor, a leading writer in the field, then chooses the best twenty or so pieces to publish. This unique system has made the Best American series the most respected — and most popular — of its kind.

Look for these best-selling titles in the Best American series:

The Best American Comics

The Best American Essays

The Best American Infographics

The Best American Mystery Stories

The Best American Nonrequired Reading

The Best American Science and Nature Writing

The Best American Short Stories

The Best American Sports Writing

The Best American Travel Writing

Available in print and e-book wherever books are sold.
Visit our website: *www.hmhbooks.com/hmh/site/bas*

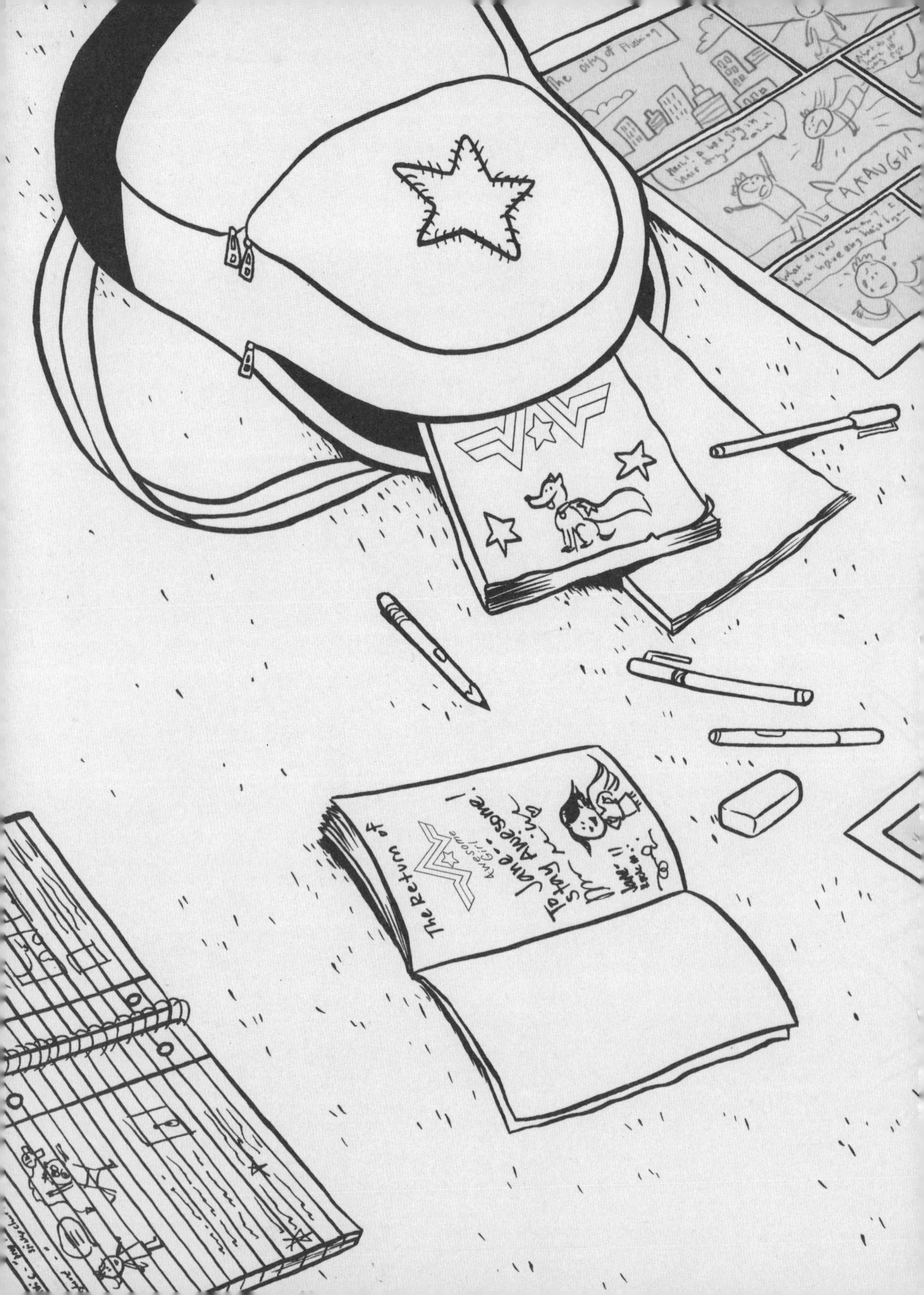
The Return of
Awesome Girl
Totally Jane Awesome!